# *In Passion* For the World

A history of
Seventh-day Adventist
Education


Floyd Greenleaf

**Pacific Press® Publishing Association**
Nampa, Idaho
Oshawa, Ontario, Canada
www.pacificpress.com

Designed by Tim Larson
Globe photo by Getty Images ©
Vintage photos supplied by author



Printed in the United States of America by
Pacific Press® Publishing Association.


www.pacificpress.com

Photo credits: Except for those listed below, all photos in this book were furnished by the General Conference of Seventh-day Adventists, Office of Archives and Statistics:

W. W. Prescott (page 38): Ellen G. White Estate.
Classroom building, Adventist International Institute of Advanced Studies (page 384): Photo by the author.
School of Theology, Sahmyook University (page 387): Photo by the author.
Plaque at Montemorelos University (page 420): Photo by the author.
Zaokski Seminary (page 445): Photo by the author.
Group photo of Faith and Learning Seminar (page 512): General Conference Department of Education.

ISBN: 0-8163-2114-0

05 06 07 08 09 · 5 4 3 2 1

# A Note to the Reader

The abbreviation, AST, appearing in the end notes, represents the General Conference Office of Archives and Statistics. The abbreviation, RG, identifies the specific Record Group number where information is located.

I have omitted references of sources for most of the historical background that appears in many chapters. For these passages containing general information that is part of the common domain I have depended extensively on general college history texts. *An Encyclopedia of World History,* William Langer, ed., was my standard source for names, dates, and incidental information. *A Chronology of Seventh-day Adventist Education,* 1972 edition, Walton J. Brown, compiler, is the source for names and dates pertaining to Adventist education.

The names of denominational administrative units, especially General Conference divisions, sometimes vary inconsistently even in the papers the divisions published. The names in this book are the most prevalent forms of nomenclature in use at the time when they appear chronologically in the narritive.

# Contents

# Foreword

Tucked against a knoll on the outskirts of Pune, India lies Salisbury Park, a small Seventh-day Adventist community whose old stone church and gabled buildings belie an unusually persistent English ambience. It was early summer when we drove over the crest and circled around to one of the larger buildings. Already the dusty soil lay brown and thick on the drive. Before we came to a stop we couldn't help but notice the flowers and shrubbery and the old trees that towered above the walkways, all emblematic of an attempt by an older generation to decorate the enclave with nature's best and to make it homey.

We spent a couple of hours wandering, talking, and paradoxically, even reminiscing about this place that we had never seen. We were in gentle competition with the clock, but as we turned to go our driver suggested that we visit the far side of the community, away from the buildings.

"There's a cemetery that you might be interested in," he said. "You should see it."

Of course we would go, and in a few moments we were wandering among the headstones, many of them set in place decades ago. The names stood out, most of which my inflexible North American tongue could not pronounce, but easier ones as well like Cherian and Lowry, both Indian and Caucasian, buried together on the edge of Salisbury Park. It was a quietly moving experience, walking among those markers and contemplating the convictions that led people from such divergent origins to dedicated careers and finally to the same resting spot.

On our way back among the trees and walkways we passed by the sign, Salisbury Park.

"By the way," I asked, "Where did the name come from?"

"The missionary."

Yes, I should have known. The missionary. Homer R. Salisbury, more commonly H. R. Salisbury. I had met him before. He was the one who, by the time he was twenty-seven, had put in a stint of teaching in South Africa and completed a course of study in London. He was the young biblical language and church history teacher at Battle Creek College. He was the one who, before his thirtieth birthday, linked up with others to make Battle Creek College the center for Adventist elementary education even while older and wiser heads warned that it was a madcap idea.

Salisbury was the one who publicly contradicted General Conference dignitaries with statistics showing that the expense of running church schools did not drain money from more conventional and more traditional church projects as they had darkly warned. And at the same time, notwithstanding their pessimism and his public contradiction, he was the one who retained their respect. He was the one who at age thirty-one went to England to establish the forerunner of Newbold College. He was the one who sent Washington Foreign Missionary Seminary off to a productive start.

And Salisbury was the one who went to India in 1913 to take charge of the tiny, embryonic Seventh-day Adventist church. Two years later as he sailed back to that field aboard the *S. S. Persia*, German torpedoes hit his ship. Salisbury was the one who gave his life belt to a fellow passenger. And Salisbury was the one who died in the Mediterranean, only forty-five years old. A stunned General Conference conducted a memorial service in Takoma Park on January 22, 1916 and four weeks later the *Review* carried his life sketch. When the Oriental Watchman Publishing House published *Images* in 1993, a pictorial history commemorating the hundredth anniversary of Adventism in Southern Asia, Salisbury was the one the Indian editors honored with a full-page portrait.

H. R. Salisbury. Yes, I knew who he was. Some time before the Mediterranean swallowed him up, he poured out his soul in an untitled poem expressing the compelling burden of his heart. "Stir me, O stir me, Lord," he wrote, "I care not how;"

But stir my heart in passion for the world;
Stir me to give, to go, but most to pray;
Stir, till the blood-red banner be unfurled
O'er lands that still in heathen darkness lie,
O'er deserts where no cross is lifted high.

Stir me, O stir me, Lord till all my heart
Is filled with strong compassion for these souls;

Till thy compelling 'must' drives me to prayer;
Till thy constraining love reach to the poles,
Far north and south, in burning, deep desire;
Till east and west are caught in love's great fire.

This book is about Seventh-day Adventist education. It is also about purpose, conviction, dedication, commitment, and mission. Whether it was the commitment that propelled the ox carts through the African wilderness to Solusi or the mission of the Loma Linda University Medical Center Heart Team, a single thread weaves it way through the tapestry of Adventist schools–the conviction to reach the hearts as well as the minds of the people of the world. In a sense Adventist education fulfilled Salisbury's stirring.

As my research revealed the story which this book recounts and the chapters took form on the screen of my monitor, I was constantly aware that I was also searching for an apt title. It was not until I was in the final stages of the manuscript that Salisbury's words struck me as the very phrase for which I was seeking. By itself, *A History of Seventh-day Adventist Education* would have been an accurate description of the book, but Salisbury's phrase, *In Passion for the World,* encapsulates the *raison d'etre* of Adventist education and gave life to the title. And so the title, *In Passion for the World: A History of Seventh-day Adventist Education.*

I have written from the viewpoint of a participant in Adventist education. I attended Adventist schools and spent my career in denominational classrooms. At various times I found opportunities to visit many Adventist campuses. As helpful as these experiences were, it was necessary to research extensively before writing this book. As my study unfolded, three distinct periods of Adventist education emerged. The first was the era of origins, extending from the nineteenth century beginnings until about 1920, the years when the first generation of schools appeared and the church took its first steps toward organizing a system of education. The second period, from about 1920 to approximately 1945, or the end of World War II, I have called the Interim, a time of notable expansion, but primarily of solidification and wrestling with the issues of maintaining an identifiably Adventist system of schools. The third period, 1945 to the beginning of the twenty-first century, was a time of fulfillment and challenge, when spectacular growth and struggles with problems were at times divisive and overpowering, and tested the mettle of Adventist education.

I have tried to describe both the narrative and the primary issues of Adventist education. In order to provide a setting, I have also included essential historical background about the regions of the world where Adventist workers established schools. It is instructive to remember that denominational education did not just happen, but in some way related to the history and the socio-political environment everywhere it went. While the narrative is interesting in itself, it is understood best as it furnishes the stuff of which the issues are made. Either one without the other would make an incomplete book.

This book is not a critique of Adventist education. It is largely a positive view of what took place, but, as the story develops, readers will learn that not everything that occurred in Adventist education was positive. On balance, the account is positive in part because education itself is a positive activity, a venture to better the human condition. In the case of Adventist education "better" takes on a significantly spiritual meaning, and that aspect of the account becomes fundamental to the book. Recurring themes crop up and at the risk of becoming repetitious I found it necessary to repeat them at appropriate junctures not only for the sake of emphasis but because they are inherent to the story and the issues themselves.

My acknowledgments begin with thanks to the General Conference Department of Education for financial support of this project. Humberto Rasi, at the time the director of the department, planted the idea for the book and furnished valuable counsel at various junctures of its production. His associates, Garland Dulan, who succeeded him as director in 2003, and Enrique Becerra and John Fowler also gave me extensive time and help. Andrea Luxton, who joined the department in 2003, also provided help. John Fowler deserves special thanks for arranging a research trip through Asia.

My leading source of information was the General Conference Office of Archives and Statistics where Bert Haloviak, director, and his assistant, Eucaris Galicia, showed generous support for my research. Tim Poirier, vice director of the Ellen G. White Estate, also made materials in that facility readily available. Alan Hecht, director of the Rebok Memorial Library at the General Conference, and his assistant, Anne Muganda, provided much help in locating and utilizing secondary sources.

Many persons gave me research materials. Enrique Becerra, General Conference Department of Education; Dae Yun Cho, Sahmyook Nursing and Health College; Gordon Christo, Spicer Memorial College; Daniel Chuah, Hong Kong Adventist College; Justus Devadas, Department of Education, Southern Asia Division; Karen and Paul Essig, Lakpahana Adventist College and Seminary; H. G. M. Fernando, Seventh-day Adventist High School, Kandana, Sri Lanka; R. S. Fernando, retired worker, Sri Lanka; John Fowler, General Conference Department of Education; Bert Haloviak, Office of Archives and Statistics, General Conference of Seventh-day Adventists; Julian Melgosa, Adventist International Institute of Advanced Studies; Liberato B. Moises, Adventist University of the Philippines; Robert Nixon; Office of Legal Counsel, General Conference of Seventh-day Adventists; Richard Osborn, Pacific Union College; Humberto Rasi, General Conference Department of Education; Vicente Rodriguez, retired educator, Cuba; Marvin Robertson, retired educator, North America; Beverly Rumble, General Conference Department of Education; Edison Samaraj, Oriental Watchman Publishing House; Milton Siepman, retired educator, Africa; and Masaji Uyeda; North Asia-Pacific Department of Education.

I am especially indebted to my many interviewees, whom I have listed in the bibliography. Some of them were members of institutional faculties or offices of education who demonstrated kind hospitality during my tour of Asia to gather information and helped to make the trip profitable.

I owe many thanks to Humberto Rasi, Gary Land, Richard Osborn, Gordon Christo and Milton Siepman for their critiques of the manuscript.

Despite my attempt to prepare a reliable account of Seventh-day Adventist education, errors may appear. For them I am responsible.

# *Part One*

# The Beginning Years, 1872-1920

The nearly fifty-year span from 1872 when the first denominational school was founded on to 1920 was a period of beginnings for Seventh-day Adventist education around the globe. Wherever the church established a presence, local leaders were prone to set up printing presses, emphasize health-care, and if possible, offer some level of education.

In 1872 Ellen White published the first of her many statements that described the character of Adventist education. Her counsel placed denominational schools in the middle of nineteenth century educational reform but spelled out criteria that gave Adventist education a unique stamp and a unifying rationale. By 1920 every major field around the world operated its own school to train church employees, thus education became the primary factor in denominational self-perpetuation.

The beginning years were years of struggle. Ellen White provided the foundational principles of Adventist education, but societies of the world formed the context in which these ideals found applications. Implementing the principles was sometimes clumsy and characterized by debate over organization, identity and purpose, but in 1920 a system existed, albeit young and somewhat faltering.

Seventh-day Adventists emerged from World War I facing a new and uncertain world in which their task of spreading the biblical gospel had become extremely more complicated. One of their most carefully guarded tools was an education system that had successfully passed its first tests, thanks to the tenacity and faith of hundreds of teachers and institutional leaders who had founded a sisterhood of colleges in North America and a generation of training schools around the world, most of which were supported to varying degrees by lower schools.

How well the new system worked depended in part on how well the founders had conceived their task.

## Chapter 1

# The Head, Heart, and Hand

*A monument reminds Adventists of the first church school that their spiritual forebears organized in 1853 at Buck's Bridge in upstate New York. Martha Byington, the teacher, was the daughter of John Byington, who later became the first president of the General Conference. The Buck's Bridge school lasted only three years.*

For many Seventh-day Adventists it has become almost second nature to think and talk about their schools. But it has not always been so. For nearly a decade after 1844 disappointed believers continued to hope that Jesus would still return to this earth very soon, too soon to worry about such mundane matters as education.

Martha Byington broke out of this mold in 1853 when she began a church school for the children of five families in Buck's Bridge, New York. The school lasted three years with a different teacher each year. This first known experiment in Adventist education occurred seven years before the Seventh-day Adventist denomination organized, hence there was no such thing as official support. Parents were on their own to organize schools spontaneously if they wanted them badly enough.[1]

A year after the Buck's Bridge school began, twenty-six-year-old Ellen White bore her third son, and with motherhood on her mind she admonished parents in the columns of the *Review and Herald* to take the behavior of their children more seriously. "Parents stand in the place of God to their children," she said, "and they will have to render an account." Two examples which she pointed out for specific attention were Sabbath observance and reverence in church. Her article, "Duty of Parents to Their Children," did not ask for formal education, but she issued a clear call for parents to teach their children deliberately in the home, an activity that she later tied closely to schools and learning.[2]

Three years later her husband James became more explicit in a three-part article beginning in the August 20 issue of the *Review*. Inspired by a writer in the *Michigan Journal of Education* who blistered the public schools for sometimes leaving children unattended and permitting vulgar behavior and profane language on school premises, White warned Adventist readers that their children should be separated from those poisonous influences. Sabbath keepers should employ teachers for their children, he said. "What if it be extra expense?" he wanted to know. "Will parents push their dear children into channels of vice, for the sake of a few shillings?" He urged both mothers and fathers to spend more time with their children, consciously educating them in the home if they did not have a teacher.[3]

*James White, technically the first president of Battle Creek College although he never claimed the title. He exerted a profound influence on the early policies of the first Seventh-day Adventist college.*

James White knew from experience what he was talking about when he laid the initial burden of education on parents. He had begun his career as a school teacher. When his articles appeared in 1857 the Byington school at Buck's Bridge had already closed. Meanwhile, other classrooms had opened in Jackson, Michigan and Northfield, Vermont. In Battle Creek several abortive attempts to start a church school alternately raised and dashed the hopes of those whose convictions were similar to White's. In 1858 John Fletcher Byington, who had taught the third and final year at Buck's Bridge, tried to make a go of it again in Battle Creek, but he only lengthened the list of frustrations.

During the 1850s and 1860s there were other experiments with Adventist schools, all short lived. Their sketchy details only tantalize us to wonder what really happened. All of them combined did not represent a movement. They were tentative and unsteady. James White looked skeptically upon these erratic ventures, despite his earlier encouragement. He and his wife practiced what they preached by hiring private teachers for their boys as long as their purses would allow it.

If Adventists had little to show by way of schools, they would have to admit that as a people they had devoted only little time thinking through the issue of why they should invest in educational enterprises. Since the first issues of the *Present Truth* and later the *Review* appeared, printing had been the primary institutional concern of Adventists, and after 1866, they added health. Education was a family matter, not a responsibility of the church.

In urging venturesome members to open small church schools, James White was advocating primary education for children, not a training program for church employees. When it came to preparing ministers he was not enthusiastic. He was prone to tell young men aspiring to the ministry to read and study on their own.[4] Adventist historian Emmett K. VandeVere has observed that "until the early 1870's, the one clear lag in the budding denomination was its neglect of advanced education. For twenty years the denomination's finest asset, its youth, had gone relatively undeveloped and unharnessed."[5]

But these circumstances and attitudes were about to change. In 1860 Adventists organized themselves into an official church and the Battle Creek community grew larger, becoming an Adventist center. In 1868 the Battle Creek Church hired Goodloe Harper Bell, a former student of Oberlin College, to teach school for a year. The next year he continued, independently. Word traveled the Battle Creek grapevine that, unlike his predecessors, he knew what he was doing. It appeared that he might be breaking the spell.

Bell's so-called Select School that began in 1868 aroused enough attention in Battle Creek to prompt James White to wonder out loud if the denomination needed an official school after all. Although they talked about it, neither he nor the church's leaders realized any material progress for three years, but in April 1872 he and his wife began urging the Battle Creek church to consider a denominationally sponsored school.

From the congregation the idea went to the General Conference, where a three-man committee headed by the church president, George I. Butler, conveniently decided to adopt Bell's Select School as the first official Adventist school. Bell merely kept on doing what he had been doing, but when classes began on June 3, 1872 in the room above his living quarters on the corner of Kalamazoo and Washington streets, the big change was the assurance that he now had official support.[6]

Given the haphazard history of Adventist schools since 1853, Ellen White was not content to allow this latest venture to die, starved by the lack of solid backing. Although she and her husband and seventeen-year-old son, Willie, left Battle Creek on Sunday, June 23, 1872 on a trip of unknown duration to California, she took with her the burden of Bell's classroom.

When the Whites left Battle Creek they had every intention to spend the next weekend in California, but stops in Missouri and Kansas delayed them. When they reached Denver, Colorado, they were already nearly three weeks behind their original schedule because of traveling to places they had not planned to visit; nevertheless, they disrupted their travel plans even more by deciding to remain in the home of Ellen's niece and family, the W. D. Wallings, who owned a lumber business west of the city.[7]

It was from this resting place in Denver that Ellen White spelled out her ideals of Adventist education, received from an earlier vision. On July 22, a month after she left Battle Creek, she began her thirty-page statement, "Proper Education," which appeared first as *Testimony* No. 22 to the church, a statement of her visions pertaining to education, and

*Ellen G. White, whose essay in 1872, "Proper Education," spelled out the fundamental character of Seventh-day Adventist education. She produced hundreds of pages of inspired counsel on which Adventist teachers and school administrators based their decisions and charted their programs.*

later as six installments in *The Health Reformer*, running from December 1872 to September 1873.

"It is the nicest work ever assumed by men and women to deal with youthful minds," she began. Ranging from primary to higher education, sometimes not distinguishing which level she was describing, she presented an overarching view of what Adventist schools ought to be. Training differed from education, she declared, comparing the first to conditioning people to obey certain commands as though they were beasts of burden. She described such people as "well drilled soldiers," but not educated to think for themselves, to make decisions on their own and to use their God-given capacities to become individuals of principle, qualified for any position in life.[8]

Among their God-given gifts students possessed individuality that Ellen White warned teachers never to violate, but rather to exploit to the advantage of the person. In a similar vein, discipline was to be redemptive, and educational methods were to encourage success rather than a sense of failure.

Another gift was personal health which Ellen White believed was jeopardized by poor heating and ventilation in schools, benches that did not fit the shape of the human body, and long, unimaginative daily programs that burdened rather than inspired students. Cultivating the health of students was to be a fundamental of Adventist education.

Education began in the home, Ellen White went on. Parents were responsible for establishing basic values which students brought to school. One of these essential perceptions was to be a high esteem for physical labor. Well-organized schools should not only provide opportunities for work, but require it.

Another cardinal point was balance. "The world is full of one-sided men and women," she charged, "who have become such because one set of their faculties was cultivated while others were dwarfed from inaction." Mental health and old-fashioned work were related almost synergistically. "In order to preserve the balance of the mind," she declared, "labor and study should be united in the schools."

Anticipating that some might doubt the wisdom of requiring students to take time out from their study to work, she stated emphatically that they would not shortchange their professional goals. "Young men should not enter upon the work of explaining the Scriptures and lecturing upon the prophecies when they do not have a knowledge of the important Bible truths they try to explain to others." This was not all. "Ignorance will not increase the humility or spirituality of any professed follower of Christ. The truths of the divine word can be best appreciated by an intellectual Christian."

Ellen White suffered no illusion about the differences between the principles she was advocating for Adventist schools and those that were common at the time. "We are reformers," she said. She warned that Adventists could not compensate for all the mistakes of the past but they could design a form of education consistent with their faith.

Appropriately, "Proper Education" first appeared in *The Health Reformer* for it was as much a discussion of health as it was of curriculum. The term *wellness* was not yet a part of the American lexicon, but the concept was a foundational element in Ellen White's view of education. The practice of mixing work with study was to become a recurring theme in Adventist schools around the globe.

Already forty-four years old when she wrote from her niece's home in Denver, the author of "Proper Education" often enlarged on her seminal essay during the remaining forty-three years of her life, even to the point of publishing books on the topic of education, but she did not deviate from her original advice. Her 1872 statement was a landmark in the history Adventist education.[9]

## Reform in American Education

As important as Adventists regard Ellen White's opening call for change in education, it would be remiss to see her as a lone voice calling for reform. In many ways she reflected the change taking place around her. During the nineteenth century, especially after the American Civil War, the United States was awash with change that left American schools and the philosophy behind them in flux.[10]

At the root of reform was the notion that education should be democratic in character rather than elitist. Noah Webster contributed to an American style of education by publishing the first distinctive American textbooks that promoted patriotic sentiments, earning him the title of "Schoolmaster of the Republic," but his leading claim to fame was his dictionary that standardized American English, the medium in which education was to be communicated to students.

It was left to William H. McGuffey to purify American primary education by writing a series of readers that preserved generic Christian values and human virtue and portrayed them as patriotic behavior. Nineteenth-century Americans fed their minds on his homespun wisdom which helped to create an American mentality that was at once Protestant and Caucasian.

Horace Mann, however, introduced the idea that to match American needs, education was to be public and cheap, if not free and open to all. As Secretary of Education in Massachusetts for twelve years beginning in 1837 he initiated a movement to create a tax-supported, compulsory elementary school system. He also instituted the first recognizable teacher-training program. By 1850 many of his ideas had materialized.

Mann's reforms touched elementary education as nothing had before. American schools had traditionally been a concern of religious bodies, but Mann's proposals began the transition that eventually led to a secular, tax-based, democratic system allowing students to proceed from grade one to university degrees. This change was anything but sudden. A public system crowned by state universities did not come until after the Civil War, and not until the third decade of the twentieth century did American secondary education assume its own peculiar shape.

Perhaps this slow change derived in part from the fact that although the United States Constitution declared the states to be responsible for education, churches had traditionally assumed the responsibility of operating schools and time was necessary to generate a tradition of public education. During the early nineteenth century the majority of American colleges were religious institutions, many of them an aftereffect of the Second Great Awakening. In spite of these religious roots, college degrees were based on studies in the classics–Greek and Latin languages and ancient philosophy. Anything that smacked of science or technical learning was categorized as professional or vocational and not worthy of a status equivalent to a college degree.

Daring thinkers not only raised questions about the practicality of a classic education in a democratic society, but experimented with change. Oberlin College in Ohio was a hotbed of shocking innovation. The school's founder announced that education should serve not only the intellect but the body and heart as well, a view that sounded much like later Adventist pronouncements about educating the head, the heart, and the hand. In 1833 Oberlin became coeducational, threw out "pagan" classics in favor of biblically-based instruction as the foundation of a college education, introduced manual labor as part of the curriculum, and taught dietary reform.

But this flirtation with change did not endure and by the last third of the century Oberlin returned to a less radical program. Other schools implemented similar ideas, but reform did not take a firm hold until after the Civil War. By that time voices of reform were also suggesting that higher levels of instruction should become more practical to suit the needs of a broadly developing American society.

Even a cursory glance at American life furnished convincing evidence that the United States was becoming more urban and industrial, and because of immigration, increasingly cosmopolitan, while at the same time it was developing new needs in mass agriculture as a result of pushing westward into virgin lands of the West. In this post-Civil War environment reformers said that training for a profession should be elevated to the level of a college education, even replacing the classics.

The framers of the United States Constitution left education in the hands of the states to regulate, but in 1862, even before the post-Civil War industrial surge set in, Congress passed the Morrill Act which assisted in integrating vocational instruction into existing schools and granted public land to the states for the purpose of establishing agricultural and mechanical colleges and to offer specialized training in the sciences. The result was to begin to revolutionize American education by supporting the high school as a feeder for colleges and universities and legitimizing professional and practical education on a level equally prestigious as an education in the classics. In time research programs at both private and state universities, and post-baccalaureate degrees became a commonplace in American education. The leading impact of reform was a democratization of education in both form and content by building a system that theoretically provided everyone with a chance to learn. Public education tended to equalize American life.

On its face, reform in American schools was well underway when Ellen White wrote her 1872 statement. She was aware of what was taking place in American education and many of the ideas she espoused were echoes of what educators were already saying. She knew that notwithstanding all of the progress toward reform and democratizing education, the actual condition of elementary education was far from the ideal. The little red schoolhouse had become an American temple, but inside those one-room shrines teachers imposed rigid and harsh schedules that silenced and immobilized children. Physical amenities were primitive and unhygienic, and learning was by rote. Ellen White was not off the mark when she told Adventists in "Proper Education" that "we are reformers." She was calling for change with an Adventist twist to serve Adventist purposes.

### A New College at Battle Creek

By the time the Whites completed their journey to California, Goodloe Harper Bell was enjoying more success with his school than he had ever known. A large enrollment forced him to divide his students into morning and evening classes. In December 1872 the number became even larger and he moved into the church.[11]

When the school year opened in 1873 the school committee replaced Bell with Sidney Brownsberger, a twenty-eight-year-old owner of a master's degree from the University of Michigan. After more than a hundred students registered for the winter term in December 1873 the new principal herded his flock from the church to a steam-heated location in the new Review and Herald publishing building. The faculty also grew. Besides Brownsberger, Bell stayed on to teach, Uriah Smith conducted biblical studies, and translators from the publishing house offered instruction in languages. Talk of a permanent college was making the rounds.

By now unquestionably committed to the idea of a college, James White was nevertheless ambivalent about events as they unfolded. In March 1873 he and his wife returned to Battle Creek from California to attend the General Conference session where he introduced a motion to establish a school to train denominational workers. In November 1873 the General Conference announced it had collected $52,000 in cash and pledges to build a college. Together James and Ellen White pledged $3,000.

Although the Whites wanted a worker-training school, they were less sanguine about the prospects of a college in Battle Creek. James unsuccessfully argued that the Adventist community was not ready for the responsibility of accommodating an institution that could easily attract hundreds of students. The question of location also provided the stuff for more debate. A serious reading of Ellen White's "Proper Education" would lead to the conclusion that a rural location would be necessary for the school, but the final decision of a campus site weighed more heavily on other considerations.

Denominational luminaries envisioned a cluster of institutions in Battle Creek, one of which would be the college. The church's pocketbook could not afford a 160-acre farm which was available by a nearby lake, and church leaders let a chance slip by to purchase a fifty-acre plot. In the end they settled on a twelve-acre estate in Battle Creek for which they paid $16,000. Promptly they sold off several acres for house construction lots, reducing the college campus to seven acres or less. Ellen White wept when she heard the news. She knew that in their haste to acquire a convenient location church leaders had scuttled her counsel to establish a school that brought labor and study together.

At a meeting of the college board in the fall of 1874 Ellen White, newly returned from California, read her statement about proper education, emphasizing the combination of labor and study. By his own admission, Brownsberger knew nothing about the kind of education she proposed. His master's degree was in the classics, and he felt unqualified to establish a work and study program.

The college board responded with less than half a loaf. It regarded Brownsberger's academic pedigree to be too valuable a commodity to discard in favor of someone who was ready to innovate. Besides, the imposing, three-story brick building which would house the new school

*The original building of Battle Creek College was dedicated in January, 1875. Later, other additions to the campus enabled the school to become a boarding institution and to broaden its offerings.*

was nearing completion. With a compromise to begin the college with a customary curriculum to which industries would be added after further study, the school board proceeded with plans for the academic program. The school's charter permitted instruction from elementary grades through college level. Although a complete college program was not in place when classes began in September 1874, Uriah Smith, editor of the *Review*, announced in February 1875 that the name of the new school was Battle Creek College.

Understandably, Ellen White felt betrayed by the turn of events, but she and her husband continued to support the fledgling college and to work for its success. School indebtedness diminished to less than $6,000 by 1880. Under Brownsberger's leadership the number of programs increased to include a commercial department, a teacher-preparation course, and a theology program. Classes in foreign languages and health were also available, with a young Dr. John Harvey Kellogg joining the teaching faculty in addition to his duties as medical director at Battle Creek Sanitarium. In 1879 the college granted its first degrees and two years later enrollment climbed to 490.

These were undeniable marks of a dynamic institution, but the school was not without its shortcomings which in one way or another related to the failure to design a school following Ellen White's "Proper Education" model. Realistically, it was probably more than anyone could reasonably expect that an inexperienced faculty could effectively produce such an institution with a smooth program overnight. With appropriate commitment it was doable, but it would take time and ample trial and error.

Militating against industrial education was the fact that few Adventists were qualified to teach in a college in the first place, and they were not ready to launch an experiment with a reform program combining labor and formal classes. Adventist historian A. W. Spalding recounts that the college board eventually voted to install limited opportunities in industries that the tiny campus could accommodate, but Brownsberger could not bring himself to implement the action.[12] Goodloe Harper Bell, with experience at Oberlin College where students had worked, was the leading supporter of the labor-and-study ideal that Ellen White advocated, but his voice was frequently lost in debate because he did not hold a college degree.

Planting the school on a small plot of ground was not the only aspect of the college that undercut "Proper Education." From the outset Ellen White urged that classes in Bible should not supplant studies in the "sciences," as she called all other academic courses, but the Bible should be central to all instruction. At Battle Creek College biblical studies were left hanging as a curricular appendage.

In the spring of 1877 Ellen White conducted a week of spiritual emphasis on the campus, during which she stressed the importance of Bible study. "The college at Battle Creek," she reported in a written account of her visit to the campus, "was established for the purpose of teaching the sciences and at the same time leading the students to the Saviour, whence all true knowledge flows. Education acquired without Bible religion is disrobed of its true brightness and glory."[13]

An effective management of student life was also difficult. Because neither a cafeteria nor dormitories existed the administration could successfully supervise student activities very little beyond the class schedule. For much of the time students fended for themselves in a small community of perhaps six or seven thousand citizens.

Facing these circumstances, the faculty who were reluctant to design a work and study program found themselves facing innovations of another kind. College officials clamped down with strict social restrictions, extending a strong arm into students' off-campus activities. They denied men and women students the privilege of socializing and threatened them with severe reprisals if they violated the rules. To maintain this social code the school had to depend on the cooperation of families with whom the students lived. The result was not always satisfactory, but the school held the upper hand.

In an attempt to monitor students, especially during the evenings, the administration instituted a proctor system which required a few selected fellow students to keep a wary eye out for suspicious behavior anywhere they could see it and report their findings to school authorities. This ill-fated system disintegrated when the students themselves rebelled after discovering that an especially aggressive proctor was using the system to conceal his own questionable extra-curricular activities at night. Even with the proctor system gone, the college still imposed strict controls. Some expulsions occurred.

Food service was another problem. To investigate a point in nutrition in his physiology class, the ever inquisitive Dr. Kellogg contracted with a group of six male students to limit themselves to only two meals a day consisting of no more than a pound of cooked food per meal. The experiment was to last four months.

One of the six, D. W. Reavis, a Missouri farm boy who later became a church spokesman for religious liberty, confessed to "a constant, unappeased appetite," but admitted that Kellogg proved his point that one could maintain good health on smaller amounts of food than were commonly believed necessary. After this experiment Reavis helped to organize a Boarding Club, a group of students contributing to a fund to buy food which a community member would prepare for them. Such clubs became a common means for students to arrange their meals.[14] The college bulletin repeatedly described in the best possible light the lack of college-owned housing and the absence of an effective food service for students, but for all of the explanations, most students and thoughtful Adventists saw the situation as a weakness.

In all fairness Ellen White had not called for dormitories or cafeterias in "Proper Education." Her statement was an elaboration on ideas, ideals, and beliefs. She did not comment on the specific details of administration as they might affect building design, the size of the campus, the number of teachers needed to constitute a faculty, and similar issues. She referred to long hours of restricted activity for children, not the precise amount of time a child should remain in a classroom. She spoke of the need for ventilation, fresh air and light, not the ratio of window space to the square footage of a classroom. She declared the benefits of agricultural labor and study, not a specific number of hours students should work or the amount of land needed to accomplish designated jobs.

Applications of the principles she enunciated were all matters that school planners and administrators would have to infer. Notwithstanding her lack of enthusiasm for the location of Battle Creek College, many of her reforms were possible on the tiny campus. The school could be heated and ventilated well, and by good planning teachers could develop daily programs to comply with ideas in "Proper Education."

It was at the post-elementary levels of instruction that the major breakdown occurred and it took only a short time to demonstrate the school's deficiencies. Despite the absence of specificity in "Proper Education," even casual readers could justifiably doubt the feasibility of combining extensive manual labor with study in a day school such as Battle Creek College. Also, depending on the community to maintain the institution's social code was precarious at best.

### Battle Creek College: an Experiment

As the first test case in Adventist philosophy of education, Battle Creek College produced mixed results. From the day it had opened in 1874 the school was an experiment in Adventist education. Although the Whites and other founders were not in doubt about the institutional mission to prepare church workers, the curriculum did not square up well with the church's employment needs, which rendered the school's purpose somewhat unclear.

Ellen White's "Proper Education" implied that Seventh-day Adventists should establish a new kind of elementary school. A teacher-preparation curriculum at the college, called by its nineteenth-century term, the "Normal course," attracted a large number of students, but nearly all of them opted for public school teaching when denominational church schools failed to materialize. With their slender resources, the majority of Adventist congregations probably did not see their way clear to initiate small schools and employ a cohort of newly educated teachers. Students could easily interpret the circumstances to mean that at Battle Creek College they could prepare for a job, but not necessarily with the church.

In his motion before the 1873 General Conference session, James White called for a school that would train workers with language competencies to spread Adventism among non-English-speaking people. But the language classes floundered for lack of interest by the students. Rather than degree programs, White and other church leaders envisioned abbreviated, intensive courses to prepare employees for a variety of assignments in different places, but productivity was low. Also, a program to prepare men for pastoral ministry fell below expectations.

During the 1870s two emphases characterized Adventist education. The first was a continued neglect of elementary schools in favor of the college. The second was curricular, a traditional college degree in the classics in spite of the proclaimed purpose of preparing denominational employees. In spite of this deficiency, the records show that scores of Battle Creek students found their way into church work.

The school also maintained an administrative fiction in the presidency. Emmett K.VandeVere has pointed out that James White was recognized as the *de jure* president until 1880, but he protested, explaining that he was not a college-educated person and should not hold the job. His travels, his frequent illnesses and his church administrative duties as well as his obligations to the denominational publishing enterprise prevented him from exercising direct authority over the daily college program, although he strongly influenced financial practices, discipline and new programs. White may have been *de jure*, but Brownsberger was the *de facto* president.[15]

Brownsberger's lack of compatibility with the theme of "Proper Education" proved to be his undoing. Losing his grip on his program, he did not complete the 1880-1881 year, but resigned in the spring. In mid-May the board appointed an acting president for the remaining weeks of the academic year.

Not all of Brownsberger's woes were of his making. No one questioned that one of the primary objects of the school was to prepare workers, but no one seemed to know how to make it a priority item on the school's agenda or how to formulate a college program to fulfill the ideals of "Proper Education." Still a young man when he became head of the denomination's first college, Brownsberger clung to what he knew best, the pattern of the classic education, but as time transpired, he found himself increasingly in agreement with Ellen White's philosophy. As the president of Healdsburg College the next year after he left Battle Creek, he found renewed energy to implement the aspects of education that had eluded him in Michigan.

What appears to have disturbed Ellen White was that neither the school administration nor the board generated the resourcefulness to go the extra mile in trying to inaugurate the principles of a distinctive Adventist education. When the college president expressed his reluctance to implement a manual labor program, the board repeatedly appeared disposed to acquiesce to his inaction to save his academic pedigree for the school rather than to hold him accountable.

Brownsberger may have ended his career in Battle Creek on a discouraging note, but despite the flaws of the school, the college was far from a failure. No one could deny that the institution had at least partially fulfilled its purpose. Students of the 1870s entered church employment, some of them becoming recognized church leaders. While pointing out weaknesses at Battle Creek College, especially in discipline, Ellen White declared in 1880 that the school "would be one of the greatest means ordained of God for the salvation of souls." This was not only a prediction, but a present reality. "We have seen a good work done in the salvation of many who have come to our college," she said.[16]

### The Alexander McLearn Debacle

Before the college board could turn the school around, matters worsened. Brownsberger's departure opened up a search for his successor, but no satisfactory candidate was in sight. Small wonder that when the recently converted Dr. Alexander McLearn appeared at a June 1881 camp meeting, Adventist leaders believed that they were blessed by divine intervention. McLearn was fifty years old, a product of Newton Theological Seminary, and held a D.D. degree. He was an experienced clergyman who knew his profession well and he brought the necessary academic credentials to Battle Creek College, the anticipated training center for pastoral careers.

James White reacted immediately. "We should be pleased to see him holding a position of importance in the cause," he wrote in the columns of the *Review*.[17] In July the college board appointed him president to succeed Brownsberger. Spalding observes that "no greater mistake could they have made."[18]

McLearn's strong will was exceeded only by his unfamiliarity with Adventist mores. By December Battle Creek College was in shambles. The faculty were divided, the students in open rebellion, and the community in an uproar. McLearn's exemplary sermons did not compensate for his fights with Goodloe Harper Bell, the acknowledged founder of the school, or for the fact that he pitted students against the traditionalists by relaxing the social code.

Only days before McLearn took office, Ellen White had warned that because of the difficulties at the college, tongues were wagging in Battle Creek and emotions were running high.[19] In December 1881 she returned to the campus from California to attend a General Conference session, and from the desk in College Hall she read a fifteen-page indictment of college leadership. The faculty had lost control of the students. Criticism from the community was rife. An effective manual labor program was absent. But her chief complaint was the loss of institutional vision. The purpose of the school was lost. Instead of placing biblical instruction first and emphasizing ministerial education as was originally intended, school administrators were still promoting a traditional college education.

Ellen White did not disparage general knowledge or urge its removal from the curriculum, but she saw the distinctiveness of Adventist education emerging from the centrality of biblical studies. "God's purpose has been made known that our people should have an opportunity to study the sciences and at the same time to learn the requirements of His word," she repeated in 1877. "Biblical lectures should be given; the study of the Scriptures should have the first place in our system of education."[20]

At the vortex of the conflict were Bell and McLearn. The new president's liberalizing policies, especially affecting the social code, were the particular target of Bell's antagonism. When the board responded by seeking a truce between the warring factions of the faculty, the students produced an impasse by throwing their weight into the battle, primarily in support of McLearn.

Until this point in the struggle the board, led by Uriah Smith, stood by McLearn, the established leader of the college, who could not have been unaware that his days were numbered. A peace proposal from the board turned the tables by favoring Bell. Shortly, the trustees asked for resignations from McLearn and a couple other faculty members. Though officially dismissed they kept on with their duties anyway and the board practically washed its hands from the crisis, leaving the school to rock on unsteadily to the end of the year.

During her visit to the college in December 1881 Ellen White read both praise and censure for Bell. After he suddenly left the college in February 1882, the battle subsided. At the end of the school year McLearn also left. In vain the board sought for a new president. Finally, in September 1882, George I. Butler, the General Conference president, announced that Battle Creek College was closed.[21]

The first chapter in the history of Adventist education ended ten years after Ellen White published "Proper Education." Facing the ruins of Battle Creek College in 1882, a few discouraged Adventists issued a failing grade to Bell and Brownsberger, and to Uriah Smith as well, the acting board chairman whose dark role in the debacle was anything but exemplary.

But Ellen White was less reactive. To Bell and Brownsberger and their experiment she gave an incomplete instead of a failing mark. In her statement to Adventist leaders in December 1881, nine months before the college shut down, she indicated that she was already thinking in terms of an Adventist system of education and its distinctive characteristics. Her eye was on the future.

At the time Adventists were experiencing an educational stirring. Before McLearn had finished his year at Battle Creek, Brownsberger was already in California to head Healdsburg Academy, which developed almost immediately into Healdsburg College and later, Pacific Union College. In his new role he demonstrated that even the most devoted protagonist of classic education could convert to a worker-preparation program that included dormitories and industrial education. Also, within weeks after he left Battle Creek, Bell journeyed to Massachusetts, founding South Lancaster Academy, a school that would become Atlantic Union College.

The break at Battle Creek College was both philosophical and practical. Bell and Brownsberger were frequently at opposite ends philosophically, but they worked together because of their commitment to a higher goal, the belief that Adventist education could and should be effective and beneficial to the church at large. During the years these two men led the school it was never so far from the ideals of "Proper Education" that Ellen White and other church leaders completely lost hope. Although they were obviously disappointed in Battle Creek College, they always saw the school in the context of what it could become.

The McLearn experience also taught Adventist educators that established leadership and even the most revered members of college boards are not always the source of reliable advice and wise decision. Within two months after James White recommended Alexander McLearn for a position of authority, Ellen White buried her husband in Oak Hill Cemetery. He did not live to see the havoc that his poor judgment helped to cause. It was a bitter lesson, but from that experience Seventh-day Adventists learned that the philosophical and spiritual commitment of institutional leaders was never to be taken for granted.

Wise heads among Adventists saw the first ten years of their experience in education as a time of groping, often learning by trial and too much error. It was an education in itself. Adventists looked back upon their Great Disappointment in 1844 as the occasion that prompted them to question what went wrong with their understanding of Scripture. Somewhat analogous to that experience was the closure of Battle Creek College, an institution into which they had poured their money and on which they had built their hopes. This time they knew what had gone wrong. Their most serious challenge lay in finding someone to repair the damage.

---

[1]Information about early Adventist schools is scarce. Two sources are Walton J. Brown, compiler, *Chronology of Seventh-day Adventist Education* (Washington, D. C.: Department of Education of the General Conference, 1972), pp. 7, 8 and E. M. Cadwallader, *History of Seventh-day Adventist Education*, 3rd ed. (Lincoln, NE: Union College Press, 1958), pp. 5-8. Two other valuable summaries are Mary Kelly-Little, "Development of the Elementary Schools of Seventh-day Adventists in the United States." M.A. thesis, University of Washington, 1932, and George Ashlock, "The Establishment of White Seventh-day Adventist Elementary Schools in the United States, 1853-1900." M.S. thesis, University of Tennessee, 1959.

[2]*Review and Herald*, September 19, 1854.

[3]*Ibid.*, August 20, 27, September 3, 1857.

[4]Emmett K. VandeVere, *The Wisdom Seekers* (Nashville: Southern Publishing Association, 1972), p. 16. This history of the evolution of Andrews University has furnished much of

the material in this chapter. Other invaluable sources are the essays in George R. Knight, ed., *Early Adventist Educators* (Berrien Springs, MI: Andrews University Press, 1983).

[5]*Ibid.* p. 15.

[6]*Ibid.*, p. 18.

[7]Arthur L. White, *Ellen G. White*, v. 2, *The Progressive Years* (Washington, D. C.: Review and Herald Publishing Association, 1986), pp. 341-343.

[8]Ellen White's 1872 statement, "Proper Education," may be read in its entirety in *Testimonies to the Church*, v. 3, pp. 131-160.

[9]For a summary of Ellen White's evolving philosophy of education, see George R. Knight's "Ellen G. White" in *Early Adventist Educators*, pp. 26-49.

[10]One can summarize reform in American education from any reputable textbook dealing with the history of education or even standard college American history textbooks. For a short synopsis see George R. Knight, "The Transformation of Education," in *The World of Ellen G. White,* Gary Land, ed. (Washington, D. C.: Review and Herald Publishing Association, 1987), pp. 161-175. Also useful is Knight's *Myths in Adventism* (Washington, D.C.: Review and Herald Publishing Association, 1985), pp. 31-36.

[11]The story of the transition from the Select School to Battle Creek College is told well by VandeVere, *ibid.*, pp. 18-26. See also A. W. Spalding, *Captains of the Host* (Washington, D.C.: Review and Herald Publishing Association, 1949), pp. 443-447, and Arthur L. White, *ibid.*, p. 375.

[12]Spalding, *ibid.*, p. 449.

[13]Ellen G. White, *ibid.*, v. 4, p. 274. For a succinct description of the curriculum at Battle Creek College during the Brownsberger years, see Joseph G. Smoot, "Sidney Brownsberger" in Knight, *Early Adventist Educators*, pp. 78-82.

[14]D. W. Reavis' account of the proctor system and eating habits at Battle Creek are found in his memoir, *I Remember* (Washington, D. C.: Review and Herald Publishing Association, n.d.), pp. 85-90.

[15]VandeVere, *ibid.*, p. 27, 29. This detail about White's presidency of the college seems to have been either lost or ignored by church chroniclers. The *Seventh-day Adventist Encyclopedia* lists Brownsberger as the first president of Battle Creek College, beginning in 1874.

[16]Ellen G. White, *ibid.*, pp. 419, 423. See Smoot, *ibid.*, for a balanced view of Brownsberger's developing philosophy of education.

[17]James White's statement is quoted in Arthur L. White, *ibid.*, v. 3, *The Lonely Years*, p. 188. There is some question about McLearn's conversion. Arthur L. White says in *ibid.*, p. 188, that "McLearn only recently had been baptized as a Seventh-day Adventist." VandeVere in *ibid.*, p. 42, categorically denies that McLearn was ever baptized as a Seventh-day Adventist. Spalding, in *ibid.*, p. 15, says Adventist leaders welcomed McLearn as "an educator who had recently joined their church," which clearly implies baptism. Richard Schwarz in *Light Bearers to the Remnant* (Mountain View, CA: Pacific Press Publishing Association, 1979), pp. 130, 131, declares that McLearn never became a Seventh-day Adventist.

[18]Spalding, *ibid.*, p. 450.

[19]Arthur L. White, *ibid.*, p. 189.

[20]Ellen G. White, *ibid.*, v. 5, pp. 21-36; Arthur L. White, *ibid.*, pp. 187, 188.

21VandeVere provides a colorful description of the Bell-McLearn struggle in ibid., pp. 42-47. He writes another very similar account in Rugged Heart: a Story of George I. Butler (Nashville, TN: Southern Publishing Association, 1979), pp. 55-61.

# Chapter 2

# A New Direction

Battle Creek College remained empty for the entire 1882-1883 academic year. Few, if any Adventist leaders, doubted that their experiment in education needed a new direction, but probably everyone had questions about how to take the first step. Finally, in July 1883, with only weeks before a new academic year should begin, the board asked W. J. Littlejohn, pastor of the Battle Creek Tabernacle to take charge of the school.[1]

George I. Butler, General Conference president and chair of the college board, trusted him because of his strong leadership in bringing order to the 500-member church that had largely sided with McLearn and the students in the recent controversy. The Battle Creek community knew Littlejohn as a college-educated person committed to church teachings and loyal to denominational leadership. He was not Adventism's leading intellectual but church leaders viewed his scholarship as solid and reliable.[2]

Although Littlejohn was handicapped by blindness, during his two-year stint as president he enjoyed at least the beginning of a turnaround for the college. Starting with an enrollment of only eighty in 1883, the number of students rose to more than 280 before the year ended. Curricular revision emphasized denominational service. By November 1884 a hundred students had gone from the college into church employment. These were not college graduates with degrees in hand; rather, they were primarily students who had completed short, intensive courses in accounting, colporteuring, and other skills.[3]

Ellen White had scolded the college administration in December 1881 for prolonging students' education and encouraging them to spend years in their studies. "We have not many years to work," she said.[4] The new look in career preparation was a response not only to her criticism but to the desire by many other church leaders for short worker-preparation courses.

Littlejohn also tackled the question of supervising student life, a problem which had harried the previous two college administrations and made them vulnerable to community criticism. The new president used his influence as the immediate former pastor of the Battle Creek Tabernacle to extract written agreements from the congregation to support the college and to respect denominational leadership, thus closing the door to the widespread discord that had erupted from the church during the McLearn episode. Students and faculty also signed similar contracts.

To a degree the partisanship among Battle Creek Adventists was rooted in a haunting doubt about Ellen White's special role in the church at large. Reestablishing among them a commitment to her leadership was a major aspect of calming the turbulence in the community. Littlejohn played a vital role in promoting Ellen White's ministry by submitting articles to the *Review* in her defense even before he assumed the presidency of Battle Creek College.[5]

Wringing promises of cooperation from the Adventist public in Battle Creek was only part of the plan to reorganize student life. By the beginning of Littlejohn's second year a small dormitory was ready for about thirty young women whose homes were not in Battle Creek. Male students lived in college-owned houses or other private homes. The college also began to provide food service, in fact, the new administration required all students, whether residents of the community or living in college housing, to eat in the cafeteria located on the ground floor of the dormitory. Students were charged the cost of two meals a day.[6]

All of these changes in management notwithstanding, the conundrum for Littlejohn and the board continued to be the manual labor program. With no exception, Ellen White regarded the centrality of biblical studies in the curriculum as the centerpiece of Adventist educational reform, but from the outset she had promoted manual labor as a means to maintain physical health and mental alertness. In December 1881 she urged college leaders to acquire land connected with the college on which to establish farming and other projects that would enable the faculty to combine labor and formal classwork.[7]

*W. W. Prescott, president of Battle Creek College, 1885-1894, brought discipline to both academic and student life. He became the first General Conference secretary of education in 1887 and later served in editorial and administrative positions of the church. He briefly headed Avondale College in Australia.*

But access to land eluded college leaders. Repeatedly during Littlejohn's two-year presidency, the board voted to install small-scale industries and shops on the campus. Limited attempts followed to integrate manual labor into the curriculum, but in spite of the rhetorical forcefulness of board actions, the president seemed almost as helpless as Brownsberger to make these changes.

Despite this failure, Littlejohn satisfied Adventists that their venture in higher education was both effective and supportable. By the end of his two-year administration he brought peace to the troubled community and made sufficient modifications in the program to restore confidence in the school and its purpose. In July 1885 he returned to the pastoral ministry, leaving Battle Creek College in the hands of William Warren Prescott, a young editor-publisher from New England.

### Prescott's Reforms at Battle Creek College

The similarities between the new president and Brownsbeger were striking. Prescott was only thirty years old, about the same age as Brownsberger when he took over Battle Creek College in 1874. Ironically, Prescott's college degree was in the classics, as was Brownsberger's, which had been a source of curricular problems. Prescott also held a master's degree, but it was a conferred rather than an earned credential.[8]

But contrasts between the new president and those he followed were equally striking. Prescott brought a more powerful personality to the campus than any of his predecessors and the effect was almost instantaneous. His were years of progress on several fronts, but it was an uneven growth and not always what he wanted. A case in point was the ongoing problem of how to design a satisfactory manual labor program. Additional buildings during Prescott's first year provided more classrooms and space for vocational instruction, but this yet unrealized feature of Adventist education continued beyond the grasp of the faculty despite persistent board recommendations to institute it.

Like Brownsberger, Prescott did not know where to begin, but he was willing enough to try and to improvise if he needed. He inspected other institutions where the work and study plans appeared to be successful, but all of his attempts were futile at Battle Creek. To make matters worse, parents resisted the idea. Eventually students took the issue into their own hands and organized a massive debate about manual labor which resulted in striking it from the curriculum.

But students did not easily stymie Prescott. In place of a productive manual labor program the college required students to work a minimum number of hours caring for the school plant. This compromise was only a part of what Ellen White had envisioned, but it was better than nothing at all. For all of her admonition and the best intentions of the college board and institutional leaders, the question of an effective blend of work and study was the nemesis of all presidents of Battle Creek College.

The demise of the manual labor program led to consequences that Prescott wished he could have avoided. To burn up student energy and to promote health he set up a gymnasium in the basement of an addition to the main building and required students to spend one class period per day doing exercise routines. For their part, students were more interested in intramural games, primarily baseball and football. Sometimes the events became extramural.

A local journalist reported one hotly contested game in a Battle Creek newspaper, which in time reached Ellen White's desk in Australia. Prescott soon received a reprimand from her, warning against "matched games." Duly chastised, the president agreed to alter the school's recreation program, but he wanted to know what she meant by matched games. In a clarifying statement Ellen White explained that she did not intend that students should play no games at all, but that recreation should have a productive objective, and games producing sharp competition and high-pitched emotions should not be on the schedule.

By some measurements, the most profound impact Prescott had on the character of Battle Creek College was the discipline he injected into student life. While still upholding strict institutional prohibitions on courting he focused on other more positive aspects of campus living to promote order and decorum. By the time he reached the campus in 1885, enrollment had regained its pre-1882 levels, and he determined to reorganize student life by providing adequate institutional housing and to improve the food service. Two years into his presidency women students had a new dormitory that also housed expanded dining facilities. The older women's boarding hall underwent remodeling and became a men's dormitory.

Acquiring ideas from other private schools that had successful dormitory organizations, Prescott and his wife and another staff member developed the notion of school homes which students were to treat with as much dignity and respect as their own houses. In the cafeteria they would learn the etiquette of refined dining as a large family, including assigned seating and the services of hostesses. Paternalistically, Prescott and his wife set the example by dining regularly at a table in the center of the cafeteria where all students could see them.

For Battle Creek these changes were revolutionary. They did not stop at the edge of the campus but exerted a far reaching influence on Adventist education at large. "It was a plan," states Gilbert M. Valentine, Prescott's biographer, "that would eventually characterize Adventist schools around the world as Prescott proteges from Battle Creek took the idea to new schools and colleges."[9]

Another aspect of student life was the spiritual atmosphere of the campus. Pursuing the idea of a school home, the president required all students to attend daily worships in the chapel. He was the usual speaker. Frequently he also led the Friday vespers and Sabbath afternoon "social meetings," a term describing gatherings devoted to personal public testimony. Each evening the directors of the school homes provided a twenty-minute silent period intended to encourage personal meditation and prayer. Prescott's wife, Sarah, commonly known as Sadie, sometimes conducted evening worships and spent many hours mixing with students. During the Prescott presidency scores of students were baptized.

### Reform in Biblical Studies

As his years at Battle Creek College advanced, Prescott became increasingly sensitive to Ellen White's challenge to make biblical studies central to all curricula. The 1888 General Conference session at Minneapolis furnished the impetus for change which Prescott wanted. A new understanding of righteousness by faith and a view of Jesus and His substitutionary death as the focal point of all Christian belief and doctrine swept through Adventism, causing many to feel that they had poorly comprehended the meaning of Christianity. Ellen White's dictum that young men should not try to explain the Scriptures to others before they thoroughly understood them themselves took on new meaning.

Although Prescott's positive reaction to this new theological emphasis was not immediate, he shortly grasped its impact. Two and a half years after Minneapolis he organized the first churchwide gathering of educators and church leaders at Harbor Springs, Michigan to discuss the implications of theology on curriculum planning. About 100 attended to hear A. T. Jones and John Harvey Kellogg join the president of Battle Creek College in presenting a thoroughgoing review of Scripture as well as to discuss its applications to education. Ellen White also took a leading role at the conference.

Ten years later P. T. Magan, who attended the Harbor Springs meetings as the history teacher from Battle Creek College, wrote that the beginnings of an "educational reformatory movement owe their birth to this gathering."[10] The results of the discussions were detailed recommendations for a four-year ministerial training course and a four-year sequence of history classes that presented history from a biblical perspective. The plan also proposed a series of college-level Bible classes that covered the entire Bible and all Adventist doctrines with Christ as the central figure.

Church leaders had commonly urged young preachers to enter pastoral work with only abbreviated preparation. For years Battle Creek College had sought to compensate for ministerial deficiencies by offering inservice sessions, but the Harbor Springs recommendation for a four-year ministerial course elevated pastoral training, which was seen as professional education, to be equivalent to a college degree and gave the church its first systematic approach to preparing ministers.

The teachings of A. T. Jones and E. J. Waggoner, who had championed the cause of righteousness by faith at Minneapolis, now found their place in all college studies. In effect, these history and Bible classes that the Harbor Springs convention recommended were equivalent to what North American colleges and universities would later term general education, a core program that provided a common breadth to all degrees. The recommendations about the centrality of the Bible also made biblical studies a generic issue in Adventist education.

For more time than Prescott hoped these recommended changes were only on paper, but even in that form they were more than Adventist education had previously experienced. In order to make room for biblical studies in all curricula at Battle Creek College other classes would have to go, most notably the classics. From 1891 to 1894 a fired-up Prescott urged his teachers to integrate the Harbor Springs recommendations into their curricula, but they were reluctant, motivated by a fear that they would weaken the higher education quality of their program. Bible classes remained optional until 1894 when curriculum planners added Bible to existing programs without dropping anything, thus lengthening rather than revising them.

In 1894 Battle Creek College became twenty years old. Prescott dominated the second of those two decades and brought about dramatic change in Adventist education. Building upon what his immediate predecessor had accomplished, he edged the school forward, but not as rapidly as he wanted nor as far as Adventist ideals contemplated. He inspired a professionalism that Adventist education lacked before he settled in Battle Creek. He was a member of professional organizations and he consulted other colleges and encouraged his faculty to learn from them. With a view of raising academic standards he sent selected faculty to a recognized teachers' college for advanced preparation. Under his leadership traditions and practices began that gave a distinctive character to Adventist schools for years to come. Although the campus had practically given up on vocational education and a viable ministerial preparation program still awaited the church, a new direction was clearly in sight.

Adventist leaders knew that shortcomings still plagued Battle Creek College, but to the non-Adventist public, the school was something of a showpiece. In May 1891, two months before the historic meeting at Harbor Springs, a three-man delegation from the Michigan State Board of Visitors inspected the campus. Their report to the state superintendent of public instruction was short, but filled with applause for Prescott and his faculty.

Since the day Brownsberger confessed that he knew nothing about a manual labor program school leaders chaffed under the consciousness that they had not fulfilled one of the most salient aspects of educational reform expected of them. Perhaps the visitors from the state of Michigan assuaged their guilt by praising the cleanliness of the school and the commitment of students to the ideals of the institution. They did not overlook the fact that students had a sense of ownership because they contributed so many hours to the general upkeep of the campus.

Church leaders fretted because the Bible was not central, but the visitors noted that Scripture "in some form is extended through all the grades from the most elementary to the most advanced. It is a feature, so far as our experience goes, that is unique . . . At first sight it might appear that Battle Creek College is endeavoring to bring the Theological School down into the College and Preparatory School grades."

Members of the college board and other church leaders were unhappy with the curriculum, claiming that the presence of the classics produced a secular atmosphere and an emphasis on mundane values. The three men who probed the campus were not impressed with the academic rigor of the program, but they admitted that the students were not shortchanged. They observed that "the students of this Institution will never learn from their instructors the modern ideas of the power of money. In this respect the School cannot be said to belong to this age."

The Board of Visitors pointed out that a long-standing issue in American education was to determine how much instruction in Christian morals a school could impose on students without violating their individual rights. Their one-day visit was only a glimpse of how Battle Creek College faculty dealt with this question but they saw enough to comment that "a closer inspection of their experiment may prove that they are solving [it] for us all."

A final observation expressed a characteristic of Adventist schools that has never ceased to amaze North American accrediting bodies through to the twenty-first century. In appropriate ecclesiastical terminology the Board of Visitors quipped, "When we learned the meager salaries the Institution could afford to its instructors, we felt that the age of the martyrs had returned."[11]

The report may have been gratifying in some respects, but Adventist leaders realized that they measured their schools by a different set of values and purposes than those the state superintendent of public instruction understood. As much progress as Battle Creek College had enjoyed, in their view it still fell short. During the 1890s events were closing in around the Michigan campus that foreshadowed a climax to the struggles over the feasibility of the Adventist philosophy of education at Battle Creek College.

### The Sutherland Era at Battle Creek College

By the time Prescott vacated his office in 1894 in favor of George W. Caviness three other Adventist colleges were in operation, all to the west of Battle Creek. Healdsburg College in California, begun in 1882, Union College in Nebraska in 1891, and Walla Walla College in 1892 were all creating their own versions of Adventist education. In addition, South Lancaster Academy in Massachusetts, operating since 1882, was gaining a reputation in the East.

The Michigan school dwarfed the others as measured by enrollment, but the most conspicuous difference was that none was cramped onto a tiny campus as was Battle Creek. No one claimed that any one of these four schools was a perfect representation of "Proper Education" and its later elaborations, but all of them were developing programs that Battle Creek College seemed unable to accomplish. Also, in matters of making the Bible central to all study, in vocational education, and in short worker-preparation courses some students could find opportunities more to their liking elsewhere than at Battle Creek. By the mid to late 1890s both students and church leaders were making comparisons among the schools which did not always leave Battle Creek in the most favorable light.

What Emmett K. VandeVere calls the "Revolution of 1897" was the first step that brought matters to a head on the Battle Creek campus. Because Caviness did not aggressively pursue change church leaders became disenchanted with his leadership. Before the end of his third year he resigned, making room for E. A. Sutherland, a young, energetic man who had already served three years as president of Walla Walla College.

The board selected Sutherland specifically to reform Battle Creek. His success was astonishing. In rapid order curricular change finally eliminated the classics course, the Bible became central to the curriculum in reality as well as on paper, and an eighty-acre farm a mile from the campus developed into a place where students could engage in manual labor. Lecturers from non-Adventist mission projects and other schools where manual labor was integrated into the program stimulated students' loyalty to the concept of combining work with their commitment to missionary service.

There were more changes. A revival lit new spiritual fires among the students. Since 1874 hundreds of workers had left the college to hold down denominational positions, but the rate picked up sharply under Sutherland even though enrollment declined. Educating church employees became the major objective of the school. A revamped teacher-preparation course became the source of a wave of church school teachers who were rewarded with opportunities to work in Adventist elementary schools that mushroomed prolifically around the circle of Adventism.

Sutherland cooperated closely with A. T. Jones and Dr. John Harvey Kellogg in reorganizing the school to resemble the original ideas in "Proper Education." From the beginning days of Battle Creek College Kellogg's primary burden was to carry out the aspects of Ellen White's philosophy of education that pertained to health and hygiene, including diet and the manual labor component of the curriculum. But he saw Battle Creek Sanitarium as a legitimate fulfillment of the labor principle and depended increasingly on student labor. He viewed the college farm with mixed feelings because it would drain off some of his workers. Jones' target of reform was biblical studies, including ministerial education.[12]

But in Sutherland the board got more reform than it bargained for. It was not long before some Adventists began to raise their eyebrows when looking at some of his changes. To express his concurrence with the idea that students in Adventist schools should have agricultural work, he, with a couple of colleagues including P. T. Magan, personally plowed up the part of the campus used as an athletic field to make room for a garden. The new president scorned some academic procedures, which resulted in the neglect of students' records and a rejection of baccalaureate degrees as unnecessary academic baggage for church workers.

Prescott had sent several faculty to recognized schools for advanced studies in elementary education, but Sutherland did not see the issue in the same light. The reform-minded president dismissed the elementary education faculty because he believed the very ones Prescott had sponsored at the University of Buffalo and other places were tainted by exposure to non-Adventist philosophies.[13]

With somewhat of a condescending air toward other Adventist colleges the president wanted to develop Battle Creek College into *the* advanced Bible school for the church. Accordingly, he unofficially changed the name of the school to Training School for Christian Workers, but the new designation did not stick.

The school paid a price for these changes. Enrollment dropped about 200 after Sutherland's first year. By the end of his second year the curriculum no longer conformed to the school's charter. Even Ellen White intimated that the president tended to extremes, although she saw the basic direction of reform as beneficial.

Meanwhile, both Sutherland and P. T. Magan, the dean of the college, were planning to move the school to a location more congenial to a genuine manual labor program. Their desire to relocate stemmed at least partially from a growing concern in church administrative circles about the general atmosphere in Battle Creek where many felt institutionalism was smothering the spiritual vitality of the church. The two educators looked upon the prospective move as the school's salvation.

**Adventist Educational Philosophy and Berrien Springs**

In a rapid sequence of actions Kellogg agreed to buy Battle Creek College and the General Conference in session voted on April 12, 1901 to move the school. In July, sixteen freight cars moved the equipment and records of the school to Berrien Springs in the southwestern corner of Michigan. On a 272-acre plot on the bank of the St. Joseph River they reestablished the college, renamed Emmanuel Missionary College to convey the new spirit of the campus.

It is difficult to separate the move from Battle Creek to Berrien Springs from Ellen White's philosophical statements about education, upon which she continued to elaborate. In 1900 her son, Willie, observed that during the preceding two years she had written more than in all her previous experience about the principles of education, the importance of Bible study in schools and combining labor and study with agriculture as the foundation of Adventist schools.[14]

While in Australia during the 1890s her staff organized her writings about education for publication. In 1901 some appeared as section three of volume six, *Testimonies for the Church*, which reiterated many of the ideas she had broached nearly thirty years earlier. But her writing showed the evolving effect of time and experience as she cautioned school administrators to maintain financial integrity of their institutions and discussed the spiritual character of school homes. Neither of these issues existed when she wrote "Proper Education" in 1872.

Ellen White's teachings about education did not emerge from a state of prophetic isolation. While she left no doubt that divine revelations inspired her writing, she also read contemporary literature for information and additional ideas. In 1899 she wrote from her Australian home at Sunnyside to her son, Edson, to send some of her books to her from Battle Creek, among them a set of Bible commentaries and other volumes that, in his judgment, would be helpful to her, adding, "I would appreciate Horace Mann."[15] Specifically which of Mann's works she owned she did not say.

In 1899 Horace Mann had been dead for forty years; meanwhile, social sciences had developed and pragmatism had become the prevailing educational philosophy. Ellen White did not indicate how much she derived from nineteenth-century educational thought, but from her reading she better understood the principles of education that she first espoused in "Proper Education" and was able to elaborate more relevantly upon them and give a peculiarly Adventist shape to educational philosophy. Ideas that Adventist schools held in common with Mann included moral values as part of classroom instruction, the inherent right of every person to an education, the participatory character of classroom activities, and the uplifting benefit society received from an educated public. Adventist educators of her time were able to recognize both the similarities and differences between her pronouncements and contemporary philosophy.

She urged the proliferation of church schools, which had become much better defined entities within the church. She relied on the example of the school farm in Australia to support her descriptions of the role of a labor program. Expressed in the vocabulary of her time are ideas about mentoring, the democratic nature of education demonstrated by a policy of open admissions, and the social responsibility of Adventist schools in preparing people to enter private society.[16] She had come to realize that not every student would, or should, become a denominational employee.

In 1903 Ellen White published *Education* in which she explained how biblical principles should pervade an entire curriculum. Prepared for a non-Adventist reading audience as well as church members, it became the most widely read treatise on Adventist education circulated by Seventh-day Adventists. For decades it was the foundation of college classes dealing with principles of Christian education. A later volume, *Counsels to Parents and Teachers*, published in 1913, was intended primarily for church consumption. What she published near the end of her life about education reveals that her ideas evolved into a much more comprehensive–but not contradictory–view of education than when she wrote "Proper Education" in 1872.

There is little question that Ellen White and the Adventist community agreed that the location of Emmanuel Missionary College would enable Sutherland and his faculty to produce a school more nearly like her descriptions than what the institution at Battle Creek had turned out to be. By the time the college moved, her philosophy about education had crystallized in its broadened form. For her, relocation was a philosophical issue that overrode all other considerations.

Since 1898 Sutherland had urged a change in location but Ellen White had demurred. But at the 1901 General Conference session she threw her weight behind the proposal to move, even though she realized that student enrollment would probably decline even more in a new location and that the sale of Battle Creek College would bring in little money to pay for a new beginning. Describing Battle Creek as "too congested," she urged the delegates to "get an extensive tract of land, and there begin the work which I entreated should be commenced before our school was established here."[17]

Transferring the college was more than a philosophical question. During an early morning conversation with P. T. Magan on the day the vote occurred, Ellen White intimated that "great things will soon be happening in Battle Creek."[18] Delegates to the General Conference session who voted that same day to move the school had already approved proposals that would reorganize the administrative structure of the entire church. Transferring the college was the first step in dismantling the institutions at Battle Creek and moving the church headquarters elsewhere. A new era for Seventh-day Adventists was in the making.

Reincarnating Battle Creek College as Emmanuel Missionary College also ended direct supervision of the school by the General Conference. Actually, the General Conference began to relinquish its legal control in 1899 as the board struggled to liquidate institutional debt. Finally, in 1906 the final step was taken to name what would become the Lake Union as the parent organization.

Between 1882 and 1892 four other major Adventist schools opened their doors in North America, but the focus of Adventist attention had remained on Battle Creek College. This first Adventist school had begun as an enterprise by the General Conference, and as long as it existed in Battle Creek, it always operated in the shadow of church leaders who treated it paternalistically as theirs to maintain. Other Adventist schools did not experience a similar relationship, although Union College operated as a General Conference institution for thirteen years after its founding.[19]

Realizing all of this, perhaps Sutherland had a measure of justification to suggest that Battle Creek College should be officially at the top of the pack. But the facts disclosed that while Battle Creek College may have been a General Conference school, pragmatically, it was really a

*Union College opened its doors in 1892. This school has the distinction of being the only Seventh-day Adventist college in North America which began as a four-year, degree-granting institution and has occupied its original site during its entire history.*

regional institution. Seven years before the move to Berrien Springs 451 of its 716 students originated in Michigan and another 151 came from six neighboring states.[20] With concentrations of Adventists growing in other parts of the country additional schools became necessary. As a relocated college, Emmanuel Missionary College relinquished its preferred status and functioned on a more nearly equal footing with the other major Adventist schools in North America.

Even though clouded by its erratic history, Battle Creek College played an important role as the first leading venture in Adventist education. The fact that reform was always on the surface indicated that the school did not live up to its original billing. No one knew this better than Ellen White; however, she also saw the school for its positive contributions and she praised Sutherland and Magan for their attempts at change. "You are not to think that you have made a failure in the school," she told them.[21]

In the main, the philosophical debate that engulfed Battle Creek College turned on the question of its Adventist character, defined by the three issues of the centrality of the Bible in its curricula, preparation of church workers and an organized agricultural labor program. The reformers held the conviction that an agricultural setting that offered labor opportunities to students was the best environment for a school that trained workers, primarily ministers, teachers and office workers such as bookkeepers and city mission workers. Influential leaders did not believe that lengthy courses were necessary for these prospective church employees.

Attempts to provide industrial and agricultural work were spasmodic, but the students were not all idling their time away. Many worked at Battle Creek Sanitarium and the Review and Herald Publishing Association, and a large number helped to maintain the school itself. Some argued that labor was, indeed, a part of life at the college. While this was true, it was also true that the students' labor was not a component of the college program as Ellen White described it, which made all of the difference to those who promoted reform.

Adventist education was both pragmatic and idealistic. Hardly any educational program could have been more pragmatic than the belief that education should emphasize health and working skills which are critical for physical survival. Adventist educators in the nineteenth century were not the only ones who believed in this principle, but they taught it within the context of a divine plan of redemption, and thus the pragmatic character of education became idealistic. Nothing could have been more philosophically idealistic than basing an education on the belief that humans need spiritual redemption because they have fallen from the perfect state in which God created them and that schools are to serve the mission of the church–spreading the good news of redemption–rather than to become ends in themselves.

In 1901 a major chapter in the debate over Adventist philosophy of education ended, but questions still remained. The expanding horizon of the Adventist world presented a demand for an ever-widening circle of schools, and as events were to unfold, the story of Battle Creek College was only an introduction to a never-ending discussion about how best to fulfill the meaning and purpose of denominational schools.

---

[1]VandeVere, *The Wisdom Seekers*, p. 48. This volume is a major source for the material in this chapter as is Knight's *Early Adventist Educators*.

[2]Arthur L. White, *Ellen G. White*, v. 3, *The Lonely Years* (Hagerstown, Md: Review and Herald Publishing Association, 1984), pp. 220-223.

[3]VandeVere, *ibid.*, p. 50.

[4]Ellen G. White, *Testimonies to the Church*, v. 5, p. 22.

[5]Arthur L. White, *ibid.*, 222, 223.

[6]VandeVere, *ibid.*, p. 49, 50. Arthur L. White, *ibid.*, p. 223.

[7]Ellen G. White, *ibid.*, p. 23.

[8]For information about Prescott's years as president of Battle Creek College see VandeVere's *Wisdom Seekers* and Gilbert M. Valentine, *The Shaping of Adventism* (Berrien Springs, Mich: Andrews University Press, 1992), pp. 1-83.

[9]Valentine, *ibid.*, p. 28.

[10]The *Review and Herald*, August 6, 1901, carried Magan's statement which is quoted in large part in VandeVere, *Windows*, p. 172.

[11]VandeVere includes the complete report in *ibid.*, pp. 125-127.

[12]Richard Schwarz casts doubt on Kellogg's support of Sutherland's reform at Battle Creek College. See his *John Harvey Kellogg, M. D.* (Nashville, TN: Southern Publishing Association, 1970), p. 97.

[13]VandeVere, *ibid.*, p. 81.

[14]Arthur L. White, v. 4, *The Australian Years*, p. 450.

[15]Letter 243, 1899, p. 2, EGW Estate.

[16]Her entire discussion is found in Ellen G. White, *Testimonies.*, v. 6, pp. 126-218.

[17]Arthur L. White, *ibid.*, v. 5 *The Early Elmshaven Years*, pp. 92, 93.

[18]In *ibid.* Arthur L. White quotes this statement from the *Founders' Golden Anniversary Bulletin*, 21, of Andrews University.

[19]Everett Dick, *Union, College of the Golden Cords* (Lincoln, NE: Union College Press, 1967), p. 26.

[20]VandeVere, *ibid.*, pp. 58, 59.

[21]*Ibid.*, p. 91.

# Schools With Special Missions

From the beginnings of Adventist education above the elementary level the question of ministerial education was the driving factor in the design of schools. Battle Creek, Union, Healdsburg and Walla Walla colleges and South Lancaster Academy were all founded with the denominational worker in mind, mainly but not limited to ministers. On these campuses the general Adventist student as well could acquire an education, and in this sense they were generic schools.

But in facing a multi-faceted world Adventists found it necessary to develop a variety of educational institutions for specific clientele. Nineteenth- and early twentieth-century schools with specific missions included correspondence schools and institutions for immigrant children, mission schools in the American South for both Blacks and Whites, and professional programs for ministers, physicians, and persons entering health-related fields. While ultimately all of these schools held to the same essential philosophy as the generic institutions, their immediate purposes were more specific and conversely, less general.

## Ministerial Education

Although it came about gradually, a denominational sensitivity for professionalism began to emerge roughly coincident with the founding of Battle Creek College. In the mid-1870s Adventists were still a tiny group, but leaders with foresight realized that publishing and health-care enterprises could not function without professionally trained personnel. Similarly, a more education-conscious leadership sensed that zeal alone was not enough to qualify a person to preach. Not everyone concurred but leading lights in the church admitted that too many Adventist ministers lacked the professionalism which the public associated with men of the cloth. In a short time ministerial education became a prime concern.

James White, who early on had been content to allow aspiring ministers to teach themselves the skills of the pulpit, saw matters differently by the mid-1870s. His was the strongest voice promoting Bible institutes for ministers where they could hear some of the denomination's leading personalities lecture on prophecy and practical questions in the pastoral profession. Sometimes these gatherings coincided with general church meetings, such as the General Conference in session; sometimes the meetings convened at the college.

One of the early assemblies took place in conjunction with the dedication of the newly constructed Battle Creek College in 1875. About 150 responded to a general invitation to attend the month-long meetings.[1] Another occurred in the spring of 1877 in Oakland, California and featured Uriah Smith as the primary speaker with both James and Ellen White also discussing biblical and professional issues.[2]

A similar institute in November 1879 paralleled the General Conference session at Battle Creek. The lecture topics suggested that Adventist ministers lacked more than a familiarity with biblical issues and that lecturers did not intend to let the 112 attendees get by lightly. Besides the usual biblical instruction, teachers drilled the pastors daily on such rudimentary matters as penmanship, English grammar, rhetoric and "elocution." John Harvey Kellogg, the twenty-seven-year-old director of Battle Creek Sanitarium, took his turn with presentations on health reform, hygiene and physiology.[3]

The issue of ministerial education gathered momentum in the 1880s. Willie White confided to W. W. Prescott in 1888 that many Adventist preachers were deficient in good judgment but even so, some conference presidents and members of denominational committees opposed plans to improve the professionalism of ministers through education.[4]

White was not alone in his misgivings. In 1889 his mother called publicly for an "intelligent, educated ministry, not novices." Because of a progressively upward trend in educational standards generally, ministers will face challenges, she went on. "Too much haphazard work has been done, and minds have not been exercised to their fullest capacity." She further urged "higher ideas of education and of employing more trained men in the ministry."[5]

In the same statement she urged that selected young men "could, if so counseled by our leading brethren, enter the higher colleges in our land, where they would have a wider field for study and observation. Association with different classes of minds, an acquaintance with the workings and results of popular methods of education, and a knowledge of theology as taught in the leading institutions of learning would be of great value to such workers, preparing them to labor for the educated classes and to meet the prevailing errors of our time." While visiting Norway two years earlier in 1887 she participated in a resolution expressing the same counsel.[6]

The implications of this advice were profound. Church educators could rightly infer that Adventist education did not exist in a vacuum and that administrators of Adventist colleges could not provide all the advanced studies that their faculty would need. As levels of scholarship heightened and professional studies became more academic, leaders of denominational schools could anticipate increased dependence on institutions with recognized reputations to supply their professional needs. Ellen White's advice was the denomination's first official recognition that education in reputable non-Adventist schools would be necessary to educate some denominational leaders. Translated into twentieth-century terms, it meant graduate education and terminal degrees.

With his Dartmouth education Prescott did not need to be convinced about professional enhancement. In response to Willie White's recommendations he inaugurated a rigorous in-service curriculum for ministers at Battle Creek College that would last the equivalent of two quarters.[7] Known as the Ministers' Bible School and sometimes called an institute, this program amounted to an abbreviated seminary. Instruction began in the winter of 1889 with twenty-week classes in biblical languages, church history, church governance, logic and civics, besides several classes in biblical studies. Administratively, the Ministers' Bible School was not part of Battle Creek College but a separate entity controlled directly by the General Conference.

More than 150 registered for the first set of classes, with later figures reaching as high as 300. In 1893 the college erected a new annex to house the institute. This unexpectedly high enrollment indicated that many Adventist ministers not only recognized how professionally deficient they were, but that they intended to quench their thirst for professionalism in spite of negative attitudes in some circles.

Prescott planned the Ministers' Bible School well, but it was doomed on two counts. It got off to a bad start when the faculty immediately began feuding over theology, incited in part by Prescott's openly favorable stance on E. J. Waggoner's and A. T. Jones' beliefs about righteousness by faith. After Prescott brought Waggoner to the campus to teach, Uriah Smith and Dan T. Jones, the General Conference secretary, supported by the former church president, George I. Butler, created a wall of opposition that aroused far more animosity than biblical understanding.

Ellen White calmed the storm, but after she learned about the plans to build additions to the college plant she spoke out disapprovingly. She had no quarrel with the classes but disagreed with the decision to pour more money into college buildings when other fields needed schools. Construction on what came to be known as the North Addition continued, however, since her advice arrived on Prescott's desk too late to stop the building project. Prescott had felt comfortable with the institute because he believed that a twenty-week period of concentrated study met her definition of short courses that she had proposed for ministers from the beginning, but she pointed out that Prescott intended the institute for pastors already in the field and that the classes kept too many pastors away from their congregations for long intervals. Churches were suffering.[8]

Professional education to upgrade Adventist ministers already in pastoral positions halted after 1896, two years after Prescott left Battle Creek College. By that time a much more developed ministerial curriculum was evolving at the college, and other Adventist schools were also turning out ministers, but these programs did not help the pastors who were already employed and needed professional upgrading. The problem of how to educate a professional ministry continued to plague Adventist leadership for nearly forty more years until a formal seminary began.

### Schools for Immigrants

Another serious education issue related to the shiploads of immigrants who sought a new life in North America after the American Civil War. Many of them came in response to promises from railroad operatives to resettle them on cheap land in the Midwest. Among German and Scandinavian colonies in that region of the United States Adventists generated sizeable communities, in fact, they constituted the larger part of church activity in states from Kansas to the Dakotas. Immigrants conducted church services in their own languages and frequently held separate camp meetings.[9]

In 1885 a string of schools for Germans and Scandinavian minorities sprang up in Chicago, Milwaukee, Minneapolis, and Ottawa, Kansas. Among others, two prominent Adventist names associated with these schools were L. R. Conradi and J. G. Matteson. All of these schools shared a common abortive end, but they brought the international flavor of the church home to Adventists in the United States. When the Ministers' Bible School began in 1889, separate classes for German, Scandinavian, and French pastors also met. Two years later in 1891 the programs for German and Scandinavian students moved to Union College where each section was known as a department. Battle Creek College housed the French students.[10]

Most of these students spoke English in addition to the languages preserved in their homes, but many of them were losing command of their family tongues and needed language instruction to evangelize among the communities fed by an immigrant flow that showed no sign of slowing down. Some of the faculty for these language groups at Union College prepared themselves by study in both Denmark and Sweden. The different ethnic groups lived in segregated dormitory space at Union and the library accessed holdings for each language. Practically speaking, Union College was to be several colleges in one.[11]

This arrangement did not function as effectively as its designers hoped. Segregation of the student body into language groups was never

*This photo, taken from a metal etching, shows Hutchinson Seminary, the boarding school for Danish-Norwegian students in Hutchinson, Minnesota. The seminaries for Adventist students from Scandinavian and German immigrant communities offered both secondary and post-secondary classes, but declined during the 1920s and disappeared by the mid-1930s.*

meant to be complete but nevertheless, its net effect was to fragment the college. Encouraged by Ellen White, concerned church leaders began plans to establish three new free-standing institutions, one for each language group. In 1910 the Union College programs for immigrant students ended.

Clinton Theological Seminary in Missouri for Germans, Hutchinson Theological Seminary in Minnesota for Danish and Norwegian students and Broadview College in Illinois for Swedish speakers all opened as predominantly secondary level institutions but they also offered post-secondary courses in worker-training programs. Although their programs were never completely exclusive of English, over the years these schools offered hundreds of Adventists of immigrant heritage an opportunity to preserve their cultural roots and to receive an education to work among their own people while at the same time helping them to accommodate to America.[12]

These schools reached their zenith in the mid-1920s but faded rapidly. In 1925 Clinton merged with Broadview; three years later in 1928 Hutchinson followed suit, creating a multi-language campus at Broadview College. This consolidation lasted until 1934 when all the post-secondary courses moved to Emmanuel Missionary College and Broadview became a secondary school. Immigrant schools vanished.

The strongest factor in their decline was the diminishing number of immigrants who stopped coming during World War I and never resumed their pre-war level after the conflict ended. New immigration laws during the 1920s further choked off the flow of newcomers. Particularly devastating to Clinton Theological Seminary was a virulent anti-German sentiment in the United States during the war. The schools also faded in part because most of the younger generation tended to assimilate into American life. A shrinking constituency ended the need for separate schools which had already lost much of their European identity.[13]

Concentrated in eastern Canada and the New England states, with small pockets elsewhere, the French-speaking constituency in North America was smaller than either the German or Scandinavian. The original French department at Battle Creek College eventually moved to South Lancaster Academy and in 1914 to Buena Vista Academy (later known as Oshawa Missionary College) in Ontario, Canada where its support dwindled. Similar to the other immigrant programs, it ended in the 1930s. Small Russian departments operated temporarily in academies in the north central states.[14]

## Origins of Oakwood College

One minority group that Adventists could not overlook was the African-American population, officially freed from slavery but still a victim of deep-seated prejudice and hemmed in by institutionalized segregation. In 1891 Ellen White addressed the General Conference session in the Battle Creek Tabernacle with a call she entitled "Our Duty to the Colored People," arguing that the plight of American Blacks cried out for relief.[15]

But the next year a train of events began that made any attempt to fulfill this appeal even more difficult. Beginning in Louisiana in 1892, a race-relations debate erupted, finally reaching the United States Supreme Court in 1896 as the *Plessy v. Ferguson* case. By an 8-1 decision on May 18 the justices issued the "separate but equal" doctrine, which stated that the Louisiana law prescribing accommodations for Blacks to be equal but separate did not violate the United States Constitution. The case arose from public transportation, but shortly the ruling found applications in nearly every aspect of American life. Pragmatically, the court's ruling made segregation the law of the land.

One of the most notorious examples of segregation was education.

In 1895 Edson White, the older of the two sons of James and Ellen who survived into adulthood, responded to his mother's appeal by starting small schools for African Americans as part of his ministry in Vicksburg, Mississippi. Enrollment reached nearly a hundred.[16]

But bigger things were also happening for African Americans. Moved by Ellen White's urging and the advancements of Adventism in the American South that had been underway since the 1870s, the General Conference Committee commissioned O. A. Olsen, president of the General Conference, George Irwin, who directed church work in the South, and Harmon Lindsay, one of the founders of Battle Creek College, to locate a site for a school for Blacks.

The year was 1895. After the three men scoured Tennessee, they followed the suggestion of C. M. Kinney, the first Black ordained as an Adventist minister, to proceed to a farm in Huntsville, Alabama, where they found 360 acres shaded in part by beautiful oak trees but also covered with underbrush that had gotten out of hand. The large mansion was in disrepair and slave cabins still stood nearby. The men bought the property after the real estate agent's mother, who had been a patient at Battle Creek Sanitarium, helped to reduce the price by a thousand dollars.

Dubbing the place Oakwood, Olsen and Irwin went to work to convert the farm into a boarding school. The two men literally donned their overalls, mixed mortar, repaired and plastered walls in the deteriorating mansion, remodeled and added new rooms, plowed fields, and cleared out the overgrowth to make way for crops. Others pitched in, among them Solon Jacobs from Iowa, who became the first principal. A visit to Booker T. Washington's Tuskegee Institute in Alabama confirmed their conviction that they should integrate a heavy component of vocational education into the program.

Even before school officially began, Jacobs' son and daughter were already teaching night classes. When school officially started on November 16, 1896, the school had four serviceable buildings and a faculty of four. Sixteen students showed up. Within a couple of months enrollment rose to thirty-eight, including fifteen day students. Some of the early enrollees came from Edson White's school in Vicksburg. Students attended classes in the morning and spent the afternoon working for tuition, room, and board. Agriculture and construction trades filled the young men's schedules; the young women devoted their time to skills in homemaking and gardening.

Not all the neighbors were happy about these events. The idea of a school for Blacks on the outskirts of a town of about 15,000 opened up old, festering wounds. Still fresh in the memories of locals were images of Reconstruction and northern carpetbaggers. In their eyes Jacobs fit that description well, but he gave his edgy neighbors pause for thought when he organized his students to help them out of their difficulties on their farms. Prejudice slackened off.

*The print shop at Oakwood Manual Training School. In addition to a productive agricultural program, this institution offered industrial education, including training in printing.*

By 1899 Oakwood Industrial School was offering two-year diplomas for students who completed the formal curriculum, but the stress was still on agriculture and skilled trades, including blacksmithing. New buildings went up, erected largely by student labor. The campus became a monument to student diligence.

When the new century turned, dormitory students at Oakwood numbered more than fifty. Nearly half as many again had to be turned away for lack of room. In 1904 the institutional name changed to Oakwood Manual Training School and thirteen years later it became a two-year college.[17]

Louis A. Hansen, who helped to establish Adventism in the South, noted that during the early years of the century Oakwood's farm produced thousands of bushels of vegetables and other food, including sorghum, all of which helped to stock the school's larder. But the success of the school was not measured by its agricultural output, as productive as it may have been. By 1918, Hansen states, nearly all of the Black church workers were graduates of Oakwood. Ten out of fourteen graduates in 1914 entered denominational employ. By 1917 an impressive number of African Americans had continued their studies in medical missionary education. From the outset there had been little doubt that the school was there to stay.[18]

### An Appraisal of Schools for Minorities

Compared to generic institutions in Michigan, California, and other places, schools for minorities in the nineteenth and early twentieth centuries differed by their focus on a narrower constituency rather than a narrower purpose. The two objectives of providing an education in an Adventist context and training workers were paramount at Clinton, Hutchinson, Broadview, and Oakwood. All four schools inaugurated vocational education, but the agricultural program at Oakwood was the most noteworthy and productive. Founders of the German school at Clinton advertised the seminary as an industrial school, but its vocational achievements fell far short of its original billing.

Providing schools for immigrant groups and descendants of Black slaves attested to the conviction that principles of Christian education were not alien to concerns such as social acceptance and upward mobility. Emmett K. VandeVere has reminded us that while the schools for immigrants did not endure, they were successful because they denominationalized a generation of European newcomers to the United States, cultivating a sense of belonging to something in their new land.

Adventist schools for immigrants were not unique. During the years that Union College housed the German and Scandinavian departments nearly 13,000,000 immigrants disembarked in United States ports. In

1910, the year that the three Adventist institutions for European immigrants opened their doors, close to fifteen percent of the United States population was foreign born, the highest proportion during the twentieth century. By this time the majority of newcomers came from eastern, southern, and central Europe and settled in urban centers in America.

In the open society where they found themselves it was not unheard of for resourceful immigrants to form their own schools, but some did not attend school at all. Americans viewed these conditions as an opportunity. Helped by compulsory-attendance laws, public schools became one of the most effective mechanisms to Americanize the children of the millions who were flocking to this new land.

Adventist immigrant schools achieved a similar end but by different means. Their purpose was to denominationalize students while Americanizing them. By providing a forum in which immigrants could retain a modicum of their traditions they enabled new citizens to practice and promulgate their faith in a bi-cultural setting. L. H. Christian, a member of the Scandinavian community when the Adventist immigrant schools operated, points out that a large proportion of students became prominent denominational workers.

If this is true about settlers from Germany and Scandinavia, an even stronger case can be made for Blacks at Oakwood. Regarded at the time as the flotsam and jetsam of American society, Blacks in the South had made little progress after their emancipation, in fact, some saw their condition worse in some ways in the 1890s than before the Civil War. Ron Graybill, church historian and one-time member of the White Estate, suggests that race relations were visibly worse during the early years of the 1900s than when Edson White first docked the *Morning Star* in Vicksburg in 1895.[19] Not only did Oakwood's original program conform well to Ellen White's 1872 statement, "Proper Education," few could deny the social impact from its concentration on both formal and vocational education.

In the Adventist world itself, the spread of denominational education into the Black population of the American South represented more than just a new school. In the Adventist mind it was something akin to establishing a mission in the West Indies or perhaps Africa. After a trip through Tennessee and Alabama in 1904, which took her to Oakwood

Industrial School, Ellen White wrote that "efforts should be made to educate and train colored men and women to labor as missionaries in the Southern States of America."[20] Her twenty-eight-page message closed with an appeal to which she gave the title "The Needs of a Mission Field."

While she applied the term "missionary" to all witnessing ventures, in a series of ten articles written during 1895 and 1896 Ellen White portrayed the South as a mission field where the predominant ethnic, climatic, and social characteristics differed from those with which Adventists generally were familiar. It was a field, she said, where the work may be too "taxing or debilitating" for some.

After landing in Vicksburg, Mississippi in 1896 to begin a medical missionary program, Louis Hansen and his wife found sanitation and other conditions primitive at best. "Needing a fountain syringe, we supposed that all we had to do was go to the drugstore and buy one," he wrote. "But there was no drugstore, and if there had been one, the fountain syringe would have been an unknown item."[21]

The needs Ellen White described were as real as though the region lay on the opposite side of the globe. Near the turn of the century she appealed to the church to give more spiritual attention to the people of the South, referring to them as "our neighbors."[22] About the same time she stated that because of slavery and its aftermath many people in the South were as "ignorant as the heathen."[23] In a special message concerning literature for the South, she cautioned publishers to prepare books wisely. "The South is a world of its own," she reminded them.[24]

Ellen White sometimes applied her descriptions of the South to the White population, sometimes to the Black, and sometimes to both, but the ring of her appeal was unmistakable: Blacks had suffered at the hands of White authority, and it was time to stop pointing fingers of blame and go to work to undo the mischief that more than two centuries of shameful treatment had inflicted. Education would be a key factor. The church's obligation was as clear as the calls from the farthest corners of the earth and just as "missionary."

Visualizing the South in this manner belied the fact that the Seventh-day Adventist Church in the 1890s and early 1900s was a creation of the American North. In a sense, the South, although politically connected to the rest of the country, was Adventism's nearest and first mission and Oakwood Industrial School, born in the heartland of racial prejudice, was as much an educational beacon as were Adventist schools in non-Christian lands.

## The Self-Supporting Movement

Seeing the American South as a mission field also provided a context for schools for Whites. Following the Reconstruction period after the Civil War the governments of southern states furnished only scant money for public education. Illiteracy was rampant among poor Whites. It was a textbook opportunity for "missionary" endeavor in the Ellen White sense of the word. During her visit through the South in June 1904 as she churned up the Cumberland River aboard the *Morning Star*, she spotted a 400-acre farm near Nashville, Tennessee that she recommended for a school, despite its mediocre land.

The land was bought and an independent corporation, the Nashville Agricultural and Normal Institute, was organized as its legal owners. Plans for the school began immediately. The enterprise was to be separate from direct denominational control, a self-supporting institution, but would function in cooperation with the church rather than as a rival project. Among the first board members was Ellen White herself. Reputedly this was the only occasion when she consented to serve as a board member of any Adventist school.

E. A. Sutherland and P. T. Magan from Emmanuel Missionary College were among the search party for the land. They and Emmanuel Missionary College were suffering from a serious case of mutual disenchantment, partly because Sutherland encouraged reform faster than his constituency could acclimate to it. Tension was high as the school year drew to an end in 1904, and both men resigned to cast their lot with the gaining movement to establish self-supporting schools in the South. With them went a band of nine faculty and students from EMC, equally interested in becoming a part of the experiment. Among them were Bessie DeGraw and Nellie Druillard, both of whom became legendary figures in the story of Madison College and Sanitarium, as the self-supporting institution on the Cumberland River came to be known.

This experiment near Nashville was not the first Adventist school in the South. A dozen years before Sutherland and his entourage fled Emmanuel Missionary College, G. A. Colcord from Oregon, equally committed to missionary adventure, opened a small school in Graysville, Tennessee, hardly more than a hundred miles southeast of Nashville. By the time the Nashville Agricultural and Normal Institute organized, Graysville had become a boarding institution with an adjacent sanitarium and was the recognized worker-training institution in the South. In 1916 the school moved to a large farm east of Chattanooga and became Southern Junior College, another generic institution.

But the Nashville Agricultural and Normal Institute did not seek to duplicate or compete with Southern Training School at Graysville or its successor, the junior college. It aimed at a completely different student market, mainly the poor, semi-literate rural population of the South, mostly in the mountains, for whom better health and improved agricultural methods were critical. Sutherland believed that these people could not afford a formal education but were willing to work for it.

Sutherland became the first president of the Nashville Agricultural and Normal Institute in 1904. Only eleven students were on hand for the opening day of classes, an inauspicious beginning and not even a shadow of the impact the school would have on the South. Ellen White explained that this campus would become a hub of training for teachers who would fan out over the southern states, establishing similar smaller schools in which agricultural instruction would be a priority topic in addition to Bible study and health.

Time demonstrated the proof of the Sutherland-White pudding. A sanitarium went up and a nursing program began. Smaller units sprouted up elsewhere, thirteen by 1909. Eventually forty campuses in the hinterlands of the South patterned themselves after the Madison model. The programs were all similar, coordinating formal learning with large components of agriculture and an emphasis on health. During the 1920s the Madison campus launched college-level courses.

In 1915 P. P. Claxton, United States Commissioner of Education, complimented Sutherland and his colleagues at Madison for their contributions to the well-being of the American South. Declaring that one of the great needs of the region was schools tailored to the conditions of

*The first board of Nashville Agricultural and Normal Institute posed for this picture in 1904. Seated, left to right: W. C. White, Ellen G. White, Mrs. J. E. White, J. E. White. Standing, left to right: C. C. Crisler, P. T. Magan, Minnie Hawkins, Nellie Helen Druillard, W. E. Sutherland, Sarah McInterfer.*

the people they served, he said that the teachers of the rural schools "have discovered and adapted in the most practical way the vital principles of education too often neglected."[25]

The Madison experiment was only one of several practical adaptations of education in the South, but it was Adventism's contribution in resolving a national dilemma. Even though it appeared to be a nostrum for the educational ills of the South, some church leaders viewed it with misgiving. As an independent institution, Madison subsisted on donations and other money the school generated through its own enterprises. While grateful for the benefit Madison was to the church, some Adventist leaders suspected that many donors gave funds to the self-supporting program rather than to officially designated projects.

Sutherland never intended Madison to be anything but an institution that supported the church. He visualized small self-supporting units throughout the South as mission projects that would establish an Adventist presence in many places where traditional evangelistic methods would have been ineffective. He knew the church could not afford to operate these units, but in 1908 the local conference voted to assist Madison with a $19,500 appropriation. Despite this show of cordiality, it was ironical that Sutherland and his associates, who deliberately designed the program not to drain funds from denominational coffers, did not enjoy the full approbation of Adventist leaders.

Part of the problem was philosophical. The chemistry of Madison's autonomy and Sutherland's commitment to reform produced less than a stable mix. It was almost unavoidable that some interpreted Madison as more orthodox to Ellen White's philosophy of education than denominationally owned schools. Sutherland's loyalty to the church was never in question, but an undercurrent of suspicion evolved between the self-supporting establishment and the church over the theology of education.

A General Conference committee appointed to study this ambiguous relationship recommended in 1915 that the official church and self-supporting institutions work more cooperatively in fund raising, management, and student recruitment. The Autumn Council of that year adopted the recommendations and relations improved. At the world convention of Adventist educational leaders and teachers at Colorado Springs, Colorado in 1923, a representative of the self-supporting movement argued persuasively about the role the self-supporting institutions played in satisfying the needs of the South, which he described as an economically disadvantaged region. His report received equal billing to reports from other world fields, but the reality of separateness continued to haunt both sides of the dichotomous situation. Teachers were free to shuttle back and forth from denominational to self-supporting schools, but the time they spent in the Madison system did not accrue for retirement benefits.[26]

It was well into the post-World War II era when changed economic conditions overtook the self-supporting establishment. Southern Junior College, which became Southern Missionary College in 1944, was flourishing with a growing system of secondary feeder schools. A rising standard of living throughout the South reduced the demand for self-supporting schools and increasingly, the self-supporting schools assumed the academic character of their denominational counterparts.

Conferences took over the management of some self-supporting schools while others closed. Falling on hard times, Madison College itself defaulted to denominational control, but in 1964, after one year of new management, its post-secondary program ended while it continued as a denominational day academy for the Greater Nashville area.[27]

The self-supporting concept declined but did not die. By 1970 only a handful of secondary schools remained a part of the movement, but they were stronger and continued to attract a loyal clientele. With Madison College gone these schools continued as less expensive alternatives to denominationally owned academies and became a part of the feeder system to denominational colleges.

A new wave of independent schools appeared in the late 1970s, but they bore only token if any relation to the mission mindedness of the original self-supporting movement born on the banks of the Cumberland River in 1904. Motivating many of the new campuses were separatist theological goals that were deliberately competitive to the denominational establishment and which inflicted a divisiveness to the North American church.

## Health Education

Another major strand of Adventist education appearing in the nineteenth century consisted of a variety of professional programs in health and medicine at Battle Creek. All of them revolved around Ellen White and Dr. John Harvey Kellogg.[28]

Both of these leaders envisioned a combination of health ministry and evangelism as the gospel in action. From 1864 onward Ellen White issued a steady stream of messages promoting this idea. In 1876 a youthful Dr. Kellogg, recently graduated from Bellvue Hospital Medical College in New York and newly appointed medical superintendent of the Western Health Reform Institute, took immediate steps to fulfill her advice. While Battle Creek College was the recognized school to prepare denominational workers, Kellogg began to convert the Health Reform Institute into a parallel center for education in health sciences. Officially changed to Medical and Surgical Sanitarium, the institution became popularly known as Battle Creek Sanitarium.

As a member of the instructional faculty of Battle Creek College, Kellogg offered courses in health and hygiene and taught private class-

*Posing in front of Dr. J. H. Kellogg's home in Battle Creek is the first group of Seventh-day Adventist physicians to graduate from the University of Michigan at Ann Arbor after taking pre-med at Battle Creek. The date was 1895. This curricular sequence was the forerunner of American Medical Missionary College, founded at Battle Creek, also in 1895.*

es to students interested in entering medical school. Always a dynamic presenter, he stirred up enough interest in health to announce in 1877 that the sanitarium would begin a School of Hygiene. He left little doubt about his purpose to unite medical care and evangelism. "Sickness is everywhere," he said, "and there is no more successful method of removing prejudice than to be able to enter the sickroom and relieve the afflicted."[29]

Between seventy and eighty students enrolled for the twenty-week course which began in January 1878. In addition to general treatment and remedies for illness, students studied anatomy, physiology, chemistry, physics, and "mental philosophy." Immediately, talk started about the possibility of offering medical degrees, but Kellogg quashed such ambitious rhetoric, explaining that his course was not a school of medicine. Medical schools commonly lacked effective instruction in hygiene and only at best, his graduates might be able to teach such classes. Hundreds of students went through the School of Hygiene during the few years that Kellogg kept the course going. Many of them spent entire careers in medical missionary work, which was in keeping with Kellogg's original intentions.

Although Kellogg received most of the accolades, others assisted in developing health education programs, among them Dr. Kate Lindsay. After a short career in nursing, she enrolled in the University of Michigan School of Medicine, graduated at the head of her class in 1875 and joined the medical staff at Battle Creek. Known as Dr. Kate, she and Kellogg convinced the sanitarium board to establish a school of nursing in April 1883. An anemic response prompted a second call for students in October. Meanwhile Dr. Kate, the acknowledged founder of the nursing program, doubled the length of the course to six months, and after the first cohort of students graduated, she increased it to two years.

Kellogg had little to do with the Nursing School, leaving Dr. Kate and another physician, Ann Stewart, to conduct most of the classes. Ever mindful of the ideal of medical missionary work, Lindsay left Battle Creek in 1895 to join the medical staff at Claremont Sanitarium in Cape Town, South Africa.

But an impatient Kellogg was not satisfied with these successes. In 1888 he and his wife initiated another project, a School of Domestic Economy, which corresponded to later home economics courses. The twenty-five week course was designed for girls and focused on personal hygiene and homemaking skills including cooking and tailoring according to principles of health.

Kellogg intended to repeat the course twice annually, but the Health and Temperance Missionary School which he inaugurated the next year absorbed the School of Domestic Economy. In effect, this new missionary training program also revived the former School of Hygiene and combined it with a growing denominational interest in combating alcohol and tobacco. For ten years the Health and Missionary School turned out practical nurses, health lecturers, experts in healthful cooking, and other personnel trained to promote physical well being. Specific courses lasted up to a year. The purpose was to provide evangelistic and health education workers for the growing number of treatment rooms and clinics outside the United States as well as inside, particularly the American South.

Through these educational activities as well as medical care that the sanitarium offered, Kellogg developed an international reputation as an apostle of healthful lifestyle. A list of patients and guests at the sanitarium included national politicians, captains of industry, and leading personalities in a variety of professions and in the arts and sciences.

### An Adventist School of Medicine

Kellogg's crowning educational act came in 1895 when he created a school of medicine, American Medical Missionary College. The idea of educating Christian physicians had been in the making for more than twenty years. In 1872 Ellen White issued a call for doctors who would practice their profession in the spirit of reform that had motivated the church to establish the Western Health Reform Institute. Thirteen years later she described the work of a physician as critical to the total ministry of the church.[30]

During the years between these two statements Kellogg promoted medicine, first by teaching pre-med classes informally for students planning to attend medical school and then offering a more organized pre-medical course. By 1885 he had prepared about twenty students to enroll in schools of medicine. Frequently these Adventist medical students spent their summers working at the sanitarium, which was a means for them to maintain a connection with the denominational health-care program.

One of Ellen White's primary concerns was the spiritual aspect of medical ministry. It troubled her to encourage students to study medicine at secular institutions where she felt they would risk maintaining their commitment to Adventist principles of health reform. In 1889 the church announced a plan to give financial assistance to medical students, both men and women, who would commit themselves to a career in medicine, but the response was small. Suddenly in 1891 matters changed when thirteen men and seven women signed a pledge to support health principles that Ellen White propounded and promised after graduation to engage in medical ministry as the General Conference prescribed. After completing pre-med courses at Battle Creek, they entered medical school at the University of Michigan at Ann Arbor, about seventy-five miles east of Battle Creek.[31]

Battle Creek Sanitarium provided a large dwelling in Ann Arbor that served as a rooming house for Adventist medical students, supervised by a small staff. On Sabbaths they conducted their own Sabbath school and church services, and during off hours on week days they acquired clinical experience by engaging in medical missionary work. Church leaders from Battle Creek kept a paternalistic eye on the medical students, reminding them of the ideals of medical ministry and their obligation to the church.

In addition to furnishing the home, the sanitarium paid the tuition and fees for those in this cohort of future physicians who could not afford the cost of a medical education. The church had never gone to comparable lengths to educate ministers. This show of support was a tacit message that the church regarded medical ministry to be crucial to Adventism and, despite its high price, was willing to spend the funds necessary to promote it.

To provide additional clinical experience for medical students Kellogg founded a dispensary in Chicago in 1893. About 700 received medical attention during the first five weeks of its operations. A second dispensary broadened medical students' training even more, but despite these successes, church leaders led by Ellen White were still nervous about the medical education itself.

In June 1895 the denominational agency in charge of health, the Seventh-day Adventist Medical Missionary and Benevolent Association, decided the time had come to establish a Seventh-day Adventist medical school. Events moved rapidly. The next month, in early July, the Illinois legislature granted a charter to American Medical Missionary College, frequently abbreviated to AMMC. Kellogg was its president. Plans called for a four-year course divided between Chicago and Battle Creek Sanitarium. On October 1, 1895, about four months after the initial decision, forty-one medical students began their studies in the new school.

Although Ellen White had been urging for a viable medical ministry led by physicians consecrated to Adventist principles of health reform, to some extent Kellogg derived his inspiration for medical missionary work from his acquaintances in New York, primarily George D.

Dowkontt. An English-born doctor who had devoted his life to international medical missionary efforts, he headed the International Medical Missionary Society, an organization that influenced many medical students to work in New York City missions similar to those Kellogg later established in Chicago. By 1894 Dowkonnt's society sent more than eighty doctors to India, Africa, and China.

Hardly had American Medical Missionary College begun before church leaders detected what they regarded as ominous danger signs. A year after the school opened, Kellogg dropped "Seventh-day Adventist" in favor of "International" in the title, "Medical Missionary and Benevolent Association." In 1898 he announced that AMMC was unique in that it was the only school of medicine in the United States whose purpose was to produce medical and philanthropic workers without sectarian control.

While its drift away from denominational control was becoming more apparent, American Medical Missionary College continued to function with moral support from the church. But by 1907, the year that Kellogg's membership in the church ended, the church ceased to recognize it as a Seventh-day Adventist institution. Excellent performance by graduates of AMMC on the Illinois State Board examinations helped to pave the way for the school's admission to the Association of American Medical Colleges, but administrative problems developed, and in 1910 it closed, officially merging with Illinois State University. During its fifteen-year life more than 185 students graduated with medical degrees.

Since its founding in 1866 the Western Health Reform Institute and its successor, Battle Creek Sanitarium, had been driven by a vision for a ministry of medical care based on health reform. Kellogg capitalized on these ideas to build a many-faceted institution, but both to its advantage and disadvantage, the future of the institution lay very much in his hands. His indefatigable leadership and his stature in the medical world were undeniable blessings to the sanitarium as it metamorphosed almost inexorably into an educational center.

That the church could lose such a critical institution pointed in part to organizational flaws. As the church evolved after its founding in 1860, semi-independent organizations developed to oversee categories of activities, such as production and distribution of literature and Sabbath schools. After 1901 these semi-independent units, with the exception of Kellogg's International Missionary and Benevolent Association, became departments of the General Conference. Under the aegis of this powerful entity Kellogg gained legal control of the sanitarium and its educational ventures and built an empire of health work that rivaled the size of all other denominational enterprises combined. As his relationship with the church deteriorated, General Conference leaders could do little to prevent what had been intended to be an educational center for health and medical ministry from becoming an independent, private project.

Kellogg's defection from the Seventh-day Adventist church was a drama that partially played against the backdrop of denominational reorganization and the church's removal from Battle Creek. Ellen White had noted the direction of Kellogg's life and profession, and in 1904 threw her support behind negotiations for a resort hotel near Redlands, called Loma Linda. A bargain price of less than $40,000, only a fraction of its value, was enough incentive to make the Southern California Conference the owner of the estate which conference leaders planned to convert into a health-care institution.

In November 1905 the newly transformed estate went into operation as Loma Linda Sanitarium. A nursing school was also part of the institution. The next year the nursing school separated from the sanitarium, broadened its offerings to include missionary training, and took the name College of Evangelists. W. E. Howell, president of Healdsburg College, became president of the new school in Southern California.

Almost immediately a few church leaders, Ellen White among them, anticipated a denominational medical school. Recalling the unlikely circumstances surrounding the purchase of the Loma Linda property, she told a camp meeting audience in Los Angeles in 1907 that God had accomplished the purchase even though "rivers of difficulties were full and overflowing their banks." Her urging continued with a special message to the 1909 General Conference session, specifically calling for an educational center to concentrate on training nurses and physicians.[32]

That same year the school changed its name from College of Evangelists to College of Medical Evangelists and received a charter to offer academic and professional degrees including nursing, medicine, and dentistry. The first class of medical students enrolled during the 1909-

1910 year and in 1914 the first class of physicians graduated. Meanwhile the sanitarium and the college merged under a single administration and the board turned to physicians to lead the expanding medical college. Drs. George K. Abbot and Wells A. Ruble, both graduates of American Medical Missionary College, served as president of CME from 1907 to 1914.

Questions about management of the medical school were crucial to church deliberations after 1909 when it became evident that more than a nursing school was in the future of Loma Linda. It was clear that the Southern California Conference, in whose name the property was originally purchased, could not afford the kind of institution Ellen White described. In a series of actions during 1910 the Pacific Union Conference in North America pledged its financial support to the medical school and agreed to participate in its management. The General Conference would be the official parent organization and would also bear some financial responsibility. In a single phrase, Loma Linda became a General Conference institution subject to direct church control. That status has never ended.

**Distance Education: a Correspondence School**

A denominational correspondence school added to the diversity of Adventist education in 1909. The roots of this enterprise reached back to Goodloe Harper Bell, who returned to Battle Creek in 1884 after two years in South Lancaster, to engage in editorial work, to write, and to teach privately. Among his projects was a correspondence school. To accompany his lessons and to inspire his students in their home study he published a small journal, *The Fireside Teacher.*[33] Correspondence classes were also among the offerings of Walla Walla College, beginning in 1897. Students had a choice of ten different classes spread across Bible, language, history, and psychology. The purpose of Walla Walla's enterprise was to enable students to acquire basic education before enrolling as college students.[34]

Frederick Griggs, head of the General Conference Department of Education, founded the denominational correspondence school in 1909 after attending an educational conference where reports of success by correspondence schools motivated him to establish a similar program for the church. In July of that year he launched the school with W. E.

Howell as principal. Within three months more than sixty students enrolled. At first known as the Correspondence School, it soon became the Fireside Correspondence School, reminiscent of Bell's *Fireside Teacher.* It was no accident that the first two principals and the first president who headed the correspondence school until 1946 had taken correspondence courses under Bell in Battle Creek.

Griggs did not see a school of correspondence as competition to existing schools. "We have workers in all parts of the world," he told the 1918 General Conference session, "who desire to continue their studies in connection with their work, as well as thousands of parents and young people whose circumstances forbid their attending one of our resident schools, but who desire to pursue their education under Christian teachers."[35] At the time Griggs reported an enrollment exceeding 1,600.

This new venture was hardly a year old before it raised questions about valid credit. At the 1923 Colorado Springs Convention C. C. Lewis, second principal of the Fireside Correspondence School, recalled that the founders of correspondence classes did not intend to provide an introduction to college as was the case of the Walla Walla correspondence classes, but an alternative to traditional education. But, "at the same time," he said, "it was inevitable that sooner or later some who had studied by correspondence would present themselves at our resident schools and desire credit for work they had done through correspondence." In 1910 the General Conference Educational Convention approved correspondence credit at face value; five years later a General Conference policy permitted students to take one half of their college or secondary graduation requirements by correspondence.[36]

Similar to many other features of Adventist education, the correspondence school was an Adventist version of an idea already in practice. In 1923, when C. C. Lewis spoke at Colorado Springs, the University of Chicago had a thirty-year tradition of correspondence classes and the University of Wisconsin enrolled 20,000 students in 500 different correspondence classes. Griggs predicted in 1918 that Adventist students were only beginning to realize the possibilities of the Fireside Correspondence School, a statement that the long history of that institution fulfilled more successfully than anyone imagined.

**Adventist Specialized Schools—an Evaluation**

The success of the first generation of specialized schools in Adventist education was uneven. From twenty-first century hindsight perhaps one of the most puzzling questions was the inability of educators and church leaders to implement a productive ministerial education program on par with the image that the profession evoked. While pastoral training may have been central to Adventist education, church leaders themselves differed on the issue of appropriate preparation. Because the demand for ministers was high in an evangelistically oriented church, expediency often outweighed professional training, and many Adventists entered pastoral work without the background that ideally they should have had.

Historically, the new medical school probably attracted the most attention not only because of its connection with the "right arm of the message" but also because it represented the most ambitious educational venture of the church. But not to be overlooked was the importance of education for minorities, especially African Americans, which expressed social implications that were in keeping with the ideals of the global mission that was developing in a church, which, in the years surrounding the turn of the century, was still emerging.

---

[1]VandeVere, *Wisdom Seekers*, p. 25.

[2]Arthur L. White, *Ellen G. White*, v. 3, *The Lonely Years*, pp. 56-58.

[3]*Ibid.*, pp. 127, 128.

[4]Valentine, *Shaping of Adventism*, pp. 42.

[5]Ellen G. White, *Testimonies to the Church*, v. 5, pp. 528, 529, 584.

[6]For a description of the Norwegian resolution see Arthur L. White, *ibid.*, 368, 369.

[7]Valentine, *ibid.*, 49-52.

[8]Valentine's and VandeVere's accounts of the institutes have provided the substance for these passages about the Bible institutes at Battle Creek College.

[9]Everett Dick, *Union, College of the Golden Cords* (Lincoln, NE: Union College Press, 1967), p. 4.

[10]Brown, *Chronology*, pp. 11-13.

[11]E. M. Cadwallader, *A History of Seventh-day Adventist Education*, pp. 277, 278; Dick, *ibid.*, pp. 26, 327.

[12]Marley Soper, "Unser Seminar," *Adventist Heritage* (Summer 1977), pp. 44-54; L. H. Christian, *Sons of the North* (Mountain View, CA: Pacific Press Publishing Association, 1942), pp. 170-182; Virginia Steinweg, *Without Fear or Favor* (Washington, D.C.: Review and Herald Publishing Association, 1979), pp. 79-88.

[13]Soper, *ibid.*

[14]*General Conference Bulletin*, 1913, no. 4, p. 59, 1922, no. 6, p. 142.

[15]Ellen White's appeal appeared first in leaflet form. It became a part of *The Southern Work* (Washington, D.C.: Review and Herald Publishing Association, 1966), pp. 9-18.

[16]See Ron Graybill, *Mission to Black America* (Mountain View, CA: Pacific Press Publishing Association, 1971), pp. 44, 45, 100, for an interesting description of Edson White's night schools in Vicksburg.

[17]Brown, *Chronology*, p. 140; the *SDA Encyclopedia,* v. 2, 1996 ed., p. 233; Schwarz, *Light Bearers,* pp. 242-244; and Charles E. Dudley, Sr., *Thou Who Hath Brought Us . . .* (Brushton, NY: TEACH Services, Inc., 1997), pp. 184-190.

[18]Louis A. Hansen, *From So Small a Dream* (Nashville, TN: Southern Publishing Association, 1968), pp. 152, 207; Dudley, *ibid.* For a broad view of Oakwood College, see *Adventist Heritage* (March 1996). The entire issue is a centennial memorial of the school.

[19]Ronald D. Graybill, *E. G. White and Church Race Relations* (Washington, D.C.: Review and Herald Publishing Association, 1970), pp. 53-69.

[20]Ellen G. White, *Testimonies to the Church*, v. 9, p. 199. A description of her visit to Oakwood is found in Arthur White, *Ellen G. White*, v. 5, p. 347.

[21]----------, *Southern Work*, p. 93; Hansen, *ibid*., pp. 14, 15.

[22]White, *Testimonies to the Church*, v. 7, p. 56.

[23]*Ibid*., p. 224.

[24] ----------, *Counsels to Writers and Editors* (Nashville, TN: Southern Publishing Association, 1946), p. 146.

[25]Hansen, *ibid*., pp. 182-190.

[26]*Ibid*.; Merlin L. Neff, *Invincible Irishman* (Mountain View, CA: Pacific Press Publishing Association, 1964), pp. 59, 72, 73; E. C. Waller, "The Rural Schools of the South and their Present Needs," *Proceedings of the Educational and Missionary Volunteer Departments of the General Conference of Seventh-day Adventists in World Convention*. Washington, D.C.: Review and Herald Publishing Association, 1923.

[27] For general information about Madison College, see Ira Gish and Harry Christman, *Madison: God's Beautiful Farm* (Mountain View, CA: Pacific Press Publishing Association, 1979). Other details are found in Arthur White, *ibid*., v. 5, pp. 340-347, and VandeVere, *Wisdom Seekers*, pp. 104-118.

[28]The major sources for this passage about health education are: Dores E. Robinson, *The Story of Our Health Message* (Nashville, TN: Southern Publishing Association, 1965), pp. 236-402; Richard Schwarz, *John Harvey Kellogg* (Nashville, TN: Southern Publishing Association, 1970), pp. 95-108; Richard A. Schaeffer, *Legacy, Daring to Care: the Heritage of Loma Linda* (Loma Linda, CA: Legacy Publishing Association, 1990), pp. 125-155.

[29] Robinson, *ibid*., p. 241.

[30]These two messages may be read in their entirety in *Testimonies to the Church*, v. 3, pp. 165-185, and v. 5, pp. 439-449.

[31] For summaries about the Adventist school of medicine, see Robinson, *ibid*., pp. 249-402, Schwarz, *ibid*., pp. 103-107, and Schaeffer, *ibid*., pp. 150-155.

[32]Ellen White's message is published in full in *ibid*., v. 9, pp. 173-178.

[33]Allan G. Lindsay, "Goodloe Harper Bell: Teacher," in *Early Adventist Educators*, Knight, ed., p. 65.

[34]Cadwallader, *ibid*., p. 266.

[35]Frederick Griggs, "Report of the Department of Education to the 1918 General Conference Session," Record Group 51, General Conference Archives and Statistics. Hereafter this source will be cited as RG 51, AST.

[36]C. C. Lewis, "Relation of the Fireside Correspondence School to Our Colleges and Academies," in *Proceedings*, p. 397.

# Chapter 4

# THE MOVEMENT OF 1897

Battle Creek College and its sister institutions were products not only of the church and Ellen White's philosophy of education but also of nineteenth century United States. It was only natural that Adventist colleges reflected many of the specific reforms with which educators were experimenting at the time. Similarly, the state of education at lower levels in North America formed a context for Adventist primary and secondary schools. To understand this educational milieu is one of the keys to an understanding of the evolution of Seventh-day Adventist education.

## North American Education, a Context for Adventist Schools

Nineteenth century America was geographically large, culturally diverse, but intellectually unfulfilled. While settlers were still taming the western wilderness, moneyed classes were creating blue-blooded cultural enclaves in eastern cities. The country hungrily adopted the technology of the Industrial Revolution before 1850 but nearly self-destructed in a violent civil war because different regions could not agree on a philosophy of nationhood. The rest of the civilized world viewed this new country whimsically, condescendingly, and sometimes warily.

American schools mirrored these conditions. Education was not well defined. Colleges issued degrees, mainly in the classics, but other than saying that college-bred people were well educated, few knew what degrees in the classics were good for in a society that had limited intellectual traditions. Agriculture was the prevalent means of livelihood, but during the latter half of the century the country rapidly industrialized. How well one could argue the niceties of classical philosophy in the office of a factory owner or a railroad magnate became irrelevant.

How students arrived in college classrooms in the first place or how they prepared for a life work was not an organized process. Schools and curricula, built on a system of neatly arranged grades, were uncommon until late in the nineteenth century. The high school, which became almost synonymous with teenagers during the twentieth century, was still an institution of the future during most of the nineteenth.

Since the early phases of the Industrial Revolution children were part of the labor supply, sometimes working ten hours a day to bolster family income. Farms were equally guilty in devouring juvenile energy. The concept of childhood and adolescence as pre-adult phases of life that deserved specific treatment was not an idea that very many had considered. For the entire nineteenth century American society expected children to have jobs at least by the time they became teenagers. They could attend school to learn what they could until it was time to go to work. The emphasis was on the work, not the learning experience.

Secondary schools existed, frequently called academies, but they were mainly in the Northeast and served society's upper crust. By the 1870s a smattering of public high schools with selective admissions and elitist curricula catered to middle-class, urban families. The public high school as it came to be known had not yet arrived.

But changes were gestating. One of the first signs of this embryonic movement came in 1852 when Horace Mann pushed a compulsory school-attendance law through the Massachusetts legislature, the first in the United States, but it applied to elementary-age students only. Other states followed. Enforcement was less than exemplary, but it was a beginning.

A combination of smitten consciences and scientific awareness created the greatest impetus for change. Darwinian evolution and its explanations of the origin of life gave rise to a wave of investigation about the human organism as something to be understood scientifically, not just theologically. The nature of the human mind and how to educate it had always been a question of philosophical curiosity, but even though many Christians denied it and Adventists would later face off against it, evolutionary theory claimed to wield scientific clout and hence its impact on social issues was profound.

During the latter half of the nineteenth century the social sciences were born and philosophies about human development emerged. Relying on the earlier philosophy of the French Jean Jacques Rousseau, the Swiss Johan Pestalozzi, and the German Friedrich Froebel, a generation of educators in the United States led by John Dewey debated the nature of childhood, children's needs, and their role in society, all of which spawned new educational practices.

By the late 1890s a pragmatic trend in American education, known as progressive education, became the prevailing philosophy. It was a broad rubric that sheltered differing and sometimes contradictory ideas, but the common notion was to reject fixed principles of education and integrate more practicality into education in order to satisfy both personal and societal needs. It did not impact every classroom immediately, but it gathered momentum and until the mid-twentieth century it was the impelling force in shaping classroom methods and teaching techniques.

Progressive education saw children as individuals in their own right who had interrelated social, physical, and psychological needs that were peculiar to their age. On the strength of this belief, activists urged policymakers to use governmental regulatory authority to protect children. During the forty years straddling the turn of the century a genre of social legislation spread across Europe and the United States, among which were child labor laws that forbade children to be exploited in the labor market.

The practical effect of these changes was to create a class of idle young. Lawmakers were quick to see that if children could not work they should be in school. By 1900 more than thirty states followed Massachusetts by enacting compulsory school-attendance laws. Ten years later the states had organized about 200,000 school districts to oversee the public schools.

The quality of education and the content of curricula varied enormously among these educational fiefdoms. Ostensibly the states controlled education, but in reality the fate of schools lay in the hands of powerful local leaders, who were often the principals and teachers themselves. Despite their contrasts, schools developed commonalities, among them a trend to classify students better according to grades and to develop an articulated sequence of teaching materials appropriate to each grade level. By the turn of the century a majority of American children attended school; however, only a fraction remained after age fourteen and a still smaller number graduated from high schools.

With respect to high schools, in 1893 the Committee of Ten, appointed by the National Education Association to study education, recommended a uniform curriculum for all secondary students in the United States. The standard fare consisted of English, history, mathematics, science, and foreign language. College presidents dominated the committee–the president of Harvard chaired the group–and it was clear that in advocating such a bookish curriculum they were thinking of high schools as a preparation for college while reformers viewed high school more practically as a place to learn skills in homemaking and job training.

As a part of a new mood of national awareness and readiness for war, Congress passed the Smith-Hughes Act in 1917, which provided federal money for agricultural, trade, industrial, and home economics education for teenagers above fourteen. Probably inspired as much by the prospect of receiving government money as the new ideas themselves, the next year the National Education Association conveniently changed its collective mind about the recommendation from the Committee of Ten. The NEA's Cardinal Principles of Secondary Education now endorsed health, vocation, citizenship, ethical character, home membership, worthy use of leisure, and a command of basic academic skills (literacy and mathematics) as the seven broad curricular objectives of high schools. The NEA also recommended a variety of curricula to meet the variety of needs that teenagers brought with them to high school. Classes in health, physical education programs, and vocational education courses appeared.

Public secondary education in the United States was a relatively new phenomenon and its purpose and character were left to innovation. By

1920 the high school was well on the way to achieving its identity as an American institution but it was not yet a completely defined tradition. It had long since become a public, tax-supported service and commonly offered multiple tracks that gave teenaged students an option for college preparation, or as an alternative, courses in business, agricultural, mechanical, or industrial education. The college preparation track closely resembled the curricular recommendation from the Committee of Ten, but the high school diploma was also an admission ticket to the world of work.

Protagonists of change thought their progress had moved with glacial slowness, but looking backward forty years from circa 1920 they could point to laws that took children out of the labor market, required them to attend school, and made school a more inviting and practical place. Within the schools themselves the curriculum had dramatically changed to become a saner treatment of childhood and youth.

It was within this state of flux that Seventh-day Adventists developed their elementary and secondary schools. In the United States much of the new thinking about educational purposes emerged from the Protestant, democratic, and pragmatic character of North American society to which Adventists believed they were special couriers of a redemptive message. As different as they planned their schools to be, in time they came to realize that the spiritual values that their separateness embodied did not mean they should ignore either the educational reform taking place around them or the immediate needs of Adventist children or teenagers. All of this held true for the generic Adventist college, schools with special missions, and elementary and secondary schools.

Ellen White had written in 1872 that until children were eight to ten years old they should run free as lambs, implying that only after that age should they be in school, the nature of which she described in "Proper Education." Her essay did not deliberately instruct Adventists to establish schools, but no one could read her climaxing comment, "we are reformers," without realizing that she was advocating Adventist primary education in addition to higher levels of schools. For twenty-five years the response from the Adventist world was close to inert. Schools that produced workers were the educational priority for the church; church schools as educational projects of individual congregations were rare.

As the progressive education movement gathered strength, some Adventists expressed a growing consciousness that they were neglecting the education of their young. Sporadic attempts to establish church schools punctuated the early 1880s. In the columns of the April 14, 1885 *Review* S. N. Haskell, one of the founders of South Lancaster Academy, called for students to attend the New England school where one of the institutional goals was to prepare teachers who could conduct summer schools for Adventist children. The purpose of these summer classes was to inculcate spiritual meaning into the students' education before they returned to their district public schools in the autumn. Teachers had already held successful summer schools in Vermont, New York, and New Hampshire.[1]

The summer schools were not church schools in the full sense of the term but they were harbingers of a trend. Three years later Ellen White mildly chastised the church leaders for not establishing church schools in several large California cities where Adventists were becoming more numerous. Later from Australia she penned one of her most quoted counsels regarding the education of children. "In some countries," she wrote, "parents are compelled by law to send their children to school. In these countries, in localities where there is a church, schools should be established if there are no more than six children to attend."[2]

There was little question that the United States fulfilled that description. This time enough Adventists heard what she said to make a difference. During the ten years before 1895 the denomination established eighteen church schools. Two years later what some have called the Movement of 1897 began at Battle Creek, which marked the real start of elementary education for Seventh-day Adventists.

### The Movement of 1897 Begins

The Movement of 1897 emerged from the confluence of a number of forces. During the 1890s Ellen White's counsel became more explicit. She no longer regarded it only as a piece of good advice to encourage churches to establish schools, she saw it as an obligation devolving upon the shoulders of Adventist parents. Among those who took her seriously was E. A. Sutherland who became president of Battle Creek College in the spring of 1897. Energetic and promising, he was only thirty-two years of age but already had three years of experience as president of Walla Walla College.

*This torn photo pictures the faculty of the elementary school at Battle Creek College in the 1890s. Frederick Griggs is standing on the right in the rear. The teacher-preparation course that these faculty offered was one of the strongest programs at the college.*

At the same time Frederick Griggs, two years younger than Sutherland and a teacher at Battle Creek since 1890, returned to the Michigan campus from the University of Buffalo where he had taken advanced studies in education. At Battle Creek College he was charged with the responsibility of establishing the first genuine teacher-preparation program for Adventists.[3] Other supporters were P. T. Magan, dean of the college and the same age as Griggs, and twenty-six-year-old Bessie DeGraw, a graduate of Central Missouri State Teachers College with brief experience as a high school principal and teacher at Walla Walla College. J. E. Tenney, an older faculty member, served the college as a public relations officer.

DeGraw offered most of the classes in teacher-education, but Sutherland taught history of education. Both drew heavily on Ellen White's advice to establish church schools. During the spring and summer of

1897 calls arrived at the college from northern Michigan, Indiana, Pennsylvania, and Wisconsin for teachers to open church schools. In October Sutherland asked for student volunteers to interrupt their education to teach.[4]

Among the eight or ten that agreed to venture out were Bertis Wolcott and Mattie Pease who were experienced public school teachers that had enrolled in Battle Creek College to recycle themselves as teachers in Christian schools. They went to Pennsylvania and Indiana, but Maud Wolcott, a nineteen-year-old cousin of Bertis and native of Battle Creek, unaccustomed to the rigors of rural life, volunteered on nothing but conviction. Winter arrived by the time she was ready for her assignment, which took her through fifteen-foot snow drifts to Bear Lake, Michigan where settlers were still clearing forests to create new farmland. In this unlikely place she spent the next six months teaching in a home school while living in a small room in the farmhouse. The walls of her room were papered with pages from *The Youth's Instructor*. Heat came from a small wood stove.

More than a half century later the young teacher recalled both her fright and her determination. After meeting the family that formed the nucleus of the school, "I sat in their midst and smiled at them," she said. "Tears ran down my cheeks. Half the night I spent in tears." She was to teach in the front room of the farmhouse, and when she faced her thirteen rural students on the first day she began with a song, "Let the Sunshine In."

Young Maud Wolcott learned that education was a two-way thoroughfare, even for teachers. She ice skated with her students and joined their snowball fights. "They gleefully taught the city girl to ride horseback, to glide across frozen lakes on an iceboat, and to enjoy the unique experiences of the nearby maple sugar camp," she remembered. "Equipment was homemade: tables, benches, and a blackboard supplemented by old-fashioned slates and limited paper supplies.[5]

Others wrote similarly about hardship and deprivation. Mattie Pease held classes in one end of a church in the coal mining region of Indiana. Bertis Wolcott conducted school in a dwelling that also served as a mini-dormitory for students who came from a nearby town. Furniture and other equipment were improvised. Wages were small, ranging from five to fifteen dollars a month.[6]

Despite these discouraging beginnings the church school movement spread to the west coast where churches depended on either Battle Creek or Healdsburg College to prepare teachers. Alma McKibbin began reluctantly in Centralia, California in September 1898 in a small room added on to the church building. A three-year drought had reduced the countryside to dust and people were destitute. Farmers had sold their horses to the soap factories because they could not afford to feed them.

After starting to school on opening day McKibbin returned three times to her room to pray before she mustered enough courage to make the mile walk to her classes. Thirty-six students crowded into twenty seats. Her equipment was all portable: a Bible, a notebook, and a pencil. She had a broken table for a desk and the students all drank from a common tin dipper. One student was older than the teacher.[7]

As primitive as these schools were, Sutherland and his colleagues saw them as monuments to Christian education. The four schools in the Battle Creek region during the 1897-1898 academic year multiplied to fifteen the next year and to sixty the third year. By 1900 Adventists in North America were operating 220 elementary church schools.[8]

*This Adventist church school in Grand Island, Nebraska in 1917 suggests that teachers were innovative and able to keep their pupils busy with a wide variety of learning activities.*

This success was not without its snags. A third of a century later A. W. Spalding recalled that the Movement of 1897 faced "strong prejudice within the church." Only a few believed in the possibility of a church school system but many were "convinced of its folly," he said.[9] The chief doubters were the members of the General Conference Committee. The church's leaders summoned Sutherland, Magan, and Griggs to a lecture that essentially blamed them for diverting money from more needy causes, primarily missions outside the United States, to establish elementary schools.

But this show of authority did not intimidate the young leaders of the Movement of 1897. Sutherland kept up a steady correspondence with Ellen White in Australia who responded encouragingly to counter the pressure from the General Conference. "There should be schools established wherever there is a church or company of believers," she told Sutherland. "Too much is centered in Battle Creek."[10]

Sutherland and company were not the only ones to receive a verbal shellacking from the General Conference office. As a twenty-seven-year-old Hebrew and church history professor at Battle Creek College, H. R. Salisbury, had watched the Movement of 1897 unfold. Sixteen years later in 1913, after a teaching career in South Africa and England and then as secretary of the General Conference Department of Education, he could not resist telling the world church in session that he and his colleagues had been right after all about promoting church schools even if they had not acted with the good will of some of their colleagues.

"Twelve years ago . . . I was told that if educators advocated the starting of these schools throughout this country," he said, "the money required . . . would greatly reduce our mission offerings, and retard our work in foreign fields." After producing statistics which showed that exactly the opposite had occurred, he concluded that "this proves that the success of any department which is a rightful part of this organization will in no way retard the work of any other department, when each is doing its own appointed work."[11]

As committed to elementary education as the young faculty at Battle Creek College were, they were not unanimous. Griggs, who was head of both the secondary and teacher-preparation programs, envisioned a two-year course for prospective church school teachers. He could tolerate a few volunteers who interrupted their studies to answer calls such as those in 1897, but he regarded a regular practice of sending out unprepared teachers as unprofessional and ultimately damaging to students and schools.

Sutherland defined teacher-preparation differently. He favored a teacher-education program consisting of abbreviated, intensive courses, a practice that Ellen and James White had urged for ministers from the outset of Battle Creek College. The mushrooming church school movement could not wait for new teachers to complete a two-year curriculum. Sutherland also mistrusted teachers who were "tainted" with secular ideas. While Bessie DeGraw had graduated from a state teachers' college, she had cleansed herself by attending Battle Creek College and had been part of the Sutherland reform program at Walla Walla. In contrast, Griggs and some colleagues in teacher-education had attended the University of Buffalo for the express purpose of studying the leading educational trends of the times and adapting them to Battle Creek.

Within two years the clash of philosophies climaxed. Sutherland's reform program allowed scant room for notions imported from Buffalo or any other secular place, and at the end of the 1898-1899 school year, Griggs left Battle Creek to become principal of South Lancaster Academy. His colleagues who had also been part of the study-leave program at Buffalo left under pressure as well, some of them to conduct church schools. While the incident had some of the makings of a purge, it was a rather bland one. Sutherland and Griggs parted company, but neither sacrificed his convictions, and until their deaths in the 1950s they both cast long shadows in the continuing development of Adventist education.[12]

## The Start of an Adventist Curriculum

The Movement of 1897 and its ensuing events raised the crucial question of an Adventist curriculum. Typically in the latter half of the nineteenth century the states provided study guides for schools and encouraged teachers to follow them, but in the end the teachers themselves or principals decided class content. As the century advanced the curriculum itself broadened to include more practical classes, but classroom techniques did not always follow apace. One of the more popular contemporary theories held that the mind grew through exercise much as a muscle develops; accordingly, teachers obliged their students with interminable drill from textbooks. The amount of rote knowledge that children could amass became the measurement of achievement.

Ellen White described such children as well trained but not well educated. From the beginning she also had advised that the Bible must be central in all instruction from the college through all of the descending learning levels. Adventists interpreted her words variously. At one extreme were those who taught that the Bible should be the only textbook. At the other were those who believed that biblical instruction should be the most important aspect of a curriculum that otherwise virtually duplicated what was taught in the local public school.

Most Adventist educators were somewhere in between, but they differed among themselves and groped for solutions to the problem of how to construct a biblically centralized curriculum. The answers came from two sources, the teachers who daily grappled with the problem in the classrooms and authors who produced textbooks.

Adventist teachers realized that their schools were to be different, meaning biblical, spiritual, practical, and still remain academically respectable, but the Movement of 1897 caught them ill prepared. Mary Kelly-Little, a Seventh-day Adventist graduate student at the University of Washington in the early 1930s, described the response by Adventist teachers as a revolution in education. "It represented a complete break with the prevailing methods and curricula of the times," she wrote.[13] Bible and nature were central and teachers developed activities around the study of these two topics that embraced the entire range of subject matter.

Statements by the teachers are graphic descriptions of their own struggles to innovate a biblical curriculum. "[W]e had so few books," Maud Wolcott described her year at Bear Lake, Michigan, "but this led us to a thorough knowledge of the Bible, music, and practical things. The pages of nature, God's first book, were spread around us on every side. . . Healthful living was a prime subject. Teaching cooking, I experimented in making buckwheat light bread instead of pancakes."[14]

More than thirty years later her husband, A. W. Spalding, defended her attempt to teach everything from the Bible. She taught reading from the Bible, he said. For spelling, she chose biblical words. Students practiced penmanship by copying texts of Scripture. To add variation to arithmetic classes, she developed problems of measurement of biblical objects, such as Noah's Ark and the New Jerusalem. To make math practical, she asked her students to measure the woodpile and the market value of potatoes the autumn harvest had brought in. "She may have been frightfully unscientific, but she managed to create a varied interest in the Book of books," Spalding commented.[15]

Alma McKibbin, who had planned from her childhood to be a teacher, was under no illusion about her lack of readiness to teach in an Adventist school. She was also conscious of the curricular dilemma that she and her peers faced. "If I knew how to teach a church school, you would not need to ask me," she told the pastor of the Centralia, California church in 1898 when he requested her to become the local church school teacher. "I would be pleading with you for the privilege. The task is spiritual work. The principles are so different from public school teaching that I do not know how to carry them out, and there is no one to teach me. There are no textbooks of any kind, no course of study, no educational leaders, no one to give a bit of advice or counsel."[16]

McKibbin's recruitment as a teacher resembled a military conscription rather than a voluntary commitment. The pastor refused to listen to her protests and the school board tersely handed her an ultimatum describing the terms of her eight-grade classroom. "Do not use public school books that teach evolution or have myths or fairy tales in them. Do not double grades, and above all things do not get behind the public schools in any subject."

Confronted with such herculean tasks, she used *Our Little Friend*, *Gospel Primer*, *Christ Our Saviour*, and the Bible. She took her students outside to construct relief maps on the ground. They dug out bodies of water and molded dirt into mountain ranges. Each night she wrote a nature lesson and two Bible lessons. One of her students spent Sundays gathering specimens for nature classes.

In her school among Indiana coal miners Mattie Pease used gospel readers and Ellen White's writings for reading, mission reports in the *Review* for geography, conference statistical reports and the story of Solomon's temple for arithmetic. On the first day of classes in Bertis Wolcott's Pennsylvania church school students brought whatever books the family happened to have, some of which their grandparents had used. "There were scarcely two of a kind, except their Bibles," Wolcott, said, "so that was the book we were compelled to use the most."[17]

Teachers in the Movement of 1897 and their immediate successors demonstrated their talents to innovate, but leaders of Adventist education could never expect to design an effective system by depending on improvisation. Conditions did not always remain as grim as the first generation of teachers described them, but curricular standardization did not develop immediately.

### Adventist Textbooks

Actually, Adventist educators had entered the business of textbook writing as early as 1881, sixteen years before the Movement of 1897 began. A set of guides and course outlines for college-level Bible classes appeared in 1883 to assist teachers who were largely left to their own devices, but the needs of the elementary school posed the most acute problem in defining Adventist curriculum.

Goodloe Harper Bell was the first to produce a textbook, *A Natural Method in English*, published by the Review and Herald in 1881. The uniqueness of Bell's book lay in his explanation that the natural method of learning proper English was to derive the rules of grammar inductively from a variety of examples. His book was so popular that it sold out within a few months. He later expanded on the original edition and prepared manuals to accompany the text.[18]

Always an educator, Dr. John Harvey Kellogg wrote *First Book in Physiology and Hygiene* in 1887, a book intended for children. He made the spiritual implication of his topic clear. "Ought we not to take such care of our bodies as to keep them in that perfect and beautiful condition in which our kind and good Creator gave them to us?" he asked. The title of his text betrayed his intentions to produce at least a second book, which, indeed, he did in 1894, appropriately entitled *Second Book in Physiology and Hygiene.*

By the time he rewrote his manuscript he apparently realized that physiology, even as simply as he described it, belonged to more advanced levels of instruction. He aimed his second edition at students at high elementary or secondary levels. In neither book did he explicitly advocate vegetarianism, but discussed some of the adverse effects of a diet of flesh foods and indicated that vegetable foods provide all of the nutritive elements that humans need. In light of his animated debates with fellow Adventists about a meat diet, Kellogg showed remarkable restraint in his textbooks.[19]

Before the Movement of 1897 began, James Edson White wrote *The Gospel Primer* to raise money to finance his river boat mission to the Black population of the South. He designed the book as a teaching tool for illiterates. The small book was reminiscent of *McGuffey's Reader*, beginning with the alphabet, each letter illustrated by a biblical word, followed by simple versions of Bible stories. Widespread sales provided White with funds; meanwhile, the book found its way into some of the early Adventist church schools, among them Alma McKibbin's classroom in California.[20]

Coincident with the emphasis on elementary education that began at Battle Creek came a veritable library of new textbooks. Between 1896 and 1898 Goodloe Harper Bell published *Bell's Language Series*, a five-volume set beginning with language lessons from nature and revelation, proceeding with grammar, rhetoric, and ending with English and American literature. This set went beyond the elementary level to introduce advanced students to Christian principles of evaluating good literature. Eliza H. Morton, a former teacher at Battle Creek College, wrote *Elementary Geography* in 1900, following the next year with *Advanced Geography.*

E. A. Sutherland took time from his administrative duties to author *Bible Reader* in 1900, which went through two revisions by 1904 with co-author Bessie DeGraw. The books were total adaptations from the Bible and were written for the beginning reader. "God made a man," the first lesson began. "God made Adam. Adam was a man." As the pupils progressed through the year they sometimes read about the natural conditions of the earth, always with a biblical twist. "Men wonder where coal comes from. I can tell. The waters of the flood covered large trees with rocks. These trees made coal, and we burn the coal today," Sutherland and DeGraw informed their young readers.

In 1901 Sutherland also prepared *The Mental Arithmetic For the Home and School.* He relied upon recent trends in math instruction to determine the level of difficulty integrated into his text, but he decried the content found in public school texts, such as deriving math problems from tobacco farming and the production of alcoholic drinks. He regarded his book as part of a reform by presenting practical problems that would edify the elementary-age student.

Arithmetic problems Sutherland found aplenty from building construction, tithe-paying, sales of Adventist literature by colporteurs, human anatomy, healthful living habits, and biblical objects and stories. "In each half jaw there are 3 teeth called grinders, or molars; how many molars in a full set of 32 teeth?" he queried in Lesson XX. In a lesson about chronology he derived a dozen questions from the stories of Noah through Jacob, complete with Bible texts for reference. In a ten-page sequence he took students through a school construction project, instructing them how to measure out a scaled floor plan and to calculate the cost of lumber and other building materials.[21]

Marion E. Cady, president of Healdsburg College and a graduate of Battle Creek College and former science teacher at Union College, published *Bible Nature Studies* in 1901, a book that brought a spiritual quality to the study of nature. He did not intend his book to be a text for children but a manual for teachers and parents. Among its features were an index of scriptural verses about nature, profuse biblical references in the text, and a culminating view of the earth made new. Mattie Pease remembered that this book gave her much needed help in preparing nature classes.[22]

Realizing that some teachers did not offer Bible classes because they had no instructional materials, and convinced that without Bible classes Adventist schools would have no reason to exist, Alma McKibbin let some of her colleagues copy her Bible lessons by hand. "At last Professor Cady insisted that I have my lessons printed," she said. "And so once more I must do what I did not know how to do–write books and publish them. The Healdsburg College Press printed my first books at my expense." McKibbin tied the first copies together with a shoestring. They became the first Bible textbooks for Adventist schools. Orders came as far away as Australia.[23]

In larger Adventist centers church school teachers worked no less assiduously to revolutionize their curriculum. Mrs. H. B. Noland, supervisor of the Battle Creek elementary school, designed a curriculum that integrated woodwork, agriculture, home-making arts and sloyd[24] into a schedule of traditional classes. Students studied English, physiology and geography from books by denominational authors Bell, Kellogg and Morton. A traditional history book was part of the program, but the teacher emphasized religious liberty and other issues to make the study relevant to Adventist children.

Arithmetic problems came from calculations in gardening and woodwork. Constructing models of Moses' tabernacle was a favorite project for sloyd. In their cooking classes the children prepared their own meals by using some of the vegetables they grew in their gardening classes. They also earned small amounts of money from their agricultural work which helped them to pay for tools that they used in gardening.[25]

Sarah Peck, a Battle Creek-trained teacher who had begun schools for children in South Africa before becoming a literary assistant to Ellen White in Australia, left one of the most detailed explanations of the line of reasoning teachers followed in creating a biblically centered curriculum, the case in point being geography. Writing in 1899, she described how she had divided the general topic into six subsections and then scoured the Bible and Ellen White's writings to find geographical terms.

The shape of the world, its surface features and seasonal cycles, the symbolic meaning of geographical terms in prophecy, changes in nature that sin had caused, and any other comment from the Bible or Ellen White about the earth became legitimate objects of study in her geography classes. In order to understand the implications of the gospel commission, human geography also became a part of class discussion. Students drew their own maps and learned the essential characteristics of the countries of the earth. "Do you think that . . . the light that the Lord has given us caused the study to be of an inferior nature?" Peck asked rhetorically. "Science itself became magnified and beautified, when seen through the powerful microscope of God's Word," she said.[26]

Not all of the first generation of Adventist textbooks were as biblical as Peck described the study of geography, but authors demonstrated that they would go to great lengths to derive curriculum content from the Bible and denominationally oriented information. Very early in the twentieth century church school teachers had at their disposal a selection of books concentrating on Bible and reading but extending to math, health, and nature study, and in the next decade, science.

As well-intended as these first textbooks were and as much work as they represented, perceptive Adventist educators saw that they were inadequate. "Little had been accomplished in the publication of textbooks until after . . . 1906," Frederick Griggs, the executive secretary of the General Conference Department of Education, remembered in 1909.[27] If denominational schools were to be successful, authors would need to produce material more precisely sequenced for the elementary grades. Between 1907 and 1912 the *True Education Reader Series*, authored primarily by Sarah Peck, but assisted by Katherine B. Hale and M. E. Cady, standardized reading in Adventist church schools. During the same years Alma McKibbin's four-volume series of *Bible Lessons*, to which four other advanced volumes were added, became the accepted Bible textbooks. In 1908, 1910, and 1913 Cady revised his original nature studies book into three volumes for the fourth, fifth, and sixth grades.

*Alma McKibbin wrote some of the first textbooks for elementary school Bible classes, which church schools as far away as Australia and other countries also used. Later editions and revisions were part of the elementary school curriculum as late as the 1940s. Pictured here in 1964, she peruses some of her early work.*

With Griggs' support, committee work on these textbooks began in 1903. Sarah Peck, one of the leading elementary educators on the Pacific coast, took personal command of textbook revision. By 1907 four educators had spent much of their own money and vacation time to design books for the readiness levels of each elementary grade, putting "the crib low enough for the lambs to reach," Peck said. During the 1920s McKibbin and other authors further refined the Bible textbooks. Speaking at Colorado Springs in 1923, Peck admitted that teachers had too long been using "wonderful, but altogether too mature" books, including Ellen White's writings, to teach reading.[28]

Although they were quickly outmoded, the earliest books were the a first step in developing a defined Adventist curriculum. Revisions and improvements followed almost immediately, and while not perfect, they were a quantum leap in both professionalizing and developing an identity in Adventist church schools.

The textbook revisions of 1907 and onward were also an implied acknowledgment that the first teachers who restricted students exclusively to the Bible had misunderstood Ellen White's counsel to make the Bible "central" in Adventist education. Central and exclusive were not equivalent terms. In the curriculum that included the new textbooks the Bible was not the only source of content but it remained at the heart because it formed a framework to understand knowledge. Less than a decade after the Movement of 1897 Adventist teachers had developed sufficient professional skills to produce these textbooks. The term "worldview" was yet not a part of the Adventist educational vocabulary, but curriculum designers sought to construct a biblical context in which students would understand information and comprehend themselves as Seventh-day Adventists.[29]

Not only was the practice of using the Bible as the only textbook extreme, Adventist educators also concluded that it would be too much to expect Adventist books to be the exclusive academic diet in denominational education. In 1916 M. E. Cady wrote that the "larger proportion of the text-books used in all schools are secured from regular text-book publishers."[30]

Notwithstanding the prevalence of non-Adventist textbooks, the identity of denominational education continued to go beyond books to values and responsibilities, broadly categorized as Christian and related to the home. Cady wrote that parents were expected to report weekly evaluations of their children from a list of forty-six items pertaining to home duties, personal hygiene and health, and self-paced spiritual activities, ranging from getting out of bed promptly in the morning to studying Sabbath School lessons. The link between the home and the school had been a part of Ellen White's thinking since she published her first article about parents' duties toward their children in 1854, but from the vantage point of the twenty-first century questions arise about how intrusive elementary schools could reasonably be.

A major point in Adventist elementary education reform was to delay formal education until children were older than the customary age for them to begin school. When reporting to the world convention of educators in 1923, Sarah Peck declared that while revising textbooks a decade and a half earlier the four authors discovered their work to be easier when they designed their manuscripts for pupils whose parents had followed Ellen White's advice to keep children out of school until they were eight or ten years old. Failure to follow this counsel, Peck said, was a departure from the faith.

While Ellen White had, in fact, given parents such counsel, she did not regard it with such inflexibility as her friend described it. In April 1888, she not only criticized denominational workers in Oakland, California for not establishing a church school for their children, but advocated a kindergarten to direct young minds in the right way.

The kindergarten movement, attributed to Friedrich Froebel in the 1830s, had not yet made much of an impact in the United States, but the idea was known. Of course a kindergarten was not to be construed as a formal classroom, yet it was a place where education would begin. The implication is clear that in Ellen White's view some level of education was appropriate for children of pre-school age.

Sixteen years later during a discussion by the board members of the local church school in St. Helena, California about their policy to deny admission to children under ten, Ellen White not only suggested that seven- or eight-year-old children should attend the school but startled them by saying that some children as young as five were ready for education. Having children in school, she pointed out, was better than leaving them to run the streets with no control, which was the practice among some families in the community.[31]

At first sight Ellen White's later statements appear to be a contradiction of her earlier advice to allow children to run as free as lambs until they were eight or ten. The context of her "free as lambs" remark in 1872 indicates that ideally, parents would be teaching their children at home, how formally she did not explain, but a deliberate educational program was to be in effect. "*Parents should be the only teachers of their children until they have reached eight or ten years of age*," she had said. "*As fast as their minds can comprehend it, the parents should open before them God's great book of nature.*" (Italics supplied.)[32]

Taken in context, Ellen White's advice over the years enunciated the principle that all children differ from one another and readiness for formal education is determined not by blanket rules but by understanding the individual child. She excoriated poorly ventilated and poorly equipped schools that restricted activity which growing children needed for health and physical balance. To be free as lambs did not equate to lack of supervision or the absence of all learning experiences. If parents were to be teachers, they would have to teach, but by not fulfilling this duty, schools became a necessity. With a curriculum that was becoming increasingly accommodating to children's needs and with nature study a key element in the study program, which in itself presupposed extensive outdoor activity, schools ceased to be the damaging environment for young children that Ellen White had once perceived.

### A Look Back at the Movement of 1897

The Movement of 1897 and later events constituted a defining moment in Adventist education. Teachers and leaders in education were compelled to think about elementary knowledge and academic skills in a manner that heretofore had lain beyond their ken. The first schools held little in common with public education at the time, and, it might be observed, had little in common with each other except that education was to reflect the conviction that the Bible was the Word of God and the basis for all belief.

Many of the first church schools were clumsy at best but they functioned anyway and inspired an ever widening horizon of confidence. Given the number of those early schools, the first wave of educational literature was prolific and creative, but it was also the product of novices. From out of this unlikely mix teachers emerged who, by trial and error, forged a curriculum based on a pragmatic balance between their professional skills and their ideals. In less than two decades after the first volunteers left Battle Creek College to initiate the Movement of 1897, an identifiable elementary system of schools was in operation.

The two decades following the Movement of 1897 not only identified Adventist elementary education, they also contributed to the development of secondary education. That elementary education did not adequately prepare students to enter college was a given, but in the late nineteenth and early twentieth centuries American education lacked a well-articulated college preparation program. The public high school filled the gap between the elementary and tertiary levels, but even by 1920 the public high school was not a completely matured concept.

By defining Adventist elementary education, the church school movement determined the upper limit of elementary schooling in the Adventist world, and thus provided an academic beginning point for Adventist secondary schools. Denominational colleges with their longer history had already established their own entry levels, thus defining the upper limit of secondary education.

Perhaps the most important aspect of the Movement of 1897 was the soul that it breathed into Adventist education. Until the advent of the church schools, Adventist officialdom saw education more as a means to prepare denominational professionals than a method to evangelize the young, in spite of Ellen White's advocacy of saving children to the church. Although the church had officially encouraged church schools, educators sometimes received only begrudging support from many influential church leaders. Nevertheless, the contingent of young educators at Battle Creek College persisted in enlarging the circle of education to include children as well as students preparing for denominational employment.

Adventist leaders had long strategized to devote their money to evangelism. They visualized projects in medicine and public health, literature production and distribution, and powerful preaching as methods to reach the public with the gospel, but the Movement of 1897 set in motion a chain of events demonstrating that the education of the young was one of most successful evangelistic tools the church possessed.

It had been a long way from Maud Wolcott's Bear Lake school on the northern Michigan frontier in 1897 to the system that existed in 1920. It was the spirit of ministry that she and others like her exemplified that had kept the Movement of 1897 alive. The young nineteen-year-old neophyte remembered that she was "ever besieged by eager children" and had no privacy except in her stark, second-story room with its improvised wall paper and wood stove. "It was there, perhaps, that I learned to be a mother-teacher," she said.[33]

Similarly, Alma McKibbin symbolized the pulsating soul of Adventist education. After she had become a recognized personality in denominational circles, Pacific Union College named a newly erected building in her honor and invited her to the campus for its opening. She was overcome with emotion and nostalgia. As she stood to receive her well-earned accolades she confessed she could not see the beautiful architecture or the nicely equipped classrooms. "I saw that little old room at the rear of the Centralia church with its bare rafters and the studding and the nails on the side where the boys and girls hung their coats and hats, and the tin dipper and the water pail and the broken stove that smoked," she said.[34]

Above all, the Movement of 1897 was a labor of love.

---

[1]Cadwallader, *ibid.*, p. 286.

[2]Ellen White, *Testimonies to the Church*, v. 6, p. 199.

[3]Arnold C. Reye and George R. Knight, "Frederick Griggs: Moderate," in *Adventist Educators*, Knight, ed., pp. 185, 186.

[4]Cadwallader, *ibid.*, p. 292; Mary Kelly-Little, ibid., pp. 18, 19, 27.

[5]Maud Wolcott Spalding, "Volunteers of '97," *Journal of True Education* (June 1953), pp. 8-10.

[6]Cadwallader, *ibid.*, p. 295; Kelly-Little, ibid., p. 19-22.

[7]Mary Hunter Moore, *They That Be Teachers,* pp. 12ff, quoted in Cadwallader, *ibid.*, pp. 296, 297; Alonzo Baker, *My Sister Alma and I* (Mountain View, CA: Pacific Press Publishing Association, 1980), pp. 47-50.

[8]Cadwallader, *ibid.*, p. 290.

[9]Spalding's comments cited in Cadwallader, *ibid.*, p. 302.

[10]For a description of this debate between Sutherland and church leaders, see Warren S. Ashworth, "Edward A. Sutherland: Reformer," in *Early Adventist Educators*, pp.165, 166; H. R. Salisbury, "Report of the Department of Education to the 1913 General Conference," RG 51, AST.

[11]Salisbury, *ibid.*

[12]Arnold C. Reye and George R. Knight, *Early Adventist Educators*, p. 192 ; VandeVere, *Wisdom Seekers*, p. 81.

[13]Chapter III, "The Movement of 1897," of Mary Kelly-Little's M.A. thesis provides an insightful description of the personalities and nature of the early curriculum development in Adventist church schools. Cadwallader, *ibid.*, chapters XXXVIII and XXXIX also furnish valuable information. Alma McKibbin's *Step by Step* (Washington, D.C.: Review and Herald Publishing Association, 1964) is a short memoir of this phase of Adventist education.

[14]Maud Wolcott Spalding, *ibid.*

[15]Spalding's January, 1931 *Review and Herald* article cited in Cadwallader, *ibid.*, pp. 301-303.

[16]Alonzo Baker, *ibid.*, p. 47-51.

[17]Kelly-Little, ibid., pp. 20-23.

[18]Kelly-Little, ibid., p. 13.

[19]J. H. Kellogg, *First Book in Physiology and Hygiene* (New York: Harper and Brothers, 1887, 1888), p. 10; and *Second Book in Physiology and Hygiene* (New York: American Book Company, 1894), pp. 29-31.

[20]J. E. White, *The Gospel Primer* (Battle Creek, MI: International Tract Society, 1895).

[21]Walton J. Brown provides a chronological list of books pertaining to Adventist education in *Chronology*, pp. 238-250. For comments on Bell's English series see Allan G. Lindsay, "Goodloe Harper Bell: Teacher," in *Early Adventist Educators*, Knight, ed., pp. 67, 68. E. A. Sutherland, *The Bible Reader, Number One*, rev. ed. (Berrien Springs, MI: Advocate Publishing Co., 1903); and *The Mental Arithmetic for Home and School* (Battle Creek, MI: Review and Herald Publishing Association, 1901).

[22]M. E. Cady, *Bible Nature Studies* (Mountain View, CA: Pacific Press Publishing Association, 1901); Kelly-Little, ibid., p. 23.

[23]McKibbin, *Step by Step*, p. 80; Baker, *ibid*., p. 57.

[24]Sloyd was a contemporary term for handicrafts which usually referred to wood carving but could include cardboard construction.

[25]Kelly-Little, pp. 28-31.

[26]*Union Conference Record*, July 28, 31, 1899.

[27] *General Conference Bulletin*, 1909, no. 6, p. 79.

[28]Reye and Knight, *ibid*., pp. 186, 187; *General Conference Bulletin,* 1909, no. 6, p. 79; Sarah E. Peck, "Textbooks For Our Church Schools," *Proceedings of the Educational and Missionary Volunteer Departments*, pp. 414-422. See Brown, *Chronology*, for specific publication dates of textbooks.

[29]George Knight devotes an entire chapter to the question of an Adventist curriculum in *Myths in Adventism* (Washington, D.C.: Review and Herald Publishing Association, 1985), pp. 139-151. Regarding the question of textbooks, see Warren S. Ashworth, "Edward A. Sutherland: Reformer," in Knight, *Early Adventist Educators*, p. 169.

[30]M. E. Cady, "Seventh-day Adventist Schools on the Pacific Slope," M. A. thesis, University of California, 1916, pp. 18, 19, 117.

[31]Peck, *ibid*., p. 419; Cadwallader, *ibid*., p. 288; Arthur White, *Ellen White*, v. 5, pp. 312-317. See also Ellen White, *Selected Messages*, v. 3, pp. 214-226 and *Review and Herald*, April 24, 1975.

[32]Ellen White, *Testimonies*, v. 3, p. 137. Italics supplied.

[33]Maud Wolcott Spalding, *ibid.*

[34]Cadwallader, *ibid*., p. 298.

# Bridging the Atlantic

As it developed in North America, Adventist education as a movement became a paradigm for Seventh-day Adventists in the rest of the world. No specific school served as *the* model, but because North Americans constituted the majority of Adventist workers around the world and they took their ideas about education, organization, and general methodology wherever they went, they dominated the church and its educational institutions worldwide. Of course, adaptations of the paradigm were frequent, necessary and expected, but a North American shape was always visible.

## Early "Missionary" Activity

It was no accident that education and mission movements of Seventh-day Adventists developed a close relationship. Adventists understood "missionary" with a broad meaning, someone who engaged in the work of carrying the gospel to other people. The word "missionary" as it appeared in the name of the denomination's first school of medicine at Battle Creek and later in names of other educational institutions such as Emmanuel Missionary College was a deliberate choice of words. These names expressed an underlying purpose of Adventist education–to prepare people formally to carry the gospel. In that sense, all students preparing to become church workers planned to be missionaries.

Over time, however, the term more often identified people who traveled to another country or at least left their native environment to work elsewhere. Adventists conceived the idea of a global mission movement in the early 1860s. In 1874, the same year that Battle Creek College was born, J. N. Andrews sailed with his two motherless children for Switzerland. He was the first Adventist worker from the United States on an official assignment outside North America and is called the first Adventist missionary.[1]

But Adventist mission work in Europe was already under way before Andrews went to Switzerland. M. B. Czechowski, a Polish immigrant to the United States who accepted Adventist teachings about 1850, preached unofficially in central and eastern Europe for a dozen years before his death in 1876, organizing groups of Sabbath keepers with whom church workers later made contact. One of his converts, James Erzberger from Switzerland, traveled to the United States in 1869, was ordained to the ministry, and returned to his homeland the next year, preceding Andrews by four years.

Erzberger was the first ordained Adventist minister in Europe. Unlike Czechowski, he labored with a valid credential but he had no specific assignment. As defined by the broader meaning of the word, he was a missionary because he carried the gospel, but the church views Andrews as the first missionary, partly because he went with an officially designated task and partly because he left his native environment to work in a field that was foreign to him. As an Adventist presence spread around the world the term "missionary" became increasingly linked to service beyond one's homeland.

Church leaders, especially James White, envisioned Battle Creek College as a place to promote missions and to educate missionaries. At White's urging modern languages were part of the curriculum, which he thought would equip students to become workers in other countries. Several practical problems combined to thwart this plan. To train someone to use a second, learned language competently in preaching, writing, and publishing required more time than the short courses which the Whites encouraged. Because the church lacked trained language teachers the school depended on translators employed at the Review and Herald Publishing Association as part-time teachers. But students showed little interest in language study and the classes floundered.[2]

Until a generation of fluent linguists appeared the church found it more practical to rely on speakers of languages who had converted to Adventism to conduct mission work. Through the nineteenth century the most prominent Adventist workers to non-English speaking peoples outside North America were not the products of an educational program to prepare Adventist missionaries, but were immigrants to the United States or native speakers from immigrant stock.

L. R. Conradi, a German immigrant who converted to Adventism after arriving in the United States, returned to lead Adventist work not only in Germany but widely throughout eastern Europe as well. J. G. Matteson, who became an Adventist nine years after emigrating to the United States from Denmark, published the first non-English Adventist paper in 1872, and in 1877 began a productive eleven-year career in his native country and Norway.

O. A. Olsen, Norwegian-born but brought to the United States when five years old, returned to Scandinavia in 1886 from where the church called him to become General Conference president in 1888. Frank Westphal, born into the German-speaking immigrant community in Wisconsin, began pioneering the spread of Adventism among German colonies in Argentina, Brazil, and Chile in 1894. In 1901 his brother, Joseph W., followed him in the same territory.

These breakthroughs were significant for Adventists, but English was still the *lingua franca* of Adventism. South Africa, Australia, New Zealand, India, and English-speaking enclaves in Argentina, Chile, Central America and the Caribbean were some of the early targets of missionary endeavor.

In 1889 and 1890 Stephen Haskell, accompanied by twenty-two-year-old P. T. Magan, conducted a world tour of Adventist missions, a trip that Arthur White declares opened Haskell's eyes to the importance of schools in countries outside the United States. Speaking at the General Conference session in March 1891, Haskell pointed out that it was necessary to educate church workers in their home environments rather than to send them elsewhere where they would lose touch with their roots. Two days later W. W. Prescott disclosed that numerous calls for schools were coming to the General Conference, one of them from Australia. The combined Adventist membership of that island and New Zealand had already reached 700.[3]

Until approximately 1920 the spread of Adventist schools beyond North America was a four-pronged movement. The first was in Europe where national workers either established their own schools or quickly took charge of them from missionary founders. The second prong extended into Australia, South Africa, and South America where England, the Netherlands, Spain, and Portugal had taken their language and customs to create substantial colonial extensions of European life and culture.

The third and fourth prongs represented Adventist education on the mission frontiers, one penetrating lands populated by Christianized, non-Caucasian people, the other to what Adventists commonly called "heathen" peoples because, for the most part, they were non-Christian and westernized only to varying degrees. The four prongs were not sequential but rather differing aspects of the Adventist educational movement. However, a flow of workers developed first from Europe and then from colonial extensions of Europe to the frontiers.

## Adventist Education in Scandinavia

No less than in North America the beginnings of Adventist education outside the so-called "homeland" abounded with poignancy, dedication, and sacrifice. Sweat and tears were common. A case in point was the church at Jerslev, Denmark. In 1893 this congregation began a church school that decades later claimed to have the oldest, continuous record of any Adventist church school in Europe.

*Scandinavia was the location of the earliest Seventh-day Adventist schools in Europe. This church school in Jerslev, Denmark held the distinction of sixty years of continuous operation when L. Mark Hamilton visited the school in 1953.*

On the eve of its sixtieth year L. Mark Hamilton, education secretary for the Northern European Division, visited the old school, calling it a shrine and confessing that he felt he should have left his shoes at the threshold. "To me this was holy ground," he said. When he asked the old timers in the church about their sacrifices and struggles over those sixty years, "their memories somehow failed them," he observed. "Those trials of faith and finance appeared singularly dim and unimportant."[4]

Schools in Europe began as early as 1883, first in Denmark and later Norway, partly as a result of the work of J. G. Matteson. During her European ministry, 1885-1887, Ellen White encouraged Adventists to establish schools in Scandinavia to educate church workers. Sometimes the courses were short such as a single, six-week class in Stockholm, Sweden that Matteson and J. M. Erickson taught for prospective colporteurs.[5]

One of the obstacles to solid educational beginnings in Scandinavia was a small church membership. A paucity of students made separate training schools for Danes, Norwegians, and Swedes impractical. This circumstance, combined with cultural and linguistic similarities among the three groups, seemed to justify a single regional school, but enough differences among the national groups prevented effective integration. Adventist education in Scandinavia advanced, but before 1920 its progress was erratic.

A permanent educational program for Scandinavia began in 1888 when a mission school opened in Copenhagen, Denmark for the purpose of preparing colporteurs and other workers. The following year a dozen students gathered in the same city to begin the Philadelphia Mission and Colporteur School which continued for five years before transferring to Frederikshavn on the eastern coast near the northern tip of Denmark.[6]

At this site Scandinavian workers dedicated a new school on August 31, 1894. Classes began in October with sixty students. Known as both Frederikshavn Hojskole and Frydenstrand, it was the recognized institution for Adventist students from all three Scandinavian countries, and thus the first Adventist union school in Europe, although union conferences had not yet become a common administrative entity within the church.

This experiment in a joint school for all Scandinavian students lasted only four years. In 1898 it closed for five years. Its revival in Copenhagen in 1903 began another uncertain phase. Within a year it moved twice, returning eventually to Frederikshavn where it once again became the Frydenstrand school. Meanwhile, Swedish Adventists took matters into their own hands and established a separate school, Nyhyttan Mission School at Jarnboas, on an old estate about 120 miles west of Stockholm. The intention was to admit Finnish students as well. Total enrollment of both Swedish and Finnish students was only fifteen the first year, a weak showing but enough to keep classes going.

A year later the school became Nyhyttan Industrial School, a typical denominational title, but in this instance the change was a signal that the school's leading purpose was to provide a practical education rather than to train workers. A low enrollment forced a one-year closure in 1905, but the school rebounded the next year, reverting to its original name which designated it as a missionary school. Briefly, Nyhyttan became an all-Nordic school, enrolling students from Norway, Denmark, as well as Sweden and Finland. Students were mature adults and, as a later director of the school described them, enrolled for the "express purpose of going out as Bible-workers and ministers."[7]

The location of the school was idyllic. The buildings occupied a prominence overlooking a valley through which a river flowed from the central Swedish watershed to Milar Lake, the large body of water west of Stockholm. Thick pine and birch forests covered most of the 500-acre estate. "Nature seems to speak to us in her sweetest tones," calling students "to listen to her benediction of peace," Swedish Conference President S. F. Svenson said rather romantically. During the summer months the school plant doubled as a sanitarium. Enrollment was not large, but encouraging. Forty-two attended the 1908-1909 year, most of whom entered denominational work as colporteurs after the school year ended.[8]

It was with encouraging news from Nyhyttan that delegates to the Scandinavian Union met at Orebro, Sweden in 1908. Inspired by the need for permanency in their schools, the Norwegian and Danish conferences agreed to join in a union school at Skodsborg, the site of a large health-care institution that occupied a former royal estate near Copenhagen.

This action left little time to prepare for the new school year, only weeks away. When classes began in October the teachers and students found themselves in rented space. Before the year ended enrollment reached thirty-four from Norway, Denmark, and Iceland. But events showed that the move to Skodsborg was as impermanent as the schools at previous locations. A new school building went up on the sanitarium grounds, but within five years classes moved to still another site, Naerum, where the school remained until 1930.

The year 1908 was a turning point in Adventist education for Scandinavia. After establishing a school at Skodsborg church leaders no longer attempted to house students from all countries in one institution but separated them into more practically managed groups. Because of the close similarities in their language, Norwegian, Danish, and Icelandic students could attend one school with minimal problems. This compromise served the Scandinavian Union until 1921 when the Norwegian constituency grew large enough to support a separate school.

Less workable was the combination of Finnish and Swedish students on a single campus. At best it was an arrangement of convenience. Long a pawn in Swedish and Russian rivalry over control of the Baltic, Finland had been a Swedish possession for years, enabling Finns to absorb Swedish language and culture. In the first decade of the twentieth century between fifteen and twenty percent of the Finns spoke Swedish but their country at the time had switched hands and was part of the Russian Empire. In an enrollment of forty-two at Nyhyttan in 1908, four students came from Finland and one from Russia. Continuing this Finnish connection, during the years 1913-1917 the school organized a special department for students from Finland although some Finnish students attended the Adventist school in Germany.

"We had to be content with a small Finnish department in the Swedish school," a Finnish worker later recalled, but in 1918, a year after the country gained its independence, the Finland Mission established its own school at Hameenlinna, eighty miles north of Helsinki. It was a beginning, but a tiny one beset with years of struggles for survival while the constituency grew sufficiently large to support a well developed institution.[9]

The beginnings of Adventist education in Scandinavia was a story of secondary-level instruction designed to prepare denominational workers. Primary education barely existed. A school in the Vesteralen region of Norway, north of the Arctic Circle, operated from 1892 to

1918. In 1909 Denmark reported two church schools, one of them at Jerslev. The priority for education was to produce denominational employees who would participate in some phase of evangelism.

L. Mark Hamilton measured the success of the Jerslev, Denmark church school not only by the number of workers who began their education there but also by the large proportion of students who remained members of the church. But the Jerslev case was a rarity in Scandinavia. Of the dozen union conferences in Europe in 1920 the Scandinavian Union was the fourth largest with nearly 7,500 members spread among more than 170 churches, but they operated only three church schools with no more than a hundred students. The vision of the church school as a learning center for Adventist children and thus a branch of evangelism had not caught on.

### Missionsseminar Friedensau

A regional school that served a multinational constituency had been necessary in Scandinavia, but its shortcomings were increasingly apparent and as the Adventist population grew, schools for single national groups became more feasible. By contrast, in Friedensau, Germany one institution became an international hub for education in central and eastern Europe.

Founded as Missionsseminar Friedensau in 1899, the school claimed its roots in a school that began in Hamburg ten years earlier. It was there that a small colony of twenty-five Adventists settled in 1889 to establish the International Tract Society, a branch of the Imprimerie Polyglotte, the Adventist press in Basel, Switzerland. This new publishing venture was international, specifically serving Russia and producing Adventist literature in several eastern European languages. Simultaneously, the group began a training school to prepare workers to sell the materials that the Hamburg branch produced.

Located sixty miles upstream from the mouth of the Elbe River, Hamburg was Germany's leading port city in the north and a strategic site for a printing establishment, but after a decade of activity, church leaders realized that it was not a suitable place for a training school for ministers. In 1899 the German Conference purchased a ninety-three-acre estate near Magdeburg, about a hundred miles southeast of Hamburg, to which they moved the school.[10]

*The main building at Missionsseminar Friedensau, Germany, near Magdeburg, one of the most productive Seventh-day Adventist training schools for church workers and missionaries prior to World War I.*

Called Klappermuhle because it included an old water mill and farm buildings, the estate quickly became known as Friedensau and the home of a thriving Adventist center. Events moved with surprising speed. In October 1899 a food factory began operations. The next month Otto Lupke started classes with seven students and in January a nursing school opened its doors.

An Adventist community, reminiscent of Battle Creek without the publishing house, was evolving on the old Klappermuhle estate. Buildings were going up, including a sanitarium, begun in March 1900. The solid structures were unquestionable indications that the German Adventists intended to remain in Friedensau a long time, but their expectations became undeniable in 1902 when they staked out a cemetery, *prima facie* evidence that they believed they would be there even after they died. Obviously, they would sooner or later need a burial place, but they delayed that eventuality as long as possible by emphasizing a healthful lifestyle by gathering regularly on the sanitarium grounds for sessions of *gymnastik.* The total Friedensau program integrated the notion of wellness with spirituality and education.

The emphasis on health was not a passing whim. Otto Lupke declared that from the beginning the aim of Friedensau's founders was to establish an industrial-missionary school that educated students for medical missionary work. They were consciously following Ellen White's advice, but legal restrictions also made health a necessary part of the program. Because various states in the German Empire, especially Prussia, did not recognize Seventh-day Adventists as a denomination the church could own no property. The German Society for the Promulgation of Health-reform was the legal entity through which the German Union held Friedensau's land and buildings.

Nursing education received a strong emphasis. The health food enterprise, a nursing home for the aged, and the sanitarium were important items on the Friedensau agenda. In less than a decade all three of these institutions became income-generating enterprises whose financial values far exceeded the amount of original investment. These statistics provided encouragement to German leaders, but Lupke steadily maintained that Friedensau's primary aim was education, and that health-related institutions played a supporting, not the primary role in preparing ministers and nurses for denominational service.

The school was an economic success but students commonly found themselves in financial trouble. It was routine for them to complete their studies with a debt of $100 to $125, a formidable amount at the time which they could not expect to pay back from their slim earnings as denominational employees. To alleviate this situation conference presidents awarded bonuses to newly hired graduates after each year of service if their labor was satisfactory. This practice enabled new workers to liquidate their debts in two or three years and also kept the school from accumulating a backlog of uncollectible accounts.

Life at Friedensau was for the hardy. Until new buildings went up holes in the roof of the original buildings let in the snow and rain. Students ate their meals in a workroom that doubled as the drying room for the laundry. The forenoons were for studying and classes; in the afternoons students worked, sometimes until night. The curriculum included practical lines of work, including agriculture, homemaking, woodworking, tailoring, blacksmithing, farm work, and forestry.

Graduates lost little time entering denominational work. By 1903, only four years after Missionsseminar Friedensau began operations, many alumni had gone to German East Africa as missionaries. At the end of the first decade of operations 350 students had graduated from the program, all of whom engaged in some form of missionary work. In 1911 thirty-nine Friedensau graduates were serving as missionaries in eight countries scattered over five continents including North America. Nineteen were in German East Africa. German-trained nurses streamed from the sanitarium to the mission fields where German workers commonly labored.

While Adventist education in Scandinavia seemed to move inexorably toward separation into national groups, the international character of the Friedensau program was deliberate. This characteristic had actually begun in Hamburg where students from Russia, Switzerland, Hungary, and Scandinavia enrolled. In addition to German-speaking Europe, Lupke recognized that the school served Slavic Europe as well, an area that stretched from the Baltic to the Balkans and farther east into Russia. He foresaw that Friedensau graduates would also serve in German and Dutch colonies in Africa, Asia, and Australasia.

In 1907 the school established a Russian department to accommodate students from that field. Of the 140 students enrolled in 1908, a dozen were non-Germans. In 1909 students enrolled not only from Russia, but from western Europe, Scandinavia, eastern Europe, the Balkans, and the Middle East.

Besides denying the church the right to own land and buildings, the law required students to attend public schools until they were fifteen years old, which effectively proscribed church schools for Adventist children. This restriction also precluded a teacher-preparation course at Friedensau. From the outset Adventist schools in Germany limited themselves to professional training.

The peak of Friedensau's activity was a pre-World War I phenomenon. It enjoyed economic prosperity, rapidly becoming *the* Adventist center for central and eastern Europe and one of the most productive and well-known educational institutions in the Adventist world for training denominational workers. It provided a location for German camp meetings; in connection with the 1911 summer gathering the General Conference Committee conducted one of its sessions on the campus. But in 1914 the tide shifted. With the outbreak of World War I Germany found itself fighting a two-front war. The imperial government conscripted ministerial students and commandeered part of the campus to house wounded soldiers. In 1917 the school closed.

Friedensau did not recover easily. In October 1919 regular classes resumed, but enrollment did not reach prewar levels. Partly as a result of the war the school lost much of its international character. In the aftermath of war a vanquished Germany forfeited its colonial holdings which had furnished a ready-made destination for Friedensau graduates entering mission service. German East Africa, the most favored mission field for Missionsseminar alumni, was particularly hard hit. All missionaries except one in that field were German, and when British forces occupied this colony during the war Adventist workers were interned, which halted church work. Permission to resume mission activities after the war was slow in coming; meanwhile ministers from South Africa patched the church together until permanent arrangements repaired the damage.[11]

Ironically, church growth also contributed to decline at Friedensau. German Adventists inherited other mission fields for which they could educate workers, but the rapidly increasing membership in Germany resulted in reorganizing the German Union into three unions, each with its own training school by 1921. Following this organizational shuffle Friedensau became the institution of the East German Union rather than the school for all of German-speaking and Slavic Europe.

## Adventist Education in France and the Latin Union

One of the contradictions of Seventh-day Adventist history occurred in the very region where J. N. Andrews planted the first official mission in Europe. It was in response to a burst of interest in Adventism that he and his colleagues established a press and administrative offices in Basel, Switzerland. An impetus for growth and organization radiated throughout Europe, but actual gains were meager in what came to be known as the Latin Union, or those countries whose culture and language derived from Latin antecedents. In this region of Europe Adventist workers concentrated their first efforts in western Switzerland, northern Italy, and adjacent portions of France.

The history of Adventist education in Latin Europe revolves around the struggle to begin, and once started, to maintain institutional permanency. For nearly two decades after Andrews' arrival in 1874 efforts to establish education in this region were non-existent; for more than a decade beginning in 1892 they were ineffectual. Among the known attempts were schools in several Swiss communities: La Chaux-de-Fonds in 1892 and 1895, Peseux in 1893, Le Chateau de Perles in 1896, and Geneva in 1901.[12]

The school at Perles was a boarding institution which Swiss Adventists established after several fathers chose imprisonment over paying fines for not sending their children to school on Saturday. The school drew both German- and French-speaking students among whom was eight-year-old Jean Nussbaum. His mother regularly took in laundry to pay fines because he did not attend school on Sabbath. No one could foresee it, but in a striking twist of irony young Jean, who had to leave home to maintain his freedom of conscience, later became a Paris physician who befriended popes and world leaders and exerted a towering influence in religious liberty matters in Europe.[13]

B. G. Wilkinson, the newly elected president of the Central European Conference, was the main force behind a school in Geneva, which opened in 1901 as a ten-week course for students above seventeen years of age. The following year he became the first head of the Latin Union and transferred the school to Paris, at the same time broadening the curriculum to include math and science and lengthening the course to twenty-four weeks, lasting from October 1902 to April 1903. Three other teachers assisted him.

Although Wilkinson's Geneva and Paris schools produced seven church workers, they did not constitute an established institution. Permanent ministerial training was an elusive thing that appeared as an outgrowth of nurses' education, which started at the Basel Sanitarium in 1895. Nine years after this institution began, it relocated at La Ligniere, an estate near Gland, Switzerland, about twenty miles from Geneva. Here, with an established educational program in place, albeit in nursing, the school almost immediately expanded by adding ministerial training. Under the title of the Latin Union School, classes began in 1904 with Jean Vuilleumier the first principal.

It was a small beginning. "Our little union school at Gland, Switzerland, is filling a long-felt want," L. P. Tieche, president of the Latin Union, reported to the General Conference five years after the institution began. Although the Latin Union included Italy, Belgium, Portugal, Spain, and parts of North Africa, it was clear from Tieche's description that the school was intended for French-speaking Europe. "The future success of the work in France depends in a large measure upon the proper training of our young people," he said. "I am certain that there are brighter days before us in the French field."[14]

But advancement was slow even though Tieche characterized the training school as "prospering" as it finished its ninth year. Enrollment reached forty-six and included students from nearly every country in the Latin Union besides England, Germany, and the United States. "This school has already furnished the field with a number of young, efficient workers," Tieche said. Wartime pressures forced the school to close temporarily in 1914; after reopening two years later, it closed again in 1918.[15]

Compared to Tieche, H. H. Dexter, president of the French-Swiss Conference, was less sanguine about education in the Latin Union when he reported to the General Conference session in 1918. Overwhelmed by the skeletal condition of the Latin Union in the final months of World War I, he declared that Italy, France, Spain, and Portugal all needed schools and complained that the Latin Union had no secretary of education. The union had only one school at Gland, he lamented, where the medium of instruction was French and all students had to learn that language to attend.

For two years after the war what remained of the Latin Union School drifted to Nimes, France for one year and back to Gland for another year before settling in 1921 at Collonges-sous-Saleve, a village straddling the French border on the outskirts of Geneva. The school itself was located above the town on a slope leading up to a near perpendicular rock cliff. Students had a panoramic view of Geneva, the Jura Mountain range across the valley, and Lake Leman, where the Rhone River began its serpentine course to the Mediterranean.

Here the school, renamed Seminaire Adventiste du Saleve, would remain. It was a spectacular location, but it lacked the opportunities for work that were typical of Adventist campuses. Nevertheless, seventy-six students enrolled for classes in 1921, an encouraging omen after thirty years of moving from pillar to post. Dexter's call for schools in other countries in the Latin Union would not be fulfilled for many years

*After more than twenty years of truncated efforts to establish a permanent school in southern Europe, church leaders moved their small training center from Switzerland to this site at Collonges-sous-Saleve, France, a location with a panoramic view overlooking Geneva.*

to come, but the choice spot under the Saleve had finally become a permanent home for the school that served the French-speaking constituency in the Latin Union.

Similar to Scandinavia and Germany, Adventist education in this field was limited to a worker-training institution. Adventist elementary church schools were virtually unknown in France and the Latin Union. Compulsory primary education in France assured a relatively high rate of literacy, and, according to Tieche, Adventist families had no problems keeping their children out of school on Sabbath, but this privilege appeared to be more the result of attitudes of civil authorities at the moment than a national policy. It was enough, however, to cause church-sponsored elementary education to appear unnecessary.

## The Roots of Newbold College in England

To its advantage England shared the *lingua franca* of the church, which made it easy for many prominent Adventist personalities to work in the United Kingdom. For nearly twenty years well-known leaders such as J. N. Loughborough, M. C. Wilcox, S. N. Haskell, W. A. Spicer, and E. J. Waggoner, were associated with the Adventist church in England. Membership languished despite this distinguished leadership. In 1897 when W. W. Prescott, only three years out of the presidency of Battle Creek College, added his name to the list of denominational luminaries as superintendent of the Adventist church in England, the number of Adventists had crawled up to 590 since 1878. Less than a year after his arrival Prescott organized the British Conference and became its first president.

This small, slow-growing Adventist community hardly justified a prediction for a bright future. Operating funds were minuscule. The only institution was a small publishing house. Circumstances were less than encouraging for a school, but education was in Prescott's blood, and shortly he inaugurated an evening school in London and later, another school in Surrey.[16]

No one envisioned either of these schools as the start of an enduring institution. Each lasted only a few months and appeared to have been something akin to a field school of evangelism, a school following public meetings for the purpose of training workers for additional evangelism. Prescott explored possibilities for a permanent school, raised funds for it, and led the British Conference to vote an official approval for an institution to prepare missionaries, but he returned to the United States in 1901 before fulfilling his goal.

It was left to H. R. Salisbury, teacher of Hebrew and church history at Battle Creek College, to found the school that eventually became Newbold College. Under his direction classes began at Duncombe Hall, North London, in January 1902, following some months of planning. The institution may have been permanent, but its location was not. During the next nine years it moved four times: in 1903 to Holloway Hall, also in North London; in 1905 to Manor Gardens, Holloway; in 1907 to Stanborough Park in Watford; and finally in 1910 to new facilities on the Watford estate. In the midst of this shuffle it acquired the name of Stanborough Park Missionary College.

All of these locations were in the Greater London area of South England. As long as the school remained in London itself before moving to Watford it bore little resemblance to the traditional ideal of Adventist schools. It was situated in one of the largest cities in the world where a student labor program revolving around agriculture was not even a consideration. In fact, the school had no industries at all nor any student housing. Students lived wherever they could find a room. In effect, this early edition of England's training school was a day school.

However, there were mitigating factors. For the most part students were mature rather than youngsters; some were married and they seized the opportunity to become colporteurs. Finding London to be a lucrative market for denominational literature, many earned enough to pay their entire expenses by spending Sunday on the streets selling papers. This arrangement bode well for the school because cash flowed into institutional coffers while the school did not have the financial burden of maintaining a cafeteria and hostels.

With the move to Stanborough Park in Watford the school developed more of a traditional Adventist identity, but it ended the financial convenience of a day school in the city. At Stanborough Park the school provided housing, but students faced financial problems. Some continued in literature sales, but transportation back and forth to London on Sunday absorbed so much of their earnings that colporteuring ceased to be a profitable venture. Others found work in the press and a new food factory, but student income lagged and many ended the academic year in debt.

For Principal H. C. Lacey, who took charge of the school when it moved to Stanborough Park, arranging enough work for students to pay for their education was his most serious problem. No matter the problems, prospective students were clamoring to enroll; the school could accept only about half of those who applied. Because the essential outlook was positive, church leaders laid plans for a set of buildings that would transform the school into a worker-training institution for the British Isles.

Considering its tentative beginnings and its uncertain development, Stanborough Park Missionary College enjoyed surprising success. Similar to Friedensau, it developed an international reputation and a solid commitment among its students to missionary service. Lacey characterized the institution as a combination of an intermediate school and a college that offered extensive language study because graduates would be working in many non-English-speaking fields. Between 1905 and 1909 attendance averaged about seventy-five, mainly from the British Isles but also from continental Europe, Africa, and North America. By 1909 fifteen workers had gone from the school to French-speaking

Canada, Switzerland, the Netherlands, Argentina, Egypt, India, and British East Africa. Thirty of the workers in the United Kingdom were former students.

Without question Stanborough Park Missionary College was not cast in the mold of a traditional Adventist training school. Its proximity to a large city was contrary to the generally accepted Adventist ideal of establishing schools in rural settings; further, it had no industries or an agricultural program. Nevertheless, it benefitted from circumstances that few other training schools enjoyed, the proximity of nearby London churches in which advanced ministerial students could gain invaluable experience as acting pastors. A half dozen congregations were turned over to the school as ministerial training labs. The story of the English training school during its early years demonstrates that a successful worker-preparation program could function in a suburban environment when one of its leading purposes was to reach the masses of the city. In unique ways Stanborough Park experienced an awareness of Adventist responsibilities to urban populations.

Church activity picked up in England after the formation of the first conference in 1898. Four years later the British Union organized; by 1920 membership reached nearly 3,500. With the advent of a small sanitarium in Stanborough Park in 1912, nursing education became an another option for students. "Already there is an increased demand for nurses training," W. J. Fitzgerald of the British Union said in 1913.[17]

A growing problem for students at Stanborough was official recognition of their education. The church readily accepted the credentials of the school's graduates who became denominational workers, but an increasing tendency of students to attend the Adventist school for a pre-university education made official recognition of Stanborough Park's program desirable. To accommodate these students the school added courses in 1915 to prepare them for the London University Matriculation and Intermediate Examinations in Arts and Sciences.

Like all Adventist schools in Europe, Stanborough Park suffered the effect of World War I. Military conscription cut deeply into potential enrollment and the number of students stagnated at about the same level it had reached when the school moved to Watford in 1907. As the end of the war neared, the burden of preparing workers for mission service also weighed heavily on the school. Vast portions of Africa, including German East Africa, had fallen under the responsibility of the British Union, raising the importance of Stanborough Park Missionary College as a center for workers for much of the British world.

In 1919 the British Union added 163 acres to the school's campus and the program enlarged to include agriculture and other small industries. By 1920 enrollment in the secondary and limited post-secondary departments mushroomed to more than 200. Despite the slow beginning of Adventist education in the British Isles, at the beginning of the post-World War I era Stanborough Park emerged as the strongest of all Adventist schools in Europe.

## Impact of Early Adventist Education in Europe

Although the original impetus and undergirding philosophy for Adventist schools emanated from North America, the first generation of Adventist schools in Europe performed an important function in the developing history of Seventh-day Adventist missions. Bridging the Atlantic with Adventist education was a mission movement in itself. The schools in Scandinavia originated as institutions primarily to serve the fields in which they were located. By contrast, institutions in Germany and England developed an international influence as educational centers for missionaries as well as workers for local service. After its re-founding at Collonges in 1921, Seminaire Adventiste du Saleve assumed a similar role, preparing workers for French-speaking populations in Europe, Africa, and the Americas.

Typically, the colonial configuration of the world fields beyond Europe helped to determine which schools would become primary sources of missionaries. These were not strict jurisdictional lines, for the dictum "from anywhere to everywhere" was the *modus operandi* that the Adventist missionary movement followed. However idealistic that motto sounded, it was a matter of common sense to recruit missionaries whose native language and citizenship would facilitate travel, residence, and missionary activity in a given colonial region.

The significance of these trends lies in the fact that participating in and even managing Seventh-day Adventist missionary activities was a responsibility that many shared. For decades Adventist speakers and writers referred to the "homeland," which more often than not meant North America, but the record shows that there was more than one homeland. Missionaries of European origin regarded their native countries as the homeland as well, and in those few instances when it occurred, they regarded themselves as missionaries even when they went to North America. By becoming international centers Adventist schools in Europe fostered a tradition of global exchange. From their beginnings they contributed much to the concept of internationalism upon which the church thrived.

---

[1]The best source for summarized data about leading personalities in Adventist history is the *Seventh-day Adventist Encyclopedia.*

[2]VandeVere, *Wisdom Seekers*, pp. 31, 32.

[3]Arthur White, *Ellen White*, v. 4, p. 13.

[4]L. Mark Hamilton, "A Shrine at Jerslev," *Journal of True Education* (June 1953), pp. 28, 29.

[5]Brown, *Chronology*, pp. 10, 11; Delafield, *White in Europe*, pp. 193, 194; C. Gilund, "East Nordic Beginnings," *Journal of True Education* (June 1953), p. 30.

[6]See accounts about Scandinavia in *General Conference Bulletin*, 1909, no. 1, p. 6; *ibid.*, no. 8, pp. 119, 120; *ibid.*, no. 9, p. 126; *The Advent Survey*, Sept. 1932, pp. 5, 8; C. Gilund, *ibid.*; Brown, *Chronology*, pp. 12-14, 94, 180; *Statistical Report for 1920.*

[7]*The Advent Survery*, Sept. 1932, p. 8.

[8]*General Conference Bulletin*, 1909, no. 8, p. 119.

[9]*The Advent Survey*, Sept. 1932, p. 5.

[10]Johannes Hartlapp, ed. *Chronik Friedensau.* (Friedensau: Theologishe Hochschule, 1999) is the best source of information about the German school. See also Wilhelm Muller, "Friedensau—Citadel of Faith," *Journal of True Education* (June 1953), pp. 31-33; *General Conference Bulletin*, 1909, no. 2, pp. 26, 27; *ibid.*, no. 6, p. 84.

[11]*Ibid.*, 1918, no. 7, p. 101.

[12]This description of the schools in French-speaking Europe depends on Robert Gerber and J. C. Guenin, *Journal of True Education* (June 1953), pp. 18, 19; *General Conference Bulletin,* 1909, no.11, p. 165; *ibid.*, 1913, no. 6, p. 98; *ibid.*, 1918, no. 9, p. 132; Brown, *Chronology*, p. 159.

[13]Gertrude Loewen. *Crusader for Freedom.* (Nashville: Southern Publishing Association, 1969), pp. 25-27.

[14]*General Conference Bulletin*, 1909, no. 11, p. 165.

[15]*Ibid.*, 1913, no. 6, p. 98.

[16]Adventist education in England is summarized from Valentine, *Shaping of Adventism*, pp. 97-108; A. J. Woodfield, "Rise and Progress of Educational Work in England," *Journal of True Education* (June 1953), pp. 26, 27; *General Conference Bulletin*, 1909, no. 3, p. 30; *ibid.*, no. 6, pp. 83, 83; *ibid.*, no. 7, pp. 95, 96; *ibid.*, 1913, no. 6, p. 97; *ibid.*, 1918, no. 7, p. 100; Brown, *Chronology*, p. 136; *Statistical Report*, 1920.

[17]*General Conference Bulletin*, 1913, no. 6, p. 97.

# Chapter 6

# Circling the World

Beginning in the 1890s Adventists established a galaxy of training schools in South Africa, Australia, and South America. The long presence of England, Spain, and Portugal in these lands had created substantial extensions of European culture so that schools bore some identifying marks of their European counterparts. Events in denominational education were dramatic. Comparisons are not easy, but in some respects founders of Adventist schools discovered it to be easier going in the English colonies for a variety of reasons. Literacy rates were higher, the original cultural setting of Adventism was more similar to English society than to Latin, and economic development was more advanced.

As they evolved, Adventist schools in the various Anglo regions resembled each other because of their common British context. Institutions in Latin America were also similar to each other because Latin traditions prevailed. Each of these two broad regions formed large blocks in which Adventist workers could establish similar practices, develop lines of exchange and communication, and cultivate mutual support.

## South Africa's First Adventist School

It was in South Africa that Adventists founded the denomination's first permanent worker-training school outside the United States, Claremont Union College, the forerunner of Helderberg College. Adventist education in this English colony owed its start to Peter Wessels, scion of Dutch settlers in the Orange Free State, who gave abundantly from the fortune that had fallen into his hands from the sale of family land containing diamond mines. Young Wessels began independently to observe the seventh-day Sabbath in 1885; soon thereafter he made contact with Adventists and became a member. With others of his family he visited Battle Creek, attended the college, and returned home determined to establish a cluster of like institutions in South Africa.[1]

In Claremont, a suburb about a dozen miles from Cape Town, a three-story structure went up, large enough to accommodate 120 students. Although Wessels was Dutch the school was in English territory and the plan was to serve both language groups with primary and secondary education and a one-year missionary course. About sixty-five enrolled when school opened in February 1893.

Although the enrollment was only slightly more than half of what the facilities could accommodate school leaders maintained a rosy outlook because of Wessels' largesse which appeared to be limitless. One of the early students recalled that at the outset the school's benefactors donated enough money so students did not have to pay fees. This generosity was both a blessing and a curse. The school depended on this money instead of establishing a work program, but when the flow of funds slowed, the school began a financial reversal. Many of the locals viewed physical labor with a certain disdain, which militated against the traditional Adventist practice of integrating labor and academic activities.[2]

Another negative issue centered on the problem of reconciling the vocational character of Adventist education with the academic purpose common to all British land, that of preparing students for external examinations which were tests for either recognition of secondary education or matriculation in a university. This question was a clash between the purposes of Adventist education and the European system of standardized testing. It lay far beyond Wessels' deep pocket, and was exacerbated by the fact that about half of the original enrollment was non-Adventist.

*Mainly because of the largesse of Peter Wessels, Seventh-day Adventists in South Africa built Claremont Union College, the first college outside North America. It began classes in 1893.*

Years would pass before Adventist educators discovered how to make them compatible; meanwhile, some South African parents chose to send their children to traditional schools because they desired an education geared to these external examinations. The net effect was a consistently lower attendance at Claremont than the school's founders had hoped.

Yet the school made an impact. Its program included some student labor, although on a small scale, and a missionary-preparation course. Students who enrolled in this program were often unconcerned about external examinations because their careers with the church did not require an officially recognized academic credential. Even with these denominational characteristics Claremont's program at first was primarily nonsectarian.

These mixed conditions did not prevent church leadership in South Africa from regarding the school as a training institution, but it was a role that grew with time. After Claremont's twenty-fifth year of operation Education Secretary Frederick Griggs referred to the institution as a worker-training school. Between 1909 and 1913 the South African

Union offered a denominational position to every graduate, most of whom accepted. "There has been an increasing spiritual awakening in the educational department of our work," stated the South African Union report to the General Conference.[3]

The general program was a matter for the school to decide, but beyond its control were severe economic problems that descended on South Africa in the wake of the Anglo-Boer War. This conflict, fought out between 1899 and 1902, climaxed nearly a century of friction between British authority in the Cape Colony and the Boer (Dutch) republics of Transvaal and Orange Free State. The aftermath of war produced a deep economic depression that nearly destroyed Claremont Union College. Many students stayed away because the school had no genuine industry in which they could earn money to pay their fees, which reduced institutional revenue.

Claremont's indebtedness reached $10,000, a daunting sum for such a small school whose meager treasury could barely stay abreast of taxes and interest. Only the flinty action of the South African Union leaders averted disaster. In 1911 church workers pledged to pay off the debt, thus shifting the burden away from the school to sacrificing individuals. Within two years they had liquidated more than 40 percent of the debt.[4]

Part of the strategy for financial revival called for a brush manufacturing industry operated by student labor, a plan that, if successful, would have helped to resolve the absence of industrial education and at the same time provide additional revenue for the school. As good as the idea was, it was too little and too late.

Plans for financial recovery could not prevent yet another problem, the threat of urbanization creeping ever closer to the campus from Cape Town. Convinced that city environment spelled anathema to their schools, South African Adventists decided it was time to move, an action that Griggs announced to the 1918 General Conference.

Demolition workers tore down the twenty-five-year-old buildings that were a monument to Wessels' generosity. The school sold some of the remains, but as many construction materials as possible went to the new location, a former Zulu mission at Spion Kop, near Ladysmith in Natal, almost a thousand miles away. The reborn institution, South African Training School, opened in 1919, "established on a farm, after

God's own plan," a General Conference Department of Education report stated in 1922 with an obvious tone of relief. Enrollment improved, but hovered around 100.[5] Only time would tell whether this move was truly advantageous.

**Avondale College at Cooranbong, Australia**

In some respects no school in the Adventist world attracted more attention than Avondale in Australia, the institution which its historian, Milton Hook, calls the "experiment on the Dora."[6] In October 1888 Australasian Adventists voted to establish a school in Melbourne, but two and a half years later when Stephen Haskell reported his world tour to the General Conference session the plan had not yet materialized. The request from Australia for a school still lay before the delegates in Battle Creek. Five days after Haskell spoke they voted to open "as soon as practicable, an English Bible school" in Australia which would be the first phase of a permanent school for students of all ages.[7]

In December 1891, only months after the General Conference action, Ellen White and her son, Willie, steamed into Melbourne, Australia on a mission that her grandson-biographer describes as specifically intended to help establish the new school, but historian Emmett K. VandeVere suspects that other motivations were also at work. Following the 1888 General Conference session the church divided into two theological camps, one that actively promoted the teachings of righteousness by faith and the other that looked askance at this new emphasis as though it were heresy. Ellen White was in the first group. To diffuse the volatile attitudes between the two factions, General Conference President O. A. Olsen scattered the major proponents of both groups. Ellen White went to Australia; E. J. Waggoner took a position in Great Britain; Prescott went on a world tour; and Uriah Smith, who had stood firmly on what G. I. Butler called the old pillars of the faith, traveled to the Middle East.[8]

It was true that Ellen White demurred when the General Conference Committee requested her to go to the island continent in the South Pacific, but in the end she went in recognition of the authority of the General Conference. Once in Australia she took advantage of every opportunity to design a school that fulfilled her expectations of "Proper Education." Her attempts to reform Adventist education in the United

States had produced much less than ideal results, she believed, and she was bent on developing the Australian school into a showcase. Six years later, in 1897, with the institution already in operation, she wrote that "no breezes from Battle Creek are to be wafted in. I see I must watch before and behind and on every side to permit nothing to find entrance that has been presented before me as injuring our schools in America."[9]

The events from 1891 to 1897 demonstrate how meticulously she watched "before and behind." Two weeks after her arrival in Melbourne delegates to a session of the Australian Conference voted to proceed with the school. Eight months later on August 24, 1892, a completely American faculty began classes in rented quarters in Melbourne. During the two years this Bible school functioned, more than a hundred students, including some from New Zealand, attended to train as colporteurs and Bible workers. The courses were short.

Less than a year and a half after the school in Melbourne opened, a search for a rural location began. The committee finally settled on the 1,500-acre Brettville estate near Cooranbong. The land bordered Dora Creek, not far from the Australian east coast about 750 miles north of Melbourne in New South Wales. The price was attractive but the colonial Department of Agriculture reported that the land was "sour." Viewpoints wavered but Ellen White insisted that the soil would produce, and by the end of 1894 the union committee, fatigued by both searching and debate, decided to follow her advice and purchased the 1,500 acres.

Subduing the land was the special project of the Industrial Department, the first organized unit of the school, which Milton Hook describes as "a euphemism for twenty to twenty-five valiant young men engaged for the most part in land-clearing."[10] Teachers and students lived in Healey's Hotel in Cooranbong, which the Australasian Union rented. Ellen White and others lived in tents on the property. A new sawmill on Dora Creek cut logs into lumber and in August 1895 the first fruit trees went into the ground.

The settlers were literally hacking the school out of the woods and appeared to be winning the battle against the soil, but they faced other problems. A legal fight erupted over the title to the land and the court ordered the school to pay nearly $2,000. Since 1892 Australia had been suffering a debilitating economic depression and money was hard to come by. Neither the school nor the Australasian Union had the funds to pay the judgment. Eventually a different law firm extricated the school from this setback, but Avondale's financial woes were not over. Money was still scarce. Two members of the South African Wessels family provided $7,500, two-thirds of which was a loan; the General Conference allocated $3,000; and Ellen White gave $1,000. The building plan was under way.

W. C. Sisley, an Adventist builder who had served as a consultant to denominational projects in England, Denmark, Germany, and South Africa, arrived to draft construction plans. Early on, the union committee decided to call the school Avondale College, a name that gave way to Avondale School for Christian Workers even before the institution formally opened. When classes actually began in April 1897 only ten students registered, but within six weeks fifty enrolled. The staff numbered seven, including C. B. Hughes as principal and the veteran Stephen Haskell as the leading Bible teacher.

The school grew rapidly. In 1898 enrollment reached seventy; by 1900 it topped a hundred. By that year two dormitories, a central building for classes, and "The Chapel" comprised the campus. A community church served the growing colony of Adventists. Also on the grounds was "Sunnyside," a home built for Ellen White. When enrollment climbed to 200 in 1905, students and faculty joined to erect another building to house the additional students and the cafeteria. Before 1910 the Australasian Union and the school added the Avondale Health Retreat, a health food factory, and a printing press to the Adventist center. In 1913 the elementary school moved into its own building.

There were no loafers at this 1,500-acre experiment on the Dora. During the school's initial phases all teachers and students put on their work clothes for a three-hour, afternoon work shift in the kitchen or laundry and shops, or in agricultural assignments. Besides the fruit orchards the school operated a small dairy and poultry farm and an apiary. In late 1898 and again in April 1899 government dignitaries visited the campus. Meanwhile, in February 1899 a fruit expert, writing in *The Agricultural Gazette of New South Wales,* commended the success of the school's orchards. For the founders of the institution it was a pleasant irony that only four years had passed since the colonial

*Students at Avondale School for Christian Workers, some time before 1908. This school became the best source of missionaries to the South Pacific islands.*

Department of Agriculture had warned that the land was unsuitable for farming.

Arthur White records that half of the first students were under sixteen years of age. Besides Bible, the original curriculum included domestic science, which translated mainly into cooking, baking, and food canning, and classes in history, English, speech, penmanship, math, physiology, geography, and music. To these classes faculty later added nature study, bookkeeping, Latin, Greek, science and "pedagogics."

After the dedication of the church in 1897 Ellen White was ebullient, declaring that the Avondale School for Christian Workers was the best "in every respect" among denominational schools.[11] Adventists generally acknowledged that more than any other educational center, the Australian school fulfilled the ideas she spelled out in her 1872 statement and later writings.

Avondale became a symbol of Adventist education. It was there that Ellen White wrote prolifically about the philosophy of education, much of it under the title, *Education*, a book published in 1903. It was to the

Australian campus that W. W. Prescott journeyed in 1895 after editing *Christian Education*, a small volume about education assembled from Ellen White's writings. In 1897, after his frequent and lengthy conversations with her during the previous two years, he compiled a second collection, *Special Testimonies on Education.*

By 1900 most of the original founders of Avondale School for Christian Workers were gone, leaving the school in other hands. Fourteen years after its founding, the institution became Australasian Missionary College, reflecting the responsibility that the school held in preparing workers for the South Pacific islands. The original resolution at the 1891 General Conference approving a school for this field contemplated an institution in which students from Polynesia would enroll. During the early years enrollees came from Tasmania and New Zealand, but it was the sense of mission *to* the smaller islands of the South Pacific rather than actually serving them as a constituency institution that gripped the Australian school.

The name change was well deserved. "Can you imagine a Seventh-day Adventist mission school or mission hospital in the Pacific Islands without the influence of Avondale College?" wrote Pele T. Alu years later.[12] An example of the school's commitment to missions was Alu's home, Tonga, a set of islands lying 2,500 miles east of the school, where Avondale graduates began arriving in 1904. The first was Ella Boyd, a teacher. The E. E. Thorpes and the G. G. Stewarts followed in 1912, the H. L. Tolhursts in 1915, and the B. E. Hadfields in 1919.

All exemplified the spirit of mission that Avondale imbued its students, not only for Tonga, but for the rest of the South Pacific as well. In the Solomon Islands workers from Australia helped G. F. Jones establish schools, one of which produced Kata Ragoso, a son of a chief who became one of the most well known Adventist national leaders among the islands before World War II. For some, the commitment of mission demanded supreme sacrifice. Pearl Tolhurst, wife of H. L. Tolhurst, was the first former Avondale student to die in mission service, a victim of the 1918 world epidemic of influenza.[13]

Within a decade after Avondale officially opened, two other worker-training schools for Caucasian students sprouted up in Australasia. About fifteen miles east of Perth, the most populous center in the southern corner of Western Australia, Darling Range School began in 1907 as a secondary school. The founder, H. R. Martin, began with a donation of one pound in Australian currency with which he bought an axe, a grindstone, and a digging fork, and started to hew out the school on land given by Charles E. Ashcroft, an early Australian convert to Adventism. With his tools Martin built what would become West Australasia Missionary College, and later, Carmel College.

About 3,500 miles to the east, midway in North Island, New Zealand, Pukekura Training School admitted its first students in 1908. Four years later it moved 200 miles south and successively became Oroua Missionary School, New Zealand Missionary School, and Longburn College. Both Darling Range and Oroua remained secondary-level institutions.[14]

In 1918 Frederick Griggs referred to the schools in Western Australia and New Zealand as "subordinate" institutions, while Australasian Missionary College, the "principal" training school, had received recognition by the government as a secondary school. Plans were on foot to introduce "full college work" at Cooranbong, but that step would not come for many years. In 1920 Australasian Missionary College enrolled more than 220 students, the overwhelming majority in the elementary grades. Of its thirty-five graduates that year thirty-one entered denominational employment. Membership in Australasia slightly exceeded 8,000, an increase of more than 7,000 since the first Bible school began in Melbourne. Few could doubt that education had played a key role in this growth.[15]

### River Plate College

Adventist education in South America began in Argentina, the largest of the countries in the southern half of the continent known as the cone. During the latter half of the nineteenth century and into the twentieth millions of European immigrants settled in this region. Spaniards and Italians were the most numerous, but there were also substantial enclaves of German farmers and English entrepreneurs.[16]

Since his arrival in Argentina in 1894, Frank Westphal, the mission director, concentrated first on the English and German population. An increasingly common topic of conversation among his fellow workers was the need of a school to train workers. Their talk assumed a more urgent tone in September 1898 after Luis Ernst, a Spanish- and

German-speaking Uruguayan showed up, unannounced, at an annual gathering of church members in the province of Entre Rios, Argentina, declaring he had arrived to attend school.[17]

While young Ernst was surprised to find no school, Westphal and his colaborers were somewhat chagrined but interpreted his arrival as a signal that they should delay the school no longer. Although non-Adventists and even some church members scoffed at the idea of a school in the middle of wheat lands of Entre Rios, farmers donated land, money and time. Some came as far as 300 miles to work on the project, located in the rural community of Diamante. During the next year and a half economic depression and locusts plagued the 250-member Russo-German constituency, but they built their school anyway. In April 1900 classes began.

Preceding this school Adventist workers had made a few halting attempts at Adventist education in Argentina. Beginning in 1893 there had been small schools in Buenos Aires; another in Crespo, near Diamante; and two colporteur-training courses in the neighboring Santa Fe Province, the first in Chaco in the north and the second in Las Tunas, less than a hundred miles from Diamante. This last venture, begun in 1898 by N. Z. Town, is the date taken for the actual founding of the Argentine training school, called Colegio Camarero after it began operations at its new location. Town's courses formed the nucleus of the curriculum which was an ungraded assortment of classes intended to prepare literature salesmen. Not until Walton C. John arrived in 1908 did the school have an experienced educator as principal. Organizationally, 1908 was a turning point for Colegio Camarero.

The names of many of the early students–Santiago Mangold, George Block, Ignacio and Pedro Kalbermatter, and Luis Ernst–were not only evidence of the bi-cultural society which the school served but they were "elderly," as Professor John described them. With the admission of children, curricular change was necessary, which resulted in organizing the school into an academy, a term that North Americans understood as a secondary school. The institutional name changed to Colegio Adventista del Plata, often shortened to CAP or its Anglicized form, River Plate College.

The early curricular experience at CAP illustrated an issue common to many Adventist schools in their initial phases. Church leaders, fac-

*Colegio Adventista del Plata in Entre Rios Province, Argentina, soon after its founding. Often called CAP, it was the first Adventist training school in South America.*

ing a dearth of workers, often encouraged short courses without the niceties of academic credit and degrees. The purpose of instruction was to equip men and women for immediate employment: selling literature, occupying practical positions and in some cases, even pastoring churches.

Parents tended to see Adventist schools differently, more as replacements of state schools where their children could receive an education in Christian surroundings. As an alternative to public education, in their view Adventist schools were to offer a curriculum of equivalent substantive quality.

Fulfilling both expectations produced varying degrees of tension. One set of critics objected to the secular academic baggage that slowed the "cause" while a second band of critics complained that without legitimate academic integrity Adventist schools would become a laughingstock and would shortchange students. In part, this issue characterized the debates about the program at Battle Creek College and also contributed to the curricular struggles in the Movement of 1897 with its ensuing experiments in denominational textbooks.

This question was especially pronounced in Argentina. Speaking to the 1909 General Conference, J. W. Westphal, director of Adventist missions in South America, confessed that besides unsatisfactory conditions in the physical plant, the school had suffered from inadequate teaching since its beginning. After Professor John's arrival "the work of the school has been more thoroughly organized, systematized, and graded," Westphal said.[18]

Before John's arrival the school was notoriously deficient in equipment. Westphal wanted to "incorporate" with the government, meaning receiving official recognition, the equivalent of accreditation, but he confided to General Conference Secretary W. A. Spicer in 1908 his doubts that the government inspector would approve a school without such rudimentary items as maps, charts, or a library.[19] While John upgraded the school he also reshaped the school to conform to Argentine national standards, which he said, were similar to those in the United States. A six-grade elementary curriculum followed by a four-year missionary course became the academic design of the school.

There was good reason for the similarity in education between Argentina and the United States. Domingo Faustino Sarmiento, Argentine president from 1868 to 1874, had once been a teacher. He was also an admirer of Horace Mann and an ardent believer in his educational reforms in Massachusetts. During his administration he employed more than sixty North American primary teachers to start elementary schools in Argentina. By the end of his presidency the number of Argentine elementary schools exceeded 1,600 and enrollment figures dwarfed comparative statistics from all other Latin American countries. Sarmiento regarded education as his greatest gift to his country.[20]

By the time Adventist schools appeared, Argentina had developed its own tradition of education which established a relatively high standard of effectiveness. But the Argentine system was imperfect and many prospective students were left out. J. W. Westphal noted in 1913 that most of the students who enrolled at CAP came without any education and that two or three years of instruction were not enough to prepare them for productive service to the church.

After five years of the new academic regimen that Walton C. John inaugurated, Colegio Adventista del Plata had produced only one candidate for the ministry, but it was turning out canvassers, teachers and nurses. Prospective nursing students simply transferred to the other side of the campus to River Plate Sanitarium for their professional training. The minimum entry level for nursing students was an eight-grade education.

Continuing the colporteur-oriented program that N. Z. Town established in Las Tunas in 1898, about ten to fourteen booksellers went out from the school each summer, some grossing as much as $400 and earning scholarships to pay for their education. By 1913 those early classes begun by Town in 1898 had evolved into extra-curricular institutes during which Max Trummer, the German-born head of literature sales and a graduate from the German program at Union College, drilled both men and women in the art of salesmanship. From the earliest years literature production played a major role in South American Adventism. Westphal attributed much of the success of this program to students.

According to John, Adventist students were also making a name for themselves in professional teaching. After completing their studies at the Adventist school, some enrolled at the state normal school to prepare for teaching careers. One of them, Camilo Gil, found employment back at River Plate College as the Spanish teacher, a position with more than ordinary importance as the school sought to educate German-speaking students in Spanish literacy. By 1913 Argentine Adventists could also report the beginning phases of a church school system, only three schools, but each with an enrollment between thirty and forty.[21]

H. U. Stevens, a former teacher from Union College with a master's degree from the University of Chicago, became director of CAP in 1912, followed by J. S. Marshall in 1919. As the leading Adventist educational center in South America, Colegio Adventista del Plata had grown from its original forty acres to 160 and recorded an enrollment of 170 by 1920. Stevens and Marshall honed the academic offerings into four programs: teaching, secretarial, ministerial and Bible work.[22]

This growth had not taken place without struggles. Hordes of locusts sometimes wreaked havoc on crops that were to furnish both food and income for the school. During the early years financial reversals in the national economy nearly brought the program to a standstill. J. W. Westphal, who kept a searching eye on financial matters, admitted that indebtedness sometimes reduced the net worth of the institution below its investment value. Meanwhile, Chilean Adventists, who were administratively part of the same mission field as Argentina, were also working against formidable odds to establish a school in their territory, an effort that would dilute whatever support the central office could give to the Argentine campus.

**The Chilean Training School**

The Chilean project began when a convert from the German community donated land in Pua, near Concepcion in southern Chile, on which Adventists worked intermittently from 1902 to 1906 to found a school. Frank Westphal, who spent the years 1900-1904 in the United States, returned to South America in 1904 to find the Chilean school in stalemate. Now assigned to Chile and administratively responsible to his younger brother, he bent all of his efforts to make the new school work.[23]

Similar to Argentina, the motivation for the Chilean venture was to train colporteurs. In 1906 elementary classes began with six students. Long conversations between the Westphal brothers produced as much financial support as the South American treasury could supply, but advancement for the Chilean school was slow. During its early years it was as much a mission school as a training institution. Children made up the majority of the enrollment, many coming from English and German homes. Some students were Indians from nearby reservations. Teachers conducted their classes in English, German, and Spanish.

Argentina and Chile split a Thirteenth Sabbath overflow offering in 1912 with one-third devoted to the financially starved school in Pua. In the same year faculty added a three-year secondary curriculum and a three-year colporteur course. By 1913 enrollment reached fifty and the principal reported that the school was successfully turning out colporteurs. After his tour of South America in 1916, W. W. Prescott described the Spartan campus as generously as honest words would allow, but he observed that "this school ought to have better facilities, and we hope that they can be provided in the near future."[24] In 1918 the school became Chilean Adventist College, sometimes called the Pua Training School; two years later its enrollment reached fifty-six, only five of whom were secondary students.

These modest successes enabled the school to continue but it balanced uncertainly between success and bare survival. Its poor showings in enrollment and finances were not so bad as to cause its closure, but church leaders in the parent organization, the Austral Union, withheld their full confidence. General Conference Education Secretary W. E. Howell visited the campus in 1920, only to offer a pessimistic view of the school's future at Pua. Within months plans were on foot to move the campus northward to an improved location near Chillan where a warmer climate, a nearer constituency, and better land spoke of a more promising future.[25]

In some respects the Argentine and Chilean schools paralleled each other. Both schools sprang from German origins and even though the trend toward an Hispanic atmosphere was inevitable, faculty at both schools were obliged to hasten the process. On a visit to South America in 1910 L. R. Conradi, General Conference vice president in charge of Europe, noted that Principal John at River Plate College was "competent to give Spanish instruction," and that the eighty students were chiefly German and Spanish.[26] By 1920 both the Chilean and Argentine schools had shed much of their original German character to become predominantly Hispanic.

But the existence of two training schools in a single union conference raised administrative questions. Conventional wisdom concluded that the sister republics of Chile and Argentina needed only one institution. Church leaders in South America sometimes speculated that the Chilean school should merge with the Argentine campus. But it was the lack of denominational workers in Chile, not Argentina, that originally convinced J. W. Westphal that that country needed a school, and the best way to remedy the deficiency was to follow the common Adventist practice of training workers in schools in their territory if at all possible. Even though Chile and Argentina shared a common border, a common official language, and a cultural heritage, nearly a thousand miles separated the constituencies that supported the schools. It was unrealistic to suppose that Chileans would, in large numbers, cross the Andean cordillera and hundreds of miles of rolling plains to attend the Argentine school.

A small constituency that was unable to shoulder the financial responsibility of a school caused slow growth at Pua, which in turn spawned many headaches and second thoughts for church leaders, but the purpose of the school was to correct that problem by preparing church workers to increase the church population. Hanging on to the small, poorly equipped school in the face of grim circumstances seemed to be the best alternative for church leaders. The move from Pua that began in 1920 was the pivotal moment in the history of the Chilean school. Once settled into its new location it began a development into a strong and productive institution.

### Brazil College

Establishing a training school in Brazil was also a lagging process. Adventist penetration of Brazil began in 1892, and similar to Argentina, the movement began among the German colonists in southern Brazil where colporteurs had sold Adventist literature. In 1896, at the behest of H. F. Graf, the Adventist leader in southern Brazil, William Stein, a bilingual Brazilian citizen of Swiss-German descent, began what was called the International School at Curitiba in the southern state of Parana. It offered instruction in both Portuguese and German. A year later Stein and his wife moved to Gaspar Alto, about 125 miles farther south in the state of Santa Catarina, to teach at another school that more clearly filled the role of a training school. Known as the Brusque School, it developed into a small boarding institution on a sixty-acre plot.[27]

Neither of these schools enjoyed a long life. The founders of the Brusque School may have intended it to be a center for training workers, but in 1903 it gave way to a third institution at Taquari, 250 miles still farther south in Rio Grande do Sul. Here the familiar pattern of forming an Adventist community around institutions was in process. A small publishing enterprise turned out both German and Portuguese literature and a self-supporting physician set up practice in a modest clinic. The leading personalities of these endeavors were exclusively German: H. F. Graf and John Lipke, both German-born immigrants to the United States; F. W. Spies, American-born with literature sales experience in Germany; and William Stein.

To many the training school in Taquari appeared promising. Lipke, the teacher and a former student at Battle Creek, described it as an industrial school with a two-year course to train teachers, ministers and Bible workers. Its program was also typically Adventist–classes in nature study, physiology, geography, arithmetic, music, grammar and writing, sewing and other hand work. Students paid $4.60 a month for tuition and meals and worked four hours daily on the thirty-acre plot which housed a stable, barn and apiary.[28]

One of the major issues in developing a central school to train Brazilian workers was the need to generate a Portuguese-speaking constituency. Church leaders recognized that the heavy emphasis on the German community was only a phase that would eventually bow to the greater needs of the rest of the nation, but effecting that transition remained more problematical than it was in Argentina or Chile. After attending a meeting of workers at Taquari in 1906, W. A. Spicer wrote that the "keynote of the conference meeting was the carrying of the truth to these Portuguese-speaking peoples." "German people were urged with all diligence to acquiring that tongue," he observed. "Our work in Brazil must turn to the Portuguese."[29]

The first signs of a move in that direction appeared the next year as the Adventist community at Taquari began to break up. The press moved to Sao Paulo, which was not only a transfer out of German surroundings, but into the large southern metropolis that perceptive Adventist leaders saw as an emerging Brazilian emporium. In its new location at Sao Paulo the press continued a bilingual policy with a growing stress on Portuguese. The school continued in Taquari for three years until 1910 when church leaders sold the property, which, for the time being, closed down the worker-preparation program.[30]

Like the Brusque experiment in training workers that began in 1898, the Taquari school lasted less than ten years. The practical effect of the shutdown was akin to a bridge-burning strategy because it ended the practice of training German workers and forced mission and union presidents to concentrate on the forthcoming central school where they would educate the Portuguese population.

However, as widely acknowledged as was the need for a school, Brazilian church leaders did not feel compelled to act before they thought they had a sufficient base of support. Without openly saying so, they were inferentially saying that before re-establishing the school, Brazil would have to wait until the Portuguese-speaking constituency was large enough to furnish sufficient students to fill a training school. But the training school would furnish workers to build the constituency, and so the impasse continued.

It was in the midst of this debate that Conradi visited South America, observing that as workers became more capable in Portuguese, the Portuguese-speaking membership increased.[31] F. W. Spies, head of the Adventist church in Brazil, admitted that the Brazilian constituency was too scattered to support a school, but that the plan was to found an institution in the vicinity of Sao Paulo. For "several years," he said, which probably meant since the close of the Taquari school, church leaders had prepared prospective workers by frequently gathering young men for short courses. Because the Brazilian literacy rate was only sixteen percent, the education of a corps of Portuguese-speaking denominational employees would not be a quick process.[32]

Explain their wait for a school as they would, some believed that they had waited long enough. Among them was Spies' own wife, Izadora, who stood up in a workers' meeting in 1914 to chide her co-laborers for postponing the moment of truth. "Let us not hesitate," she urged.[33] Her words fired up the ministers who immediately set about to end the delay. About fifteen miles from Sao Paulo the group found a parcel of land without mail service, electricity or water. It was accessible by oxcart, at least in the dry season. Believing that this location fulfilled Ellen White's counsel that Adventist schools should be isolated from the distractions of the cities, they purchased the property and went to work.

The opening day of the new school arrived on May 6, 1915. Eighteen students enrolled in classes and a labor program, both of which were barely evolving. The school's development followed the pattern of Avondale: the first students lived in primitive conditions, in this case, tents, and participated in conquering the land and erecting the buildings. Under the direction of J. H. Boehm, who with his wife, managed the construction, housing, and food service, the workers dug clay to burn bricks for construction, cut lumber, dammed up a stream, and installed a hydraulic ram to pump water. Their first buildings were barns, sheds and chicken houses, but before the livestock arrived, the students and workers moved in. After constructing dormitory space they developed the farm.

A party of General Conference dignitaries toured the site in late December, eight months after construction began. Among them was

W. W. Prescott who described the place in laudatory terms reminiscent of Australia's Avondale School for Christian Workers which he had witnessed at a comparable stage of development. By the time of Prescott's visit students were occupying the partially completed buildings. Prolific fruit orchards and gardens provided an abundant food supply and the scenery was pleasant. Plans called for living quarters for more than seventy students, but construction advanced only on a pay-as-you-go schedule, which slowed progress but avoided indebtedness. Prescott obviously liked what he saw.[34]

The training schools at Brusque and Taquari had functioned in relative obscurity, but in Sao Paulo the developing campus created a stir. The idea of an industrial institution was new to Brazilians who saw the enterprise as somewhat of a curiosity, but they were willing to help. The agriculture director of the state and the head of the local horticulture station were both friendly, giving a variety of seeds and about 1,400 ornamental and fruit trees to develop the campus. To store food for a herd of imported Wisconsin cattle Boehm built two silos, a novelty that Brazilians had never seen. Directors of the nearby annual state fair regularly requested the school's farm manager to send samples of silage to demonstrate effective methods of feeding cattle.

Two years after its beginning, the school faced a stir of a different kind when a military contingent arrived on campus to investigate gossip that the school was really an ammunition factory to help revolutionists. Playing into the hands of the rumormongers were many years of unrest, caused by army generals who were out of control and fighting each other to settle old personal accounts. After the beginning of World War I, the situation became even more complex because of pro-German attitudes among the German colonists in southern Brazil that ran counter to the pro-Allied stance of the government. The leading personalities at the school could not conceal their identity. John Lipke, superintendent of the Sao Paulo Mission, shared teaching responsibilities with Paul Hennig, the secretary of the Brazil Union and a former teacher at the German Seminary in Clinton, Missouri. The J. H. Boehm couple hailed from the German Adventist community in Kansas. This obvious German presence was a ready-made target for whisperers.

After the soldiers searched the campus and found no ammunition, the faculty invited them to stay for a chapel service featuring the school choir that sang a number of hymns, including Psalm 46, "God is our refuge and strength, a very present help in trouble." The soldiers replied with their own rendition of the national anthem, then left the school as friends and in peace.[35]

Oliver Montgomery, president of the newly organized South American Division, was duly impressed after a visit to the campus in 1916. "The establishment of this training school marks the beginning of a new era for the work in Brazil," he said, voicing not only his, but the opinion of his colleagues as well. Enrollment statistics bore them out.[36]

In the early matriculations more female students showed up than the school planners expected, forcing male students to live in the attic of the unfinished main building, but this inconvenience only served as a stimulus to hurry student housing. The second year thirty-five enrolled, and fifty-six registered for the third year. Nineteen became student colporteurs after the third year. In 1920 enrollment reached 125; by that time the school had produced thirteen denominational workers.[37]

The pioneer character of the school was unavoidable, but in 1919 Thomas W. Steen and his wife, Margaret, experienced North American educators, arrived to inject as much academic advancement into the program as the still simple circumstances would allow. Church leaders in Brazil regarded the new principal's work as a reorganization. One of the first moves was to shorten the cumbersome name from Seminary of the Brazil Union Conference of Seventh-day Adventists to a more succinct Adventist Seminary. A new wave of construction added dormitory space. E. C. Ehlers, whose parents entered missionary service from Hamburg, Germany, joined Hennig as Bible teacher. Margaret Steen taught music, and Mrs. W. E. Murray, husband of the secretary of education in the South Brazil Union, conducted the normal program. In 1922 the first class graduated and the following year the institutional name changed again to Brazil College.[38]

From its beginnings in Brusque, Adventist education in Brazil had been uncertain and sometimes truncated, but nearly twenty years after the first school, Izadora Spies' urgent call had struck a responsive chord, and the results were permanent.

### Parallels Among Adventist Schools

A number of parallels characterized Adventist institutions in North America and Europe, the Anglo colonies and Latin America. In addition to the usual purposes of educating church workers and preserving Adventism in the minds and hearts of students, these Adventist schools represented the philosophy spelled out by Ellen White, but to varying degrees. Most of them functioned in rural settings, incorporated student labor into their organized programs, and made the Bible central in their curricula. By blending physical labor into the learning process and sometimes providing instruction in lines of ordinary work that people customarily did not associate with formal education, Adventist schools demonstrated that even menial tasks had an inherent dignity and value. Hence, what the Adventist world understood as training schools for denominational professions the public often knew as industrial schools.

Adventist schools were not the first to promote vocational education, but their participation in a movement to raise it to the level of formal education contrasted sharply with traditional philosophy that justified education on the basis of academic reasons. Adventists could not take all the credit, but sooner or later this pragmatic aspect of education caught the eye and the respect of thinking individuals. Frederick Griggs noted in 1909 that the practice of integrating agricultural programs into formal education was gaining ground. Agricultural studies were becoming more common in both the United States and Europe. In France and Belgium classes in basic agriculture were mandatory.[39]

There were contrasts as well as parallels among Adventist schools, such as the plight of elementary education. Church schools developed unevenly. In 1918 Griggs stated that eleven church schools were operating in Brazil.[40] Two years later his successor, W. E. Howell, noted church schools "here and there" during his visit to South America, but lamented that they did not figure prominently in the educational program. In Australia and New Zealand Adventists established a moderate number of elementary schools that evolved into a small system of Adventist schools, but the practice did not catch on in South Africa or Europe. Primary education eventually flowered in South America, but as a movement, it trailed worker training schools by more than two decades. A similar lag period had occurred in the United States.

One of the most striking contrasts between Adventist education in North America and the movement in Anglo colonies and Latin America was the difference in its highest level of instruction. In the United States by 1920 it had become a practice to design ministerial training as a college degree, which placed ministerial education on a par with traditional college degrees.

At the same time no denominational institution outside the United States was classified as a four-year, post-secondary institution as measured by North American standards, which meant that beyond North America Adventist schools tended to prepare ministers less formally. They offered mixed curricula, usually consisting of secondary-level courses, to which they added worker-preparation classes appropriate to the maturity and competence of the students. The practice of defining professional education academically as a degree belonged to a later period.

A common characteristic of Avondale College and Claremont Union College and it successor, South African Training School, was their proximity to vast, non-Caucasian mission territories. The primary role of these institutions was to be worker-training schools for white-skinned constituents, but they were also to serve as training centers for missionaries to sub-Saharan Africa and Oceania.

The first schools in South America held a similar role. Europeanization had penetrated much of this continent but in the Amazon watershed and the Andean spine lived many pre-Columbian tribes who maintained their ancient customs, some scarcely touched by civilization. Others lived under a veneer of Christianity. Preparation of missionaries in large numbers for these regions was not an immediate outcome of training schools in South America, but in time their graduates entered the hinterlands.

Like Friedensau and Stanborough Park, Avondale College quickly became a missionary-producing institution, but schools in South Africa and South America developed more slowly and would not become productive sources of missionaries for years to come. Meanwhile, mainly from North America, workers shouldered the responsibility of taking the gospel to peoples in the jungles and the mountains.

With the spread of Adventist schools into westernized countries denominational education became a part of a world movement. In this process the North American paradigm underwent changes, but not radical ones. Differences in culture and rates of literacy existed from country to country, but education in all of these regions was essentially western. A broad understanding of educational values and purposes underlay all schools. It was in the third prong of the spread of Adventist schools that even more dramatic developments occurred.

---

[1] The story of Adventist education in South Africa is summarized from *SDA Encyclopedia*, 1995 ed., v. 1, p. 686, and v. 2, p. 865; Helen M. Hyatt, "Christian Education Begins in South Africa," *Journal of True Education* (June 1953), pp. 38, 39, 63; *General Conference Bulletin,* 1909, no. 7, pp. 98, 102; *ibid.*, 1913, no. 16, pp. 244, 245; Frederick Griggs, "Report of the Department of Education to the 1918 General Conference Session," RG 51, AST; Brown, *Chronology*, pp. 10-15.

[2]Hyatt, *ibid.*

[3]*General Conference Bulletin*, 1913, no. 16, p. 244.

[4]*General Conference Bulletin*, 1909, no. 7, p. 98; 1913, no. 16, p. 245.

[5]*Ibid.*, no. 3, 1922, p. 74; Griggs, *ibid.*

[6]Milton Hook, *Avondale: Experiment on the Dora* (Cooranbong, New South Wales, Australia: Avondale Academic Press, 1998) provides the best history of the school. For an abbreviated account, see Hook, "Avondale College," in *Seventh-day Adventists in the South Pacific 1885-1985,* Noel Clapham, ed. (Warburton, Victoria, Australia: Signs Publishing Co., 1985), pp. 146-165. Arthur White's *Ellen White*, v. 4 contains many details about the founding period of the school. For an insightful glimpse of the early years at Avondale, consult George R. Knight's "Early Adventist Education in Australia: A Report of Recent Research," *Journal of Adventist Education* (April-May 1982), pp. 10, 11, 45, 46.

[7]Arthur White, *ibid.*, p. 13.

[8]VandeVere, "William Warren Prescott," in Knight, *Early Adventist Educators*, pp. 125, 126.

[9]Cited in both Arthur White, *ibid.*, p. 304 and Knight, *ibid.*, p. 41.

[10]Hook, "Avondale College," in *Adventists in the South Pacific*, Clapham, ed., p. 150.

[11]Arthur White, *ibid.*, p. 322.

[12]Pele T. Alu, "The Influence of Avondale College in the South Pacific," in *Avondale and the South Pacific: 100 Years of Mission*, Barry Oliver, *et. al.*, eds. (Cooranbong, New South Wales, Australia, Avondale Academic Press, 1997), p. 25;

[13]Leonard P. Tolhurst, "Pastor H. L. Tolhurst: A Reminiscence of His Life and Contributions to the Development of the Seventh-day Adventist Church in the South Pacific," *ibid.*, pp. 67-82; Eric Were, *No Devil Strings: the Story of Kata Rangoso* (Mountain View, CA: Pacific Press Publishing Association), pp.7-43.

[14]General *Conference* Bulletin, 1909, no. 8. p. 113; Brown, *ibid.*, pp. 75, 126; *SDA Encyclopedia*, 1995 ed., v. 1, pp. 294, 295, 955, 956.

[15]Griggs, "Report of the Department of Education to the 1918 General Conference Session," RG 51, AST; *Statistical Report*, 1920.

[16]For early descriptions of the Argentine school see reports in the *General Conference Bulletin*, 1909, no. 13, p. 198; *ibid.*, 1913, no. 12, p. 183; *ibid.*, no. 20, pp. 315, 316. Walton Brown, "Young Man With A Satchel," *Journal of True Education* (June 1953), pp. 22, 46. See also Frank Westphal, *Pioneering in the Neglected Continent* (Nashville, TN: Southern Publishing Association, 1927), pp. 44-50.

[17]*Ibid.*

[18] *General Conference Bulletin*, 1909, no. 13, p. 198.

[19]Floyd Greenleaf, *The Seventh-day Adventist Church in Latin America and the Caribbean*, v. 1, pp. 103, 104.

[20]Hubert Herring, *A History of Latin America*, 3rd ed. (New York: Alfred A. Knopf, 1968), p. 727.

[21]*General Conference Bulletin*, 1913, no. 20, p. 316.

[22]*Statistical Report*, 1920; Greenleaf, *ibid.*, v. 2, p. 23.

[23] Sources for the narrative of the school in Chile are *ibid.*, pp. 26-28, 104-107; *General Conference Bulletin*: 1909, No. 13, p. 196; 1913, No. 20, p. 316; *Statistical Report*, 1920; *RH*, July 8, 1916; Brown, *ibid.*, p. 76; .

[24]*RH*, July 8, 1916.

[25]Greenleaf, *ibid.*, v. 2, pp. 26-28.

[26]*RH*, May 11, 1911.

[27]Ruy Carlos de Camargo Vieira, *Vida e Obra de Guilherme Stein Jr.* (Sao Paulo, Brazil: Casa Publicadora Brasileira, 1995), pp. 148-156; F. H. Westphal, "Preaching the Truth in Brazil," *The Home Missionary* (July 1895), pp. 134-135; articles in *RH*: October 6, 1896, April 6, 1897, April 20, 1897, June 21 and 28, 1906; Brown, *ibid.*, 16, 17, 110.

[28]*RH*, June 6, 1907.

[29] *Ibid.*, June 21 and 28, 1906.

[30]*Ibid.*, October 15, 1908.

[31]*Ibid.*, May 25, 1911.

[32]*General Conference Bulletin*, 1909, no. 14, p. 206; *ibid.*, 1913, no. 14, p. 215.

[33]John H. Boehm and Gedeon de Oliveira, "It Was an Ammunition Factory," *Journal of True Education* (June 1953), pp. 20, 21.

[34]*RH*, February 10 and 16, 1916; *ibid.*, February 22, 1917; *ibid.*, July 25, 1918.

[35]Boehm and Oliveira, *ibid.*

[36]*RH*, February 22, 1917.

[37]*Ibid.*; *ibid.*, July 25, 1918; January 29 and August 5, 1920.

[38]*General Conference Bulletin*, 1922, no. 9, p. 215; Brown, *ibid.*, p. 110; *RH*, August 5, 1920.

[39]*General Conference Bulletin*, 1909, no. 6, p. 79.

[40]*Ibid.*, 1918, no. 3, p. 41.

# Chapter 7

# On the Frontiers in the Christian World

The first decade of the twentieth century was pivotal for the church. Administrative reorganization, dismantling Battle Creek, reestablishing the church headquarters in Washington, and the Kellogg debacle were salient events, but frequently lost sight of is the missionary awakening that swept through the church and its effect on Adventist education. The consciousness that Adventism was a global movement that had a crucial dependence on education weighed heavily on members of the General Conference Committee who gathered in Gland, Switzerland in May 1907 for their biennial session.

Since the General Conference session in 1905 church leaders had been traveling the world, and part of the baggage they brought back was a multitude of requests for workers. H. R. Salisbury said the situation "rivaled anything that had been before demanded of them."[1] It was not merely the lack of personnel to fill missionary positions that challenged the committee, but the needs for workers in regions where culture, climate, and social habits were alien to western minds and bodies. Besides schools in the United States, institutions in Australia, Germany, and England were furnishing missionaries, but the task was overwhelming and the members of the General Conference Committee re-

*H. R. Salisbury and wife, Lenna Whitney Salisbury. He headed the first training school in England before becoming president of the Washington Foreign Missionary Seminary in 1907. He died in 1915 when the ship on which he was sailing was torpedoed and sank off the Egyptian coast.*

alized the church was unprepared to respond effectively to petitions for workers.

In the face of unprecedented requests, the committee voted to convert Washington Training College, which had been operating only three years, into Washington Foreign Missionary Seminary that would offer classes especially designed to prepare workers for "heathen" lands. It was to be an institution controlled but not operated by the General Conference. The committee tapped Homer R. Salisbury, who had just completed six years developing the school in England, to be the president of the revamped Washington school.[2]

The new missionary school in Washington was highly touted around the Adventist world. Its courses were demanding and left no time for students to work for pay as in the generic institutions; consequently, Missionary Volunteer societies, also created at the Gland meeting, raised a hundred scholarships for students to attend the seminary. Students enrolled with a general appointment to serve as missionaries. They did not all take the same classes, but tailored their program according to the needs of their appointments and how well prepared they already were. General Conference personnel served as advisors to make sure students enrolled in the right classes.

The program included pastoral training and Bible instruction, supplemented by Greek and Hebrew. Classes in French, German, Spanish, Chinese, and Hindi were available, indicating the missions that the new seminary targeted. A hybrid nurses' course more similar to a program in public health than hospital or sanitarium nursing offered instruction in tropical medicine, general diseases, dietetics, hygiene and physiology. Orientation to non-Western societies and some industrial training, especially in printing, rounded out the curriculum.

The new seminary paid little heed to traditional academic matters. It admitted people with only limited education on equal footing with college graduates and offered no academic credit. Only a mile from the General Conference office building, the school operated under the watchful eye of church leaders who might interrupt students' preparation to send them away "almost at a moment's notice," Salisbury said, to respond to an especially urgent call from a remote corner of the earth.

Not everyone went to a distant or "heathen" land. Some entered the ministry in North America. Before two years elapsed seminary students had gone to Norway, China, Bengal, North India, South India, Burma, Australasia, British Guiana, Peru, Ecuador, Guatemala, and Jamaica. "We have them here under tentative appointment for every continent as well as the islands of the sea," Salisbury explained. "I trust we may duly appreciate what it means from this time on to send of our best by scores."[3]

The seminary received accolades from General Conference leaders, but it turned out to be a well-intended experiment that lasted only seven years. During that short period about ninety mission appointees went out, nearly thirty in 1913 alone, the majority of them to Asia and Latin America. At the close of the 1913-1914 school year the seminary ended its operations and the school reverted to its original charter as a liberal arts institution, renamed as Washington Missionary College. The Foreign Missionary Seminary as a separate school may have dropped out of sight, but at the time church leaders had the understanding that it would continue functioning as a department of the restored college.

Only speculation can answer why the seminary was short-lived. Preparing for mission service did not lose its luster, but a mood to convert the ungraded school into a college was gathering momentum. It was commonly recognized that classes at the seminary were of post-secondary quality, which induced delegates to the 1913 General Conference session to vote to redefine the seminary as a two-year college with the option of becoming a four-year institution. The action put an end to the ungraded courses and effectively destroyed a notion persisting from the beginnings of Battle Creek College that quick, practical results from short courses without academic trappings were the best method to prepare for a denominational career.

No matter the high hopes that so animated Salisbury, the new seminary was ambitious and concentrated, perhaps too much so. But he admitted that part of the dilemma the church faced was the need for better educated workers to lead Adventist missions. The seminary curriculum was intended to provide the improved education, but expecting students to become conversant with Hebrew and Greek Scripture, to learn a foreign language, and to develop a utilitarian knowledge of both nursing and printing, all in a short course, presupposed extreme cramming even by those with exceptional learning skills. The two ideas of short courses on the one hand and thoroughness on the other did not square well with each other and it is likely that the unrealistic level of expectations for the seminary was quickly manifest.

Another possible factor in the seminary's demise was an ever increasing consciousness that a key to successful missions was to develop competent national workers rather than to depend indefinitely on North American or European missionaries. From the earliest days missionaries with foresight advocated the education of natives in order to supply workers for mission fields. In this broad scheme of self-support, training schools in the missions themselves became progressively more important than seminaries for missionaries. The need for missionaries would continue as the frontiers of missions expanded; nevertheless, the first generation of missionaries was aware of the fundamental validity of self-support and promoted it.

Washington Foreign Missionary Seminary also attempted to isolate the education of missionaries from the mainstream of Adventist education in a manner similar to medical education. No one doubted that missionaries needed some specific preparation but it was questionable that the total package of missionary education was so different that it required a separate institution. The mission movement was almost synonymous with Adventism, and while it depended on education to survive, it survived best when it became part of the mainstream of church activity rather than separating it into a unique institution.

For whatever reasons, Washington Foreign Missionary Seminary did not endure, while the principles of missionary education became an inherent part of generic institutions. Following the example of Emmanuel Missionary College, itself founded for the express purpose of preparing missionaries as broadly construed, other Adventist institutions adopted the word "missionary" as part of their names. In time the practice spilled over from North America to schools from Europe to Asia and Australia, which evidenced a denominational recognition of the missionary character of Adventist education.

### Adventist Education in Jamaica, West Indies

One of the closest frontiers for Adventist education was the West Indies, almost next door to the United States. Beginning in the seventeenth century this region had been the scene of bitter rivalry among Spain, Holland, France, and England who competed for island holdings. Corsairs engaged in frequent shootouts and sailed with impunity on Caribbean waters. In this international melee Jamaica fell to the English in the mid-seventeenth century and became the center for stepped up buccaneer activity and slave trade. Eventually the island developed into a prime sugar-producing colony which British plantation owners turned into rich profits at the expense of their Black slaves.

To a lesser extent other colonial islands in the Lesser Antilles that arched down from Jamaica to the coast of Venezuela shared this history. The abolition of slavery by the British in 1834 brought legal freedom to the Blacks but prosperity eluded them. To complicate matters, the sugar industry fell on bad times. Personal incomes sank.

The first Adventist workers who dared to venture into this exotic but plagued region were colporteurs in the late 1880s. In short order they fanned out from British Guiana to the east coast of Central America. The most prosperous field was Jamaica where they found a few readers who soon began observing the seventh-day Sabbath on their own. When A. J. Haysmer and his wife, the first permanent Adventist missionaries, arrived in 1893 they found a handful of Sabbath-keepers suffering from endemic poverty.[4]

Membership growth was slow at first, but more encouraging in Jamaica than the rest of the English-speaking Caribbean. Talk about schools picked up in 1898 with the arrival of a twenty-two-year-old Battle Creek graduate, George F. Enoch, who complained that the quality of Jamaica's schools was poor and that they violated the North American principle of separation of church and state. Churches in fact did operate schools with tax money and teachers took the liberty to instruct students according to the beliefs of the church which happened to house the school. At times Adventist children suffered because of their beliefs. Enoch's answer to this situation was to establish Adventist schools.

Haysmer, who after a dozen years in Jamaica, was about to return to the United States in 1905, did not disagree, but was less a crusader. A few church schools began. To the General Conference session that year he spoke encouragingly about the nearly 1,100 baptized members on the island, scattered about in twenty organized churches and nine companies, but he also admitted that "the extreme hard times" in Jamaica had forced churches to close their schools because they did not have money to pay their teachers. The students reverted to the government schools that Enoch found so unsatisfactory.[5]

But practically while Haysmer was speaking Enoch spearheaded a move to establish a training school for the English-speaking West Indies, which, he glowed, would train workers for such far away places as Africa. The reason for his optimism was Willowdene, an old sugar plantation at Bog Walk near Kingston that the Jamaica Conference bought to convert into a school. Enoch predicted it would become a veritable forest of fruit-producing tropical trees and that the prospective school could not only sell fruit but manufacture and export Panama hats.

Compared to the size of membership in other locations, Haysmer's figure of 1,100 appeared to be a constituency large enough to support a small training school, but not so in Jamaica, not even with the collaboration of other English-speaking fields in the West Indies. But Enoch's rosy outlook won the day and in what had become a typical Adventist venture, J. B. Beckner, president of the Jamaica Conference, and a group of fourteen students moved to the school site in 1906 to clear the land and begin instruction as soon as was feasible. C. B. Hughes, who had experienced similar conditions at Australia's Avondale, arrived the next year to start classes, but it became painfully clear that Enoch had built an air castle. Willowdene's land was not suitable for the kind of farm that he and others dreamed of.

In 1907 Enoch transferred to India and the school moved to the 507-acre Riversdale, another estate near Kingston, which renewed hope for a dairy farm, vegetable gardens, and coconut groves. The 1909 enrollment of thirty-six included nine girls. Students came from as far away as Barbados and Panama, but only three were able to pay the $8.40 monthly fee. The rest depended on work, which meant that the school would have to produce salable items to avoid giving a free education to its students. Although Hughes cultivated the good will of officials in the agricultural department of the colonial government, he was working against an unforgiving economy. With rhetoric that was a model of understatement, he described Jamaica as "poverty stricken," acknowledging "perplexities peculiar to our work," and forecasting "much hard labor" before the school would be ready.[6]

At issue was more than a depressed economy. Geography, communication, and ethnic differences all militated against a viable parent organization to support a training school. In an effort to organize the growing church in the Greater Caribbean, church leaders threw the entire region together in 1907 under the title of the West Indian Union. This entity was geographically fragmented into islands and small countries that sprawled from British Guiana in the southeast corner westward across the Caribbean to Central America. Politically, some of the populations were independent, some were colonies. Collectively they spoke French, English, Dutch, and Spanish.

The first president of this conglomerate was thirty-year-old Urbanus Bender, commonly called U. Bender. He was not long in discovering how impracticable his job was. Because direct communication among many of the separate fields did not exist he spent an inordinate amount of time on the water and sometimes found it necessary to travel via New York to make connections from one island to another. By 1913 his energy was depleted and he left the field, making room for Haysmer who returned from Alabama to replace him.

Steadily the language areas of the West Indian Union broke away into separate missions, finally leaving hardly more than a phantom organization. In 1918 Haysmer gave way to G. A. Roberts, president of the Jamaica Conference, who found himself presiding over the formal demise of the West Indian Union the next year.

In 1911, Bender, only four years into the decline of the West Indian Union and beset with organizational problems and a diminishing financial base, notified the General Conference that he had closed the school at Riversdale. The shrinking West Indian Union could not afford the operating subsidy that the institution required. At least for the time being, Oakwood Manual Training School in Huntsville, Alabama served the English-speaking fields of the Caribbean. In 1913 Oakwood's enrollment reached about ninety, "principally from the Southern States and the West Indian Union," the school's report said.[7]

But this was a makeshift solution that turned out to be as unworkable as the schools at Bog Walk and Riversdale. Haysmer let the issue lie, but immediately upon becoming West Indian Union president, Roberts organized a school board to resurrect the school, even rehiring Hughes as principal.

Hughes and Roberts set about to repair the Riversdale property until a virtual injunction came from General Conference Assistant Secretary J. L. Shaw who spoke not only with authority from the church headquarters but also from experience as a former principal of Claremont Union College. Church leaders in Washington had soured on the Riversdale estate and insisted on a new location for the school. They also disagreed with Hughes' intention to pattern the revived program after the Huntsville model, advising instead a more traditional school for workers with less emphasis on training for ordinary jobs.

Hughes had never intended to relegate the worker training program to second place in the curriculum. He confirmed that preparing workers would be the leading purpose of the school, but also made the point that the church should provide an education for Adventist students even if they did not plan to enter denominational employment. Resolving the question of a new location took more time than coming to a meeting of the minds on the issue of curriculum, but Roberts and Hughes finally found space to rent in Mandeville, fifty miles west of Kingston at a higher and more liveable elevation where they began classes in 1919.

With this move the previously truncated plan for a West Indian Training School passed its final test. Membership in Jamaica was on the increase and school enrollment also rose commensurably. More than eighty students completed the third year. A better balance between the number of students who depended on labor and those who could pay at least part of their way improved the school's financial condition. In 1922 the formation of the Inter-American Division eliminated many of the administrative misadventures that had previously weakened the Caribbean church, and a stronger organizational structure supported the school. West Indian Training School had finally begun its journey to become Northern Caribbean University.

Compared to other educational movements on Adventist frontiers, the conditions surrounding the origins of West Indian Training School were unique. Although a British holding, Jamaica was relatively close to North America, which brought influences from both the British Empire the United States upon it. Adventists could view Jamaica as similar to the American South. Kingston, Jamaica's capital, was closer to the growing Adventist population in parts of the South than to the corners of the original West Indian Union. Jamaicans had emerged from slavery only a generation before the emancipation of North American slaves, and like the Blacks in the southern states, they suffered acute poverty. In both Jamaica and the American South education became a means of preparing a former slave population to occupy its legitimate place in society. Besides their role as institutions to educate denominational workers, both Oakwood and West Indian Training School played a part in that movement.

### F. A. Stahl and the Indian Movement in Peru

From the South American republic of Peru came a dramatic sequence of events during the early years of the twentieth century that became one of the most publicized stories of Adventist education. To some extent, this riveting experience emerged from the history of the country itself. Driven by stories about a hoard of gold in a fabled mountain kingdom, in 1522 Spanish *conquistadores* climbed into the Andes to confiscate all the wealth they could lay their hands on, successfully wrenching the land from its Inca rulers and subjecting the indigenous peoples to Spanish authority. In the process accompanying curates baptized the mountain dwellers into a nominal practice of Catholicism.

To govern this region the Spanish crown set up a viceroyalty headquartered in Lima. It brooked little variance from the official line, which, in practical terms, meant that the landowners, the army, and the church collaborated in a governing triumvirate of power. The halls of the viceregal capital where officialdom circulated glittered with opulence. Independence in 1824 eliminated the authority of the Spanish crown but changed little else except that Peruvians spent much of the nineteenth century scuffling among themselves to stabilize their newly founded republic and floundering to establish a viable economy.

These developments brought no rewards to the descendants of the pre-Columbian peoples who still inhabited the Andean highlands, many of them concentrated around Lake Titicaca. Reduced to illiteracy and poverty, they lived in silent subservience in a system that had closed around them.

Adventist missionaries as well as some native South Americans speculated about the need to enter Peru and even ran reconnoitering sorties into its largest cities, but until 1906 their efforts were erratic and they all departed with the same story–religious intolerance made open evangelism impossible and clandestine meetings necessary. The Peruvian constitution forbade public worship except for Catholic services. A smattering of Adventist believers, mainly in Lima, were left on their own, but when a liberal-minded judge ruled that non-Catholic worship in an unmarked building was a private gathering and thus did not fall under the constitutional prohibition, the wall of isolation cracked.[8]

F. L. Perry and his wife, the first permanent Adventist workers, arrived in 1906. In spite of the consensus that Peru was destined to be a hard field, Perry began his ministry with public meetings and literature distribution. Some papers were dropped off in the Lake Titicaca region. By 1908 word came down from the mountains that Manuel Camacho, an Aymara Indian convert near Puno on the northwestern shore of the Lake, was conducting a school for his fellow tribespeople and he wanted help. He was one of the few Indians who had been able to escape the unpromising circumstances of Indian life. Besides speaking both Aymara and Quechua, languages of the two leading Indian tribes in the region, he also held a teacher's certificate that he had acquired in schools on the western slope of the Andes.

Help was soon on the way. Inspired by stories drifting out of South America, F. A. Stahl and his Swedish-born wife, Ana, both graduates of the nursing course at Battle Creek, paid their own travel expenses from Ohio to South America to begin work in La Paz, Bolivia. In 1910, a year after their arrival, they transferred to Lake Titicaca and immediately laid plans for a mission station consisting of living quarters, a building for Camacho's school, and a clinic. The mission linked education and health as parts of a single movement. Stahl's successful travels around the Lake, treating ailments and injuries and conducting classes in hygienic living helped to build confidence in Camacho's school.

Construction of the mission went slowly with Indians carrying construction materials on their own shoulders from Puno twenty-one miles south to La Plateria, the site of the clinic and school. By 1912 Stahl reported that the mission was near completion. Newspapers in the region, particularly in Puno, lauded the Stahls' medical work and the school as symbols of modernization and social advancement. This recognition triggered an angry reaction from the bishop in Puno who saw La Plateria as a threat to his longstanding control over the Indians. In March 1913 he precipitated an attack on the school and landed several Indian converts, including Camacho, in the Puno jail.

Repercussions shook all of Peru. At the same time, liberal politicians were seeking to amend the national constitution by striking provisions that recognized Catholicism as the state religion and prohibited non-Catholic worship. Their efforts coincided with a reform movement at the University of San Marcos to liberate the Indians from their subservience. After his release from jail Camacho himself met with the Peruvian president to discuss these events and the issues at stake. The upshot was support for a proposal to revise the constitution that passed both houses of the Peruvian Congress in September and October 1913. Two years later the proposal survived a tumultuous session of Congress to pass its second reading before becoming law.

Camacho and Stahl had not conspired to revise Peru's constitution, but their activities had given substance to the arguments for change. From time to time hostilities continued against La Plateria, but the law was on the side of the mission. With the aid of Indian assistants, Ana Stahl added school teaching to her medical activities. Appeals for schools from Indian villages around Titicaca descended on La Plateria where attendance reached more than a hundred.

In 1916 John Howell, a young teacher from the United States, arrived to take over the school at La Plateria. In short order he acquired a

Peruvian teacher's license, which gave him authority to appoint teachers. By the end of the year he had established eight schools in the Titicaca area, all headed by Indian teachers. During the summer off-season they gathered at La Plateria for additional preparation. The school was evolving into a training center, although it was not advanced to the point of becoming an official Adventist training school.

Before the end of 1916 Oliver Montgomery, the new president of the South American Division, visited La Plateria and organized the Titicaca Mission with Stahl as superintendent and Howell as secretary-treasurer. Conducting clinics and schools was their leading activity. In less than two years under the new Titicaca Mission the number of schools rose to nineteen with an enrollment measured in the hundreds, most of them at outstations.

This was the period of the Broken Stone Mission, an oft-repeated account of an Indian chief who asked Stahl for a school but wanted a means to identify the teacher who would eventually arrive. Stahl broke a stone in two pieces, gave one part to the chief and assured him that the promised teacher would bring the other half with him for identification purposes. The actual matching of the stones never occurred, but the story persisted in Adventist circles that the teacher and the chief matched the stones to fulfill Stahl's original promise, creating an unfounded myth. Stahl lost his half during an Indian raid, and by the time he sent the promised teacher the Adventist movement around Lake Titicaca was so well known that no identification was necessary.

At best no one could call the outstation schools anything but primitive. They were devoid of equipment and the seats were only mud or stone elevations around the inside wall. But primitive or not, the schools were symbols of advancement and the Aymaras kept coming. Instruction was in Spanish. The schools also became gathering places for Stahl's clinics.

Both the local and national government were taking notice of the positive effects of the combination of medical and educational work. Soon after the constitutional revision went into effect local dignitaries wanted to organize La Plateria into an official town as an example of a community that functioned according to Christian principles. As good as this sounded, Adventist mission leaders demurred, realizing that the

*Pomata Mission Station in the Lake Titicaca region of Peru where John Howell and F. A. Stahl established scores of schools for the Aymara Indians. The stark landscape was typical at the high elevations of this region.*

negative inference on the previous centuries of Catholic rule was obvious and would stir up animosity rather than serve as an inspiration.

By 1918 Peruvian leaders in Lima came to regard the school at La Plateria as a model school and invited three Adventist missionaries to explain to the government the methods their teachers used in their schools. At the same time the chairman of a congressional committee sought out the head of the Inca Union to gather information about training Indian teachers.

There was little wonder why members of the Peruvian government and Congress were impressed. Occasionally, individual Indians broke out of the caste system that doomed them as a race, but the Titicaca Mission was developing a program that trained Indians to educate themselves and improve their own well being. By the end of 1918 Indian teachers were in charge of twenty-five of the twenty-six schools within a 150-mile radius of La Plateria. Leaders of the Titicaca Mission claimed they could have ten more schools in operation if they had the teachers. Adventists believed that it was not simply coincidental that two more reform bills were pending in the Peruvian Congress, one of which would allow Protestants to form associations to own property and carry on religious activity.

A training school was an obvious need, but for the time being it was beyond the purse of the Titicaca Mission. Consequently, La Plateria filled that role. Even though its elementary program did not include actual professional education, in 1918 General Conference Secretary of Education Frederick Griggs referred to the school as a training center, but immediately qualified it as one for Indian students only.

After his visit to Lake Titicaca in 1920, W. E. Howell, who had replaced Griggs, wrote that he was "overwhelmed" by both the needs of the region and the accomplishments of Adventist schools in the mission. During the four years since John Howell took charge of the education program the number of schools had soared to forty with fifty-six teachers, most of whom were Indian. Adventist membership stood at 2,000. The school had proved itself as *the* evangelizing tool.

In 1921 the education movement spread to the Quechuas, a neighboring group of indigenous people who for years had been agitating Titicaca Mission for schools. Of the 130 calls for new schools that inundated the mission in 1921, sixty originated from this tribe, but the mission managed to fill only two of these requests. E. H. Wilcox, the new superintendent of the mission described the "school work" as "one of the biggest problems we have to deal with."[9]

In 1922 the long anticipated training school became a reality. Colegio Adventista del Titicaca opened near Juliaca, about thirty miles north of Puno and fifty miles from La Plateria. Its three years of secondary level instruction was a quantum leap from the six-grade program that La Plateria offered. Although the new training school did not claim La Plateria as its antecedent, no one could deny that a connection existed.

One of the important elements of Adventist education among the Peruvian Indians was its spontaneous beginning. Missionaries built on what Manuel Camacho himself began, and they continued to oversee educational planning and to manage La Plateria, but they could not personally head all of the schools. The success of the program around Lake Titicaca depended on the development of Indian teachers.

A major reason for relying on the Indians was the rarefied air in the Andean highlands. Missionaries suffered respiratory and related problems they developed after continuous life at elevations exceeding

12,000 feet. After the 1918 General Conference Oliver Montgomery found Titicaca Mission in an "embarrassing" condition because of numerous health problems among the missionaries, some having spent months at a time recuperating in more congenial climates. Some of the families at Titicaca Mission were missionaries from Argentina, such as the David Dalingers, the Pedro Kalbermatters, and the R. A. Nelsons, but they also suffered from the inhospitable environment of Lake Titicaca.

In only few locations did health care and education become as closely coupled as at Titicaca Mission. Schools and clinics each benefitted from the success of the other. Both instilled a sense of personal worth and dignity in students and patients. The Stahls consistently taught a hygienic life style, a supplement to the school curriculum that was an early version of a public health program. They ministered to the immediate needs of the body, providing relief from suffering that a people living on the edge of society had come to regard as normal. The schools themselves were a parallel movement, bringing light to the mind. During the early years the Stahls' medical efforts probably drew more attention than the Indian schools, but education grew to be the primary mission activity.

The experience of F. A. and Ana Stahl among the Titicaca villages inspired the establishment of the Stahl Center for World Service at La Sierra University where a museum memorializes their work and perpetuates their ideals of service. Directed by Charles Teel, Jr., research at the Center has concluded that Adventist education changed the fabric of Titicaca society by helping to abolish a feudal and abusive system.

The missionary couple had not deliberately planned or foreseen this political outcome, but they arrived at an opportune moment. Immediately prior to their arrival, during the final years of the nineteenth century and the early years of the twentieth, many thinkers in South American countries exhibited increased sensitivity to such matters as personal freedoms, justice, and social equality and their agitation was forcing a liberalizing trend. Stahl's clinics demonstrated a compassion where previously there had been very little, and Adventist schools showed that an education with sincere motives could make a difference. The impact on the Peruvian constitution did not result from hobnobbing or lobbying for special favors, but the Stahls stimulated honest thinking by observant Peruvians who wanted their country to become part of the twentieth century.[10]

Adventist education among the Aymaras had developed well enough to inspire similar ventures in the neighboring Andean republics of Ecuador and Bolivia. Also, the Stahls transferred to the jungles surrounding the headwaters of the Amazon in northern Peru where they tried to replicate what they had done at La Plateria, but education for indigenous peoples in all of these locations remained only a shadow of the dimensions it achieved in the Titicaca Mission.

## The South Pacific

Another frontier of Adventist education presented itself in Fiji, a large island group in the South Pacific lying about 2,000 miles northeast of Sidney, Australia. Europeans learned of these islands in the mid-seventeenth century, but not until the nineteenth did they begin regular contact, and then to exploit sandalwood resources. Missionaries quickly followed, but their influence did not immediately put an end to the barbarities that erupted among people that practiced cannibalism. Out of this chaos Cakobau, a local chief, emerged as the Fijian king. In 1874, only three years after he had risen to the top, he and the chiefs under him requested the British to annex their land. In the process Cakobau agreed to adopt Christianity and Fijians discarded their war clubs in favor of trading opportunities.

In the peaceful era that followed, Christianity, albeit somewhat diluted, became the accepted way of life. About 120,000 people lived in Fiji when the first Adventist missionary arrived in 1891. The native Fijians numbered approximately 100,000, or possibly less, while the rest of the population was mixed, with no more than 3,000 Europeans, mainly English, controlling the country and about an equal number of Polynesian immigrants as laborers. Thousands more indentured workers from India worked on the sugar and fruit plantations.[11]

John I. Tay was the first Adventist to set foot in Fiji. Five years later, in 1896, J. E. Fulton, originally from Nova Scotia but educated in the United States, arrived. Except for one year, he spent the next ten in Fiji and had already begun a school for Fijian youth when he wrote that "the education of the native youth for missionaries has been the aim of all successful missionary efforts in all denominations," adding that "the strength of the white missionary has been quite largely directed toward educational work."[12]

*J. E. Fulton, a pioneer worker in the South Pacific who established one of the first schools to educate islanders in their own environment rather than to send them to Australia.*

Although he was not openly calling for a local training school, his hint was hardly concealed and expressed a view that differed from opinions heard at Avondale School for Christian Workers. From Sunnyside, her home on the Avondale campus, Ellen White was urging church leaders to bring natives from the islands to the Australian school for an education. The plan was to send them back home as trained workers.

Her advice was feasible in parts of the South Pacific, but when Fijians tried to follow her advice they encountered more obstacles on their way to Australia than they could overcome. Wesleyan missions controlled education in Fiji, and local chiefs collaborated with them to require a special permit for Fijians who wanted to leave their home towns. The colonial government would not overrule these local ordinances. In addition, the New South Wales government in Australia would not permit Fijians to enter the country unless they had a competitive grasp of English. Rather than entangling students in reams of red tape, Fulton advocated an advanced school in Fiji, but even for that option to succeed, changes would have to occur in both the colonial and local government.

Facing these restrictions, Fijians at Avondale were a rarity. In 1901 E. H. Gates, president of the Australasian Union, personally took a student from Fiji to Australia, but the young man was a son of an English plantation owner, not a Fijian. Two years later some "Bless the Lord" responses came from the audience at the General Conference session when Gates announced that the Fijian governor had softened enough to

*Seventh-day Adventist schools became a commonplace in the South Pacific islands. This school at Nukualofa on the island of Tongatapu, Tonga, included both native and Caucasian students.*

allow "another" native to go to Avondale. In 1905 two Fijians were studying in Australia, but by that time Fulton's suggestion of a training school in Fiji was beginning to materialize, partly because membership was rising.

By 1905 about 200 Sabbath observers, not all of them baptized members, worshiped at various places in Fiji. Fijian literature was flowing from the Australian press, and a monthly church paper gave a sense of unity to members on the islands. Gates told the delegates to the General Conference session that workers in Fiji had acquired about 500 acres of land for an industrial school which would become an educational center for prospective workers for other Pacific islands. Fulton called for General Conference support, saying he could put everything in operation for $1,500.

Classes in the new school began in 1904 at Buresala on the island of Ovalau. Avondale graduate S. W. Carr was principal. Five years later a girls' school opened as well. In 1908 the General Conference Committee observed that Fiji had ten churches and 133 baptized members, which amounted to the best showing of any place in the

Pacific islands. "The training school work has been the great factor in Fiji, developing successful native laborers," the committee minutes said.[13]

Enrollment did not rise encouragingly, but church leaders kept the school alive and viewed it as an integral institution in the South Pacific. In 1909 thirty students enrolled; in 1920 the figure dropped to twenty. It was a small beginning, but isolated as it was, this humble school on a distant island would develop into Fulton College, one of the major Adventist educational centers in the South Pacific.

### Planting a School in the Philippines

The borders of the Australasian Union, which included the South Pacific islands, also swung north to encircle the Philippines where Adventism arrived late as compared to other major regions in Asia. This archipelago remained as an Oriental vestige of the Spanish Empire until 1898 when it became the property of the United States as one of the spoils of the Spanish-American War.

But the end of the war did not bring peace. Many Filipinos, already fighting the Spaniards, regarded both Spanish rule and American occupation with equal hatred, and it was not long before shooting broke out between Philippine guerrillas and the Americans. Before the United States Army could squelch this new outbreak it lost more than a thousand men chasing insurrectionists through the jungles. The Philippines were only half subdued in 1901 when a civil government headed by W. H. Taft, a future United States president, imposed an Americanization process that transplanted the United States public school system in the Philippines, complete with English language instruction and North American teachers. By 1920 school attendance reached about a million. By that time the majority of the teachers were Filipinos, many of them educated in the United States.

Although political conditions in the Philippines were inviting, Seventh-day Adventists did not run opportunistically to the islands immediately after the United States took possession of them. Nor did the Philippines attract missionaries from Australia in the same way as places like Fiji, Tonga, and the Cook Islands. During his scouting visit to the Philippines in 1905, G. A. Irwin, president of the Australasian Union, reacted cautiously to the mixed conditions he found.[14]

After more than four centuries of Spanish hegemony, the Philippines were nominally Catholic, but the southern part of the archipelago was Muslim and in other regions many mountain tribes were "heathen," using the jargon of the time. Estimates placed illiteracy at seventy-five percent in Manila and nearly ninety percent in other areas. Following the war, Protestant missionaries from many denominations pounced upon this new field, organized an evangelical society, and divided up the islands into ecclesiastical spheres of influence. American dollars, which were paying for an infrastructure of roads, communication, and education, kept the economy hot; even six years after the war in 1905 inflated war prices hung on and showed no sign of subsiding. For most Adventist workers with less than modest earnings the cost of living was out of reach.

At Irwin's urging, a small Adventist beginning occurred, but for three years it reached hardly anyone outside English-speaking circles. This changed in 1908 when the L. V. Finsters arrived who aimed their efforts at the Filipinos themselves. Success was slow. Not until 1911 did Finster baptize anyone, but he followed the ceremony with classes to train the new converts to conduct personal evangelism. By 1912 Adventists claimed about a hundred baptized Filipinos.

In 1909, even before any Filipinos became members, J. E. Fulton suggested that the church should have a school in the Philippines. The quickening pace of church growth after 1913 was all the inspiration Finster needed to convert his early classes into formal education. In 1917, with the help of three teachers, one of them a Filipino, he launched a twelve-grade school at Pasay on the fringe of Manila, next to a small Adventist publishing house. Thirty-six students enrolled, a third of them girls. They met on the ground floor of a small building above which in the second story the male students lived while the girls lived in a separate building. The ubiquitous Adventist work plan was also part of the program with students building furniture, working in gardens, and erecting houses.

Growth at the new Philippine Academy was meteoric compared to other institutions on the frontiers of Adventist education. The school began with three teachers and added three more the second year after enrollment jumped to eighty. By the time the first class graduated in 1920 the school had registered an estimated 180 students and employed a faculty of ten. Hardly before anyone realized it, Philippine membership grew to about 2,200, and the training school became one of the largest outside North America.

### A Comparison

Similarities characterized education on these Adventist frontiers in Jamaica, Peru, Fiji and the Philippines. Although beginning at different times, by 1920 the idea of an Adventist training school was a firmly established aspect of mission activity. Education also began as one of the leading evangelistic tools of the church. In some cases the school was *the* primary method of creating a denominational presence and developing an effective mission. Also common to all four countries was the tendency by the public to view education as a movement of social uplift.

The Christianization process had advanced to varying degrees in all of these mission frontier countries and, as a rule of thumb, acquaintance with Christian traditions worked to the advantage of Adventism and Adventist education. But the Christianity already existing in these countries was not always a blessing. To some extent, workers suffered prejudice in all of these fields but only in Peru did it turn violent. It was a singular irony that the stiffest opposition to Adventist education occurred where it was most closely linked to humanitarianism, but in the end the combination of education and humanitarianism in Peru directly influenced structural change in the political establishment.

With the similarities there were differences. Unlike Jamaica, Peru and Fiji, the Philippines were a holding of the United States and there is little question that Adventist education benefitted from the American occupation. Of all the frontiers of Adventist missions, schools advanced most rapidly in these islands where it was part of a deliberate and well funded effort by the United States to raise the literacy level of Filipinos.

---

[1]*General Conference Bulletin*, 1906, no. 21, p. 361.

[2]This description of the Foreign Missionary Seminary is summarized from *General Conference Bulletin*, 1906, no. 21, pp. 361-363; *ibid.*, 1909, no. 6, p. 79; *ibid.*, no. 20, pp. 325, 326, 344; *ibid.*, no. 21, pp. 361-363; 1913: *ibid.*, no. 20, p. 310; General Conference Committee Minutes, February 20, 1913 and March 16, 1913, AST.

[3]*General Conference Bulletin*, 1906, no. 21, p. 362.

[4]The sources for this account of the West Indies are Greenleaf, *The Seventh-day Adventist Church in Latin America and Caribbean*, v. 1, pp. 48, 143, 166, 176-178. See also, *General Conference Bulletin*, 1905, no. 4, p. 19; *ibid.*, 1909: no. 20, pp. 339, 340; 1913: *ibid.*, no. 5, p. 79.

[5]*Ibid*, 1905, no. 4, p. 19.

[6]*Ibid.*, 1909, no. 20, p. 240.

[7]*Ibid.*, 1913., no. 5, p. 79.

[8]This account of Adventism in Peru relies on F. A. Stahl, *In the Land of the Incas* (Mountain View, CA: Pacific Press Publishing Association, 1920); *Review and Herald* articles published from letters of missionaries between 1906 and 1921; also *General Conference Bulletin*, 1909, no. 21, pp. 355, 356; 1913: *ibid.*, no. 12, p. 184; *ibid.*, no. 14, pp. 211, 212; *ibid.*, 1918, no. 3. p. 41; no. 5, pp. 66, 67; and Greenleaf, *ibid.*,v. 1, pp. 115-120, 304-311. E. H. Wilcox, *In Perils Oft* (Nashville, TN: Southern Publishing Association, 1961), a memoir of the Titicaca region, provides valuable insights but no chronological data of the period under study.

[9]*RH*, October 20, 1921.

[10] Stahl Center for World Service, La Sierra University.

[11]For this section on the South Pacific see *Missionary Magazine* for the following articles: J. O. Corliss, "Missionary Work in the Pacific Islands," (April 1898), pp. 118-122; Allen Moon, "Our Work in Polynesia," (April 1898), pp. 115-118; J. E. Fulton, "The Fijians," (May 1898), pp. 163, 164; J. E. Fulton, "School Exercises In Fiji," (November 1898), pp. 414,415; E. H. Gates, "A Trip Through Fiji," (June 1900), pp. 255-258; J. E. Fulton, "Missionary Labor in Fiji," (February 1902), pp. 64-66; *General Conference Bulletin*, 1901, no. 1, p. 10; *ibid.*, 1903, no. 9, pp. 141, 142; *ibid.*, 1905, no. 3, p. 9; *ibid.*, no. 2, p. 16; 1909: *ibid.*, no. 8, p. 113; *ibid.*, no. 16, p. 262; *ibid.*, 1913, no. 10, p. 150; General Conference Committee Minutes, April 22, 1908, AST; *Statistical Report*, 1920.

[12]Fulton, "School Exercises in Fiji," *Missionary Magazine* (November 1898), p. 414.

[13]General Conference Committee Minutes, April 22, 1908.

[14]The information about the beginning of education in the Philippines comes from *General Conference Bulletin*, 1905, no. 6, pp. 13, 14; *ibid.*, 1909, no. 8, pp. 114, 115; Spalding, *Christ's Last Legion*, pp. 103, 104, 526; Brown, *Chronology*, p. 147 ;"The Philippines," *Missionary Magazine* (June 1895), pp. 213, 214; *Statistical Report*, 1920.

# Chapter 8

# Frontiers in Africa and Asia

Perhaps to the North American Adventist there was little if any difference between frontier missions in non-Caucasian countries that had been Christianized and missions in non-Christian lands. But as demanding as were the tasks that lay within the Christian community, even greater challenges faced Adventist education among non-Christian peoples. At times exotic beyond expectation or primitive beyond imagination, life in these distant corners of the earth intrigued the Adventist world and pulled a generation of workers from their comfortable western surroundings to live on the other side of the globe. Many spent their lives in their adopted lands.

Stories about these pioneers forged a stock-in-trade view of Adventist mission life that lingered for decades in the Adventist mind. The picture of a European type, living in a small home with little furniture, meager food, and no plumbing, or garbed in jungle attire, standing beside a picture roll, teaching a group of half naked listeners approximated more often than not what Adventists saw in their minds' eye when they heard the word *missionary*. To a great extent this popularized image of Adventist missionary life owed its existence to missionary activities on the frontiers, some of them in non-Christian parts of the world.

The picture was at least partially valid, for there were indeed cases of primitive living and teaching groups of listeners in the wilderness where missionaries created islands of civilization in remote locations. But the view was not universally true. Ancient and rich cultures characterized some non-Christian regions although the masses often lived in poverty and illiteracy. Many missionaries lived in urban locations but they lived simply.

At its heart the Christianizing process was a matter of teaching as broadly understood, and education was informal as well as formal. Adventist schools figured prominently in missionary activity. Although it bore an Adventist stamp, education took on new forms wherever missionaries went in non-Christian lands. A respect for change and improvement in personal well being and in living conditions formed the practical impact of the message of salvation through Christ.

## Solusi—an Adventist Legend

Few projects grabbed the imagination of Adventists as dramatically as Solusi Mission in Africa. Its story became an Adventist legend, probably, as educator and author E. M. Cadwallader has explained, because Solusi was the first mission "established by Seventh-day Adventists among a primitive, pagan people."[1] Africa had also been the location of the first so-called Adventist college outside North America, partly because of the generosity and vision of Peter Wessels. It was he and his brother, John, who urged the church to carry the gospel to the "Kaffirs."

Heralding Christianity to Black Africa was part of the colonial penetration of Africa that Europeans began as early as the mid-seventeenth century. Until the nineteenth century the movement of civilization proceeded slowly. Dutch and British settlers were the early rivals in the south, but through the nineteenth century Germans, Portuguese, Belgians and French joined the colonial movement.

Outsiders were no strangers to Africans. For centuries Muslim adventurers had pushed into the interior from the north and east, trafficking in slaves, gold, agriculture, and native products and establishing Arab communities, some of them hundreds of miles inland from the coast. Indian traders were also common along the east coast. For Africans, the Europeans were only another alien element whose primary economic activities during the nineteenth century were slave trading, cattle raising, agriculture and mining. Free-wheeling entrepreneurs trekked far into the interior to establish mining concessions and to found communities where Africans could buy trinkets, fabrics, tools and household goods. Many settlers staked out personal holdings to exploit the agricultural potential of the continent. Moved by religious idealism, mission societies followed this economic activity by importing Christianity.

It was in this setting that the Wessels brothers donated $15,000 to buy land for a mission among their neighbors to the north. An interview between A. T. Robinson, president of the South Africa Conference, and Cecil Rhodes, head of the British South Africa Company, led to an acquisition of 12,000 acres of land near Bulawayo in Matabeleland, later known as Southern Rhodesia, which became the Zimbabwe of the late twentieth century.

The land itself was a gift, but Adventists were to pay an annual quit rent of about $60 in order to keep it. Rhodes negotiated the deal on the heels of his crushing defeat of the powerful Matabeles. Doling out land was part of his empire-building scheme to colonize the region with

*W. H. Anderson, a graduate of Battle Creek College, and his wife and daughter stand before their mud house at Solusi Mission. Anderson was the first teacher at Solusi, the earliest Seventh-day Adventist educational mission among "heathen" peoples.*

Europeans. Missionaries, he believed, would be much more effective than militia in subduing the land and bringing peace to warring tribes.

As missionaries to this part of Africa, Adventists were late comers; both Protestant and Catholic missions had been in the back country for decades. A group of seven Adventist workers ventured out in 1894 to claim the land that Rhodes offered and establish the mission. Traveling as far as the train from Cape Town would take them, they completed their 1,500-mile journey by oxcart. The party included Peter Wessels and two former students of Claremont Union College, Fred Sparrow and I. B. Burton. The next year a second group arrived, also having plodded by oxcart for several weeks to begin mission operations. In this second party were W. H. Anderson and his young wife, fresh from Battle Creek College, who recalled that as they passed through Bechuanaland natives begged them to stay and establish schools among them. "Day after day, and over and over again, we were compelled to turn a deaf ear to the entreaties for teachers," he said. Anderson knew that Africa was ready for an educational movement.[2]

The work began at Solusi Mission in 1895 with a physician, A. S. Carmichael, treating the sick and G. B. Tripp serving as general supervisor. Gradually Anderson began teaching the local people whose language was not yet reduced to written form. Students were mature men. Tribal leaders were reluctant to allow women to enroll in school because they feared that education would generate a spirit of independence and would ruin traditional African home life.

Less than a year after Anderson began his teaching, the Matabeles rebelled against Rhodes' empire-building plans. The missionaries fled to Bulawayo while friendly tribespeople protected their homes and belongings during the five-month siege. When the mission staff returned in September 1896 they picked up where they had been interrupted. Attendance at church services rose, but trouble fell upon them immediately.

A post-war famine became both a scourge and a blessing. Food prices soared and survival was difficult, but it provided a chance to teach agriculture with special meaning. Solusi workers turned the mission into a vegetable farm that kept their pantries filled. The surplus they sold in Bulawayo for much needed cash. The famine and its attendant disease produced a population of young orphans whom the missionaries took in. These victims of war and hardship shared the homegrown food and became eager students in the school. Shortly they developed into the first generation of native African teachers. But disease took its toll. Before the end of 1896 five workers died. Among them were Tripp, the mission director, and Carmichael, the physician.

Whatever the difficulties, the missionaries had no intention of leaving. In 1899 F. L. Mead, who had replaced Tripp, organized two nearby missions, one with a school at Umkupuvula, about twenty-five miles from Solusi. Other outstations sprouted up. Teachers were natives who had finished the third grade level course at Solusi. "These out-schools were well filled," Anderson wrote. "Our native boys would teach school in one village during the forenoon, and then walk two miles to another village to teach there in the afternoon, returning home at night about sunset. Thus our work was expanding in every direction." Founding schools where students could learn the gospel became the evangelistic method in Africa.[3]

Solusi itself rapidly developed into a central training station for the Adventist community in Black Africa. Outstation schools implemented a third grade education similar to the original program at Solusi. The courses in satellite locations were preparatory for the most promising students who continued their studies at Solusi. Inspired by these successes, missionary teachers founded other similar schools. One of the earliest was Somabula Mission, begun in 1901 by F. G. Armitage and his wife, who scouted the region by oxcart for several weeks before settling about 200 miles northeast of Solusi near the town of Gwelo.

In 1903 Anderson ventured into Batongaland, a region that became Zambia, the home of tribes so brutal and vicious that even David Livingstone himself years before had doubted that anyone could change them. Anderson's purpose was to honor his promise to Lewanika, king of the Barotses, that he would establish a school among them. At first resentful of the incursions of the Whites into Africa, the Barotse king changed his mind after traveling to London as a royal guest at the coronation of Edward VII. Anderson's four-month, 300-mile odyssey nearly cost him his life, but he recorded a claim to a 5,000-acre tract that became Pemba Mission, later known as Rusangu Mission, a school patterned after Solusi.

After about two decades of operation, Solusi's campus consisted of a brick classroom building with a corrugated iron roof, blackboards fashioned from linoleum painted black, and a couple of maps. Arranged among the campus flower beds were a church, dormitories, a kitchen and dining room, living quarters for Whites and African workers, a store, a blacksmith shop, and a tool shed. A herd of cattle produced milk and butter, flocks of hens furnished eggs, and 300 acres of cultivated land bore fruit and corn. Nearby Bulawayo was a market for many of the farm products. Besides their work in the school industries, many students sold literature to pay their expenses. Among the gold mines in Southern Rhodesia they found many who bought something to read even if they were illiterate.

The instructional faculty included one White teacher assisted by two African teachers. Already Black Africans were assuming the responsibility of training educators. "The natives are far more efficient as laborers for their own people than is the European, who can never understand the working of the native mind," Anderson observed.[4] English was the medium of instruction for several reasons. The school was in English-held territory, and very early Africans with an eye for their own future realized that advancement depended on their competence in English. Missionaries preferred English because they had difficulty learning African vernacular.

In 1910 Solusi traded 4,000 acres of its land for territory on which to establish Inyazura Mission, the first mission in Mashonaland. By 1917 the Solusi system grew to more than a thousand church members. The several training schools in what was called South Africa enrolled nearly 700 prospective African workers. More than 3,000 pupils studied in the outstations. These schools were crude by any standard, but they were a beginning and better than nothing for the illiterate tribespeople who attended. Among Adventists Solusi became *the* example of a successful educational mission in a primitive setting.

Anderson and fellow workers referred to schools in Africa as training schools, but these centers were not comparable to training schools as the West knew them. Curricula in the African schools were rudimentary at best. For the time being they were training schools for an illiterate society. Not until the general level of literacy rose in Africa did Solusi and its system of outstations develop an instructional program at the secondary level, and later, post-secondary.

Europeans may not have been strangers to Africans in the nineteenth century, even deep in the interior, but in the late nineteenth century the sub-Saharan continent was still an uncivilized land. Yet, change had impacted many Africans. Some of them burned with resentment, regarding Christianity as merely another commodity that Whites peddled along with cloth, pots and pans. However, in growing numbers others became keenly aware that education was a means to enjoy at least a small measure of the comforts that the Whites had.

Adventist missionaries brought with them Ellen White's instruction to mesh an agricultural program with education, especially in rural and economically disadvantaged areas and, if necessary, to carve self-supporting institutions out of the wilderness. Also, they were to educate church workers within the context of their own culture. If Avondale School for Christian Workers in Australia, emerging simultaneously with Solusi, exemplified her advice as applied in Western society, Solusi was the prime illustration in a non-Western, primitive area.

The decision to use education as a means to spread the gospel was not original with Adventists. Other denominations had already implemented these ideas in Africa before Solusi existed and Adventists benefitted by their experience. Among the notable examples was a Church of Scotland industrial mission in neighboring Nyasaland where one of its students, James Malinki, earned a teacher's certificate in 1890. Ten years later he established a chain of schools for fellow Africans which he turned over to Seventh-day Adventists after he converted to Adventism. Among them was what became Malamulo Mission.

Until 1920 Malinki served as a supervisor of all Adventist village schools in Southern Nyasaland.[5] His influence in evangelizing his home country was extensive. "In Nyasaland, we have a training school as large as one of our colleges in America," W. H. Anderson wrote in 1919. "We are developing workers as fast as we can; yet we are absolutely unable to supply the great, insistent calls that are multiplying all about us."[6]

The practice of establishing Adventist schools spread to other parts of Africa. Completely independent of the Solusi system was Waterloo Industrial School, begun in 1909 in the British protectorate of Sierra

Leone on the southwestern shore of Africa's hump. It functioned as a training center for West Africa. In the same year, about 500 miles east of Cape Town near Grahamstown, Maranatha Mission School opened. Eight years later it relocated a hundred miles northeast in Butterworth and became Bethel Training School which began graduating students from its theology department in 1920.[7]

Cecil Rhodes' argument that missionaries would be effective carriers of civilization proved true. Bulawayo, thirty-five miles from Solusi, was a community of 7,000 Europeans in 1898, an unquestioned civilizing influence but hardly a model of Western values and culture. By contrast, Solusi was a school that transformed Africans into teachers who radiated out among the villages. While they taught Adventism they also taught literacy and instilled a sense of personal worth and dignity. Developing Solusi from a raw mission to a training school had taken only about four or five years, including the interruptions caused by war and famine. If Solusi played a significant part in African Adventism, it also had figured in the development of Africa itself.

## Adventist Education Enters China

No less important to the movement of Adventist education were early schools in China. By the nineteenth century this land was losing its grip as the dominating influence in the Orient. Similar to Africa, European entrepreneurs were active in China, wringing concessions from the imperial government to sink mines, build railroads, and lease seaports. In the face of Western military superiority China lay almost prostrate. During the last years of the nineteenth-century, European governments from Russia to England parceled out the country into spheres of influence in which they arrogated special political privileges to themselves. Japan also joined the scramble. Christian missionaries followed their flags, often making it difficult for Chinese to distinguish between what was political and what was religious.

To fall prey to foreign intrusion was a bitter pill for a people whose ancient culture had produced poets, artists and philosophers, contemporaneous with the Old Testament. By the end of the nineteenth century the Chinese were in a contentious mood, exasperated not only with foreigners but with their own imperial government which appeared powerless to defend them against outsiders. In 1900 their pent

*In 1902 this first group of Seventh-day Adventist workers settled in Hong Kong to learn Chinese. The next year, Ida Thompson, seated second from right, began a school for girls in Canton, the first Adventist school in China. It eventually became what is now Hong Kong Adventist College.*

up anger flared, especially against Christianity. In the ensuing Boxer Rebellion about 200 missionaries lost their lives.

Two years later in 1902 the first Adventist missionaries, J. N. Anderson, his wife, and wife's sister, Ida Thompson, arrived from the United States, landing in Hong Kong to learn the language before settling in the interior. Before the end of the year another contingent of North American workers arrived. The tiny band of Adventist workers had little money. Thompson was in China, thanks to the generosity of the North American Wisconsin Conference which had put her on its payroll. Two years after her arrival she opened a school for girls in Canton, a city of 2,500,000 in southern China, about a hundred miles north of Hong Kong. The Wisconsin Conference also agreed to support her school, and in turn, she named it Bethel Girls' School after the secondary school that had recently been established at Bethel, Wisconsin.[8]

In a house with freshly whitewashed walls, newly painted woodwork, and tile floors that were scrubbed until the white grout showed again, instruction began on May 25, 1904. Any girl could attend who provided her own books and desk and promised to study. Twenty-five came the first day. Because she could not teach in Chinese, Thompson hired a young Chinese woman educated at the local Baptist mission to translate. That first morning Thompson started with a prayer followed by teaching the song, "Jesus Loves Me." Adventist education in China had begun.

There were no teaching materials in Chinese, but like her predecessors in the Movement of 1897, Thompson and the Baptist teacher depended on the Bible as the central textbook. The class schedule ran six full days and on Saturday for only an afternoon, which the teacher devoted exclusively to Bible study and spiritual activities.

*Seventh-day Adventist education proliferated rapidly in China. On the island of Amoy this school began shortly after Ida Thompson's school in Canton. The photo underscores the growing trend during the early twentieth century in China to provide education for girls.*

As the students became more familiar with biblical matters, the Sabbath afternoon sessions merged with regular Sabbath services. By the end of the first year the students had memorized the entire gospel of Mark.

Thompson's vision of establishing a girls' school was only a tiny straw in the wind of change that was arousing China from its isolationism. An imperial decree abolished the old Confucianist system of education in 1901, replacing it with instruction in western arts and sciences. In less than a decade, education for females, previously unheard of, was a growing trend. Another encouraging sign was a prohibition in 1902 of the practice of binding women's feet.

Once the new measures set in students flocked to Chinese schools that offered courses in teaching, commerce, industrial education, and military training. Thousands of government-sponsored students also attended universities in Europe, the United States, and even Japan. In 1908 four Chinese women enrolled at Wellesley College in Massachusetts at government expense, one of the earliest cases of Chinese women studying abroad. Speaking to the General Conference session in 1909, Thompson called these developments "the index finger, pointing out to us what is before us, and that now is our time to work for the women of China."[9]

Notwithstanding these omens of modernization Thompson had faced trying times in establishing her school. Old customs did not reverse themselves overnight. Society had long denied girls an education and regarded women as subservient wives whose primary duty was to bear children. Thompson estimated that not one woman in a hundred could read. Not all Chinese looked kindly to anyone who upset their ancient practices and finding someone from whom to rent or buy a house for a girls' school had not been easy.

But Adventist education continued to grow and to benefit from modernization. In 1911 a republic replaced the Chinese imperial government, making it easier for new ideals to seep into the country. Changes in education were part of the ethos of the times. Mission schools demonstrated that a foreign presence in China could be committed to social uplift rather than a symbol of exploitation. Soon after her arrival in China in 1919, Adelaide B. Evans, wife of I. H. Evans, president of the Far Eastern Division, talked with an elderly man whose twin grandsons were attending school. "That is the great thing," he stated, reflecting a mood of pride in the new trends.[10]

In 1906 the missionaries bought the Baptist Academy in Canton. They equipped a dormitory for twenty girls and set aside one room as a prayer room. Enrollment rose to seventy, and to accommodate this increase, Thompson employed two teachers and a cook. Within a year after Bethel Girls' School opened, Edwin Wilbur, another Adventist missionary, began Yick Chi Boys' School, also in Canton. This school soon closed, but reopened in 1915 as SamYuk Middle School.

Similar to Adventist schools in Africa, the original purpose of Adventist schools was to convert students to Adventism rather than preserving Adventist children to the church–at first there were no Adventist children to preserve–but they also prepared workers. Schools provided the first effective opportunity for Adventists to reach the masses and education became the leading evangelistic method in China. "Every foreign worker in China must be an educator," Dr. A. C. Selmon, an Adventist physician in China, declared in 1909.[11] With her experience in school work Thompson became somewhat of a denominational authority in Chinese education. "We believe the school work to be one of the most effective means of carrying this gospel to the Chinese," she said.[12]

It was from the elementary and mission schools that the church realized membership gains. Teachers taught reading from the Bible and song books, and improvised lessons in geography, physiology and arithmetic. Girls practiced sewing and weaving, and mature men and women learned to write Chinese characters and prepare materials to teach the gospel.

By 1909 Adventist schools numbered about ten, found in each province where missionaries had established a presence: four in Honan Province, 800 miles north of Hong Kong; a boys' school in Fukien Province, on the southeastern coast opposite the island of Taiwan; and five schools in Kwang Tung Province, immediately north of Hong Kong. One of the boys' schools in Kwang Tung functioned as a Bible training school which produced six Chinese workers by 1909.

In less than a decade after the founding of Bethel Girls' School the Adventist population grew enough to require a school for Adventist children. More advanced training schools also became a matter of concern. Between 1909 and 1913 one of the schools in Honan moved three times, eventually settling in Shanghai where it became the recognized training center for Mandarin-speaking Chinese. In 1919 it began offering post-secondary classes and assumed the name Shanghai Missionary College. In 1922 the original schools in Canton, Bethel Girls's School and Sam Yuk Middle School, merged to form a single training school in South China. where Cantonese was the prevailing language.

The reputation of Adventist schools spread. In Hunan Province, 500 miles north of Hong Kong, a son of an Adventist pastor became one of the earliest second-generation workers after attending school in Shanghai. C. P. Lillie, a missionary visiting Adventist groups in the same province during 1918, spoke of several promising students also attending the training school in Shanghai.[13]

The girls' schools likewise had an effect. In Mrs. B. L. Anderson's school for girls on the island of Amoy about 1,000 students enrolled during the ten years after its founding in 1909. But it was at Bethel where Adventist education began that denominational schools recorded some of their striking successes for women. Among the students were young slave girls, daughters of well-to-do Cantonese, and mature women. One, aged sixty, learned to read, gave up her tobacco, and became a dedicated Christian. Another, an estranged wife of a magistrate, overcame her hatred of foreigners, learned to read, stripped her home of its images, and became a teacher in an Adventist school.

Also at Bethel a young widow of an Adventist worker continued her dead husband's commitment to the ministry by training as a Bible worker. Girls from Bethel broke with tradition by becoming colporteurs and were among the first Adventist students in China to earn educational scholarships. Adelaide Evans noted in 1920 that "more and more, too, the girls of the better classes are going to school, and learning how to help the children of their own land."[14]

Frederick Griggs separated Adventist schools in China into four categories: schools for the children of missionaries and English members, training schools for nationals, elementary schools conducted by churches for native children, and mission schools for the public. By 1916 the number of the elementary and mission schools in China reached 118 with an enrollment of 5,000. Denton E. Rebok, the young American secretary of education for the South China Union, reported about a hundred schools in his field in 1918. By 1920 seven Adventist training schools operated in China with a reported enrollment of 844. Five of the seven offered the equivalent of a full secondary curriculum. At Shanghai Missionary College nine students were classified as post-secondary.[15]

The mediocre quality of Chinese education gave an opportunity for Christian mission schools to provide an improved system of learning. Compared to other Christian bodies, such as Roman Catholics with their fifty institutions in Shanghai alone, Adventists made a very small impression. "Our plans are not yet matured, our schools are few, our teachers are wanting, our courses of study are crude . . . but we have made a beginning," Thompson said.[16]

Although new education philosophy motivated Chinese schools, adopting western teaching methodology was not rapid. Rebok discovered in his South China schools that students created a deafening roar by studying out loud, even shouting. Examinations were unheard of. In response to a specific question by Rebok, a student began to repeat the textbook, word-for-word. Rebok remonstrated, but the teacher explained that the student would eventually have to arrive at the answer since it was somewhere in the book and Rebok would simply have to wait for it.

Whatever their flaws, Adventist schools were a growing enterprise in China. While direct evangelism was gaining ground as the medium for membership growth, education had earned its spot as a tool of progress for the church. By 1920 Adventist schools in China enrolled more students than in any other country outside North America. Also, the foundations of a permanent educational system were underway.

### Singapore Training School

Within the orb of China was Singapore, a British colony on a small island at the southern tip of the Malay Peninsula. In 1819 the British East India Company founded a trading post on the island, which was then under the control of a Malay sultanate. With this toehold in Malaysia the English commanded the Straits of Malacca, the shortest sea route from India to the Orient. In 1867 Singapore became a crown colony. Chinese merchants were the most numerous of a population of entrepreneurs who gravitated to the city from other locales, including Europe, the Arab world, India, Malaysia, East Indies and Southeast Asia. Caucasians brought Christianity, Islam claimed a large number of followers, but Buddhism was the leading religion. By the turn of the century Singapore had become the home of a cosmopolitan population and a wealthy entrepot of Southeast Asia.

Adventists made only inconsistent gestures toward Singapore until 1904 when G. F. Jones and his wife, former missionaries to the Pacific islands, moved to the city. Accompanying them was a colporteur. E. H. Gates, president of the Australasian Union, regarded Singapore as a "wicked city," but nonetheless an especially strategic and opportune location to spread the gospel. The recently arrived workers agreed. Scarcely had they begun their work before they spoke in terms of a medical outreach and a printing press. "Our laborers there are kept exceedingly busy," Gates wrote.[17] Among the first converts were Chinese, Ceylonese, and Europeans, symbolic of the international character of the city. Two years after the Joneses arrived, Singapore became the headquarters for the newly formed Malay Mission.[18]

Typically, the workers' vision did not stop with intentions to establish a publishing center. In 1905 they began a church school. Two years later it assumed the name of Eastern Training School, whose small but certain existence formed the foundation for a training school that opened in 1915 with eighty-two students. Almost overnight this school became the center of a ring of mission schools in Sumatra, Java and Borneo, and similar to Philippine Academy, it suffered immediate growing pains. By its third year the newly named Singapore Training School enrolled 142 students and increased its faculty to six, but it was still short handed.

"Already," Frederick Griggs wrote in 1918, "22 students have gone from this school into the work of our cause as canvassers, teachers, ministers and Bible workers."[19] The school did not maintain the spectacular growth it showed during its first years, but it remained a permanent fixture in Southeast Asia. From its original location the school moved twice by 1920, the last transfer to Serangoon Road where permanent buildings went up for what would become Southeast Asia Union College.

## Korea

Another example of a major step in Adventist education came out of Korea, called Chosen after 1910 when Japan began its thirty-five-year occupation of the country. The cultural heritage of this geographical appendage of China was mostly a mixture of Buddhist and Confucian tradition. Its nineteenth century history was checkered with conflict. Koreans repeatedly braced themselves against Chinese and Japanese interference and systematically sought to uproot Christianity, which had gained a substantial foothold. In 1895 Korea gained a short-lived independence.

In 1905 the W. R. Smiths arrived as the first Adventist missionaries and remained for twenty years to lay the foundations for education, publishing, and a widening circle of churches. "As most of you know," Smith told the 1909 General Conference session, "we have a small school at Soonan, in a building 60 x 12 feet." Crammed into those 720 square feet were a school for boys, a school for girls, a "little printing press," and a dispensary for Dr. Riley Russell, who was less than a year out of medical school. The combined school enrollment was about a hundred.[20]

Smith's description of the "small school" that he had begun two and a half years earlier could hardly have been less auspicious for what would become Sahmyook University with more than 5000 students, the largest school in the Adventist world at the end of the twentieth century. Soonan, the original home of this venture, was a suburb of the northern city of Pyongyang. The school began in December, 1906 as Euimyung School, a school for boys. Two years later Smith started a girls' school, and after another two years, the two merged to become Chosen Industrial School.

The development of this training school was relatively rapid. When the Chosen Conference organized in 1917 the school added a two-year ministerial course; two years later, following the formation of the Chosen Union Mission, the institution changed its name to Chosen Training School, a secondary level school. By 1920 its enrollment reached an estimated 124.

The original building in Soonan was a donation by the government with the condition that Adventists conduct a boys' school. At the time, Frederick Griggs noted, Korea was also feeling the influence of modernization, and the school made it possible for Adventists to reach the people. He also credited the school with being a "large benefit to the . . . rapidly growing Chosen Conference" by producing church workers.[21]

Among these denominational employees was K. O. Lee, who at age twenty-five was one of the first two Korean nationals to become a baptized member. Immediately after his baptism he enrolled in the Soonan school, became one of its teachers in 1908, and later, head of the mission where the training school was located. After fifteen years of church presence in Korea, the Adventist community grew to more than a thousand, organized into a union mission composed of three smaller missions. Similar to the Adventist community in China, Koreans also turned to education as a means to reach the public. In 1920 the twenty churches in Korea operated twenty-two schools.

Educational practices from the earliest days at Soonan were clearly born out of Adventist tradition, but they were new to Korea and in some instances, set precedents for educational change in the country at large. Among the firsts for Korea was education for girls as well as co-education, a break from Confucian tradition. Dormitory life for students was another precedent, and the school was also among the first to promote the dignity of labor by integrating vocational training into the curriculum.

### Meiktila, an Experiment in Burma

Probably in no other country in the Orient did Adventists enjoy more immediate benefits from the winds of modernization than in Burma. Upper Burma was mountainous, drained by the Irrawaddy and other rivers that washed a huge delta southward into the Indian Ocean. The country's neighbors, India, China, and Siam, later called Indochina, had been intermittent threats to Burmese autonomy, but it was to the British that Burma lost its identity during a series of nineteenth century wars. By the mid-1880s it had become a tribute-paying protectorate in the British Empire.

The story of Adventist education in Burma revolves around one man, Robert Bruce Thurber, who with his wife, entered the country in 1909 on a mission to establish a school. He brought five years of experience in Adventist schools in Ohio and Michigan. His destination was

Meiktila, 300 miles north of Rangoon in central Burma within the drainage basin of the Sittang River.[22]

According to Thurber, the Chinese and Indians were the dominating agents of change in Burma, perhaps even more influential than the West. In Meiktila a group of educated Burmans concluded that Burmese men must learn to work if the country was to hold its own in a changing world. About the same time they learned about Adventist philosophy of education, including the dignity of labor, from a government worker who had studied briefly with Adventist missionaries. Teaching skilled trades was contrary to the educational traditions of Burma, but inspired by their convictions and the prospects of a technical education, they formed an association, elected officers, raised money, and asked Adventists in Rangoon to establish a school for them. Adventist leaders saw their request as an opportunity to establish an Adventist presence.

Thurber began cautiously, knowing that he had agreed to provide a vocational curriculum. "We deceived no one," he wrote, "nor expected to do so; for the natives generally know what the chief purpose of the missionary is. We would do just as we agreed . . . Yet we would all the time hope and pray and work to the end that some boys would see in passing the greater good of the heart education that Christianity affords."[23]

Thurber hired a Chinese woodworker, brought in two Burmans to teach in the vernacular, and began classes with twenty boys ranging in age from eight to twenty-five. Enrollment quickly rose to thirty. Despite support from the locals, Thurber soon ran out of money and he and other workers staged a fund raising campaign to buy land and build a school with shops that would produce a self-supporting program. Two years later he moved into a new school building on the shore of Meiktila Lake. Others buildings went up, creating a boarding school with more than a hundred students.

Except for vocational training in Burmese jails, Meiktila Technical School was the only school in the country where students could learn a skilled trade. They studied Burmese and English in the morning and spent their afternoons in the trades classes, making furniture, shoes and products from cane weaving. Some of their work reached government offices. Most of the students were Burmans, but Chinese, Indians, and Eurasians also enrolled, as did Karens, a mountain people of Burma with their own language.

After five years Thurber knew that his program faced serious financial problems and would not survive without change. He had already rejected an offer of a government subsidy after studying the experience of mission schools of other Christian bodies that had accepted government grants-in-aid. The support he turned down was indeed tempting; it would have amounted to half the cost of the buildings and teachers' salaries, but the condition for this money was a government-outlined curriculum that prepared students for external examinations but did not allow time for classes with biblical content. Courses of study, textbooks, and teachers' qualifications all fell under government control.

Thurber tried to maintain the school's independence by developing a self-supporting school that offered technical and Christian education. Students taking courses in trades skills did not pay tuition, in fact, the school paid them a small wage for their work. Only those students who enrolled in what Thurber called the "literary" curriculum paid tuition. The school was dependent on these student fees and sales of its industrial products for income.

As hard as Thurber worked the school fell short of government standards and thus remained unrecognized. After five years he could no longer avoid the truth that "the school was slowly sinking." Meanwhile, the idea that Burma would benefit from an emphasis on vocational education became a national topic, prompting a conference in Rangoon to discuss the issue. The meetings resolved nothing but broke up with educators resigned to what they deemed the impossibility of integrating technical education with the prescribed government curriculum.

This impasse ended after the district commissioner of education unexpectedly visited Meiktila Technical School. After examining the entire campus he concluded that Thurber was doing "just what that conference in Rangoon said couldn't be done."[24] The government Education Department almost immediately offered official recognition to Meiktila, urging Thurber to take public money. After negotiating concessions allowing him to continue teaching skilled trades in place of some academic subjects and to withdraw from the arrangement at the end of any school year, he accepted the government's offer. The grants-in-aid that Thurber's program received paid half of the teachers' salaries and enabled Meiktila to continue.

Meiktila served the primary purpose of providing a technical education to Burmese young men but it also offered enough traditional courses to function as an Adventist training school. Leaders in Southern Asia viewed it as the chief Adventist educational center in Burma. In 1918 Griggs noted that during the nine years since it began about sixty students had been baptized. Some of them left for additional study in India. Others went farther into the mountains among the Karens to teach in village schools that Adventist missionaries began in 1915. By 1920 enrollment at Meiktila Technical School reached 155 and a school for girls had also opened in the same community.

The Meiktila experience is one of the earliest cases of Adventists confronting the issue of government subsidies to sectarian education. Two decades earlier the gift of land which became Solusi Mission had raised a storm of protest in some Adventist circles. Some religious liberty leaders claimed that accepting the donation was a breach of the principles of separation of church and state. Arguing that God impresses men in high places to assist His work on earth, Ellen White settled the debate by advising in favor of the gift, explaining that the cry to reject the land came from a distorted understanding of the issue.

Grants-in-aid were also a form of government support but they represented a different question. They were sustained financial support of sectarian schools from the public treasury, and probably a clearer case could be made against them, at least as North Americans understood the circumstances. But Thurber was in Burma, not the United States. Further, the British colonial government did not actually prohibit classes with biblical content; instead, it prescribed curricular controls that made additional instruction of any kind so difficult as to be infeasible.

Thurber did not oppose government money as a violation of the principle of separation of church and state, but rather on the principle that Adventist schools were not to implement curricula that had no room for Bible classes, which would have deprived them of their denominational identity. Only when he received assurances that Meiktila could retain its character as an Adventist school while receiving grants-in-aid did he accept government money.

In 1914 when Thurber made his decision, Adventist policy-making was primarily a process based on North American experience. At that time the question of accepting government support for education was not an issue in North American politics, hence, there were no North American precedents to follow, but in principle, Adventist leaders sought to avoid any connection with governments that could threaten denominational freedoms whether or not an immediate danger existed.

Adventist schools contemporary with Meiktila were institutions with simple purposes–to prepare workers to engage in some form of evangelistic activity, but Meiktila had begun as a response to a public request and from its inception its objectives were mixed. Thurber unapologetically pursued a dual purpose. By his arrangement with the British colonial government he showed that it was possible for sectarian schools to accept public money, but the circumstances indicate that government education leaders rationalized their support for Meiktila as a school that fulfilled a public service rather than as support of an Adventist training school.

From the vantage point of the twenty-first century Thurber's decision to accept grants-in-aid looms large, but in 1914 it was not an epochal point in the history of Adventist education. It remained only an innocuous footnote in Adventist history, practically unnoticed in his memoir, *In the Land of Pagodas*, published in 1921 as part of the reading fare for the entire denomination. No one foresaw the political and social complexities facing Adventist education in years to come and that the issue of government subsidies would appear time and again in the Adventist world, becoming progressively more thorny as Adventist schools spread around the globe.

## Adventist Schools in India

One of the daunting tasks of Adventist missionaries was to establish schools in India. Often called the subcontinent, the India of the nineteenth century was a much larger land than the India of the late twentieth century. It lay across the underside of Asia, stretching from the Islamic Middle East to the Buddhist Orient while bulging upward against China on the north. It was home to hundreds of millions, divided into many ethnic groups, each speaking its own language and maintaining its own cultural heritage. Islam and Hindu were the two major religions, but many Buddhist traditions survived from India's ancient past. The population divided into castes, ranging from the Brahmins, heirs of a wealthy and cultured past, to the illiterate, squalid untouchables.

More so than in most parts of Asia, India was the place where the East and the West met. Under the manipulative control of the English East India Company, a quasi-governmental agency, this congeries of peoples step by step fell into English hands. England annexed some portions of India but left others as client states. In 1858 the English Parliament handed over the governing authority of the East India Company to the crown, but little changed. English domination typically meant little interference in local matters but total control of larger issues, including economic affairs. Restiveness was common among Hindu and Muslim, who were sometimes mutually suspicious, but joined in resentment over colonial policies. English retribution for lack of compliance with colonial authority was usually swift and sometimes brutal.

But England's harsh paternalism had its brighter side. In India during the late nineteenth century there were universities, hospitals, railroads and telegraph lines; nevertheless, it was still an undeveloped country. Literacy among the male population was low by Western standards, probably no more than ten percent, and among women, less than one percent. Yet the emblems of Western culture were having their impact. Indians in small numbers were edging into the system. Some became middlemen and manufacturers, and a small professional middle class evolved.

It was in 1892 that Adventist colporteurs began selling literature in India's large cities. In 1895 Georgia Burrus, the first permanent Adventist worker, arrived in Calcutta, the largest center in northeastern India. Before the end of the year others joined her and the following year they opened a school for girls in the mission house in which they lived.[25]

Accounts differ, but in rapid succession missionaries started other schools in Calcutta and a school for missionary children. These small ventures bore a striking humanitarian character–one was an orphanage, another a kindergarten. Twenty years after Burrus' arrival, workers had established boarding schools, industrial schools and mission schools from the Himalayas to South India.

Visiting these schools was the purpose of General Conference Secretary of Education H. R. Salisbury's four-month tour of Asia prior to the 1913 General Conference session. "In India we now have a score of boarding-schools and village schools," he summarized after his trip, "with an attendance of nearly nine hundred students." This figure included Meiktila Technical School. About two-thirds of the enrollment were day students.[26]

Although missionaries were in charge of the larger schools, for good reason they depended on Indians who did most of the teaching. Student enrollment was too great and the variety of languages too numerous to expect missionaries to teach effectively, although some of them had become proficient in the vernacular. Salisbury counted schools in six languages besides English and Burmese. Some schools, such as those at Panvel near Bombay and at Karmatar in Bengal, were educational centers surrounded by outstations where Indian teachers conducted village schools.

Although some schools were segregated between boys and girls, in others the enrollment was mixed, both ethnically and in gender. In the first school Salisbury visited, girls outnumbered boys by two and a half times. Students were Christian, Muslim, Hindu, and in some instances, Jewish. The chief men of the village appeared not at all concerned about this mix; they welcomed Salisbury with speeches of appreciation for the school.

But a sense of brotherhood was not powerful enough to surmount the caste system. At Kalyan near Bombay, Indian teachers conducted two schools to accommodate different castes. In this community mission workers had access to only one building for a school; significantly, the higher caste occupied it while the lower caste met under a tree. At the school in the Himalayan community of Garhwal the L. J. Burgesses provided separate food preparation and eating areas for students of different castes. Here, Salisbury observed, the daily teaching of the Bible "has begun to drive out the darkness of superstition and ignorance from the hearts of the boys."[27]

At Mussoorie, also in the Himalayas, Edith E. Bruce operated a school intended for both the Anglo-Indian community and European children. It offered a curriculum that met the requirements for external examinations. As teachers discovered elsewhere in the British Empire, integrating Bible and vocational classes and a student labor schedule into an established program was not easy, but they succeeded well enough to become the testing site for the Trinity College examination in music.

The proliferation of Adventist schools between 1896 and 1915 underscored two trends that characterized Adventism in India. The first was a recognition that formal preaching was a peculiarly Christian activity, not as well suited to introduce biblical teachings in non-Christian societies as was education. This same aspect of Adventist education was also apparent in other countries where literacy rates were low. In these regions many native people experienced enough exposure to education to associate the skills of Western culture with personal enhancement and social advancement. Thus Adventist schools became a vehicle to convey not only biblical teachings and spiritual conversion but basic education as well.

That many Indian people accepted Adventist schools primarily as a means to acquire an education rather than to adopt Christianity became obvious at the Bengali school in Karmatar. At first the parents of the fifty or more Muslim and Hindu students seemed more willing for their children to associate with each other for the sake of education than to listen to instruction from the Bible. But biblical topics and Christian practices were part of the educational package, and in time their objections vanished and some opened their doors to Christianity.

The second trend in Adventism in India was its fragmented character, which became obvious as each of the Adventist schools functioned separately instead of part of an overall administrative structure. With a paucity of members scattered over the subcontinent, language and ethnic differences tended to isolate regions from each other with each language area representing a mission in itself. Oversight of India rested first in the hands of the General Conference and later the Asiatic Division. Changes in this arrangement occurred only when membership constituted a critical mass sufficiently large to justify regional and local church organization.

Adventist education reflected these conditions, which had long been a cause for concern. After visiting much of the world field between 1907 and 1909, Frederick Griggs characterized Adventist school work in India as "desultory," and called for permanent schools in Tamil-speaking South India and also in Burma, which at the time, was part of the Greater Indian field.

The first steps to turn the "desultory" nature of Adventist education around occurred in 1910 with the formation of the India Union Mission, which became an administrative umbrella for smaller missions composed of geographic clusters of language groups. With this beginning of regional administration came concepts of additional organization, including training schools for workers.

Among the early workers in India to reach the conclusion that education was the preferred method of evangelism were G. G. and Bertha Lowry, who sailed for India in 1909. They settled in Tamil-speaking South India where the momentum of Adventism had shifted from the Bengali area around Calcutta. In the same year that the Lowrys arrived, J. S. James, leader of Adventist missions in South India, established a school at Nazareth, which became the leading school in the region until Lowry established the South India Training School at Coimbatore in 1915.

Also in 1915 I. F. Blue, a former professor at Union College in the United States, founded the Indian Christian Training School at Lucknow in North India, the seat of the India Union Mission. Workers viewed Lowry's and Blue's schools differently, the one at Lucknow as an institution for the entire India Union in contrast to Coimbatore as the educational center for South India.

Whatever status the two schools had, circumstances favored South India Training School. It was the only Adventist school in the entire country where Indians could earn a secondary education. The first year's enrollment at Coimbatore outnumbered the Lucknow students three to two; the second year with forty-three students South India nearly doubled the Lucknow enrollment. The improvised conditions of the school plant at Coimbatore could hardly accommodate this growth and Lowry began a search for a new location. After the close of the 1917 school year he moved to rented quarters in Bangalore where he remained until he could erect buildings on a permanent location about six miles from the center of the city.

Two major changes marked the move to Bangalore: a new principal, E. M. Meleen from North America, replaced Lowry, and the teaching staff separated boys and girls into different schools, a policy that remained until coeducation at that level became an acceptable practice. From opening day onward the program in South India was a blend of Anglo and Indian effort. Lowry made certain that some of his staff were Indian. While teachers used vernacular languages for all classes in the lower standards, they taught in both English and vernacular in the middle levels. English was the exclusive medium in the upper, or secondary standards.

In 1920 South India Training School tentatively began offering post-secondary classes, a simple, one-year course to train ministers. Enrollment was fifty, thirty boys and twenty girls. This figure represented a drop from previous levels, but enrollment was beginning to divide among six other schools in the South India Mission that attracted a combined total of nearly 300 students. Among them was another school at Nazareth. These schools were developing stronger programs and undoubtedly some students were remaining in local centers rather than traveling to Bangalore. Taken as a whole, Adventist education in South India revealed that the concept of a system of feeder schools supporting a central training school was taking shape.

Events were not as kind to Indian Christian Training School at Lucknow. Hardly had operations begun when illness struck the principal, forcing him to withdraw while an interim replacement kept the new program going. Meanwhile, little optimism developed for the intended union training school as it could not overcome a consistently low enrollment. Other schools in North India were developing into competitors rather than feeder schools. Adventist educator E. W. Pohlman has suggested that language problems appeared to be more difficult to resolve in North India than in South India, which contributed to the lack of growth at Lucknow. For a combination of reasons the school closed in 1919 after only four years of operations. Following this shutdown Adventist schools in North India shuffled from place to place and frequently changed their names. These unsettled conditions allowed South India Training School to emerge as the leading Adventist educational enterprise in India. This development had not been deliberate, but no one can dismiss G. G. Lowry's foresight as mere happenstance. It was he who seized the opportune moment to begin a defined training school. Once taken, that step proved to be a turning point for Adventist education in India. A central publishing house and a central church administration were already in place. Within five years after it began, South India Training School injected a strong element of organizational unity to the church by becoming the most prominent educational center to train personnel for all of Adventism in India.

## A Review of Adventist Education Until 1920

By 1920 Adventist education had spread from its North American origins to nearly every major world field where the church maintained a presence. In remote regions it had spawned training schools *apropos* to the cultural level of each society. In most undeveloped lands education served as a leading evangelistic tool to reach the public, which was a contrast to developed, Christian societies where preaching was the prominent means to convey the gospel.

In undeveloped countries classrooms became congregations and preaching gave way to the more intimate practice of teaching. Playing into the hands of Adventist missionaries and other Christian bodies as well was the intellectual and social ferment of the times that produced a mood of acceptance, even eagerness at times for a Western education. Yet Adventist schools did not enjoy universal approbation. Some native people resented Adventist education because of its sectarian character and also because it appeared to be part of a larger imperial movement. Even after their exposure to Adventist education some Africans chose to retain their ancient traditions, some Chinese stuck by Confucianism and some Indians remained Hindus. But teachers would argue that education gave people a choice to accept Christianity and that it would be unrealistic to suppose that every student would adopt it.

That the evangelistic goals of Adventist education sometimes rode on the coattails of a colonial movement that was not religious in itself did not seem to worry Adventist missionaries, in fact, they often cast themselves in the context of a movement of social uplift. Principles such as education for women, the dignity of work, and self enhancement were part of early Adventist educational concepts on the frontiers. Adventist schools may have imperfectly exemplified these notions, but they contributed to the abolition of caste, recognition of gender equality, and the destruction of ethnic walls of separation. Even in the face of centuries of tradition, thinking people in non-Caucasian lands could not deny the validity of these principles.

One of the key issues for Adventist educators was preventing the needs of social uplift from blurring the Adventist identity of their programs. Thus, Adventist education embodied not only social benefits and fostered personal well being, but associated these blessings with the redemptive mission of Christianity. With a compelling sense of mission they inculcated the conviction that native students bore the responsibility of educating their own people. It was the purpose of Adventist schools to prepare couriers of this gospel who would take these ideas with them.

On this point schools on the frontiers did not differ from schools in North America or anywhere else. To prepare workers had been the prime objective of Adventist education since James and Ellen White prodded Battle Creek College into existence. While the idea of preparing workers was central, the conditions were different. A six-year elementary curriculum at Solusi bore little substantive resemblance to a baccalaureate degree from Walla Walla College, but the two were alike in depending upon similar commitment and engendering similar spiritual goals.

Only the earliest of Adventist training schools beyond North America were twenty-five years old by 1920; most of them were considerably younger, and others just beginning their history. Yet they all demonstrated an evolving sophistication with the passage of time and by 1920 some were venturing toward post-secondary status. In part this trend resulted from rising educational standards in their home countries as well as an intensifying belief that Adventist workers needed a constantly improving education.

By 1920 more than 3,700 students attended training schools outside North America. More thousands attended mission schools, outstations, and church schools. Although Adventist education was far from a mature movement, its formative days were over.

---

[1]E. M. Cadwallader, *A History of Seventh-day Adventist Education*, p. 194. Besides Cadwallader, for this passage about Solusi I have relied on W. H. Anderson, *On the Trail of Livingstone* (Mountain View, CA: Pacific Press Publishing Association, 1919); Arthur L. White, *Ellen White*, v. 4, *The Australian Years*, pp. 183-186; A. W. Spalding, *Christ's Last Legion*, pp. 377, 378; Alberto Sbacchi, "Solusi: First Seventh-day Adventist Mission in Africa," *Adventist Heritage* (Summer 1977), pp. 33-43; Brown, *Chronology*, p. 167.

[2]Anderson, *Trail of Livingstone.*, p. 43.

[3]*Ibid.*, p. 144.

[4]*Ibid.*, p. 334.

[5]For a novelized account of Malinki's life, see Josephine Cunnington Edwards' *Malinki of Malawi* (Mountain View, CA: Pacific Press Publishing Association, 1978).

[6]Anderson, *ibid.*, 344.

[7]*SDA Encyclopedia*, 1995 ed., v. 1, p. 194; v. 2, p. 311.

[8]For these paragraphs about China, see Ida Thompson, "Bethel Girls' School," *With Our Missionaries in China*, Emma Anderson, *et. al.* (Mountain View, CA: Pacific Press Publishing Association, 1920), pp. 43-63; Anna Lee, "To the Dragon Gate, Adventist Schools in South China and Hong Kong, 1903-1941," *Adventist Heritage* (Spring 1983), pp. 52-60; *General Conference Bulletin*: 1909, no. 5, pp. 66-68; "History of Hong Kong Adventist College," *Hong Kong Adventist College Catalog*, 2001-2003.

[9]*General Conference Bulletin*, 1909, no. 5, p. 66.

[10]Emma Anderson, *Missionaries in China*, p. 304.

[11]*General Conference Bulletin,* 1909, no. 5, p. 68.

[12]*Ibid.*, p. 67.

[13]Anderson, *ibid.*, pp.91-94, 294.

[14]*Ibid.*, p. 304; Herbert Ford, *For the Love of China: The Life Story of Denton E. Rebok* (Mountain View, CA: Pacific Press Publishing Association, 1971), 54.

[15]*Ibid.*, p. 57; Frederick Griggs, "Report of the Department of Education to the 1918 General Conference," RG 51, AST; *Statistical Report,* 1920.

[16]*General Conference Bulletin*, 1909, no. 5, p. 66.

[17]*General Conference Bulletin, 1905*, no. 3., p. 10.

[18]The information about Singapore comes from *General Conference Bulletin*, 1905, no. 3, pp. 9, 10; *ibid.*, 1909: no. 6, p. 262; *ibid.*, no. 8, p. 113; *ibid.,* 1913, no. 10, p. 154; *ibid.,* 1918, no. 3, p. 42; *Statistical Report*, 1920; Brown, *ibid.*, p. 169.

[19]Griggs, *ibid.*

[20]*General Conference Bulletin*, 1909, no. 10, p. 147. For other data about the beginnings of Adventist education in Korea, see *ibid.*, no. 6, p. 8; *ibid.*, no. 16, p. 262; *ibid.*, 1913, no. 5, p. 71; "Report of the Department of Education to the 1918 General Conference Session," RG 51, AST; *Statistical Report,* 1920; Brown, *ibid.*, p. 154. Also, *SDA Encyclopedia*, 1994 ed., v.10, p. 917; website, www. syu.edu as of April, 2002.

[21]Griggs, *ibid.*

[22]For information about Adventist education in Burma, see Robert Bruce Thurber, *In the Land of the Pagodas* (Nashville, TN: Southern Publishing Association, 1921); *General Conference Bulletin*: 1909, no. 17, p. 277; *ibid.*, 1913, no. 1, p. 169; *ibid.*, no. 12, p. 181; *Review and Herald*, May 15, 1913; "Report of the Department of Education to the 1918 General Conference Session," RG 51, AST.

[23]Thurber, *Land of Pagodas*, p. 139.

[24]*Ibid.*, p. 261.

[25]The beginnings of Adventist education in India is a summary from George Roos Jenson, *Spicer Memorial College . . . A Dynamic Demonstration of an Ideal* (Pune: Oriental Watchman Publishing House, 1965), pp. 1-35; Edison Samaraj, ed., *Images 1893-1993: the Seventh-day Adventist Church in Southern Asia* (Pune: Oriental Watchman Publishing House, 1993), *passim*; Edward W. Pohlman, "First the Blade, then the Ear," unpublished edition Spicer Memorial College, (published version in *Eastern Tidings*, September 15, 1945); *General Conference Bulletin*: 1909, no. 6, pp . 80, 81; *ibid.*, no. 17, p. 273; *ibid.*, 1913, no. 11, pp. 171, 174; *Review and Herald*, May 8, 15, 1913; Brown, *ibid.*, pp. 17, 18, 20, 22, 23, 27, 28, 172; *Statistical Report*, 1920.

[26]*RH*, May 8, 1913.

[27]*Ibid.*, May 15, 1913.

# Chapter 9

# The Administrative Agenda

In 1920, as Seventh-day Adventists stood at the gate of the post-World War I era it was apparent that Adventist education had reached a milestone. Since 1872 it had fashioned its own shape, and an administrative structure evolved that was assuming the dimensions of a world system. Some of the events were hit or miss, but in the main, these developments were not just a coincidence. Although contrasts separated schools around the world, a remarkable similarity connected them, deriving more from philosophical ideals than objective realities.

Chief among the unifying influences was the General Conference Department of Education, itself an office that evolved within the system while at the same time developing patterns of control and accountability for educators. Like much of Adventist history, the roots of this process were in Battle Creek. Who was responsible for guiding the newborn education movement was a question that the Battle Creek Church thrashed out in 1873 after Goodloe Harper Bell's Select School became a success. The congregation gave moral support to the school but requested the General Conference to accept responsibility for its operations.

The reason for this action was a prevailing conviction that because the school was to train workers for denominational employment, the General Conference should control it. It would thus become the official Seventh-day Adventist school, authorized to prepare church employees, not merely the creation of a single congregation.[1]

### The Educational Society and Secretary of Education

Soon after the Battle Creek school became a college the General Conference organized the Educational Society to handle affairs of education. The immediate purpose of this body, incorporated as a legal entity with stockholders in March 1874 with James White as president, was to own the fledgling institution and to become its constituency to which the board was answerable, but its practical function was a supra-board of the college. Naturally, the General Conference Committee expected the school to fulfill the needs of the young denomination and from time to time voiced sentiments about educational philosophy and issued statements that amounted to attempts to control the school through both the board and the Society.

Enough educational activity was astir by 1887 for the General Conference Committee to persuade W. W. Prescott to fill a newly created post, secretary of education. Two years later the General Conference session voted to ask the education secretary to supervise all church schools and to appoint assistants in the conferences at his discretion. These actions were the first steps in the swing of authority away from the Educational Society into the hands of people whose primary duty was education and who, in some cases at least, were experienced in the profession.[2]

Although Adventist education was still embryonic, the actions of 1887 and 1889 were none too soon. In 1882 other training schools began in California and New England, raising questions about relationships among schools and ultimate accountability. Ellen White had been urging churches to establish schools for children since her original advice in 1872, but they were a rarity with only a few in operation by 1887. In the 1880s South Lancaster Academy in Massachusetts began to publicize itself as a center to train teachers, which supplied some impetus to the notion of church schools.

As secretary of education, Prescott was not the head of a General Conference department. No department existed. He functioned more as an advisor or supervisor-at-large and liaison between the General Conference officers and the field. He took his new responsibility seriously, although he did not have much time for his new role since he was president of Battle Creek College, and remained so for seven years after his appointment.

Prescott gave his attention to the training schools—colleges and academies—while the colleges assumed the task of designing teacher-preparation courses and advising the few elementary schools that were in operation. While still president of Battle Creek College, Prescott also became president of Union College in 1891 and Walla Walla College in 1892, but principals on each campus actually ran those two new schools. This administrative arrangement was only temporary; each school soon installed its own president.[3]

Prescott left Battle Creek College in 1894, and three years later he dropped educational work altogether to fill other church administrative positions. With his departure the office of secretary of education nearly disappeared. The job of keeping tabs on Adventist education fell to L. A. Hoopes, the thirty-eight-year-old General Conference secretary who had taught briefly at the University of Nebraska and Union College. Though he was no alien to education, his appointment suggested that watching over Adventist schools was only a matter of coordination that one could do as a sideline to a full-time job.[4]

Hoopes could take little credit for the rapid growth of Adventist schools during his four years of benign neglect. Hardly had he settled into his office in 1897 when the Movement of 1897 began in spite of resistance in the General Conference. Four years later the number of church schools in the United States exceeded 220 and training schools had sprouted up in Europe, South Africa, Australia, and South America, besides other mission schools in Africa and India. An educational movement was underway that required more attention than a part-time coordinator would or could give it.

### From Educational Society to Educational Department

The organization of Adventist education underwent a thorough shakeup beginning in 1901, many of the events culminating at the three General Conference sessions of 1901, 1903, and 1905. Delegates gathered in Battle Creek for the 1901 session in a mood to reform, sensing that they faced an organizational crisis affecting the entire denomination. Before leaving town they completely overhauled the church administrative structure. One of their prime targets was the traditional method of handling church activities through incorporated societies or associations headed by presidents who had become little "kings," to use Ellen White's term.[5]

A. T. Jones, president of the Educational Society at the time, hardly qualified as a little king because leading personalities in the schools were prone to seek advice directly from Ellen White, the acknowledged source of Adventist educational philosophy. The powerhouses in Adventist education were Prescott, Kellogg, and Sutherland. All were reform-minded and threw their full weight to effect change, but each with his own theme.

Prescott's main concern was to make sure that the Bible would be the center of all curricula, Kellogg hoped to design education around health, and Sutherland sought ways to ignore academic trappings and incorporate agriculture as the fundamental element in an education program that trained missionaries. All disagreed with one another on some questions, but all three found considerable common ground and ample support from Ellen White on which to base a rationale for the stands they took. Of the three, Prescott was the most scholarly and well versed in Ellen White's statements about education.

It was one of the last significant actions of the outmoded Educational Society at the 1901 General Conference to act on a proposal to move Battle Creek College. Moving the school was a matter of reform itself. It touched off a slate of other actions advocating more church schools, financial integrity of all schools, improved supervision by local school boards, appointment of conference superintendents of education, more thorough preparation of prospective teachers, and more emphasis on foreign language instruction and premedical courses in the training schools.

The most telling blow was to organize the Educational Department as the overseer of Adventist education. In effect, this action replaced the Educational Society whose authority was limited to Battle Creek College; it also revived the office of secretary of education that Prescott once held. The new department was intended to be a standing committee directly responsible to the General Conference president instead of a semi-independent, incorporated body with property-owning rights headed by a corporation president.

Two days after the 1901 session ended, in the quieter atmosphere of a conference room, the new General Conference Committee, led by A. G. Daniels, appointed J. H. Kellogg to chair the Educational Department, assisted by P. T. Magan as secretary. The original list of departmental duties consisted of seven items, five of which posed no questions: the responsibility to be the "reference" point in all matters of education, to promote plans for education, to act as a book committee, to advise about teacher-preparation courses, and to serve as an intermediary among the schools.

After a lengthy exchange, however, the committee flatly rejected the sixth proposal that the department should supervise the reorganization of Battle Creek College in its new location in order to assure the church that it would be a school to train missionaries. Similarly, the committee threw out the seventh proposal asking the department to take on general supervision of church schools and conference schools.

The actions of 1901 were only a partial prescription to cure the organizational ailments of Adventist education. The General Conference had gained direct access to denominational education, which most leaders regarded as an improvement, but the Educational Committee was still in the hands of people who could give only part-time attention to their new responsibilities. Kellogg, as the mover and shaker in a mind-boggling succession of educational and medical projects in Battle Creek, and Magan, as the dean of the new Emmanuel Missionary College, which was still on the drawing board, were both very busy already, but as members of the new department, each had thrust another iron in the fire. How much the General Conference could expect from these men was open to question.

Another aspect of the 1901 actions defined the relationship of the General Conference to Adventist schools. The General Conference Committee designed the new Educational Department as an umbrella under which Adventist education would function. Basic relationships among schools, promotion of education, definitions of categories of Adventist schools, and broad curricular matters, including books, were the department's realm. All of these were essentially policy items. The Educational Department deliberately chose not to have direct supervisory contact with schools, which restricted the function of the newly created department to a global policy-making and advisory role. This status differed from the previous Educational Society, which as the legal owner of Battle Creek College, possessed the right to become administratively intrusive.

Kellogg's and Magan's tenure as chairman and secretary of the Educational Department lasted one year. Prescott succeeded Kellogg, with Sutherland as secretary, but again, both were gone after another year. Such fluidity elicited skepticism in place of the high hope surrounding the Educational Department when it began. By the time of the General Conference session in 1903 it appeared that the education movement had escaped reform after all.

Meanwhile, Adventist schools were appearing at a quickening pace, and persuasive voices were debating the strength and the flaws of the new order. Discussions at the 1903 General Conference session began innocently enough with a report about the need for missionary zeal to permeate Adventist schools when M. E. Cady, president of Healdsburg College, seized the floor to criticize the state of affairs in education. Without expressing a lack of confidence in the philosophy of Adventist education, he lashed out, "I am persuaded that what we need more at this time than a study of the principles is a study of organization."[6]

*As president of Healdsburg College and one of the first union directors of education in the United States, M. E. Cady supported Griggs' organizational plans, wrote textbooks for lower instructional levels, and by 1916 earned a master's degree in education.*

Because other issues crowded into the General Conference sessions, leaving no time to plan for education, Cady pressed for a convention of education leaders to discuss problems of curricular cohesion and rational development of institutions. Little had happened in education, he went on, excoriating the practice of naming a college president or some other prominent person already holding another position as head of the Educational Department. He doubted that "we have any man that has broad enough shoulders to take charge of these different lines of work."

Pointing out that, unlike other church programs, education was underrepresented in denominational councils, Cady called for more members from education on the General Conference Committee. "The Educational Department," he said, " is the supply department for the work of the third angel's message. You look to our institutions, to our colleges, to our academies, for young men and women to go out and fill the calls that come from foreign fields and from this country also."

Cady's blistering indictment was honest but not acrimonious. He pointed no accusing finger, but admitted he shared responsibility for the chaos in education. He also wore two hats, he said, one as a college president, the second as secretary of education in the Pacific Union and it was to be expected that he would favor the college. Immediately after he finished speaking the meeting adjourned.

Days later recommendations reached the floor that embodied all of Cady's suggestions. The document precipitated a prolonged discussion over the essence of the goals of Adventist educators. After reaching a meeting of minds, Daniells and the promoters of change compromised to give the General Conference president another year to make the existing Educational Department productive. L. A. Hoopes, who had left the General Conference in 1901 to become president of Union College, replaced Prescott as chairman of the Educational Department, and Frederick Griggs, principal of South Lancaster Academy, became secretary. According to the organizational formula, the secretary, not the chairman, would be the sparkplug of the department.

Daniells kept his word, allowing this latest arrangement one year to prove itself before elevating Griggs to be chairman of the department, a choice filled with irony. A decade earlier at Battle Creek College Griggs had been one of Prescott's disciples both in organizational matters and in seeking ways to professionalize the institution. He, with several other college faculty, had attended the University of Buffalo to acquaint himself with current educational practices, but Sutherland as a reform president of Battle Creek College regarded him as tainted and made him an unwelcome member of the staff. Knowing that if he stayed at Battle Creek he would waste his time, Griggs left, spending the intervening years as principal of South Lancaster Academy where he put his ideas to work and developed a reputation in his own right.

### Griggs and an Adventist System of Education

When becoming chairman of the Educational Department in 1904, Griggs took with him the responsibilities of running the department which he had done as secretary. With his backing, a proposal to sharpen up the organizational framework for Adventist education went to the 1905 General Conference. The document described a sixteen-grade system of education composed of primary schools, intermediate schools, and colleges and laid down a string of specific policies rather than the usual platitudinous recommendations which General Conference delegates hoped church leaders and educators would follow.

It was evident that the age of Kellogg, Prescott, and Sutherland was over. Kellogg was on the threshold of defection from the church, Prescott was weighed down with General Conference responsibilities, and Sutherland, whose reforms had gone sour at both Battle Creek and Berrien Springs, had forsaken denominational employment to found a self-supporting system of education in the American South. Griggs, the professor purged from Battle Creek, had returned to discover himself to be the leading voice in Adventist education.

*During the years from 1904 to 1918 Frederick Griggs was one of the strongest voices in Seventh-day Adventist education. He became the leading designer of a rational organization of denominational schools and urged a serious upgrading of teachers' credentials.*

For the first time Adventists found themselves grappling with the concept of a denominational system of education. This idea was at the heart of the 1905 actions, "a harmonious system of education," the document described it.[7] Insofar as possible common books and examinations and curricular uniformity would be a key in unifying Adventist schools, but even more crucial would be manuals that spelled out Adventist philosophy of education and methods of operating schools. Presiding over this structure would be a twenty-five-member Department of Education with representatives from all the world fields. Delegates approved the proposal with no amendments.

Two years later in 1907 Griggs left South Lancaster Academy to become the first full-time chairman of the Department of Education. In 1909, the title of chairman disappeared and the head of the department became secretary of education. With this last change the General Conference Department of Education reached the basic form it would retain.

Putting a rational organization of Adventist education into effect had not been easy. It began uncertainly, as part of the general church reorganization in 1901. In one fell swoop delegates to the 1901 General Conference session revamped the entire denominational infrastructure, but votes did not automatically create smoothly running systems. Some actions did not go far enough, others were misguided. In their over zealous mood to do away with kingly power that had been accumulating in Battle Creek, reformers even abolished the title of president of the General Conference, substituting instead the term "chairman" of the General Conference Committee. This, the church soon decided, was too much. Without any doubters, the church needed time to settle into its new format and to effect additional change.

The years immediately following 1901 were a time for new precedents. Adventists in South Africa and Australia had experimented with departmental organization, but North Americans did not know how the new church departments were to function. They were not only unacquainted with departments, they feared them as tools of overcentralization. That the new Educational Department floundered during its first years was not surprising, given the newness of the idea and the powerful individualism of leading personalities in education.

Also, a new level of church administration, the union conference, became the standard administrative unit in the reorganization package of 1901. Until a *modus operandi* evolved that accommodated this new layer of administration, no one could foresee how the new system would work. Daniells hoped that the unions would translate into a new era of Adventist administration. During the organizational discussions at the 1903 General Conference he and W. C. White were the most vocal promoters of the new unions in the United States as the regional focal points of administrative authority which would free the General Conference to function as the mission board for the denomination. This did not mean that the world headquarters had abdicated leadership, but its role would become more advisory rather than directly involved in details of local interest.[8]

The practical upshot of this process was to grant union presidents in North America a *de facto* status unlike that of their peers in the rest of the world. In some respects North American union presidents presaged the modern division president. As the General Conference withdrew from its direct supervisory role in education, the responsibility for operating the major training schools and colleges landed on the doorsteps of the unions. Probably no one foresaw in 1901 that in time the major educational institutions in North America would become symbolic not only of the education system that the 1905 recommendations envisioned, but also of the new, practical authority vested in the unions as well.

In 1903 General Conference officers were beleaguered with problems of moving the church headquarters from Battle Creek to Washington, D. C. Daniells, Prescott, and W. A. Spicer spent inordinate time working out the details of this relocation and raising money to make it possible.

The educational system was only evolving and still experimental when Griggs took full-time charge of the Department of Education in 1907. In spite of the firmness of the policies voted in 1905, these new actions were still ideals to be achieved and to a great extent the viability of the system depended on how effectively Griggs managed it. Even before he moved to Washington, assistants in education were appearing, though, as Cady pointed out in 1903, their help was frequently weak.

Nevertheless, all of this was a beginning. By 1900 five state conferences in the United States had appointed superintendents of education. Practically overnight the unions appointed their superintendents. By 1920 leaders of education were the rule in North American conferences rather than the exception. As the discussion of organization unfolded and schools appeared in other parts of the world, divisions and unions outside North America created the office of superintendent of education and by 1920 official leaders of education held office in Argentina,

Australasia, China, England, Germany, India, Japan, Korea, Peru, the Philippines, South Africa and the West Indies.

### Redefinition of Schools

A mix of several issues surfaced during the organizational debates affecting education. For years beginning in 1901 denominational leaders discussed a clearer definition of Adventist schools, which involved graded instruction and the purpose of different categories of schools. By implication, these discussions also involved the importance of an integrated agricultural work program in Adventist education, an idea that had been a vital part of Ellen White's original pronouncements in "Proper Education" as well as in her later statements.

At the turn of the century church schools, intermediate schools, and training schools were the terms describing what developed into elementary, secondary, and post-secondary institutions, but during the early years of the century a clear distinction separating each of these levels was lacking. The provisions voted at the 1905 General Conference reflected an attempt to correlate Adventist schools to popular educational models by changing the terminology to primary schools, intermediate schools, and colleges. The first category would carry students through seven grades, intermediate schools were to offer grades eight through ten, and colleges consisted of grades eleven through sixteen.

These were not rigid lines of demarcation but rather rules of thumb, which led to confusion. Adding to the vagueness was the Adventist academy, which was a non-degree-granting training school with a secondary-level curriculum whose graduates were presumably ready for denominational employment.

By 1913 more changes were evolving. Because of the lack of precise definition, many church schools tended to increase their offerings upward to include eight grades, and some intermediate schools were also extending themselves upward as far as the twelfth grade, at the same time calling themselves academies. At the 1913 General Conference session resolutions relating to upgrading buildings and teaching equipment encroached on the definitions of the schools themselves, that is, the number of grade levels in each category of schools, which in turn, would determine which students were expected to attend what schools and the curricula they would study. Also in question was the use of specific terms to describe categories of schools. For example, an intermediate school that had expanded upward to include twelve grades might be categorized as an academy on par with a traditional academy that functioned as a training school, but the purpose of the two would differ.

The waters were murky and the debate was prolonged and punctuated with considerable disagreement. Below the surface of the verbal exchanges were implications of territoriality. Conference and union leaders were concerned about the impact of the proposals on their fields and wanted to offer as much education as they could for students in their own constituencies. While delegates reached no conclusions about how to classify Adventist schools, it became clear that there was an upward trend of the demarcation lines among the schools and that the secondary level was carving out its own niche between the primary school and the college with cutoff points at grades nine and twelve. Part of the reason for the upward movement was the desire to permit local church schools to retain students through the eighth or tenth grades until they were old enough to leave home and live in a dormitory.

By 1920 secondary education became a more clearly defined body of class work and demarcation lines hardened enough to designate "academy" as the accepted term describing an Adventist secondary school, although intermediate schools continued primarily as projects of local church constituencies. Junior colleges had also entered the scene as post-secondary schools distinct from degree-granting institutions. In this settling process, academies were losing their role as recognized training schools.

### The New System and Adventist Tradition

These changes affected the Adventist philosophical tradition of agricultural projects integrated into work and study programs. As early as 1901 the church tagged the intermediate schools as agricultural, but as the concept of a secondary-level boarding academy grew, agricultural programs shifted away from intermediate schools which were usually operated as day schools by individual congregations. Academies included agricultural work programs, but the size of both dairy and produce farms varied from one institution to another.

How much land would be necessary for agricultural projects was debatable. Of the fifty-three colleges and secondary schools in North America categorized as Adventist "educational institutions" in 1920, the amount of land averaged 180 acres per school, admittedly enough to carry on a sizeable agricultural program. But of more importance was the fact that fourteen, or more than a fourth of the institutions in North America, reported holdings of less than twenty acres, three with no land at all.

Adventist educational institutions outside North America averaged even less acreage. Seven of the forty-two schools in the world fields had no land, and an additional eighteen had less than ten acres, but a work program of some sort gave Adventist schools a distinctive stamp. Even on the small campuses some agricultural projects were possible.

The original purposes of an agricultural program were to provide activity for students in order to avoid an excessively bookish mentality and to give prospective denominational employees practical training that would be useful in reaching people at their own social level. Agricultural know-how would also benefit missionaries in establishing farming projects at institutions in underdeveloped regions of the world where food production was the leading means of livelihood. But Ellen White also promoted the idea of training in skilled trades, such as specialized lines of construction work and small scale manufacturing.

As the case of Meiktila Technical School in Burma demonstrated, programs of student labor did not always require large acreage to exert their practical educational value. Small manufacturing enterprises also grew into businesses that supplied schools with supplemental income. It became a judgment call to determine what a given school should emphasize and the amount of land needed to implement a labor program. An absence of an extensive agricultural project comparable to the one at Avondale did not mean that a school was rejecting the principle of student labor. On its twelve-acre campus Washington Foreign Missionary Institute stressed practical nursing and printing skills rather than agriculture in contrast to Emmanuel Missionary College with its 400-acre farm. Both institutions legitimately claimed to prepare missionaries.

As important as Ellen White regarded an agricultural labor program, she did not lay down a single philosophical formula for all

Adventist schools. In 1907 she explained that there was "no exact pattern" for schools.[9] Although she advocated that training schools were to be free from urban influences, she also enunciated the principle of taking education to the communities where students lived in large numbers.

In 1903, while the debate about defining Adventist schools was heating up, she advised pastors to establish church schools in cities for families who could not leave urban areas or send their children to training schools. "And in connection with these schools," she added, "provision is to be made for the teaching of higher studies, where these are called for."[10] The three landless secondary schools in North America in 1920, Harlem and Temple academies in New York City, and Boston Intermediate Church School, were well within this instruction, as were the seven city schools scattered from Hawaii to China to India.

Rather than an agricultural program, the single, most weighty concern was a biblically based curriculum with a view of training students for service. Schools were to serve the ultimate purpose of the church, which was to fulfill the commission to spread the gospel.

### Conventions for Educators

A series of educational gatherings also helped to crystallize the education movement and nurture the idea of a system. At a meeting in College View, Nebraska in 1903 educators agreed that each union conference should own and operate a training school, preferably at the college level. Intermediate schools were to be the property of local conferences, and individual churches would assume responsibility for primary schools. In addition, the Educational Department recommended to reincarnate itself as the Department of Education with new organization to represent the world field more adequately.[11]

Three years later representatives from all categories of schools in both North America and Europe met again at College View to outline an Adventist curriculum encompassing the first through the sixteenth grades. Motivating this gathering was the belief that Adventist education was a continuum and that students everywhere should move from one grade to the next at a more or less uniform rate which would permit them to advance through elementary and secondary levels anywhere they happened to be and be able to enter post-secondary training schools at the same or a similar point in their academic careers. Marked differences persisted in the classrooms, however, causing problems in promoting students. In 1908 principals of advanced schools convened to iron out these wrinkles and to discuss improved curricular articulation among all levels of instruction.

Personnel from academies and colleges met in 1910 and 1912 to define an Adventist college, to strengthen instruction in Bible and the sciences, and to prepare guidelines for libraries at training schools. In 1911 education superintendents gathered to address the needs of elementary education, specifically to improve methods of supervising elementary schools, to develop uniform testing of learning, and to establish standards of teacher certification.

These organizational decisions formed a basis for Adventist schools around the world. Representatives from European schools participated in the educational council in 1906. Griggs' penchant for organization led him to a biennial session of the Asiatic Division in 1917 to introduce the newly adopted educational policies and to pattern the administrative structure of Adventist schools in the Orient after the North American model. After the meeting S. L. Frost, secretary of education for the division, took the new order to other parts of Asia.

As important as the notion of system was to Griggs, he was not advocating strict uniformity around the world. Although he lauded the actions in Asia for basically following the North American model, he was quick to recognize that "our school curricula throughout the world should be adapted to the school system of each country. There has been a strong tendency in the past to conduct our school work in all parts of the world upon the American plan of organization. This is not always wise, and we are pleased to see our schools thus adapting their work to meet the educational conditions of the country in which they are situated."[12]

Institutes for teaching and administrative faculty were not new to Adventist education. As early as 1888 Prescott gathered thirty delegates to a teachers' convention to discuss how to integrate Bible into the curriculum. The centrality of biblical studies was the theme at the 1891 convention at Harbor Springs, Michigan. Three years later in 1894 Prescott continued the same discussion, adding general professional qualifications of teachers to the agenda.

The organizational debates following the 1901 General Conference overshadowed teachers' meetings, but instructional and administrative faculties continued their gatherings. By that time specializations determined the agenda and who should attend a given meeting. Education itself was the topic in 1917; Bible and history teachers met in 1919; and management of dormitories was the theme in 1920.

The net effect of education councils and teachers' institutes was to generate a sense of ownership among educators in a system they helped to build. Griggs worked hard at cultivating a participatory mood. Gatherings especially for teachers provided a forum to discuss professional issues. Recommendations for organization usually passed through an approval process, but they originated in the field of education rather than in the offices of general church administration. The underlying spirit was to encourage educational reform and progress among the educators themselves and to institutionalize recommendations through a ratification process that reached the top of the administrative scale of the church.

## Institutional Indebtedness

A concern over institutional finance also fueled the debate about education. When Seventh-day Adventists turned the corner into the twentieth century many institutions were so deeply in debt and marinating in red ink that denominational stability was threatened. The causes for school debts and the amounts of the obligations varied from place to place, but typically, school administrators from the late 1880s through the 1890s depended on borrowed money both to start institutions and to meet day-to-day costs, a financial management practice that Arthur White calls "irresponsible."[13] It was unavoidable that economic dislocations in the United States during the 1890s also made matters worse and contributed to financial uncertainty.

Indebtedness spread to schools in South Africa, Australia, England, Scandinavia, and Germany, but the schools in the United States were the primary culprits. Union College and Battle Creek College bore the largest financial burdens. Defaults on land deals in the aftermath of its original construction nearly buried the school at Lincoln, Nebraska, while at Battle Creek building expansion followed by a sharp decline in enrollment during Sutherland's presidency brought the church's first college to its knees. Loans were the easy answer for schools, but with most of their income deriving from rock-bottom tuition rates, schools were hard put to keep up with their financial promises.

Ellen White advised that tuition should provide operating expenses and that if necessary, tuition should go up to cover costs. Salary cuts for teachers and donations even by teachers themselves were other options to meet expenses. Whatever school administrators did, she warned, they should devise an "entire change" in their "demoralizing" practices of financial management.[14] Estimates differ, but by 1900 the total school debt reached around $330,000 with an annual interest rate exceeding $16,000. It was a moment of gloom. "I believe it almost came to be a settled fact that those debts never could be paid," P. T. Magan reflected. "It was practically impossible for our schools to continue to run."[15] The majority of the schools could not even pay the interest on their loans.

From Australia came Ellen White's offer to donate the profits from her recent manuscript, *Christ's Object Lessons*, to help pay school debts. She asked the Pacific Press and the Review and Herald Publishing Association to circulate the book at cost and salesmen to forego their commissions. The General Conference organized the Committee on Relief of the Schools with S. H. Lane, president of the board of the Publishing Association, as chairman and P. T. Magan as secretary.

The campaign began in 1900 and advanced quickly. At the 1901 General Conference session Magan reported more than $57,000 to apply to the debts. Two years later, Daniells told the General Conference session that debt reduction approximated $200,000. It soon reached $300,000.

The sale of *Christ's Object Lessons* was a blessing but it was a bailout rather than the new administrative policies that Ellen White advocated, and as might be expected, indebtedness recurred. By 1906 twenty-one leading schools carried nearly $140,000 in debts, which amounted to about 21 percent of their assets. By 1911 this ratio had worsened to more than 43 percent, or a half million dollars of debt.

Daniells was displeased with the financial direction of Adventist education and proposed a systematic fund-raising campaign to help the schools. Already in effect was the fifteen-cent-a-week plan which had originated in North America, calling on each member to give that amount above tithe to support denominational missions. Daniells proposed raising the weekly quota to twenty cents and to devote the extra five cents to eliminate institutional debts. Schools whose financial obligations exceeded more than half of their assets would receive help first. In order to receive aid schools could not add to their debts or increase their operational expenses. If schools found it impossible to function they were to close. The debt relief plan applied to sanitariums and publishing houses as well as schools and was to go into effect on July 1, 1913.

The General Conference Committee went to the 1913 General Conference session primed with facts and arguments to see their proposal through, but for the delegates it was a heavy dosage of strong medicine. Twice they referred it back to the committee on finance before it finally passed. The bone of contention was the original wording that made the General Conference responsible for the financial integrity of schools in the United States and Canada. In the end delegates left the proposal intact except for transferring the burden of accountability from the General Conference to the North American Division working through its unions. The General Conference would collect the money but turn it over to North America for distribution. This detail was a not-so-subtle reminder that the North American unions, not the General Conference, had control over the schools within their territories.

The action also hinted that unacceptable debt ratios were more than a question of efficient management. The preamble to the new twenty-cent-a-week plan admitted that denominational leaders had not carefully laid out a rational scheme of financial support for any of their institutions, which was an implied admission that to expect schools to rely totally on tuition income was not realistic.

Meanwhile, school debts had swelled to more than $750,000 but remained at 43 percent of institutional assets. Three years later, at the end of 1916, schools had lowered their debts while increasing their assets, resulting in a debt ratio of 23 percent. Encouraged by the success of the twenty-cent-a-week plan and inspired by the burgeoning needs of missions, the Autumn Council of 1917 raised the goal to twenty-five cents a week and earmarked one dollar in twenty-five for the five senior colleges and the nine junior colleges and academies qualifying as missionary training schools. The importance of the new medical school at

Loma Linda became obvious when the council voted to give it an amount equal to all other schools combined.

When reporting to the 1918 General Conference, Griggs spoke with evident optimism about the impact of the fund raising and of additional plans to provide a regular operating subsidy to the major schools in North America. School finances were moving in the right direction, which, it was hoped, would enable schools to invest in improved facilities.

But tight financial conditions would not go away. Operational losses continued as schools tried to comply with the Adventist tradition of supplying equipment for industrial training in addition to meeting ordinary costs. In April 1919 the General Conference Committee agreed to new proposals doubling the amount of subsidies to training schools beginning in January 1920.

Adventist educators in North America began the post-World War I era not yet having found the key to manage their schools without losses. Publishing houses sold tangible products priced according to a profit-making market; sanitariums sold services connected to physical survival for which people were willing to pay, but the leading articles that Adventist schools sold were values, knowledge, and preparation for mostly denominational jobs that offered enormous spiritual satisfaction but small remuneration. The salable products of the church's schools were intangible. Also, they were priority items for only a narrow market. The price tag was minimal which kept institutional income low.

From the beginning, the argument for an integrated student labor program was to train well rounded Adventist workers, but it took more time to recognize its accompanying virtue–it frequently provided schools with additional operational income. Developing and refining Adventist education, even before 1920, presupposed substantial sums of money to provide an academically defensible system of schools, but the schools themselves were economically incapable of generating their own capital. It was a hard and long delayed lesson of Adventist educational economics that tuition income alone is insufficient to operate a school for the Adventist public. By 1917 denominational policy acknowledged for the first time that systematic subsidizing was necessary, but the subsidizing program itself remained undefined.

No matter how committed Adventist parents were to church-sponsored education, for years a consciousness that Adventist schools faced a steep uphill struggle haunted denominational educators. Ever since Ellen White's "Proper Education" in 1872 Adventist statements pertaining to education frequently contained the goal of not allowing denominational schools to fall behind in the "common branches," which betrayed a sense that the established public education system had set the standard for achievement and Adventist schools were the ones that had to measure up. Public education was tax-supported and cheap for the consumer, and in spite of the argument that their children needed a biblically centered education many parents chose the less expensive option—public schools—and depended on active church membership to maintain their spiritual values.

I. H. Evans, president of the North American Division, confided to the delegates at the 1918 General Conference that only 50 percent of Adventist youth attended Adventist schools. Even that figure reflected enrollment increases after a calculated campaign had bolstered attendance by more than 27 percent during the 1916-1917 academic year. Adventist school facilities, Evans argued, were already large enough to accommodate the growing number of potential students from the enlarging Adventist population. The problem was how to induce students to attend. But when he suggested that the church should find means to allow every Adventist of school age to enroll in a denominational school, he predicated his appeal on the need for more denominational employees rather than the need of young Adventists for a Christian education.

The tension between these two purposes had always been present in Adventist education and would always remain. Both purposes were legitimate, and while not mutually exclusive, either one could become overbalancing if allowed to ignore the other. By 1920 it had become evident that Adventist education depended on both purposes. The church could not prosper without programs to prepare students for denominational employment, but it was also vital to recognize that an the Adventist constituency viewed church-sponsored education as an opportunity to the general students who simply wanted an Adventist education. The problem was how to devise a way to deliver education to both groups of students in an affordable manner.

## The Debate Over the Number of Colleges

Although the Educational Department after 1901 deliberately rejected a supervisory role over schools, church policy and financial needs sometimes involved the General Conference in detailed decisions. Church leaders were appalled by institutional indebtedness. In part they blamed the schools for engaging in unbridled competition for students, sometimes pitting secondary schools against colleges in the same union. At the same time these schools vied for money and were quick to incur debt to remain in operation. Some complained that North America had too many schools.

Motivated by the dual need to prevent schools from undercutting each other with costly duplication of programs and to lessen debt loads, delegates to the 1913 General Conference session voted controls, among them recommendations to reduce Adventist senior colleges in North America from five to three. The other training schools would become junior colleges. The proposal singled out Mount Vernon College in Ohio to revert to a twelve-grade secondary school and permitted Washington Foreign Missionary Seminary the option of becoming a senior college at an undetermined time in the future, whenever the school deemed it appropriate to resume its pre-1907 status. The proposal also redefined the role of secondary schools.

Before the proposal went to the General Conference session the heads of the colleges had agreed to the plan, but it sparked stiff opposition, especially from the Columbia Union president whose territory was home for both Mount Vernon College and the Foreign Missionary Seminary. Pointing out that prospects for a college to emerge from the Seminary were indefinite, he declared that the plan snatched a college from his territory and alleged that if implemented, the proposal would increase rather than reduce debt. The final decision rested with the North American Division.

As a college Mount Vernon had experienced indifferent success. In 1893 it had started as an academy, but began to offer college degrees in 1905. Until 1912, fewer than a half dozen students had graduated from four-year programs. The school was heavily in debt. Meanwhile, the Seminary, despite its non-academic program, was offering the equivalent of college classes and attracting relatively large enrollments. It was obvious that the prospects for a successful college were greater in

Washington than Mount Vernon, Ohio. Over the reluctance of the union president, in 1914 Mount Vernon lost its college standing, but the Columbia Union retained a four-year college by hastily rechristening the Foreign Missionary Seminary as Washington Missionary College, a degree-granting institution beginning with the 1914-1915 year.[16]

### The Beginning Years in Review

By 1920 Adventist education had met a plethora of organizational issues. Philosophically, denominational educators had wrestled with, among others, the essence of a church-related system, the application of philosophical uniformity in the context of global diversity, and the reconciliation of spirituality to secular professions. Pragmatically, they had dealt with problems of viable organization, curricular continuity, fiscal integrity, relationships to government controls over education, and professional qualifications of faculty.

The need for church-related graduate education had also come up. The Battle Creek College bulletin for 1881-1882 advertised M.A. and M.S. degrees, but it became painfully evident that the statement was an imprudent and unilateral expression of presidential hope rather than reality. Battle Creek did not actually issue graduate degrees and the bulletin dropped the matter. After discussing how to improve the qualifications of teachers, those attending the 1894 teachers' institute outlined a denominational teacher-preparation program leading to doctorates, a proposal that died aborning.[17]

By 1920 Seventh-day Adventists founded a broad spectrum of schools, the diversity of which indicated the important role that the church saw for education. Not only was education *per se* an integral part of their program but the presence of a biblically based curriculum in a variety of educational ventures became the central identifying mark of denominational schools. It was a philosophy that had universal applications.

The early struggles of Adventist education were bittersweet. In 1920 Adventist schools were still searching for their own professional identity, but they had already produced a couple of generations of church workers, some of whom were approaching the final years of their careers. Graduates of Adventist schools had circled the globe. Measured in terms of denominational purposes, they had accomplished much with little. Humble but respectable beginnings in Adventist education marked the years from 1872 to 1920; the next two and a half decades would show how substantial those foundations really were.

---

[1]VandeVere, *Wisdom Seekers*, pp. 18-22.

[2]The General Conference action cited in Cadwallader, *History of Seventh-day Adventist Education*, p. 285.

[3]VandeVere, *ibid.*, pp. 66, 67; Cadwallader, *ibid.*,p. 311; Valentine, *Shaping of Adventism*, pp. 45-49.

[4]Sources for the discussion about organization of the Department of Education are *ibid.*, chapters 1-8; Cadawallader, *ibid.*, pp. 310-314; Reye and Knight, "Frederick Griggs: Moderate," *Early Adventist Educators*, pp. 184-204; Brown, *Chronology*, pp. 187-230; Richard Schwarz and Floyd Greenleaf, *Light Bearers; A History of the Seventh-day Adventist Church* (Nampa, ID: Pacific Press Publishing Association, 2000), pp. 253-256; Walton J. Brown, "Education—Eden to Eden," *Journal of Adventist Education"* (October-November 1982), pp. 5-7, 45; *General Conference Bulletin,* 1901, no. 1, ext. 9, p. 207, ext. 14, p. 305; *ibid.*, 1903, no. 8, pp. 114, 115; *ibid.*, no. 12, pp. 177-185; *ibid.*, 1905, no. 4, pp. 19, 20; *ibid.,* 1909, no. 15, pp. 221-225; *ibid.*, 1918, no. 2, pp. 26, 27; General Conference Committee Minutes, 1901.

[5]I have depended on the following sources for the passage about the issues in education, 1901-1920: *General Conference Bulletin*, 1901, no. 11, ext. 9, p. 207; ext. 10, p. 219; ext. 14, p. 306; *ibid.*, 1903, no. 12, pp. 177-186; *ibid.*, 1905, no. 4, pp. 19, 20; *ibid.*, 1909, no. 15, pp. 221-225; *Statistical Report*, 1920.

[6]For Cady's entire speech, see *General Conference Bulletin*, 1903, no. 8, pp. 114, 115.

[7]*Ibid.*, 1905, no. 4, pp. 19, 20.

[8]See *General Conference Bulletin*, 1903, no.5, p67; no. 7, pp. 100, 101; no. 10, pp, 158-160; no. 12, p. 180.

[9]Knight, *Early Adventist Educators*, p. 45.

[10]*Review and Herald*, December 17, 1903.

[11]For summaries of meetings of educators see Frederick Griggs, "Report of the Department of Education to the 1909 General Conference Session," RG 51, AST; H. R. Salisbury, "Report of the Department of Education to the 1913 General Conference Session," RG 51, AST; Griggs, "Report of the Department of Education to the 1918 General Conference Session," RG 51, AST; "Teachers' Meetings—1917-1968," RG 51, AST; Valentine, *Shaping of Adventism*, pp. 43, 44, 74, 75.

[12]Griggs, *ibid.*

[13]Arthur L. White, *Ellen White*, v. 5, p. 198. For further information concerning institutional finances, see White's entire chapter, pp. 198-208; Spalding, *Christ's Last Legion*, pp. 42, 43; *General Conference Bulletin*, 1901, ext. 10, pp. 209-211; *ibid.*, 1903, no. 2, p. 19; *ibid.*, no. 12, pp. 183-186; *ibid.*, 1913, no. 20, pp. 330, 331; *ibid.*, 1918, no. 2, p. 26; no. 4, p. 58; General Conference Committee Minutes, January 21, 22, 1913; November 5, 1917; September 22, 1918; February 18, 1919; April 30, 1919, AST.

[14]Arthur L. White, *ibid.*, p. 199.

[15]*General Conference Bulleting*, 1901, no. 1, ext. 10, p. 209.

[16]The Mount Vernon story is derived from VandeVere, *Wisdom Seekers*, p, 131; *General Conference Bulletin*, 1913, no. 6, p. 95; *ibid.*, no. 20, p. 311; *ibid.*, no. 21, p. 324.

[17]For comments about these two skirmishes with graduate education, see VandeVere, *ibid.*, p. 41; Valentine, *ibid.*, p. 44.

# Part Two

# THE INTERIM YEARS, 1920-1945

For Adventist education the twenty-five years from 1920 to 1945 were an interim separating the establishment of the first generation of training schools from a later era when they would become institutions of higher education. Simply put, the interim was the age of the training schools, which ringed the globe in 1920. Commitment to an overarching philosophy that produced similarities in curriculum and organization held these institutions together in a newly conceived and still developing system that had the makings of a global organization but was still skeletal. The schools shared commonalities but were not uniform because they reflected the societies in which they functioned and addressed cultural needs around them. During the interim years the original schools fleshed out and experimented with genuine post-secondary education, new schools organized, and education spread to additional regions.

While these trends represented an accomplishment of new goals for Adventist educators and helped to give shape and definition to the newly born system of denominational education, church educators encountered new challenges in carrying out their agenda during this quarter-century.

The period began with the world trying to settle down after World War I, but problems were everywhere. The equation of international power changed. Public moods shifted. Countries spent two decades coping with economic problems left over from the war that contributed to the most serious financial dislocations the world had seen. Some countries experimented with new political systems that were not always congenial toward ecclesiastical activities. Old political sores kept festering and finally, an even worse war broke out.

All of these conditions impacted Seventh-day Adventists. The war of 1914-1918 engulfed the world church, and its institutions faced recovery at nearly every turn. Restoration and growth were difficult in the international tensions that marked the 1920s and 1930s. New expectations in academe brought unanticipated complexities to issues of internal management of a global system of Adventist education. In 1945 the church faced another round of rehabilitation from war while at the same time its educational institutions were poised to launch a wave of change that was unthinkable only a decade earlier.

# World Challenges During the Interim

As a context for Adventist education in Europe and English-speaking countries during the interim years, denominational schools spent much of the period redefining themselves in a modernizing world. Outside the United States the training school had become the single most important educational venture, and while church leaders focused on it as a worker-preparation institution, schools at lower levels also underwent dramatic change.

## Developments in Enrollment and Institutions

Most of the growth in Adventist education between 1920 and 1945 occurred at the elementary level. Enrollment in primary schools increased from 23,500 to 123,500, or more than five times. This rate exceeded the growth in the Adventist population which tripled during the same period to reach 576,000. Most of the increase took place in the fields outside North America where elementary enrollment ballooned from 6,000 to more than 100,000. In its totality, Adventist education grew more rapidly outside North America during the twenty-five years after1920, but the bulk of denominational education at the secondary and post-secondary levels still existed in North America.[1]

Between 1920 and 1945 elementary enrollment in North America improved from 17,500 to 23,000, increasing the average size of elementary schools from twenty-four to twenty-eight students. The Movement of 1897 and its aftermath brought wide attention to Adventist elementary education in North America, which by the end of World War I had developed many of its own textbooks and curricular materials. By 1920 Adventist educators had drawn the general profile of elementary education, but they continued to revise curriculum and teaching tools as much as was financially practical for a small system.

In the United States one of the leading trends in education at large during the 1920s was the emergence of the defined high school as the standard secondary educational unit, the step that bridged the gap between elementary school and college. Related to this development was the growing practice to rely on colleges for training in professional careers, although vocational high schools and trade schools continued to emphasize technical education. These movements had been underway since the nineteenth century but did not achieve their ends until after World War I.

Adventist education reflected these trends. Denominational secondary schools, or academies, inherited their general character from the habit of visualizing schools as institutions to prepare students for a denominational profession. By 1920 North American Adventists operated thirty-six free-standing academies that offered grades nine through twelve. Most of the enrollees were pre-college-age students, but many of the schools also offered vocational or professional courses, prompting church leaders to regard them as training schools and many of their graduates as readily employable.

Long before 1945 this view changed. The academy lost its reputation as a training school by stressing college preparatory classes and evolving into the Adventist version of the typical North American high school. By the end of World War II the number of North American academies grew to sixty-three, fifty of them free-standing as either boarding or local day schools. Thirteen functioned as the secondary-level component of colleges.

In the United States Adventist education did not develop a counterpart to the vocational high school or trade school. Even after academies became college preparatory schools they continued to offer vocational education and frequently required their graduates to complete a minimal amount of this so-called non-academic credit, but these classes were usually only introductory courses echoing the denominational tradition of providing instruction in selected practical skills instead of complete programs to prepare students for the skilled labor market. Most boarding academies also offered a variety of labor opportunities, many of them in agriculture and small-scale industries.

Increasingly during the years after 1920 what used to be vocational education at the secondary level shifted to the college campus. In the North American Adventist community a general broadening of post-secondary curricula took place to accommodate this change as well as new programs in professional education. The number of sixteen-grade colleges also increased. Motivated largely by apprehensions about institutional indebtedness, the General Conference Department of Education attempted in 1913 to limit North America to three, sixteen-grade colleges, but "the suggestion did not meet with hearty approval," North American President I. H. Evans recalled with wry understatement.[2]

Church leaders were not convinced the schools were graduating enough prospective denominational employees; consequently, they preferred expansion rather than constriction. The idea of a complete, college-level training school in each union carried the day over the recommendation from the Department of Education. It was evident that the desire by leaders in the conferences and unions for a steady flow of future workers overrode their financial worries.

Five colleges offering grades thirteen through sixteen were in operation in 1920; by 1945 the number climbed to eleven, including Canadian Union College in Alberta and the self-supporting, independent Madison College in Tennessee. Atlantic Union College matured to senior college status in 1922 and Madison followed in 1937. The other four, Canadian Union, Oakwood, La Sierra, and Southern Missionary colleges, appeared in quick succession between 1943 and 1945. The three seminaries for immigrant groups shrank out of sight by 1934 while junior colleges remained at Keene, Texas and Oshawa, Ontario, Canada.

During the years following 1920 the North American Adventist intermediate school, or junior academy, also found its identity. In early Adventist education any school was "advanced" if its program extended beyond the elementary level; consequently, intermediate schools became advanced institutions along with academies and colleges. However, with clearer definitions developing during the organizational years after 1901, the intermediate school became an extension of the local church school. It offered limited secondary classes but ordinarily not beyond grade ten. An urban church, or perhaps two or more churches, usually organized intermediate schools that they often called junior academies. By 1945 fifty-eight of these intermediate schools served municipal congregations in Canada and the United States.

The growth of Adventist education varied from field to field around the world. As the largest single segment of the world-wide program, North American schools served as the testing grounds for many educational techniques and curricular materials, but other fields developed their own niche in the denominational schema. To systematize the global program, the terms *elementary*, *secondary*, and *college*, as defined in the United States, became the measuring rod to ascertain equivalent instructional levels in all Adventist schools, while the design of curricula and the institutions themselves conformed to the educational standards required in the countries in which the schools were located.

In Adventist jargon, the term "training school" carried over from earlier years to describe all institutions that prepared students for denominational employment, regardless of their instructional level. In 1920 Adventist post-secondary education outside North America existed only in England and China with a total of thirty-three students. By the end of World War II this level of classes proliferated to twenty-six of the 128 Adventist training schools in the world fields and the number of college-level students grew to 1,570.

## Struggles in Europe

But the story of Adventist education during the twenty-five years following 1920 is more than numbers; it reflects the economic and political turbulence of the era. As the period unfolded in Europe there were setbacks as well as accomplishments. The importance of these events emerges from the relationship of education to the church's larger world program.

Adventist education in Europe had begun in the northern half, mostly in the northwestern quadrant of the Continent, and schools in that region remained stronger than in southern Europe. Before World War I they were influential in the denomination's budding mission program. European Division President L. H. Christian attributed this influence to the fact that European powers in that region had accumulated an enormous amount of global wealth, transplanted their culture to many remote places, and controlled much of the world's traffic. Even though the Seventh-day Adventist church was born in the United States, he saw European ascendancy as a major power behind the spread of Adventism.[3]

Christian visualized the best days for European Adventists as in the future. "Before the war," he told the 1922 General Conference session, "Europe trained and sent out many workers into the home and foreign fields. In the course of a short time, we should be able to do this again, as our training schools are started."[4] He foresaw a strengthened educational program that followed old colonial lines, especially in Africa. European countries had cast long shadows around the world, and Christian anticipated that in order to spread the gospel, means and money would once again stream from Adventists living in continental countries to the rest of the colonial world they already controlled.

There were others who shared Christian's views. J. F. Simon, education secretary in the European Division, reminded his colleagues that during the first two decades of the twentieth century Germany had produced 1,000 missionaries and England, 200. He lamented that only 640 of an estimated 20,000 Adventist youth in Europe were enrolled in training schools in 1922, but predicted a renewal in mission training. "A reformation is sweeping a part of Europe today," he said, "and it has come about through the work of our schools."[5] With a new campus in Collonges, France, and new schools emerging in Germany, it momentarily seemed that conditions bode well for a new beginning.

These optimistic phrases did not express the reality of Europe whose woes did not slacken with the end of the war in 1918. Economic troubles, followed by the rise of totalitarian regimes with bellicose policies frustrated the rehabilitation of Europe which dragged on, deep into the post-World War I era. "Europe stands bleeding and staggering by her appalling loss," Christian said in a much different tone in 1926, eight years after the war.[6] Hope that Adventists could simply resume their activities was dulled; nevertheless, Christian clung to his vision of a restored worker-training program in Europe. His hope was not entirely misconceived. Between 1922 and 1930 Northern Europe sent out 122 workers to Africa and other lands, and more than a hundred went from Seminaire Adventiste, many of them to French-speaking Africa.[7]

### Seminaire Adventiste and Newbold College

Despite repeated expressions of the need for additional training schools in southern Europe, Seminaire Adventiste in Collonges, France continued as the sole training school for Latin Europe. After the formation of the Southern European Division in 1929 the French school functioned more or less as a division educational center, at times offering work in Italian and Spanish, and even Yugoslavian and German.

Enrollment in the French training school hovered just above the 100 mark, increasing only slowly during the 1920s and 1930s, which re-

*After several relocations, the training school in England took the name of Newbold Missionary College in 1931. In 1946 it settled on an estate in Binfield, near Bracknell, Berkshire, west of London. Pictured here is Moor Close, the estate manor, which became the ladies' residence hall.*

flected sluggish membership growth in the region of Europe the school served. In 1940, after wartime restrictions made it impossible for Italian students to travel to the French campus, a small school opened in the Italian Mission headquarters in Florence, but the war hampered its growth. In 1945 it enrolled only thirteen students.

In Scandinavia, part of the Northern European Division, Adventist education continued uninterrupted during the twenty-five years after 1920, with two schools rebuilding at new sites. From a generally rising level of educational expectations came the conviction that Adventist workers needed improved academic and professional preparation. By 1930 leaders in Northern Europe voted to establish a senior college in England where graduates from all other schools in the division could earn a college degree.

The following year Stanborough College relocated and changed its name to Newbold Missionary College. H. L. Rudy, the division education secretary, regarded the baccalaureate degree essential for workers going from Europe to Africa, and a knowledge of English equally important. "Newbold Missionary College naturally suggests itself for senior standing in view of these and other considerations," he declared, addressing educational leaders in Northern Europe in 1932.[8] His view of Adventist education turned out to be more optimistic than realistic. Fulfillment of his hope was long in the making, a delay that belied a general underestimation of the herculean tasks that Adventist leaders faced following World War I.

In 1945 schools in France and England, and some in Scandinavia were still reporting enrollments exceeding a hundred and continued to furnish workers for European countries and the world fields. They all had begun to offer post-secondary classes, but while their accomplishments were encouraging they were not outstanding. Faced by mounting hardships during the interim years and the uncertainties of World War II, these institutions held their own and did not close, as did Adventist schools elsewhere on the Continent.

## Progress and Setbacks in Germany

In Germany, Missionsseminar Friedensau, closed during the last year of World War I, resumed classes in 1919. After World War I German Adventist membership rose rapidly, and with the creation of three

*As a result of rapid membership growth in Germany, Seventh-day Adventists established schools in each of the three German unions. At Marienhoehe, immediately south of Frankfurt, this property was purchased for a worker-training school. Under political pressure it closed during the era of national socialism, but reopened after World War II. Picture taken about 1968.*

German unions in 1920 came two additional training schools, the first at Kirchheim, near Stuttgart to serve southern Germany. In 1924 it moved to Marienhohe in Darmstadt, near Frankfurt. The second was in the Rhineland at Neandertal, near Dusseldorf, which served the western part of Germany. Combined enrollment of all three schools reached nearly 500 by 1930.

The development of national socialism in Germany gave rise to new problems, and while G. W. Schubert, president of the Central European Division, described the "present government" as positively as he could to the 1936 General Conference session, his generous words could not mask the threat that the new totalitarian regime posed. In 1934, two years before he spoke, Neandertal closed in the face of political pressure, and in 1939 Marienhohe shut its doors. After these two casualties Friedensau again became the sole training school for Germany, a role it fulfilled until 1943 when, for the second time, the German army commandeered the school to use as a military hospital. In 1945, at the end of World War II, German Adventists were prostrate with a shattered church organization and no school.

One of the major developments in Europe after 1920 was the spread of Adventist education to the eastern parts of the Continent. The schools were small and often operated erratically, but they were the beginning of denominational traditions of education that led to larger accomplishments after World War II. Because of its eastern location, before World War I Missionsseminar Friedensau attracted more students from Eastern Europe than any other Adventist institution on the Continent. Hostilities that broke out between Germany and Russia in 1914 caught forty Russian students at the German school with no place to go. Under the protecting hand of L. R. Conradi, president of the European Division, they remained on the campus, sequestered as it were, until after the war when they returned home, well educated to become church workers.

### Adventist Education Enters Eastern Europe

Conradi was quick to explain the experience of Russian students at Friedensau as evidence of providential leading, but with growing membership in both Germany and Russia, the German school could not continue as the training school for all Adventists from the eastern Baltic to the southern Balkans. By 1922 educational stirrings–small, short-term classes–were taking place in Poland, Latvia, Yugoslavia, and even communist Russia, and by 1925 classes also started up in Romania and Czechoslovakia. In 1926 the Russian school grew encouragingly to thirty students.

Institutul Biblic, founded in Moldavia in 1925 in northeastern Romania, was an especially important event for Adventists in that country. Romanian Adventists numbered only about 2,000 in 1920, but a rapidly growing membership proved the country to be a productive field for conversions. By 1930 only in Germany and Russia were Adventists more numerous. In 1931, with estimates as high as 10,000 Adventist children eligible for school, Institutul Biblic moved into a new, sleek masonry building in central Romania near Brasov in the Transylvanian Alps. Adventists enjoyed their new facility for only a decade before the occupying German army confiscated the plant in 1941. Romanian Union leaders obtained authorization to conduct a school in the capital city of Bucharest, but the back of Adventist education in Romania was broken.

The other small efforts in Adventist education in Eastern Europe coalesced in three countries, Poland, Latvia, and Yugoslavia. Poland, for centuries trampled upon by military campaigns from both the east and west and often the victim of territorial dismemberment, emerged from World War I again with redefined borders and multiple language groups from which Adventists drew their membership. Begun in Warsaw in 1926, the Polish training school moved the next year to Bielitz in the southern part of the country to begin again on a farm that allowed an agricultural program to supplement the worker-training classes.

Leaders of the Polish Union School had their hands full. The variety of languages made instruction difficult. Besides Polish, students spoke Czech, German, Russian, and Ukrainian. The school settled on Polish and German as media for the classroom, but pressure to teach in other languages was always present. Public suspicions of Protestant education and an unfriendly government that threw heavy tax burdens on the school added to their problems.

"Perhaps no school in this [Northern European] Division has had the difficulties that our Polish school has experienced," H. L. Rudy observed in 1932.[9] After 1926 it closed and reopened twice before World War II forced its third and final closing in 1939. Enrollment was consistently low, but after six years of operations it had prepared thirty-six church workers.

In Riga, capital of the Baltic republic of Latvia, Advent Missionary Seminary operated several small industries in addition to its worker-training program, which led the government to recognize it as an industrial school. Latvia and Estonia furnished most of the students, but a small number also came from Lithuania. Enrollment in 1930 was seventy-three, but typically the school matriculated few students, a cumulative total of about 330 during its first decade. By 1932 more than eighty of its ninety-one graduates had entered some phase of church work. In what was an oft-repeated story in Europe, the outbreak of World War II, which in the case of the Baltic republics included their absorption into the Soviet Union, ended the sixteen-year life of Advent Missionary Seminary.

*One of the many attempts to establish Seventh-day Adventist education in eastern Europe after 1920 was this small school in Zagreb, Yugoslavia. This photo shows students in 1936 gathered in the dining hall, which doubled as a classroom.*

In Yugoslavia a tiny school limped along from the 1920s until 1931 when it became the Yugoslavian Training School in Belgrade. The next year Yugoslavian church leaders reestablished it in the Yugoslavian Mission headquarters. Fourteen students enrolled in 1935; in 1940, twenty-nine. Two years later it closed, another fatality of the war.

Events in Europe only partially fulfilled aspirations for a rejuvenated Europe and the resumed role of Adventist education as a source of denominational workers for the world fields. In Germany and Eastern Europe Adventist education suffered acutely. In 1945 the educational institutions in Germany were gone, and schools in Romania as well as those in Finland, Latvia, Poland, and Yugoslavia were either not functioning or reduced to a shadow of their prior operations, which had been small from the start. In Russia Adventist education hardly had a beginning and with hardening lines of domestic policy under communism, a formal school was only a wish. The collapse of training schools in Germany and Romania and the stillborn attempt in Russia dealt severe blows to the church, for membership growth in these countries was the most robust in Europe following World War I. These growing constituencies could have supported effective schools.

### Advancements in Australia and New Zealand

Australasia, a region that lies afloat in the South Pacific below the Asian mainland, also shared many of the political and economic setbacks that characterized the twenty-five years following 1920, but Adventist education in this region developed a hardy independence and a strength of its own. Three related trends were preeminent: the role of Australasian Missionary College as the principal educational institution in the field, the development of an elementary and secondary education system, and the establishment of training schools in the South Pacific islands. Also of importance was English as the leading international language in the region.[10]

Central to the expansion of Adventist education in the South Pacific was Australasian Missionary College. From the days of its inception, this institution's overriding objective was to prepare church workers, many of whom intended to have a mission career in the South Pacific. The urgency of mission opportunities among the islands overshadowed any desire for official institutional recognition, but events inexorably pushed the school in that direction. The first indication took place in 1936 when the Council of Public Education in the neighboring state of Victoria recognized the college's teacher education program.

This action came late, for professional education courses had been a part of the school's curriculum for years. In 1921, the General Conference *Statistical Report* categorized these classes as post-secondary; after 1924 the same source listed Australasian Missionary College as a fourteen-grade school, and in 1936 a sixteen-grade institution. Whatever the classification of the professional courses, Australasian church leaders consistently referred to the school as one of the five secondary-level institutions in the division. During the 1920s and 1930s the number of students enrolled in these professional courses fluctuated, but usually did not exceed the secondary enrollment which remained the largest sector of the campus.

Although the Victoria Council of Public Education recognized the teacher-preparation program in 1936, the school did not become a degree-granting institution. The professional education studies were taught at a level of difficulty appropriate for post-secondary classes, but the program in its entirety lacked the breadth of a baccalaureate degree curriculum, thus it constituted professional training rather than a professional degree.

Students validated their professional competence with certificates after passing public examinations in their fields. The school gained additional stature during the late 1930s when business and accountancy students recorded some of the highest examination scores in Australia and New Zealand. Access to these external tests, combined with recognition by the state of Victoria for the teacher-preparation course, gave graduates from professional courses at Australasian Missionary College something that roughly corresponded to an accredited post-secondary education as measured by educational standards in the United States. But because the programs did not lead to degrees, the Australasian school lacked official senior college status.

Regardless of the technical standing of the school, as the decade of the 1930s wound down, little question remained that the Cooranbong campus was considerably more than a secondary school. In 1946 E. B. Rudge, president of the Australasian Division, declared that the "home field" in his division had a senior college and two junior colleges, referring first to Australasian Missionary College and secondly to the two secondary schools, West Australia Missionary College in Carmel and New Zealand Missionary College in Longburn.

The reputation of the Cooranbong campus as the "pattern school" also hung on. It was an image that General Conference Education Secretary W. E. Howell, who took office in 1920, repeated as he called for educational reform among Adventists. E. E. Cossentine, a former principal at both the Australian and New Zealand campuses, was nothing short of effusive when describing the state of Adventist education in Australasia in 1930 and how much the Australasian Division depended on its own schools for workers.

Recalling that enrollment in the three major institutions approximated 500, Cossentine ventured that nearly all of the students were "preparing to give this message." "Hardly any of our workers come from outside our division," Cossentine went on. No more than a half dozen North Americans were left in Australasia. No one could visit the Australian school, he said, "without realizing the divine wisdom that carried us to that secluded place where we have been able to train so many missionaries for our island work."[11]

At the end of World War II, Rudge estimated that the schools in the Australasian Division had produced about a thousand church workers, some of whom occupied positions in the General Conference and other parts of the world. Church leaders harbored no doubts about deriving their money's worth from Australasian Missionary College and its sister institutions.

Paralleling the development of training schools in Australasia was a movement to establish elementary church schools. Australasian educator Trevor Lloyd attributes the elementary program to Ellen White's nine-year ministry in Australia, spanning the 1890s, when she lived on the Avondale campus and wrote profusely about education. Although Australasian Missionary College began as a worker-training school, about a third of its students were elementary level, thus the traditional primary school movement as well as what would become higher education began at Cooranbong. By 1906 Adventist elementary schools spread to every state in Australia. In 1902 New Zealanders established their first church school at Ponsoby in South Island.

Teachers taught in small quarters, frequently in a room attached to a church, and improvised their curricula and instructional materials similarly as had the teachers in the Movement of 1897 in the United States. As Sarah Peck showed in her account of the development of a geography curriculum based on the Bible, teachers attempted to use the Scripture as the source for a wide range of substantive class work. Some of these early Australasian schools depended on Alma McKibbin's first published textbooks.[12]

By 1921 Adventist congregations in Australia, New Zealand, and Tasmania, at the time called the "home" territory of Australasia, operated twenty-seven church schools with 725 students. Almost all of the thirty-six teachers for these small enterprises were home grown in the training schools, primarily Australasian Missionary College. These numbers were not large, but Adventist membership in the three home fields was about 7,300, a figure comparable to North American membership in the mid-1870s when elementary education was still hardly more than an occasional topic of conversation. Adventist elementary education in North America began only after a circle of training schools had opened and nearly a generation of students had passed through Battle Creek College. In contrast, the Australasian church school movement began and developed simultaneously with the training school in Cooranbong.

The parallel development of elementary schools and a training school in Australasia contributed to the concept of an educational system linking all Adventist schools together. As the two tracks developed, comparatively quickly a flow of students began with the boarding schools in New Zealand and West Australia drawing students from their regions and in turn feeding the enrollment at Avondale.

Australasians did not find it easy to finance their church schools. Between 1917 and 1921 teachers' earnings increased one-and-a-half times, causing some alarm among Australasian Union leaders who realized that if churches raised tuition commensurably, the cost of Adventist elementary education would become prohibitive. The solution lay in a three-way cooperative arrangement. Local congregations assumed responsibility for a third of the cost of their church schools, the conference paid another third from tithe paid by church-operated restaurants, and the Australasian Union paid the final third from operating gains of its institutions. By 1922 the plan produced better equipment and more qualified teachers.

This financial system was more than a stopgap; it was an innovation unique in the Adventist world, founded on the notion that the entire denominational program formed a single system and shared the same financial base. "Australasia is to be congratulated on having solved the perplexing problem of the proper support of church schools," W. E. Nelson, General Conference education secretary, commented in 1936. "These schools are subsidized from the profits of the food industry."[13]

As the Adventist population increased in the Australasian home fields church school teachers cautiously began offering secondary-level classes. Developing out of this experimentation was the intermediate day school. In 1931, after a teaching career extending back to early World War I years, William Gilson became education secretary of the Australasian Division and led the movement to develop secondary day schools which also prepared students for external examinations.

Even with the strong financial support that Australasian schools enjoyed, the system did not grow as rapidly as might be expected. By

1941 the elementary and intermediate schools consisted of 1,200 students, only a forty percent increase in about two decades. By the end of World War II additional growth was only slight. Part of the problem stemmed from the lack of a professional program on the Cooranbong campus for secondary teachers, a deficiency deriving from British higher education which did not accommodate Avondale's students in its examination system to validate secondary teachers. Too many instructors in Adventist secondary day schools found themselves teaching classes for which they had no college-level preparation. For students whose academic future rested on their success in public examinations, this deficiency posed a serious problem in Australasia and would not be resolved until later in the post-World War II era.

## The South Pacific Islands

It was in the South Pacific islands that Adventist education made some of its most notable advancements in the Australasian Division. In 1901 the General Conference assigned the task of furnishing workers for this oceanic field to the field itself, which in practical terms meant that Australians and New Zealanders would form the pool of nurses, teachers and ministers. From Australasian Missionary College and Sydney Sanitarium, located about a hundred miles from the college, these workers flowed in large numbers to Pacific outposts where they established schools and clinics in a manner similar to the missions begun by Stahl in Peru.

By 1920 Fiji, a centrally situated island group in Oceania, was already one of the leading locations for Adventist missions and schools. Education picked up elsewhere during the 1920s, ranging across 7,000 miles of water from Papua, British Guinea, in the west to Pitcairn Island in the east. The first inroads were not always easy, but by 1922 C. H. Watson was able to tell fellow Adventists that "there is not now any place where we may not enter with the advent message."[14] Before the decade ended it was evident that producing missionaries was not the exclusive domain of the school in Australia. Fijian workers from Buresala Training School were filling positions as far away as Papua and native islanders staffed the thirty-nine schools in the Solomon Islands, home of a "strong training school." Plans for Adventist education were on foot in the New Hebrides. Samoans were asking for a school, and a teacher was already in India, preparing to take charge of a school for Indian immigrant laborers in Fiji, which opened its classes in 1930 at Suva on the main Fijian island.

The 1920s brought steady upgrading of facilities and personnel until the training schools in Fiji and the Solomon Islands achieved secondary-level status. Not to be overlooked was the school in Tonga which passed through several phases until a boarding institution opened in 1921. Steady increases in enrollment and employment of professional teachers led to official recognition by the Tongan government in 1937.

Together with Europe the Pacific islands suffered from World War II. Many but not all Adventist schools were within the ring of the war. Mission workers evacuated Tonga while native Paul Fua took over the training school. Not so fortunate was Put Put Training School in New Guinea where no one had a chance to save the campus. Invading forces devastated the buildings, which had been in operation only since 1936. Besides destroying tangible property of the denomination, the war also snuffed out lives of some educational workers.

As military action moved northward out of the South Pacific, more nearly normal activities resumed. Losses had occurred but official statistics show that as a whole, the system of Adventist elementary education actually grew during the war. In 1945 ten of the fifteen island missions were operating 299 church schools for nearly 6,000 students. The Solomon Islands alone accounted for 185 schools.

The twenty-five years after 1920 witnessed dramatic change in Adventist education in the South Pacific. Although Watson said in 1922 that mission workers could enter most of the region uninhibited, four years later in 1926 J. E. Fulton, president of the Australasian Division, declared that evangelism was beset with a "dense wall of heathenism" and "impenetrable night."[15] Freedom to preach and teach did not automatically translate into immediate civilization or easy conversions.

However, fifteen years later in 1941 the rhetoric was noticeably different. Civilization still had not penetrated every nook and cranny of the Pacific, but island governments were establishing educational standards of their own and requiring Adventist schools to hew the line. E. B. Rudge did not complain about this turn of events, in fact, he admitted that these requirements had lifted the standard of Adventist schools. After citing an enrollment of 5,000 in the island schools, he confessed that "more and more we are coming to recognize our dependence upon . . . the successful education of the native youth."[16]

Homer O. Stilson, an Adventist medical officer in the United States military serving in the South Pacific, wrote during the last year of the war that in those regions where European workers had left, indigenous teachers educated in Adventist training schools had held the church together. The war had not been pleasant, but it showed how far Adventist schools had progressed and that the sense of dependence on indigenous leadership that Rudge acknowledged had come none too soon.

**Helderberg College**

World War I left its scars in more places than Europe. An example was German East Africa where prior to the war Missionsseminar Friedensau had furnished enough workers to establish sixteen mission stations. During the war German and British military units battled each other fiercely in this colony. Estimated losses were as high as 60,000 among the African population. Fighting units even dug trenches across Adventist mission grounds and blew up mission buildings. In the territorial shuffle after the war German East Africa became Tanganyika, a British trust territory in which Adventist missions were the responsibility of the British Union and Stanborough College.

Meanwhile, the school in South Africa continued to fill a significant place in Adventist education. Church leaders in South Africa hailed its move from a suburb of Cape Town to a rural site at Spion Kop in Natal in 1919 as a moment of progress, but a new set of problems at this location became even more thorny than the original ones causing the transfer. The new issues were mainly financial. The school could not shake its debts, which African Division President W. H. Branson called "staggering," and its agricultural program, once deemed so important, became an additional financial drain following several droughts. By 1926 the school's property shrank to about a fifth of its original 2,200 acres. Another nagging problem was its thousand-mile separation from the heart of South Africa, which increased operational expenses of the school.[17]

Instead of progress at Spion Kop, the school maintained only a precarious existence. It took only eight years to convince church leaders to move again, this time to a 400-acre farm in Somerset West, thirty miles from Cape Town. At this new location the school became Helderberg College. While in Natal, Spion Kop College began to offer post-secondary classes, but enrollment never reached expectations, and only thirty-two students graduated. Following the school's renewal near Cape Town, students began showing up in record numbers. The first year enrollment shot up from seventy-seven to 134 with the number of post-secondary students nearly doubling.

After only two years at Somerset West, the school was producing enough graduates to fill most current needs for church workers, which also reduced Africa's dependence on missionaries. Branson calculated that more than half of the White employees in the African Division were products of Adventist education in South Africa.

The move to Somerset West also proved to be an antidote for debt. Utilizing student labor extensively, school administrators built much of the campus by 1936, but "only as funds have been available,"General Conference Secretary of Education W. E. Nelson said. "Not a shilling of debt of any kind."[18] By the end of World War II enrollment reached 275, about half in the secondary grades, but more than seventy enrolled in college-level courses.

The turnaround at Helderberg had been impressive, but not trouble-free. The school offered a junior college course, which prompted more than a third of the graduates to migrate to the United States to complete their education and earn a degree. Many of them did not return. In an attempt to stanch the flow of workers out of the country Helderberg faculty tried to redesign the theology program to integrate it with degree-completion programs in North American schools, but their efforts were unsuccessful. The notion of trans-oceanic affiliations was pre-mature.

The pivotal question with which Helderberg was dealing was its lack of degree-granting authority. In order to earn an official degree or to enroll in a university, graduates of Helderberg would have to pass examinations from a recognized institution such as the University of South Africa, which presupposed a curriculum designed to prepare students for the tests. But Helderberg's programs of studies were to equip students for denominational employment, and until faculty found a way to fit worker-training and external examinations into a single study track, diplomas from the Adventist school commanded no official recognition.

Ruth Gorle, English teacher at Helderberg, showed that through persistent and disciplined self-paced study, graduates of Helderberg could break this mold and earn graduate degrees from recognized universities, but it was too much to expect everyone to follow that course. For students seeking a career in the ministry, a recognized degree was not critical, at least at the moment. Thus for the time being the lack of recognized degrees was only onerous rather than a threat to the church. However, educational aspirations of students were rising along with society's progressively higher expectations in professional education, which in time would force the issue.

**Changes at Solusi**

Adventist education spread through Africa along the lines of church growth and organization, first moving northward from its beginnings in South Africa. Penetration southward from northern regions of the continent also occurred as European countries and their African colonies were paired in the same administrative division of the General Conference, but Solusi Mission had given the English-speaking south a head start in reaching Africa's interior. During the years following World War I it continued to be the showcase training school for the continent.

Several indicators pointed to Solusi's success, one of which was the employment of national workers. Soon after the school started, Africans began to take their places among the faculty of the school. By the 1930s about a third of the staff were Solusi alumni, the others were graduates of Helderberg or workers from the United States.

Solusi's program remained at the elementary level, but it evolved beyond basic educational skills of reading, writing, and arithmetic. Young women in the first four instructional levels, Standards I-IV, took village crafts and introductory classes in homemaking, and later could elect a three-year homemaking course. All male students in the lower standards trained in agriculture, construction, metalwork, and woodwork, acquiring enough skill to become self-supporting workers among outlying villages. In the early 1930s formal teacher-evangelist courses began for students who had passed Standard IV. This three-year program emphasized professional preparation in religion and teaching besides more industrial education.

These accomplishments in Adventist education-evangelism were not without distractions. Solusi could not shed its reputation in Adventist circles as a school that spawned questions about the relationship between sectarian institutions and government. The debate began when Cecil Rhodes' original gift of land triggered sharp discussion among church fathers in Battle Creek. As time progressed the school prospered and fears of government intrusion appeared unfounded, partly because Rhodes was happy to leave education for Africans in the hands of missionaries who operated schools. He never intended to interfere with school policy.

This *laissez faire* attitude changed after World War I as the Rhodesian government became more paternalistic and issued regulatory policies. Inspectors began periodic visits to Solusi and outstation schools, eventually making annual stops. School leaders and church officials did not believe that this probing threatened them inasmuch as they profited from government grants-in-aid that followed successful inspections. This money was a boon that helped to keep Solusi financially afloat and also bore part of the construction cost of new buildings when the school upgraded its program to become the central training school for the Zambesi Union.

About 1940 the situation became more complicated. In keeping with its policy of increased involvement in education, the Rhodesian government began erecting its own schools and employing teachers. In public schools salaries were higher, working hours fewer, and responsibilities less demanding. Teachers trained at Solusi readily saw that teaching positions in government institutions offered a more lucrative professional career than church employment and took advantage of the opportunity.

Adventist mission schools could not compete against these odds. The impact was both immediate and negative, and the practical effects amounted to a curricular crisis at Solusi and an employment problem in church administration. Evangelism in Africa at the time revolved around mission schools, and Solusi's only program, the evangelist-education course, was the source of evangelistic workers for much of the south-central part of the continent. However, beckoned by better pay and easier working conditions, enough Solusi graduates opted for jobs in public schools to reduce significantly the number of potential church workers.

Solusi found itself educating teachers for the government system, and depending on government grants-in-aid for survival, which planted question marks in the minds of some Adventists. They argued with some logic that, in effect, Solusi had become a government training school. The issue was debatable, for Solusi remained above all a contributor to the well being of the church, which, in turn, contributed to the well being of Africa. All of this had been a goal of the mission from its beginning and had been compatible with Rhodes' objective, which explained why the church received the gift of land in the first place. But some believed that Solusi was diluting its peculiar Adventist mission. At stake was not how to relate to an intrusive and hostile government, but rather how to untangle some of the strings that were tied to financial help from a friendly one. It was a question that Solusi would not resolve until well into the post-World War II era.

As the earliest educational experiment in Africa, Solusi was a model for other training centers, some making their appearance before World War I. Following the organizational model of North America, E. D. Dick, education secretary for the African Division beginning in 1926, implemented a division-wide policy of designating one school in each of the six unions as a central training institution and lesser schools as preparatory centers. Because Solusi was the largest and most promising school in the Zambesi Union it became the central institution for a union that sprawled over much of south-central Africa, including Northern and Southern Rhodesia, the Congo, and the Bechuanaland Protectorate.

By 1930 each of the six unions in the African Division had a training center similar to Solusi, the major ones at Malamulo in Nyasaland, Bongo in Angola, Gitwe in Urundi (Rwanda and Burundi), and Bethel, which had moved from Grahamstown to Spion Kop in South Africa when the European school relocated at Somerset West. It would transfer back to its original location in 1937.

When reporting to the 1926 General Conference session, W. E. Howell, General Conference secretary of education, described the impact of African schools on church membership as "Pentecostal." Given the rates of church growth at the time, his superlative was not an exaggeration. Four years later W. H. Branson referred to "hundreds" of graduates of African training schools who were teaching and evangelizing among their own tribes.[19]

Enrollment in mission schools exceeded 14,000 in 1930; in 1941 it approached 26,000. At one mission school more than 400 students were baptized in a single year. By the end of World War II about fifteen training schools were scattered across Africa from Tanganyika in the north to Natal in the south and on to the hump of West Africa. The majority of these schools enrolled students by the hundreds. The largest, Malamulo, had nearly 700 students.

## The Interim in Brief

During the interim years Adventist leaders commonly described denominational education in terms of advancement and progress. In Europe some campuses closed because of the trial by fire through which they passed before and during World War II, but institutions became more numerous in the United States, Africa and Australasia. By 1945 Adventist schools in these fields represented the full range of denominational education–the most elementary to the most advanced. Especially in Africa and the South Pacific the frame of reference for education was evangelism. Denominational leaders consistently measured their success by the numbers of baptisms and church workers that the schools produced.

The growth of the educational movement in Africa was spectacular during the interim years, which Adventist leaders could interpret as a demonstration of the widespread hunger among Africans for personal advancement as well as an indication of evangelistic success. Similar attitudes characterized the South Pacific although the numbers were smaller. While missionaries still maintained control in Africa and the South Pacific, by 1945 natives had assumed much of the teaching responsibility in individual schools. The shift of authority from the Caucasian to the non-Caucasian was well under way.

---

[1] The statistics in this and the following paragraphs about schools in North America and the world fields have been adapted from *Statistical Report*, 1920-1945.

[2] *General Conference Bulletin*, 1918, no. 2, p. 26.

[3] For Christian's views on this topic, see *General Conference Bulletin*, 1922, no. 9, p. 217, no. 13, 293; 1926, no. 3, pp. 9-15.

[4]*Ibid.*, 1922, no. 9, p. 217.

[5]*Ibid.*, no. 15, p. 380.

[6]*Ibid.*, 1926, no. 3, p. 9.

[7] For education in Europe, see *Ibid*, 1922, no. 5, p. 118; *ibid.*, no. 9, p. 217; *ibid.*, no. 13, pp. 293, 318; *ibid.*, no. 15, p. 380; *ibid.*, 1926, no. 3, pp. 9, 14; *ibid.*, 1930, no. 2, pp. 37, 45; *ibid.*, no.5, p. 82; *ibid.*, no. 6, p. 105; *ibid* ., no. 7, p. 115; *ibid.*, no. 14, pp. 250, 251; *ibid.*, 1936, no. 3, pp. 168-170; *ibid.*, 1941, no. 2, p. 41; *Statistical Report*, 1920-1945; *The Advent Survey*, October 1930, pp. 3, 4; *ibid*, September 1932, the entire issue devoted to Adventist education in Europe; Hartlapp, *Chronik Friedensau*, pp. 20, 34; Yugoslavian Training School *Bulletin*, 1977-1978; Brown, *Chronology*, pp. 114, 131, 160.

[8]*The Advent Survey*, September 1932, p. 3.

[9]*Ibid.*, p. 2.

[10]Sources for Australasia are *General Conference Bulletin,* 1922, no. 14, pp. 326, 327; *ibid.*, 1926, no. 11, p. 21; *ibid.*, 1930: no. 12, p. 208; *ibid.*, 1936, no. 7, p. 149; *ibid.*, 1941, no. 9, pp. 219, 220; *ibid.*, 1946, no. 4, p. 92; *Statistical Report*, 1920-1945; W. E. Howell, "Report of the Department of Education to the 1926 General Conference," RG 51, AST; Brown, *ibid.*, pp. 66, 70, 75, 98, 126; Homer O. Stilson, "Mission Schools Carry On," *Journal of True Education* (February 1945), pp. 12, 13; Trevor Lloyd, "Church Schools," in *Seventh-day Adventists in the South Pacific 1885-1985*, Noel Clapham, ed., pp. 168-185; Milton Hook, "Avondale College," *ibid.*, pp. 146-165; Oliver, Barry, Alex Currie, and Doug Robertson, eds. *Avondale and the South Pacific, passim.*

[11]*General Conference Bulletin*, 1930, no. 12, p. 208.

[12] *Union Conference Record*, July 28, 31, 1899; Alonzo Baker, *My Sister Alma and I*, p. 57.

[13]*General Conference Bulletin*, 1936, no. 7, p. 149.

[14]*Ibid.*, 1922, no. 14, p. 327.

[15]*Ibid.*, 1926, no. 11, p. 21.

[16]*Ibid.*, 1941, no. 9, p. 220.

[17]This passage about Africa is summarized from *General Conference Bulletin.*, 1926, no. 7, p. 23; *ibid.*, 1930, no. 4, p. 75; *ibid.*, 1936, no. 7, p. 148; *ibid.*, 1941, no. 2, p. 40; *Statistical Report*, 1920-1945; *Southern African Division Outlook*, August 1, 1932, p. 5; *ibid.*, November 1, 1935, p. 2; "Report of the Department of Education to the 1926 General Conference Session," RG 51, AST; memorandum, 1938, RG 51, AST; Interview, Milton Siepman, January 8, 2002; Cadwallader, *History of Seventh-day Adventist Education*, pp. 194-203; Drusilla Hertogs, *Ruth Gorle, Makhumalo: Mother of Teachers* (Published by the author, no date); Brown, *ibid.*, p. 105, 107.

[18]*General Conference Bulletin*, 1936, no. 7, p. 148.

[19]Howell, "Report of the Department of Education to the 1926 General Conference," RG 51, AST; *General Conference Bulletin*, 1930, no. 4, p. 25.

# Chapter 11

# The Interim Years in Asia

To understand the story of Adventist education in Asia one must see it as part of Western penetration into the East. Military action reached only the western fringes of this part of the world during World War I, missing the dense populations in the Asian heartland, but the conflict helped to stimulate urges of national consciousness that fermented, yeastlike, wherever western civilization had spread during the years of imperial expansion. Similar to North America, Europe, and the South Pacific, Adventist education in Asia bore the marks of the human context in which it existed. During the interim years the training schools in Japan, Korea, and Southeast Asia played important roles in Adventist education, but most of the headlines came from China, the Philippines, and India.

## Adventist Education in China during the Interim

The experience in China presents a unique chapter in the story of Adventist education. While two world wars and the Great Depression were the dominant politico-economic events in Western countries during the first half of the twentieth century, China struggled with its own troubles, severe internal turbulence that rendered the country nearly prostrate. Persistent agitation by a young and ambitious generation of reformers brought about the demise of the Manchu dynasty. China became a republic in 1911, but a very unsettled one as warlords, nationalists, and communists fought among themselves for hegemony. China was an ancient land undergoing struggles for nationhood, and these see-saw struggles produced waves of competing sentiments that swept alternately across China for much of the time after the 1920s until the communist revolution settled the matter following World War II.

The leading figures in these events were Sun Yat-sen, Chiang Kai–shek, and Mao Tse-tung. The first two married sisters from the wealthy Soong family, Christians by persuasion and friends of Dr. Harry Miller, a career Adventist medical missionary to China who also served as president of the China Division during the 1930s. Sun Yat-sen led the Kuomintang, the Nationalist party, and while not a communist, he allowed communism to gain considerable influence in his party during 1923 and 1924. After Sun's death in 1925 Chiang Kai-shek emerged as China's acknowledged leader and by parrying communists and smashing opposition from fratricidal warlords remained so to the end of World War II. Communism's flirtation with popularity ended in 1935 when Mao, the leader of the communist movement, finally retreated with his followers to northwest China, quietly waiting for a more opportune moment to grab power.

Weakened by internal disorder, China became easy prey. In 1931 Japan occupied Manchuria and in 1937 invaded and ravished the eastern fringe of China. For the time being Chinese communists and Nationalists buried the hatchet to fight their common enemy. Much of the western world had been at war for two years when Japan's attacks in 1941 on the holdings of the United States and other western powers in the Pacific sucked Europe and America into the Asian maelstrom.

During the twenty-five years after 1920 China progressively adopted elements of western life although internal conditions did not reflect a wholesale acceptance of occidental culture. No part of Adventist education better reflected these new moods in China and the debilitating international political scene than the major training school in China. In 1919, barely ten years since its founding, it had already moved from its original location in Honan Province to Nanking and then on to Shanghai where it assumed the name of Shanghai Missionary College and began offering college-level classes.[1]

S. L. Frost, education secretary for the Far Eastern Division, disclosed in 1922 that in the three years since the college had operated in Shanghai enrollment had grown to new levels and that 171 of the 270 students were earning nearly all of their educational expenses in school-owned industries. Of the remaining students a large percentage earned a part of their expenses, some as much as three-fourths.

*Denton E. Rebok began a lengthy career in Seventh-day Adventist education in China during the World War I years. He reestablished the training school near Nanking and introduced a strong agricultural and industrial program. He later served as president of the Theological Seminary in Washington, D. C.*

These figures were impressive, but D. E. Rebok, president of the school, determined to improve them by adding agricultural training as a key part of Adventist education in China. In 1925 church leaders in China moved the school back to Nanking and changed its name to China Missionary Junior College, a move that they explained was an attempt to promote both rural education and industrial training in keeping with traditional Adventist philosophy. In Shanghai industrial training was a successful part of the program , but the school was not rural. Under Rebok's direction students on the Nanking campus raised tons of strawberries to be shipped to the Shanghai market, produced metal beds for numerous commercial customers, and ran a thriving print shop and operated other enterprises in food processing and weaving.

The industrial and agricultural character of the school at Nanking proved to be its savior from political problems that were brewing. Communist influence in the Kuomintang revived in 1930, and with it came an attempt to implement an accreditation program requiring all schools to register with the government and to eradicate non-Chinese elements from their curricula, including Christianity. As a gesture of patriotism, all students were to participate in what approached adoration of Sun Yat-sen, generally regarded as the father of republican China.

Adventist schools refused to comply. Pressure mounted, and just as the issue was about to snap, Dr. Harry Miller, president of the China Division, explained to one of his patients, H. H. Kung, who was Chiang's minister of labor and industry, why China Missionary Junior College would close rather than buckle under the new restrictions. Kung advised Miller to reorganize the school as an industrial training institution registered with the ministry of labor and industry rather than to continue as an entity subject to the ministry of education. Immediately the school redefined itself, jettisoned its name in favor of China Training Institute, but continued its program unchanged and unmolested.

By and large the crisis was over, but not all Adventist schools fared as well as China Training Institute. Some temporarily closed. In an unanticipated gesture of helpfulness, the ministry of education advised one Adventist "middle school" that if it followed denominational traditions of practical education it could continue its operations unhampered. In 1936 Miller told delegates to the General Conference that practical education had not only saved the central training school but many lesser institutions as well from government restrictions while at the same time affording an opportunity for hundreds of Chinese students to earn an education.

The traditional image of an educated Chinese was a cultured person educated in Confucian principles who led a reflective and sedentary life aloof from the masses, but China Training Institute catered to the poor, some of whom went from the school to become physicians and professionals with graduate degrees. The school promoted human dignity in a different manner and demonstrated that academic achievement and physical labor were not mutually exclusive. The proof was not only in the tangible products that came from the campus, but also in the school's uplifting impact on students.

This concept of education was something new for China, and influential Chinese took notice. Hardly had the initial crisis with government registration subsided when Madame Chiang personally asked Paul Quimby, religion and history teacher at China Training Institute, to join the Kuomintang as a special advisor to the government on educational matters. To fulfill her request would require him to work full-time for the government.

Quimby resisted, realizing that an alien, a Christian no less, joining the Kuomintang was diametrically opposed to the prevailing Chinese mood to purge the country from foreign influences, but Miller urged him to join the Nationalist government anyway to help resolve deep-rooted problems in Chinese education. Quimby's reluctance evaporated when Madame Chiang remonstrated, "Mr. Quimby, you are from Chiao Tou Chen [China Training Institute]. You know the answers to these problems. That's why you are here."[2] She later confided to him that being a Christian herself and with her husband's partiality toward Christianity, she wanted Christian principles to become a part of Chinese education.

Miller later related that China Training Institute lent one of its professors to the government for three years and a dozen more Adventist educators could find immediate employment in government schools if they were available. He was not exaggerating. In 1935 Chiang offered Miller and the China Division a completely endowed school to operate for the government. It was now the doctor's turn to demur.

But before Chiang could make good on his offer international events caught up with him. The Japanese invasion of China in 1937 targeted Nanking, the seat of Chiang's Kuomintang. China Training Institute was also a probable target, only miles from Nanking on the railroad leading to Shanghai. Quimby, who had returned to the college as president, closed the school, leaving it to the invaders who reduced the campus to rubble, killing three Chinese workers. Although the physical plant was gone, the immediate reaction of the China Division was to reestablish the faculty and classes in Hong Kong jointly with the South China Training Institute.

The South China school was the newest edition of Canton Training Institute, which was a descendant of the first girls' school and a boys' school of the Ida Thompson era. Known as Canton Training Institute, it functioned as one of several middle schools in the shadow of the college at Nanking. By 1935 it became one of the larger Adventist schools in China. The South China Union, the largest union in the China Division, assumed control of the institution and changed its name to South China Training Institute. To protect it from the turmoil in much of

China, in 1937 it moved approximately 150 miles south to the British crown colony of Hong Kong.

At the time of this move the destroyed college from Central China joined the South China school at its new site. Although this was supposedly a joint operation of two schools with the title of China and South China Training Institute, for practical purposes it was a single institution. This arrangement continued in temporary quarters until it occupied a new campus on a forty-acre plot at Clear Water Bay in the New Territories northeast of the city of Hong Kong.

The desired protection in the British colony lasted only three years. After the Japanese captured Hong Kong in 1942, school authorities lost little time separating the two institutions and moving them to safer locations. While the former Nanking school followed the Nationalist government to Chungking to join the West China Union Training School, the old Canton section transferred back to nearby southern China where it remained until after the war, functioning under its resumed title of South China Training Institute.

During most of these wartime years about a hundred students graduated, a living testimony to the leadership of James Wang, who, with help from fellow Chinese P. T. Ho and C. I Meng as well as missionary T. S. Geraty, kept the school going. Between 1945 and 1950 two attempts to revive the school at its old Nanking campus failed. In the wake of the communist revolution in China, church activity disappeared and the school became only a paper entity with a dissolved constituency, but Chinese Adventists kept its memory and traditions alive as part of the South China Training Institute, reconstituted in Hong Kong as the sole survivor of Adventist schools in China.

In 1945 Adventist education in China could look back on more than forty years of history. The first schools were evangelistic tools to reach the public, but with the development of post-secondary education in Shanghai in 1919 and an evangelistic program based on formal lectures and preaching, the leading purpose of Adventist schools metamorphosed into worker-training institutions whose primary products were teachers and ministers.

China was a country whose vast geography and vernacular differences separated the people into regional groups, but Adventist education embarked on its post-World War I era with remarkably strong traditions. Calamitous events or not, it not only survived, but grew. In 1920 Adventist membership exceeded 3,500 with the largest concentrations in southern and central China, but small numbers of members lived in Manchuria and in the northern and western regions of the country. More than seventy of the eighty-three Chinese congregations operated church schools. Six schools offered enough advanced courses to be classified as training schools, one of which was Shanghai Missionary College, a unifying element in this fractured land and only one of two Adventist post-secondary institutions outside North America.

In 1930, with approximately 10,000 members, China separated from the Far Eastern Division to become the China Division. By 1940 Chinese Adventists approached 20,000, scattered among nearly 300 congregations that maintained 116 church schools. Despite the war and the occupying Japanese army, Adventists in China operated seventeen training schools, including a nursing school, a correspondence school, a school in Shanghai for Russian members, and a secondary school for children of missionaries.

The Adventist educational movement in China benefitted from the services of some of the church's better educators. Harry Miller, though first and foremost a physician, was a man of versatile talents who never lost sight of education as a critical part of the church. D. E. Rebok gave twenty-three years of his career to China, much of which he spent as president of the training school at Nanking. Quimby's skills propelled him into government circles. Frederick Griggs, one of the denomination's foremost personalities in education, served as president of the China Division from 1936 to 1938.

### Philippine Academy Becomes Philippine Union College

Compared to China, successes in the Philippines were paradoxically similar and different. When Philippine Academy at Pasay on the outskirts of Manila opened its doors in 1917 Adventist training schools outside North America had been in operation for twenty-five years, but the late arrival of the Philippine school did not prevent its swift rise to prominence. It soon became one of the leading Adventist schools not only in Asia but in all of the world fields. Students flocked to the tiny four-acre campus. The school began with thirty-six students in a twelve-

*Philippine Union Academy was one of the most rapidly growing training schools outside North America. Just four years after its beginning it graduated this first class of secondary students. In the 1930s it became the first Seventh-day Adventist degree-granting institution outside North America.*

grade curriculum. Three years later the first class graduated and by 1922 enrollment reached 230.[3]

In order to keep pace with a rapidly growing student body, school administrators pursued a continual building program. After five years of operations the school expanded to accommodate 250 students, including dormitory space for a hundred students and facilities for a library, chapel, labs, and food service, besides faculty housing. Some limited industries provided student labor opportunities.

As good as all of this sounded, I. H. Evans, president of the Far Eastern Division, confessed that not a single school in his field was adequately equipped with library materials, science labs, or even buildings. Nevertheless, there was no let up in growth at Philippine Academy or the expansion of its program. In 1925, only eight years after founding day, church leaders authorized the school to become a junior college. The two-year phase-in began the next year. After two complete years as a fourteen-grade training school, total enrollment, including elementary and secondary students, reached 319, which lifted the institution to fourth among the ninety-four Adventist training schools outside North America.

From the beginnings of Adventist presence in the Philippines, a rapidly increasing constituency fed the growth of the training school. In 1925 when the academy ascended to college status, church membership in the Philippines exceeded 6,000 and was accelerating. The Philippine Union claimed the highest baptismal rate of any union in the Far Eastern Division. At the same time, the division, with more than 19,000 members, ranked third in size among the denomination's seven divisions, and in a moment of ebullience with an eye on the need for workers throughout his field, Division Education Secretary S. L. Frost wished out loud that all of the training schools in his field could make the transition to colleges.

Frost's exuberance was not far off target, at least as it affected the Philippines. During the four years before 1930 membership in the American-held islands nearly doubled, prompting I. H. Evans to predict that this trend would soon make the Philippines one of the largest unions in the Adventist world. The pressure for a steady and certain supply of workers was one of the keenest needs of the field.

Philippine Junior College was not long in outgrowing its four-acre plot in Pasay. The idea of relocating the school in a rural setting on a larger campus with additional facilities became progressively more plausible. In anticipation of this eventuality the Philippine Union purchased a sixty-five acre rural plot in Baesa in Caloocan City, again near Manila. School administrators stretched the investment value of every dollar of General Conference assistance by relying heavily on student labor to build a new campus.

In 1931 the school moved to its new site. The next year, before the smell of newness had hardly worn off, Philippine Junior College received approval to become Philippine Union College, the first Adventist institution outside North America to achieve senior college status and degree-granting authority. Only fifteen years had elapsed since the school began in 1917.

The first graduates from four-year programs received their degrees in 1935. Pride in the school was evident. With a tinge of triumph W. P. Bradley, secretary of the Far Eastern Division, told the 1936 General Conference session that Philippine Union College was a senior college offering general and professional courses with the largest college enrollment of any resident school outside North America. W. E. Nelson, General Conference education secretary, remarked that "the greatest educational progress has been made in the Philippines" when commenting about Adventist schools in the Far Eastern Division.[4]

Actually, the only four-year degree available was a bachelor of science in education, but it was enough to give the new college an edge over all other Adventist institutions in Asia in teacher-preparation programs. The net effect was to recognize Philippine Union College as the center for advanced education for the Far Eastern Division.

This role became the burden of college President L. M. Stump when he appealed to students during an assembly talk to look beyond the Philippines for likely careers of church service. Thirty students pledged to become missionaries and formed the first foreign mission club in the short history of the school. The school "is becoming a base from which workers can be sent to other fields," Bradley said.[5] On the eve of World War II post-secondary enrollment climbed to 145, the largest of all Adventist colleges outside North America and nearly double the size of the school next in line. It was still the only four-year post-secondary Adventist institution beyond the United States.

During the years from 1917 onward the evolution of Philippine Union College overshadowed all other educational news coming out of the islands, but Filipino Adventists did not overlook education at other levels. In 1922 S. L. Frost intimated that elementary schools were appearing, only three at the time, but enough to be a straw in the wind indicating that Adventist education was spreading throughout the Philippines. By the time the central training school became a senior college in 1931, three academies were also in operation. In the north Northern Luzon Academy evolved from an elementary school, and East Visayan Academy on the island of Cebu and West Visayan Academy on Iloilo served Adventists in the central Philippines. All three schools functioned as training centers as well as feeder schools for Philippine Union College.

By 1940 these three schools reported a combined secondary enrollment of nearly 300 besides hundreds more elementary students. In addition, ninety elementary church schools dotted the islands, attracting more than 2,600 pupils. Nearly one church in every four supported a church school. The heavy emphasis on teacher-preparation courses at PUC had paid off.

But by 1940 other issues were looming in the Philippines. Observers of events in the Orient saw Japanese military incursions on the Asian mainland as omens of trouble for other strategic sites, especially the far extremity of the Pacific rim of defense for the United States in which Manila was the key. Tension turned to shooting in December 1941, eventually forcing Americans into a retreat. Philippine Union College passed into local hands. With the help of Filipino faculty, Reuben G. Manalaysay held the school together, continuing classes until peaceful times returned except for the school year of 1944-45.

The thriving educational establishment in the Philippines was in part a byproduct of the United States presence in the islands. One of the major objectives of public policy was to educate Filipinos for self-government, which included preparing Filipino teachers for Filipino schools. Adventist practice paralleled this trend once Adventist membership became large enough to warrant a training school. Adventists in the Philippines also benefitted materially from American control of the economy and from democratic principles that became a part of Philippine life.

The hegemony of the United States was not the only explanation for the hurried advancement of Adventist post-secondary education in the Philippines. Adventist leaders in the Philippines were North Americans, but they were quick to point out that Filipinos were apt students who needed only a taste of education to whet their appetite for professional life. Since Philippine Academy had become Philippine Junior College nationals had served the institution in substantial numbers. By the mid-1930s when the school became a senior college, they were in the majority, even serving as religion teachers to prepare a Filipino ministry. When nationals took over the college during the war, it was not a case of turning the school over to rank novices. Anglo leadership returned to the college after the war, but the Manalaysay presidency was a harbinger of future trends.

## Japan's Threefold Educational School

Elsewhere in the Far Eastern Division Adventist schools sometimes faced steep uphill struggles. Unlike the Philippines and China, Japan had a high literacy rate but this achievement proved to be no advantage for Christian education of any stripe. The imperial government had preempted the field with a system of primary schools that offered effective education in Japanese culture which left little room for interlopers such as Adventist schools.[6]

Adventist education in Japan began in 1897 but the first training school did not open until 1908 near Tokyo. This enterprise remained small before closing in 1917. Two years later it reopened, seemingly with a rejuvenated program, but growth was still slow. "Our . . . school work in Japan is not large," S. L. Frost acknowledged in 1922. "We have one training school and one primary school."[7] Enrollment was about fifty, divided into two sections according to gender.

Inspired by a $2,500 donation from a Thirteenth Sabbath overflow offering in 1924, Japanese Adventists matched it ten times, enabling them to give the school a new beginning. In 1926 they transferred the section for male students out of Tokyo to a rural location across Tokyo Bay, leaving the women's half of the school at its urban site. A redesigned program that added post-secondary courses and an agricultural component brought a new institutional name, Nihon San Iku Gakuin, or "Japan Threefold Educational School."

W. P. Bradley, division secretary, described the change with exhilaration, stating the school was "blazing the way" by introducing something new in Oriental education–a learning program that incorporated student labor. Visitors, ranging from farmers and professionals to government functionaries, toured the campus to see, to praise, and to marvel, Bradley said.[8] As encouraging as these courtesies were they did not overcome the deeply rooted hostility for Christianity that smouldered in the imperial government. Threefold education was a novelty for the Japanese but its impact was something less than a revolution in the government schools.

A laggard rate of membership growth kept development slow at the training school. "The Japanese people make good Christians, faithful and true," I. H. Evans stated in 1930, but he confessed that of all the fields in the Far Eastern Division, Adventists succeeded least in Japan.[9] By 1935 membership barely topped a thousand and school enrollment was less than seventy-five.

As the imperial government flexed its military muscles in Asia, problems mounted for Adventist education. In 1910 Japan had annexed Korea; in 1931 it occupied Manchuria and in 1937 invaded eastern China. In early 1940 non-Japanese church workers withdrew from Japanese-controlled regions and national workers shouldered the responsibility for church and institutional leadership.

Accompanying these military actions were rumblings emanating from Tokyo that threatened a merger of all Christian bodies into a single movement, which would smother denominational identity. This unification occurred in October 1940, but Adventists were one of a score of denominations that did not comply, leaving the church vulnerable to intensified pressure. The college struggled to remain alive under the direction of two successive Japanese presidents, H. Yamamoto and K. Otsuki, but in 1943 a government decree shut the institution down. It remained closed until 1947.

## Uncertainties in Korea

A near replica of events took place in Chosen, or Japanese-occupied Korea. Under Japanese controls, the training school in Soonan began the post-World War I era as Chosen Union Training School. During the immediate years after 1918 rebellion and student strikes favoring independence pockmarked the country. The training school "had to share with others in the matter of strikes," C. L. Butterfield, superintendent of the Chosen Union, said, admitting that enrollment dropped during the disturbances.[10]

By 1922 quieter political times cooled students' fiery spirits and helped bring on an enrollment revival. Enlarged facilities financed by the same Thirteenth Sabbath overflow offering that had benefitted San Iku Gakuin in Japan enabled the Korean school to double its student housing capacity. By 1930 the school rebounded with more than 250 students, mostly elementary, but with a small post-secondary enrollment.

School growth stemmed from other causes as well. Korean Adventists had endured "sad times," as I. H. Evans reflected on the state of affairs in Chosen, but membership increased much more rapidly than in Japan, more than tripling Japanese numbers by 1935. This growth translated into more students to educate. Also different from Japan was the Korean practice of maintaining a relatively prosperous system of lower schools which fostered the idea of a training school for the advanced students. Adventist leaders were gratified by the number of Korean students who entered church employment.

But the upward trend in education did not last. In 1931, presumably because of political pressure from the occupying Japanese, theological classes moved from the Soonan campus south to Seoul under the direct tutelage of Chosen Union personnel. Between 1932 and 1937 formal ministerial education stopped altogether, while a secondary school operated at Soonan. In 1939 ministerial education resumed in Keijo, the Japanese form for Seoul, and the secondary school moved to the same city, but enrollment suffered from the interruption. A year later responsibility for church affairs devolved into local hands and American and European workers evacuated from Japanese-controlled areas. For two years beginning in 1940 school principals Lee Sung Eui and Chai Tai Hyun headed the school, but anti-Christian political pressure forced it shut in 1942. As in Japan, the school remained closed until 1947.

### Prosperity and Reversal in Singapore

Of all the training schools in the Far Eastern Division, Malaysian Union Seminary in Singapore received the least publicity. Serving a polyglot field extending from the Straits of Malacca to the eastern shores of the Netherlands East Indies, its enrollment continued to rise during the 1920s. Students came from Thailand, known at the time as Siam, from the British-controlled Malay States, and from Borneo, Java, Sumatra and the Celebes, all parts of the Netherlands East Indies. English became the medium of instruction, although teachers spoke Chinese and Malay in the lower levels.

After a quick and optimistic beginning the school had an up and down experience. By 1921 enrollment dropped from more than 140 to sixty-five, but after settling in a permanent site on Upper Serangoon Road, student numbers picked up. More than 350 enrolled in 1930, a figure that dropped to fewer than a hundred the next year when the Netherlands East Indies separated from the Far Eastern Division to become part of the Central European Division. A new school in Dutch-held Java attracted only a fraction of the lost enrollment.

This erratic experience did not lessen the importance of the school in the eyes of church leaders, who consistently regarded it as one of the five major training schools in the Far Eastern Division and deserving of junior college status. Showing remarkable resiliency, the Malayan Seminary, as it was renamed, regained its cosmopolitan character and in 1935 registered about 150 students who spoke thirty-six different languages, according to W. P. Bradley. Five years later the enrollment reached a near-capacity 360. Elementary-level courses predominated, but secondary enrollment was encouraging enough to support a small department to offer one year of post-secondary classes.

Still another blow was about to hit the school. As one of the most strategic ports in Asia, Singapore was in the direct path of the Japanese military as it swept down the Asian coast in 1941. In February 1942 the Japanese flag was flying over Singapore and much of Southeast Asia, including the Netherlands East Indies. This time the Seminary closed and European and American workers fled, some of them not in time to avoid capture and internment. From 1942 to 1945 the school did not function.

### Adventist Education in China and the Far East—a Comparison

Besides the common trials of war, Adventist education in the China and Far Eastern divisions experienced other changes during the twenty-five years after 1920. Nationalization succeeded best in the Philippines, but in all of the main schools local teachers were conducting many of the classes before the war erupted, including extensive coursework in religion and theology, regarded as key responsibilities in producing church workers. According to E. L. Longway, acting president of the China Division as it emerged from the war, national leadership during the war was "perhaps the greatest item that should be credited to the right side of the ledger."[11]

Because most of the schools in China managed to stay on the friendly side of political lines during the war, they remained open and produced workers, but the Far Eastern Division enjoyed no such luxury. At war's end this field was suffering badly from Japan to Singapore because of a dearth of workers. All schools had closed and no graduates had entered church employ for four years.[12] Record keeping during the war years was next to impossible, but official denominational statistics show that elementary education in the Far Eastern Division maintained its level as measured in total enrollment. By contrast, the China Division sustained more than a thirty percent loss. In these two fields trends of growth in elementary schools occurred before World War II.[13]

### Complexities in Southern Asia

Compared to events in the Far Eastern and China divisions, the development of Adventist education in the Southern Asia Division was small and quiet, at times almost unnoticed. One reason for its lack of attention was the long delay between the first denominational schools and the establishment of a central training school. Adventist secondary schools were relatively numerous in Southern Asia, but the field did not establish an official training school until 1937.[14]

India was the dominant country in this division which included a ring of neighbors strung out from Afghanistan in the west to Burma in the east, and north and south from Tibet to Ceylon. Ethnic, linguistic and religious differences separated not only the countries but split India itself into pockets that were as alien to each other as distant nations.

As new Adventist missions appeared in Asia they fused into the Asiatic Division that sprawled thousands of miles from western India eastward through China and even Australia and the South Pacific. In 1919 this cumbersome arrangement fell apart, with India and its peripheral neighbors joining to constitute the Southern Asia Division. The major missions in India became unions.

As a rule of thumb among Adventist missions, a recognized training school appeared soon after the church established a toehold, but events were different in Southern Asia. Membership growth was slow and schools tended to serve the local mission. Each union developed its own training school with programs at both the elementary and secondary levels. Under this organization the South India Training School became the educational center for the South India Union although it was emerging as the strongest educational center for India. E. M. Meleen, who had taken charge of the school in 1918, spent nearly his entire six-year principalship developing the new campus at Krishnarajapuram near Bangalore with other lesser schools in the field supplying students for advanced work at the union school.

Although South India Training School, or SITS, was a single institution, it functioned in two parts, segregated by gender. By 1922 it was offering a limited number of post-secondary classes, although it was officially a secondary school. Two years later the campus became coeducational, a mark of changing times in India.

These early years of the South India Training School coincided with widespread nationalist agitation throughout India which church leaders viewed with mixed feelings. W. W. Fletcher, the first head of the Southern Asia Division, saw the new political trends as a threat to Christianity, but he could not varnish over his restrained admiration for the leader of Indian nationalism, Mohandas K. Gandhi, whom he described as a "quaint and frail figure," a "wonderful spectacle," stirring India as it had never been moved before and forging a new, intensified national consciousness.[15]

Gandhi was aware of Adventist beliefs and the nature of Adventist education. During his twenty-year sojourn in South Africa before World War I he had established Tolstoy Farm, a combination school and refuge for Indians living in Transvaal, where he experimented with a simple diet, vegetarianism, cross-ethnic education, coeducation, and a program combining training in agriculture and skilled labor with traditional instruction and spiritual development.[16]

Without introducing himself as an Adventist, G. F. Enoch, a career missionary to India, later visited the leader of Indian nationalism, thinking to impress him with the virtues of practical education as Adventists practiced them, especially at the South India Training School. But he could not trick Gandhi. Before he finished his remarks the Indian leader interrupted him to ask if he was a Seventh-day Adventist. Years later the Indian leader visited the Krishnarajapuram campus and joked that he had experienced the peanut-butter fad with Adventists.

Although Gandhi was congenial and in agreement with many of the ideals of Adventist education, the political trends he represented made little or no room for Christianity. He was frequently at odds with British authority. For the time being Adventist leaders found it advantageous to keep some distance between themselves and the nationalist movement.

By the end of the 1920s India's Adventists recognized the South India Training School as their most advanced learning center which continued offering post-secondary classes through the decade. Union leaders agreed to a resolution in 1929 stating that it was financially unfeasible for all union schools to offer classes beyond the secondary level and in their opinion the Krishnarajapuram campus would be the ideal location to send students for post-secondary work. This resolution was not an official action establishing a division school but rather a consensual statement recognizing the preeminence of South India Training School in what, in effect, was a consortium of supporting schools. The South India Union continued to manage the school, but the action paved the way to its later official designation as a division institution.

Official action or not, South India Training School reacted by eliminating elementary courses and concentrating on secondary and post-secondary classes. In 1930 only thirty-six enrolled, all officially secondary students. As the decade progressed, the school's drawing capacity grew with students registering from all parts of the division, including Burma. By 1935 the student body was largely post-secondary, although still less than fifty. Enrollment was predominantly male, but women formed a growing part of the school. Since its early days a dairy, a poultry farm, and a printing press were the leading industries.

College historian George R. Jenson has pointed out that while enrollment was less during these years, the numbers represented actual growth because students were exclusively in the upper standards, including college-level, which constituted a new trend in Adventist education in India. This general upgrading and the industrial and coeducational programs caught the eye of Mysore state government officials who visited the campus from time to time and encouraged school leaders in their work.

At its biennial meeting in 1937 the Southern Asia Division Council voted to make official what had become obvious by finally designating the South India Training School as the division college to train vernacular workers. Appropriately, the management of the training school passed from the South India Union to the Southern Asia Division. At the same time the institution took the name of Spicer College to honor W. A. Spicer, General Conference president from 1922 to 1930 who spent a brief term in India near the beginning of his career.

This action culminated a twenty-two year evolution. Some of the leading personalities included G. G. Lowry who established the school, E. M. Meleen who developed the Krishnarajapuram campus and later, as a leader in the South Indian Union, continued to shepherd education in general and the school specifically. N. C. Wilson, president of the Southern Asia Division, led the division to take the final action. Among the Indian workers who served the school were L. G. Mookerjee and E. D. Thomas, the first nationals to become ordained ministers in the Southern Asia Division. Mookerjee held many positions of responsibil-

*E. D. Thomas, one of the first ordained native ministers in India, held leadership positions at the South India Training School, which developed into Spicer Memorial College.*

ity, among them religion teacher and press manager at the training school. Thomas at one time was an assistant principal of the school and business manager.

Enrollment continued to climb after the school became the division educational center, topping seventy by 1940, the majority of whom were postsecondary students. After a prolonged search, college and division leaders moved the college from Krishnarajapuram north to a larger and more central site on the outskirts of Poona, which would allow for easier access and institutional expansion. In 1945 the school changed its name to Spicer Missionary College and the next year it achieved senior college status.

The evolution of Spicer College was above all else a process of emergence, a natural outcome of events and conditions that favored its growth into its role as the division school. This process was slow, reflecting small membership increases in the division. In 1940 Southern Asia was the smallest of all the world fields with fewer than 5,000 members.

The notion of a divisional system of education that furnished students to the top institution was integral to the emergence of the South India Training School. It became unofficial policy after the 1929 resolution recognizing the *de facto* role of the Krishnarapajuram campus as the leading school in India, a status that received additional strength when school leaders discontinued instruction in the elementary standards in order to focus on secondary and college level classes. In this respect Southern Asia's school was different from all other Adventist training schools outside North America. While those institutions grappled with the issues of offering instruction at all levels, South India Training School was the first to concentrate on its primary objective of preparing church employees by limiting itself to advanced education.

In some ways no other field outside North America had better equipped itself to centralize its adult educational program than the Southern Asia Division. A multiplicity of ethnic and linguistic groups had required a multiplicity of schools, and the 1937 action creating a division junior college also perpetuated the existing practice of restricting all other schools to elementary and secondary status. At the time about twenty such schools were scattered throughout the division, many of them boarding institutions. Some were staffed entirely by Indian teachers. Five were in Burma, among them Meiktila, which served as the central training school in that country. One was in Ceylon. Also in India were several score of church and village schools.

The organization of Adventist education into a workable system did not mean that the schools had breached the ethnic and linguistic differences in India's society. The question of how to touch this multitudinous and variegated land with Christianity weighed heavily on the minds of church leaders. E. D. Thomas described the gargantuan task to delegates to the 1936 General Conference when he reminded them that India's overwhelming rural population was scattered among 750,000 villages. "If Jesus at the beginning of His earthly ministry had begun to visit these villages," he said, "spending only one day in each village, He would still have to spend 118 years in order to complete His task."[17]

That Adventist schools had played a crucial part in Southern Asia's evangelism was common knowledge. As G. G. Lowry had envisioned it, the mission school was the most important vehicle to carry the gospel to India's masses. But the mission schools had not been easy to establish or to maintain. I. F. Blue, superintendent of the Northwest India Union, recounted in 1922 that he had "stripped the field" of every Indian worker who could teach and even employed some Hindu and Muslim teachers to conduct Adventist schools, mainly for children of church members or "inquirers."

Village preachers were also teachers who maintained a school during the day and preached in the evenings. The schools themselves were primitive with no equipment, sometimes meeting under a shade tree, but they accomplished their task. "By serving the community in this way as teacher and preacher," Blue said, "soon the worker has a little company meeting regularly for Sabbath school; and after thorough teaching, they are ready for baptism. Little lights spring up in the way."[18]

During the twenty-five years after 1920 this plan remained, but with it also came a greater emphasis on church schools. H. A. Morrison, General Conference secretary of education, observed in 1941 that compared to other fields, Southern Asia operated a large number of elementary and secondary schools. "If evangelism can be promoted by other means than through the school," he remarked, "the minimizing of the mission school may be desirable."[19]

In addition to the system of vernacular schools in Southern Asia, missionaries utilized Vincent Hill School at Mussoorie in northern India as a convenient place to send their children rather than returning them to their home countries. The school originally catered to the English and Anglo-Indian communities. After operating at two locations, it moved to Mussoorie in 1922, opening with eighty students. At this third site, known as Vincent Hill, about 150 miles north of Delhi in the foothills of the Himalayas, the school outgrew its initial objective and within five years became a junior college.

Division and union leaders came to regard Vincent Hill School and College as a division training school for what they euphemistically called the English work. Most of the students were elementary, but by 1935 total enrollment surpassed 130 with thirteen college students. Division President A. L. Ham recalled in 1946 that Southern Asia had been able to employ nearly all of the graduates from this school.

The Vincent Hill campus grew steadily until after World War II, but whatever impact it had as a supplier of denominational workers, the ultimate need was indigenous leadership, which by definition, would come from the vernacular schools. The post-secondary enrollment at Spicer had long since exceeded the number of college students at Vincent Hill, and by 1945 the school for the English work began to decline. In 1951 the college section closed and soon after the curriculum became Americanized. The school no longer prepared English-speaking workers, but educated children of missionaries.

## Adventist Schools in Asia Compared

In many Asian countries where Adventists established schools ancient traditions of philosophy and learning were common, and the concept of education was not new. But illiteracy was high because native education and learning were elitist and shut out much of the population. The Western form of education which Adventists as well as other Christian bodies brought differed from indigenous customs. The primary purpose of Adventist schools was to contribute to denominational aims of spreading the gospel, but an inherent part of its effect was a democratizing process, making education available to the masses.

Asian countries lacked democratic traditions, but to varying degrees they accepted some democratic ideals, among them a trend toward social equality which gradually became more visible during the interim years. It is safe to conjecture that Adventist schools succeeded in part in Asia because they contributed to national goals.

Japan did not fit this description well. A system of state education was already in place when Adventist education arrived, and thus in the public eye Adventist schools became competitors rather than vehicles of advancement. In this island nation Adventist education had to survive solely on the merit of its Christian character.

Irrespective of the differences among Adventist schools in Asia, during the interim years native leadership rose much more rapidly in Asian schools than in Black Africa or the South Pacific islands. Like their counterparts in Europe, Adventist schools in Asia suffered from World War II, but in 1945 they were no longer the frontier enterprises that they had been in 1920.

---

[1] Information about China has come from *General Conference Bulletin*, 1922, no. 15, p. 359; *ibid.*, 1930, no. 3, p. 52; *ibid.*, 1936, no. 3, p. 55; *ibid.*, no. 13, p. 260; *ibid.*, 1946: no. 8, p.185; *Hong Kong Adventist College Bulletin*, 2001-2003; *Statistical Report*, 1920-1940; John Oss, *Mission Advance in China* (Nashville, TN: Southern Publishing Association, 1949), pp. 187-193; Paul Quimby with Norma Youngberg, *Yankee on Yangtze* (Nashville, TN: Southern Publishing Association, 1976), pp. 77-160; Raymond S. Moore, *China Doctor* (New York: Harper & Brothers: 1961), pp. 155-161; Herbert Ford, *For the Love of China*, pp. 53-93, 111-118; Brown, *Chronology*, pp. 78, 154.

[2] Quimby, *ibid.*, p. 100.

[3] For data about the Philippines, see *General Conference Bulletin*, 1922, no. 15, pp. 356, 358; *ibid.*, 1926, no. 10. p. 30; *ibid.*, 1930, no. 3, pp. 61, 62; *ibid.*, 1936, no. 6, pp. 54, 55; *ibid.*, no. 7, pp. 134, 149; *ibid.*, 1941, no. 2, p. 40; *Statistical Report*, 1920-1945; Brown, *ibid.*, pp. 91, 138, 147, 184.

[4] *General Conference Bulletin*, 1936, no. 7, p. 149.

[5] *Ibid.*, no. 3, p. 54.

[6] I have gathered information about Japan, Korea and Malaysia from *General Conference Bulletin*, 1922, no. 15, pp. 344, 358; *ibid.*, 1926, no. 4, p. 14; *ibid.*, 1930, no. 3, pp. 61, 62; *ibid.*,

no. 7, p. 114; *ibid.*, 1936, no. 6, p. 54; *ibid.*, 1941, no. 7, p. 155; *ibid.*, no. 8, pp. 186, 187; *ibid.*, no. 9, p. 216; *Statistical Report*, 1920-1945; Sahmyook University *Bulletin*, 1999-2000; Brown, *ibid.*, pp. 154, 156, 169.

[7]*General Conference Bulletin*, 1922, no. 15, p. 358.

[8]*Ibid.*, 1936, no. 3, p. 54.

[9]*Ibid.*, 1930, no. 3, p. 61.

[10]*Ibid.*, 1922, no. 15, p. 344.

[11] *General Conference Bulletin*, 1946, no. 8, p. 182.

[12]*Ibid.* no. 7, pp. 155, 157.

[13]*Statistical Report*, 1920-1945.

[14]Data dealing with Southern Asia comes from *General Conference Bulletin*, 1922, no. 1, p. 4; *ibid.*, no. 2, pp. 44-46; *ibid.*, no. 13, p. 303; *ibid.*, 1930, no. 11, p. 190; *ibid.*, 1936, no. 5, p. 101; *ibid.*, 1941, no. 2, p. 40; *ibid.*, 1946, no. 3, p. 53; *Statistical Report*, 1920-1945; Spicer Memorial College *Bulletin*, 2001-2002; Jenson, *Spicer Memorial College*, pp. 26-72; Samaraj, ed. *Images 1893-1993*, *passim*; Pohlman, "First the Blade, then the Ear," unpublished edition, pp. 32-40; R. S. Lowry and M. G. Champion, "A Providence in India," *Journal of True Education* (June 1953), pp. 34, 35; Brown, *ibid.*, pp. 172, 181.

[15]*General Conference Bulletin*, 1922, no. 2, p. 44.

[16]An informative source of Gandhi's views are in his autobiography, *Gandhi, an Autobiography: the Story of My Experiments with Truth.* Mahadev Desai, trans. (Boston: Beacon Press, 1993 ed.). See particularly pp. 328-340.

[17]*General Conference Bulletin*, 1936, no. 5, p. 101.

[18]*Ibid.*, 1922, no. 4, p. 88.

[19]*Ibid.*, 1941, no. 2, p. 40.

# Latin America and the Caribbean in the Interim

Removed from the combat theaters of both world wars but not immune to the impact of war and the Great Depression of the 1930s were the two sister divisions, South America and Inter-America. In these two territories educational development contrasted sharply. The Inter-American Division did not organize until 1922. Prior to that date the region was in organizational disarray and only after repeated frustrations had church workers been able to establish a single training school in Jamaica. In 1920 this fledgling institution was still feeling its way. By the time South American Adventists organized a division in 1916, training schools were already functioning in Argentina, Chile, and Brazil, and in 1919 a fourth campus opened in Peru. Although this last campus originated during the beginning years, it was really a school of the interim.[1]

### Argentina's Colegio Adventista del Plata

All four South American institutions were called training schools, but differences in their strength and reputations were inevitable. Colegio Adventista del Plata, or CAP, the first training school in South America, early developed the unofficial standing as the leading school in the field. It was closest to the managerial hub of Adventist work and although its financial footing was not prosperous it was better off than other training schools in South America during its formative years. In 1926 its future brightened when it became a junior college, but through the rest of the 1920s and the following decade enrollment did not increase as school administrators hoped. In 1920 enrollment stood at 172; twenty-five years later the number of students rose to 287, an increase of less than sixty percent even though membership in its supporting constituency, the Austral Union, quadrupled during the same period.

Fluctuating economic conditions were partly to blame for slow growth at CAP. Another contributing factor was the habitual departure of prospective ministerial students from the campus to enter pastoral work after they completed secondary school. This practice provided congregations with pastors quickly, but it undercut the primary source of potential post-secondary students. Sooner or later the Austral Union would feel the pinch for better educated ministers.

The school enjoyed unique success with its teacher-preparation and agricultural programs. J. S. Marshall, principal and president from 1919 to 1934, and his wife Marian, who supervised the teacher training curriculum, began following the government's certification program in 1927. Seven years later when they left the campus, they had pulled sixty-two students through the government examination process to earn life teaching certificates in Argentina. During the late 1920s the school farm gained national acclaim for its dairy and agricultural products.

Church leaders and administrators of Colegio Adventista del Plata ended the quarter century after 1920 with a debilitating debate about the school's location. Its founders had deliberately put the campus in the country where it would serve the surrounding German-speaking Adventist population, but as church membership increased and the school became Hispanized, pressure built up to move the institution closer to an urban center. Repeated criticism argued that students were staying away from a rural school accessible only by muddy roads.

But other pressures were at work. By 1941 the school had suffered a string of operating losses and could not afford capital improvements. As the canons of World War II began firing, a defense-minded Argentine government issued a set of decrees announcing tighter controls over education. At the time Adventist leaders in South America were discussing the feasibility of "officializing" the school, which would make it a nationally recognized pre-professional institution, but the new regulations raised questions about Saturday classes, military training as part of the curriculum, and restricting faculty to Argentine citizens. The government also frowned on coeducational boarding institutions.

A plot of land just north of Buenos Aires was being readied for a new campus for CAP, but faced with a near-impossible political situation in Argentina if the school proceeded with plans to officialize, some leading voices in the Austral Union began a campaign to transfer the school to Uruguay. Church leaders stalemated, however, not being able to decide between Argentina with its threats and Uruguay, separate from the heart of the Austral Union. The upshot was a decision once and for all to remain at the original location in Entre Rios Province, the least problematic site, away from the capitals of either Argentina or Uruguay.

The decision was a turning point for the school. Officializing the school did not occur, but the conclusion cleared the air from the uncertainty that had clouded the campus for years. In 1945 the post-secondary enrollment was only twenty-nine, but with the divisive debate behind them, administrative faculty and Austral Union leaders could concentrate on upgrading the school plant and extending its program to transform the institution into the school they had been dreaming about ever since it became a junior college.

## Success at Brazil College

While the Argentine school was struggling with its identity, Brazil Seminary developed a post-secondary program that made it the most prominent school in the South American Division by 1945. Although its campus was rural and accommodated a thriving agricultural program, it was also close to Sao Paulo, one of Brazil's major cities, which led some leading denominational personalities to believe that the school's location was one of the best in the Adventist world. By 1920 enrollment reached 136, mostly secondary students in worker-training programs.

Probably motivated by an economic downturn and the need for more assurance than the slim financial resources on which the school depended, Brazil Seminary President T. W. Steen instituted a cash-in-advance payment plan in 1921. His action aroused widespread skepticism among church leaders in Brazil who warned that it would strangle enrollment. The upshot was neither as successful as Steen hoped nor as bad as the critics portrayed it. School authorities made exceptions for about a fourth of the students who needed to work. Enrollment indeed dropped somewhat, but the school enjoyed unprecedented financial well being, which was one of Steen's primary goals.

Whatever the virtues of the cash-in-advance plan, it did not last. It was almost axiomatic that Adventist schools would incorporate labor programs and that students should work. The notion of requiring students to pay a year's fees in advance appeared to deny a long accepted philosophy. Further, the origins of Brazil Seminary and the size of its agricultural projects presupposed that the school needed the students to work. Within three years the campus was back to the more traditional practice of providing institutional labor as a means for students to gain an education.

Through the entire interim between 1920 and 1945, and long thereafter, the training school near Sao Paulo was, in effect, an inter-union campus, serving Brazil's three unions and depending on financial support from all of them, although the school was associated more closely with the South Brazil Union. After 1923 the institution more often went by the name, Brazil College. During the 1930s enrollment rose and fell according to the economic fortunes of the country, but gradually it edged upward. Unofficially it began offering post-secondary classes, and in 1940 the General Conference *Statistical Report* listed it as a junior college, the fulfillment of long standing Brazilian aspirations.

The school's new status symbolized the rising tide of national consciousness that washed over Brazil during the 1930s. A movement among Brazilian church leaders to split from the South American Division and form a separate Brazilian Division got nowhere, but they had more success in nationalizing Brazil College. From the school's beginning North Americans supervised theological studies. Their language skills were frequently less than professional and rapid turnover made for discontinuity. After Brazilian theology teachers took charge in 1931 the program stabilized and the number of ministerial students increased. In 1939 Domingos Peixoto succeeded to the presidency, the first national to head a major training school in South America. By that time the faculty was largely Brazilian.

Enrollment at Brazil College caught up with attendance at River Plate College in the mid-1920s, but the pattern during the 1920s and 1930s showed more fluctuation and fewer students in Brazil than in Argentina. In the 1940s, however, trends reversed. In 1945 when the Brazilian school celebrated the thirtieth anniversary of its founding, more than 500 students registered, nearly 300 in secondary classes and 127 in post-secondary courses. Brazil College had become the largest Adventist school in South America.

### Training Schools for Andean Indigenous Peoples

Most of the issues that the Argentine and Brazilian schools encountered during the years after 1920 pivoted on the question of making certain that training programs conformed to Adventist educational philosophy and were productive according to church needs. While these questions were omnipresent at Adventist schools, at times public problems became all absorbing. Such was the case in the Inca Union, consisting of Ecuador, Peru, and Bolivia.

For some of the Peruvian intelligentsia, the Adventist system of schools for the indigenous population in the Lake Titicaca region was a social service, a means to integrate the mountain people into the mainstream of society. While Adventists acknowledged the legitimacy of this purpose, for them the schools were an evangelistic tool, a miraculous accomplishment whose crowning event was the opening of a training school for the Aymara Indians in Juliaca in 1922.

A Thirteenth Sabbath offering that year provided funds for new construction, and in 1924 the school moved into a new building. Although it was officially an elementary school by North American standards, Peruvian education authorities classified some of its instruction as secondary. Enrollment grew encouragingly and from the Aymara mountain villages came more calls for primary schools than the training school could handle.

To manage these petitions leaders of the Inca Union and the new Titicaca Normal School required the requesting villages to furnish liv-

*The graduating class of 1927, Titicaca Normal School, poses in front of the main building. This school represented one of the most dramatic successes in Adventist education in South America.*

ing quarters for teachers and buildings for the schools they wanted. Additionally, villagers also had to establish an equipment fund equivalent to US$50 and guarantee at least eighty students. The schools also began charging small fees. Even with these new conditions hardly a letup occurred in calls for village schools.

By the mid-1920s graduates of the training school were numbered in double digits, who almost without exception found employment as teachers in the widening circle of outlying schools, some of which were in neighboring Bolivia, taught by Bolivians who attended the Titicaca campus. Especially important to the educational program in the Andes were the summer sessions when teachers in the village schools gathered for more training. Nearly 290 attended the summer session of 1925-1926. With these figures in their hands, South American church leaders regarded Titicaca as one of the five training schools in the division, although the curriculum and labor program, which included sheep herding and rug making, differed from those at the Argentine and Brazilian schools.

All of this activity came to a sudden halt in 1928 when Augusto B. Leguia, Peru's president, accused Titicaca Normal School of jeopardizing national unity and issued a decree closing the school. He also threatened the same treatment for all similar schools–meaning Adventist schools–and proposed that the government should build and operate Indian schools and require all schools to use approved textbooks. Adventists interpreted Leguia's actions as an imminent danger. South American Division President Carlyle B. Haynes declined a full explanation when he reported to the 1930 General Conference session, saying that matters were too sensitive to discuss openly. What he did not divulge was that he and his colleagues were dealing with an alleged desecration of the Peruvian flag on the Titicaca campus.

The more Adventists protested, the firmer Leguia became, arguing that he had not acted in violation of religious freedom, which he acknowledged the Peruvian constitution guaranteed, but to protect national integrity. He whispered to confidants that he did not intend to send Adventists packing, but that he had, indeed, aimed his decrees directly at the training school. In spite of his tough talk, no other Adventist school closed, although at the time no one knew how far the Peruvian president would take his threats.

Haynes urged Adventists around the world to pray, and what many interpreted to be a quick case of divine intervention, a *coup d'etat* overthrew Leguia and installed a president who had once been a patient in the nearby Juliaca Clinic and was sympathetic to Adventists. In December 1930 the new Peruvian chief executive reopened the training school while administrators tried to put their program back together. But the school suffered lingering damage; enrollment plunged to fewer than fifty by 1932. Recovery was slow but sure, and by 1940 the student body exceeded 160. Enlargement of the curriculum was also part of the new growth.

Questions of government controls did not go away. In 1943 the school faced new demands by inspectors who imposed a prohibition of coeducation. This time the school did not shut down but modified its program to arrange a compromise with state officials. By 1945 Titicaca Normal School had become a leading secondary school in the South American Division with an enrollment exceeding 230.

Ironically, about the same time Titicaca Normal School closed in 1928, the Bolivian Board of Instruction published a complimentary article about educational methodology at the Peruvian school. Bolivian

Adventists read the article, remembering that their students had encountered problems crossing into Peru to attend Titicaca Normal School. After Leguia shut the school down, the Bolivian Mission decided to open its own program to train indigenous teachers for village schools patterned after those in Peru which Bolivian education leaders had just praised. A modest beginning at Collana, high in the Andes, in 1929 drew twenty students, a figure that grew to about seventy the next year.

Enthusiasm ran high, but church leaders did not conceal their doubts about the future of a campus staked out at a cold, barren, near-14,000-foot elevation. Two years after the school opened it moved to Cochabamba, a more inviting site at 8,500 feet. This change was an improvement, but a war between Bolivia and Paraguay siphoned off potential enrollment into the army, and economic dislocations sapped the school's resources. School directors hung on, attracting a gradually rising number of students and introducing secondary-level classes in 1938. By the end of the decade the campus established itself as a training school in its own right with an enrollment of more than 150. The school's first decade and a half was a study in tenacity for what would become a major educational institution in South America after 1945.

### The Forerunner of Universidad Peruana Union

Also a part of the Inca Union was Instituto Industrial, the forerunner of Universidad Peruana Union, which began in four rented rooms in the suburbs of Lima in 1919. H. B. Lundquist, who had been in Peru for only a year, took the initiative in responding to a need to educate not only local Adventists but also children of workers. From the first day of classes, church officials regarded this new enterprise as a training school, but its first years were difficult, if not disappointing, and a far cry from the institution it would eventually become. The first year Lundquist offered elementary-level classes to fifteen students; about twenty enrolled the second year, and thirty-five the third.

Unlike the schools in Argentina, Chile, and Brazil, the Peruvian venture functioned at first without land, but it was known as Lima Industrial Institute. To satisfy the Adventist custom of including labor opportunities, Lundquist encouraged students to sell literature, but he also equipped a limited carpentry shop. Three years after its founding the school transferred to a small rural location where agricultural opportunities were possible.

After only two years at the school, Lundquist moved on to church administrative positions, leaving others to resolve the serious problem of cramped quarters. His successors resolved this matter in 1926 by relocating again on a seventy-acre site on the edge of Lima. The new location was large enough to establish a dairy farm, but this improvement did not compensate for another major weakness of the school–its lack of graduates. Until 1928 only one student finished the complete course. Similar to students in Argentina, many entered church employment before completing their studies, only in this case, they did not even finish a secondary course.

The school also struggled with a small enrollment. In 1928 when the school began its tenth year only forty students attended. The next two years brought a turnaround as enrollment more than doubled. It may have been coincidental, but these were the same years that Titicaca Normal School was closed. It was apparent that students became more decisive about their commitment to worker-training courses while uneasiness concerning the government's attitudes toward Adventist education permeated the Inca Union.

Although enrollment rose, when compared to River Plate and Brazil colleges, the training school in Lima was small. Facilities also were mediocre at best, but the enrollment surge had a much needed positive effect. Students tended to remain in school longer, with more of them graduating–twenty-six between 1928 and 1939. Lundquist observed near the end of the 1930s that an increasing number of former students were filling positions of responsibility and the number of imported workers was diminishing notably, both trends attributable to the impact of the training school.

The struggles of the Peruvian school during the 1920s and 1930s underscored the tenacity of South American Adventists to prepare national church workers. South American Division President P. E. Brodersen confessed to the 1926 General Conference session that missionaries from North America could never produce desired results because they required years to acclimate to life in their new environment and to learn a new language in which they more often than not communicated imperfectly. "Our schools are our only hope," he said. "The possibility of successful evangelism for South America lies with our national evangelists."[2]

Instituto Industrial had become the recognized training school for the Inca Union, but hardly had its prospects brightened before they began to dim. In 1942 the Peruvian Ministry of Education clamped down with enforcement of legislation prohibiting coeducation, the same law that inspectors would apply the next year at Titicaca. Attempts to petition their way out of this dilemma proved as futile as had earlier conversations about the closure at Titicaca. In 1940 enrollment reached 235, but by 1942 when the prohibition on coeducation went into effect, all that was left were some night classes. This crippled program hobbled along for two years, finally developing into separate schools according to gender. Urbanization of the region surrounding the school and public works construction projects also reduced institutional acreage. It required no insight to conclude that the school's days were numbered and it would have to move.

In 1945 both the boys' and girls' schools fulfilled accreditation requirements with the Ministry of Education, at the same time receiving permission to merge into a single institution and move to a new campus at Ñaña, about twenty miles above Lima. The anti-coeducation law still applied, but in the case of the new school, appropriately known as Union College, it demanded only separate classrooms and dining facilities. With a promise of financial assistance from the December 1945 Thirteenth Sabbath offering, school officials began classes at the new site in the same year.

### Developments at Chillan, Chile

Adventist education in Chile seemed to have received a new lease on life when the training school moved from Pua to Chillan in 1922, but discouragement soon set in. The Chile Conference was unable to provide sufficient financial support and the school's labor program was skimpy. Debate about moving again quickly surfaced, but by 1926 a firm decision to remain at Chillan scuttled further talk.

J. M. Howell, a firebrand who had begun his mission career as a teacher in the Titicaca schools, took over the Chilean training school in 1925, immediately setting about to use the variety and quality of farm

*The Seventh-day Adventist training school in Pua, Chile, began as a school to serve both German- and Spanish-speaking students. It struggled as one of the poorest schools in South America until it relocated at Chillan in 1922. This picture shows the school two years before the move.*

products as a means to impress the public as well as the Adventist community with the values of Adventist education. Within five years he had turned the school around and established it as a productive source of denominational workers. In 1933 his successor added post-secondary classes to the curriculum, but enrollment at this level remained low even though total attendance topped 300 in 1940.

Militating against the development of a college-level program was an organizational obstacle. The school originated because church leaders in Chile deemed it necessary to prepare workers for Chile on Chilean soil; however, it became evident during the 1930s that while the original argument might be strong enough to rationalize the school's existence, it was not powerful enough to sustain it. The Austral Union still looked to River Plate College as the primary educational institution for the union, leaving the Chilean school as more or less a project of the Chile Conference where membership was perennially sparse. By 1940 it was only 2,500, too small to support an effective training school on par with CAP in Argentina.

In 1939 an earthquake devastated much of the Chillan campus. For years the school reeled from the blow, operating in makeshift arrangements with repairs coming slowly. Enrollment held up, however, and the rebuilt plant featured the most comfortable structures in its history. In 1944 a two-year ministerial course finally received the backing of the South American Division, effectively ending efforts to send ministerial students from Chile to Argentina. Enrollment did not immediately shoot upward, but the action was a watershed for Chillan, for it was a tacit acknowledgment that the Austral Union had two training schools, which, at least on paper, were academically equal.

### Elementary and Secondary Schools in South America

While the training schools were becoming well-established institutions in the South American Division, elementary education also grew. Village schools for indigenous Andean tribes constituted a major part of this movement, but these projects were deliberately evangelistic in purpose and thus not of the same character as the traditional elementary church school for children.

Teacher-preparation courses were staple curricular items at the training schools, and although not every graduate from these programs entered denominational employment, it was apparent that South American Adventists intended to educate themselves in their own schools. In 1916 the Austral Union took on the responsibility of translating Alma McKibbin's Bible textbooks for use among church schools. At the time only a few schools existed, but by 1925 more than 1,100 students were attending thirty-eight elementary schools in Brazil and the Austral Union. The largest number of church schools in South America appeared in central Argentina, including the national capital, doubtlessly a result of the heavy stress on teacher-training at River Plate College.

During the 1920s and 1930s the idea of Christian education put down deep roots throughout the division. By 1945 South American churches operated nearly 190 schools with more than 8,000 students in addition to the Andean indigenous schools.

The evolution of college-level programs on the central campuses drew attention to the distinctions between the purpose of training schools and secondary education, and the need to keep them separate. Among larger concentrations of Adventists boarding academies sprang up in the 1930s–Buenos Aires, Argentina; Taquara, Brazil; and Petropolis near Rio de Janeiro. By 1945 at least seven secondary schools were functioning in Brazil, Argentina, and Uruguay.

Taken in its entirety in 1945 Adventist education in the South American Division had spread more broadly and materialized into a better developed system of post-secondary schools than in any division outside North America. Its network of elementary schools was among the largest in the Adventist world.

Striking similarities existed among the education programs in South America, Africa, and the South Pacific. To use Australasian terminology, a westernized home territory characterized all three divisions on which the church depended for its educated leadership. On the shoulders of the home territories also rested the responsibility of preparing a corps of workers to reach out to indigenous peoples within their divisions. Education was the major medium for this process, thus the outlying indigenous schools were unmistakably evangelistic ventures. In contrast with South Africa where a widespread Adventist educational movement at the secondary and elementary levels did not exist, lower schools in Australasia and South America developed with the training schools and created an educational system.

### The Educational Setting in Inter-America

In the region that in 1922 became the Inter-American Division training schools were latecomers to the world of Adventist institutions. E. E. Andross, the first president of the division, set the tone for education soon after he arrived in 1922. In rhetoric that few others matched, he told the 1926 General Conference session that "our hope for the future of our work in this field lies in the training of a large number of consecrated young men and women in our denominational training schools in the field," adding that the church needed workers "born in the tropics, whose mother tongue is the vernacular of the people, who know their people as no foreigner can know them, and who are accustomed to climatic conditions that are often fatal to a foreigner."[3]

In the English-speaking sectors of the Greater Caribbean Adventist missions got off to an early start, even thirty years before Andross arrived, but training schools did not follow quickly as they did in other fields almost as a matter of course. A lack of effective church organization and the absence of parent organizations to give financial support to schools combined to make educational centers nearly impossible. Administrative cohesiveness was difficult when vast stretches of water, undeveloped communication, and different languages separated much of the region into pockets that for years defied effective organization.

One of Andross' greater contributions to Inter-America during his fourteen-year presidency was a solid organizational and institutional infrastructure which resulted in productive membership growth and the establishment of institutions. Once begun, Adventist education developed rapidly, making up for lost time, as it were, proceeding in the wake of membership increases among the three major language groups, English, Spanish and French. Much of the school construction occurred during the late 1930s and early 1940s, drawing funds from the Adventist purse that some believed should have gone into evangelism.

But Andross had insightfully regarded the expenses of education as an investment and his administrative legacy paid rich dividends. By 1940 Inter-America's membership became the third largest of all divisions outside North America. At the end of World War II every major administrative component of the division operated its own training school.[4]

**Growth of West Indian Training College**

Jamaican Adventists had managed to overcome early organizational deficiencies of the region to establish a training school in 1915. It had an uncertain beginning, but in 1920 it was still alive, the only Adventist school of its kind in the Greater Caribbean. Once West Indies Training School hurdled its original obstacles, it made remarkable progress. In 1923 the first class of secondary-level students graduated, and the next year faculty added college-level courses and changed the institutional name to West Indian Training College. Already at least ten students had entered denominational employment.

Opportunities for student labor had been the nemesis of previous educational attempts in Jamaica, but the wife of the conference president solved this issue when she embarked on a fund raising campaign in the mid-1920s. The first $5,000 she scoured up was enough to build a sheet-metal shop and a bakery, buy a press, upgrade the furniture factory, and improve the water reservoir.

Her strategy turned out to be not only a blessing for students who needed to work but a stroke of good public relations as well. Student-produced commodities made their way into the Jamaican market, bringing cash to the school and at the same time arousing inquiries about the campus. "Our ideal has been threefold development, a heart-head-hand education," Principal W. H. Wineland reflected, adding with a touch of honest pride, "this was a new educational idea for citizens of the island, but many of them fell into sympathy with our plan, and seemed to appreciate our educational program."[5]

Wineland was not overdrawing the situation. Visitors began touring the campus weekly, some of them influential in Jamaican politics, and when commencement occurred in 1927 about a thousand attended, most of them non-Adventists. Even the governor of Jamaica was impressed enough to invite the entire college staff to a special dinner in one of Kingston's leading hotels.

During the years of the Great Depression the school approached a financial crisis that threatened its reputation as a unique educational institution in Jamaica. The school relied on income from the industries to fund most of its operating expenses, but even with these opportunities for work, many students were unable to pay for their education. Student accounts receivable mounted, and in turn the stack of accounts payable grew. A considerable amount of the blame went to the industries themselves, since they held extensive receivables from customers. When R. S. J. Hamilton arrived on campus in 1938 as president and chief financial officer, he found the school unable to pay its bills and some local merchants threatening to sue.

Part of the indebtedness came from church-related loans, which the Inter-American Division wrote off as appropriations. Hamilton engineered other adjustments in financial policies, essentially taking a firmer line with both students and customers of the industries. In short order he turned the institutional financial statement around, and the school averted financial embarrassment.

It was while the school struggled to maintain its financial integrity during the 1930s that its identity as a post-secondary institution strengthened. Earlier, in 1924, with attendance surpassing a hundred and prospects progressively brightening, the school became a junior college. This upgrading was part of the strategy to keep both students and their money in Jamaica by removing the temptation from students to enroll in a North American college. Jamaicans who traveled to the United States frequently did not return. But even after institutional upgrading the number of post-secondary students remained small, only twice reaching six before 1932. As the country sank into the financially disastrous 1930s, overall enrollment plummeted and cuts in personnel occurred, but ironically, college-level enrollment rose to unprecedented double digits. In 1936 the school registered twenty-five college students.

By 1945 enrollment was approaching 200 and the reputation of West Indian Training College as the only institution in Inter-America for English-speaking students that offered post-secondary courses was well established. Its industrial auxiliaries had been the financial backbone of the institution and remained one of its greatest selling points.

### Caribbean Training College in Trinidad

A second training school for the English Caribbean opened in Trinidad in 1927. To prepare for this event the Inter-American Division council created the East Caribbean Union, which would become the parent organization. Andross estimated that between 700 and 800 youth in the new union would be eligible to attend.

Following the denominational tradition of involving students in preparing the campus, Principal C. J. Boyd, a veteran schoolman from the United States with experience in Australasia and elsewhere in Inter-America, led his original faculty of six and a crew of students in land clearing and construction. The school sprouted from the soil of "La Realista," a 260-acre estate near Port of Spain that offered only a house and a couple of sheds for shelter as the work started. For the first year the labor detail occupied most of the students' schedule, leaving time for night classes only.

Through the interim years this new school exhibited two major shortcomings, low enrollment and a lagging construction program that fell short of campus needs. Andross' hope that hundreds of students would attend vanished as enrollment remained less than 100 until 1940. Explanations were many, but the obvious issue was widespread poverty on the island. The collapse of the sugar industry long before Adventism reached Trinidad left the population virtually penniless, a condition that had improved very little before the school opened. Also problematical was the lack of adequate financial support from the East Caribbean Union. Although it was the parent organization, it was almost as new as Caribbean Training College and had not built up a strong financial base on which the school could depend. Capital funds were hard to come by which showed up in a lack of adequate buildings. After a dozen years the division education secretary referred to the school as still unfinished.

Partially compensating for these problems were the managerial talents of R. S. J. Hamilton, school director from 1930 to 1938. He left a legacy of a sound industrial program, financial integrity, and respectable academic traditions. By promoting institutional industries and a variety of agricultural projects, he was able to derive nearly eighty percent of the school's operating budget from auxiliary income, which lessened the dependence on cash payments by students. It was a practice that he developed well and took with him when he transferred to West Indies Training College in 1938.

The school's industries brought popular respect to the campus, which was an accomplishment in itself. Initially, the school met with prejudice, but thinking Trinidadians came to realize that the type of education Caribbean Training College offered was adapted to people's needs. Trinidad's Agricultural Society conducted some of its meetings on the campus, and a leading newspaper published congratulatory comments about the labor opportunities the school offered to students.

The primary industry was a broomshop, the only one on the island, which gave Caribbean Training College a monopoly of the broom market and created island-wide attention. It also cultivated support for the school, which reached the columns of Port of Spain's newspaper, the *Trinidad Guardian*, when editors expressed confidence that the college would not let the island down when a shortage of broom corn threatened the factory during World War II .

Enrollment may have been slim, but Hamilton stretched his dollars and left the school in 1938 with no red ink on the financial statement. The school also benefitted from his academic skills and personnel management. He was the first person with a graduate degree to head an Adventist school in Inter-America. During the eight years he headed Caribbean Training College only one change occurred in the faculty, which brought stability and academic continuity to the campus.

West Indies Training College had quickly risen to post-secondary status, but Hamilton was content for the Trinidad school to remain a secondary-level training school and to establish academic respectability within that limitation. Not until 1944, six years after he left the

*The training school in the West Indies was the first Seventh-day Adventist school of its type in the Greater Caribbean. It was the first in the Inter-American Division to offer post-secondary classes and developed a reputation as a unique institution in Jamaica. This photo taken in 1953.*

campus, did the college board vote to participate in the British external examination program. College historian Glenn O. I. Phillips describes this decision as among the most momentous since 1927, since it was a key move in upgrading to post-secondary level the next year.[6]

Compared to West Indies Training College, progress at Caribbean Training College was more conservative but it was also more evenly paced, and by the end of the interim years in 1945 the school was on the threshold of a new and prosperous future.

### Educational Ventures in Central America

Most of the English-speaking population in the Inter-American Division occupied islands in the eastern Caribbean, but a significant number also lived in a narrow corridor extending along the eastern coast of Central America and outlying islands from present-day Belize to Panama. This area had been a destination for early Adventist missionaries, but not until after World War I was there a large enough constituency to supply students for a school.

It was in 1921 when West Caribbean Training School opened its classrooms at Las Cascadas, literally on the banks of the Panama Canal.

The land and buildings were originally United States government property used during canal construction, which the North American government wished to jettison. The Central American Union negotiated a generous lease for what amounted to a ready-made campus, complete with faculty housing, recreational facilities, paved roads, electrification, sanitation, and water supply.

For Central American English-speaking students there would be none of the prolonged and anguished working and waiting for financial support that the schools in Jamaica and Trinidad experienced. After remodeling the interior of the buildings, the school was ready for occupancy. Students could sit in their classrooms and watch ships traverse the canal. Enough land was available for a booming agricultural business, and buildings for shops gave students ample opportunity to work. As a part of the Canal Zone, the school enjoyed a unique financial blessing–duty-free status. Within five years enrollment at this utopian campus reached 125.

The old adage "if it's too good to be true, it probably is," never had a better fulfillment in Adventist education. Within ten years the school was dead. Loss of its duty-free status was a contributing factor, but only an annoyance in comparison to termites that chewed the buildings beyond repair. A rebuilding campaign was not out of the question, but the telling blow was a decision by Central American Union officers concluding that their territory was essentially Hispanic, not English, and that the union needed a training school for Spanish-speaking students more than for the English. Helping to convince them were curricular problems that set in early at Las Cascadas when a growing number of Spanish-speaking students enrolled, making a bilingual program necessary and expensive.

In Costa Rica the Central American Union officers found property at La Sabana where they transferred the Spanish half of the Panamanian school in 1927. Two training schools were more than the union could afford, and in 1931 the Central American Union voted to close the Panamian campus. While it lasted West Caribbean Training School was a success. From its classrooms came at least forty graduates, some of them lifelong denominational workers, including Linda Austin, who put in an entire career at Caribbean Training College.

La Sabana was only the first stop for the school which eventuated into Central American Adventist University. Here enrollment stagnated and prospects for plant expansion were dim. Five years later the school moved to Tres Rios near the Spanish colonial city of Cartago, its location until 1950. During the interim years after 1932 it remained a secondary school, changing its name to Spanish-American Adventist Academy in 1932 and to Central American Vocational School in 1945.

At Tres Rios enrollment immediately picked up, increasing every year even during the Great Depression. By 1940 attendance approached a hundred. Also at Tres Rios the school's ministerial training program flourished under the leadership of Braulio Perez, a Spanish-born, Argentine-educated minister with a poetic command of the language and a predisposition to evangelism, a combination that soon made him one of the best known personalities in Latin American Adventism and the speaker of the Spanish Voice of Prophecy.

## A Training School is Born in Colombia

Adventist education in Central America symbolized a growing consciousness among leaders in the Inter-American Division that the Hispanic population dwarfed the English and French combined, and that even though Adventist membership at the time was larger in English fields, the future of the division lay in balanced growth among the three major language groups. "Our purpose now is to build up strongly the schools in the Spanish fields," W. L. Adams, division education secretary, wrote in 1938, more than a decade after the Central American Union established its training school.[7]

But schools could operate only as rapidly as membership grew and money allowed, which became obvious as a side issue of the Central American school. The original decision to move the Spanish portion of the Panamanian school to Costa Rica included a footnote that designated the new campus as the educational center for students from Colombia, a republic on the northwest corner of South America that was geographically half of the Colombia-Venezuela Union, which organized the year the school transfer occurred. Because the new union was unprepared to establish a training school of its own Colombian students were expected to enroll on the campus in Costa Rica. The idea was well intended but impractical. Similar to Chilean students who resisted crossing the continent to attend school in Argentina, Columbian students did not jump at the chance to travel north into Central America for an education.

For years Colombia-Venezuela remained the smallest union in Inter-America with most of the membership in Colombia, but in 1937 with approximately 1,700 members, classes began for a dozen students in Medellin, an Andean city 200 miles south of the Panamanian border. It attracted little attention, moving to a less urban setting in 1938, and again in 1941 to a panoramic fifty-acre site, still near Medellin, which would become its permanent campus. By the time of this final move, the school enrolled about eighty students.

At this location the school assumed a new shape. An experienced North American construction engineer supervised the erection of a set of new, brick buildings and the farm yielded a wide variety of fruits and vegetables. Until its last move, Colombia-Venezuela Training School was blessed by a faculty with little turnover, which went far in establishing an effective academic program and attracting a growing number of students. Former students were already entering denominational employ when the move took place in 1941. Leadership changes occurred more frequently after that date, but by 1945 enrollment stood at 150, of whom more than 80 percent were secondary-level students.

### Cuba's Antillian Union College

The construction of a new campus in Colombia coincided with building projects at both Caribbean Training College in Trinidad and the Spanish-American Academy in Costa Rica. Added to this list of new school plants was Antillian Union College in Cuba, which moved from Bartle to Santa Clara in 1940. This spate of school construction drained funds from other uses, but given the tardiness of education in the Inter-American Division, it was hardly arguable that the expenditures were extravagant.

Of the five unions in the field, none resembled the makeup of the entire division more than the Antillian Union, consisting of the largest islands of the Caribbean with populations representing all three of the major languages, English, French, and Spanish. A single training school for this union was not even a consideration. Nearby Jamaica already had its West Indies Training College and during the 1920s and 1930s a school for each of the Spanish and French populations struggled into existence.

The Spanish school began in 1922 at Bartle, close to the eastern end of Cuba. Optimistic talk during the next decade and a half could not hide real problems at the campus such as limited acreage, inadequate water, poor soil, and lack of accessibility, all of which had blunted enrollment growth. During those first fifteen years the highwater mark was sixty students. The school began its sixteenth year in 1937 with a new principal, J. S. Marshall, who, speaking from the vantage point of a sixteen-year success story of administration at River Plate College, admitted the unvarnished truth about the impossible conditions at Bartle and urged a change.

Marshall timed his advice well. The division council had just voted to upgrade to a junior college to serve Cuba, Puerto Rico, and the Dominican Republic, but the new principal knew that a school with only four classrooms and no library would never pass muster. He also knew that the division had earmarked a portion of a Thirteenth Sabbath offering in 1939 to upgrade the school, but money would not fix the problems at Bartle and he was unwilling to spend another peso for a dying cause.

Marshall's counsel sank in. By the end of 1939 the Antillian Union had purchased 150 acres of promising land at Santa Clara, near the middle of the island, and laid plans for a new campus. Work proceeded with no delay, and in 1940 classes began at the new site.

Similar to other Adventist schools, the farm brought favorable publicity to the campus. Truckloads of produce were regular contributors to the food markets in Santa Clara, and in 1945 sixty Cuban school administrators who were attending an education convention visited the school to learn what an agricultural program could accomplish.

Marshall stayed on through the entire change, giving the newly christened Antillian College ten years of administrative stability. From the moment he had stepped onto the campus in 1937 enrollment began to climb, and in 1945, with more than 150 students, he added post-secondary classes to the curriculum. It was the first instance of college-level courses for Hispanic students in Inter-America.

## A French-Speaking Campus in Haiti

No such drama accompanied Adventist education in the French-speaking sector of the Antillian Union. In 1921 Hermanie Roth, sister of the head of the Haitian Mission, launched a small beginning for eight secondary students on a fifteen-acre estate near Cap-Hatien on the northern coast. Six years of virtually no growth followed before adding elementary classes, which increased enrollment, but the operation remained small. French-speaking teachers were at a premium, and the school stagnated, even closing during 1929 for lack of adequate faculty. Four more years of halting operations with an enrollment less than thirty-five told the leaders of the Haitian Mission that they could expect very little from the school unless they moved to more inviting surroundings.

In 1933 the school moved 130 miles south to the Haitian capital, Port-au-Prince, where it became a day school and functioned in two urban buildings, the smaller one serving as a woodshop and a press. The school also changed its name to College Vertieres. The move brought a rebirth, at least in terms of attendance. Two years later enrollment went over a hundred. After two more years during which attendance doubled, the government recognized it as a complete secondary school. Briefly it offered a limited amount of post-secondary classes, but for all of its growth, the vast majority of students were elementary. By 1940 enrollment began to recede and in 1945 it dipped to 130.

*Seventh-day Adventist education developed slowly in Haiti because of widespread poverty and sparse membership in the French-speaking Caribbean. During the 1930s a small training school occupied rented space in this building in Port-au-Prince.*

The lack of French textbooks and teaching materials left the school with an improvised program, and with enrollment decline College Vertieres lost its training school character. The Haitian Mission, the school's parent organization, was hardly capable of providing necessary support. In 1945 Haiti's membership was the largest component in the Antillian Union, but its tithe income and mission offerings ranked at the bottom or next to last, revealing one of the most poverty-stricken populations in the islands.

These obstacles prevented Haitian Adventists from maintaining a promising educational program, but Herminie Roth, her brother and sister-in-law, A. G. and Hazel Roth, had stuck by the school for most of the interim years, exemplifying the tenacious conviction that Adventist education was going to succeed. As bleak as the outlook was in 1945, it was a substantial advancement from of its position in 1921, but the school's prosperous years were still in the future.

## Dramatic Break-through in Mexico

By some standards, Inter-America's most dramatic breakthrough in Adventist education took place in Mexico. In this next-door neighbor to the United States a bloodletting revolution broke out in 1910, giving the country a new constitution that among other things, confiscated church property. Remembering that priests had initiated Mexico's independence movement and strong ties to the church had been part of the political milieu, devout Mexicans viewed this new revolutionary order as a contradiction of their history. Others saw the revolution as a means of standing up to their imperious northern neighbor and joked that they lived under a double curse–their country was far from God and too close to the United States.

Adventists in Mexico saw little humor in this irreverent candor. Their missions, including an attempt at education, were beginning to jell when the conflagration erupted. When the battlefield smoke blew away, Adventists faced a new political environment in which official hostility to religion was common, open evangelism was not possible, and religious education was very difficult. The battle to draft a constitution ended in 1917, but bands of armed malcontents stalked the country with impunity until well into the 1920s. Meanwhile, a succession of presidents during more than two decades left little doubt that they intended to enforce the new constitution as it affected religion.

Through the 1920s and 1930s Adventists made repeated efforts to establish a training school in or near Mexico City, but they uniformly brought indifferent results and always frustration. Several schools for

Adventist Mexican-Americans in the Hispanized borderlands of the United States offered an alternative, but they proved to be impractical. The most notable venture was a "Spanish Department" at Arizona Academy during the 1920s, but even the school's invitations to Adventists south of the border brought only a negligible number of students. In 1935 Adventist leaders in Mexico purchased a large house in McAllen, Texas, almost within a stone's throw of the international line, planning to establish a training school for prospective workers. Before their hopes materialized the building burned down, leaving the Mexican church with only the insurance money.

This seemingly impregnable wall barring a successful school began to crack in 1938 when Raimundo Garza, a recently converted physician and a professor of medicine in the northern city of Monterrey, began to speculate about the possibilities of nursing education. He could not dismiss the evangelistic potential of his clinic in the basement of the local church which brought about 5,000 patients in contact with Adventists, and he with other doctors decided to conduct a brief training course for nurses to establish similar clinics in other churches. Successful training institutes in 1940 and 1941 led to a formal request for a bonafide nursing school.

Meanwhile, the 1940 national election landed a new president in the national palace who personally viewed religious activities much less harshly than his predecessors. Garza's reputation and political connections were crucial, enabling church leaders to put their foot in the door and request permission to establish a school, which, they openly admitted, would prepare church workers, but with a strong emphasis on agricultural and industrial education. They already had their eyes on a 200-acre estate in Montemorelos, fifty miles south of Monterrey. Shortly it was theirs, with approval from the state of Nuevo Leon to begin a training school.

After a hasty and incomplete construction program, the school opened in November 1942 with eighty-five students, an astounding opening enrollment compared to other schools in Inter-America. The academic emphasis was on ministerial training, but the institution assumed the most innocuous name possible, Agricultural and Industrial School, and within months the state approved the elementary and secondary curricula.

The impact on the Adventist community in Mexico was profound. Division President Glenn Calkins wrote that "the building of this school is the greatest single factor that has ever taken place in Mexico in connection with our work."[8] After an Adventist presence of nearly a half century, Mexico finally acquired a genuine training school. No less than Mexican President Manuel Avila Camacho himself and governors of two neighboring states visited the school in April 1943 to express their interest in this project of practical education. Camacho personally lent a hand to bring in a manager of the dairy farm who would also teach classes in agriculture.

The very existence of Mexico's Agricultural and Industrial School signaled the beginning of a new era when political winds would blow from a different direction and sweep away official resistance to religious activity that had long been the order of the day. In 1945 the new school was just settling onto its campus, but in the years to come this unique venture would become Montemorelos University, one of the best known institutions in Adventist educational circles.

### Review of the Interim in Inter-America

Adventist education in Inter-America was a movement of the interim years. Besides the single training school in Jamaica in 1920, only in the West Caribbean Conference–consisting mainly of churches in Central America–had church schools made an impact. In this field were ten elementary schools that enrolled 500 students; throughout the rest of the territory that would become Inter-America only three schools with sixty-six students were functioning. Twenty-five years later the number of church schools rose to 131 with more than 180 teachers and nearly 6,000 students. Two secondary schools apart from the training schools were in operation, New Hope College in Jamaica and Panama Academy in Panama, both for English-speaking constituencies.

During the interim years the Inter-American Division established six training schools, one in each of its unions. Four of the campuses were in Spanish-speaking regions, thus making good the intentions of the division leaders to promote a balanced program among the major language groups within their territory. The seven training schools in the division constituted the largest number of such institutions in any division outside North America, although only two of them, the campuses in Jamaica and Cuba, offered post-secondary classes.

In its twenty-three-year life before 1945 the Inter-American Division became the largest field beyond North America, and South America the third largest. In 1945 one Adventist in every six lived in these two sister divisions. Adventist education had advanced to higher levels in other fields than in the South American and Inter-American divisions, but each of these two fields had succeeded in establishing an infrastructure for a system of education that would achieve unforeseen productivity in the post-World War II era.

---

[1]Sources for education in South America are *General Conference Bulletin*, 1922, no. 9, p. 215; *ibid.*, no. 11, p. 251; *ibid.*, 1926: no. 7, p. 12; *ibid.*, no. 8, p. 8; *ibid.*, 1930, no. 9, p. 147; *ibid.*, 1941: *ibid.*, no. 2, p. 40; *Statistical Report*, 1920-1945; *Review and Herald*, May 3, 1934; February 2, 1939; December 21, 1939; *South American Bulletin*, April 1927, p. 7; Floyd Greenleaf, *The Seventh-day Adventist Church in Latin America and the Caribbean*, v. 2, pp. 22-68, 271-300; Brown, *Chronology*, pp. 76, 77, 79, 81, 83, 110, 113.

[2]*General Conference Bulletin*, 1926, no. 7, p. 12.

[3]*Ibid.*, no. 10, p. 9.

[4]The story of Adventist education in Inter-America comes from *General Conference Bulletin*, 1922, no. 11, p. 270; *ibid.*, 1926, no. 10, p. 9; *Review and Herald*, February 11, 1926; May 10, 1928; June 23, 1938; August 22, 1940; August 7, 1941; *The Inter-American Messenger*, June, 1924, p. 3; July 1924, p. 3; *Statistical Report*, 1920-1945; John E. Weaver, "Observations and Impressions of Inter-America," *Journal of True Education* (October 1943), pp. 3, 4, 28; Greenleaf, *ibid.*, pp. 69-99, 237-252; Glenn O. I. Phillips, *The Making of A Christian College: Caribbean Union College, 1927-1977* (Port-of-Spain, Trinidad: The College Press, 1977), pp. 9-43; Brown, *ibid.*, p. 75, 76, 111, 160, 161, 183, 184.

[5]*Review and Herald*, May 10, 1928.

[6] Phillips, *ibid.*, p. 43.

[7]*Review and Herald*, June 23, 1938.

[8] Glenn Calkins to T. J. Michael, June 21, 1943, AST.

# Debate Over Accreditation

The interim years between 1920 and 1945 may be called the era of the Adventist training school. In some regions of the Adventist world this institution was a well-established entity before 1920, but globally, the training school was only entering into its own at the beginning of the post-World War I era. During the quarter century after 1920 the concept of the training school dominated Adventist education and church leaders viewed this institution as the key unit in the denominational school system.

**The Complexion of Adventist Education during the Interim**

Prior to the organizational movement of 1901-1918 denominational schools more often than not evolved according to however local church leaders interpreted Ellen White's advice about education. But an ever-widening circle of training schools coupled with the rapid growth of elementary education as a result of the Movement of 1897 created a need for organization. The system existing at the beginning of the post-World War I era was not perfect, but it represented a serious attempt to provide both structure and definition to what at the beginning of the century had been a series of loosely related events in establishing Adventist schools.

The changing world environment was already testing the young system, and during the twenty-five years after 1920 extensive debate revolved around Adventist schools as institutional administrators and church leaders sought a meeting of the mind on how to perpetuate what they had begun. Among the major points in their discussions were questions of how to maintain the Adventist identity of schools, how to improve the systematization of Adventist education, how to relate to accreditation, and how to handle graduate study by Adventist teachers. These issues affected the entire world of Adventist education, but in North America where denominational schools were more developed the problems were singularly acute.

Denominational leaders most often gauged the success of training schools by their impact on the evangelistic objectives of the church, but there were other considerations. Often neglected was the social impact of Adventist education, which was partially associated with colonialism, a movement that had opened up vast regions of the world to Western traffic, much of it in places where denominational schools sprang up. Although colonialism declined during the years between the two world wars, it did not disappear entirely and remained a force in the mission program. Missions and missionaries often found their way paved with the political conveniences that "mother" countries provided.

While the colonial movement was primarily a spread of economic and political power, it was also a vehicle for ideas. The Adventist church was not an imperial power, but the education it established became a catalyst to mix Western values with non-Western cultures quite apart from its religious character. The idea of upward social mobility was inherent to denominational education and obvious to both colonizers and to many of the colonized. That Adventist evangelistic goals occupied common ground with Cecil Rhodes' view of missionary activity as a means to spread literacy and to educate indigenous peoples into the mainstream of the world was hardly a unique coincidence.[1]

Besides literacy, Adventist schools laid heavy stress on health, working skills, and personal well being, all aspects of individual enhancement. The general public saw this emphasis on personhood in a secular sense, but Adventists most often put it in a religious context, which made it difficult if not impossible to separate personal development from evangelistic success resulting from education. This was especially true of health. In countries where the levels of education and standards of living were low, Adventist education thus assumed both a spiritual and a humanitarian character. Adventist schools were usually more successful when host countries, either colonial or independent, were predisposed to accept the social benefits of education–literacy, improved public health, and productivity.

Adventist membership increased notably around the world during the years after 1920, especially in the developing world where the need for educated national leaders intensified. The role of Adventist schools as training schools became critical. Church leaders tended to laud schools most when high percentages of their graduates entered denominational employment. They ordinarily put these numbers in an evangelistic setting, but they also recognized that educating national workers for leadership was a practical necessity and references to the social and nationalistic character of this trend were also heard occasionally at Adventist gatherings.

Through the 1920s the number of students in the world fields who became church workers was consistently greater than the number of graduates from training schools because it was common for students to enter denominational employment before completing their education. During the 1930s this practice slowed and by 1940 the number of students outside North America who became church workers was less than seventy percent of the graduates of training schools.[2] It is doubtful that a single factor caused this trend, but among others, it was a silent indication that while most students still sought a denominational job, an increasing number of students entering Adventist schools in all probability simply desired an Adventist education. The fact that education was a means of personal enhancement was setting in.

The fact that the schools were producing more workers but that they represented a diminishing percentage of training school graduates also raised the question of why Adventist schools existed and how well they were fulfilling their purpose. It was an issue that was as old as Battle Creek College. While church leaders believed that the underlying reason for Adventist schools was to prepare church workers, statistics suggest that not all of the students or their families agreed that church employment was the only justification for an Adventist education.

It was plausible for many students to believe that the mission of Adventist schools was to provide an education for Adventist youth, whether they intended to enter denominational employment or not. It was not a matter of students rejecting their religious convictions if they chose to work elsewhere than for the church, but rather only a question of where they would fulfill their careers. Ellen White herself referred to the need to educate Adventist youth to enter private employment. Speaking about the need to educate all Adventists of student age, she advised "they all need an education *that they may be fitted for usefulness in this life, qualified for places of responsibility in both private and public life*" (italics supplied). Assuming responsibilities in private life hardly describes denominational employment.[3]

Church leaders encouraged all youth to attend Adventist schools, but it was neither feasible nor wise to demand a commitment to become a church worker as an entrance requirement to training schools. Although the need for new employees was at times dire, admittedly, the church could not employ all students who completed courses in Adventist schools. As employment needs broadened in North America during the interim years, college curricula also expanded, making a wider selection of careers available and increasing the likelihood that students would enroll in order to earn an education in an Adventist environment rather than to become a denominational employee. In subtle ways this question related to the discussions of educational organization from 1901 through 1918. It was also connected to later debates surrounding accreditation and the identity of an Adventist system of education.

## Adventist Education Begins a New Professionalism

When Frederick Griggs moved from the General Conference to Michigan in 1918 to become president of Emmanuel Missionary College, he left behind one of the better organized departments of the church. He was the prevailing influence in Adventist education during the organizational years and the face of education in 1918 was primarily attributable to him.

But at the end of World War I the world was not the same place when Griggs began his organization program. Socially, politically, economically and philosophically, arresting change had taken place and church leaders did not foresee that during the next two and a half decades the world would continue to change radically as it passed through history's severest financial dislocation before plunging into an even more brutal war than the one from which they were trying to recover at the moment. At the same time the concept of professionalism took a quantum leap, which directly impacted education generally. In order to survive, Adventist education would have to adapt to conditions that no one had imagined before the organizational movement began.

Beyond the actual mechanisms of organization, one of Griggs' more noteworthy contributions was to inject a mood of balance into Adventist education. While he was unquestionably committed to Adventism and its educational goals, he believed that educational needs were basically human needs that transcended denominational tags and that Adventist schools and teachers should not isolate themselves from the broader field of education beyond the church.

Griggs supported the goal of Adventist education to produce church workers, even encouraging students in 1918 to enter denominational employ when they were mature enough to handle the work whether or not they had completed their courses. With some ambivalence, he simultaneously urged for greater numbers of college graduates in responsible positions of church work. Griggs' comments demonstrated that he was willing to acquiesce to present needs, but he taught that college degrees should embody the improved professionalism that he believed the church needed.[4]

In Griggs' opinion attendance by Adventist teachers at non-Adventist institutions for advanced studies was a means of assuring official approval of Adventist education and its credibility. His view was an admission that education as a social institution existed prior to Adventist schools, and that in the economically developed countries Adventist institutions would have to meet standards which they did not establish. At the same time he saw Adventist education as unique and believed that it should remain so, but he also maintained that it was not incompatible with much of the general body of information about the human being and instructional techniques which non-Adventist educators were developing. Denominational teachers could use instructional materials that have an Adventist character, but psychologically, Adventist students did not learn differently from non-Adventists. Griggs taught that it is necessary for Adventist teachers to understand the essential methods of teaching that were basic to all successful learning programs.[5]

From the days of Ellen White's "Proper Education" Adventist educators aimed to develop a unique curriculum that could stand up under public scrutiny, but they wanted to accomplish this goal on their own terms, even ignoring whatever educational controls might get in their way. Griggs took a different position and successfully persuaded the General Conference session in 1905 to approve a recommendation from the Department of Education stating that "our training-schools be advised to so plan their work that the State examining boards, such as the Regents of New York, can give credit for any work done in these schools."[6]

The implications of this resolution were profound. Griggs was not proposing that Adventist schools surrender their identity but that Adventist identity could legitimately accommodate the authority of the state to control education and that it would be advantageous for denominational schools to comply with standards that the state established. The action also implied that students in Adventist training schools would have the assurance that their education was legitimized by government authority.

That the same principle applied to schools at lower instructional levels was a given. It was also a given that Adventist schools around the world would fulfill whatever legal restrictions that governments placed on them. Progressively more Adventist leaders in education came to view state control of education as legitimate and compliance as beneficial and just. At the time, in 1905, government approval was the most powerful recognition that schools could have.

## The Appearance of Accreditation in the United States

For most of the Adventist world the 1905 General Conference action was only a confirmation of accepted practice in the world fields. Adventists established their schools and continued to operate them through the interim years as the laws of host countries allowed. Post-secondary education in the United States, however, faced the growing power of extra-legal accrediting associations. These bodies were useful to education because the states defined college degrees differently; some states even allowed colleges to establish their own definitions of degrees. Because states exercised reciprocity in many matters, including education, it was important for baccalaureate degrees to reach at least a modicum of equivalency from state to state. Accrediting bodies were of two categories, regional associations that examined schools within a cluster of states, and professional or specialized associations that assessed specific fields of study. Under the purview of both accrediting systems were definitions of minimal levels of academic quality, financial capabilities of institutions to do what they advertised, and adequate instructional facilities. The credentials of college teachers thus fell under their jurisdiction. Although their primary target was postsecondary institutions, they also accredited schools at lower levels. Schools could function without accreditation, but it became increasingly apparent that the professional world depended more and more on regional or specialized accreditation to validate education.[7]

### Adventists' First Encounter with Accreditation

Adventists first felt the crunch of accreditation at the College of Medical Evangelists. In 1911 the American Medical Association nearly killed the school by assigning it a "C" rating, which was the lowest evaluation a medical school could receive and remain in operation. In effect, CME was blacklisted and forced either to improve or close. The expense to upgrade was enormous, prompting some to urge limiting the school to the first two years and sending students to recognized schools to complete their medical degrees.[8]

This idea collapsed when church leaders reviewed Ellen White's advice to establish a medical school and to fulfill whatever obligations were necessary to educate physicians. In 1917 CME rose to a "B" rating, and five years later acquired an "A" rating. Much of the reason for the "C" rating stemmed from unsatisfactory facilities, but by 1918 the question extended to student admissions when the American Medical Association warned that the school should accept students from accredited schools only. The College of Medical Evangelists also felt the heat from the National Board, the national examination body for physicians, to graduate competent doctors, which by implication, involved admission of qualified students to medical school.

Immediately the onus was on Adventist colleges to achieve accreditation, but even without this pressure from the medical profession, some schools were already seeking recognition from state universities and toying with the possibilities of regional accreditation. As early as 1905 Union College received accreditation from the New York Board of Regents and the next year agreed to an affiliation with the University of Nebraska. At least for the time being, this recognition met the needs of pre-med students at Union. In 1911 the University of Washington accredited Walla Walla College's secondary school.[9] To satisfy entrance requirements at CME, Adventist colleges sought recognition as junior colleges, but this remedy worked only temporarily. By 1928 entrance requirements to medical school increased to three years of college. Two years later the regional accreditation body for the north central states, the North Central Association, balked, arguing that degree-granting institutions that were accredited as two-year colleges were an anomaly and not in keeping with credible educational practice.

The water became even more muddy when the teaching profession raised its standards for certification of elementary and secondary teachers by demanding teacher-preparation courses to be accredited. At the same time nursing schools also required nursing students to take their preparatory work, either at the secondary or post-secondary level, in accredited schools.

### W. E. Howell, Opponent of Accreditation

Adventists reacted ambivalently. For the most part, educators favored accreditation, but some church leaders harbored doubts. Initially, they objected because of the high costs of upgraded facilities and faculty, but beginning in 1918 their attention turned to fears of losing the Adventist character of education. The strongest warning came from General Conference Secretary of Education Warren E. Howell. He had been a member of E. A. Sutherland's first faculty at Emmanuel Missionary College, president of Healdsburg College, president of Loma Linda College of Evangelists, and since 1914, the assistant secretary in the General Conference Department of Education.

After Howell succeeded Griggs in 1918 his office became the launching pad for a campaign of resistance to accreditation. At his recommendation the annual Spring Council in 1919 passed a resolution which prohibited Adventist schools from seeking "recognition from higher educational institutions or organizations outside our denomination." Six months later at the Autumn Council the Department of Education backpeddled to say that Adventist schools should not "follow the standards of secular and other educational systems" except as required by law or to "draw features of merit" to serve church purposes.[10]

*W. E. Howell, General Conference secretary of education, 1918-1930, exerted strong pressure to avoid secular accreditation of Adventist institutions and graduate study by Adventist teachers at non-Adventist institutions. However, he aggressively promoted the denominational identity of Adventist schools, helping to establish the Board of Regents and an Adventist accrediting system which has served as one of the strongest unifying influences in Adventist education.*

It was obvious that the hard line of resistance was already softening because of pressure beyond denominational control. It was also obvious that if schools could draw features of merit to serve church purposes the policy became so open-ended that anyone could rationalize its applications as one might desire. The policy to prohibit accreditation had turned out to be no policy at all, largely because of its impracticality.

Motivating Howell was a fear that accrediting bodies would require Adventist schools to relinquish their distinctive curriculum which was designed to inculcate denominational teachings and to prepare church workers. He and some church leaders interpreted accreditation as one of the most sinister threats to the church, believing that the forces of accreditation were conspiring to put small institutions out of business, especially sectarian schools.

State legislation helped to feed these fears. In 1920 and 1924 Michigan voters quashed attempts to legislate all parochial schools in the state out of existence. Soon after the first referendum, quick action by Adventist religious liberty activists and others averted an order to strike religious instruction from all elementary schools in the state. A similar and more celebrated case occurred in Oregon in 1922 when the legislature proscribed all private elementary schools. A court injunction stayed the law, and in 1925 the United States Supreme Court ruled the measure unconstitutional.[11]

Warnings from Howell and the Religious Liberty Department rightly referred to these events as dangers to Adventist education, but the proposed laws also reflected the wave of conservatism sweeping across the United States after World War I. Understood under the rubric of "normalcy," this conservative trend gave rise to isolationist policies and open prejudice toward ethnic and religious minorities. In this reactionary milieu the Ku Klux Klan was reborn. In part, the Oregon legislation was directed against education by and for Asian immigrants, portraying it as un-American. It was during this same period that legislation restricting immigration contributed to the decline of the three seminaries for German and Scandinavian Adventists in Missouri, Minnesota, and Illinois.

Howell's apprehensions extended to secular graduate education. He discouraged post-baccalaureate study as bookish and inappropriate preparation for Adventist workers, and suggested that in many cases, secondary education was sufficient to equip denominational employees for service. Accreditation of Adventist colleges presupposed more Adventist professors with post-baccalaureate degrees earned at non-Adventist institutions. Howell believed that almost by definition these teachers would dilute the purity of Adventist teachings and the ideals of Adventist education.

Through the decade of the 1920s Howell sounded his alarms during visits to Adventist college campuses, at General Conference sessions, and at Colorado Springs, Colorado in 1923 where he presided over a world convention of Adventist educators. At the 1922 General Conference he delivered a lengthy indictment of the shortcomings of Adventist schools, "How Can We Preserve the Sacred Traditions of Christian Education?", concluding with an apology for the bluntness of his rebuke, but at the same time salving his conscience.

At the two-week convention at Colorado Springs the following year he addressed teachers from around the world six times, each speech circling back to the burden of his heart–Adventist education had lost its simplicity and its direction. The powerful constant in his presentations was his progressively stronger emphasis on the evangelistic purpose of

Adventist education and his pleas to restore the original Adventist identity to denominational schools.[12]

Howell's ardor did not discourage a small but growing number of educators from enrolling in graduate studies either for a master's degree or in some cases, a doctorate, but they were on their own and met with suspicion by many church leaders. One of the most notorious cases was M. L. Andreasen, head of the Bible department at Union College, who left General Conference President A. G. Daniells standing alone on the street corner while he boarded a trolley to attend a graduate class at the University of Nebraska where he was studying for a master's degree in history. Later in the same day while Andreasen listened silently, Daniells took him to the proverbial woodshed for his brazenness. But the experience did not change Andreasen's mind. In 1922 both he and his daughter graduated on the same day with master's degrees.[13]

*Because he believed that the future of the College of Medical Evangelists and Adventist higher education was at stake, P. T. Magan became one of the earliest supporters of accreditation of Seventh-day Adventist schools by regional and specialized accrediting bodies.*

One of the strongest voices urging Adventist schools to achieve accreditation was P. T. Magan, at the time dean of the College of Medical Evangelists. Although personally suspicious of accreditation, he ratcheted up the pressure on denominational colleges to seek recognition, but at the same time he continued to accept premed students from unaccredited campuses in noncompliance with recommendations from the American Medical Association. He realized that he could not continue this contradictory practice indefinitely and that Adventist education would not survive without accreditation, and in 1926 he issued an ultimatum–Adventist colleges would either meet the criteria for accreditation or Adventist students would go elsewhere no matter how determined their expectation to attend the College of Medical Evangelists.

Howell grudgingly gave way to the inevitable, but he and other leading lights tried to isolate the evils of accreditation to those academic programs in which legal or practical ramifications were too strong for Adventist schools to avoid. In 1926 the Department of Education recommended that only pre-med and elementary education programs seek accreditation, and only then after approval by either the General Conference Committee or the committee of the world division in which schools in question were located. The proposal passed with little or no discussion. The twofold practical effect was to verify that, in fact, accreditation was necessary but that only a minimal number of Adventists would study in secular graduate schools.

### A System of Adventist Accreditation Begins

As reluctant as this action was, it changed the direction of the tide. Two years later the General Conference created the Board of Regents as the executive arm of a new entity, the Association of Seventh-day Adventist Colleges and Secondary Schools. The purpose of this body was to administer a denominational accrediting program. The new system went into effect in 1929, accompanied by the hope that it would preempt the need for regional accreditation.

In what amounted to a capitulation by Howell, the new rules stated that each college should have at least eight departments, each chaired by a professor with "post-graduate work," but not specifying graduate degrees. In the case of the two-year normal course, however, the teaching faculty were to have at least one year of graduate study and the head of the program was to own a master's degree.[14] Obviously, because no Adventist graduate school existed, department heads and other teachers would have to attend secular institutions in order to qualify for their positions.

Howell's changed stance was a key to the new educational regimen. However forcefully he had opposed accreditation since succeeding Griggs in 1918, he was willing to admit that Adventist education needed it after all. Because Adventist schools were critical to the denomination and because legal and professional restrictions were closing in on education generally, Howell concluded that denominational schools could not afford to arouse doubts about their legitimacy. In 1930 he advocated that Adventist schools should seek recognition "to give them a standing above question in the educational world."

Howell persisted to argue that public regulation of education deprived Adventist schools the freedom they should have "in continuing to function fully in the service of the third angel's message," but in matters of adequate buildings and equipment, financial integrity, balanced curriculum, teachers' qualifications and the size of their teaching loads, denominational schools could meet accreditation criteria without "bringing in any of the teaching content that is contrary to our faith, and without compromising any of the principles held dear by us in the history of our educational work."[15]

**General Conference Debates Accreditation**

Hardly had the new Board of Regents' accrediting plan begun before it became apparent that it was no substitute for the regional accrediting bodies. The stage was set for further change. In 1930 C. W. Irwin succeeded Howell as the secretary of education. Irwin brought a pedigree to his new post that made him a near-perfect candidate to handle the polarization that marked Adventist education. On the side of orthodoxy he was the son of former General Conference President George Irwin, schooled at Battle Creek and for five years the principal of what became Avondale College, the model school of Adventism. On the flip side of the coin he was independent enough to complete a master's degree from the University of Nebraska during the 1920s while his predecessor was roundly criticizing graduate education.

Less than a year after Irwin took charge of the Department of Education, the Spring Council appointed him to chair a survey commission to study Adventist higher education and to recommend necessary changes leading out of the dilemma that had deadlocked the system during the previous decade. The nine members of the investigating group were all General Conference personnel including the president and two vice presidents and six others holding the title of secretary at some level. Among them was Howell.

The commission's report, delivered in September, 1931, said little about the spiritual dangers of accreditation and graduate study at non-Adventist institutions, focusing instead on financial and other practical matters. Its primary conclusion held that the North American Adventist constituency was too small, measured in both membership and revenues, to afford its existing post-secondary program.

The upshot was a recommendation to divide the North American Division into five regions with constituencies ranging from 18,000 to 29,000 and to reduce the number of degree-granting colleges from seven to five–one in each proposed region. The plan included six junior colleges, two in Canada and four in the United States. Outside this post-secondary system but still a part of the education program were the seminaries for Scandinavian students, Oakwood Junior College, and the College of Medical Evangelists. All five senior colleges were to offer the complete pre-med program and the six junior colleges could offer pre-med only after achieving accreditation with both the denomination and regional associations.

Even with these arrangements, the commission admitted that the size of supporting constituencies for Adventist colleges would be among the lowest in the country, which spelled financial trouble. Ironically, in the face of this grim outlook, the commission recommended that the denomination establish its own graduate school to avoid postbaccalaureate studies by Adventist teachers in non-Adventist institutions.[16]

A month later the spiritual aspects of the issue resurfaced as the Autumn Council debated the report extensively, turning from the financial questions to leave the number of senior colleges intact and adding caveats to protect Adventist education from secular influences which leaders feared would seep into denominational schools through teachers holding secular graduate degrees. The church would recognize compliance with accreditation requirements as an "emergency" and allow Adventist teachers to earn advanced degrees from secular institutions only after they were screened to determine their spiritual readiness for graduate study. Also added was a limitation of pre-med curricula to the senior colleges and three of the six junior colleges. Schools were to spend money only from operating gains or donations when preparing for accreditation and teachers holding doctorates were not to be called "doctor."[17]

Despite its chary tone, this action opened the door to accreditation. At the time the world was suffering the throes of the Great Depression and church revenues were sinking. In order to maintain itself, the General Conference was depending on its operating reserves which were rapidly dissipating. Church leaders had good reason for their caution about finances, but the limitation on spending also was a means to discourage accreditation on pragmatic grounds rather than on spiritual arguments.

Pacific Union College was the first to acquire denominational accreditation under the terms of the new Board of Regents and immediately sought accreditation from its regional accrediting body, which it received in 1933, again the first Adventist college to receive such recognition.[18] W. E. Nelson, PUC's president who navigated the college through these exploratory waters, succeeded Irwin as General Conference secretary of education the next year, but once in Washington he assumed a far more conservative stance toward accreditation than he had taken as a college president.

Only weeks after moving to the General Conference, Nelson asked all college presidents to report how much money they had spent to upgrade college facilities and to help teachers in graduate study, and to differentiate between the amounts they would have spent anyway and the amounts resulting from plans to accredit their programs. The presidents submitted some figures but they found the inquiry nearly impossible and their written comments were not instructive to the new education secretary. With a tinge of sarcasm Thomas Steen, president of Emmanuel Missionary College, told Nelson that "no human being now alive knows the answer," at least as it pertained to EMC.[19]

At the 1935 Spring Council General Conference President C. H. Watson planned to forestall the accreditation movement by issuing a presidential fiat that reduced the number of Adventist schools approved for regional accreditation. But William Landeen, president of Walla Walla College, had been working quietly for accreditation with the Northwest Association of Colleges and Secondary Schools and before Watson finished his statement he opportunely announced that WWC had been approved by its regional association.[20]

Landeen's disclosure derailed Watson's proposed limitation, but the General Conference Committee appointed another educational survey commission to study thoroughly the operations of Adventist colleges, including the needs for plant improvements, adequacy of curricula, and overall costs. A fact-finding committee probed every campus, compiling data about class size, numbers of students per teacher, teaching loads, effectiveness of curricula, library holdings, and a host of other statistics.

The data unmistakably confirmed the conclusion of the 1931 survey: the Adventist membership in North America was too small to support the existing Adventist colleges. As a result colleges were not operating efficiently. Many classes were too small to justify their existence, which yielded small revenues and increased operational expenses. The commission also complained that ministerial education in junior colleges was poor, underfunded on most college campuses, and on the decline generally.

In summary the report stated darkly that "It is evident that our colleges, when rated alongside standards or criteria of the accrediting associations . . . rank well toward the bottom of the list in all of the important financial factors of amount expended per student, total receipts, and the proportion of income from subsidies and outside sources . . . That all the accrediting associations are progressively building toward the favorable development of the larger and stronger institutions, and to the circumscribing, if not the discouragement, of smaller colleges with more limited constituencies and financial backing, is suggested, if not actually in evidence, in the standards and criteria of their recognition programs."[21]

The 1931 report of the survey commission appeared to concentrate on financial aspects of accreditation at the expense of spiritual questions, but the 1935 report erased the conclusion that spiritual concerns were really dead. Beginning with a declaration of the "peril" that recognition brought to Adventist schools, the 1935 commission recommended that because the cost of accreditation would "embarrass the financial resources of the denomination," and the professional needs of the church required only two regionally accredited colleges, that only Emmanuel Missionary and Pacific Union colleges "be authorized to acquire and maintain accreditation in regional associations."

The report precipitated a wrenching debate at the Autumn Council. W. H. Branson, General Conference vice president for North America, confessed that, in his view, the 1931 commission had overreacted in allowing all Adventist colleges to apply for accreditation. He stated that accreditation would destroy the principles of Adventist education and undermine the goals of the church. College administrations and college graduates were ignoring the safeguards against these deleterious influences. Young Adventists were enrolling in secular graduate programs on their own rather than waiting to be chosen. Avoiding accreditation would allow colleges to return to the business of preparing missionaries rather than preparing students in the art of living, which was a threat to the identity of Adventist schools.

Speaker after speaker echoed Branson's sentiments. The strongest remarks came from General Conference President C. H. Watson who declared that accreditation was necessary for some purposes, such as implementing a pre-med program, but he would prefer closing CME rather than to destroy Adventist education by "going worldly" through extensive accreditation. Several admitted that misgivings and fears had silently accompanied their consenting votes in 1931, and they were grateful for an opportunity to undo the wrong they had committed.[22]

On the other side of the debate was Howell, six years separated from the Department of Education, who spoke little but reminded the audience that while he had strenuously opposed accreditation in previous years, experience showed that Adventist schools could not survive without it. He went on record to support the principles of accreditation with "limitations." He did not spell out what he believed would be appropriate limitations–and no one could read his mind–but his brief remarks indicated that he probably realized that to be a defined and defensible system, Adventist schools could not sidestep accountability and that accreditation was the method of accountability to which Adventist education would have to adjust in the best possible manner. Gone were his inflammatory comments about denominational schools losing their identity and their purpose.

The most vehement observations came from H. H. Votaw, associate secretary of the Department of Religious Liberty, who disagreed with the General Conference president with rare bluntness. He argued that if accreditation was a means to destroy Adventist schools, as many speakers had claimed, the Autumn Council could not justify selecting two schools for recognition, which allegedly would lead to their spiritual destruction, and permit a third school to continue its accredited status while the other campuses remained untainted.

"Let us face the thing," Votaw said, "do one thing or the other. I cannot see it any other way, between sending boys and girls to hell from three schools or six . . . We had better take more time to study before we vote. I cannot see any connection between any speeches the President of the denomination has made and the report of this commission. One says it is wrong, and the commission says we will do it for three schools. If this comes up for a vote I am going to say 'NO' long enough for my vote to register 'No.' "[23] Some union presidents, who were also college board chairmen, agreed that Adventist colleges needed to conform to denominational principles, but admitted their confusion over the zig-zag route the accreditation process was taking.

The recommendation went back to the commission for restudy, but the next day the document returned, virtually unchanged. After another plea by Branson, it passed, but with modifications that contained the seeds of its own demise. Colleges other than Pacific Union and Emmanuel Missionary could accredit their junior college programs with regional associations, a decision that presumably would protect professional education on all campuses, but it raised questions about how college administrations would isolate the impact of accreditation from the upper halves of their campuses.

*M. L. Andreasen at one time served as principal of the Danish-Norwegian Seminary in Hutchinson, Minnesota. He later became president of Union College and helped to lead the movement for graduate study by Adventist teachers and for accreditation of Seventh-day Adventist colleges by regional bodies.*

The 1935 action lasted less than a year before the General Conference Committee reversed itself again during the world session in May 1936, this time opening up the way for accreditation for all denominational colleges. The action occurred after M. L. Andreasen, president of Union College, and his board chairman informed the General Conference Committee that the North Central Accrediting Association refused to approve the institution as a junior college, which would have cut the school in half, academically. Because the school offered four-year degrees it would have to apply for accreditation as a senior college or not at all. Lacking accreditation, Union would lose all of its professional programs. An *ad hoc* committee that included Branson, Watson, and J. L. McElhany, a General Conference vice president, took only one day to recommend granting Andreasen's request to apply for full accreditation. Earlier, Walla Walla College had faced a similar situation. It was clear that the 1935 measure could not work.[24]

Before the 1936 General Conference session ended F. M. Wilcox, editor of the *Review*, addressed the delegates with a parting shot about the evils of accreditation and graduate study. It was the final hurrah for the campaign against accreditation. The following year at the world convention of Adventist educators in Blue Ridge, North Carolina, H. A. Morrison, who had replaced Nelson as the new secretary of the Department of Education, dismissed the issue of accreditation with only a couple of paragraphs in his prepared address. Admitting in his opening remarks that accreditation for the sake of prestige could be harmful, he noted that Adventist colleges were pursuing regional recognition.

"This ought not to affect in any way the objectives or purposes in these schools," he said. "Yet we must recognize that it adds one more point of contact with the influences about us concerning which we must be ever on the alert . . . Experience has taught many of us that these rating agencies are not interested in having us change our objectives, but are interested in our doing a high quality of work along the lines of our own choice and in accordance with our own purposes."[25]

## The Aftermath

Questions about the merits of accreditation still haunted the minds of many but the debate was over. Shortly the number of Adventist senior colleges in North America rose to eight, excluding Oakwood and Madison colleges which were administratively outside the North American Division. By 1945 all of the Adventist degree-granting institutions in North America were accredited by their regional associations.

The debate about accreditation was the most acute struggle that Adventist education had experienced up to that time. The formula for resistance contained several ingredients that produced a potent mix. Many church leaders believed explicitly that Adventist education was unique and that the only way to preserve its character was to isolate it as much as possible from external influences. They viewed accreditation as a menace because it subjected them to control by people who did not share their convictions.

One of the major points of disagreement was secular graduate education, which was unavoidably linked to faculty upgrading. The fundamental philosophy of Adventist education was an uncompromising belief in Scripture as the source of truth and the rule of life. This did not mean that all knowledge is revealed in the Bible, but that discoverable information is accurately recognized only within the parameters of biblical understanding. By contrast, secular education taught that the principles of truth as well as information are discoverable and that inquiring minds must search for them, which implied skepticism, questioning, and testing while pursuing the search.

Many leading Adventists held that it was improbable if not impossible for Adventists to study any academic field in a secular setting without damaging their sense of commitment to *a priori* beliefs and that after an inevitable absorption of secularist principles, Adventist teachers with graduate degrees would contaminate Adventist campuses. Because of these perceived dangers denominational leadership attempted to control which and how many Adventist teachers would expose themselves to the inexorable spiritual toxins of secular graduate study. They watched with alarm when teachers struck out on their own or when young, unseasoned persons ventured to the tree of knowledge of good and evil without first passing an official screening.

While no one questioned the uniqueness of Adventist education, a growing number of Adventist educators believed that there was no place on earth to escape erroneous philosophical notions. Fallacious philosophy permeated all levels of intellectual activity, even touching the man on the street who was as vulnerable to misleading ideas that were part of a pedestrian life as were students in higher education. They believed that information in and of itself was neutral, and that the challenge to gather and to understand knowledge within the spiritual context of Adventism would strengthen, not weaken faith. For them the intellectual temptations of secular education were an occupational hazard that required alertness, but the danger did not equate to a prohibition. There was never a claim that the teaching profession would suffer no casualties at all if Adventists enrolled in graduate programs, but graduate education did not automatically chill Adventist fervor or produce apostasy.

Antagonists of accreditation prolifically cited statements by Ellen White that warned against secular influences and adopting worldly standards. Supporters of accreditation pointed out that Ellen White's instruction to meet whatever requirements were necessary to maintain a flow of Adventist students into the Adventist medical school also applied to the increasing array of restrictions in other professional fields of study that were critical to denominational operations. Neither side convinced the other with its arsenal of historical support. If this aspect of the debate demonstrated anything, it showed that it was both tricky if not dangerous to quote the founder of Adventist educational philosophy posthumously as though she were present and speaking to a specific situation.

Much of the debate revolved around the question of balance between idealism and pragmatism. In the heat of the struggle the General Conference president spoke his conviction to close down the medical school rather than to submit to worldliness, but P. T. Magan pointed out that without accreditation Adventists would resort to physicians to lead the denominational health movement who were schooled entirely in the atmosphere they sought to avoid. Listeners could not miss the point: idealism was necessary, but in the matter of professional education, following the principle of a higher good rather than complete withdrawal from society was crucial to Adventist education.

In part, the debate derived from a collision between two views of the purpose of Adventist education. Some church leaders saw schools primarily as a means to prepare students for denominational employment, but others, including the students themselves, visualized education more as a means to prepare for employment anywhere. Only begrudgingly if at all did the first group agree with accreditation. They doubted that church workers needed the extensive academic baggage that higher education was developing and which accrediting bodies were demanding, and they were prone to oppose accreditation as an interference to their purposes.

But church workers could not continue indefinitely with these nineteenth century norms. Higher education and professional education became more academic after 1920 and in order to function credibly Adventist institutions needed professionals with valid credentials. It went without saying that Adventist students who simply wanted to study in an Adventist school for a profession benefited from these circumstances. Their number was growing and from their point of view accreditation was a means to achieve the assurance that their education was legitimate.

Given the outcome of the struggle, it is easy to tag those who campaigned against accreditation as short sighted and misguided. But when the debate first erupted accrediting bodies themselves were still evolving and no one knew how far their influence could or would reach. The associations did not delineate specifically all the details of what schools should do to achieve accreditation; they evaluated an institution only after it applied for recognition. As experience showed, fears that regional associations would proscribe religion in Adventist classrooms were ill-founded, but Adventist leaders had no assurances at the time that a biblically based education would meet with approval by professional educators who promoted secular ideals.

It was undebatable that financial questions also played a key role in the battle. The cost of facilities and faculties commensurable to the rising expectations of higher education was severe. Adventist leaders who conducted the survey commissions of 1931 and 1935 confirmed what the accrediting bodies were trying to tell Adventist colleges all along: their financial status was among the weakest in the country and institutions with such precarious economic footing could not afford facilities to conduct successful post-secondary education as commonly understood, irrespective of religious implications for the church.

One of the great fears that drove denominational leaders was that compliance with accrediting standards would force them to drain money from evangelism to pay for what they thought was unnecessary institutional change. That the colleges were already financial problems and inefficiently run, as the 1931 and 1935 surveys showed, only added to their argument. For many church leaders accreditation jeopardized formal evangelism, the heart of the denominational *raison d'etre*.

What appears to be a major misconception, or perhaps a rationalization, occurred in 1931 when the General Conference Committee instructed the Department of Education to portray graduate education for college teachers as an "emergency" measure which the Adventist public was not to construe as an endorsement of secular education or a blanket approval for study at non-Adventist institutions. It is unclear if the members of the highest decision-making body in the church really thought their "emergency" would disappear once the colleges achieved accreditation or if they sensed that this was truly an ongoing condition, and that as institutions grew and generations passed, the need for larger numbers of faculty with graduate degrees would never end.

The emergency myth cloaked denominational approval of accreditation for years. Despite H. A. Morrison's calm approach to accreditation at the Blue Ridge convention in 1937, a recommendation from that gathering echoed the exact words of the 1931 General Conference Committee action, referring to the situation as an emergency.

Not often discussed were Adventist attitudes toward state regulation of education–which were legal provisions–as compared to extra-legal controls imposed by the voluntary accreditation system. Despite the flare up during the 1920s to eliminate parochial education in some states, Adventist leaders seldom questioned the legitimacy of the regulatory authority of governments. More often than not Adventists actively pursued recognition by arms of governments that controlled education. Outside the United States Adventist education faced government intrusiveness, but the difference in the reaction by church leaders turned on one fact: state controls were legal and unavoidable while regional accreditation in the United States was voluntary. But voluntary or not, the system of regional accreditation eventually developed enough clout to produce an impact that rivaled legal regulation.

One of the amazing chapters in Adventist higher education is its achievement of accreditation notwithstanding all of its institutional inadequacies. There was no more convincing argument that the ideals of sacrificial Christian service were paramount objectives in Adventist education than the college faculties who received salaries that were less than competitive. Also, Adventist school administrators claimed that without endowments, prestigious faculty, or research labs and libraries, denominational colleges could produce graduates with respectable professional competence to meet the needs of the public workplace as well as denominational employment. Regional associations agreed that the work ethic so prevalent on Adventist campuses provided an institutional tone in keeping with denominational ideals of commitment and service.

The debate over accreditation was primarily a North American issue because voluntary accreditation did not exist outside the United States. The struggle was polarizing and spirited, but after 1936 the denomination set about to acclimate to the practical results of its new educational imperative, which simply put, meant coming out of its isolation to become a recognized education program while retaining its Adventist identity. By 1945 when accreditation had become the norm on Adventist campuses, there was probably no greater acknowledgment that the principles of Adventist education were valid than the simple fact that regional associations had, after all the doubting, recognized Adventist colleges.

---

[1]For a thought provoking discussion of the relationship between Adventist education and upward mobility, see Malcolm Bull and Keith Lockhart, *Seeking a Sanctuary* (San Francisco: Harper & Row, Publishers, 1989), pp. 254-268.

[2]*Statistical Report*, 1920-1945.

[3]Ellen White, *Testimonies*, v. 6, p. 207.

[4]Griggs, "Report of the Department of Education to the 1918 General Conference," RG 51, AST; Reye and Knight, *ibid.*

[5]For this aspect of Griggs' career see Reye and Knight, "Frederick Griggs: Moderate," *Early Adventist Educators*, pp. 184-204.

[6]*General Conference Bulletin*, 1905, no. 4, p. 20.

[7]The accreditation debate is summarized from Joseph G. Smoot, "Accreditation: Quality in the SDA College," (*Journal of Adventist Education*, February-March 1983), pp. 10, 11, 44, 45; William G. White, "Flirting with the World," (*Adventist Heritage*, Spring 1983), pp. 40-51; William G. White, "Another Look at Those Pioneers of Adventist Accreditation," *Focus* (winter 1978), pp. 10-13; Everett Dick, Union, *College of the Golden Cords* (Lincoln, NE: Union College Press, 1967), pp. 153-168; Virginia Steinweg, *Without Fear or Favor: the Life of M. L. Andreasen* (Washington, D. C.: Review and Herald Publishing Association, 1979), pp. 94, 95, 134-138; Terrie Aamodt, *Bold Venture: a History of Walla Walla College* (College Place, WA: Walla Walla College, 1992), pp. 67-69, 75-76, 81-87; George R. Knight, *Myths in Adventism.* (Washington, D.C.: Review and Herald Publishing Association, 1985), pp. 37-45; Michael Bull and Keith Lockhart, *Seeking a Sanctuary* (New York: Harper and Row, 1989), pp. 230-243; Walter Utt, *A Mountain, A Pickax, A College* (Angwin, CA: Alumni Association of Pacific Union College, 1968), pp.87, 88; Doris Holt Haussler, *From Immigrant to Emissary* (Nashville: Southern Publishing Association. 1969), pp. 89-99; *60 Years of Progress: Walla Walla College* (College Place, WA: Walla Walla College Press, 1952), p. 249.

[8]Carol Small, *Diamond Memories* (Loma Linda, CA: Alumni Association, School of Medicine, 1984), pp. 15, 16, 139-141.

[9]Aamodt, *Bold Venture*, p. 67; Dick, *Golden Cords*, p. 155.

[10]General Conference Minutes, April 30, 1919, AST; *ibid.*, October 14, 1919.

[11]General Conference Bulletin, 1922, no. 3, p. 76; *ibid.*, 1926, no. 9, p. 17; Lloyd P. Jorgenson, "The Oregon School Law of 1922: Passage and Sequel," *Catholic Historical Review* (LIV, 1968), pp. 455-466; Paul M. Holsinger, "The Oregon School Bill Controversy, 1922-1925," (*Pacific Historical Review*, XXXVII, 1968), pp. 327-341.

[12]Howell, "Report of the Department of Education to the 1922 General Conference Session," AST; *ibid.*, 1926, 1930; Howell's presentations in *Proceedings of the Educational and Missionary Volunteer Departments of the General Conference of Seventh-day Adventists in World Convention.* (Washington, D.C.: Review and Herald Publishing Association, 1923).

[13]Steinweg, *Without Fear or Favor*, pp. 94, 95. Dick in *Golden Cords*, pp. 157, 158, names Howell, not Daniells, as the snubbed visitor.

[14]"Standards for Accrediting Colleges," April, 1929, RG 51, AST; "Two-Year Normal School," *ibid.*

[15]Howell, "Report of the Department of Education to the 1930 General Conference Session," *ibid.*

[16]"Meeting of the Survey Commission of Board of Regents," September 29, 1931, *ibid.*

[17]General Conference Committee Minutes, October 23, 25, 1931, *ibid.*

[18]Utt, *A Mountain, a Pickax*, p. 88.

[19]Memo, Nelson to college presidents, September 20, 1934. RG 51, AST. Steen to Nelson, September 24, 1934, *ibid.*

[20]Aamodt, *Bold Venture*, pp. 85-89.

[21]"Report of the Fact-Finding Committee Appointed by the Educational Survey Commission," October 23, 24, 1935, RG 51, AST.

[22]See the twenty-one-page transcript of speeches, RG 51, AST. For the recommendations as voted, see General Conference Committee Minutes, October 31, 1935, *ibid.*

[23]*Ibid.*

[24]General Conference Committee Minutes, May 25, 26, 1936; Aamodt, *Bold Venture*, p. 85.

[25]*Report of the Blue Ridge Educational Convention, August 17-25, 1937.* (Washington, D. C.: General Conference Department of Education, n.d.), pp. 18, 19.

# Trends Toward Modernization

As the major preoccupation of Adventist education during the 1920s and 1930s, the debate about accreditation stimulated more than its share of pros and cons, often overshadowing other administrative questions that church educators faced. Among the issues were an evolving educational system, the financial stability of Adventist colleges, denominationally sponsored graduate education and the development of baccalaureate nursing education. In one way or another these matters related to accreditation, and because Adventist schools in North America were in the vanguard of denominational education, the aftereffects of these issues rippled into the world fields.

**W. E. Howell's Contributions to Systematization**

W. E. Howell's misgivings about accreditation and graduate study were well known, but his opposition did not mean that he was unfamiliar with educational issues or against systematization. He was a disciple of system and assiduously pursued an Adventist identity for denominational schools. When he began his career as the General Conference secretary of education he believed that Adventist schools could best preserve their identity by isolation from outside influences, but his twelve years in office taught him that processes of systematization were by definition organization and that organization, in turn, led to the very results that accreditation proposed.

Howell undeviatingly held to his view that Adventist education had three simple objectives that distinguished it from all other learning programs: 1) to save Adventist children to the church, 2) to prepare denominational workers, and 3) to pioneer evangelism in non-Christian and developing countries.[1] Contrary to the prevailing view among church leaders, he consistently maintained that the preservation of Adventist children to the church took precedence over preparation of workers, although in practical application this distinction mattered little. To inculcate these ideas into the minds of Adventist educators Howell widened the practice of conventions, bringing to Adventist education a sense of a global movement with denominational identity.

In 1922 Howell's recommendations to the General Conference session included a proposal to provide employment security to teachers, an issue that was within the scope of accreditation issues. The question had been the leading topic on the agenda of the Department of Education during the session and simply read that heads of colleges serve terms of four years and academy principals for two years, and that teachers have continuous employment after their third year. Removal would be possible for "sufficient reasons, and upon due notice."

Immediately after Howell read his proposals, W. H. Branson, at the time president of the African Division, invited him to "defend his resolutions," but the secretary of education shot back that they didn't need defense inasmuch as they were based on employment policies already practiced in ministerial ranks, and that teachers and officers of educational institutions should have equal opportunity to carry out their functions.[2]

This tart exchange between Howell and Branson indicated the lesser rank that education personnel occupied in the denominational schema, a situation that the secretary of education viewed as inimical to systematized progress in Adventist education. Delegates to the session approved the recommendations although the new measures had little immediate impact on actual employment practices. Nonetheless, they were a beginning of eventual improvement in the status of teachers.

Professional gatherings were another tool Howell used to systematize education. Before he succeeded Frederick Griggs, teachers' conventions and institutes had taken place for the most part in North America, in part because Adventists lacked a critical mass of professional educators in any single field outside the United States that would make such gatherings practical. One notable exception to this pattern occurred in 1916 when Griggs conducted a meeting in Shanghai for teachers and church leaders in China.

This first teachers' convention beyond North America exemplified how the systematizing process would take place in Adventist education. "The educational field work was organized on the same general basis as that obtaining in the North American Division Conference," Griggs afterwards wrote, but he added that extensive adaptation was necessary to compensate for cultural differences.[3] The North American model meant that agriculture, other industries, and health education were integral parts of instruction. Curriculum design for the purpose of preparing church employees received special emphasis at the Shanghai meeting, and decisions served as a norm for other countries in the Far East.

During his years as secretary of education Howell followed the precedents set in Shanghai. In the wake of World War I the General Conference was deluged with needs to rehabilitate the church in Europe, including a rejuvenation of education. Even with these acute conditions crying for attention, the General Conference Committee sent Howell to South America in 1920 as a member of a delegation to represent church headquarters at divisional meetings in March. As a part of the session he conducted a convention for denominational educators and later visited the major schools in the field.

At the Autumn Council that year Howell submitted a slate of recommendations which, for the first time, embodied a coordinated approach to institutional development in the South American Division. At the same time the Council also passed a similar list of recommendations affecting Europe, and in 1921 Howell made his belated tour of the Continent to inspect new and developing schools.[4]

By 1926 either Howell or his associate, C. W. Irwin, had traveled to Africa and Southern Asia, both regions where Adventist educators gathered for the first time in professional meetings. In Shanghai denominational teachers and administrators met together again, this time for the first education convention in the Far Eastern Division. Both Howell and Irwin also attended separate institutes in Europe in successive years. During 1926 and 1927 Howell's calendar scheduled him for five trips outside North America.[5]

**World Education Conventions**

Howell's crowning convention took place from June 5 to 19, 1923 when he brought the entire Adventist educational fraternity together at Colorado Springs, Colorado for its first world convention. One of the more substantive presentations came from Sarah Peck, Howell's associate secretary of education for elementary schools, who declared a need for a complete set of denominational textbooks for elementary grades. She urged colleges to reorganize the teacher-preparation curriculum to include more courses in academic subject areas and to integrate the new curricula into baccalaureate degree programs.

Among her other recommendations was a request for the colleges to introduce special courses to prepare better qualified supervising teachers and education superintendents. Recalling Ellen White's advocacy of Adventist education, she repeated Howell's point of view that teachers were as relevant to the mission of the church as were ordained ministers and suggested that their salaries should reflect that status.

Administrative flaws in Adventist education as of 1923 were hardly secrets, but Peck's forthright speech made them common knowledge, and during the ensuing years the issues about which she spoke occupied a large space on the denominational agenda. But it was apparent that Howell had other reasons for the Colorado Springs gathering than to discuss general administrative questions. His globetrotting both before and after the convention revealed that one of his goals was to cultivate a global system of Adventist education, focusing on his convictions about its distinctively spiritual character.

The leading impact of the Colorado Springs convention was inspirational if not evangelistic. The overwhelming majority of attendees represented North American entities, but Howell gave delegates from the world divisions prime time to recount their struggles and to describe the spirit of sacrifice in their fields, which underlined his opening statement that Adventist education in these regions had been "planted in weakness, with meager facilities, with slender staffs."[6] A retinue of denominational leaders offered encouragement and counsel. The delegates listened to updates on state legislation hostile to private education, especially the Oregon School Law, but the central message was Howell's repeated advice to shun both accreditation and graduate education and to maintain the identity of Adventist education by separation from the world. In Howell's view commitment produced effectiveness, and both were virtues that superseded formal, advanced training which he believed was often superfluous.

In 1937, fourteen years and three secretaries of education later, Adventist educators from as many world divisions as practical assembled at Blue Ridge, North Carolina for their second world convention. Similar to the Colorado Springs meeting, it was predominantly a North American affair. Again, the question of a distinctive Adventist education was paramount. But the mentality of the delegates was one of acceptance of the reality of the secular educational world at large and to define the role Adventist education played in it rather than to suppose that denominational education should preserve itself by isolation. The specific aim was to update the standardization process in Adventist schools in keeping with educational expectations of society and curricular trends in general. Accreditation and graduate education, old nemeses for Howell, received matter-of-fact treatment from H. A. Morrison, the General Conference secretary of education. By 1937 accreditation was a given and graduate education had become a necessity, even at secondary levels of instruction. The essential attitude was to accept these new conditions of Adventist education, but some delegates continued to echo Howell's original concerns.[7]

Colorado Springs and Blue Ridge were epic moments in espousing a global view of Adventist education, but the 1937 meeting was the last attempt to convene delegates from Adventist education at all levels from around the world. Growth of the education movement raised the cost of the meetings to prohibitive levels and hostile international conditions made world conventions impractical. The North American practice of departmentalized gatherings that concentrated on such matters as administration of dormitories, specific academic disciplines, or levels of instruction such as elementary or secondary spread to the rest of the world. General Conference representation at these gatherings kept the idea of a denominational system alive.

## The Concept of a Global System

The concept of a global system of education also continued through means of the denominational accreditation system. After four years in office Howell observed in 1922 that Adventist education was "ripening into somewhat settled lines." He recognized that elementary and secondary schools rested in the hands of local congregations and conferences but colleges fell into a different category. He declared "that they are in fact denominational and world institutions, and that we must think of them in world terms . . .[I]t seems to me beyond dispute that their policies should be determined by the responsible body of the whole."[8]

By controlling the colleges the General Conference could also determine much of what occurred at lower levels of instruction. There could be no misunderstanding that Howell intended that the General Conference Department of Education, contemporaneously known as the "General Department," would become the educational hub of the church around which all education revolved.

The formation of the Association of Seventh-day Adventist Colleges and Secondary Schools and the Board of Regents in 1929 expressed Howell's conviction about a system. Within a year after the Board of Regents began, it issued its own criteria for upgrading colleges and academies to qualify for denominational accreditation. Initially, these standards were not demanding and applied only to North American schools, but over time they tightened and in 1954 the purview of the Association expanded to the world fields.

The impact of the Board of Regents was mixed. The innovation failed to become a recognized accrediting body as Howell and others hoped, but even though it was a toothless organization in the eyes of the larger world of education it was a seminal action in self-policing and upgrading Adventist education irrespective of rulings by regional accreditation bodies. The Board of Regents' instruments for school evaluation constituted a single measuring rod which educational leaders applied to all secondary and tertiary schools, and the Department of Education used it effectively as a systematizing procedure to establish Adventist norms in school operations and curriculum.

Ironically, actions by the Board of Regents turned all of Howell's past warnings about accreditation and graduate education upside down. Among the first requirements sent to the colleges were criteria establishing departments headed by teachers with graduate education and in some cases, graduate degrees.

Howell succeeded in advancing systematization but he did not achieve the levels he envisioned. His view of Adventist colleges as world institutions and his goal to place them under General Conference control was unrealistic. Policies that gave each union in North America authority over the college in its territory had been in effect since the early years of the century and had become an ingrained tradition. Attempts by the General Conference Department of Education to supersede union authority had failed in 1913 when a recommendation to reduce the number of colleges met with resistance. Again, as the accreditation debate peaked in the 1930s, union presidents who chaired college boards sometimes quietly encouraged college administrations to seek accreditation in spite of General Conference recommendations to the contrary.

It is safe to say that Howell visualized North American colleges as the primary source of international workers and since the General Conference was in charge of missions, it followed that the world headquarters should design a system of education and control the postsecondary campuses. It is open to question whether Howell or anyone else was clairvoyant enough to foresee Adventist institutions around the world maturing into the major centers they eventually became, reducing at the same time the influence of North American higher education. From purely a speculative point of view Howell and other church leaders could not imagine the dimensions of Adventist education three-quarters of a century later probably because they believed the imminence of Christ's second advent prevented such mind wanderings. Whatever may have been the case, they had no way of knowing that the concept of a system of education as it related to the control of Adventist higher education would be a major struggle in the years to come.

Regardless of future pitfalls, the concept of a system was unmistakably present in North American post-secondary education nonetheless. Colleges were not autonomous in matters pertaining to salary schedules and retirement policies. Employees could shuttle from one institution to another and maintain a single service record as though they worked continuously for a single employer. Institutional administrators and church leaders alike assented to denominational teachings and Adventist mores as part of their operational practices, specifically affecting employment. For the time being the notion of a system, even at the tertiary level, was stronger than its counter influences.

### Persistent Financial Woes

During the interim years persistent financial woes continued to gnaw on the vitals of Adventist education. The earlier rescue program based on the profits from a worldwide sales program of Ellen White's *Christ's Object Lessons* had benefitted Adventist schools, and a subsidy plan that in some ways was a denominational substitute for an endowment was furnishing relief money, but in 1920 North American schools still faced a debilitating debt load.

In Howell's words at the 1922 General Conference session schools had the reputation of being the "biggest money-sinkers and debt-makers we have."[9] As a preventive remedy he pushed through a policy requiring all schools to operate on the basis of annual budgets rather than the hand-to-mouth method that had so long characterized Adventist schools. To advocate his point he cited several cases when colleges and academies realized sizable savings by simply organizing their annual income and expenses into a budget.

Admitting that educational institutions inherently had only limited ability to generate capital, Howell suggested that literature sales by students could, in effect, become an institutional industry that would supply a major source of cash to barren school treasuries. He even predicted that institutions could liquidate their debts and operate in the black on the strength of income from literature sales. Howell's suggestions about student colporteurs did not produce a bonanza among secondary schools and colleges in North America, but for a significant number of students both in the United States and around the world literature sales became an effective means to finance their education.

Denominational schools beyond the United States were more prone to function on a pay-as-you-go policy, which resulted in fewer debts but at the same time prevented them from having as many amenities as they needed. Schools in North America were prone to borrow funds and by the time Howell left office in 1930, the combined debt of Adventist schools was approximately $575,000, an increase of more than $150,000 since 1921 but a decrease since the mid-1920s when institutions owed more than a million dollars.[10]

The problem did not stem simply from lack of annual budgets. General Conference Treasurer W. T. Knox observed in 1922 that while debt ratios improved during the recent half dozen years and school finances were in better shape, the actual volume of debt was increasing. The subsidy plan, whose first object was to provide relief from debt, was not accomplishing its purpose as well as denominational leaders intended. Institutions tended to use relief funds to pay ordinary operational expenses or even as capital to expand facilities.

The situation worsened during the Great Depression. During the six years after 1930 schools reduced their debt only marginally while at the same time writing off more than a half million dollars in uncollectible student accounts. Even after this wholesale cancellation, schools retained nearly $600,000 in student receivables. Summarizing these bleak conditions, W. E. Nelson, General Conference secretary of education, uttered doubt about one of the identifying marks of Adventist education–institutional industries to provide student labor and bring in cash to the schools. Successful commercial industries depended on skilled workers, he argued, and students, who at best were part-time workers, graduated about the time they became productive employees. Nelson believed that school industries were working at a disadvantage because they were constantly training a large portion of their workers.

The Great Depression aggravated this situation because more than ever before Adventist students became more dependent on institutional labor opportunities to pay for their education. By the end of the 1934-35 academic year students' earnings from campus jobs at all schools amounted to about half the total charges for tuition, food, and dormitory rooms. Recognizing that this amount was, for practical purposes, a subsidy to students, Nelson commented that "We believe that this is a larger amount than it is safe for our schools to supply."[11] According to Nelson, operational losses on the campuses occurred largely in the work sector. Secondary schools and junior colleges were the leading offenders. Commercial industries on the campuses generated a degree of cash for schools, but services such as maintaining the plant and grounds and assisting teachers with their paper work were outright costs for which the schools paid from tuition revenue, thus these jobs were expenses for which there was no compensating income. Although no one explained why secondary schools and junior colleges were more prone to lose money in their labor programs, the younger average age of the students made productive industrial labor less likely and employment in services more likely than in senior colleges.

The financial health of Adventist schools in North America paralleled the United States economy. Severe losses occurred between 1929 and 1936, but the next five years saw denominational education turn around with annual gains approximating $300,000 for the entire North American system. Indebtedness decreased and institutional net worth went up. Except for three academies, all colleges and secondary schools were debt-free by 1945 and the colleges were commonly realizing operational gains between two and four hundred thousand dollars a year. "This is a new experience for our educational work," Secretary of Education H. A. Morrison wrote.[12]

Coincidental or not, the opposition to accreditation also followed the economic patterns of the country. W. E. Nelson nearly drew blood in 1934 when he inquired about college expenditures to upgrade plant and personnel, but his probing came as the United States economy bottomed out during the Great Depression and habitual losses threatened the very existence of institutions. Although the accreditation debate at the 1936 General Conference session revolved around the philosophical question of maintaining the spiritual identity of Adventist education, arguments against accreditation lost much of their punch after schools were able to afford the costs of upgrading their programs. Adventist campuses were not flush, but during the five years after 1936, schools spent a half million dollars on equipment and plant improvements, including new buildings, all of which were needed anyway, but these changes helped schools to meet accreditation criteria.

## Background of Adventist Nursing Education

One of the leading issues in the processes of systematization and accreditation of Adventist education was the development of nursing education. This issue was a textbook example of how a field of vocational education transformed itself into a baccalaureate program. The first nurses' training program was a six-month course that began at Battle Creek Sanitarium in 1883, but became a two-year program the next year. As other sanitariums went into operation the common practice was to establish a school of nursing as an educational appendage of the institution. The courses were thus under the control of a health-care center rather than a school and ordinarily required two or three years to complete.[13]

Entrance requirements were minimal, sometimes pegging the entry-level age around twenty but demanding little academic background, often no more than an elementary education. The courses included formal classes in health, anatomy, and other pertinent topics, but student nurses spent the bulk of their time tending patients. Typical to the training were introductory periods when student nurses worked in domestic departments, such as housekeeping, laundry, and the dining room and kitchen.

The purpose of these programs was to prepare nurses for mission service at a clinic or sanitarium. Entrance requirements frequently included screening to ascertain the commitment of prospective students to missionary work. Classes in religion formed a core which would prepare future nurses to give Bible studies. This pattern of nursing education spread throughout the Adventist world. By 1910 ninety sanitariums operated schools of nursing, forty-two of which were outside the United States.

These formative phases for Adventist nursing occurred while the profession at large started to reform itself. Hardly had the twentieth century begun when denominational nurses felt the effects of change. A resolution voted at the 1901 General Conference session recommended that all Adventist schools with sufficient equipment should organize a pre-nursing course based on a cluster of sciences and health-related topics that would form the skeletal program.[14] Three years later some states imposed a three-year minimum requirement on all nursing education programs, which forced Adventist nursing schools in the affected states to meet the new standards.

Change was also in the offing for denominational nursing as it touched the nature of the profession itself. Adventists conceived of nursing as health-care designed for sanitariums that implemented natural remedies and alterations in lifestyle, all leading to patients' well being. Denominational sanitariums around the world followed this model. It became an integrated part of the church's evangelistic plan. But health-care in general was moving toward what would become critical care that included drugs and prescribed medicines and the education of professional nurses with clinical experience compatible with new techniques.

A sanitarium was an ideal setting to fulfill the denominational purpose of preparing missionary nurses, but hospitals that offered critical care were becoming more common environments for nursing education generally. It naturally followed that the kind of nurse typified by Adventist programs differed from the nurse that other nursing schools produced. Distinctions also showed up between Adventist programs in larger sanitariums where a large patient census and a greater variety of equipment permitted better clinical training than was available in small sanitariums with a limited number of beds and equipment.

To compensate for their inadequacies and to cultivate more similarity among Adventist programs of nursing education, nursing schools at small sanitariums affiliated with larger sanitariums. However, medical leaders in the church did not as easily settle the question between missionary nursing as Adventist sanitariums offered it and professional nursing that hospitals conducted. In 1907 the debate over this issue broke wide open at the second Medical Missionary Convention when two leading Adventist physicians read papers that took differing points of view.

Loretta Kress portrayed the issue as an either-or question: missionary nursing and professional nursing were mutually exclusive and Adventist nursing schools should remain faithful to their calling. However, W. W. Worster saw common ground between the two aspects of nursing. He suggested adding *materia medica*—classes in the use of drugs and medicine—to the nursing curriculum, and argued that professionalization of Adventist nursing did not translate into a loss of missionary fervor but simply helped to produce more competent care-givers.

Worster's paper opened pandora's box and for decades to come denominational nurses, physicians, and church leaders debated the point of view he represented and its implications. However committed sanitariums were in training missionary nurses, changes in denominational nursing education were beginning to appear that hinted of Worster's views. In 1909 the General Conference recognized legitimate differences between missionary nursing and ordinary nursing by recommending an "advanced" course for nurses in addition to the short program for missionaries. The following year a training period of thirty-six weeks incorporating eight hours of formal classes per week became the standard in Adventist sanitariums.[15] Four years later in 1914 the General Conference recommended that all Adventist schools of nursing should either reorganize their programs according to minimum standards as the denomination set forth or close.

### The Shift in Nursing Education

At the beginning of the interim years for Adventist education in 1920, denominational nursing had changed but by and large it retained the essential mold it received at Battle Creek when the first two-year program started. During the next twenty-five years, however, Adventist nursing education underwent dramatic alteration that transformed it from a sanitarium-based course to a college-based program with recognized academic standing.

The first step in this turnabout occurred in 1922 when Kathryn L. Jensen, the newly appointed, thirty-year-old assistant secretary of the General Conference Medical Department, recommended that the Department of Education should recognize the schools of nursing as legitimate parts of the denominational education movement. Additionally, the medical and education departments should study ways to convert classes in nursing education into college credit.

For the next nineteen years Jensen pressed hard to accomplish her recommendation. Much of her inspiration originated from sources outside the denomination, such as recommendations from the National League for Nursing–the NLN–which was the most prominent watchdog over nursing education after reorganizing itself in 1912 from its original format as an association for superintendents of nursing schools. In 1917 the NLN published a standard curriculum for nursing schools.

Six years later the Goldmark Report, a historic study of nursing education financed by the Rockefeller Foundation, recommended an increase in nursing programs to five years and academic programs that offered baccalaureate degrees for nurses.

The Goldmark Report was leading more rapidly than nursing schools were willing to follow. As for Adventist nursing education, it found itself wedged into the accreditation imbroglio after other recommendations from the profession advised nursing schools to accept into nurses' training only those students who had taken their preparatory classes in accredited colleges. With this single provision nursing education not only eliminated the academically unprepared who had only an elementary education but also joined the medical profession in promoting general accreditation by regional associations. Repeatedly during the struggle over accrediting Adventist colleges, some church leaders and educators referred to this recommendation as a compelling reason to support approval by regional accrediting bodies.[16]

Armed with data from professional sources, Jensen spent much of the 1920s assessing the quality of Adventist nursing and standardizing curricula. Her colleagues in the Medical Department continued to promote the concept of missionary nursing, which she also supported unequivocally in her assessment instruments by presenting mission service as a primary objective of Adventist nursing. But she went farther, arguing persuasively that professionalization as defined by the NLN and other nursing associations would enhance rather than threaten Adventist nurses' training.

As the pendulum swung away from sanitarium-based nursing toward professionalization two major problems confronted Adventist nursing education. The first was a challenge to continue with their sanitarium training schools that were becoming outmoded. The upshot was a diminishing number of Adventist nursing schools. By 1926 the total shrank to twenty in North America; four years later the figure dwindled to thirteen with thirteen more in the rest of the world. L. A. Hansen, an assistant director of the General Conference Medical Department in 1930, commented that standardizing curricula and careful supervision of nursing programs had benefited nursing schools, but the reality of fewer, more effective programs also implied that only the larger Adventist sanitariums were able to compete in the professionalization process.[17]

The second problem centered upon affiliations with nondenominational hospitals to compensate for clinical deficiencies in sanitarium nursing schools. This question proved to be increasingly thorny. To meet the standards of professional nursing, Adventist nursing students spent one or more clinical rotations in nondenominational hospitals. This affiliation, though necessary for purposes of personal certification, forced nursing students out of their Adventist environment and into the hands of secular instructors.

Church leaders opposed this practice, viewing it similarly as sending academy and college teachers to non-Adventist universities to attend graduate school. They warned that student nurses exposed to education in secular medical institutions risked losing their commitment to the missionary objectives of their profession. Jensen met these warnings by showing from surveys of Adventist nurses that these fears were unfounded, but they persisted anyway.

Step by step through the interim years nursing education nudged closer to Jensen's ultimate goal to elevate nursing from its status as vocational education to an academic field of study worthy of a college degree. A precursor to baccalaureate nursing appeared first in 1919 at the self-supporting Madison College which granted a bachelor of science degree to nurses who attended a full year of college classes after completing the three-year nursing course at the sanitarium. Following extended preliminary study, in 1924 Washington Missionary College launched the first denominationally sponsored degree programs for nurses that required five years to complete, three years on the college campus and two at the sanitarium. This regimen led to a bachelor of science degree with an emphasis in teaching to qualify nurses as professional teachers in nursing schools.[18]

Neither of these programs equated to a baccalaureate degree in nursing as appeared two decades later. Instead, they were cooperative ventures between the college and the sanitarium, with the college recognizing the legitimacy of nursing education as partial fulfillment of the requirements for a college degree. To facilitate the trend toward degrees Jensen organized summer institutes for nurses who had completed their training and already owned nursing certificates. By 1925 these classes carried college credit and were opened to general college students in addition to nurses.

Nurses who completed these summer institutes and degree programs were known as graduate nurses–nurses with a college degree as distinct from nurses with only certificates from the sanitarium nursing schools. The idea of a graduate nurse in denominational circles was not new; it dated from a General Conference action in 1909 recommending that the sanitariums in Loma Linda and Washington should offer a fourth year of study beyond the nursing certificate to supply graduate nurses for the Adventist health system.[19]

Jensen's innovation was to conduct the additional instruction on college campuses and to offer college credit. In effect, this program transferred the graduate nurse program from the sanitariums to the colleges. From Washington Missionary College summer institutes spread to Pacific Union College in the mid-1930s, and by the end of the decade educators were studying formulas to measure nursing clinical experience in college credit hours.

When the Association of Seventh-day Adventist Colleges and Secondary Schools was born in 1928, Jensen formally requested membership for the nursing schools, which had long since come to be known as training schools. Working partially from standards of professional nursing education, she was instrumental in preparing criteria for accreditation of Adventist nursing schools which the Board of Regents approved, and in 1932 nine of the sanitarium nursing schools became members of the new Adventist education association.

Ten years had passed since Jensen first asked the General Conference to recognize nurses' training as a part of the denominational education movement, but until the actions of 1932 the sanitarium programs were answerable to the Medical Department. With the Board of Regents now in control, nursing education became a joint effort between the medical and education departments.

Kathryn Jensen left the Medical Department in 1940, leaving behind a profound impact on Adventist nursing education. For two decades she guided a sanitarium-oriented training program that still bore its nineteenth-century stamp into the twentieth century of professional nursing. From the beginning at Battle Creek the philosophy of sanitarium nursing and missionary nursing were nearly synonymous, and some saw the shift to hospital nursing as tantamount to a rejection of a tried and true denominational principle. But as time passed the larger Adventist sanitariums took on much of the character of hospitals and some changed their names accordingly, often calling themselves "sanitariums and hospitals." Little doubt remained that this change in institutional status paved the way for modifications that Jensen advocated.

While promoting scholarly respectability in her profession, Jensen consistently maintained spiritual integrity as the critical aspect of denominational nursing. With her measured approach, issues such as affiliations with nondenominational hospitals, compliance with nursing standards supported by the National League for Nursing, state registration, and membership in professional nursing associations never became explosive problems as did the debate over accreditation of colleges, even though they were as potentially controversial.

In 1944 the Board of Regents set in motion the final step to convert hospital-based, professional nursing education into a college program, or collegiate nursing as its originators called it. In 1946 Union College instituted the first baccalaureate nursing program, and by 1950 three other institutions developed similar programs. According to Muriel Chapman, chronicler of Adventist nursing, these new programs placed Seventh-day Adventist nursing education ahead of the majority in North America. Although the Goldmark Report of 1923 recommended that colleges assume control of nursing education, only a smattering of schools actually accomplished it. Adventist schools of nursing did not transfer their programs to college campuses until more than twenty years after the Goldmark statement, but even at that, Adventist colleges were at the front of the national trend.

### Adventist Nursing Education in the World Fields

Adventist nurses' training in the world fields was also affected by these trends in the United States, but events in North America did not dictate the future of nursing in other countries. Many of the programs outside the United States were simple if not primitive, as were many of the early nursing schools in small American sanitariums. Similar to the United States, the number of sanitariums outside North America offering nursing training diminished after the first decade of the twentieth century.

The General Conference action in 1910 that established a thirty-six-week training year and curriculum also applied to Adventist sanitariums in Europe. Significantly, the resolution did not include sanitariums in other parts of the world where nurses were in training even though the ideal of the missionary nurse was the dominant theme around the world. European and North American nursing schools were seen as sources of missionaries to the world in contrast to simpler and more localized programs in regions where educational standards were not as high. As the concept of graduate nurses evolved in Adventist nursing education, the Medical Department recommended that larger sanitariums in other countries, Friedensau in Germany and Skodsborg in Denmark, specifically, should offer a fourth year of "post-graduate" study.[20]

During the twenty-five years after World War I advances in medical technology and practice raised expectations in health care, even in developing countries, and government regulation of medical practice and health-care institutions increased. Adventist schools of nursing beyond North America were not answerable to the Board of Regents, even after nursing schools in the United States joined the Seventh-day Adventist Association of Colleges and Secondary Schools, but periodic inspections by personnel from the General Conference Medical Department became a tool to spread North American standards as well as to maintain a denominational identity in nursing education.

In some cases, among them institutions in Australia, the Philippines, Argentina, and for a limited time in Shanghai, sanitariums and traditional training schools were near to each other or even occupied the same campus, but academic control of nursing was not an issue in the world fields. With the exception of Philippine Union College, Adventist colleges outside the United States did not grant degrees during the interim years. Eventually, baccalaureate nursing entered some of the world fields, but in 1945 the era of college-based nursing education outside North America was still a thing of the future.

## Adventist Graduate Education

Closer to the problem of accreditation than nursing education was the question of an Adventist graduate school. The idea of postbaccalaureate education had been with Adventists since the early years of Battle

Creek College, but after 1928 the issue became a part of the debates about systematization and accreditation.[21]

For one academic year, 1881-1882, Battle Creek College under Sidney Brownsberger offered master's degrees to individuals who had graduated with a bachelor of arts or bachelor of science degree at least three years previously and had successfully engaged in scholarly pursuits. Recipients did not earn the master's degree on the strength of a formal program of studies but in recognition of the candidate's professional accomplishments. Brownsberger's sudden exit from the campus also ended this graduate degree program. A plan to establish a denominational graduate school that offered master's degrees and doctorates came from the second institute for Adventist teachers in 1894, but nothing materialized. "It was," as Gilbert Valentine says, "an idea born out of time."[22]

These truncated attempts did not stop discussion about the matter. Union College "toyed" with master's degrees, according to college historian Everett Dick, beginning to offer them in 1907. A graduate council selected candidates who, as in the case of Battle Creek College, did not have to complete a prescribed course of study but had to own a bachelor's degree and demonstrate productive professional skills.

In the main, the denomination functioned almost in a state of denial regarding the necessity of advanced education. Contemporaneous with the early years of Battle Creek College Adventist leaders, including Ellen White, spoke often about the urgency to fill the field with workers; consequently, they favored short courses that hurriedly produced church employees with hardly any attention to academic baggage. Adventist education was still in its organizational phase during the first two decades of the twentieth century, but after a mood of systematization set in, Secretary of Education Frederick Griggs told the 1909 General Conference session that the denomination needed to raise its standards of education. "It is a fair proposition that a teacher ought to be educated at least a year or so ahead of those he is to teach," he said. "The trouble is, we are not graduating enough young people from the higher grades."[23]

Griggs applied this principle to secondary-level grades, stopping short of the colleges, but weeks later when he became president of Union College he left no doubt that he believed that graduate education was a necessity for college teachers. Describing Union College as the most suitable location for a denominational post-baccalaureate program, he received board support to raise an equipment fund to begin graduate studies for teachers in Adventist colleges.

Griggs' plans went the way of previous attempts to inaugurate an Adventist graduate degree program, but after the College of Medical Evangelists began its face off with its accrediting body, educators and other church leaders could no longer dismiss the issue off-handedly. The question involved ministerial education as well as the preparation of college teachers. From the days of James White concern that Adventist pastors should be better educated was the motivation behind a series of Bible institutes for ministers, which translated into the practice of relying on inservice training to educate pastors.

This method was too informal to be permanently successful and during the era of World War I education for the ministry became a matter of serious concern. Notwithstanding the effort to raise theology to the level of a college degree, the General Conference found it necessary in 1913 to recommend that conferences restrict ministerial licenses to men who had completed a minimum of twelve grades of school. Licensed ministers who had not yet reached this level should attend a training school or enroll in the denomination's correspondence school to achieve the prescribed education before ordination. The implication of this action was unavoidable: of the leading professions which church employment offered–medicine, nursing, teaching, and pastoring–the ministry suffered the poorest academic preparation.

In 1918 the General Conference adopted a proposal by the Department of Education that outlined the content of the bachelor of sacred theology degree for senior colleges and a two-year ministerial diploma program for junior colleges. The plan also provided an affiliated status with a college for ministerial hopefuls who were still in secondary school, thus giving them a special standing. The fact that, in part, these measures were intended to help ministerial students avoid military service during World War I did not detract from the organizational impact on ministerial education.

The 1918 action also dealt with the selection process of Bible teachers. An *ad hoc* committee later proposed that Adventist colleges "ought to be emphatically Bible schools," with the schools of theology being "preeminent" in their influence on the entire campus and its organization.[24] The 1919 Spring Council voted its support of schools of theology that were to grant distinct degrees and would be headed by a dean who supervised a separate faculty. These schools were to be unique but not autonomous units of a college. By the beginning of the interim years it was clear that the General Conference had assumed control of the education of Adventist ministers and accorded a role of primacy to ministerial education on Adventist campuses.

Shortly after implementing this plan, Emmanuel Missionary College initiated an earned master's degree program in theology, conferring five graduate degrees between 1922 and 1925. Again, it was Frederick Griggs, now transplanted on the Berrien Springs campus as college president, who oversaw this project.

During the 1920s W. E. Howell's opposition to accreditation by secular bodies and his resistance to graduate education in non-Adventist institutions became proverbial, but finally concluding that accreditation and graduate education were issues that were not going to disappear in the face of Adventist opposition, he capitulated. If his attitude accomplished anything, it helped to whip up support for a denominational graduate school. Discussion about an Adventist graduate school hypothetically portrayed a program that would offer master's degrees in a variety of academic disciplines which, it was hoped, would obviate the growing tendency of denominational teachers to enroll in non-Adventist schools. An education council in 1929 proposed that in view of demands on Adventist schools, the church should establish a free-standing graduate school with eight departments including professional education and the common disciplines in the arts and sciences.

As a parting word in 1930, in his last report as secretary of education, Howell conceded that Ellen White's counsel given more than forty years previously supported the notion of graduate education. "If we can establish our own graduate school for advanced study by our college teachers," he elaborated, "it will give us a complete system of our own, and remove the necessity of attending a school of the world to maintain a recognized standing in the educational field."[25]

The commission to survey Adventist colleges in 1931 followed up with a recommendation that the denomination should establish a program offering a master's degree on the campus of a centrally located senior college. Other colleges might offer post-baccalaureate classes but not post-baccalaureate degrees. For the time being, the report stated, doctorates were beyond the resources of an Adventist graduate school.

It took a year for the General Conference to digest this proposal, but in 1932 the Autumn Council approved a joint recommendation from denominational officers and the Department of Education to establish a graduate school of theology on the campus of a senior college. The graduate degree was to be a master of theology, but students could select minors in church history, secular history, biblical languages, and English. This action was a compromise that narrowed the previous recommendations for a graduate school down to a seminary for ministers and Bible teachers. Because of the Great Depression funding for the proposed school was difficult, and a year later the General Conference changed its mind, voting instead to offer twelve-week summer sessions in Bible and history.

When thirteen faculty and about forty students gathered at Pacific Union College in 1934 for the first session of this new academic venture, the concept of a complete graduate school had shrunk to what the General Conference called the Advanced Bible School that offered post-baccalaureate classes but no graduate degrees. In this reduced format Adventist graduate education continued for two years before the General Conference consented in 1936 to establish a separate graduate school on its own campus in the vicinity of Washington, D. C.

The new school would offer graduate work in Bible and religious history and organize a graduate degree program. In 1937 M. E. Kern, who held the title of dean of the Advanced Bible School since 1934 became president of the program that had been reorganized into the Seventh-day Adventist Theological Seminary. When he assumed his new post he added a winter quarter to the class schedule. By 1945 a four-quarter academic year had gone into effect. Meanwhile, in 1941 the Seminary moved into its new quarters, a separate building adjacent to the General Conference offices. The following year the Seminary finally authorized the master of arts in religion.

Adventist historian and archivist Bert Haloviak has noted that during the first decade of its operations the seminary emphasized programs for teachers more than evangelism. This trend was not a happenstance. Kern stated in 1936 that Adventists were rightly "a very active people."

*In 1934 the long struggle to upgrade Seventh-day Adventist theological education produced the Advanced Bible School which became the Theological Seminary in 1937. In 1938 Seminary faculty and students gathered for this photograph. Among the faculty, seated, are Charles Weniger, second from left; M. E. Kern, president, fourth from right; and M. L. Andreasen, second from right.*

But, he warned, "there is a real danger that thorough, reverent Biblical scholarship shall be sacrificed on the altars of plans and promotion. We need to focus our attention anew on the searching of the Scriptures."[26]

That the Seminary provided nutriment for the intellectually undernourished ministry became evident. Since the 1920s an internship plan had kept ministerial recruits in something close to evangelistic perpetual motion, but in 1944 the General Conference modified this practice by recommending a balanced program of evangelism and seminary study leading to the bachelor of divinity degree. This action was a turning point in the evolution of the Seminary, for it broadened the purpose of the graduate program from preparing well-educated Bible teachers to include the art of effective congregational pastoring. It also linked the college ministerial curricula to the graduate programs at the Seminary, forming a single educational chain.

In 1946, D. E. Rebok, who followed Kern as Seminary president, recalled thirteen years of graduate school operations by noting that more than 1,200 students had enrolled since 1934. Only thirty-four had earned the master's degree, but the overwhelming majority had benefitted from one or more quarters of intensive study. A survey of more than 150 ministers in nine North American unions indicated that the stress on higher education was having its impact. More than ninety percent had completed some college-level education with approximately sixty-three percent having graduated from college. Rebok summarized the purpose of the Seminary in four parts: to provide professional training for pastors, to prepare Bible and history teachers, to offer refresher courses for workers from the world fields, and to give special preparation to mission appointees.

By the end of World War II the international impact of the Seminary was undeniable. After the spring quarter of 1946 Rebok announced that twenty-two percent of the enrollment since the Seminary's beginning came from countries beyond North America. Offering classes to students from the world fields, he said, was "a means of strengthening the bonds which bind our worldwide work into a unified, aggressive movement which must encircle the globe."[27]

Rebok also voiced what had become almost axiomatic in Adventist education: centralized control of ministerial education was a self-evident truth of denominational life that needed no explanation beyond its own obviousness. "It is only reasonable and logical," he said, "that every organization or institution should train its own leadership."[28] Until the General Conference recommended specific curriculum content for ministerial education in 1918, the training of ministers had been fragmented among the institutions and local fields, and from some points of view, professionally disappointing. To rectify this problem the General Conference, with the approval of its constituency, pushed through a denominational model of ministerial education. By this action the church adopted the policy of centralized control of pastoral training.[29]

During the interim years colleges followed the 1918 model imperfectly, but by the time Rebok spoke, twenty-eight years later, the recognized formula included a graduate degree as the standard level of academic achievement for ministers.[30] Rather than an immediate requirement, for practical reasons this policy was a recommended ideal to which the denomination worked. The corps of Adventist ministers would not accomplish it even by the end of the century, but it was no less an ideal which benefitted them enormously. It was this aspect of leadership training that Rebok referred to as the logical prerogative of the church, not the undergraduate programs on the college campuses where most ministers still received their basic, or introductory preparation. In 1946 no one saw reason to challenge Rebok's statement, but it was to be a major point of debate decades later.

The Seminary was a success but it served a narrower purpose than the educators of the 1920s hoped. It did not fulfill the denominational need for a broader graduate school, which left teachers in fields other than Bible, biblical languages, and church history with no other alternative than to attend non-Adventist institutions in order to earn academic credentials that accreditation required. But the Seminary played an important role beyond its immediate purposes. As a legitimate, denominationally sponsored post-baccalaureate institution it broke the arguments that lingered in the minds of many who believed that intellectual pursuits hampered the advance of the gospel.

During the interim years from 1920 to 1945 Adventist education underwent a far-reaching transformation. At the end of World War II Adventist schools were still only a fraction of the broad educational spectrum and largely unnoticed by the educational world, but the struggles of the interim years had developed a new maturity among them. The debate over accreditation brought legitimacy, financial burdens forced administrators to develop modernized management, conventions and gatherings introduced improved professionalism, baccalaureate education enlarged its circle to include vocational programs such as nursing, and graduate education provided intellectual respectability. These developments occurred in North America, but in the years to come they would impact the entire world of Adventism.

---

[1]See Howell's reports to the General Conference sessions of 1922 and 1930, AST, RG 51; *General Conference Bulletin*, 1922, no. 7, p, 162, no.11, p. 271, no. 12, p. 282.

[2]*Ibid.*

[3]Griggs, "Report of the Department of Education to the 1918 General Conference Session," AST, RG 51.

[4]General Conference Committee Minutes, January 11, 1920; October 27, 1920; May 25, 1921; *The Advent Review and Sabbath Herald*, July 1, 1920. Howell described his tour in a series of articles entitled, "School Notes in South America."

[5]Howell, "Report of the Department of Education to the 1926 General Conference Session," AST, RG51.

[6]One can read the entire proceedings of the Colorado Springs gathering in *Proceedings of the Educational and Missionary Volunteer Departments of the General Conference of Seventh-day Adventists in World Convention.* (Washington, D.C.: Review and Herald Publishing Association, 1923).

[7]For a complete account of the 1937 world convention, see *Report of the Blue Ridge Educational Convention, August 17-25, 1937.* (Washington, D. C.: General Conference Department of Education, n.d.). For a list of meetings of North American educators, see Brown, *Chronology*, pp. 231-238 and "Teachers' Meetings, 1917-1968," AST, RG 51.

[8]*General Conference Bulletin*, 1922, no. 3, p. 76.

[9]*Ibid.*, p. 75.

[10]For information about school finances, see *General Conference Bulletin*, *ibid.*, no. 1, p. 26; no. 3, pp. 75, 76; 1926, no. 3, pp. 13, 14; 1936, no. 7, pp. 147, 148; 1941, no. 2, p. 41; 1946, no. 4, p. 90.

[11]*Ibid.*, 1936, no. 7, p. 147.

[12]*Ibid.*, 1946, no. 4, p. 90.

[13]Muriel Chapman's *Mission of Love: A Century of Seventh-day Adventist Nursing* (Silver Spring, MD: Association of Seventh-day Adventist Nursing, 2000), pp. 1-124 is the leading source for this section about Adventist nursing education.

[14]*General Conference Bulletin*, 1901, no. 1, extra no. 14, p. 306.

[15]General Conference Committee minutes, June 17, 1909; March 25, 1910.

[16]One of the most notable instances was W. E. Howell's admission in his report to the 1930 General Conference session when he included nursing with teaching and premed classes as the ones that required accreditation. "Report of the Department of Education to the 1930 General Conference Session," AST, RG5.

[17]*General Conference Bulletin*, 1926, no. 11, p. 7; Chapman, *Mission of Love*, p. 79.

[18]*General Conference Bulletin*, 1930, no. 4, p.74.

[19]*Ibid.*, 1909, no. 16, p. 243.

[20]*Ibid.*; General Conference minutes, March 25, 1910.

[21]For this account of graduate education I have used General Conference minutes, October 20, 1913; November 20, 1918; April 30, 1919; October 19, 1932; October 24, 1933; June 10, 1936; *General Conference Bulletin*, 1909, no. 15, p. 223; 1936, no. 8, p. 174; 1946, no. 7, pp. 166-168; Howell, "Report of the Department of Education to the 1930 General Conference Session," AST, RG 51; "Meeting of the Survey Commission of Board of Regents," September 29, 1931, AST, RG 51; VandeVere, *Wisdom Seekers*, pp. 4, 157; Valentine, *Shaping of Adventism*, p. 44; Dick, *Union College*, pp. 179, 180, 181; Milton E. Kern, "Graduate Work in Bible and History," (*Journal of True Education*, December 1940), pp. 6, 7, 30; Bert Haloviak, "A Brief Sketch of SDA Ministerial Training," unpublished manuscript, 1988, AST; Ronald Knott, "For a Beginning, 'Most Satisfactory': A History of SDA Graduate Education," (*Journal of Adventist Education,* February-March 1983), pp. 20-23,38-41.

[22]Valentine, *Shaping of Adventism*, p. 44.

[23]*General Conference Bulletin*, 1909, no. 15, p. 223.

[24]General Conference minutes, Nov. 20, 1918.

[25]Howell, "Report of the Department of Education to the 1930 General Conference Session," AST, RG 51.

[26]*General Conference Bulletin*, 1936, no. 8, p. 174.

[27]*Ibid.*, 1946, no. 7, p. 168.

[28]*Ibid.*, p. 167.

[29]General Conference minutes, September 9, 1918.

[30]For the specific wording of the policy, see General Conference minutes, October 30, 1944.

## *Part Three*

# YEARS OF FULFILLMENT AND CHALLENGE, 1945-2000

In many ways the years after World War II were years of fulfillment. In 1945 the age of the training school as the typical Adventist campus in the world fields was in decline and the era of degree-granting institutions was on its way in. Many of these new schools depended on North American academic strength at the beginning of their new status, but before the century ended they were operating on their own cerebral power. The transition from training school to degree-granting institution was not always easy or as ideal as the denomination wanted, but it happened anyway and by the year 2000 Adventists could point to a circle of institutions around the world that would have been unthinkable a half century earlier. Graduate education, so long regarded as an intellectual detraction at best and feared as a secular malignancy at worst, became common.

In other ways, however, the years after World War II were years of challenge. The concept of system that Griggs and Howell promoted so vigorously during the first thirty years of the century encountered serious tests, not always successfully. By the end of the century the denomination's 12,000,000 members sprawled unevenly around the globe, making a centrally administered system difficult. Some believed a system to be impractical if not impossible. Instead of the General Conference, the administrative divisions of the church became the key points of management of denominational education. At the beginning of the new millennium the church and the education establishment had a full agenda of unfinished business relating to the issues of system.

To maintain an identifiably Adventist philosophy of education in a world that bore scant resemblance to the nineteenth century when denominational education began formed the crux upon which all other issues balanced. There was no scarcity of opinions about how to go about the business of Adventist education, but effective solutions to problems were increasingly hard to come by. Nevertheless, by the year 2000 Adventists owned one of the largest parochial networks of education on the planet and they could say that, after all things considered, Proper Education had fulfilled itself well.

# From Colleges to Universities

Few trends impacted Adventist education as forcefully as the development of graduate education. It legitimized Adventist postbaccalaureate learning and raised the bar of academic achievement. But it did not happen overnight. The Theological Seminary did not match earlier recommendations to establish a graduate school for secondary and college teachers in the arts and sciences, and as events turned out, the Seminary would be in its second decade of life before Adventists would feel a substantial effect of denominationally owned graduate education.

## The Seminary Becomes Potomac University

Meanwhile, for many years after its founding, the Seminary played a dual role for the Adventist ministry. M. E. Kern, Seminary president from 1937 to 1943, explained to his board in 1940 that his faculty had divided their classes into two categories, the first, a master's degree program, and the second, non-credit courses for students who did not plan to earn master's degrees or were not academically prepared for graduate study. This second function was essentially providing inservice or continuing education for ministers and Bible teachers.

The College Bible and History Teachers Council, also meeting at the Seminary in 1940, concurred with this academic format. D. E. Rebok reported at the 1946 General Conference session that over a span of thirteen years, dating from the first summer session in 1934, only thirty-four students, or less than three percent of the Seminary's enrollees, had earned a graduate degree. These numbers revealed that the primary contribution of the Seminary had been to continue the inservice tradition that began in the days of James White. The natural conclusion was that the Seminary had not yet made its mark as a graduate-level institution.[1]

But change was in the air even as Rebok spoke. General Conference recognition in 1944 of graduate study at the Seminary as the logical sequence to undergraduate ministerial education was a step toward another General Conference recommendation nine years later in 1953 to mandate a master's degree as part of the ministerial internship program. This new requirement was to go into effect in 1955. The 1953 action also raised Seminary entrance requirements to ensure that prospective students were academically equipped for graduate study and not enrolling merely for inservice courses. It also recommended a Ministerial Training Advisory Committee that would determine the content and format of ministerial education at both the four-year colleges and the Seminary and would correlate baccalaureate ministerial courses with graduate education. Taken *in toto*, these provisions not only established a master's degree as the standard degree for the Adventist ministry, but they also tightened the grip of the General Conference on ministerial education. Reflecting on these changes, Charles E. Weniger, dean of the Seminary, editorialized that the "Seminary has come of age."[2]

Ministerial education was finally making up for years of lost time. The Adventist pastorate in North America was finally on schedule to reach an academic level that matched the expectations of the Christian community. Meanwhile, the idea of an Adventist graduate school for teachers remained in limbo. To handle denominational needs for graduate study in the arts and sciences the Board of Regents placed post-baccalaureate programs in the hands of college administrations to implement when they deemed necessary. However, before offering graduate programs colleges were to submit their proposals for approval by the General Conference.[3]

Not surprisingly, this haphazard approach to upgrade teachers' credentials did not work well. It left the serious problem of professional development dangling and bred a spirit of rivalry among the colleges. In 1954 the General Conference charged a committee to investigate and control graduate programs, but activity among the schools and the teachers themselves was moving too rapidly for denominational bureaucracy to seize the initiative.

Spurred by a reminder that the General Conference Department of Education had recently recommended five years of study for secondary teachers and that many states were requiring the same standard for elementary teachers, the 1954 Autumn Council asked the General Conference to "reactivate" the committee on graduate study in order to provide an Adventist graduate school. At the time, the committee to be reactivated was less than four months old, which suggested that the topic had been something less than a priority item. A second committee likewise accomplished little.[4]

The next year General Conference President R. R. Figuhr scrapped both committees, dumped their open-ended assignment, and commissioned a new committee to investigate the status of and the need for graduate education and to prepare a specific proposal. The committee discovered conditions that were probably more acute than anyone suspected. A survey of Adventist institutions disclosed that only about 250 of the near 1,100 secondary teachers in North America owned graduate degrees but that the stream of denominational teachers attending universities of the land had grown from a trickle twenty years before to a torrent of 400 by 1955.

It was evident that teachers were not waiting for church leaders to handpick the spiritually reliable to attend graduate schools of the world. With a tinge of alarm the editor of the *Journal of True Education* stated that a rising number of Adventist youth were going to universities because they were "unable to understand why it is not permissible, when so many Adventists are enrolling there for graduate work." These data left little question that graduate education was a marketable commodity within the denomination.[5]

At the Autumn Council in 1956 the Committee on Graduate Study presented its proposal. It called for a university consisting of the Theological Seminary and a school of graduate studies that would offer graduate degrees in theology and education and later would embrace other fields. The new university would affiliate with Washington Missionary College. Because graduate courses were already appearing on Adventist campuses in the western states a special coordinating committee would coordinate those programs.[6]

For the next two years a profusion of committees worked out the details for the proposed graduate institution, establishing a new administration and faculty and selecting the name Potomac University. These were relatively simple tasks compared to the question of locating the new campus, a snag on which the university planning group found itself impaled for months. Suggestions ran the gamut from erecting a new university building in Takoma Park to developing a new campus to which Washington Missionary College would move and serve as the undergraduate school. Winton Beaven, dean of Potomac University, recalled that the committee inspected nearly fifty tracts of land but that "something was wrong with every one of them . . . It went on and on and on."[7]

### Andrews University Is Born

The answer came unexpectedly when Floyd Rittenhouse, president of Emmanuel Missionary College and the newly elected president of Potomac University, persuaded the stymied committeemen in Washington to sell out their present holdings and reinvest on the Michigan campus. By this time Washington Missionary College was virtually out of consideration as an affiliated undergraduate institution because of seemingly unsolvable problems connected with moving the campus, and no nearby land was available to make an affiliation of WMC with the graduate school workable. On October 24, 1958 this now overheated topic reached the voting stage, and delegates to the Autumn Council cast their ballots in favor of moving to Michigan and integrating Potomac University with Emmanuel Missionary College.

The decision to transform the Michigan campus into a university rang with a triumphant tone, but denominational leaders and educators, regardless of how much work they had already accomplished, quickly discovered that they had much to learn about creating a university as understood in American education. Administrative changes were legion and new roles had to evolve. Three divisions comprised the new institution, the college or undergraduate school, the graduate school, and the Seminary. Until the Berrien Springs campus could be readied to accommodate the Seminary, Potomac University continued to operate in Takoma Park as a separate school. The physical and legal merger of the two institutions did not occur until 1960, only weeks after the board chose to name the new campus Andrews University, memorializing J. N. Andrews, the first Adventist who officially worked outside North America.[8]

At the time of the merger, statistics demonstrated that earlier actions to develop a valid graduate-level campus rather than an inservice and continuing education agency had yielded results. The anemic showing of only thirty-four master's degrees granted by the Seminary between 1934 and 1946 grew to more than 850 from the Seminary alone by 1960, and over sixty more from the short-lived graduate school of Potomac University.

As the seat of theological education for the entire Adventist world, Andrews University became a General Conference institution, no longer under the aegis of the Lake Union. Until its move from Washington, the Seminary had operated with its own board, but at Andrews it became a part of the larger university. One of the sticky issues was to design an institution that offered an academically respectable program of graduate studies and at the same time allowed the Seminary to retain the status of primacy that leading churchmen intended for theology on Adventist campuses.

The graduate program began with degrees in mathematics, English, education, history, and religion. During their first visit in 1961, examiners from the North Central Association found ample reasons to doubt that the institution had become a genuinely integrated university, and they denied accreditation. Rittenhouse engineered sufficient corrections to achieve preliminary accreditation in 1963, but at the same time he fell from the good graces of denominational leaders and a few months later the university board dismissed him. He had been a popular and respected personality in both denominational and secular circles, and this abrupt change raised more questions about the university's administration and governance, prompting North Central to slap the university with probationary standing.

*From his office as a General Conference associate secretary of education, Richard L. Hammill promoted the establishment of a Seventh-day Adventist graduate school and university. He served as president of Andrews University, 1963-1976 and later as a vice president of the General Conference. He was a leading force in developing theological education around the world and the establishment of the Geoscience Research Institute.*

It was Richard Hammill's thirteen-year presidency, from 1963 to 1976, that brought stability and growth to Andrews University. The new president had been a successful college teacher and administrator, and since 1955 as a member of the General Conference Department of Education he was a leading participant in all the major discussions and committee actions relating to graduate education.

Forced into another self-study, the university practically started its accreditation campaign over again, but by 1968 Hammill's indefatigable efforts in building an adequate campus and assembling a representative faculty paid off. Ten years after the vote to merge Potomac University with Emmanuel Missionary College, the North Central Association granted full accreditation to Andrews' master's degrees in English, history, mathematics, biology, business administration, education, and the master of arts in teaching. The Seminary remained outside the purview of North Central but sought accreditation from a theological association, eventually the Association of Theological Schools in the United States and Canada.

During the last three decades of the century Andrews University developed numerous graduate programs and organized component schools. The number of liberal arts disciplines offering a master's degree diminished, but many departments cooperated with the School of Education to offer a master of arts in teaching, a professional degree in secondary teaching with supporting graduate-level work in an academic field. The dominant trend was the spread of graduate degree programs to the professions, including physical therapy, nursing, social work, and business administration. The School of Education developed sequences for both the doctor of education and doctor of philosophy degrees. In addition to a variety of degrees at the master's level, the Seminary offered the doctor of ministry, doctor of philosophy, and doctor of theology degrees.

To enhance its ethos as a university, Andrews invested in special collections. One of the major projects was to establish the Adventist Heritage Center as a part of the James White Library, a department that housed publications and documents by and about Seventh-day Adventists. By the beginning of the new century the Center had become one of Adventism's richest sources for information about the denomination with its more than 30,000 books and theses, a similar number of unpublished records, about 750 linear feet of private papers, and other graphic items, recordings, artifacts, and rare books. It also became part of a larger entity, the Center for Adventist Research which functioned as a branch of the White Estate.

*Aerial view of Andrews University in 1973, created by merging Potomac University with Emmanuel Missionary College, thus transforming the sixty-year-old rural college campus into the denominational center for theological studies.*

A notable contribution of Andrews University to the academic world was the Seminary's involvement in archeological digs in the Holy Land. From these expeditions the university inherited a significant collection of artifacts displayed in the Siegfried H. Horn Museum, named after the German-born professor of archeology who began these projects in 1968 at Heshbon. Later professors continued the investigations in Jordan. Helping to coordinate these activities was the Institute of Archeology.

The university did not heavily emphasize study in the sciences, but the Museum of Natural History became the repository for thousands of birds, mammals, marine life specimens, insects, and botanical items. Also catering to the denomination's intelligentsia was the Andrews University Press, established in 1969, which published scores of scholarly works in archeology, education, and theology.

Enrollment in graduate studies on the Michigan campus justified the transfer from Washington. The graduate school at Potomac University opened in 1957 with about thirty students; seventeen years later in 1974 when Andrews celebrated its centennial, nearly 550 students were enrolled in post-baccalaureate programs. Total university enrollment approximated 2,300. The number of students continued to rise, exceeding 3,000 during the decade of the 1990s.

### Loma Linda University Grows from CME

The committee report in 1956 that set in motion a string of decisions resulting in Potomac University also recommended separate action concerning graduate education in the western states. During the late 1950s and into the next decade most of the denomination's attention centered on Andrews University as the locus of Adventist graduate education, but simultaneously Loma Linda University was in the making in California. These two graduate institutions developed along contrasting lines. Andrews was born from a deliberate plan calling for a denominational graduate school to supply post-baccalaureate credentials for Adventist teachers. Contrariwise, Loma Linda emerged almost by default from the College of Medical Evangelists as an institution of health sciences.[9]

The California school originated as an educational unit authorized to offer academic and professional degrees, including dentistry. At the time, 1909, the intention was to prepare physicians, but the next year the school added nursing when Loma Linda Sanitarium and its nursing school merged with the medical college. The administration also added other programs which, by 1941 included medical technology, physical therapy, and medical radiography. The organizational *modus operandi* allowed these programs to function as separate schools with more autonomy than academic departments on a baccalaureate campus, which meant that administrative structure similar to a university was present from the beginning.

The programs beyond the School of Medicine did not constitute baccalaureate education, but all of them developed under the auspices of an institution that held a college charter. Meanwhile, the academic character of CME became progressively evident, especially after the American Medical Association gave its full approbation to the School of Medicine. The net effect of all of these influences was a drift in the direction of a health sciences educational center.

This trend was not lost on the administration of the College of Medical Evangelists. In 1944 CME proposed to reorganize itself into what amounted to a university, actually, an institution with separate colleges, including a graduate school. The General Conference turned the plan down, labeling it as "inadvisable," although praising the "progressive spirit" at CME and at the same time recommending a committee to conduct a feasibility study for a school of dentistry.[10]

Movement toward a university speeded up after World War II when a short-lived graduate school supervised residencies for medical students and offered a master's degree in medical science to residents who completed a thesis. While this program did not endure, the school of dentistry became a reality in 1953 which added to the administrative complexity of the institution. Meanwhile, the urge to introduce a traditional graduate school which would grant post-baccalaureate degrees and sponsor research gathered momentum. Before the General Conference would agree to reorganization, however, the 1953 Autumn Council requested a blue ribbon committee to study the objectives of the institution.

Chaired by R. R. Figuhr, General Conference president, the committee reported at the Autumn Council in 1954 with recommendations that were a watershed in the history of the College of Medical Evangelists.

The document committed the institution to a "spirit of sound research and a desire to participate in the advancement of knowledge," and agreed to add a graduate school which would oversee graduate education and related research.[11]

Because CME was already organized along university lines, deans or directors headed the component schools which customarily published separate bulletins. Faced with the prospects of a university on the West coast, church leaders addressed their overriding concern which was to bind all of the separate parts of the institution together in a manner to preserve its longstanding purpose as a training ground for personnel to operate the denominational health-care system within the evangelistic goals of the church. A six-paragraph statement affirmed this role–a school that prepared professionals both to heal bodies and to preach the gospel–and directed each of the various schools to include declarations embodying the essence of these spiritual objectives in its bulletin.

In 1954 graduate education began by inaugurating a master of science in nursing, the denomination's first graduate program in nursing. Only six years had elapsed since Loma Linda had begun its baccalaureate nursing program. In 1955 the General Conference approved a recommendation that authorized CME to offer a doctor of philosophy degree in three basic fields of science taught in the School of Medicine. The following year the General Conference extended its approval to include two more doctoral fields. All doctoral programs were to begin at the discretion of CME's administration. By the 1954-1955 academic year the institution had become a university except in name.[12]

From its inception graduate education at the College of Medical Evangelists focused on sciences relating to health or the medical profession, although church leaders justified CME's graduate school as a means to offer graduate degrees to Adventist teachers. The practical effect of this reasoning was to broaden the purpose of the College of Medical Evangelists to include science education as well as health in its offerings. CME was probably better prepared than any other Adventist institution to enter the field of science education since it could establish research facilities more easily than four-year colleges, which gave it an advantage over Adventist schools that contemplated graduate programs in science.

*School of Dentistry, Loma Linda University. One of the major steps in developing the College of Medical Evangelists into Loma Linda University was a new school of dentistry that began classes in 1953 and moved into this new building in 1955. This addition filled a major gap in Seventh-day Adventist health education.*

Despite this advantage CME was not the first Adventist school to initiate postbaccalaureate programs on the West coast. Graduate classes began as early as 1940. In 1944 the General Conference noted the trend and advised schools not to add courses until the denomination could develop a plan, especially in religion since the Seminary was the preferred school. The church's first official reaction to graduate education came the next year and permitted individual colleges to establish graduate programs on a supply and demand policy, but institutions were to acquire approval, program by program, for postbaccalaureate studies. In compliance with this arrangement, in 1948 Walla Walla College received approval to offer graduate studies in biology. With graduate education in general left more or less to the initiative of individual campuses, the General Conference concentrated on developing the Seminary.[13]

By the mid-1950s agitation about graduate education had come to a boil in Washington and CME convinced the denomination that graduate studies at the doctoral level were advantageous in the sciences. The floodgate for graduate study opened. In 1957 Walla Walla's authorization to offer graduate education extended to chemistry and history. Again, the supporting rationale was to provide graduate study for Adventist teachers. The following year La Sierra College gained approval to grant master's degrees in education to elementary and secondary teachers. These gestures were clear indications from the West that the embryonic Adventist university in Washington, D. C., oriented toward ministerial education, did not furnish the broader program of graduate studies that the denomination needed.[14]

Events in the West culminated in another series of historic resolutions at the 1959 Autumn Council. The heart of the actions was to grant university status to the College of Medical Evangelists and to authorize whatever reorganization was necessary to implement the decision. This action only made official what had been in operation for some years, but in addition it created a consortium of "participating colleges"–La Sierra, Pacific Union, and Walla Walla, in addition to the College of Medical Evangelists–to coordinate all of the graduate education in the West according to a rational plan. The central and overseeing responsibility in the consortium belonged to CME, but General Conference approval was still the ultimate step in governing graduate education. Church leaders foresaw that this new post-baccalaureate bloc in the West would overlap the expectations they held for Potomac University, which had recently found its new home in Michigan, hence geographic limitations to the service areas of both new universities were necessary.[15] The next year CME took the name of Loma Linda University.

### The Merger of La Sierra and Loma Linda

For several years the members of the consortium cooperated by submitting their requests for graduate programs for approval, but the educational water was becoming murky. Instead of functioning as the central institution in a consortium, CME competed by offering baccalaureate degrees and expanding its offerings in general studies that supported its degree programs at both the baccalaureate and graduate levels, thus preempting the need for corresponding programs on the college campuses.

As early as 1953 a division of religion became a major component of the medical college. By 1962 Loma Linda gained General Conference approval to grant master of arts degrees in a limited number of traditional liberal arts disciplines. The university's continuing incursions beyond the health sciences as strictly defined into the province of the "participating colleges" came to an end when La Sierra College and Loma Linda University merged in 1967 with La Sierra becoming the Riverside campus of the university. With this linkup the evolution of a medical school into a conventional university was complete.[16]

Similar to the merger of Potomac University and Emmanuel Missionary College, this experiment brought congratulatory reaction, but the union in California turned out to be a marriage of dissatisfied unequals. Each campus was eager to retain enough autonomy to prevent a genuine partnership. La Sierra campus professors complained because their salary was considerably lower than their peers on the Loma Linda campus. By the late 1980s accreditation problems descended on the joined schools and university restructuring became a common conversation piece. In part the issue turned on the question of whether Loma Linda should be a multiversity or a health sciences university, but the institution could not easily sweep under the rug the unequal status of the campuses as revealed in salary differences. By the spring of 1990 the dissolution of the merger appeared to be the most likely solution to satisfy the regional accrediting body, and following the 1990 General Conference session the two campuses separated, each pursuing its own purposes with clearer resolution.[17]

To facilitate this separation the Pacific Union agreed to resume ownership of the La Sierra campus, which in short order became La Sierra University. This new entity retained the several master's degree and doctoral programs in education which it had developed while a part of Loma Linda University. But the split was not clean. Before the merger Loma Linda had established degrees that arguably were legitimate on baccalaureate campuses, and following the dissolution it reestablished its claim to some of these common programs. An awkward situation developed with two Adventist universities, less than twenty miles apart, offering virtually duplicate programs in some fields. While the separation helped to clear the air from issues with the Western Association of Schools and Colleges, it intensified the rivalry between the neighboring campuses.

As ill-fated as it was, the merger of La Sierra and Loma Linda was in keeping with earlier statements by church leaders that encouraged the health sciences institution to assume a role in educating teachers. Failure of the merger did not mean that developing programs of science education was a case of poor judgment. From the day of its founding, Loma Linda was an educational institution. Master's degrees and doctorates for teachers in the sciences were conceivably legitimate programs. A doctorate in biology, a critical academic field for Adventists, was and continued to be a part of Loma Linda's offerings after the two campuses reverted to their individual identity.

But health sciences were at the heart of Loma Linda University, and its reputation evolved from academic medicine and health, not in education. To touch the public in matters of health was a product of its commitment to scholarly investigation. Its celebrated heart team exported good health and good will to scores of communities around the world, most notably in developing countries.[18] Although the university incited some negative headlines in 1984 when doctors inserted a baboon's heart in a human baby, the neonatal heart transplant research project matured into one of the world's most successful heart transplant programs for children. Loma Linda's proton treatment facility placed the university on the forward edge of technological therapy for cancer.

Repeated investigations into nutrition and health helped Adventists to validate scientifically much of their teaching about diet. Personnel from the Loma Linda University Medical Center repeatedly shared their expertise with hospitals and physicians in developing countries–India and China, for example–to improve medical training procedures. In some cases these connections facilitated a medical education for Adventist students in emerging countries by enabling them to study in their own universities rather than to spend considerably more money to enroll in Loma Linda. Exchange agreements with health-care centers brought physicians from other parts of the world to learn new techniques at the Adventist center in California.

## The Meaning and Role of Adventist Universities

The Adventist university was a milestone that denominational education did not reach by happenstance. Its place in Adventist education became a much discussed topic, frequently in the context of how to reconcile it with denominational educational goals that church leaders for decades had associated with the virtues of simple and limited schools. At earlier stages of denominational institutions, they were prone to discourage advanced education on the basis of how they understood Ellen White's example and counsel, but a newer generation also quoted her in support of graduate schools and universities. One of the most oft-cited passages was her statement in 1889 that selected students should attend "leading institutions of learning," which many others had also interpreted as counsel favoring postbaccalaureate education.[19]

Ellen White also advocated a well educated and cultured ministerial corps, prepared to reach all social strata of the public. This advice took on new dimensions when church leaders applied it to the late twentieth century. With increasing clarity Adventist educators had come to see the unity of knowledge and were quick to point out that possessing information about the universe, whether in the arts or the sciences, is ultimately an intellectual highway to spiritual understanding.

In 1955 Keld J. Reynolds, who was to become the first dean of Loma Linda's graduate school, told an assembly of medical students and faculty at CME that the American university was a blend of professional training and traditional arts and sciences, and in view of the secularism invading western education, especially in Europe, the Adventist medical school had a unique opportunity to inculcate values of faith with learning. Seven years later he advised his colleagues at Loma Linda University that as Adventists were entering into two ventures of graduate education, "it is imperative that the church know what it is doing. Before that, it is imperative that we know what we are doing, and why we are doing it, and what results we hope to achieve."[20]

Reynolds admonished universities to keep their objectives always in focus, reminding them that they were to foster investigative attitudes and that the intellectual horizons of students must broaden while their immediate studies became more centralized. He warned against the temptation of watering down postbaccalaureate study and weakening the graduate degree.

Richard Hammill, whom historian Emmett K. VandeVere describes as perhaps the one who had "explored the need for, and the concept of, a Seventh-day Adventist university more than any of his fellow educators,"[21] caught the essence of a university when he declared it is an institution dedicated to the *discovery* of knowledge in contrast to a four-year college where the primary goal is to *transmit* information.

"University studies," Hammill wrote, "are far different from the concept held by some that such studies are just an additional year or so of college. The program of study in a good university must involve an entirely different approach on the part of both the teacher and the student." University students, he elaborated, must not be content just to sit at the feet of their teachers, and university teachers must not be content just to read books. Both must reach beyond the borders of what is known in order to *contribute* to the body of knowledge about humanity and the world. Hammill believed that a university is a place for asking questions and that both teachers and students must learn by constantly examining and inquiring.[22]

Godfrey T. Anderson, for fourteen years president successively of CME and Loma Linda University, added that as seekers for truth scholars were the *sine qua non* of a genuine university. Their search creates a "priesthood of a scholar," he said, and "all truth is God's truth." In Anderson's view the "scholar is the enemy of all tricks, all humbug, all sham, all pretense, all phoniness." Scholars relate to truth with honesty. "This is the kind of scholarship which makes a university respectable."[23]

Those who initiated Adventism's first ventures into universities clearly understood the implications of the term *university* in the context of educational practice in the United States. Before Adventist universities went into operation the sole academic responsibility of college teachers was to offer classes, usually so many that to engage in scholarly investigations was a rare phenomenon. Faculty pursued research as personal projects if they pursued it at all. The fact that Adventist teachers seldom conducted serious research substantiated Hammill's assertion that colleges characteristically transmitted information rather than discovered it.

The generation of Hammill, Reynolds, and Anderson intended to launch a new era in Adventist education by designing institutions that would, by policy, support scholarly investigation. Hammill predicted that instructional loads for teachers would become smaller to allow time for research. Larger budgets for investigation materials and investments in libraries would become routine. Publication facilities to make known scholarly findings by university professors would become a necessity. This new era would measure graduate degrees by their qualitative difference from baccalaureate classes rather than simply by the number of hours spent in a classroom. It envisioned graduate students and faculty more as a community of scholars rather than a campus of lecturers and listeners.

Notwithstanding some significant research by faculty at the denomination's new universities, the campuses did not evolve into research institutions commonly understood in American education. Postbaccalaureate education at Andrews, La Sierra, and Loma Linda universities focused on preparing professionals in ministry, education, medicine, dentistry, and health-related fields rather than scholarly investigation. Professors were teachers first and researchers second.

But in keeping with original intentions the policies of Adventist universities encouraged scholarly investigations and contributed to those projects with both time and money. No longer was an Adventist researcher a unique specie. Loma Linda most nearly achieved the status of a research university by receiving millions of dollars annually in grant money for the purpose of scientific studies.[24] These changes produced a sharp distinction from higher education as Adventists had known it in the past.

Adventist graduate education did not begin with the advent of denominational universities, nor did it continue only on those campuses. Even before and continuing through the era of the joint university campuses at La Sierra and Loma Linda, graduate education at Pacific Union College and Walla Walla College remained but did not expand. By the end of the 1990s several Adventist colleges in the United States were offering master's degrees, most often in education, but in other scattered fields as well, almost exclusively in fields of professional studies. Some of them changed their name to university, primarily for marketing reasons, but they did not embody an appreciable advancement in scholarly goals which the generation of Reynolds, Hammill and Anderson had visualized as appropriate for a university.

Another question about Adventist graduate education was the extent to which it resolved the problem of satisfying accreditation criteria by offering graduate degrees to upgrade the credentials of denominational teachers. In 1929 W. E. Howell rationalized the original recommendation for an Adventist graduate-level institution by arguing that the church could select a few of its more promising and dependable educators and send them to the proposed school to earn master's degrees, thus meeting the demands of accrediting bodies. Denominational schools could then continue operating, unhampered, as training schools for workers.

Events did not allow such a simplistic resolution to the accreditation problem. More than thirty years elapsed between the recommendation for a graduate school and its actual launching date. During that time educational standards veered upward steeply. After World War II and onward, many Adventist college professors taught on the strength of a master's degree, but the doctorate become the standard credential and college administrations turned up the pressure to improve the ratio of doctorates on their faculties. When the universities went into operation it had become clear that Adventist education could not afford a broad spectrum of doctoral programs or even very many respectable master's degrees in academic fields.

Additionally, to avoid academic inbreeding, accrediting bodies advocated an institutional faculty representing degrees from diverse institutions rather than a single university. This unwritten law of accreditation made it unwise for Adventist college teachers to depend on one or even two denominational universities for their degrees. The result was doctoral programs on only a limited scale at Loma Linda, La Sierra and Andrews to meet denominational needs, primarily in theology, pastoral ministry, education and biology.

The principle of academic inbreeding did not apply to elementary or secondary schools. Credentials based on graduate degrees from any accredited institution satisfied state departments of education to which the lower schools were responsible. Secondary teachers could earn master's degrees in a small number of substantive fields at Loma Linda and Andrews, but the number of these options declined from a variety that was already limited, making it necessary for many Adventist teachers to attend non-Adventist graduate schools.

In offering doctoral studies in professional education Adventist universities made one of their most significant impacts by providing training for superintendents of education and administrators, although some who earned doctorates in education found employment in college departments of education on Adventist campuses. Many teachers in elementary grades studied for master's degrees at Adventist universities with financial support from their sponsoring conferences. A limited number of graduates from the Seminary's doctoral programs also taught in college departments of theology, and graduate programs in nursing furnished some teachers for Adventist nurses' training courses. Beyond teaching, the ministry, and nursing, graduate degrees in a variety of other professions, ranging from public health to business and architecture, gave young Adventists the chance to prepare for a career on a denominational campus. Regardless of these achievements, Adventist graduate education did not develop the dimension of what it was in large universities.

Some have argued that the heavy stress on graduate education in the professions combined with the decline of the initial emphasis on the philosophy of graduate education as Hammill and his contemporaries saw it has perpetuated the traditional Adventist utilitarian view of education. Seventh-day Adventists have never had either the will or the wherewithal to establish universities committed to the exploration of ideas. In many ways they have paralleled the trend among most Christian denominations that operate colleges and universities with the belief that erudition becomes valuable only when it has a pragmatic application. Historian Mark A. Noll has expanded on this notion in *The Scandal of the Evangelical Mind*, suggesting that "evangelicals do not, characteristically, look to the intellectual life as an arena in which to glorify God because, at least in America, our history has been pragmatic, populist, charismatic, and technological more than intellectual."[25]

Perhaps the educators who founded the Adventist university overstated their case, but it is worth remembering that higher education in the United States has also followed a utilitarian trend beginning in the nineteenth century. At that time practical education was regarded as reform. Yet, for all of its utilitarianism, the intellectual level of Adventist higher education rose substantially because of the Adventist university and its influence on the colleges. Within the Adventist world, research occurred, investigators published their findings, and scholars contributed to the body of knowledge about the universe. The university transformed the character of Adventist education because it represented the conviction held by a generation of educators in the 1950s that by more emphasis on critical thinking and whatever investigation was feasible, truth would ultimately strengthen, not disappear.

According to one line of reasoning Adventist universities in North America were the culmination of the accreditation controversy. Resistance to regulation had been powerful. Many church leaders saw accreditation as truckling to secular authority, but in the end more reasoned voices prevailed. Providing qualified teachers as measured by a recognized standard was a valid explanation in its own right and conformed to Ellen White's enunciation of the principle, long before Adventist universities were born, of academic preparation appropriate to the professional and intellectual needs of the church.[26]

Adventist universities helped to change denominational education by leading the trend for a greater sense of professionalism. Through the latter half of the twentieth century an increasingly higher number of graduates entered the broader job market rather than church employment; consequently, the belief that denominational schools were to provide competitive academic experiences took on new meaning. As a result, in their student recruitment campaigns, Adventist colleges and universities found themselves compared with secular institutions.

## Adventist Universities Spread

The trend toward universities did not end with Andrews and Loma Linda. University status spread to the world divisions, beginning in 1973 when Colegio Vocacional y Profesional in Montemorelos, Mexico converted to Montemorelos University. By the end of the twentieth century thirty Adventist institutions in nine of the eleven divisions were classified as universities, many of them offering graduate degrees. In contrast to the United States where the term *university* carried no legal significance, elsewhere the term symbolized official recognition as a degree-granting institution in most of the other countries. For Adventist schools that received this recognition, the status of university was mandatory.

Most of these universities were in developing countries. With their new degree-granting authority their mission was to become a local source for higher education which would avoid sending future denominational employees half way around the world to the United States to earn a degree. Thus, research was not central to their mission although it did not inherently conflict with their purpose. In part, these young institutions earned professional reputations by helping to establish academic respectability in the nation-building process. By acquiring university status they represented a maturing educational establishment both for the denomination and society at large.

Adventist universities were institutions of varied character. However widespread they became, the Adventist world continued to recognize the campuses in Michigan and California as the unofficial academic centers in the denomination, but the development of other universities provided legitimization of Adventist education that the former colleges and training schools lacked.[27]

Both Andrews and Loma Linda universities were and continued to be General Conference institutions with General Conference personnel chairing their boards and subsidies from the General Conference supporting their operations. Denominational needs determined their roles, which meant that while they entered the circle of universities their purposes remained limited. It was never the intention of the church to compete with the ivy league, but within the range of their institutional missions the goal of both institutions was to excel. As they stood on the threshold of the twenty-first century, the universities could look back upon approximately forty years of tradition-building which, on occasion, had caused both debate and controversy, but without denial, had added a new chapter to Adventist education and helped to shape denominational education in the world fields as well.

---

[1]Kern to Seminary Board, 1940 (no specific date), AST, RG 51; College Bible and History Teachers to J. L. McElhany, August 23, 1940.

[2] Charles E. Weniger, "The Seminary Comes of Age," (*The Journal of True Education*, June 1954), pp. 36, 37; *General Conference Bulletin*, 1946, no. 7. pp. 166-168.

[3]General Conference minutes, October 30, 1944.

[4]Ibid., July 1, October 26, November 11, 1954.

[5]Richard Hammill, "New Developments in Adventist Graduate Education," (*Journal of True Education*, February 1957), p. 3. Also see General Conference minutes, April 5, 1955; Ronald Knott, "For a Beginning, 'Most Satisfactory'," (*Journal of Adventist Education*, February-March 1983), p. 22.

[6]General Conference minutes, October 28, 1956.

[7]The minutes of the various university planning committees, 1956 through 1958, are found in AST, RG 51.

[8]For a colorful account of the merger, see VandeVere, *Wisdom Seekers*, pp. 243-251.

[9]For the story of Loma Linda University, see *From Vision to Reality 1905-1980* (Loma Linda, CA: Loma Linda University, 1980), and Carol Small, ed. *Diamond Memories* (Loma Linda, CA: Alumni Association, School of Medicine, 1984).

[10]General Conference minutes, October 30, 1944.

[11]Ibid., October 22, 1954.

[12]Ibid.; ibid., January 25, 1955.

[13]Ibid., April 14, October 30, 1944; October 26, 1948.

[14]Ibid., October 25, 1957; October 24, 1958.

[15]Ibid., October 25, 1959.

[16]Ibid., October 24, 1958; October 8, 1962; October 17, 1963.

[17]Ron Graybill, "Loma Linda–a multiversity or a health science university?" (*Spectrum*, v.19, no. 5 1989), pp. 2-7; John Whitehair, "Loma Linda put on probation for two years," (*Ibid.*, no. 4), p. 62; Pacific *Union Recorder*, March 5, 1990, May 21, 1990; General Conference minutes, August 30, 1990.

[18]For an insight into the work of the heart team, see Herbert Ford, *Affair of the Heart* (Nashville, TN: Southern Publishing Association, 1970).

[19]Ellen White, *Testimonies*, v. 5, pp. 583, 584. See A. L. White's background material about the same statement as it applied to European schools. *Ellen White*, v. 3, *The Lonely Years*, pp. 368, 369.

[20]Keld J. Reynolds, "'Universitas'–The Idea of Higher Education," (*Journal of True Education*, October 1956), pp. 16-18; Reynolds, "Patterns of Graduate Education," (*Ibid.*, October and December 1962), pp. 7-9, 30 and 19-22.

[21]VandeVere, *Wisdom Seekers*, p. 254.

[22]Richard Hammill, "What Is a University?" (*Focus*, January-February 1965), pp. 1-3.

[23]Godfrey T. Anderson, "The Christian Scholar and the Church," (*Spectrum*, winter 1969), pp. 7-14.

[24]Leslie R. Martin and James R. Wilson of La Sierra University discuss the benefits of research in "The Critical Role of Research in Adventist Education," (*Journal of Adventist Education*, April/May 2002), pp. 37-40.

[25]Mark A. Noll, *The Scandal of the Evangelical Mind* (Grand Rapids: William B. Erdmanns Publishing Company, 1994), p. 55.

[26]Ellen White, *Testimonies*, v. 5, pp. 583, 584.

[27]*World Report 2000* provides a list of Adventist universities, division by division.

*Chapter 16*

# Higher Education in Asia and the Pacific

Developing training schools outside North America into a system of postsecondary schools became one of the primary issues in Adventist education after World War II. The driving force in this movement was a determination to furnish recognized credentials, first to ministers in order to fulfill public expectations for formal preparation of clergymen, and often to teachers to comply with legal requirements in the teaching profession. The trend evolved unevenly, but the stress was ordinarily on ministerial education, in which the General Conference maintained a strong, controlling hand based on actions beginning in 1918. This authority remained a critical element in the transition from training school to degree-granting institution.

## Theological Education outside the United States

Except for Philippine Union College which became a degree-granting institution in the mid-1930s, training schools represented the highest level of education in the rest of the Adventist world until after World War II, although a score or more began offering limited post-secondary classes during the interim years. Occasional students from the world fields journeyed to the United States to attend a college, but only a few could afford the expense and the time. Many training schools served union constituencies and developed a local character, but others cultivated an international complexion because they were education centers for larger regions or General Conference divisions and drew students from different countries.

Worker-training courses, usually meaning ministerial education, followed a denominational-institutional design rather than a systematic and recognized pattern for baccalaureate degrees. Training schools could issue diplomas to students graduating from these courses but these documents were of limited value outside the denominational employment market. As the post-World War II era advanced the Adventist Board of Regents granted an increasing number of institutions the authority to offer four-year degrees in theology, but until the schools received official recognition by the appropriate government agency, these degrees still lacked credibility. Schools sometimes earned government approval for specific programs, such as teacher-preparation, which validated the credential of graduates in education, but ministerial students were the ones most often left with no recognition.

All of this meant that the legal validity of diplomas varied from place to place. The situation could become especially complicated for training schools that served an international constituency. Students from one country who enrolled in post-secondary courses in a neighboring land needed assurance that the institution was recognized if their diplomas were to mean anything in their home country. On the basis of denominational reciprocity, the Seminary would accept these degrees as preparation for graduate study, but this was an in-house arrangement that did not guarantee official recognition outside Adventist circles. Degrees based on denominational approval did not equate to government recognition.

The Theological Seminary touched Adventist education at its most tender spot, ministerial training, which became a key factor in elevating training schools to recognized, degree-granting institutions. One of the stated aims of the Seminary was to provide advanced education for church workers around the globe, but because training schools did not offer the necessary prerequisites for graduate education, most personnel from the world fields were eligible only for non-degree, inservice courses.

Coupled with this deficiency was the fact that during the early years of the Seminary many ministers from North America did not have time to complete a master's degree. These conditions accounted for the tendency of the Seminary to function as an inservice center rather than a true postbaccalaureate institution. Refresher classes were better than none at all and they had a unifying effect on the Adventist ministry, but students who completed them had little more than their transcripts to validate their academic experience inasmuch as they did not fulfill a defined program of studies.

The practical effect of graduate programs in theology at the Seminary was a widening gap between North American institutions and training schools in the world fields. In North America ministerial education was synonymous with a baccalaureate degree which earned even more strength after the granting institution achieved accreditation, while in the world fields most training schools fell short of the degree. This difference became even more pronounced in 1953 when the Seminary raised its entrance requirements to restrict enrollment to graduate-level students, which effectively cut off students from most of the world fields unless they held a degree that the Seminary would accept by reciprocity. Unless training schools around the world converted into recognized degree-granting institutions, pastors and ministerial students in most of the world fields would have to content themselves with less than a baccalaureate education and would not benefit from the Seminary.

## Transition from Training School to Higher Education

The first institution outside the United States to earn degree-granting authority was Philippine Union College which took the step even before the Seminary began. Spicer Missionary College in India was next in 1944 while World War II was in its final stages. By 1973 every major training school outside North America that survived World War II became a four-year, post-secondary school. As Adventist membership increased, new tertiary schools appeared. By the end of the year 2000 the chain of post-secondary denominational institutions around the world lengthened to ninety-four, seventy-nine of which were outside North America. During the final quarter of the century some of these institutions inaugurated graduate education.[1]

Although circumstances differed from institution to institution, some general patterns emerged. Schools received their status as four-year, postsecondary schools by General Conference authorization which usually applied to the theology curriculum first and secondly to teacher-preparation courses. It was not the rule, but from time to time schools offered postsecondary classes unofficially before authorization came. On the basis of reciprocity graduates of these schools could enroll in the Seminary.

The majority of Adventist postsecondary schools appeared in the developing countries, most of which had weak educational traditions. A mentality of self-awakening permeated these societies. In most cases their new sense of nationhood fostered education as a means to improve their standing in the sisterhood of nations, but sometimes governments were cautious about recognizing Adventist schools, wanting to make sure that they were compatible to their strategy for nation building.

That this mood would impact the Adventist world was a given. The growth of Adventist higher education around the world, while under the general oversight of the General Conference Department of Education, also occurred at the pleasure of host governments that functioned within the framework of post-World War II nationalism. Whether they planned it or not, Adventist schools in the developing world often became instruments of nationhood.

General Conference approval may have permitted institutions to grant degrees in ministerial education, but governments did not uniformly recognize them. Holders of these unrecognized degrees encountered little difficulty as long as they remained in denominational employ, primarily pastoral work, but their careers could suffer if conventional wisdom expected pastors to study in professionally recognized institutions. Students seeking degrees in careers that governments regulated were at a disadvantage unless the schools they attended had acquired official status. Teaching was one of the most frequent examples of a regulated profession.

In some instances schools could not grant theology degrees independently from government approval; in such cases ministerial education lagged. Some schools attempted to compensate by affiliating with a North American Adventist college. This practice provided a vehicle for credible degrees, but these arrangements were not always feasible because regional accrediting associations in the United States sometimes attached conditions to their approval that would effectively block any link between an American campus and a struggling school in a developing country.

Educational jargon sometimes added confusion. Many training schools took the title of *college*, which simply meant a school in most countries outside the United States. As used in the United States *college* and *university* were not synonymous but both referred to postsecondary institutions with degree-granting authority through the doctoral level. In some countries both colleges and universities were postsecondary but universities had a legal right to grant degrees while colleges did not. Again, perhaps a college was authorized to offer postsecondary classes but a university was much larger with a larger number of academic fields. Also, different understandings of secondary education affected the definition of postsecondary education.

*Typical of a new generation of Seventh-day Adventist schools sprouting up after World War II was Mount Klabat College in Indonesia, beginning in 1965. This 1969 photograph shows faculty housing and West Hall during the early phases of campus construction. By the year 2000 enrollment on this campus reached about 1,600.*

Besides these conditions education became more technical after World War II and denominational leaders did not always sense a clear direction in handling this complex mix as they sought to systematize denominational education. Because Adventist higher education was born in the United States, North American education became the measuring rod to determine equivalent values of academic credit when students transferred from one country to another. With the advent of world institutions that deliberately attracted students from around the globe–Andrews and Loma Linda universities–it became even more necessary that baccalaureate degrees from schools in all world fields were comparable to each other.

In 1972 the General Conference Department of Education published the first of four editions of *Patterns of Seventh-day Adventist Education* which, among other data, detailed the levels of instruction, program by program, in Adventist schools around the world. With the advent of degree-granting authority in institutions in the world fields, *Patterns* became less needful, and the Department of Education initiated *World Report: Adventist Education Around the World*, which summarized statistically the categories of Adventist schools and their curricula, division by division. These publications demonstrated that the Adventist accrediting system had generated a similarity of educational practices in denominational postsecondary education. Against this complex background some selected examples demonstrate the historical development and variety of Adventist higher education in Asia and the South Pacific.

*Middle East College, Beirut, Lebanon, founded in 1939 as a junior college, was the only Seventh-day Adventist postsecondary institution in the Muslim Middle East. In 1946 it became a four-year institution and at one time served as the only college in the Afro-Mideast Division.*

## Graduate Education in the Philippines

The first request to offer graduate education outside the United States came from Philippine Union College in 1939 where Adventist education had developed rapidly along North American lines partly because of four decades of United States presence in the islands. The intent was to organize a graduate school to offer credentials for nationals who would teach at the college. General Conference leaders were not ready to take this step and nothing came from the request, but after it reappeared in 1948 and again in 1952, church leaders authorized a limited amount of graduate study during the summer and stipulated that a full graduate program should follow only after the institution underwent a thorough self-study.[2]

Between the original request in 1939 and its repetition in 1948 a world war interrupted the school and the Philippines gained independence. In 1949 Philippine Union College planted an extension program on an academy campus in the southern island of Mindanao. This school eventuated into Mountain View College, but at the time it offered only junior college classes, but the need for credentialed postsecondary teachers was increasing. National leadership took over Philippine Union College about the same time the third request to offer graduate classes reached the General Conference in 1952. One of the prominent issues at PUC during the 1950s was curriculum development, and after adding several degree programs, the school received authorization from both the Philippine government and the General Conference in 1957 to offer a master's degree in education.

With enrollment soaring above a thousand and students enrolling from all regions of Asia, Philippine Union College was an unquestioned fulfillment of the announcement by W. E. Nelson, General Conference secretary of education, at the 1936 General Conference when he declared that "It is planned that this school shall also be the training center for advanced work for all countries in the Far Eastern Division."[3] Candidates for the new master's degrees began graduating in 1959; by 1964 the General Conference approved a graduate degree in religion, which allowed Adventist ministers in Asia to earn a master's degree at considerably less cost and trouble compared to spending time at the Theological Seminary in the United States.

In view of the unique role PUC played in Adventist education in

Asia, an organized seminary and graduate school became common talk even at General Conference levels, and in 1972 a newly organized Seventh-day Adventist Theological Seminary graduated its first student. A year later the Association of Theological Schools in South East Asia accredited the graduate program. The seminary was still an arm of Philippine Union College, but it 1978 when the school moved from a suburb of Manila to Silang, an hour below the national capital, it separated from the college to become an institution of the Far Eastern Division. Accordingly it changed its name to Asia Adventist Theological Seminary but also functioned as a graduate school. Its new title indicated that its service area extended far beyond the boundaries of the Philippines to serve all of Asia.[4]

Before the move to Silang an arrangement with Loma Linda University introduced a master's degree in public health, but for the most part the graduate program developed on its own. In its new location and with its new identity the seminary thrived. In 1988 seminary Dean Werner Vyhmeister added a doctoral program to its lengthening list of graduate degrees, but the impracticality of operating two institutions on a single campus was becoming obvious. Philippine Union College was daily stung by the loss of its graduate program because it hosted the seminary on its campus and shared common facilities. When friction and misunderstandings became too serious to pass off as incidental, moving the seminary away from the college appeared to be the best resolution. In 1989 dignitaries from the government and the church broke ground for a new campus for the seminary about fifteen miles from PUC.

*Kata Ragoso, a son of a native chief on the island of New Georgia, Solomon Islands, was a product of Adventist schools. He provided effective leadership to Seventh-day Adventists during World War II and helped to translate the Bible into Masori.*

Two years before groundbreaking a presidential decree enabled the seminary and graduate school to reorganize under a new name, the Adventist International Institute of Advanced Studies. As an international institute, AIIAS fell under different regulatory legislation than universities or colleges, which gave administrators more flexibility in employing non-Filipino faculty and institutional officers. The new graduate program caught on handily and AIIAS attracted students from many parts of Asia and also offered extension classes on Adventist post-secondary campuses from Bangladesh to Korea.

By 1990 AIIAS had expanded its offerings to thirteen master's degrees in education, business, institutional administration, nursing administration, public health, and religion, and three doctorates from the seminary, including a doctor of philosophy degree. Plans were under way for doctoral programs in education. Also in 1990 AIIAS graduated its first students from the graduate school and its first doctorates. Six years later the school became a General Conference institution. Although some Philippine Adventists persisted in seeing AIIAS as a Filipino school, it was designed for an international clientele, but operated on Philippine soil.[5]

The development of a separate graduate education program was a bitter pill that became totally unpalatable for Philippine Union College after AIIAS moved to a separate campus. Practically speaking, the college reverted to an undergraduate institution operated by the North Philippine Union, a status that was several cuts below the reputation the school had developed since the mid-1930s as the leading Adventist school in Asia. AIIAS functioned without an undergraduate base on its campus, but the Adventist colleges in the region, including PUC, understood that they would serve in that role. The graduate library, which the Far Eastern Division had bankrolled for the graduate school, went to the new campus, but PUC received classroom and residential buildings that had once belonged to the seminary.

Arguably, Philippine Union College reverted to undergraduate status when the graduate school and seminary organized into a separate institution several years prior to opening the new AIIAS campus. The two entities functioned on the same grounds, which benefitted the college because students continued to gravitate to the campus from many parts of Asia. Filipinos easily perceived PUC as a postbaccalaureate school, which it earlier was. The move of AIIAS to a separate campus was painful, not only because PUC had become an undergraduate school, but because it no longer enjoyed the reputation that the graduate programs had brought.

Soon after the break, Philippine Union College set plans in motion to become a university in its own right and recover the reputation it had lost. In order to meet the criteria for universities set by the National Accreditation Federation, Philippine Union College improved its ratio of doctorates to twenty percent and established a research center. Government approval in 1996 resulted in a name change to Adventist University of the Philippines, or AUP. By the time of this change, the school had restored its graduate program and was offering master's degrees in education, religion, biology, nursing, and business. In 2002 it announced a doctoral program in science education with emphases in biology and math, and another doctorate in education with fields in administration, psychology, and English.[6]

The desire by Philippine Union College to regain what it saw as its lost status was neither a secret nor merely a whim of the moment but rather an urge to preserve its traditions. Decades previously, church

*The major classroom building on the campus of the Adventist International Institute of Advanced Studies, Silang, Cavite, Philippines. This unique Seventh-day Adventist institution offers only graduate degrees and employs an international faculty. Its enrollment is largely Asian.*

leaders had supported its development into the focal point for Adventist education in Asia. The original motivation for graduate education in the Philippines was the need for credentialed teachers. In the revived graduate program at AUP, professional education was still the cornerstone of advanced studies.

University administrators were enthusiastic about the new university status and graduate education, but there were doubters. Six decades since Nelson's declaration to the General Conference session in 1936 had brought changes in both professional needs and denominational organization that required different solutions than those conceived in the 1930s, hence the separated AIIAS. One prominent question asked if an institution with less than a fourth of its faculty holding doctorates and a library with fewer than 40,000 volumes was competent to offer doctoral programs on the scale that AUP advertised. Others argued that AUP was reinventing the wheel by offering programs in competition to a sister institution only fifteen miles away, even though the two campuses were accountable to different administrative units of the church.

The financial strength of the school was also in question. Since the seminary and graduate school moved to a new campus AUP no longer benefitted from subsidies that came from the Far Eastern Division, or in its reorganized form, the Southern Asia Pacific Division. The university was one of three tertiary institutions in the North Philippine Union Mission, and it remained to be seen whether this single parent body could muster enough financial support for the ambitious program that the school contemplated.

## Sahmyook University

Adventist higher education made astonishing advancements in South Korea. Asian turmoil had scarred this country–more than three decades of Japanese occupation, cut athwart at the thirty-eighth parallel after World War II and divided into two politically hostile camps, each a symbol in the parrying contest between communist and capitalist philosophies. In 1949 the Adventist training school reestablished itself on a 200-acre rural site northeast of Seoul, only to be driven out less than a year later by invading forces from North Korea. When the school reoccupied its ravaged campus in 1951 the Korean War was still see-sawing along the North-South frontier, only a stone's throw away, as it were.[7]

Reestablishment also brought a new name, Korean Union Training School, which the Koreans called Sahmyook Seminary, a term analogous to the Adventist concept of educating the head, the heart, and the hand. Three years later the government recognized it as a postsecondary institution and in 1961 the Ministry of Education authorized it to grant degrees in theology. Within another year the Korean government granted permission to organize industrial programs as part of a junior college curriculum specializing in agriculture and home economics.

While school leaders felt blessed, they had not yet received approval by the denominational Board of Regents either as a degree-granting or even a postsecondary institution. These events meant that Korean Union College, as it came to be known, had advanced more at the lead of the South Korean Ministry of Education than the General Conference Department of Education. But the church could not easily refuse friendly gestures from the government, which left little choice for the Korean Union than to upgrade the school as rapidly as possible to satisfy the accrediting criteria of the Board of Regents. In 1964 the General Conference issued its approval to KUC as a four-year postsecondary school.

By the end of the decade the campus was well into a transforming construction program. The 1970s brought curriculum broadening. After the government approved the teacher-preparation program in 1967, the college added an English language department, followed by a nurses' education course in 1973 as part of the junior college. Before the decade ended the junior college organized departments in dairy science and food and nutrition. Building on older courses in home economics and agriculture, the college developed departments in business and pharmacy.

Enrollment gains required more construction which left no questions about institutional aims. In 1985 a new library opened with shelf space for 350,000 volumes and seating for a thousand students. In the same year more than 2,100 students enrolled, making Korean Union College second only to Loma Linda University as the largest postsecondary campus in the Adventist world.

*The School of Theology, Sahmyook University, Seoul, Korea. At the beginning of the twenty-first century, Sahmyook University had become the largest tertiary institution operated by Seventh-day Adventists with an enrollment approximating 5,500 students.*

Expansion in the 1990s continued at a phenomenal pace. Typifying its advancement, the institution changed its name in 1992 to Sahmyook University. Academic departments proliferated in both the traditional arts and sciences as well as contemporary vocations, embracing among other fields, computer science, environmental landscaping, and international language. In 1993 the university opened a branch on the Russian island of Sakhalin.

Government approval in 1980 of a master's degree in theology was the first step toward a graduate school that began the same year. By 1998 the graduate school was offering master's degrees in pharmacy, nursing, chemistry and biology. Government recognition of the graduate school of theology as a seminary came in 1989, which enabled the university to offer a doctor of philosophy in theology. The government also approved a school of management in 1996 as part of graduate-level offerings.

At the beginning of the twenty-first century enrollment exceeded all previous expectations and gave Sahmyook University the distinction of being the largest Seventh-day Adventist school in the world. In round numbers 5,500 students attended, 2,000 in two-year programs, 3,000 in four-year degree programs, and 500 in the graduate school. About eighty-five percent of the faculty held doctorates. Not only had institutional growth been spectacular within the Adventist community, it had also caught the eye of the government. In 1994, when enrollment was still less than 3,000, the government accrediting agency rated Sahmyook ninth among all institutions in the country, both public and private, based on an evaluation of its facilities, faculty, program, and finances.

Trends in Korean life played a role in developing Sahmyook University, and the history of the institution suggests that school officials consciously sought to contribute to a new Korea. One matter revolved around the increase in the Christian population. At the close of the twentieth century South Korea was still predominantly Buddhist, but it was nearly one fourth Christian. This development indicated that traditional religion was less important than the spirit of nationhood in the South Korean mentality, a mood that paved the way for Adventism. Sahmyook's step-by-step advancement with government approval empowered the school to grow rapidly, not only as a theological center but also as an institution that served the needs of the Korean college-age population.

Sahmyook's speedy growth to become a recognized university offering a variety of graduate degrees was more a response to national needs than a calculated design by denominational leaders to develop a powerful university, but Korean Adventists had succeeded in planning an institution that conformed to national standards while retaining an Adventist character. While adjusting to Korean needs, Sahmyook reached back to its beginnings to substantiate claims to have helped to shape the new Korea by introducing progressive ideas into education, among them coeducation, professional training for women, dormitory housing for students, vocational and technical education, and the notion of service as an educational goal.

An important aspect of this process was the location of the campus. Originally, the surroundings were rural and in conformity with the denominational tradition of planting training schools in the country. Agriculture was part of its program, and even after the institution gained official recognition, the junior college curricula centered on the dairy and the arts of homemaking.

But South Korea became an industrial force to be reckoned with. By the late 1960s and early 1970s the economy was generating unprecedented prosperity. Technology and other professional studies superseded agriculture as fields of study. Education became an item of high demand and with more wealth at their disposal Koreans found education more easily accessible. As Seoul's population spread to the gate of Sahmyook's campus, the school lost its rural character but adapted to national trends. At the beginning of the twenty-first century the agricultural program still existed in abbreviated form, but the vocational emphasis was on preparing students for urban living.

Church leaders and university officials alike agreed that one of the contributing factors of Sahmyook's growth was its location on the edge of the national capital. Korean students, they argued, would gravitate to the Adventist university from all parts of the country in order to attend an urban school but they would not enroll in an agricultural institution in the country.

University officials used these circumstances to serve evangelistic purposes. Kei Hoon Shin, a former president of Sahmyook University, once pointed out that in the new Korea the church had to devise means to take the gospel to Korean youth and that schools were the most effective way to accomplish that task.[8] As a result, evangelism developed into a major campus activity and Sahmyook became what some might call a mission university, a large, modernized edition of the traditional mission school.

By the end of the century the institution had become one of the most productive evangelistic agencies in Korea. Of the 5,500 students only about 10 percent lived in dormitories; the majority were commuters. Typically, about three-fourths of the freshmen enrolled as non-Adventists and were organized with other non-members into groups which became "parishes" for students in the School of Theology, who gave special attention to their spiritual needs. By the end of the 1990s this personal evangelism netted nearly a thousand baptisms each academic year. Evangelism also became a prominent part of the nursing school associated with Seoul Adventist Hospital where the majority of the 300 students also enrolled as non-Adventists, but at graduation about eighty percent had become members.

Adventist higher education at Sahmyook University differed from its counterpart at Adventist University of the Philippines. The Korean institution was more prone to cater to public needs and even though it had become a university, it tended to interpret its role as reminiscent of the traditional mission school. In the Philippines graduate education emerged from the need for credentialed teachers, and later pastors, whereas ministerial education was always the priority concern in Korea. A teacher-preparation program at Seoul figured prominently during the late 1960s, but by the end of the century this course attracted only a small proportion of the student population. The program may have dwindled, but it was effective. In the year 2000 Korean Adventists operated eight secondary and ten primary schools which required nearly 400 teachers. Every teacher in the system held certificates from both the state and the denomination.

The stress of Sahmyook's graduate school remained on the School of Theology, but taken as a whole, the university was geared to professional fields that did not necessarily lead to denominational employment. This tendency produced a similarity with colleges in the United States where students could prepare for an enlarging variety of careers.

## Trends in India

Probably no set of circumstances in Asia were more problematic than those that surrounded Spicer Missionary College in India. This institution had been a strong worker-training center that became a four-year postsecondary school but it did not have recognized degree-granting authority. Indian independence in 1947 gave rise to a powerful movement of national self-awareness and within the Adventist community the intention to convert the college into a recognized degree-granting institution developed into a priority goal for the Southern Asia Division. The education of ministers was an important part of the college program, but the campaign for recognition was also closely tied to the need for credentialed teachers in Adventist elementary and secondary schools, which were more numerous in India as compared to most world fields.[9]

These denominational schools maintained a strong Adventist identity, but they were poorly equipped and managed. The finger of responsibility pointed to Spicer where teachers trained. The prospects of ameliorating the teacher-preparation program at Spicer worsened when India tightened its regulation of education, requiring Adventist teachers to hold valid credentials which the Adventist school could not grant.

In 1959 R. S. Lowry, secretary of education in Southern Asia, tied all of the problems together into an impassioned call to improve the college at all costs. Based on his sense of the direction which independence was leading India, he was convinced that education at Spicer and in the lower schools was to be not only Adventist, it was also to be Indian, and that it must be professionalized to meet the increasingly higher educational goals of the new nation. Lowry viewed the situation as a crisis and singled out improvements at Spicer, including recognition for its programs, as the crucial point in church affairs in Southern Asia.

Recognition was not a new problem. The state government had consistently denied degree-granting authority for Spicer as it customarily did for all private institutions. Following a suggestion in 1956 to affiliate Spicer with an Adventist college in the United States, Duane Johnson, associate director of the General Conference Department of Education, cautioned that the American school should have unquestioned approval by its regional accrediting association and the word "missionary" must not be part of its name. After weeks of bandying the idea among themselves, educators in both India and the United States gave it up as infeasible.

Johnson's caveats revealed much about Indian independence. His warning to avoid the word missionary signaled that Indian leaders did not believe their country needed Christian missionaries to teach them values. India was notorious for poverty and illiteracy but it was also home for philosophical religion and a well-educated upper class. Intellectualism was not alien to the country. Some of India's best had been students in England's leading universities and had become the leaders of independence. Johnson's recommendation that unchallenged accreditation by an Adventist college was to be a precondition for affiliation with Spicer was a warning that Indian officialdom knew the meaning of valid higher education and that India was not opening itself as a market for imported, second rate education. Spicer Missionary College changed its name to Spicer Memorial College in 1955 to honor William A. Spicer, a recently deceased General Conference president who had spent mission time in India, but dropping the "missionary" from its name was an omen that the institution was in harmony with Indian moods.

Approval by the University of Poona became the next option, but it fizzled when the university laid down conditions, which in effect, would require Spicer to relinquish control of its Adventist identity in matters of curriculum and personnel. Although these conditions were according to policy, not a sinister plot to gain control of the campus, compliance was impossible for an Adventist institution. Without any means to provide recognized education to Indian Adventists, the source for teachers, nurses, and physicians would dry up, leaving much of the denomination's program leaderless. Almost as a corollary, Adventist youth, many of them children of church workers, began to avoid Spicer by enrolling in universities in large numbers to study for professions with no intention to prepare for denominational employment.

Some church leaders viewed this trend as a lack of loyalty to the church. After a six-week visit to Southern Asia in 1976, Ethel Young, associate director in the General Conference Department of Education, tersely recommended a requirement for all workers to send their children to denominational schools. As it would apply to elementary and even secondary levels, it was possible for church workers to comply, but Indian parents, denominational workers or not, could not force their children to attend a college that was an academic dead end for students except as they planned careers in some phase of denominational employment that did not require a recognized credential.

The problem was very complicated. One of its complexities was the commonly held view in India that schools were an effective evangelistic tool. R. S. Lowry, who became division president in 1962, instituted a practice of planting schools in as many communities as possible in order to establish an Adventist presence. Frequently these schools spawned companies of believers and eventually churches. Evangelistically, the schools were paying handsome dividends, but their increasing number only added to the problem of preparing credentialed teachers. Without teachers evangelism would suffer, and so the problems fed on each other.

One of the root issues in upgrading Spicer was the inability of Adventist workers to enter Indian universities for advanced studies because of their unrecognized degrees from the Adventist college. Enrolling in graduate programs in the United States was possible but required years of strenuous work. Moreover, the paucity of funds prevented church leaders in India from providing financial support to prospective Indian educators studying in American schools. When Spicer attempted to fill some of its teaching positions with missionaries, immigration authorities sometimes denied visas, but in spite of this obstacle some well qualified classroom professors made it to the campus, primarily from other Commonwealth countries.

That it would be possible to find a way even partially through this maze was something attributed to Lowry. Realizing that time was running out on the expatriate worker, he scraped up enough money to sponsor a handpicked cluster of promising Indian workers in North American graduate schools–not always Adventist institutions–on condition that they return to Southern Asia after acquiring a graduate degree. Among them was M. E. Cherian, a 1949 alumnus of Spicer, who earned two master's degrees, one at Andrews University and the other at the University of Maryland. After returning to India he enrolled in 1963 in the University of Poona to study for a doctorate in political science, the first Spicer graduate that the university admitted. At the same time he became president of Spicer.

Cherian's reputation broke the ice, and the University of Poona regularly began admitting Spicer graduates despite their unrecognized degrees. The university also began matriculating students with unrecognized degrees from at least two other Christian institutions. By 1990 nearly a hundred Spicer alumni were studying for master's degrees and twenty-five or more were engaged in doctoral studies in a wide variety of liberal arts and professional fields. Spicer and the Adventist community benefitted from this unexpected breakthrough, but the arrangement with the university was only a gentleman's agreement, and before the century ended the university withdrew Spicer from its most favored list, explaining that the presence of students from an unrecognized school proved to be an embarrassment. Students from the other Christian schools had already lost their enrollment privileges. Meanwhile, in 1980 an affiliation with Andrews University went into effect that enabled Indian students to enroll in graduate studies at Spicer in theology, education, and business. Some Spicer graduates also traveled to Andrews for doctoral studies and the Philippines for master's degrees.

In the field of medicine and health other breakthroughs occurred. Since the days of R. S. Lowry a special arrangement coupled with denominational financial contributions to the Christian Medical College in Vellore near Madras opened the way for Adventist students from India to study medicine in their own country with minimal cost. A similar affiliation with another Christian medical institution in the Punjab opened up more seats for Adventist medical and paramedical students. In 1984 an agreement between Loma Linda University and Kasturba Medical College near Manipal on the southwest coast of India set up a teacher exchange program between the two institutions and established a center for greater numbers of Adventist students to enroll in the physicians' course. By 1990 Adventist students at Kasturba branched into dentistry and pharmacy and students at Vellore were entering a variety of allied health fields and the sciences.

Despite these accomplishments the blanket recognition that would regularize Spicer's program proved as elusive as it had always been. The need for Adventist teachers in Adventist schools became even more acute as church membership soared in the latter years of the century and the number of denominational schools mushroomed. Spicer's inability to supply recognized credentials for teachers was a key factor that fed a trend to hire non-Adventist teachers. This practice became common in the 1980s. As the Southern Asia Division entered the twenty-first century nearly forty percent of the teachers in the elementary and secondary schools were not members of the church and approximately ninety percent of the students were not Adventists.

Sharp debate arose about the direction and purpose of Adventist education in India. Critics charged that Adventist schools had lost their identity and had become a public service instead of institutions where church members could send their children to study in a denominational environment. The high ratio of non-Adventist teachers generated doubt that the schools were genuinely Adventist, especially when occasionally non-Adventist teachers taught Bible classes. In the eyes of many the church had chosen financial stability over evangelism, for they believed that the primary purpose of these schools was to furnish operational funds to the church.

Defenders of the system admitted that Adventist schools were a public service, even a business, but argued that they were contemporary forms of the traditional mission school in which Adventist philosophy permeated irrespective of the high percentage of non-Adventist faculty. They pointed to membership growth that was ever spiraling higher than they had imagined even a decade and a half earlier as evidence that schools continued to be an effective evangelistic tool. The schools were a method to reach the homes of the middle and professional classes. Through them the denomination was gaining a reputation as one of the finest educational agencies in India in a manner similar to the reputation of denominational health-care units where neither the clientele nor the medical staff was restricted to church members.[10]

During the last years of the twentieth century Adventist higher education duplicated some of the trends in elementary and secondary schools. In quick succession five post-secondary schools sprang up, all evolving from Adventist high schools. In 2002 all but one were affiliated with local universities and thus advertised recognized programs. Somewhat analogous to the day schools, these colleges functioned as public service institutions, specializing in such professions as business, computer science, and allied health. Enrollment ranged from fewer than fifty to approximately 400, and in the largest schools the students were predominantly non-Adventist. Bible classes as Adventists knew them became elective courses.

These new ventures reflected a growing desire among Indian youth for professional education and the willingness of the Adventist community to contribute to change that was overtaking the country. It was against this background that the church's intellectual leaders in India insisted Adventist education must be understood.

Standing at the gate of the twenty-first century Adventist education in Southern Asia was thriving, but it undeniably differed from the traditional pattern of Adventist schools. It was inevitable that controversy would swirl around the question of whether or not denominational schools in India truly typified Adventist education. It was evident that protagonists on either side of the debate remained unconvinced by the others' arguments. Despite these issues, given India's fierce nationalism, forged in the crucible of independence, the church was blessed in retaining its educational heritage, a benchmark of its existence.

The condition of Adventist post-secondary education in India was mixed. The traditions of study and vocational experience continued to attract favorable attention. Despite their unrecognized education, Spicer graduates had long since earned the right to sit for external examinations which opened opportunities for them to enroll in other schools in India. At the beginning of a new century faculty at Spicer with master's degrees from these schools were a commonplace. About twenty percent of the faculty held doctorates from several different institutions, including Andrews University and AIIAS. More than twenty-five academic tracks led to bachelor's degrees, including a program in both western and indigenous music. Through affiliation Spicer offered graduate degrees in theology, education, and business and in 1996 the School of Religion introduced the doctor of ministry degree with an emphasis in missions, which placed cross-cultural evangelism at the top of its academic priorities.

Spicer's experience illustrated some of the issues that Adventist higher education faced in the developing world after World War II and the persistence that denominational educators needed in order to resolve them. Affiliations helped, but a maturing Indian democracy also produced improved conditions. Even though it lacked official recognition, Spicer was still atop the academic pyramid of denominational schools in India. Regularizing its program remained one of the critical questions in Adventist education in the subcontinent.

### Avondale

It was not Spicer but Australasian Missionary College, or AMC, that was the first school to affiliate with a denominational college in North America to compensate for its lack of official recognition. Except for students completing the two-year elementary education program accredited through the state of Victoria, graduates of AMC worked without recognized credentials because state governments in both Australia and New Zealand consistently denied degree-granting charters to private institutions. With a view of improving the theology program, the Board of Regents ranked AMC as a four-year post-secondary school in

1951, which did not change its official standing within the Australian system, but ministerial students could now earn the equivalent of a baccalaureate degree, although an unrecognized one.[11]

Because the Australian sequence required five years of secondary courses followed by three more at the post-secondary level, Australian Adventists concluded that an affiliation with a college in the United States would be the most effective way for students to earn a recognized four-year degree in theology. The affiliation was to be an adaptation of the practice by universities in the United States to conduct extension campuses combined with the policy of the University of London, which supervised students around the world in programs of external studies. In this case Australasian Missionary College would link to Pacific Union College whose faculty would go to Australia on temporary assignment to teach and oversee the curriculum that Australasian students followed.

The essence of affiliation was to design a course of study in Australia whose content and level of difficulty equated to degree requirements at Pacific Union College. By completing this program Australasian students would earn a four-year degree from PUC but take all of their classes in Australia. As it materialized, the affiliation agreement allowed AMC to retain its identity as an Australian school. Pacific Union College did not control the curriculum in Australia or demand that Australasian Missionary College meet accrediting standards of the same association which recognized PUC, which would have practically converted the Australian school into a North American institution.

In addition to ministerial education, the affiliation applied to the preparation of secondary teachers, where a gaping hole existed in the Australasian Adventist school system. Unlike AMC's recognized two-year elementary education program that furnished Adventist primary schools with credentialed teachers, the college had no authority to prepare students to teach in substantive areas in secondary schools. The result was a dearth of qualified teachers in Adventist high schools.

The affiliation with Pacific Union College went into effect in 1954 and lasted until 1990. It functioned well for theology students who were able to begin a sequence of studies coordinated with graduate studies at the Seminary, but prospective secondary teachers were still tied to the local certification system in which a degree from the United States carried less weight than one from Australia or New Zealand. Often teachers with education degrees from the Adventist college found it necessary to start over again by earning their credential a second time from a recognized school.

Two trends within Australia helped to resolve this problem. In their certification procedures state governments became more prescriptive which made Australian degrees much more advantageous. At the same time Australia eased its restrictions on professional schools, especially teacher-preparation institutions, by forming the Colleges of Advanced Education, an association that upgraded professional schools to degree-granting institutions. Long before the affiliation with Pacific Union College ended, Avondale College–newly renamed in 1963 from its older name, Australasian Missionary College–became a College of Advanced Education and in 1974 began offering an officially recognized bachelor of education degree. With the door opened, the school added degrees in business and nursing. But the system was still left wanting because Australian and New Zealand universities tended to withhold full recognition to graduates of a College of Advanced Education who enrolled for graduate studies.

For Adventist students in at least some professional fields this problem disappeared by the end of the twentieth century when Avondale expanded its programs to include master's degrees in business, education, nursing, and theology with all programs recognized by either New South Wales accrediting agencies or the Commonwealth Register. These curricular additions enabled Australasian students to earn recognized credentials in a variety of fields open for both denominational and private employment.

### A Summary of Asia and the Pacific

By the year 2000 the four General Conference divisions in Asia and the Pacific were operating twenty-seven post-secondary institutions located in Bangladesh, Myanmar, Indonesia, Taiwan, Hong Kong, Korea, Japan, the Philippines, and Fiji. Together these campuses reported more than 20,000 students. Programs in business claimed about 4,700; health, 2,800; and theology, 2,000, the total of these three fields amounted to almost half of the entire enrollment. The rest of the students registered in a wide variety of programs in the arts, sciences, vocations, and teaching.

The meaning of these statistics is clear. Since 1945 Adventist education had graduated from its training school status to become a major enterprise. The most academically advanced Adventist degrees were available in ministerial education and teaching, but the broad spectrum of fields indicated that denominational schools had become much like their predecessors in North America, campuses where students could prepare in an Adventist environment for a variety of careers.[12]

Other numbers indicate that the concept of the mission school did not die with the development of higher education. Approximately 6,900 non-Adventist students enrolled in the tertiary schools in Asia and the Pacific in the year 2000, and during that academic year almost 1,300 were baptized, which translates into a conversion rate of nineteen percent. Besides the level of instruction, the major difference between the pioneer mission school and the contemporary post-secondary institution was that the campuses were in the hands of nationals. Adventist educators in Asia and the Pacific were quick to admit flaws in their system, but the half century after 1945 had brought more change than they had envisioned.

---

[1]See Brown, *Chronology*, for the dates when training schools became four-year institutions. For statistics on tertiary schools, see *World Report 2000* (Silver Spring, MD: General Conference Department of Education, 2000).

[2]General Conference Minutes, November 30, 1939, April 27, 1948, February 21, 1952.

[3]*General Conference Bulletin*, 1936, no. 7. p. 149.

[4]*Review and Herald*, February 20, 1969, June 22, 1972, August 23, 1973, April 28, 1977; *Adventist Review*, July 6, 1978; *Academic Bulletin, 1998-2000*, Adventist International Institute of Advanced Studies; Minutes of the Seventh-day Adventist Theological Seminary–Far East, October 12, 1976, AST, RG 51.

[5]*Adventist Review*, August 11, 1988; Far Eastern Division *Outlook*, December 1988, February 1989, October 1990, March/April 1991; interviews: Oliver Koh, May 17, 2002; Julian Melgosa, May 18, 2002.

[6]*Adventist University of the Philippines Bulletin, 1997-2000*; interviews: Elizabeth Role, May 17, 2002; Liberato B. Moises, May 17, 2002; John Fowler, May 19, 2002.

[7]Sources for events in Korea are General Conference Minutes, January 23, 1964; July 27, 1967; September 29, 2000; *Review and Herald*, June 23, 1969; *ibid.*, October 31 and December 5, 1974; *Adventist Review*, October 13, 1994 and September 28, 1995; *General Conference Bulletin*, 1950, no. 10, pp. 237, 238; no. 11, p. 15; *ibid.*, 1962, no. 3, p. 29; *ibid.*, 1985, no.

5, p. 27; Far Eastern Division *Outlook*, February-March 1987; *ibid.*, November 1994; *Sahmyook University Bulletin*, 1999-2000; Masaji Uyeda, "Northern Asia Pacific Division," 2001 GC Report; and interviews: Masaji Uyeda, June 3, 2002; Jin Hong Shin, June 4, 2002; Kei Hoon Shin, June 4, 2002; M. K. Oh, June 5, 2002; Dong Seung Park, June 4, 2002; Dae Yun Cho, June 4, 2002; D. K. Nam, June 5, 2002; H. H. Lyu, June 4, 2002; Si Young Kim, June 4, 2002;Y. K. Chung, June 4, 2002.

[8]Interview, Kei Hoon Shin, June 4, 2002.

[9]The paragraphs relating to India are based on R. S. Lowry, "Summary of Observations, Impressions and Recommendations from the Education Department on Tour in the Southern Asia Division, August 4 to October 7, 1953," AST, RG 51; "Division School Inspection Reports–1955," ibid.; R. S. Lowry, "Report of the Quadrennium Ending 1959," ibid.; L. R. Rasmussen to E. E. Cossentine, December 6, 1956, ibid.; R. E. Rice to P. W. Christian, April 3, 1957; ibid.; Duane S. Johnson to W. R. Beach, February 1, 1957, ibid.; Duane Johnson, to L. R. Rasmussen, October 3, 1957, ibid.; other miscellaneous letters among General Conference, Walla Walla College, Southern Asia Division, and Spicer Memorial College, 1957, ibid.; Richard Hammill to R. R. Figuhr, February 6, 1961, ibid.; Ethel Young to R. S. Lowry and C. H. Tidwell, June 11, 1974, ibid.; the Self-Study by Spicer Memorial College, 1976, ibid.; W. J. McHenry, "Southern Asia Division Report," (*Journal of Adventist Education*, February-March 1980), pp. 15, 20, 21; *Southern Asia Division Tidings*, November 1990 pp. 3-7, 14; *Spicer Memorial College Bulletin, 2001-2002*; George Roos Jenson, *Spicer Memorial College*, pp. 61-117; Justus Devadas, "Report Presented at the Asia-Pacific Education Leadership Seminar, April 4-10, 2002. Interviews: Justus Devadas, May 24, 2002; Y. R. Samraj and wife, May 25, 2002; Gerald J. Christo, May 26, 2002; Charles Tidwell, January 2-27, 2002; John Fowler, February 7, 2002; Samuel M. Gaikwad, May 27, 2002; Gordon Christo, May 28, 2002.

[10]See Edison Samraj, "A Framework For Approaching Non-Christian Students In Our Schools," in *Maturing of Adventism*, Edison Samraj, ed. (Pune, India: Oriental Publishing House, 1995), pp. 141-172; John M. Fowler, "Caring and Excellence," (*Journal of Adventist Education*, Summer 1990), pp. 70, 72, 73, and "The Mission School: Catalyst or Catastrophe?" (*Ibid.*, December 1993-January 1994), pp. 37-40.

[11]George L. Caviness, "Upper Biennium Education at Australasian Missionary College," (*Journal of True Education*, April 1957), pp. 24, 25; Milton Hook, "Avondale Campus," in *Seventh-day Adventists in the South Pacific*, pp. 146-165; *Avondale College Handbook*, 1999-2000; "The Plan to Affiliate the Australasian Missionary College and Pacific Union College for Curriculums in Ministerial Training and Secondary Teacher Training Leading to a Baccalaureate Degree," AST, RG 51; "Recommendations to the A.M.C. Boar of Managment and the Australasian Inter-Union Committee," ibid.

[12]These statistics adapted from *World Report 2000.*

# Higher Learning: Europe, Africa, and Latin America

Similar to its counterpart in Asia and the Pacific, the development of Adventist tertiary education also spread to Europe, Africa and Latin America. The details varied, but sometimes the movement represented the effectiveness of affiliations and extension campuses that had played an important role in Australia and India. As the first instance of an affiliation between a North American institution and one in a world field, the experience of Australasian Missionary College and Pacific Union College demonstrated that if the conditions were right, an official connection between schools on different continents could be a successful means to export baccalaureate and perhaps post-baccalaureate education to the Adventist world.

Whether or not affiliations or other official arrangements joined North American institutions with campuses elsewhere, schools in the United States continued to set the educational pace for the Adventist world. Globally speaking, after World War II theological education, teacher-preparation, and business were the fields of study most in demand, which accounted for the tendency of Andrews University to become the most prominent mentor in Adventist higher education around the world, but Loma Linda also played a vital role in advancing education in medicine and health. As the story of denominational education in Europe, Africa and Latin America show, the conditions were not always right for affiliations or extension centers, which left some Adventist schools responsible for their own academic reputations. Such was the case in Europe.

### Adventist Higher Education in France and Germany

In 1948 the General Conference Department of Education conducted two councils in Europe to revive education after World War II and to systematize the schools in the Northern European and Southern European divisions. A major point of consensus was to continue preparing students for external examinations that would validate their education, but the schools were not to sacrifice their identity as Adventist training schools in the process. Seminaire Adventiste du Saleve in Collonges, France was to become the educational center for the entire Southern European Division with lesser schools sending their graduates to France for the most advanced courses available in the field.

General Conference approval of Seminaire Adventiste as a four-year, post-secondary campus came in 1955. With this new authority the school began offering a complete post-baccalaureate program in theology, but because the school lacked government accreditation beyond the secondary level the degrees were of little if any value outside denominational circles. In 1963 the French school requested the General Conference to recognize its theology degree as equivalent to a master of arts in religion as defined by American standards. Neither this petition nor discussions of a cooperative plan allowing students to begin a graduate degree in France and complete it at Andrews University produced concrete results.

It was not until the theology department affiliated with the University of Strasbourg in 1983 that ministerial graduates earned government approved theology degrees. The arrangement to issue theology degrees under the umbrella of the University of Strasbourg amounted to accreditation by a reputable institution and allowed graduates to pursue further studies in other universities. The same arrangement recognized a fifth year of theological study as a master of theology. The school of theology at Seminaire Adventiste defined its four-year program as equivalent to the North American master of arts. In 1996 the school became Saleve Adventist University. Later Saleve Adventist University added a master's degree in leadership administered by Newbold College in cooperation with Andrews University. A master's degree in youth ministry through the good offices of the University of Wales, Lampeter and Newbold College also became part of the offerings on the Collonges campus.[1]

Larger than Saleve Adventist University was Friedensau University in Germany. The restoration of Adventist education in Germany after World War II brought a renewal of ministerial education at Marienhohe Seminary in 1948, itself having revived that same year after a hiatus of nearly a decade beginning during the era of national socialism. Similar to the French school, the German seminary did not seek affiliation with a North American school. A request to the General Conference from Marienhohe to offer graduate studies died in stalemate. In 1994, five years after the collapse of the German Democratic Republic, the ministerial training program transferred to Friedensau in former East Germany where a seminary that had functioned during the post-World War II socialist years received recognition in 1990 as a university. This merger resulted in a single ministerial education program for Germany. By the end of the decade enrollment exceeded 200 and the program included master's degrees in theology and social work.[2]

### Newbold College

These experiences in France and Germany confirmed that denominational leaders in Europe held the long established practices of European education and university traditions in high esteem and that an affiliation with an American university yielded few benefits. But equally as strong was the growing sentiment among church leaders that the Seminary at Andrews was the world center for Adventist theological studies and that a systematic organization of seminary education should be the ideal for all the world fields.

Probably no case in Europe better illustrated this conviction than the story of Newbold College in England. In 1950 the Northern European Division council voted to establish this school as the division educational center, which meant that it would offer the equivalent of a four-year theology program for students from the British Isles, the Netherlands,

Scandinavia, Poland, West Africa, and Ethiopia. Although these fields had their own training schools, Adventist membership was too slim to support a degree-granting institution for every country. In 1953 Newbold began a new phase of its history as the division's senior college and, by definition, an international institution.[3]

The plan was well intentioned but it ran amuck inasmuch as the school shared a problem common to nearly all private post-secondary schools in the British system–it lacked degree-granting authority. This problem intensified as pressure was mounting in Europe for Adventist ministers to carry not only a degree but credentials from recognized theological programs. Also of concern was a tendency by immigration offices in former English colonies to deny visas to Newbold graduates on mission appointments because they did not own degrees from a recognized institution.

From its early days the school in England had been a leading source for workers who could enter colonial territories around the world on the strength of an English passport, but after World War II the mentality in these countries stiffened. Sometimes they did not permit such easy travel. Newly independent governments were prone to make sure that holders of visas who were planning to live and work in their countries were prepared professionally to contribute to nation building. A recognized degree would provide the necessary credential, but Newbold degrees could not qualify. To rectify this problem, in 1955, only two years after becoming a senior college, Newbold negotiated an affiliation with Washington Missionary College to allow its theology students to earn an accredited degree.

Church leaders in the Northern European Division planned that other schools in their field would form a network of feeder institutions for Newbold. Students would take two years of classes in their own country and complete their degrees in England with two additional years of study. For practical purposes this arrangement redefined the schools in Scandinavia and the Netherlands as junior colleges instead of training schools because they lost their ministerial education programs. Between the years 1956 and 1964 theology students from England and others from as far away as New Zealand and Jamaica took advantage of the affiliated degree program; 102 students graduated with a baccalaureate degree in theology. Additionally, the Theological Seminary conducted refresher classes without academic credit as extension centers at other European locations.

But problems arose when attempting to superimpose an American degree on a European educational framework. Questions surfaced in 1964 when V. Norskov Olson, the Danish-born president of Newbold College, proposed to extend Newbold's program beyond theology to majors in religion and history with several different minors. He also proposed that Andrews University establish a master's degree in theology on the English campus to enable European ministers to stay abreast of advancing trends in their profession. These changes required alterations in the affiliation with Washington Missionary College, which had since become Columbia Union College.

As a result of these suggestions a candid exchange broke out among Adventist educators in Scandinavia, the Netherlands, and England on the topic of comparable levels of education in Europe and the United States. The crux of the issue was the conflict between the European system on the one hand that followed regimented curricula and external examinations in order to advance upward through the system, eventually into a university, and on the other hand the Adventist theology degree, a baccalaureate program built on secondary preparation, American style, that lacked well defined counterparts in Europe.

Europeans argued that their secondary education carried students more academic distance than American secondary schools and that European degrees represented more penetrating scholarship than American degrees. While the American bachelor's degree was accepted in Europe, ministers who earned it in the affiliation program at Newbold were at a disadvantage if they tried to pursue graduate studies in a European university. European educators feared they would weaken their programs in the junior colleges if they made curricular changes to accommodate what they believed were lowered admission requirements at Newbold. These changes, they affirmed, would jeopardize their government-approved curricula which prepared students for external examinations.

This negative reaction did not mean that heads of schools and faculties in the Nordic countries and the Netherlands were opposed to teaching religion and preparing ministers. They lamented the loss of ministerial training from their campuses when their programs transferred to

England after Newbold became a senior college, and they perceived decline in their schools as a byproduct. But in what was becoming an oft-told tale, they saw denominational schools as places where youth in the church could earn an education in an Adventist environment rather than institutions that were predominantly worker-training schools, and they felt obligated to protect the validity of denominational education as it fit into the schema of their countries, which would benefit the majority of Adventist youth who attended.

The debate did not end quickly nor did church leaders retreat from their aim to center their theology program at Newbold. Schools in Scandinavia and the Netherlands maintained their government-approved curricula but the denominational need for advanced theological education carried the day. Andrews University initiated a regular extension school on the Newbold campus in 1964. In 1972 this arrangement grew into the Postgraduate Year which allowed Newbold students to take a year of graduate classes and transfer to the Andrews campus to complete a master's degree. To add substance to this graduate program an Ellen G. White and Seventh-day Adventist Research Centre opened on the Newbold campus in 1974, the first of its kind outside the United States.

By the 1990s Newbold students could chose one of three routes to a degree. Through its revised affiliation with Columbia Union College students could earn bachelor of science degrees in accounting and management. An agreement with the Open University Validation Services made bachelor of arts degrees available in biblical studies and humanities. The affiliation with Andrews offered bachelor's degrees in English, history, Islamic studies, and behavioral studies, and master's degrees in education, religion, and pastoral ministry.

Newbold resolved the conundrum of degree-granting authority by blending American and English education through affiliations and the Open University system. Through these means Adventist youth were able to choose from a comparatively broad set of offerings to acquire an education on a denominational campus. At the beginning of the twenty-first century ministerial education remained the strongest of all fields; about one of three students enrolled in theology, the program that had started the school on its road to senior college status. With only a small number of church schools in the Northern European Division–in the year 2000 three secondary and nine elementary in the British Isles and a handful scattered throughout Scandinavia and the Netherlands–a teacher-preparation course was not a critical issue.

In 1950 the vision for Newbold was to develop an international campus. A half century later the school retained that character, in part because of the decline of worker-training courses in other schools in the division and in part because English was the *lingua franca* of the denomination. The college gained a preeminent role among denominational schools in Europe by accepting students from many Adventist post-secondary campuses on the Continent into the Open University Validation Services program, thus providing an alternative graduate study track for church workers.

## A Summary of Adventist Education in Europe

By the year 2000 Adventists operated fourteen post-secondary schools in Europe with a total enrollment of nearly 2,100. Because many of them offered narrow academic programs–primarily ministerial training–enrollment tended to be small; one reported only fifteen students. Eight schools enrolled fewer than a hundred and the largest approximated 500. As a rule these schools had to find their niche as legitimate institutions within the system of the country in which they were located.

Of financial benefit to some of these schools such as those in France and Spain was the Adventist Colleges Abroad program, a consortium of Adventist schools that arranged for students from the United States to attend a non-American college either to earn a large segment of credit toward an academic major in a foreign language or simply to have an experience of living abroad for a year. Known as ACA, the program brought much needed cash to the host campuses.

## Solusi After World War II

During the nineteenth century, England transplanted its educational traditions throughout its Empire, and even after newly independent countries dismantled the colonial system after World War II, vestiges of these educational practices lingered. Such was the situation at Solusi in Southern Rhodesia where Adventists experienced their first major test in establishing post-secondary education for Africans.[4]

*Russell Staples, president of Solusi College, congratulates a graduate of the school as Maurice Hodgen, professor of education, looks on. Solusi was the first Seventh-day Adventist school for Africans to upgrade to baccalaureate status. In 1995 it received a charter as a university.*

For fifty-three years after its founding in 1895 Solusi offered only elementary-level education. In 1948 the General Conference elevated the school to secondary level, and four years later authorized it to become a four-year post-secondary institution. More than any other factor stimulating this fast-moving change was the recognition that the colonial system was crumbling throughout Africa and that the Southern African Division needed to establish an institution to prepare Africans to take charge of denominational affairs in their own countries. The responsibility to convert Solusi into a viable post-secondary school fell initially on the shoulders of C. Fred Clarke, science and math teacher at Helderberg College in South Africa, who transferred to the Rhodesian campus as principal.

The school proclaimed its new status by changing its name to Solusi Missionary College in 1954, but when Clarke arrived that same year he discovered little that resembled a post-secondary school. Before him was a deteriorating school plant, a diseased dairy herd ready for the slaughterhouse, dysfunctional water and sanitation systems, a deplorably equipped academic program, a treasury emptied of its money but saddled with ample debt, a faculty with critical vacancies, and interpersonal problems on the staff that bore racial overtones. Little else but his belief in miracles kept him going for the next seven years, but in 1961when he handed over the keys to his successor, Russell Staples, Solusi had graduated its first class of theology students from the four-year post-secondary program. At the time Solusi was the only private school in the Federation of Rhodesia and Nyasaland to offer this level of education to Africans.

Staples had joined the Solusi faculty earlier as part of the upgrading process, and when he took over the school he stepped into office with informed opinions about the school's future. He also faced troubling political events that sowed seeds of uncertainty on the campus. Solusi's inception as a senior college coincided with the formation of the Federation of Rhodesia and Nyasaland, an attempt to hold together English territories in south-central Africa under a single government. In 1963 this ill-fated union disintegrated and out of the territory came Rhodesia and the new countries of Zambia and Malawi. During the same year in the wake of these events and other swiftly changing conditions, a series of All-Africa conferences of churches, youth, and heads of independent states convened in rapid succession to strategize for a new continent.

Adventist leaders could not ignore these happenings. Accordingly, in 1963 prominent denominational personalities from all parts of the continent assembled at Solusi for a Conference on African Trends. The six-day agenda was packed with topics dealing with change in Africa under the motto "A Changeless Christ for A Changing World." This gathering came none too soon. Less than two years later a government of European minority rule seized Rhodesia and unilaterally declared independence. The nature of this new government alienated much of Africa and made travel difficult for Solusi students from all parts of continent. Fighting between discontented Africans and the government threatened the safety of the school and in 1978 Solusi closed to allow the storm to blow over. By the time the school reopened in 1980 the majority Black population had gained control of the country, changed its name to Zimbabwe, and instituted new reforms.

Staples did not stay at Solusi long enough to watch all of this excitement personally. In 1967 he left but not before changing the direction of Solusi's development. His foremost contribution was to reject a proposal to correlate the theology degree with the program of external studies outlined by the University of South Africa, which he admitted looked good on paper but was beset with pitfalls. At Bethel College, a well known Adventist school for Blacks in South Africa, a similar plan was in operation for art, but Staples warned that applying it to theology would bring chaos to Solusi. He and his faculty wanted no connection between an Adventist theology program and the University of South Africa. One of the main reasons was the fact that Solusi was an international school whose students came from countries vehemently opposed to the South African policy of apartheid. Adventist ministers carrying credentials from the University of South Africa would be as politically incorrect as one could become in Africa. Staples also pointed out that an alignment with the University of South Africa would produce divisiveness on the campus. Students studying for external examinations often berated their peers enrolled in internal degree programs, and vice versa. According to Staples, whether or not to issue recognized degrees was not the question; what was debatable was whether the degree should be an Adventist degree from an affiliation with Andrews University or an African degree from the University of South Africa. Staples convinced his colleagues that the connection should be with Andrews in order to maintain a strong Adventist character in the school.

Affiliation did not come easily. Richard Hammill, the new president of the freshly hatched Andrews University, spoke optimistically about the possibility, but Andrews' accrediting body, the North Central Association, balked, not permitting the new university to entangle itself in such an arrangement unless the African campus became a complete extension school. The fact that Andrews itself was struggling with accreditation problems did not help.

The needed improvements at Solusi were daunting, involving every aspect of the plant, equipment, and curriculum. Progress was slow and costly. Not until 1978 did the first African college professor land a position at the college. In 1981 library accessions finally reached 20,000 books. Long before Solusi's administration checked off all of the items on its long list of recommended improvements, discussion about affiliation dissolved.

The tide turned in 1984. A visiting delegation from Zimbabwe's government the previous year did not bring the long coveted official recognition, but government accolades were nevertheless profuse. Andrews University followed with an inspection team, which recommended affiliation, and in October 1984 the connection became effective. It was a milestone, but did not completely resolve the problem of unrecognized degrees. Zimbabwe's Ministry of Education was still not satisfied with Solusi's improvements and withheld its approval, at the same time refusing to recognize degrees from Andrews even though most African countries did not question the United States institution.

Another decade passed before Robert Mugabe, president of Zimbabwe, visited the campus in 1995 to receive an honorary doctorate and to announce a university charter for Solusi, complete with degree-granting authority. Solusi became the second private school in the country to achieve this status. The president lauded the new university, but cautioned that evangelical zeal for conversions to Adventism should never be an excuse to deny admission to eligible applicants. His counsel was actually a policy statement by the government supporting Solusi University's freedom to maintain its religious identity, but at the same time expecting it to contribute to national well being.

The original thrust of higher education at Solusi came from theology, but degrees spread to other fields. At its centennial graduation the largest single group earned degrees in business. This trend was deliberate. Adventist education in Africa had revolved around basic education and theology with little attention on the financial aspects of church administration. In 1968 Solusi expanded its curriculum to include business in order to correct this deficiency. As time would show, this curricular development would also fit well into the educational aims of Africa in general.

Figures in the year 2000 indicated that Solusi had complied with its mandate to be part of Zimbabwe's nation building. More than half of its 842 students were non-Adventist. Also more than half enrolled in business or business-related curricula, many undoubtedly aiming for careers outside denominational employment inasmuch as the church did not have that many job openings for graduates in those fields. Teacher-preparation and ministerial education, the two long-standing professions in the church, attracted about a fourth of the students.

## The University of Eastern Africa, Baraton

Denominational interest in Solusi stemmed from its long history as the first Adventist school for underdeveloped people. Its evolution into a university was one of the great successes of Adventism in Africa, but more recent schools were no less important. Probably none received as much attention as the University of Eastern Africa, Baraton, in Kenya.

The urge for a post-secondary institution in this country reached near coercive levels in the 1970s, not only because of substantial membership increases in East Africa but also as a result of an international crisis. Since 1970 Middle East College in Lebanon had been the educational center for the newly fashioned Afro-Mideast Division, of which East Africa was a part. Political volatility in Lebanon forced the school to close in 1978, which, although temporary, provided the impetus for a tertiary institution in a less risky climate. Because Adventist membership in Kenya was among the highest in the division, the country became a likely location for a school.[5]

Events moved rapidly. Working through an Adventist member of parliament, the Kenyan president agreed to lease a former agricultural station to the church which the division would convert into a post-secondary school. A hurried master plan depicted a total campus, complete with student housing, academic facilities that extended to agricultural and vocational instruction, a 120,000-volume library and an Ellen G. White Research Centre, and a university press to publish results of scholarly research. During the construction of the school, developers saw to it that plant and academic equipment was not cast-away quality. Classes began in January 1980.

The impact of University of Eastern Africa (UEAB), which became the official institutional name soon after it began operations, was almost instantaneous. The library began with 5,000 donated volumes; by 1985 accessions approached 18,000. Academic offerings broadened quickly into vocational fields. Some graduates entered public education. Instructors in the dairy and agricultural program conducted experiments in cooperation with agricultural agencies in Kenya, and the library collaborated with other civic and university collections. In 1990 the school received a half-million-dollar grant from the United States government to erect and equip laboratories for auto mechanics and auto body repair and to offer bachelor of science degrees in auto technology and in teaching auto service.

From the beginning Kenyan President Daniel Atap Moi made it clear that the new school should have degree-granting authority, but twelve years passed before the government granted the charter. Moi was a trained educator who had entered politics, becoming minister of education before ascending to the presidency. His intentions for UEAB were never in doubt, but neither was his deliberation. While the university waited for government recognition it affiliated with Andrews University, which allowed graduates to enter the professional world with recognized degrees. After only a decade since opening day, the university graduated students from eight fields with business and agriculture at the top of the list.

In 1991 President Moi granted the long-anticipated charter. With explicit thanks to Andrews University for its mentoring role in developing the African institution, he emphasized the place of high academic standards in Kenya. "My chief concern here," he said, "is on the quality of education our youth should receive at university level. This concern arises out of my belief that universities have a role to play in the liberation of our people from hunger, ignorance and disease. Through their researches, universities should also act as catalysts for development."[6] There could be little question that Kenyan government officials viewed the University of Eastern Africa as far more than a Seventh-day Adventist worker-training institution; they gave it a mandate to become a research center and to contribute to Kenya's nation-building process.

During the 1990s UEAB enlarged its program as a higher-education school for denominational workers and professionals. The first class of baccalaureate nurses graduated in 1992 and by the end of the decade the university teamed with Loma Linda University to offer master's degrees in public health. Master of arts degrees in education were also part of the graduate program, and by 2002 the faculty of theology were on the verge of master of arts and master of divinity degrees.

Enrollment reached nearly 1,200 by the end of the century, momentarily establishing UEAB as the largest Adventist tertiary institution in Africa. Slightly less than half of the students were non-Adventist. Of all denominational post-secondary schools on the continent the enrollment at Baraton showed the most balance among fields of study. Business remained the first choice among students, but sciences and health were also popular, each attracting more than a hundred students. Theology was one of the larger departments with slightly less than a hundred enrollees.

The University of Eastern Africa owed its quick rise from a vacant agricultural station to one of the prominent tertiary institutions in the Adventist world to a number of factors. In addition to a friendly government, the foremost was a willingness by the Adventist community to design a school with an academic breadth that matched Kenya's national aims. It was a typical course of action in the developing world.

### Elements of Change in Adventist Education in Africa

The events that unfolded at Solusi and Baraton were only two of many in Africa. By the beginning of the twenty-first century the Adventist Accrediting Association had approved ten post-secondary schools that ranged across the continent from South Africa north to Nigeria and Ghana in West Africa to Kenya and Ethiopia in the northeast. Most of these institutions originated after World War II. Two offered graduate programs. In addition, several unaccredited schools were in operation and worker-training curricula were still producing church employees.

Of special note were schools in Central Africa and along the coast of the hump. Adventist University of Central Africa in Rwanda, established in 1979, became the single most important educational center for French-speaking Africans before closing in 1994, no longer able to function side by side with tribal conflict that bathed Rwanda with the blood of tens of thousands of slaughtered victims. By 1996, after hostilities had subsided, the African-Indian Ocean Division recreated the university on four campuses in French-speaking Africa, all taking the name of Adventist University followed by the campus name. Central Africa resumed operations in Kilgali, Rwanda; Cosendai opened in Cameroon, Wallace in Lukanga, Congo, and Zurcher in Madagascar. Each of the three institutions outside Rwanda developed from earlier secondary and worker-training schools dating back to 1936. Each campus operated independently with separate administrations, but a limited number of personnel migrated from school to school and a single university senate became the seat of governance for the system. In 2003 combined enrollment on all four campuses approximated 1,200.[7]

Twenty miles north of Accra, Ghana, Valley View University began with only a handful of students in 1979. A persistent and effective affiliation with Griggs University helped the school to develop a bachelor's degree in theology, and its accreditation with Ghana's National Accreditation Board permitted it to offer additional degrees in computer science and accounting. By 2003 its enrollment reached 800.[8]

Following five years of planning, Babock University in Nigeria opened its doors to seven students in 1959, known at the time as Adventist College of West Africa. An affiliation with Andrews University in 1975 stimulated growth, and in 1988 an extension program from the Michigan campus enabled ministerial students to earn master's degrees. In 1999 the Nigerian government recognized the school as a private university, resulting in an enrollment soaring above 3,000, which catapulted the campus above the University of Eastern Africa as the largest Adventist tertiary institution in Africa. By 2003 it offered four-year degrees in more than twenty fields including nursing, computer technology, theology, and a variety of areas in business. It maintained its affiliation with Andrews University to grant master's degrees in pastoral ministry and religion.[9]

Several causes contributed to this growth of denominational higher education in Africa. The demise of colonialism gave birth to a large number of new independencies, and as the church repeatedly redrew its administrative map to group these young and often struggling countries into manageable administrative clusters, schools followed as instruments of reorganization. The languages that Africa's colonial masters left behind helped to determine the lines of reorganization. Tribal differences also influenced new boundaries. Political leanings sometimes held regions together or conversely, forced separation and more reorganization.

Apart from these external forces affecting the number of Adventist schools was the internal matter of membership growth. From the 1970s onward conversions multiplied almost exponentially; by the year 2000 African Adventists numbered into the millions. The sheer weight of the Adventist population demanded schools in which to prepare denominational employees, especially ministers. Church leaders regarded the lack of educated leadership as a major crisis.

Educators most frequently targeted theology to be the strongest academic field among the schools. Across all the accredited tertiary schools, about a fourth of the students chose careers in the ministry, but total enrollment was approximately equally divided between Adventist and non-Adventist students, which meant that about half of the Adventist students were preparing for the ministry. The complete figures indicate that the trend at Solusi toward business as the favored field of study among all students held true throughout the rest of Africa. Nearly thirty percent, the largest single category, selected curricula leading to careers in the business world.

The universities in Africa were very gratifying to church leaders, but looking at Adventist education across the continent, observers could see that denominational schools were not an unqualified success. Notwithstanding the membership explosion, total enrollment in Adventist post-secondary institutions approximated 5,000 at the end of the century, a fact that gave rise to questions about the adequacy of Adventist schools to accommodate the rising tide of potential students. By comparison, in the year 2000 African Adventists numbered twenty times the membership in South Korea, but enrollment in Sahmyook University was equal to approximately eighty percent of the students in all of Africa's tertiary schools combined. It was obvious that thousands of Adventist youth in Africa were not attending denominational schools.

In an effort to systematize the needs of schools and plans for the future, in 1994 and 1995 a Commission on Seventh-day Adventist Education in Africa toured the campuses of post-secondary schools and visited the division and union offices of education throughout the continent. Commission members usually found cordial relations between Adventist education and governments, but some other aspects of Adventist education were troubling. All too frequently school plants were inadequate, underfunded, understaffed or staffed with too many unqualified persons. Plans to expand programs and school plants were optimistic to the point of being unrealistic as the commission members assessed them.[10]

But however many question marks the commission found, the single most striking feature of denominational education in Africa led back to Solusi's founding when Cecil Rhodes granted land to the young Adventist church for the purpose of bringing civilization to Africans. To varying degrees, ever since Adventists claimed their 12,000 acres in Matabeleland, denominational schools continued to play the role that Rhodes envisioned while at the same time fulfilling the church objective of preparing Africans to become carriers of the Christian gospel.

From among the tens of thousands who attended village schools to learn how to rise above the hunger, ignorance and disease that Kenyan President Daniel Atap Moi said still existed in his country in 1991, no one knows what percentage became enduring church members. But the tradition of the mission school did not die with modernizing trends. Baptisms among non-Adventist students at the end of the century approached thirteen percent. The Africa of 2000 was not the same land as in 1895, but the needs of an emerging people were still present, and it is to the credit of Adventist schools from Solusi to the University of Eastern Africa that they were able to blend the social gospel with the saving gospel to create a single message.

### An Overview of South America and Inter-America

In the American republics south of the United States a combination of events led to singular achievements in Adventist higher education that had previously been far out of reach, even for the most optimistically minded. To a large extent, these accomplishments derived from the most systematically developed educational establishments in the Adventist world. Also of importance was church membership, which began to rise significantly in the 1950s. The South American and Inter-American divisions were the largest outside North America, and by 1970 more than one of every four Seventh-day Adventists in the world lived in Latin America and the Caribbean.[11]

Adventist medical units were scattered across South America, and in Brazil and Argentina two major publishing houses produced large volumes of denominational literature. Publishing and health-care institutions lagged in Inter-America, but after 1945 a ring of hospitals sprouted up. These institutions, combined with a swiftly increasing number of churches and schools, presented a steadily growing demand for denominational employees which church leaders expected Adventist training schools to supply.

The situation was complicated by the proximity of the two divisions to the United States. A steady flow of immigrants northward added to the Hispanic population that already occupied the southern fringe and many of the large cities in the United States. This community became a fruitful evangelistic source for North America, and by the 1970s the Spanish-speaking membership in the United States numbered many thousands, constituting hundreds of congregations and creating a need for pastors.

Dating from the era of World War I former missionaries to Latin America attempted to educate Spanish-speaking ministers in the United States, but their efforts always ended as truncated good intentions. The last was a seminary near Albuquerque, New Mexico that prepared a bevy of church workers after its founding in 1942, but became the conference boarding academy ten years later. Many of the Spanish-speaking ministers in North America originated in Latin America, thus the North American Division depended on schools in Inter-America and South America for workers to shepherd one of its fastest growing sectors.[12]

Between 1955 and 1973 twelve of the training schools from Cuba to Argentina received Board of Regents approval as four-year post-secondary institutions. Eight of the campuses were Spanish, the remaining four were English, Portuguese, and French. In every case ministerial education was the motivating cause of upgrading. Because neither South America nor Inter-America designated a training school as the division educational center these institutions functioned more or less on an equal administrative footing.

But the schools were not equal. Brazil College served all Brazilian unions and until other institutions developed it functioned as a regional campus. Others, such as West Indies College in Jamaica, River Plate College in Argentina, and Antillian College in Cuba, which moved to Puerto Rico, developed strong reputations and attracted students from other parts of the Americas. Nursing programs at Montemorelos, Mexico and River Plate College also drew international enrollments.

While this system of education was well organized, post-secondary schools functioned without government recognition. Governments frequently accredited nursing education and teacher-preparation courses, which allowed graduates to receive certificates of completion, but the institutions remained unrecognized, although countenanced and even encouraged by public officials. As was the case elsewhere, diplomas from unrecognized courses were valid only in denominational circles.

As institutional development progressed Andrews University offered some extension courses in both Inter-America and South America and affiliated with West Indies College and Caribbean Union College, both of which originated in the British system and faced problems of recognition similar to Adventist schools in other former English colonies. Educational policies differed from country to country in the Latin nations, but during the 1970s and onward a string of actions in countries ranging from the Dominican Republic to Argentina brought official recognition to Adventist tertiary institutions that had already received denominational authorization as four-year, post-secondary schools. A broadening of curriculum usually accompanied recognition or followed soon after. As a rule of thumb, governments were friendly and often helpful in the process, partly because they were interested in improving literacy rates and raising basic educational standards.

### The University of Montemorelos and Inter-America

Through the 1950s Antillian College in Cuba appeared to be advancing toward legitimate post-secondary status more satisfactorily than any other training school in Inter-America, but a revolution halted the school's progress after 1959. The first training school in the division to break the barrier and receive recognition was Colegio Vocacional y Profesional in Montemorelos, Mexico. Ministerial education had always been the primary course on this campus, but a nursing school connected to the hospital on the edge of the campus had earned widespread public respect, and medicine and healthcare became key issues in the process of academic recognition.

The demand for medical personnel in Inter-America was far greater than Adventist institutions could furnish, going far beyond nurses to include physicians and technicians. In 1969 the Inter-American Division officers voted to sponsor students in medical school and technical training. Nearly at the same time the administration of the school at Montemorelos requested degree-granting authority from the state of Nuevo Leon, hinting that a school of medicine might be possible inasmuch as a hospital was part of the institutional campus. Suddenly in April 1973, without consultation with school officials, the governor of Nuevo Leon signed a decree that elevated the training school to a degree-granting institution–a university–and authorized it to establish a medical school.

State authorization struck the campus as a shockwave, but reaction by the denomination was less dramatic. Two months after the governor's announcement, an *ad hoc* committee convened on the campus to survey the readiness–or unreadiness–of the newly created Montemorelos University to take advantage of the future that had opened up before it. During its proceedings the committee repeatedly referred to the prospects of a denominational school of medicine as a case of providential intervention and indeed, many conditions were favorable to the new order. The hospital enjoyed a reputation as one of the finest in northern Mexico. Adventist membership in Mexico exceeded 60,000 and was rapidly increasing. As the largest Spanish-speaking country in the world, Mexico was probably in the best position to address the chronic lack of medical personnel in both Inter-America and South America.

Denominational approval in principle for the university came in the autumn of 1973, but on condition that the reorganized school should become an institution of the Inter-American Division and that improvements would follow both the general upgrading instructions from the

*In 1973 Mexico's Vocational and Professional Training School received state permission to become a degree-granting institution. This plaque commemorates the visit of Mexican President Jose Lopez Portillo to the University of Montemorelos in 1981 to inaugurate the new medical center as the clinical facility for the second school of medicine in the Adventist world.*

General Conference Department of Education and the specific instructions the *ad hoc* committee spelled out. A second committee composed of representatives from the General Conference, Inter-American Division, and the Mexican Union was to visit the campus in 1974 to take stock of the upgrading process before the schools of medicine and nursing began operations. The new university program was not to exceed the recommendations by the first *ad hoc* committee.

If the limitations laid down by the General Conference appeared cautious it was because the new university faced gargantuan tasks despite basically favorable conditions. The campus was lacking in adequate library and plant facilities, sufficient equipment, and qualified personnel, all serious deficiencies. A recognized teacher-preparation program was already in place and the school had begun an abbreviated accounting course, but several degree curricula and a medical instructional staff were necessary to become a university. Original plans called for five separate degree-granting schools: accounting, nursing, education, medicine, and theology. Deliberately, no graduate education was part of the plan.

These beginnings were minimal. Besides denominational funds, about $5,000,000 flowed onto the campus from the German-based Protestant Central Agency for Development Aid, enabling the university to redesign the campus and erect a set of architecturally coordinated buildings. To strengthen the theology program the White Estate established an Ellen G. White Research Center on the campus.

In spite of the importance of theology, most of the attention was on the school of medicine, which began in 1975 as only the second physician's course in the Adventist world. Loma Linda University extended a helping hand, sending instructors on short-term teaching assignments to the Mexican campus. The first class of twenty-five graduated in 1979 and the following year eighteen more completed the course. The largest single group of medical students came from Mexico, but others hailed from a half dozen other Latin American countries, and Asia, Africa, and the United States.

In 1981 Mexican President Jose Lopez Portillo spoke at the opening of a new hospital that had been integrated into the university as the clinical facility for the school of medicine. In the same year graduate education in religion began as an extension of Andrews University. By the end of the decade Montemorelos University was offering its own master's degrees in education and public health. During the 1990s curriculum expansion brought master's degrees in business and pastoral theology, specializations in ophthalmology and odontology, and a doctorate in education. The equivalent of a baccalaureate degree was available in more than fifteen fields as divergent as theology and nutrition.

Recognition, which had been so elusive during the first thirty years of the school's existence, became commonplace in the next thirty. Approval by the state of Nuevo Leon gave blanket accreditation to the university, and the school joined national bodies that oversaw higher education and private institutions. The school also maintained membership in associations that monitored professional programs.

At the beginning of the new century the number of post-secondary schools in Inter-America rose to ten, all of which achieved official recognition except Caribbean Union College in Trinidad. The Ministry of Education for Trinidad and Tobago accredited the teacher-preparation course, but an affiliation with Andrews University allowed students to earn accredited degrees in other fields. In keeping with the division's long and consistent support of elementary and secondary schools, nearly thirty percent of the 8,800 students in the institutions of higher education enrolled in teacher-preparation programs.

Enrollment on other campuses in Inter-America forged ahead, especially at Dominican Adventist University in the Dominican Republic and Northern Caribbean University in Jamaica, formerly West Indies College, rivaling Montemorelos University, but because of its stature as a division institution, the Mexican school offered a greater breadth of programs, especially in the health sciences.

### Accomplishments in Brazil and Argentina

In 1945 the best known campuses in South America were Argentina's River Plate College, the oldest Adventist educational institution in the division, and Brazil College on the outskirts of Sao Paulo. The Brazilian school was the largest in South America with more than a hundred students studying at the post-secondary level. In 1959 the General Conference authorized the school to offer a baccalaureate degree in theology. Two years later in 1961 the school became an institute, Insti-

*Colegio Adventista Brasileiro grew to be the largest of Seventh-day Adventist post-secondary schools in South America. By the 1980s the city of Sao Paulo surrounded the rural atmosphere of the campus and in 1984 the institution split, moving the theological program and related studies to a new campus while leaving the sciences and related studies on the original site. This post-World War II photograph shows the older campus.*

tuto Adventista de Ensino, which designated it as a recognized Brazilian post-secondary institution offering between five and ten programs. The campus reorganized itself into several schools with degree-granting authority, but theology degrees remained unrecognized.

At the time of its origin the school was rural, but population growth in Sao Paulo pushed the city closer to the campus, which fomented a mood in the 1970s to move the school to a different location. The upshot was a decision to construct a new campus at Engenheiro Coelho, about 120 miles from the original site, to which theology and programs in social studies and humanities would transfer, leaving health, nursing and sciences in Sao Paulo. The new campus added an Ellen G. White Research Center for advanced studies in religion and eventually developed into the largest theological center in South America, offering both master's degrees and doctorates by the end of the 1990s. In 1998 the entire complex of both campuses advanced to the status of a university center, the next to the highest rank for universities in Brazil.[13]

Official recognition at River Plate College came in piecemeal fashion, illustrating the tantalizing, if not patience-testing, pace of the development of Adventist education in some countries. The curricular stress at the Argentine school also lay on theology, but in the public eye the school's academic reputation derived from a teacher-education program dating from the 1920s whose graduates received official certificates after passing an external examination. The institution received government recognition in 1943 as a secondary school, and ten years later the teacher-preparation course became part of the secondary program and also received official recognition. It was the first time in Argentine history that a private Protestant school acquired this level of approval.

River Plate College had been offering post-secondary classes for a dozen years when the General Conference authorized it as a four-year post-secondary institution in 1958. During the 1960s and 1970s the college developed post-secondary tracks in teaching, office administration, philosophy, and music, each of which earned official approval. In 1969 a business course gained government recognition, and in 1973 Rosario University, less than a hundred miles to the south, incorporated the school of nursing into its school of medicine. A rise in Adventist membership throughout South America created a need for a nontraditional educational option, which led Home Study Institute, the Adventist correspondence school, to establish a branch on the River Plate campus in 1966.

Since 1943 River Plate had been advancing program by program toward recognition, but total institutional accreditation remained beyond its grasp. Although the campus was rural it was never out of the sight of government officials. In 1965 Argentine President Arturo Illia, a physician by profession, toured the campus, commending college and hospital administrators for their educational and medical programs, but leaving no encouragement that recognition was forthcoming. Fifteen years later negotiations for university status began with the Argentine Ministry of Education, but ten years passed before the coveted recognition came. It was a moment of ecstasy, "where for years university-level programs seemed an impossible dream," wrote South American Division Education Director Nevil Gorski.[14] With it also came a name change to River Plate Adventist University, a degree-granting institution organized into four schools: theology, health sciences, business, and a single school for humanities, education, and social sciences.

In 1994 the university began a fifth school, a school of medicine, which the government accredited in 2001. This new undertaking joined its sister institution in Mexico as the third physician's course in the denomination which would serve Latin America and the Caribbean, the home of thirty Adventist hospitals and major clinics besides lesser health-care units. As River Plate Adventist University began its second century it offered more than thirty fields of study, including a master's degree and a doctorate in theology.

### The Latin American Theological Seminary

Like its Brazilian counterpart, River Plate offered graduate degrees in theology through the Latin American Theological Seminary, most often known as SALT. During the early 1970s River Plate and Brazil colleges joined a growing number of schools requesting permission to inaugurate graduate studies in theology. Typically, these petitions received a mixed reception at the General Conference, but denominational leaders realized that they could not ignore the surge for post-baccalaureate education and generally sought ways to upgrade gradually. For several years leaders in both South America and Inter-America considered a single institution for both fields, but by 1978 they jettisoned the idea as infeasible because of the vast territory the seminary would have to serve. Instead, the two divisions substituted their first request with a second to offer graduate studies in theology at their three major campuses in Mexico, Argentina, and Brazil.

The next year, after the newly created General Conference Board of Theological Education inspected the campuses to advise on matters of upgrading, South America launched SALT to organize pastoral education programs on all campuses in the South American Division into a single administrative unit. The seminary was not an institution but an administrative office in the South American Division headquarters in Brasilia that managed theological education. Initially, SALT developed a graduate curriculum for summer classes at River Plate College and Brazil College. As the seminary matured it incorporated Northeast Brazil College and campuses in Peru, Chile, and Bolivia. Departments of religion at all post-secondary schools became branches of the seminary but continued to offer degrees in the name of their schools.

The academic aim of the seminary was not to produce theological scholars but to professionalize the South American ministry in pursuit of the church's evangelistic needs, which, besides direct evangelism, included teaching, pastoring, and church administration. Beginning in 1981 with two master's degrees, SALT added doctoral studies in theology and pastoral theology in the 1990s. The latter degree resembled the North American doctor of ministry but included more theology. In addition to the approval by the General Conference Board of Theological Education and the Adventist Accrediting Association, SALT joined theological associations that recognized seminaries in Brazil and Spanish-speaking South America. By 2002 the seminary had graduated about 600 students.

The Latin American Theological Seminary was unique in several ways. It became the denomination's supreme example of church administrative control of ministerial education. With seminary offices at the division headquarters and the seminary president doubling as a counseling secretary of the South American Division, SALT became an arm of the division, or perhaps even a second department of education assigned to theological instruction.

During the 1970s when conversations began about a seminary for Latin America, five post-secondary schools in South America offered ministerial education, one a junior college in northeastern Brazil. Politically, the division was bi-polar with one sphere in Portuguese-speaking Brazil and the second embracing the Spanish republics. Each of these regions experienced striking membership increases, which made it impractical to designate an existing institution as a single educational center for the division. SALT was an organization designed for multi-campus functions, which was especially applicable to South America but would not have been necessary in divisions such as Southern Asia where only one ministerial program existed.

By the year 2000 eight different post-secondary schools operated in South America, most of them universities. By creating a central office for theological studies and removing it from the control of the tertiary institutions, South America preserved the notion of a system of higher education revolving around theology and at the same time avoided the financial strain of supporting a sprawling university.

SALT also exerted a standardizing influence on theology education. With the best qualified instructors from various corners of South America conducting summer classes, all branch sites of SALT shared a common personnel pool. The result was a tendency of the various religion departments to become more nearly equal. Also contributing to the equalizing process were criteria with which institutions complied in order to qualify as a branch of the seminary.

About 8,400 students enrolled in South America's tertiary schools in the year 2000. While the division put its best efforts into ministerial education, the parent organizations of the schools—the unions—were responsible to acquire official recognition and develop new curricula according to regulatory legislation in the countries where the schools existed. Teacher-preparation courses and health sciences, including medicine, were the fields of study in highest demand, each with more than 1,900 students, which reflected the long history of schools and health-care institutions in the division.

In the year 2000 the Inter-American Division followed with its long-awaited seminary when the Association of Theological Schools in the United States and Canada recognized the Inter-American Theological Seminary with headquarters at the division offices in Miami, Florida. Previously, graduate studies in ministerial education in Inter-America were extensions from the Seminary at Andrews University. The new division seminary, known as IATS, absorbed these programs into a single institution, which, in a manner resembling its South American counterpart, assumed control of theological studies in all tertiary schools and exerted a similar standardizing influence on ministerial education. Headed by a dean, IATS offers graduate studies at branches at the college in Trinidad and the universities in Mexico, Puerto Rico, the Dominican Republic, Colombia, and Venezuela.

### A Summary of Adventist Tertiary Education

Seen against the tradition of training schools that dominated Adventist education until after World War II, the emergence of nearly a hundred tertiary institutions around the globe by the year 2000, most of them officially recognized, was an abundant academic harvest for

Seventh-day Adventists. Not only had baccalaureate education or its equivalent spread throughout the Adventist world, but graduate studies also became common. However, regardless of how penetrating it was, most graduate education retained a pragmatic character that derived from the longstanding denominational custom of establishing schools to prepare church employees. Given this underlying purpose, Adventist higher education tended toward the professions and applied sciences rather than erudition in letters. In this intellectual climate scholarly activity and research seldom received official support for its own sake; more often it had to serve denominational interests in some manner, even if nothing more than creating a favorable public image.

Before the majority of denominational schools in the world fields stood on their own as recognized institutions, some of them affiliated with North American colleges, which established accredited programs by proxy. Ministerial training retained its place of primacy in Adventist education. Because of its resources as the designated world center for Adventist theological education, Andrews University became the primary exporter of accredited Adventist education. Andrews also was the strongest magnet to draw church workers from all corners of the Adventist map and to educate them for professional roles in their home fields. In 1980 the Inter-American Division employed 186 administrators, teachers, and pastors who were graduates of various programs at Andrews. Ten years later the university reported eleven affiliations besides numerous extension programs.[15]

During the 1990s, as a larger number of Adventist tertiary institutions around the globe received recognition, the role Andrews University had played declined but remained strong. Its relationship with other institutions in the world fields became increasingly similar to a sibling rather than a mentor; however, official recognition of Adventist education was not universal, which made the presence of Andrews or another accredited institution a continued necessity, especially for younger, still developing schools.

As the leader of denominational academic medicine, Loma Linda University had also been and continued to be influential in Adventist institutions, but its shadow rested more on medical centers than schools. It also sought out non-Adventist sites at which it could establish a denominational presence and extend a healing hand. By 1995 it was affiliated with five university dental programs in Scandinavia and fifteen medical centers in Asia, Africa, and Russia. It also organized graduate study programs in public health that drew international enrollments among Adventists.[16]

As Adventist higher education around the world entered the twenty-first century, it was not a homogenous enterprise, but for all of its internal differences it still bore the marks of a single origin. Because of their narrower purpose training schools had been more similar to each other than were tertiary institutions. While theological education had been the central motivation in the spread of accredited post-secondary education, by the year 2000 Adventist higher education had become multifaceted to accommodate the needs of a broader spectrum of potential students.

More than a century earlier Ellen White had written from her Australian home that Adventists should establish educational centers around the world because church workers should receive their preparation in the fields in which they were to serve. In addition she advised that schools should not aim at a narrow clientele but that all Adventist youth should have the opportunity of church-sponsored education in order to become productive persons whether they entered private or public life. It was an obvious implication that Adventist education should be as broad as possible and that educators should not expect all students to be formal church workers.[17]

The approximately one hundred Adventist tertiary schools at the beginning of the twenty-first century fulfilled this counsel. Graduates marched from these institutions by the thousands, educated for church service, but post-secondary curricula also broadened to accommodate Adventist students who would enter private life. Denominational higher education was not all things to all people, but it offered an extensive repertoire of professional courses that the church community at large could not foresee in 1900.

---

[1]Keld J. Reynolds, "Two Educational Councils," (*Journal of True Education*, December 1948), pp. 20, 21; Otto Schuberth, "Southern Europe," (*Journal of True Education*, June 1954), p. 10; Pietro Copiz, "New Buildings, Exciting Opportunities," (*Journal of Adventist Education*, Summer 1990), p. 32, 33; Minutes, General Conference Committee, Southern European Division, 1963; P. Steiner to E. E. Cossentine, January 26, 1966, AST, RG 51; Min-

utes of the European Theological Education Committee, October 12, 1976, ibid.; Minutes of the Board of Theological Education, October 3, 1977, ibid.; Saleve Adventist University Bulletin, 1999-2000. Email, Andrea Luxton to Floyd Greenleaf, March 2, 2005.

[2]Minutes of the European Theological Education Committee, October 12, 1976, AST, RG 51; Minutes of the Board of Theological Education, October 3, 1977, ibid.; Johannes Hartlapp, ed. *Chronik Freidensau*, pp. 52-64.

[3]The section about Newbold College is summarized from *Northern Light*, August, 1953; November, 1953; November, 1954; April, 1955; March, 1956; August, 1959; November, 1959; no. 6, 1972; no. 5, 1974; Newbold College *Prospectus*, 1998-1999; *World Report 2000*. Archival materials from AST, RG 51: V. Norskov Olsen to E. E. Cossentine, July 23, 1964; Duane S. Johnson to Richard Hammill, July 28, 1964; Henning Karstrom to B. B. Beach, no date (c. summer 1965); Norskov Olsen to Richard Hammill, September 24, 1964; J. van Westrhenen, "Junior College-Newbold-C.U.C. Affiliation and Credits;" "General Comments from Stanborough School on the Letter re: Junior College-Newbold-CUC Affiliation and Credits;" "Department of Health, Education and Welfare, International Education Office;" "Statement of the Faculty of Toivonlinna Junior College on Its Relation to Newbold College;" Vaino Jaakkola to B. B. Beach, December 2, 1964; "Replies to the Ten Questions."

[4]Information about Solusi comes from Brown, *Chronology*, pp. 126, 167, 168; Sylvia J. Clarke, "Solusi: From Secondary School to College," (*Adventist Heritage*, Spring 1992), pp. 4-14; *Review and Herald*, June 23, 1960; March 1, 1962; February 13, 1964; *Adventist Review*, April 23, 1981; Trans-Africa *Division Outlook*, May 15, 1980; January 15, 1984; *Eastern Africa Division Outlook*, August-October 1984; January-February 1985; September-October 1985; May-July 1990; July-September 1994; April-June 1995; *World Report 2000*. Interview: Milton Siepman, January 8, 2002. Archival materials from AST, RG51: Russell Staples to J. B. Cooks, September 8, 1961; Richard Hammill, "A Report To the Board of Trustees of Solusi College and To the Southern African Division Committee Concerning the Request for an Affiliation with Andrews University;" E. E. Cossentine to Robert H. Pierson, November 1, 1965; Richard H. Davis to Richard Hammill, November 12, 1965; "Memorandum on the Future Development of Solusi College Presented to the Solusi College Board of Managers," November 15, 1965; F. G. Thomas, "Memorandum on Educational Problems in Rhodesia," March 11, 1966.

[5]For the description of UEAB see *Adventist Review*, May 3 and June 28, 1979; *Eastern Africa Division Outlook*, April 15, 1984; May-June 1986; November-December 1985; March-April 1990; August-September 1990; March-May 1991; April-June 1992; *University of Eastern Africa Bulletin*, 1998-2000 and 2000-2002; *World Report 2000*.

[6]*Eastern Africa Division Outlook*, March-May, 1991.

[7]*Directory of Seventh-day Adventist Colleges and Universities*, 2004 ed. pp. 7-10.

[8]*Ibid.*, p. 108.

[9]*Ibid.* p. 19.

[10]*Data Book of the Commission on Seventh-day Adventist Education in Africa.* (Silver Spring, MD: General Conference Department of Education, 1995).

[11]The following sources have provided information about South America and Inter-America, including the Latin American Theological Seminary: General Conference Minutes, October 30, 1958; October 25, 1965; August 18, 1966; October 4 and December 27, 1973; Interview, Enrique Becerra, February 13, 2002; *Statistical Report*, 1945, 1950, 1970; *World Report, 2000*; Brown, *Chronology, passim*; *General Conference Bulletin*, 1980, no. 3, p. 10; no. 8, p. 12; Nevil Gorski, "Doors Opening for Adventist Education," (*Journal of Ad-*

*ventist Education*, Summer 1990), pp. 60-65; Greenleaf, *Adventist Church in Latin America and the Caribbean*, vol. 2, pp. 458-468; Universidad de Montemorelos *Catalogo*, 1998-2000; "Report of the Committee Appointed to Survey the Readiness of the *Colegio Vocacional Y Profesional Montemorelos* for Upgrading to Senior College Status," June 10-12, 1973, AST, RG 51; "Report of the Accrediting Visiting Team, Seminario Adventist Latinoamericano de Teologia, 19 May to 3 June, 1991," GC Department of Education; *LATS Evaluation*, self-study report, 2002; *Report of the Visiting Committee for Latin American Adventist Theological Seminary*, 2002; *Report from the Argentinian Campus to the General Conference Survey Committee, 1997*; "Evaluation Visit to the South American Theological Seminary, February 9-17, 1997"; Minutes of the Board of Theological Education, October 3, 1977, January 4, 1978, April 21 and October 3, 1978, October 2, 1979, October 6, 1980. *Directory of Seventh-day Adventist Colleges and Universities,* 2004 ed., p. 50.

[12]For the impact of Hispanic immigration on the North American Division, see Manuel Vasquez, *The Untold Story: 100 Years of Hispanic Adventism, 1899-1999* (Nampa, ID: Pacific Press Publishing Association, 2000).

[13]The best source of information about the development of Brazil College into a university center is Alberto R. Timm, ed., *Instituto Adventista de Ensino Campus 2: 15 Anos de Historia* (Engenheiro Coelho, SP: Imprensa Universitaria Adventista, 1999). See chapter II, by Andre M. Pasini, "IAE-C2: Origem E Desenvolvimento Fisico," pp. 8-17.

[14]Nevil Gorski, "Doors Opening for Adventist Education," (*Journal of Adventist Education*, Summer 1990), p. 62.

[15]*General Conference Bulletin*, 1980, no. 6, p. 7; *ibid.*, 1990, no. 5, p. 15.

[16]Schwartz and Greenleaf, *Light Bearers*, p. 482.

[17]Ellen White's statment is recorded in *Testimonies*, v. 6, pp. 126-218. See specifically pp. 137, 139, 197, 206, 207.

# Chapter 18

# Adventist Education in Adverse Climates

One of the unwritten chapters about Adventist education after World War II is the account of hardship denominational schools faced in countries governed by socialist regimes. Before World War II Adventist schools faced uncongenial conditions in Eastern Europe, and elsewhere, for that matter, but the problems of the post-1945 era were the result of a new politico-economic atmosphere. In the aftermath of the war a wave of socialist ideology spread rapidly from the Union of Soviet Socialist Republics, washing across Slavic Europe, splitting Germany into two countries and sweeping away old centers of political power. Illiberal governments quickly seized authority to reestablish order and reconstruct shattered economies. Only ten months after the war's end Winston Churchill characterized the new order as an iron curtain that cordoned off Eastern Europe as a buffer between the USSR and Western democracies.

This region of radical socialist governments, extending about 8,000 miles from the western edge of East Germany across Eastern Europe and the Soviet Union, variously called the Soviet bloc, communist bloc, or eastern bloc, pitted itself in a struggle against the capitalist West. Although at times the conflict erupted into live warfare, it was largely a battle of nerves, popularly known as the Cold War which spread with varying intensity to the corners of Asia, Africa, and Latin America.

Radical socialism claimed philosophical roots in scientific atheism and proposed to eradicate Christianity as though it were an intellectual poison, but religion did not disappear easily, even in the USSR. In one form or another Christianity had a long entrenched history in Europe and constituted part of the cultural milieu. The same could be said about Latin America and non-Christian religions in Asian countries. When seeking to make good its threats against religion, radical socialism often found compromise necessary. The movement also declared itself to be an international train of events inevitably determined by economic conditions, but in reality it was more a combination of nationalism and anti-West politics and its character differed from country to country despite its common rhetoric.

Whatever the circumstances, because of its philosophical declarations, radical socialism exerted a powerful influence on education, producing new dilemmas for Adventist schools in affected countries. It did not take long for denominational education to feel its impact. "Unfortunately," Keld J. Reynolds wrote when reporting the two education councils in Europe in 1948, "some representatives of our Eastern European schools were unable to attend their divisional council at Florence." It is doubtful that Department of Education personnel expected events to be different. They had devoted the entire June 1948 issue of *The Journal of True Education* to pictures and commentary about the recovery Adventist education around the globe was making from World War II, but the coverage included only a single laconic allusion to the post-war political order. "Behind the curtain are other schools that are in God's hands," the editor said with veiled concern, "the unofficial reports from which are encouraging."[1]

### Missionsseminar Friedensau

Because of a divided Germany, Missionsseminar Friedensau near Magdeburg found itself in the German Democratic Republic, lumped together with Adventist education in Eastern Europe where denominational schools had operated only erratically in the prewar years. In both world wars the German government expropriated the school at Friedensau to convert it into a military hospital, a function that the Soviet army continued when it overran eastern Germany in 1945. Claiming to be the rightful owners, less than a year after the war's end Adventists in East Germany requested the Soviet military government to return the school to them.[2]

Friedensau reopened in 1947, "after great difficulty and lengthy negotiations," General Conference Secretary of Education E. E. Cossentine later commented, and a historic Adventist campus, now resuscitated, was off to an uncertain future in a communist climate.[3] Classes began on July 1 with eighteen students and five teachers. For school director Walter Eberhardt and his faculty the first year was a struggle to stay alive. Food was scarce. Kitchen equipment was both deficient and poor and furniture was lacking. To survive teachers had to work at much more than classroom instruction.

The government, whether headed by Soviet occupation forces or later the East Germans themselves, did not allow Friedensau to forget that the country was socialist. As it had been since early institutional days, the community was actually a small village of Seventh-day Adventists surrounding the school and retirement center. When a new road was under construction to connect Friedensau to nearby towns, students put in their fair quota of the work, laboring by hand to lay the roadbed. "Under socialism came many curiosities," *Chronik Friedensau* recalled. The celebration on May 8, 1953, the eighth anniversary of the liberation from Naziism, became a work bee to pull weeds and clean up the community. To observe Whitsunday the next year, a German youth congress organized egg collections on poultry farms.

Changes occurred in the student labor program. From its beginning the school was known as an industrial school with students logging between ten and twenty hours weekly in the various work departments. The program was an integrated part of their education that helped to keep the school financially afloat and helped students to pay their school fees and learn a skilled trade. Although the school changed its name several times, the labor program continued, but during the socialist years the meaning of student labor changed because education was free. The government permitted no funds to leave the country, which allowed the East German Union to accumulate relatively large reserves with which to subsidize the school completely. Even though they did not need to work, the students still put in their customary hours and earned a modest amount.

The school could not advertise religious education, but the church itself could promote classes as church projects. Under this guise the seminary offered a variety of summer and one-year classes especially for German youth to orient them in so-called laymen's activities, a term broadly construed to include instruction not necessarily religious, such as typing. Known as deacons' short courses to distinguish them from the ministerial curriculum, they continued for forty-three years, nearly the entire life of the German Democratic Republic. Eventually a new set of two-year laymen's classes offered among other subjects, nursing, typewriting and shorthand, and social work opportunities. These classes were the forerunner of the social work program that became a recognized part of the curriculum in 1989.

The purpose of the school was to offer a ministerial training course equivalent to the post-secondary program in the United States. In 1961 the school's name changed, designating it as a ministerial seminary, and two decades later changed again to Theological Seminary. Enrollment was consistently less than a hundred, but the name changes signaled not only an advancing institutional maturity but also a degree of relaxed socialist regulation and more involvement with the Adventist world. In the 1980s students enrolled from the socialist countries of Mozambique, Angola, Yugoslavia, and the Soviet Union. The school also improved its academic standing, resulting in denominational accreditation in 1984.

With the unfolding years the institution became more intertwined with church-related events in East Germany. In 1957 a Bible Conference for youth drew 950 participants to the campus, culminating in a baptism. Three years later the first workers' meeting for all ministers in East Germany convened on campus, but West Berlin preachers, though conveniently less than sixty miles away, were prohibited. During the 1960s and 1970s leading denominational personalities visited the campus, including archeology professor Siegfried Horn from Andrews University, General Conference President Robert H. Pierson, and Richard Hammill, who had become a General Conference vice president and a kind of roving minister of education. A division-wide Bible Conference for workers in 1977 attracted 300 ministers from East Germany and other socialist states in Eastern Europe. Representatives from the General Conference Biblical Research Institute and Andrews University also attended this gathering.

Friedensau's reputation reached beyond the confines of Adventism. Several bishops from the Evangelical Methodist churches and the consistorial president journeyed to the campus, as did the chairman of the Evangelical Church Council. Gerald Gotting, the president of the People's Chamber of the German Democratic Government and chairman of the Christian Democratic Party also paid the school a visit. All of these contacts, both within and outside Adventism, added up to a recognition that however surly radical socialism might be toward religion, it was evolving a sense of accommodation that contradicted scientific atheism's original assertions that there could be no compatibility with Christianity.

A strong heritage of music dating from the days of Otto Lupke, the school's first director, continued during the socialist years and helped to bring recognition to the campus. Regular concerts that audiences would expect only in large cities began in the mid-1950s, which brought noted artists to the "small village in the forest," *Chronik Friedensau* observed. In 1974 the school installed its fourth organ in the chapel, a powerful instrument that came on the occasion of the seventy-fifth anniversary of the school.

It was apparent that radical socialism was softening, at least in some respects, and it would continue this course despite uprisings in 1956 and 1968 that had incited an iron-fisted response by Soviet forces in East Germany, Poland, Hungary, and Czechoslovakia. Dissent in a newer form appeared in the 1980s, a product of glasnost and perestroika in the USSR itself, elements of a new spirit of openness with the possibility of restructuring society. At Friedensau Bible conferences for both youth and the clergy were common and visitors from denominational headquarters were frequent. Andrews University also established extension courses on the German campus.

In 1989 the Berlin Wall tumbled under the weight of a demonstrating public, and the next year the government authorized the Theological Seminary to become a university and to grant degrees in its own right. German unification followed soon after, which gave German Adventists the opportunity to consolidate their post-secondary education by merging the ministerial program at Marienhohe with Friedensau. The seminary at Marienhohe became a secondary school. By the mid-1990s the new university at Friedensau was offering graduate studies and diplomas in social work with an emphasis on international programs.

Friedensau had come full circle. A century earlier it began as Europe's strongest center to produce ministers and public health workers. It had quickly grown into an international campus. By the year 2000 it had regained its international character, and although its enrollment remained small–a margin above 200–it had become a strong Adventist educational hub in northern and eastern Europe.

The experience at Friedensau was a case of educational success in spite of a less than sanguine environment. The government of East Germany was not known for its lax attitude toward the capitalist West, but the growth of Adventist education occurred anyway and in time flourished, neutralizing the negative philosophical impact of an anti-religious government and even gaining the respect of public authority.

### Poland's Michal Belina Czechoswski Spiritual Seminary

Another example of Adventist education in Eastern Europe came from Poland which furnished one of the best examples of compromise between a socialist government and a Christian society. Before World War II Seventh-day Adventists in Poland had no legal standing, but the post-war government viewed Adventism, as small as it was, as a balancing force that socialism could use to help equalize religious influences in the country. Accordingly, Adventists received government recognition in 1946 as an official church, which meant that they could own and operate institutions.[4]

This new legal status was at least a shadow of freedom and an improvement over prewar conditions, but the new liberty was a matter of practical politics rather than freedom in an idealistic sense. Nevertheless, it was with optimism that Adventist workers began offering seminary classes in Krakow in 1947, which were really a resumption of a Polish worker-training school that functioned intermittently during the 1930s at Kamienica Slaska in the south. In 1949 the small ministerial course moved back to this prewar site.

For five years beginning in 1953 politics reversed itself and the school did not operate, but its reopening in 1958 was encouraging enough to bring a $15,000 appropriation from the General Conference to help restart the fledgling enterprise. Comforts were few. Thirty students crowded into four dormitory rooms and some teachers lived in improvised quarters in an attic. It was evident that the new school needed all the assistance it could get.

The purpose of the Adventist school was to prepare church workers. In the recent absence of a school one of the most common methods to prepare ministers had been to assign a young prospect to an experienced pastor for mentoring until he became ready to shoulder full responsibility. Adventist membership was inching upward to 3,300 and a need for formally educated ministers was probably the most serious deficiency in the three Polish conferences.

A year after its rejuvenation, the school moved to Podkowa Lesna, about fifteen miles west of Warsaw. The new site was an eight-acre estate, formerly of the aristocracy, that allowed room for small agricultural projects that would furnish fruit and garden products to the school. Here the ministerial program gelled into a five-year sequence.

At the time of the reopening in 1958, Adventist students were attending universities in Warsaw and Krakow to study for a wide variety of professions from medicine to law and various disciplines in the humanities. Education of that kind was a concern of the state. The small Adventist venture at Kamienica was not an attempt to provide an Adventist alternative to these public institutions, but the school collaborated with state education by allowing its students time to attend a nearby government school to take classes preparing them for the university entrance examination.

Although the seminary was a place to educate new pastors, the practical effect of this arrangement was to provide an Adventist study track for a few students while at the same time preparing ministers. By 1965 about thirty had graduated, eleven of whom became church workers. Despite this ratio of employing only about one in three graduates, the seminary had its desired impact. Most if not all of the ministers in Poland had been students at the seminary at one time or another. In time, curricular changes modified theological studies to two- and four-year sequences, both of which permitted time for students to continue their studies at the state university. Occasionally some were able to attend Newbold College in England for degree studies.

Enrollment remained low from the 1960s through the 1980s because students had few reasons to attend the seminary unless they planned to become church workers; however, by the mid-1980s prospects for increased enrollment rose as the school developed more academic breadth. A construction project added a new seminary complex to the campus that housed a 200-seat chapel, a cafeteria, and eight classrooms, besides dormitory space for more than sixty-five boarding students. The school offered three curricula: a three-year theology program, a Bible instructor program, and a secretarial course. Enrollment was thirty-two in these "day school" curricula, roughly the same number as in 1958 when the seminary reopened for the second time. The school also offered a two-year correspondence course in theology for laymen interested in evangelism. Enrollment in this program exceeded eighty-five.

The seminary, since the 1970s called the Michal Belina Czechoswski Spiritual Seminary, opened the new complex in 1986 with a celebration that brought several public personalities to the campus, including the Polish minister for religious affairs, the director of non-Catholic minorities, and the local mayor. Speaking before these dignitaries, the president of the Polish Union described plans to add courses in healthful lifestyle, drug prevention, and foreign languages, and to establish connections with Newbold College, Andrews University, and the theological seminary in Germany as well as to prepare students for graduate studies at the Polish Christian Theological Academy, the state supported ecumenical institution in which the government exercised the authority of appointment.

These ambitious goals were the product of liberalizing trends, but Polish politics proposed to integrate all elements of Polish society into a single egalitarian movement. Polish law decreed that religion and state must be separate, declared all churches equal, and guaranteed religious liberty to all churches, but only to those that were legally recognized. The state reserved the right to educate, but allowed legal churches to operate schools without interference, called centers of religious instruction, and to establish seminaries to educate clergy.

In reality religious influences in Poland were far from equal; consequently, the government exerted a controlling hand over religious affairs to maintain a degree of balance. B. B. Beach, a former director of education in the Northern Europe Division, observed in 1973 that "the churches in Poland are free to preach, publish and prosper, if they forthrightly co-operate in building a new socialist egalitarian society."[5] It was clearly in the context of a socialist society that the Adventist seminary functioned.

The breakdown of the socialist system in 1989 did not bring prosperity to the Polish school. The school remained a secondary institution with a worker-training course that was post-secondary but not a degree program. Of note as well was the loss of many Adventists to western countries by emigration, which caused comparatively slow membership growth, only 900 during the 1990s. The demand for a large number of new pastors tapered off. By the year 2000 enrollment dropped to the levels of the 1950s.

### Adventisticki Seminar Marusevec in Yugoslavia

By some estimates Adventist education in Eastern Europe fared best in Yugoslavia where socialism appeared to be less caustic. In 1955, thirteen years after the Yugoslavian school closed because of World War II, seminary classes resumed on a newly purchased, seven-acre property in Rakovica near Belgrade, the national capital. Pavle Borovic, a student at the seminary beginning in 1957 and later a conference worker and teacher, remembered that the Yugoslavian church submitted many requests to the government before the school reopened. The curriculum was limited to male students enrolled in a three-year theology curriculum. Space was too limited to permit a new beginning class of students each year, so each cohort had to complete its studies in order to make room for the next group. Because theology books were scarce teachers wrote their own texts which they copied with a laborious printing method.[6]

Hardships or not, the school hung on, and by 1968 its leaders were laying plans for expansion and a coeducation program that would offer women students courses in secretarial training and home economics. But growth at Rakovica became a moot question as the local civil government expropriated the school property to construct a highway, promising to pay for the land. Borovic, who by this time taught at the seminary, saw the government's action as an attempt to stop the school, but if indeed, that was the case, it backfired. Yugoslavian church leaders, including Borovic, argued that the land was extremely valuable to them and proposed an exorbitant price for compensation.

Surprisingly, the government agreed, and with the money the Yugoslavian Union leased an old castle in the northern village of Marusevec, near Varazdin, about twenty miles from Hungary and not much farther from Austria. Sufficient funds were left to repair the deteriorating castle, purchase adjoining land, erect two dormitories, student apartments, and faculty homes. The new institution opened as a secondary school only, without the seminary, but in 1974 the seminary joined the school which took the name of Adventisticki Seminar Marusevec.

Additional land acquisition by 1978 expanded the campus to approximately seventeen acres, some of it devoted to classrooms and housing for both faculty and students, and some to cultivation. By 1980 seminary enrollment reached almost fifty in three different curricula for both men and women. Secondary students numbered about 170. All were from Yugoslavia.

*After closing during World War II, the Seventh-day Adventist school in Yugoslavia reopened in 1955 and became one of the most prosperous of Adventist schools in socialist countries. In 1968 the school moved to this castle in Marusevec in northern Yugoslavia.*

As early as 1968 the seminary underwent accrediting by the General Conference Department of Education. The examining committee found much to commend but recommended more careful budgeting to improve academic equipment and library accessions. It also suggested that the school should reorganize its theology curriculum to cover four years instead of three and to align with Seminaire Adventiste in France, which would enable Yugoslavian ministerial students to complete a theology degree.

During the next decade Marusevec became the only Adventist school in the communist world to maintain a direct connection with a denominational institution in a capitalist democracy by not only linking with the French campus, but also with Newbold. It tied to Friedensau as well, which furnished a variety of options for the equivalent of a bachelor's degree in theology from schools both in and out of the European socialist community. The Yugoslavian school was also unique among Adventist seminaries in Eastern Europe by having a well organized secondary school beneath it. Similar to the Polish seminary, Marusevec also cooperated with the Yugoslavian system of higher education by designing the ministerial curriculum as an entrance prerequisite for university studies. The effectiveness of this program became evident as Adventist students fared well when taking university entrance examinations.

Marusevec benefitted from a less virulent socialist government as compared to other countries in Eastern Europe. The primary burden of the Yugoslavian government was to hold an ethnically diverse country together in a federated system rather than to maintain solidarity within the eastern bloc; in fact, early in the post World War II era Yugoslavia made it clear that Soviet personnel and influence were not welcome and that Yugoslavian communism was for Yugoslavians. In this nationalistic environment, programs such as Adventist education which joined the various ethnic groups within the country in peaceful pursuits could be perceived to be nationally beneficial. The seminary campus also became a Yugoslavian Adventist center for youth camps, ministerial retreats, seminars for parents, and conventions, all activities that fostered unity among Yugoslavian Adventists.

One such gathering on the campus in 1986 was a six-day workshop which the Trans-European Division conducted in conjunction with Adventist World Radio to improve religious radio programming. Church leaders in Yugoslavia and students alike attended. At the time Yugoslavian Adventists could not broadcast programs, but they were able to prepare radio programs in six languages which they sent to Adventist short wave stations in western Europe that were within range of radio receivers in Yugoslavia.

Within two years after the demise of radical socialism in Eastern Europe, fighting erupted in Yugoslavia and the country broke apart along ethnic lines, producing several small republics. Almost immediately, in 1991, enrollment at Marusevec dropped to a quarter of its normal level while the school became a haven for refugees. Reflecting the new political map, the Adventist Yugoslavian Union also fractured in half, and in 1992 the seminary returned to the Serbian city of Belgrade that had been the Yugoslavian capital for many years. In its relocated site the seminary became Belgrade Theological Seminary, serving a constituency of about 8,000 in the new independencies of Bosnia-Herzegovina, Macedonia, and the remaining territory of the old Yugoslavia. This combined membership approximated two-thirds of the former Yugoslavian Union.

With the departure of the seminary from Marusevec the campus reorganized as a government accredited secondary school in newly independent Croatia. Shortly the school added ministerial education to become Adriatic Union College with a constituency in Croatia, Slovenia, and Albania. By the year 2000 about eighty enrolled in the two post-secondary theology programs at Belgrade and Marusevec. Graduates of both schools were eligible to enter the Open University Validation Services at Newbold College for graduate study.

### Romanian Adventist Theological Institute

In Romania, the European country with the largest Adventist population, political conditions were deceptively congenial immediately after liberation from Nazi occupation. In 1947 the denominational training school reported an enrollment of 136, a figure that could have been larger if the campus could have accommodated more students. "Having liberty once more to preach the gospel, the young people go from village to village and from home to home, calling the people to God," the General Conference Department of Education announced.[7] But this new freedom was only an interlude between one oppressor and the next. In 1949 the government confiscated the school and the best the church could do was to maintain only a skeletal form of ministerial education in Bucharest.

Events moved quickly after the fall of the communist regime in 1989. The rate of church membership growth in Romania had been and continued to be one of the highest in Europe and by the year 2000 the restored Romanian Adventist Theological Institute had grown to be the largest denominational school in the Euro-Africa Division with about 500 students. Nearly half of them were in theological studies, but the school also offered a variety of other curricula with business and the humanities also attracting large numbers. The school's degrees were nationally recognized. In 2002 Andrews University established an extension on the fifteen-acre campus to offer a master of arts in theology.[8]

### Zaokski Theological Seminary, Russia

In the Soviet Union itself Adventist education made a late appearance. During much of the 1920s Seventh-day Adventists, like other religious bodies, practiced religion with comparative freedom. Church leaders organized short, rudimentary classes in ministerial education, but by the end of the decade official attitudes against religion hardened. In 1929 the General Conference stopped receiving official statistics of Adventist activity in the country. Officially, at least, the church came to a standstill. During the 1930s a school for Russians operated at Harbin, Manchuria, where some prospective ministers received training.[9]

Only when official Soviet policy began to relax in the 1970s did church activity start to escalate. In the next decade the Russian terms, perestroika and glasnost, expressing more openness and connection with the outside world, became part of the English vocabulary. Adventists organized conferences during the 1970s; union conferences appeared in the late 1980s, and in 1990 the Euro-Asia Division went into operation. At the 1985 General Conference session the church heard an official report about Adventism in the USSR for the first time in about sixty years. Among other optimistic descriptions of denominational affairs, Mikhail P. Kulakov, head of the Adventist church in the Soviet

*Russian Seventh-day Adventists built Zaokski Theological Seminary and began offering classes in 1989, two years before the communist government collapsed. This 1995 photograph shows the original classroom building with the library on the far side, added in 1994.*

Union, said he was "confident that the government will soon allow the church to start a theological course for its pastors."[10]

Two years later the church gained permission to reconstruct a destroyed building in Zaokski, a small community about seventy-five miles below Moscow. Led by Mikhail M. Kulakov, son of Mikhail P., Russian Adventists rallied to the task, donating time and supplies over a period of two years. The new facility, built along traditional Russian architectural lines and surrounded by a classic iron fence, opened in December 1988. Among the guests were the chairman of the Soviet Council for Religious Affairs, leaders of other churches, General Conference President Neal Wilson, and other Adventist personalities.

A theological seminary in the Soviet Union, even advertised by a road sign, was headline news that appeared on national television in the USSR, but also of interest was an agricultural program based on a fifty-acre plot where Jacob Mittleider, a well-known Adventist agriculturalist, introduced new methods of vegetable production. When the seminary opened it offered three courses: theology, music and agriculture.

The tempo of other church activities also picked up. Adjacent to the new seminary was land dedicated to a new Adventist publishing house. Adventist evangelists conducted meetings in Moscow. A radio broadcasting center was under construction in nearby Tula. Members of the Adventist Geoscience Research Institute attended a gathering of the Academy of Natural Science in the Siberian city of Novosibirsk and representation from the Theological Seminary at Andrews visited the Zaokski campus to assist with the theology program.

Though seen as a providential gift, the seminary nevertheless faced myriad problems. A phenomenal rise in the number of conversions and new congregations in Russia produced a heavier demand for ministers than the seminary could supply. Well-educated Russians who could teach were not uncommon, but a credentialed theology staff did not exist; consequently, the school depended on experienced ministers to teach classes and on visiting pastors, church administrators, and teachers, mainly from the United States, to conduct short intensive courses or even remain for an entire quarter.

Meanwhile, the newly organized Euro-Asia Division supported a campaign to upgrade promising faculty, sending them primarily to the Theological Seminary at Andrews University. Particularly acute was the lack of persons trained in accounting and business to handle church financial matters, careers that were unknown during the Soviet era. By the mid-1990s the seminary added a short business course equivalent to a minor in the American baccalaureate system. The school also affiliated with Andrews University for graduate programs in theology.

Through the 1990s Zaokski retained its original emphasis on ministerial education, music, and agriculture, avoiding major curricular additions partly because the school was officially recognized as a seminary and to add new degree programs would require re-accreditation. Adventist education at lower levels in Russia was evolving but not spreading rapidly, which meant that a teacher-preparation course at Zaokski was not practical.

Radical socialism in Europe was teetering on the edge of disintegration when the seminary at Zaokski was born, but of all the schools in the Soviet bloc, it attracted the most attention as something almost surreal, given the apparent political isolation of the USSR. Just as surreal was the membership explosion during the 1990s which raised the total from about 35,000 in 1990 to more than 135,000 ten years later. In 1999 the seminary celebrated its tenth anniversary. The next year enrollment reached nearly 350, of whom more than 200 were in theological studies, making Zaokski one of the leading Adventist theological centers in Eastern Europe.

### China

The largest country outside the Soviet Union to adopt radical socialism was China where a communist revolution succeeded in 1949, but the country did not become part of the Soviet bloc as did Eastern Europe. The stance of the new Chinese government against Christianity was more rigid than in most places in socialist Europe. Adventist education in China simply vanished and the school in Hong Kong inherited the responsibility of denominational post-secondary programs for Chinese Adventists. In 1951 the Far Eastern Division began construction on a new institution in Taiwan where the remnant of the Chinese republic maintained a free government. After passing through several phases of development, the school became Taiwan Adventist College.

The demise of the Maoist era in the 1980s also marked the beginning of more pragmatic and less ideological domestic policies in China, but Adventist education did not reappear. With Adventist membership estimated marginally less than 300,000 as the twenty-first century began, the need for trained pastors and other workers was acute, but only informal methods of ministerial preparation were available. Fewer travel restrictions allowed some students to enroll in Hong Kong Adventist College, and even attend a denominational school elsewhere.

Conditions also permitted visitors from the East Asia Association in Hong Kong, something analogous to a set of union officers without a constituency, who encouraged the growth of Adventism in China but had no role in administering the churches. Without becoming intrusive, the committee was able to exert an informal influence on Chinese workers through inservice sessions. After the formation of the Northern Asia-Pacific Division in 1999 the East Asia Association became the China Union Mission, but no differences in educational activity occurred.

## Lakpahana Adventist College and Seminary

Of all communist governments, China took the most adamant stand against Christian education. Ironically, it was its Asian neighbor, Sri Lanka, that represented one of the most benign cases of socialist influence on Adventist schools. In 1948 this island gained its independence but remained a dominion in the British Commonwealth and retained the name of Ceylon. Socialist political parties on the island originated during the period between the two world wars, but not until 1956 when the Sri Lanka Freedom Party ascended to power did the government veer substantially to the left.

Under the tutelage of the SLFP, as the party was called, socialism never assumed the radical form that characterized some of the governments in Eastern Europe. A broad spectrum of political parties continued to thrive, elections continued, and the country avoided a dictatorship. The SLFP generally favored the majority Sinhalese population which was Buddhist, a policy that tended to alienate the Tamil minority that was largely Hindu.[11]

Given this political cleavage, turmoil was unavoidable. The most serious troubles were periodic communal riots among the Tamil-speaking population that eventually led to outright hostilities. A see-saw political struggle ensued between the SLFP and its leading rival, the more conservative United National Party. Constitutional changes in 1972 and 1977 changed Ceylon's name to the Democratic Socialist Republic of Sri Lanka, which confirmed the political trends of the previous two decades.

As it evolved, socialism in this island nation was far more nationalistic than ideological, but it translated into attempted land reform, expropriation of private schools and free education from kindergarten through university, free medical care, assistance to the poor, and nationalization of industries, especially those under foreign control such as oil production. Although the SLFP lent moral support to liberation fronts in many countries, it maintained a diplomatically non-aligned relationship between the protagonists of the Cold War. Beginning in the late 1970s the government sought ways to return industry to private hands and encourage foreign investment.

Adventist education walked a narrow and discreet path through these political land mines. Less than two years after independence, the

Ceylonese government requisitioned the land on which the training school operated in Kottawa, near the capital, forcing the school to move northward in 1952 to an old coconut estate in the mountains, a dozen miles from Kandy, the island's second largest city. Some regarded the change as a blessing inasmuch as the new location was a choice property that offered opportunities for growth that did not exist in Kottawa. In typical Adventist fashion, a group of pioneer teachers and students settled on the estate to build the school from the ground up, first clearing the land that lay in abandoned confusion. The new school, named Lakpahana, meaning light of Lanka, had hardly established itself when the SLFP took over the country in 1956.

One of the government's first measures was to legalize Sinhala as the national language. This attempt to nationalize communication sparked the anger of the Tamil population who sent the country reeling in communal riots. Lakpahana, whose faculty and students were both Sinhalese and Tamil, tried to protect itself from the divisiveness in the surrounding community by literally closing its gates and emphasizing unity on the campus. Years later, in calmer moments, the government recognized Tamil as a second official language, but the mischief had been done, and conflict over this issue ignited a perennial hostility between the two ethnic groups that broke out in occasional violence and shooting. Meanwhile, in order to maintain itself, Lakpahana had to furnish teachers for both of the languages and English as well.

Another government attempt to unite the country came from the rival United National Party after it regained power in the mid-1960s. With a new sensitivity toward the Sinhalese population, the UNP replaced the Christian Sunday with the Poya Day, a Buddhist holiday, when schools and businesses would close. This new day of rest meandered through the traditional seven-day week because the moon's cycles determined its frequency. The result was a confused class schedule for Lakpahana which also closed on the Saturday Sabbath. Although it disrupted the traditional week, this calendar was more of a nuisance than a threat. Even the general population found this calendar irksome because it made difficulties for the business community which had to correlate its activities with the rest of commercial world that conducted its affairs according to the seven-day week.

The attempt to nationalize education by establishing a single language and to institute a unique Sri Lankan calendar were matters of nationalism rather than socialism, but land reform was a common socialist issue that nearly destroyed Lakpahana. During the election of 1960 the local representative to the national legislature promised to break up the estates in his area and redistribute the land to the people. Legislation to fulfill his pledge passed, and forty acres of Lakpahana's best plantation land were surveyed in preparation for redistribution, but only hours before the school was to become a victim of this expropriation, the government fell and land confiscation proceedings were immediately scrapped.

Hardly had this threat passed before the government began outright expropriation of private schools as part of its plan to nationalize education. The government claimed legality for its actions because it subsidized private institutions and was justified to control them in the name of national well being. Since the early days at Kottawa in the 1920s Adventist schools had followed the government's prescribed curricula that prepared students for external examinations that validated their education, but they had not accepted government subsidies, and from the expropriation scheme of the 1960s Lakpahana escaped unscathed.

With the passing of this crisis the worst was over for Lakpahana, but the school still faced routine government controls. Nationalization of education was part of a broader plan to improve literacy, and after independence successive governments continued the colonial practice of external examinations as a means to standardize achievement at government prescribed levels. Accordingly, in addition to its traditional Adventist curriculum, Lakpahana included preparation for both the ordinary and advanced level tests. Adventist students established a good performance record, and testing officials usually allowed them to avoid examinations on Sabbath.

Although the record spoke well for Lakpahana, the school did not earn the right to grant degrees. When Lakpahana added post-secondary courses in ministerial education and teacher-preparation, two-year diplomas were the limit of its academic authority. Several conditions worked against the school's advancement. Sri Lanka needed pastors, but the Adventist population on the island was neither large nor increasing rapidly; consequently, the demand for ministerial students was not as critical as in bigger and faster growing fields. Government controls over elementary and secondary education made it impossible to conduct traditional church schools, thus the long-standing denominational practice of establishing lower schools wherever possible and developing a system that fed students upward to a post-secondary institution did not occur in Sri Lanka. Adventist membership on the island was also poor, placing tuition out of reach of many Adventist families.

Even against these odds, enrollment at Lakpahana reached well above 300, but in the two-year diploma programs the number of students was skimpy, which prompted an evaluation team from the Southern Asia-Pacific Division to recommend in 1998 that the school should drop its post-secondary curricula. While officially the school discontinued the courses, it retained its post-secondary status and concentrated on reestablishing its lost programs. Meanwhile, furnishing even a few well-prepared pastors became problematical.

If Lakpahana's function as a post-secondary school had suffered, it was clear that its role as a mission school was as strong as it had ever been as it entered the twenty-first century. Non-Adventist enrollment stood at forty percent, overwhelmingly Sinhalese. About half of the 370 students were from the immediate community. While the school resumed its worker-training courses, they remained unrecognized. The original plan to develop a student labor program lagged inasmuch as the school developed no industries, but for the boarding students the school provided jobs maintaining the campus.

In spite of the problems Lakpahana faced through the years–or perhaps because of them–the impact of the institution on Sri Lankan Adventists was enormous. When the institution celebrated its seventy-fifth anniversary in March 1998–its origins dated from 1923 at Kottawa–nearly a thousand alumni, former staff, and friends flocked to the campus. One native Sri Lankan living in Canada and unable to attend, sent $1,000 for the school's discretionary spending. For a field whose Adventist membership slightly exceeded 3,000, this showing was remarkable. The school had furnished the island with ministers and teachers, some of whom had proceeded to other institutions of higher learning and positions of trust and leadership within the denomination beyond Sri Lanka.

While Sri Lankan Adventists regarded Lakpahana Adventist College and Seminary as their premier institution, other denominational schools on the island represented a different turn. Because traditional Adventist church schools were not feasible, Adventists in the Colombo region established two large high schools as businesses, operating them in a manner similar to church-sponsored schools in India. As entrepreneurial enterprises they did not fall under the ordinary government controls over education. Kandana Seventh-day Adventist High School and the Adventist International School each enrolled about a thousand students from primary levels through secondary school who were mainly Buddhist, but Hindu, Muslim, and Christian students also attended. Many of the teachers were Buddhist but the curriculum was denominational as were the teaching materials. The Sri Lanka Union Mission regarded both campuses as mission schools.

Reflecting on the history of Lakpahana, one alumnus wrote in 1998 that the school had "been through the ravages of terrorism and politics," but it had survived even though at times some thought the school should close.[12] From the vantage point of a half century after the training school moved from Kottawa, Adventists on the island could agree that the aggressive character of the government had produced trials from time to time, but Lakpahana had not suffered crippling damage.

### Antillian College in Cuba

Such was not the case in Cuba where a more militant socialist movement engulfed Antillian College beginning in late 1958. Since 1956 a small band of revolutionaries had been fighting out of the Sierra Maestra mountains of eastern Cuba, gathering strength far beyond its small numbers and becoming an increasing irritant to the Cuban government. The campaign moved steadily westward and during the Christmas season of 1958 the revolutionaries moved into Santa Clara, occupying the campuses of Antillian College and a public university immediately across the road. For days the rebels, led by Fidel Castro and his companion-in-arms, Che Guevara, fought it out with government forces while faculty and students watched with a mixture of excitement and fright. Planes bombed and strafed the campus, resulting in little damage, but there were some near misses among those who had to run for cover.[13]

On January 1, 1959, the Cuban government fell and the revolutionaries surged into Havana as the new masters of the island. During the battle of Santa Clara Guevara frequented the Adventist campus and two months later Castro himself also visited both the university and Antillian College. Both leaders personally assured Walton J. Brown, director of the school, that the Adventist institution represented educational ideals that the new government espoused. Understandably, a degree of security ensued, but nonetheless, an undercurrent of unease was also present on the campus.

For about two years Antillian College functioned without significant change, but this honeymoon turned sour after the Bay of Pigs episode in April 1961. In the aftermath of this failure by Cuban refugees, backed by the United States, to retake the island, the government nationalized private schools, including the Adventist campus. After the college protested, Castro apologetically reopened the school, but assigned a government supervisor to keep an eye on campus affairs.

Until 1967 Antillian College continued operations but under severe modification. In 1956 it had become the only institution in the Inter-American Division with denominational authorization to offer four-year post-secondary degrees in theology for Spanish-speaking students, and its unofficial status as the educational center for the division drew an international enrollment. After the crisis of 1961, however, the Cuban government cut off communication with the world beyond its shores. Foreign students left and the school became an exclusively Cuban institution. On the shoulders of Vicente Rodriguez, a native Cuban, fell the responsibility of director. In the wake of these events, Antillian College moved to Puerto Rico, leaving only a seminary in Cuba that could offer a two-year program.

Despite these restrictions, enrollment remained surprisingly high, exceeding 300 in 1962 and remaining above 200 through 1967. In February of that year the government expropriated the campus, including all equipment except the library books. Government officials insisted that the action was not a confiscation and that they would pay for the facilities, but remuneration never came. "Night had fallen," wrote Walton Brown. "The much loved Antillian College had disappeared."[14]

When the government allowed Adventists to reopen a tiny seminary in the former office of the Antillian Union in Havana in 1970, government limits on enrollment sharply reduced the number of students, which, through 1990 never exceed forty and frequently less than ten. After restrictions on travel and communication eased, L. H. Fletcher, director of education for the Inter-American Division, and Walton Brown were able to visit Cuba in 1982, finding the seminary barely limping, sometimes with one person shouldering responsibility for all of the teaching.

During the harsher socialist years of the late 1960s and the 1970s the church had not ceased to function or sometimes to evangelize, but harassment and religious discrimination had been common. Finally, Castro himself admitted in 1985 that Christian values were necessary to combat social problems of contemporary society. Similar to most radical socialist countries, during the 1980s Cuba loosened its grip on domestic policies and by the end of the decade Adventists successfully petitioned for the authority to offer post-secondary degrees and for non-Cuban teachers to travel to the island to conduct classes. The first class–twenty-four students–graduated from the seminary in 1990 with bachelor of religion degrees. Teachers from Montemorelos University offered the classes in several sequences of six-week intensive courses.

*Antillian College in Cuba continued to operate following the socialist revolution in 1959, but after 1961 it functioned under severe limitations. In 1967 the school closed. In this photo students gather on the campus in 1961 to conduct prayer bands.*

The government also permitted a select few of the graduates to leave Cuba for graduate study.

Since ministerial education classes resumed in 1970 Cuban Adventists hoped and repeatedly asked for a new seminary building with offices, library, and classrooms. A generation passed before a small group broke ground in 1995 for the long anticipated educational center. Maranatha Volunteers International helped to erect the building. The next year Caridad Diego, director of religious affairs in the Cuban government, was on hand to congratulate the show of solidarity of the Adventist church with its Cuban members and to hear Robert Folkenberg, General Conference president, dedicate the seminary, the first non-government educational structure to go up in Cuba during the forty-eight years since the revolution.

Cuba Adventist Seminary was still a small institution, built to accommodate about fifty students, but by the year 2000 enrollment reached nearly eighty. Its sole program was theology. Because Adventists operated no institutions in Cuba, teachers and other categories of institutional workers were not in demand. Although the seminary could offer a traditional ministerial education program, the government still controlled other aspects of education, which obviated the possibility of broadening the curriculum to other fields of study. As academically narrow as it was, the seminary filled a critical need for Cuban Adventists. At the time of the revolution in 1959, membership approximated 5,000, a figure that had risen to more than 13,000 when the new seminary went into operation in 1996. During the same period the number of recognized congregations had doubled to about 140. Trained pastors were needed.

A key factor in the revival of post-secondary education in Cuba was the role of Montemorelos University. Since the Mexican Revolution that began in 1910 the Mexican government had habitually dealt moderately with leftist political movements anywhere, and its influence was thus welcome in socialist locations where North Americans would have encountered obstacles. Especially was this true in Cuba where, in addition to being a radical socialist movement the revolution was also a stiff reaction against the United States occupation of Cuba and its controls following the Spanish-American War in 1898. With its authority as a state approved institution and at the same time the home of a denominationally recognized school of theology, Montemorelos University was in a better position than any other Adventist institution to mentor a ministerial education program in Cuba.

**A Look Back at Adventist Education under Radical Socialism**

From the experiences of Adventist education in socialist countries after World War II comes much understanding about denominational schools and their function under stress. It can be argued that the problems these Adventist institutions encountered were no more serious than those in any politically illiberal environment. From the beginnings of Adventist education in the world fields church leaders never restricted their schools to places where they could frolic in complete freedom; sometimes they established schools in uncivilized or hostile environments, but in any case they experienced at least a modicum of toleration. Sometimes illiberal governments even expedited Adventist education, sometimes they obstructed it. Stress from authoritarian states was neither new nor something denominational educators could calculate by formula.

But radical socialism exerted a different kind of threat from anything Adventist churches and schools had previously encountered because of its claims to scientific atheism, a systematic, international movement that proposed to uproot Christianity. The story of Adventist education demonstrates that quite the opposite actually occurred. Wherever socialism established a foothold, whether in Christian societies or cultures of other religions, without exception nationalistic sentiments superseded ideology.

At first glance, it would appear that Adventist schools in Germany, Poland, and Yugoslavia were none the worse for the all of the anti-Christian philosophy of radical socialism. But such a judgment should be tempered by a reminder that however successful these schools were, until radical socialism collapsed, they always swam against a swift tide. The question is a speculative one, but it is probably safe to say that in these three cases Adventist schools operated with no less freedom and possibly with less interference than before the Soviet bloc existed, although Friedensau in pre-Nazi Germany would be an exception.

Nevertheless, the pressure of a fundamentally antagonistic government remained. Pavle Borovic reminisced that spies frequented churches and evangelistic gatherings and church leaders received threats, even in Yugoslavia, but often these problems originated with overzealous officials in local governments rather than members of the state government. It is likely that this same condition existed elsewhere in the eastern bloc.

During the earlier stages of the Cold War Adventists in East Germany, Poland, and Yugoslavia were able to maintain official contact with the church at large, and not uncommonly support money from the General Conference made its way into the education centers in these countries. With the exception of Albania which suffered near complete isolation until the Soviet bloc crumbled in 1989, policies toward religion in the Eastern European countries softened sufficiently beginning in the 1970s for churches to function officially. Adventist administrative structure in these countries reintegrated itself within the official church organization and the General Conference regularly received statistical reports of membership growth and other activities.

Although seriously curtailed in Cuba, the church never stopped its functions and in China the 1980s also brought a measure of open religious practices. In these countries socialist governments reined in the church tightly, but did not destroy it. Although Sri Lanka became a socialist republic, competitive politics continued, which reduced the threat of authoritarianism comparable to other socialist governments while preserving an essentially leftist democratic climate.

These changes toward less bellicose policies did not mean that all stress was gone, but that despite the philosophical claims of radical socialism, governments could not deny the reality of Christianity. As the twenty-first century began, the international movement of radical socialism was a thing of the past although some governments remained, but unlike the countries in the original Marxist movement, these vestiges made no claims of being part of an international wave of scientific atheism. While the Marxist politico-economic movement was at its zenith, Adventist education had been part of a silent, passive, and peaceful resistance, demonstrating that the conviction stemming from the gospel commission to "teach all things whatsoever I have commanded you" was more powerful than the philosophy and politics of authoritarianism and exclusion.

---

[1]Keld J. Reynolds, "Two Educational Councils," *(Journal of True Education*, December 1948), p. 20, 21; *ibid.*, June 1948, p. 17.

[2]For data about post-war Friedensau see Johannes Hartlapp's *Chronik Friedensau* pp. 34-66; General Conference Minutes, April 1, 1946; April 18, 1947; July 7, 1949; August 17, 1961; December 9, 1965; October 21, 1976; September 8, 1977; November 19, 1981; August 19, 1982; February 25, 1988; *World Report*, 2000; Pietro Copiz, "Euro-Africa Division," (*Journal of Adventist Education*, Summer 1985), pp. 25-28; E. E. Cossentine, "The Department of Education: Report of the Secretary, 1950," AST, RG 51; email interview, Daniel Heinz, July 4-7, 2003.

[3]E. E. Cossentine, "The Department of Education: Report of the Secretary, 1950," AST, RG 51;

[4]Sources for Poland are interview, B. B. Beach, March 14, 2002; *Northern European Light*, December 1958; September 1959; April 1960; November 1962; July-August 1965; November 1965; v. 23, no. 3, 1973; v. 5, no. 5, 1978; v. 28, no. 1978; June 1986; November 1986; November 1988; General Conference Minutes, October 28, 1957; October 24, 1966; December 29, 1966; *World Report*, 2000; SDA *Yearbook*, 1991, 2001.

[5]*Northern Light*, 1973, no. 3, p. 7.

[6]Information about Yugoslavia drawn from interview, Pavle Borovic, July 30, 2003; 1977-78 *Bulletin* of Adventista Teoloska Skola; "Report of the Visiting Committee, Yugoslavian Adventist Seminary, May 24-26, 1968," AST, RG 51; "Report of the Visiting Committee of the General Conference Board of Regents and Euro-African Division Commission on Accreditation for Adventisticki Seminar Marusevec," 1978, *ibid.*; General Conference Minutes, April 11, 1974; June 4, 1981; January 21, 1988; December 12, 1991; *Light*, v. 28, no. 3, 1978; November, 1986; September 1989.

[7]Newsnote, (*Journal of True Education*, April 1947), p. 25.

[8]Interview, B. B. Beach, March 14, 2002; *Northern Light*, December 1955; April 1956; *Light*, March 1990; Adventist *Review*, July 25, 2002; *World Report*, 2000.

[9]For data about Adventist education in Russia see *General Conference Bulletin*, 1985, no. 7, pp. 2, 3; *Adventist Review*, September 14, 1989; April 12, 1990; *Light*, February, 1989; Reo Ganson, "Adventures in Russia–Adventist Education's Newest Frontier, (*Journal of Adventist Education*, December 1992-January 1993), p. 3; General Conference Minutes, July 19, 1990; September 20, 1990; November 8, 1990; March 21, 1991; May 9, 1991; September 19, 1991; November 7, 1993; Mikhail Kulakov, *God's Soviet Miracles* (Boise, ID: Pacific Press Publishing Association, 1993); interview, Harry Mayden, February 27, 2002.

[10]*General Conference Bulletin*, 1985, no. 7, pp. 2, 3.

[11]Sources for information about Sri Lanka: combined interview, U. D. Aloysius, W. D. Joseph, Peter Munasinghe, J. Willy Reith, Colombo, Sir Lanka, May 21, 2002; interview, Paul Essig, Mailapitiya, Sri Lanka, May 22, 2002; interview, Karen Essig, Mailapitiya, Sri Lanka, May 23, 2002; interview, H. G. M. Fernando, Colombo, Sri Lanka, May 22, 2002; interview, R. S. Fernando, Kandy, Sri Lanka, May 23, 2002; Donald M. Fernando, ed., *75th Anniversary: Lakpahana Adventist College* (Mailapitiya, Sri Lanka: Lakpahana Publishing House, 1998); R. S. Fernando, *The Isles Shall Not Wait* (Colombo, Sir Lanka: Associated Newspapers of Ceylon, 1987); A. W. Robinson, "Partial Account of Our Ceylon Experience," unpublished manuscript, library, Lakpahana Adventist College; E. A. Crane, "I Remember Sri Lanka," unpublished manuscript, *ibid.*; Joyce and Eric Juriansz to Friends of Lakpahana, March 27, 1998, *ibid;* Paul Essig to Joyce and Eric Juriansz, August 20, 1998, *ibid.*; Richard

Hammill to R. R. Figuhr, February 6, 1961, AST, RG 51; General Conference Minutes, June 1, 1961.

[12]Kingsley C. J. Peter, "Lakpahana–A Reflection," published in *75th Anniversary: Lakpahana Adventist College.*

[13]The Cuban story summarized from Walton J. Brown, *Oh Mi C. A!* (unpublished history of Antillian College, 1990); interview by letter, Vicente Rodriguez, April 12, 2002; General Conference Minutes, January 25, 1968; February 27, 1969; May 27, 1971; *World Report*, 2000; *Adventist Review*, May 5, 1983; March 26, 1987; November 16, 1989; March 8, 1990; September 15, 1994; December 14, 1995; December 12, 1996; *Liberty*, May-June, 1988.

[14]For a dramatic account of this phase of Antillian College, see Brown, *Oh Mi C.* A.!, pp. 83-104.

# Academic Freedom and State Aid

During the second half of the twentieth century developments in Adventist education brought an entirely new look to denominational schools. With the establishment of degree-granting institutions and graduate education around the world came new issues that were both pragmatic and philosophical. Among the leading questions were new views of the two related matters of academic freedom and academic due process. The issue of government aid raised questions about the doctrine of separation of church and state, with which institutional administrators and church leaders debated, sometimes with visible passion. Increasingly, these problems exerted external pressure on denominational control of education.

### Inductive Learning and Revealed Truth

The decision to establish universities that offered graduate degrees gave rise to keener awareness of scholarly activity and the role which the proverbial pursuit of truth played in Adventist institutions. Understood in the context of academe, a search for truth meant that institutions committed themselves to a methodical process of repeated questioning, testing, and dialogue in the belief that truth was discoverable. While this academic atmosphere was routine in education at large, it caused discomfort to many Adventists because they had long accustomed themselves to a theologically oriented educational process based on revealed truth rather than inductive search. For some Adventists it was tantamount to a denial of faith to say that Adventist higher education was engaged in a search for truth when they believed they already possessed the truth that mattered, truth that went beyond the earthly and natural to the eternal and supernatural.

It was not always easy to sort out the details of the debate. Scripturally revealed truth was theological and moral, and thus largely prescriptive. The meaning and validity of Scriptural truth rested on believers' faith in and commitment to its divine origin, which were very subjective matters. By contrast, descriptive truth was scientific, natural, objective, discoverable, and in its purest form, amoral. But this oversimplified distinction blurred because Adventists also believed that while revealed truth was supernatural in origin, it contained many discoverable realities, such as prophetic interpretation and historical facts pertaining to events and people as verified by research and archeological discoveries. In the event of apparent contradictions between the two schools of thought, the intellectually inclined found themselves impaled on the question of whether to accommodate their faith to the discoverable realities they knew or to accommodate the realities they discovered to their faith.

### Academic Freedom on the Adventist Campus

As the major protagonist of descriptive truth, secular education rejected the supernatural and subjective aspects of prescriptive truth as unreliable and held that prescriptive truth was as discoverable as descriptive truth. Adventist education did not deny the objective reality of descriptive truth, but regarded it as secondary, if not subservient, to prescriptive truth. The undergirding rationale was that God as creator was the author of both prescriptive and descriptive truth and therefore contradictions existed only as a result of inadequate understanding. A collision of the two mentalities launched a debate over academic freedom during the 1960s that helped to shape the nature of Adventist higher education from that point forward.[1]

The legal profession never reduced the idea of academic freedom to a neat definition for the courts, but as understood by the American Association of University Professors, the very notion of education presumed that teachers owned an inherent right for protection to research and publish their findings in oral and written form. Implicitly, academic freedom gave teachers the right to challenge conventional wisdom and tenets of belief, but questions were to be serious and academically responsible, not flippant or merely challenge for the sake of challenge. The protection teachers enjoyed under academic freedom was limited to their professional specialties and related topics. This freedom never gave teachers the right to say anything they pleased with impunity. The courts generally upheld this position.

University teachers founded the American Association of University Professors in 1915 expressly to promote academic freedom and due process. Known as the AAUP, in 1940 it published a seminal statement on academic freedom, with the caveat that religious institutions could legitimately proscribe certain teachings by their faculty, but in all fairness administrators should make their restrictions clear in writing before employing anyone. Thirty years later in 1970, the AAUP withdrew its endorsement of this exception with the explanation that sectarian institutions no longer needed or desired it.

It was during the years leading up to this 1970 action that the debate about academic freedom broke out among Adventist educators. Earle Hilgert, vice president for academic administration at Andrews University, warned in 1968 that the AAUP was on the verge of repudiating its 1940 exception rule for sectarian schools and that regional accrediting associations were also picking up on the same idea. He stated the obvious when he said that Adventist schools would face acute problems if accreditation bodies denied them the right to maintain their identity.

Four years prior to Hilgert's bleak prognosis, the General Conference went on record to uphold the paramount position of divine revelation as applied to knowledge. A year later, in 1965, a committee of five Adventist college and university presidents hammered out a proposed policy of academic freedom that complied with AAUP's 1940 statement, declaring that a teacher exercised academic freedom on an Adventist campus within the "framework of the appreciations, ideals, spirit, beliefs, and doctrines of the Seventh-day Adventist Church, for as a member of the church he has subscribed to its teachings and has accepted its doctrines. Outside of this faith and structure he is not at liberty to speak or teach."[2]

Until the 1960s Adventist campuses were relatively free from debate about academic freedom, but the issue had existed from the days of Battle Creek College. One of the earliest Adventist cases involving academic freedom occurred in 1889 when W. W. Prescott appointed E. J. Waggoner as a teacher in the Ministers' Bible school to introduce the new doctrinal emphasis on justification by faith. Even though Prescott also assigned Waggoner's theological antagonist, Uriah Smith, to conduct theology classes at the same time, traditional stalwarts in the denomination ignited an incendiary reaction to Waggoner's presence on the Battle Creek campus, accusing him of violating doctrinal orthodoxy. Waggoner did not remain on the campus long, but Prescott, with whom most of the church leadership sided, did not let up his support of Waggoner's views, even teaching some of the material himself.

As this fracas showed, maintaining the principle of academic freedom on an Adventist campus was probably more a matter of determining the shape of church beliefs than a guard against non-Adventist teachings. The validity of such doctrines as the Sabbath and the state of the dead were not controversial theological issues in Adventist schools, but shifting nuances on long-held doctrines could precipitate cries of heresy.

But fears of unorthodoxy figured in a case seven years after the Waggoner incident when about a dozen instructors in the teacher-preparation department left Battle Creek because the new president, E. A. Sutherland, believed they had adopted ideas incompatible to Adventism while studying at the University of Buffalo and other non-Adventist institutions. During the accreditation debate in the 1920s and 1930s a similar fear became the primary argument to discourage or even prevent denominational teachers from enrolling for advanced studies in non-Adventist schools.[3]

Through the years it became evident that some fields of study were more susceptible to controversy than others. Theology topped the list, but literature, history, science, and teacher-preparation programs were special targets. Early on, some teachers exaggerated Ellen White's advice to make the Bible the center of all study into a policy that made the

Bible the sole textbook in all subject areas, but even though that impulse subsided, a general sense remained that Adventist beliefs must be obvious in all courses. However prevalent this conviction was, denominational educators were unable to standardize it, and with no measuring rod, teachers were on their own to devise methods to integrate spiritual teachings into their courses. Sooner or later this grey area of opinion would produce problems.

In time church leaders and educators focused on theology and science as the primary fields where the question of academic freedom was most critical. In some respects, the Adventist approach to church doctrine contributed to an atmosphere of debate and thus heightened the level of controversy and emphasized the meaningfulness of academic freedom. Adventists taught that the Bible was the absolute measure of church teachings, but understanding biblical truths was progressive, which presupposed continuous study with the possibility that churchmen would revise the wording of church beliefs to reflect improved comprehension of Scripture.

Accordingly, church leaders did not reduce Adventist doctrines to an official creed, but chose instead to publish statements of fundamental beliefs that were subject to reexamination. A comparison of the three statements of Seventh-day Adventist fundamental beliefs issued in 1872, 1931, and 1980 indicates that while basic doctrines retained their essential meaning, understanding of biblical truths was indeed a process of development and that the principle of progressive understanding applies to corporate Adventism as well as to individuals. Without the freedom of discussion this kind of change would have been unlikely or even possible.[4]

### Academic Freedom and Science

During the 1930s concern mounted over science education in which the theory of evolution was becoming increasingly pervasive. Science classes in Adventist education had traditionally served two leading purposes–they taught students to appreciate nature as God's "other textbook" that demonstrated His creation, and they prepared students for careers in medicine or nursing. Adventists customarily treated evolution as a theological issue which the Bible refuted, but college professor George McCready Price had been agitating since the turn of the century that creationists should meet evolutionists on their own ground with contradicting evidence gathered from a study of geology.[5]

Price wrote prolifically and developed an international reputation among creationists. Although he taught widely in denominational schools and authored science textbooks that argued against evolution, the church was ill prepared for the piercing wake-up call it received during the 1925 "monkey trial" in Dayton, Tennessee when a court convicted John T. Scopes of violating state law by teaching evolution in the local high school. Though they won the case, creationists suffered a serious loss of respect in the public eye as Scopes' defense caricatured the biblical explanation of origins as a ridiculous idea. It became apparent to Adventist theologians and science educators that while Price had been hammering on the use of scientific evidence to oppose evolution, aside from their theological arguments which scientists rejected out of hand, the average Adventist science teacher was nearly bereft of rational explanations for a belief in the Genesis story.

A year after the Scopes episode, delegates to the General Conference session approved a resolution encouraging research and publication in geology and biology in order to stave off the advance of evolution, and four years later at the request of the Department of Education, the General Conference voted a position statement on creation. There was little question that those who wrote the proposal understood the philosophical implications of the issue. "We repudiate the materialistic interpretation of science," it read, "and believe that in all fields of scientific research we must look for the cause of natural phenomena, not in resident forces, but in the active will of God."[6]

In 1938 Adventist science and mathematics teachers began a series of conferences on the note that they should seize the initiative in researching the issue of creation in order to answer the claims of evolutionists. A growing number of science teachers held doctorates in their fields but contrary to the fears of many church leaders who had discouraged advanced studies, proceedings of the gatherings of science teachers in 1942, 1947, 1952, and 1956 indicated their unquestionable commitment to the Adventist belief in creation rather than a decline.

By the 1950s advances in radiocarbon dating posed a new challenge to creationists, apparently pushing the age of the earth irretrievably beyond the interpretation Adventists placed on the Genesis account.

Discussions that began at the 1956 meeting culminated the next year when the General Conference formed a standing committee which, in time, matured into the Geoscience Research Institute whose purpose was to fulfill the 1926 resolution to research and publish on the issue of creation. As the GRI scientists probed deeper into the questions of origins, the age of the earth and the biblical flood, they sometimes differed among themselves, especially on the question of the trustworthiness of the geologic column. It became clear that their findings were not conclusive, but only incomplete evidences pointing to the integrity of the biblical record.

It was also evident that Adventist scientists could not answer every question. How to interpret data was not always apparent. Increasingly, Adventists learned to live with the consciousness that creation was beyond scientific explanation, a matter of faith, even though some had hoped to nail it down.

The impact of these events on academic freedom in Adventist schools was profound. A degree of pluralism entered academe which affected theology as well as science. While the statements of fundamental beliefs in 1872 and 1931 recognized the creative power of God, it was not until 1980 that Adventists spelled out the doctrine of creation as a fundamental belief. Some critics complained that the heavy research of the GRI would produce skeptics, but the 1980 statement upheld the seven-day creation week, crowned by the Sabbath, but was silent on the age of the earth.

Most of this debate as it affected academic freedom took place in the United States, but as Adventist higher education spread to the world fields, denominational schools could not avoid the impact of evolution. That there were variations of the belief in creation was an acknowledged fact; what was not so certain was the influence these differences exerted on students in denominational schools and the church at large.

At the Annual Council in 2001 the General Conference approved a proposal for scientists, educators, theologians, and church administrators to conduct a three-year sequence of Faith and Science Conferences to deal with the growing debate in the church about creation. The plan called for regional discussions around the globe and two international conferences to discuss the "interplay of faith, science, and philosophy and the ways in which these challenge or contribute to the church's understanding and proclamation regarding Genesis 1-11."[7] Because the doctrine of creation itself was not under review, the Faith and Science Conferences were left with the task of clearing the air of tensions by providing a forum for exchange and thus clarifying how Adventists understood creation and how to teach a belief rooted in science as part of a confessional faith.

After three years of discussions in seven of the world divisions and two plenary sessions in the United States, the Faith and Science Conference issued "An Affirmation of Creation," a judicious but unequivocal statement explaining the position of the conferees. The statement attributed the debate not only to questions that scientists raised but also to the large number of Adventist students attending secular institutions. Among denominational scientists no support for a completely naturalistic explanation of origins arose, which meant that the issue turned on variations of belief in the Genesis account rather than the biblical story itself. The document confirmed the legitimacy of the scientific method in studying matters of faith and applauded scientists for the contributions they made to Adventist beliefs and to higher education.

As much as "An Affirmation of Creation" supported scientific studies in Adventist classrooms, it denied science the right to be the final arbiter of truth when scientists perceived disharmony between interpretations of Scripture and empirical data. It upheld the primacy of Scripture in the Adventist understanding of Genesis 1-11 and rejected the idea that the scientific method was the only means to arrive at truth, but it recommended the continual reexamination of Scripture in light of information derived from scientific investigation. Significantly, it asserted that belief in the biblical account of creation was foundational to all other teachings of Adventism and suggested that Seventh-day Adventist Fundamental Belief Six–the doctrine of creation–should be revised to be more precise regarding the creation week and creation itself as a recent cosmological event.

Members of the 2004 Annual Council overwhelmingly adopted the report, but rejected the proposal to revise Fundamental Belief Six. This show of support for the Adventist view of creation was encouraging to church leaders, but it did not erase the fact that variations of belief existed, described as "earth-age pluralism" by one attendee who was concerned that Adventist campuses would continue to tolerate "deep-time" theories of creation espoused by some science teachers.[8] The dominant theme of "An Affirmation of Creation" was its firmness on the long-standing Adventist position that faith in revealed and prescriptive truth was more influential than belief in discoverable and descriptive truth when the two were in conflict. The statement did not include the term *academic freedom* but it spoke to the question of responsibility and integrity within the teaching profession. As a fundamental belief of the church, creation remained strengthened as a limitation on the concept of absolute academic freedom in Adventist education.[9]

### The Institute for Christian Teaching

The General Conference Department of Education also undertook projects to bridge the gap between inductive learning and faith in revealed knowledge. Adopting a model from evangelical colleges in the United States, in 1987 George Akers, at the time director of the department, and Humberto Rasi, an departmental associate who became director in 1990, founded the Institute for Christian Teaching as a vehicle to promote Adventist philosophy of education. The primary activity of the Institute was a sequence of seminars for post-secondary teachers in all world fields to strengthen both their understanding and their commitment to integrate faith and learning.

Rasi believed that Adventist teachers were obligated to help students "in the rediscovery of the inherent unity that underlies all fields of knowledge," a concept that he believed secular education had lost through excessive reliance on rationalism and empiricism for explanations of the natural world. This movement had climaxed in postmodernism that declared truth to be inaccessible. "Adventist education challenges those assumptions head-on," Rasi wrote, "and intentionally seeks to restore the unity of knowledge that still exists, thus reconnecting faith, knowledge, values, and life."[10]

The seminars were something new for Adventist educators, who were typically conditioned by a traditional belief in the inherent values of Adventist education without reflecting on the philosophical issue that Rasi described. The motivating element of the seminars was a conviction that many Adventist teachers were susceptible to a dichotomous approach to their classes, eliminating faith from their teaching in secular fields. As a requirement participants in the faith and learning seminars read books and prepared papers which Rasi compiled under the title of *Christ in the Classroom* and sent to Adventist college libraries around the world. By the end of 2004 Rasi had conducted thirty-two seminars and attendees had produced about 600 essays that explained how various academic and professional disciplines could integrate a biblical world view in their college classrooms. Thirty-two volumes of these essays were available to every Adventist post-secondary institution, and about a third of them were retrievable as online documents.[11]

**The Desmond Ford Case and Recent Denominational Events**

Perhaps the most celebrated case of academic freedom in the field of theology began in 1979 when Desmond Ford, an Australian theology professor teaching at Pacific Union College, advanced views that disputed the traditional Adventist interpretation of the Mosaic sanctuary and the prophetic significance of the year 1844. After he submitted a lengthy explanation of his position, a 125-member Sanctuary Review Committee met in 1980 to discuss his understanding of the doctrine of the sanctuary. Ford did not convince the committee of his interpretation, and as a result he lost his ministerial credentials but retained his membership in the church.

Events in sectarian education at large furnished support for the position of Adventist education on academic freedom. As they unfolded, it became clear that the AAUP had underestimated the resolve of church affiliated institutions to adhere to the 1940 declaration of academic freedom rather than to buckle under pressure to accept its recision in 1970. One of the chief spokesmen in favor of religious limits on academic freedom was George M. Marsden, a member of the Christian Reformed Church and for two decades a member of the faculty at Calvin College before moving to Duke University and finally to Notre Dame in 1992. Throughout his career he argued persuasively in numerous books and articles that academic freedom was a legitimate right of church related institutions as well as individuals, and that religious scholarship was reliable and contributed to the multicultural society that the United States claimed to be. Joining the debate was attorney John Whitehead, president of The Rutherford Institute, who defended academic freedom on the basis of the First Amendment to the Constitution.

In 1997 the AAUP showed signs of second thoughts when it teamed up with Baylor University, the American Academy of Religion, and the Society of Biblical Literature to conduct a conference exploring the issue of academic freedom at sectarian colleges and universities. *Academe*, the journalistic voice of the AAUP, devoted its entire January-February 2001 issue to the topic, providing a forum for Marsden and others to state their case. Before the 1990s ended it was evident that sectarian education had safeguarded its position on academic freedom.

Within Adventist circles educators never even hinted that they would conform to AAUP's 1970 action. In 1972 the Board of Higher Education considered a statement of academic freedom which upheld "disciplined" research and teaching, and included academic due process to provide a fair hearing for teachers suspected of unorthodox instruction. Fifteen years later in 1987 the General Conference adopted a position statement that continued to uphold church doctrine as the norm for limiting academic freedom but left room for differences of opinion in some unspecified areas of belief. The action placed due process in the hands of academic institutions where, after the mid- 1990s, the boards of trustees became the legal controlling authority. In its essential principles academic freedom as Adventists practiced it had not changed from those embodied in the 1965 statement, but procedures of implementing it had altered dramatically not only as a result of influences from higher education but also as a result of the wider latitude in which Adventists understood church doctrine.

### Issue of Government Aid

The issue of academic freedom pivoted on the question of control of denominational institutions, which was also true of government aid to sectarian schools, another topic of animated discussion beginning soon after World War II ended. At the heart of the debate was the First Amendment to the United States Constitution which enunciated the "establishment clause," the cornerstone of American religious liberty which forbade Congress to legislate "respecting an establishment of religion, or prohibiting the free exercise thereof." It was this concept that Thomas Jefferson immortalized in his classic metaphor of a "wall of separation" between church and state.

Based upon this long tradition, Adventist church leaders habitually taught that Adventist schools should not accept government support. As part of the fallout from the Solusi episode, the 1895 General Conference session went on record with a resolution stating that gifts or grants, either of land, money or anything else of value from governments at any level violated the principle of separation of church and state and as a denomination Seventh-day Adventists should neither seek nor accept such favors.[12] D. Lois Burnett, of the General Conference medical department, surprised no one when she wrote in 1944 that Adventist nursing schools would not enroll students under the terms of the Bolton Act, a wartime provision to furnish financial assistance in educating nurses to serve public needs, including civilian as well as military duty. Her reasons were unapologetic: Adventist schools risked their identity as sectarian institutions if they accepted tax money either directly or indirectly.[13]

**Debate Over Governmental Aid in North America**

Despite a rigid verbal stance on this question, immediately after the war Adventist institutions took advantage of governmental largesse in distributing surplus property to private institutions. The prime example of tax-funded assistance to the church was the sale in 1948 of a former military base to the Central California Conference for a dollar, despite its fair market value of $350,000. The property became Monterey Bay Academy. Some elementary schools participated in government-supported school lunch programs. The question was complicated by the G. I. Bill, legislation that paid discharged military personnel to attend schools of their choice. These allotments were payments to persons, not institutions, but because the intention was to finance education and school bursaries eventually received much of the funds, many argued that this was a form of public aid to private education.

By the 1960s government financial involvement in private education had become common. Through federal, state, and local governments tax money and services became available to private schools in the form of reimbursement to families who did not use school busses, loans of textbooks and teaching materials to private schools, auxiliary health and counseling services to non-public institutions, vouchers to families to pay educational fees in private schools, and grants to

*Charles B. Hirsch served as president of Columbia Union College, vice president for academic affairs at Andrews University, General Conference director of education, and General Conference vice president. He vigorously promoted the Adventist accreditation system around the world and helped launch the debate about the position of Seventh-day Adventists vis-a-vis government aid for church-sponsored education.*

construct buildings and to fund research projects. Adventist schools in the United States sometimes took the money, sometimes refused it. In every case, positive or negative, the deciding factor was avoiding any possibility of compromising the Adventist identity of schools.[14]

As consistent as this practice appeared, some were dubious about the church's fundamental opposition to government aid. Charles B. Hirsch, at the time vice president for academic administration at Andrews University and later General Conference Director of Education, became one of the first to challenge openly denominational policy when he spoke out in 1965, denying that the government had any intention of usurping control of private schools when it provided money and services, but instead simply wanted to assist private education. After reviewing two decades of financial aid to private schools, he could cite no case when Adventist schools in the United States lost their independence or denominational identity as a result of accepting tax-funded support, and pointed out that any strings attached to government aid were no more than those justified under reasonable accreditation requirements.

Hirsch also suggested that the constitutionality of government aid was fluid, depending on opinions of judges whose views could change from one generation to the next. Strict separation had once been the norm but one of the growing arguments to justify granting public money to non-public schools was the doctrine of non-preferential assistance. Hirsch pointed out that if this understanding of the First Amendment and the establishment clause became the dominant one, educators could expect public money to flow to private institutions. Another variation on the First Amendment that was becoming more acceptable would permit public money to fund non-religious aspects of sectarian schools, but in no case could church-related education legitimately depend on government aid for direct religious education.

Hisrch exploded a bombshell by venturing that the reason why Adventists rejected government aid was to perpetuate the doctrine of separation of church and state as fixed and unalterable. "It is here," he said, "not in the question of control, doctrine, or moral issues, that we have the crux of the matter. It is the factor of inconsistency that will plague us . . . and yet we must recognize that the path we have followed to the present has not been a most consistent one."[15]

Not everyone agreed with Hirsch, but no one could deny the increasing volume of public money flowing to private campuses. All schools throughout the United States, both public and private, faced expanding enrollments after World War II which spawned financial dilemmas and stimulated federal involvement in education and required states to spend more on education. During the 1960s when the baby boomer generation began to enter post-secondary schools a sympathetic federal government opened its purse, and under the slogan of the "Great Society" poured out public money in unprecedented amounts to schools, especially colleges and universities. These demographic and financial conditions affected Adventist schools, but except for the G. I. Bill and other cautiously selected assistance, Adventist policy placed government aid off limits.[16]

In 1968 the issue broke wide open during a conference of North American higher education teachers and administrators at Andrews University. The debate did not settle the question, but protagonists on both sides of the question squared off and deepened the rift that separated them. Facing severe financial dilemmas, Adventist post-secondary schools acted on their own and arranged for help from the public sector in spite of an official policy that was under severe fire. One member of the General Conference Committee recalled that a stunned silence descended on the General Conference Committee when colleges disclosed how extensively they were involved in programs of government aid. In the case of the most lucrative engagement, even the chairman of the board rose to say he was not aware of the school's commitments.[17]

By 1971 Adventist colleges and universities in the United States were receiving public money in one form or another totaling almost $5,400,000. The figure rose to nearly $9,000,000 in 1978. Perhaps the most telling impact of this money was the fact that it accounted for nearly eight percent of institutional operating funds and approximated half the amount of church subsidies to Adventist higher education in North America. Government money was clearly the margin of difference to balance the annual budgets in Adventist schools. Most of the money came under the umbrella of financial assistance to students and thus was a benefit to individuals, but the unmistakable destination of the money was the institutional bursary.[18]

In 1972 the General Conference revised its earlier policy to allow institutions to accept government money but only discreetly and with a wary eye toward the risk of government control. The action, according to Roland Hegstad, a member of the General Conference Public Affairs and Religious Liberty Department, was to legitimize the growing practice of institutional applications for public money.[19]

Among Adventist educators an ambivalent attitude arose over this situation. Institutional administrators welcomed government aid because it was sure funding that allowed them to balance their budgets and to make campus improvements. On the flip side of the coin was a misgiving over institutional dependency on public money and an apprehension about demands that federal and state governments might impose on schools to control the quality and nature of an education that they were funding. An unease also arose among many who saw the process as a cancerous undermining of the doctrine of separation of church and state.

The same attitudes characterized conference and union superintendents of education and principals of elementary and secondary schools. Many of them stood to benefit from auxiliary public health services, lunch programs, and loans of textbooks, computer equipment and other teaching materials. Pressure intensified as government aid did not slacken while the sentiments on both sides of the issue became divisive.

In 1991 at Clackamas, Oregon a group of about seventy-five church leaders and educators, mainly from North America, met to discuss denominational practices and policies relating to government aid, focusing on elementary and secondary schools. Among the speakers were attorneys, educators, theologians, and leaders in the field of religious liberty. Presenters from Australia and Canada discussed the issue as it affected Adventist schools outside the United States.[20]

Opinions of the speakers varied, beginning with those who reminded the audience of the historical position of the church and the specter of government controls that always lurked in the shadows. On the other side of the question, the strongest appeal to accept tax-supported aid came from Richard Osborn, vice president for education in the Columbia Union, who argued forcefully that eschatological beliefs had impaired a rational understanding of the purposes of government aid.

The attendees were not empowered to make any decisions. Probably the most visible outcome of the meeting was its blunting effect on the belief that government aid was unbiblical. However strong the church had held to its beliefs, the question was a legal matter, and while vigilance over government interference was a valid concern, the issue came to be seen as a practical rather than a moral one. The gathering also enlightened educators concerning shifts in legal tests that courts applied to determine whether or not a given case of government aid violated the establishment clause.[21]

## Columbia Union College v. Clarke

What some Adventist leaders deemed the capstone event in the discussion about government aid was a lawsuit that dragged over the decade of the 1990s, climaxing in 2001 when a federal court of appeals approved an application from Columbia Union College to receive Maryland state funding in excess of $800,000 for math, computer science, and nursing programs. In 1992 the Maryland Higher Education Commission denied CUC's original request for public money with the explanation that the school was pervasively sectarian and to grant it money would violate the establishment clause. Court actions upheld the Commission's decision, but after additional hearings, the courts found the college not to be pervasively sectarian, which made the school eligible for state funds.[22]

The court's ruling jolted Adventists and sparked a debate about the nature of denominational education and potential repercussions of the decision. Conditioned by customary denominational thinking, many believed that being pervasively sectarian was axiomatic in Adventist schools because of the long tradition that Adventism was inseparable from all instruction. The conviction that this ideal should prevail in denominational schools was fundamental to the faith and learning seminars that Humberto Rasi conducted around the world and the message of his *Christ in the Classroom* series–a worldview of knowledge that provided a biblical rationale for all learning. Also, being pervasively sectarian was a point to be made to satisfy the criteria of the Adventist Accrediting Association.

Some held the opinion that, in order to acquire public money, Columbia Union College had minimized the spiritual character of its non-theology programs out of existence. They saw CUC compromising its institutional mission by declaring that for practical purposes much of its program was no different from what students would find at a state university. It was easy to charge CUC with relinquishing its Adventist identity and to forecast calamitous results for the school when it faced problems that legally hinged on its status as a religious college.

Others, however, saw the decision more in light of equal treatment of religious entities. According to the court, "pervasively sectarian" was legalese which meant that the primary purpose of a given class was to impart religious knowledge. Applying the court's reasoning, a chemistry teacher, for example, could include religious elements in the class syllabus and share religious points of view in class lectures and labs, but because the purpose of the course was to deliver information about chemistry rather than theology the religious aspects were only incidental and did not produce a pervasively sectarian class. Church-sponsored schools could even require students to attend religious convocations and teachers could pray before classes without becoming pervasively sectarian.

To add to the uncertainty, doubts were springing up in the legal profession about the propriety of the pervasively sectarian test in the first place. Justices and constitutional lawyers alike were complaining that to identify a pervasively sectarian campus they had to become too intrusive about the ways in which religious schools practiced their faith. They did not question the impropriety of funding actual ministerial education or general religion classes, but they were becoming increasingly reluctant to split theological hairs about other religious activities and tumble into pitfalls of inconsistency by declaring some schools eligible for public money while denying others. They were fearful of weakening the ability of the legal system to protect the rights of institutions to fulfill their legitimate religious mission under the terms of the free exercise clause of the First Amendment.

The *Columbia Union College v. Clarke* case had originated during the presidency of William Loveless, but continued into the administration of Charles Scriven who contended that in the interests of fairness CUC should receive aid inasmuch as all other mainline denominational institutions were receiving it. The application was for funds from a state program designed especially for private institutions of higher education, including sectarian colleges which had to meet measurable qualifications. In their arguments for the college, attorneys hinted strongly that Scriven's view of the issue was the critical one, neutrality rather than being pervasively sectarian was the primary question. Because other sectarian institutions had received state funding from the same source, almost by definition the pervasively sectarian test became irrelevant.

Some argued with a degree of cynicism that by relegating the pervasively sectarian test to the back seat, judges and attorneys were engaging in legal gymnastics to arrive at the neutrality test which was a much less controversial way to settle the issue. Whatever the truth, *Columbia Union College v. Clarke* was a textbook case illustrating the dynamic nature of legality. The court accepted the reality that religion itself was a pervasive influence in society and that to apply the pervasively sectarian test was too tricky to be practical. They decided that the more evenhanded response was to grant religious schools money on an equal footing, but at the same time ensuring that the funds did not finance ministerial training or theological instruction. Whether or not Columbia Union College was pervasively sectarian in the Adventist sense of the term was a philosophical issue left to the judgment of the college administration and the board.

*Columbia Union College v. Clarke* was important to Adventists because it directly involved Adventist education, but it was only one of a lengthening list of even more significant decisions that set precedents for the issue of public support of sectarian education. Viewed in their entirety and chronologically from the 1940s onward, they emphasized

Hirsch's observations made in 1965, which had also received attention at Clackamas: constitutional interpretations of the First Amendment are not moral questions but instead are legal issues that swing according to the political context and the stream of current thought in the legal profession, converting what is illegal in one decade into legality in the next.

When the United States Supreme Court ruled in June 2002 that school vouchers were not a violation of the establishment clause, Adventist leaders in education and religious liberty were officially silent. School vouchers were analogous to the G. I. Bill–money which denominational schools had accepted because it benefitted individuals who chose the schools where recipients would spend the money. More than thirty years earlier the North American Division voted not to take a position on the voucher issue because the conditions that states attached to the money varied to the point of defying any blanket policy. The NAD action instructed schools to accept or reject vouchers on the basis of the strings that the states had tied to them.[23]

### Government Aid in Australia

The debate over separation of church and state as it affected sectarian schools had a peculiarly North American flavor because of the establishment clause, but the rest of the Adventist world also had its versions of this issue. Of all countries where government support of sectarian education took place, Australia most resembled the United States, chiefly because its constitution also included an establishment clause that denied the Commonwealth the authority to enact any law to establish religion, to impose religious observance, or to prohibit free exercise of religion. Similar to the United States, education was a concern of the states rather than the federal government.[24]

Tax support for church affiliated schools in Australia was a non-issue until after World War II when the Commonwealth government began funding private education by granting money to the states, which, in turn, disbursed the money according to criteria spelled out in the legislation itself. By the 1960s and into the 1970s these grants acts opened the valve to a torrent of tax money flowing into sectarian schools. Using these funds for both operating and capital purposes, religious bodies built attractive and well equipped elementary and secondary schools that drew large enrollments.

This practice developed two rival systems of education, the first consisting of traditional Australian public schools and the second, church-affiliated schools with a dependency on state aid. Opponents to government grants alleged that nongovernment schools were a threat to the public schools because the tax support they received was in violation of the Constitution. As a practical matter they alleged that the private schools drained off the better students into elitist programs. In 1960 the Australian Council for the Defence of Government Schools–which often went by it acronym, DOGS–organized to prevent tax money from going to church-affiliated schools On the basis of the Australian establishment clause, in 1970 the DOGS sued to declare government grants illegal.

In contrast to *Columbia Union College v. Clarke* two decades later, which intended to *expand* state aid to sectarian colleges in the United States, the DOGS case–*Attorney General (Vict.); ex rel. Black v. the Commonwealth*–sought to *prevent* aid to elementary and secondary schools. Legal arguments in Australia took an all-or-nothing approach, charging that sectarian schools possessed an inherent religiosity that made it impossible to separate secular and religious instruction, and that government aid by definition established religion and therefore violated the Constitution. This line of argument differed from the American pervasively sectarian test which admitted that degrees of religious influence could exist in schools that received public funding without infringing on the Constitution.

Attorneys representing both Columbia Union College and the Australian church schools downplayed the religious aspects of their programs in order to demonstrate the legality of state aid. In the DOGS case their testimony mattered little inasmuch as six of the seven justices found that while the financial grants laws furnished aid to sectarian schools they did not establish religion as an institution of the state, which was what the Australian Constitution forbade. Education in church schools had to measure up to secular standards irrespective of its religious admixture. Religion, however prevalent it might be in the schools receiving grants, was only incidental to the purpose of the aid.

The court also argued that Australia depended on church-affiliated schools to share the government responsibility for education and if Commonwealth funding withdrew from sectarian schools, the burden of education would fall completely on the states, which would be a tax load too great for them to bear. From this argument Australians could infer that church affiliated schools helped the country to fulfill its compulsory education laws by providing education that met state criteria, thus reducing government expenses. Whatever grants they received were, in a sense, compensatory funds.

The ruling became the watershed event in Australia regarding state aid to religious education and exerted a direct impact on Adventist education. Years before the DOGS case Adventist elementary and secondary schools in Australia began receiving state aid. Before 1965 they generally refused assistance, but in a few cases public funds found their way into denominational schools in the form of payments to families. In 1965 Carmel College in western Australia accepted a grant to build a science laboratory. This was the first spurt in a stream of tax money that funded additional science projects, libraries, and other capital improvements in Adventist institutions. By 1977 more than 30 percent of both capital and operating funds for Adventist elementary and secondary schools in Australasia, including Longburn College in New Zealand, originated with the government.

Although Adventist elementary and secondary schools depended heavily on state aid, the real target in the DOGS case was the Roman Catholic system that comprised about 85 percent of the non-government schools. Nevertheless, the small fraction of money Adventists received was sufficient to categorize them among the defendants, although the suit did not name them as such.

Australian grants laws prescribed accountability from the schools that received money, but South Pacific Division Director of Education Lester D. Devine wrote that until the DOGS case schools received state aid on the basis of the "equivalency" test, which permitted schools to receive grants with few attached conditions if they spent equal amounts from nongovernment sources of revenue. In 1981 following the DOGS suit, the government ended the equivalency program and established categories of expenses for which schools could appropriately spend tax money and at the same time required stricter accountability from the schools concerning how they spent state aid. In Adventist circles this wave of regulation prompted a review of the purposes of church education accompanied by an acknowledgment that grant money would be unacceptable if it required schools to compromise their denominational identity or the purposes of the church.

At the end of the twentieth century all Adventist schools in Australia received government aid, but at a substantially lower rate than most other sectarian schools. "The Adventist Church in Australia should continue to accept government money," Devine said in 1991, "because if it doesn't, the schools are going to suffer and the quality and the total volume of education provided would be substantially diminished, and most [of] our small schools would not be viable."[25] In keeping with this policy the church restricted state aid to a margin below half of any given institution's budget, which empowered the church to maintain an upper hand in educational finance in a manner analogous to the stockholder of a business that owns at least fifty-one percent of the shares and thus claims managerial rights.

### Miscellaneous Cases of Aid to Adventist Schools

Unlike the United States and Australia, many governments established a specific church by supporting it with public money, but through constitutional provisions safeguarded the free exercise of other faiths and permitted sectarian schools to function. Whether or not established churches existed, governments commonly held that education was their responsibility and, recognizing that sectarian schools provided a public service, many countries made tax-supported assistance available to religious institutions.

The General Conference resolution in 1895 declaring government grants unacceptable to Adventists had a very short life. Ironically, the explanation of Adventists' involvement in the Solusi episode in which the denomination received 12,000 acres of land and which precipitated the 1895 resolution, became the standard rationale in any discussion about government aid, but the record of receiving public money was mixed. In order that the Adventist industrial school at Meiktila, Burma could survive, Robert Bruce Thurber accepted grants-in-aid to pay teachers' salaries as early as 1914, but only after negotiating concessions that would allow the school to retain its identity as an Adventist institution. Government aid was common in Africa and contributed much to the advancement of Solusi Mission.

Yet there was an undercurrent of apprehension. L. H. Christian, president of the Northern Division, noted in 1930 that Adventist mission work in Africa was largely education and that government policies were becoming more numerous and sometimes difficult. "Some of our schools have been given liberal grants of money by the government," he said.[26] R. E. Loasby, a delegate from India to the 1923 Colorado Springs Convention, told his audience that he declined an offer for a government grant for an Adventist school, choosing instead to establish industries in which students could work and generate operating capital for the school.

In 1965 when Charles Hirsch challenged denominational policy affecting government aid in the United States he observed that in Scandinavia, Canada, West Africa, and parts of India Adventist schools regularly accepted public money. The list of schools was actually longer. In Australasia, Korea, Japan, Hong Kong, Trinidad, British Guiana, Chile, and Argentina government aid went to Adventist schools.[27]

Hirsch admitted to misgivings and complications resulting from accepting public money in some parts of the world, but denied that government interference followed as if by formula. Church leaders who warned Adventist schools in the United States against accepting public money and services were hard put for evidence that their fears of government regulation actually materialized, but the fact that some denominational schools in the world fields had wrestled with serious challenges from governments over the question of church control of education lent credence to the cautionary attitude in the United States.

This lesson came from Lakpahana in Sri Lanka which escaped government confiscation because it had refused government assistance. Again, after communists took control of the state government of Kerala, India in 1957, they did not force government aid upon the schools, but they proposed to pay teachers' salaries and assume control of faculty appointments in schools that continued to accept grants-in-aid. The Adventist school avoided this problem because it rejected government money. Complaints also came from Trinidad where government money seemed to be at the root of problems of control of denominational schools.

## Government Aid to African Schools

Of all the places where complications arose from accepting government money, Exhibit A was the Southern African Division during the 1950s and 1960s. This region embraced nearly all of Africa below the hump. Here the problem was not an invasive policy by the colonial governments into schools as a result of financial aid, but a general policy of government regulation. Government grants were involved because private education in the English-speaking colonies had developed a near addictive dependency on them.[28]

After a generation of giving assistance to mission schools, colonial governments began to regulate education in 1931, and in 1945 they made known their intention to supervise all schools. Six years later the Beecher Report, a lengthy statement about education in Africa commissioned by the British government, recommended that colonial governments should take over all schools. In quick succession Kenya, South Africa, and the Rhodesias legislated aspects of the Beecher Report that would pave the way for government control.[29]

Government aid had usually come to Adventist schools in the form of subsidies through the mission treasuries, but according to the new plans teachers would receive their salaries directly from the government, which would sidestep the denomination and place teachers immediately under government control. Colonial governments also proposed to register all teachers in an employment pool and assign them according to the needs of individual schools, which would remove church authority to manage school staffs. It was likely that in time private schools would cease to exist.

One of the contributing factors to this issue was the modernizing trend sweeping across Africa. One church leader remarked that twenty-five years earlier a missionary teacher earning a couple dollars a month with a chalk board and thirty or forty students gathered under a tree was conducting a respectable school. But times had changed. Government aid had helped mission societies to develop a wide system of schools that for Adventists had begun as the most effective means of evangelism but had become what amounted to a part of the colonial school system.

Not all Adventist schools took grants. Statistics in 1953 showed 200 aided schools compared to 1,043 unaided in the Southern African Division, but the amount of government money for the few exceeded denominational appropriations for the many by more than 80 percent. Aided schools were better staffed and the teachers better paid, which created a rivalry among teachers to land jobs where salaries were higher. The government grant policy focused attention on the inferiority of Adventist schools that could not afford the upgrading that new expectations demanded.

Adventist leaders were alarmed. Workers in the East African Union interpreted the new proposals as a sinister plan that had been underway for years to put sectarian schools out of business, a conclusion that was not hard to imagine. That denominational schools had been a part of the modernizing movement was undeniable, but government money had enabled them to do it. Church control of aided schools had become progressively difficult as teachers receiving salaries from aid money sometimes neglected conventional Sabbath observance and ignored denominational lifestyle standards. If government regulations went into effect as feared, Adventist schools would have no authority over their faculties, and denominational identity could vanish. Church leaders faced the dilemma of whether to continue receiving public support and risk the loss of denominational schools to government regulation or refuse grants and risk the closure of church-sponsored education because of its inability to remain competitive.

The issue was potentially the most intense in the Zambesi Union in the central area of the Southern African Division where about four of every five schools were dependent on grants-in-aid. But the most shrill reaction came from the East African Union in the northeastern part of the division, where the majority of church leaders viewed government support of sectarian education as unbiblical and therefore immoral. Motivated by the hopelessness of their options and a desire to withdraw abruptly from the government program, they dispatched a frantic request for help to the Southern African Division and the General Conference. Unless massive amounts of money came from church sources to take the place of government aid they foresaw the demise of Adventist education in their territory.

Neither the necessary amount of denominational money was forthcoming nor was the church ready to buckle to financial conditions dictated by the government. In 1957 Adventist schools in East Africa,

Northern Rhodesia and Nyasaland began to terminate their relationship with the government. R. S. Watts, president of the Southern African Division, told the 1958 General Conference session that while the division had turned over many schools to the government to control and supervise, hundreds of primary and mission schools remained in church hands, "financed entirely with denominational funds," he added with a tone of orthodoxy.[30] He did not mention the fact that in Southern Rhodesia in the Zambesi Union no schools withdrew from the aid program.

With their income declining, schools charged students high tuition rates, but even so, low salaries continued as the norm and little money was available to invest in buildings and equipment. The result was unavoidable: governments evaluated Adventist schools as substandard and questioned the benefit of an Adventist education that was more expensive and offered less than public schools.

Five years into the austerity program F. G. Reid, president of the Zambesi Union, categorically rejected the view that the issue was a moral one. The historical trend of Adventist education had led to a commitment to mass education, and the denomination could pour huge sums of money into what was virtually a part of the public school system only by diverting funds from other legitimate church projects. Reid saw this possibility as both unrealistic and prejudicial to the church. In 1962 he wrote that to refuse government money was worse than receiving it. By continuing to accept grants Adventists would be able to preserve a degree of denominational influence and recover the lost reputation of their schools. This choice, he argued, should be the course to follow as long as possible and would allow the church to meet each problem in the best way that circumstances permitted at the time. As he understood the issue, it was a pragmatic answer to a pragmatic problem. By the early 1960s many of the schools were already returning to government aid, lending support to Reid's judgment.

Colonial rule in Africa collapsed with domino-like rapidity during the 1960s, and questions about education passed on to indigenous governments. As the new independencies gained power, each one approached the issue differently but by the middle of the decade some patterns of similarity emerged. The fledgling African countries deemed education to be a responsibility of government and continued giving grants-in-aid, but, in keeping with the spirit of the Beecher Report, regulation descended on schools as a matter of policy, not as interference resulting from accepting public money. Government money became a means that private schools used to meet regulatory legislation which applied to all schools, aided and unaided alike.

Sometimes regulation could become a more thorny issue than grants-in-aid. New governments tended to exercise direct supervision of teacher-preparation programs and to prohibit unaided schools from offering these courses, which meant that in some cases Adventist institutions had to accept government money in order to educate teachers for denominational schools. Frequently authorities also separated secondary schools from institutions that trained teachers. Governments were also prone to regulate enrollment, establish tuition charges, and designate the location of new schools. To control private education governments sometimes used official recognition which did not always follow a consistent pattern or indicate academic quality.

African students were quick to learn the value of government accreditation and enrollments could fluctuate sharply according to official approval. A case in point was Babcock University in Nigeria where enrollment jumped from 250 to about 1,000 in a single year because of sudden recognition by the government. Meanwhile, the number of students at Bethel College in South Africa plummeted from about 300 to fewer than fifty because the government withheld recognition.

In Kenya Kamagambo Training School faced an uncertain future because of new regulatory measures. The problem improved, partly because by 1965 fourteen former or current church members were elected to the national legislature and helped to establish cordial relations between Adventists and the new government, creating an atmosphere in which denominational schools could function and continue to receive aid.

In Africa government support of sectarian education proved to be a tradition too ingrained give up. By the end of the century the majority of Adventist elementary and secondary schools were free from grants but heavy dependence remained in Malawi, Zimbabwe, and the former Congo, and in the Southern Africa Union nearly all denominational secondary and elementary schools operated partially on government funds.[31]

### Adventist Policy at the End of the Century

At the end of the twentieth century about one of five Adventist elementary schools around the world received public money as did nearly a quarter of the denomination's secondary schools, but state aid followed a checkered pattern determined by political circumstances and the need for money. Besides Africa and Australia, schools in Europe, Japan, Korea, and parts of Indonesia were frequent recipients, and scattered cases existed elsewhere, including the French Antilles, Chile, and Argentina.[32]

With low costs and simple goals characterizing early Adventist education, church leaders did not envision that they would ever face the intricate problems that government financial assistance brought. But denominational schools were forced to conform to professional standards in order to survive, which drove operating expenses upward. After struggles with recurring debt and world depression, school administrators learned that students could not afford the real cost of a competitive education and government aid in one form or another appeared to be part of the solution.

In 1948 M. L. Andreasen, theologian and former college president, reflected with ironic humor that "We have learned a new thing: As the students cost more than they pay in, the more students, the harder it is to run a school financially. We used to think that many students would help us. But each one costs more than we take in. So one thousand students are worse than five hundred. That is a new one. And so all our schools are running in debt."[33]

The debate over state aid remained an issue as Adventist education entered the twenty-first century, but opposition, especially in the United States, was slackening. North American colleges and universities commonly applied for and received government money for equipment and research. Loma Linda University received millions annually. Government confiscation or lethal regulation of Adventist schools as a result of accepting public money appeared to be more of an apprehension than a reality. The General Conference Public Affairs and Religious Liberty Department had no record of Adventist schools closing because they accepted public money. It was true that denominational schools in Angola, Mozambique, and the Maritimes provinces in Canada closed, victims of their governments' axes, but closure was the result of government policy, not a consequence of accepting government money.

These incidents pointed to the likelihood that governments could find ways to close or control sectarian schools without using grant money as an excuse, although this was not an absolute. In some regions schools could refuse government money but would then become subject to taxation. In such instances schools became entrepreneurial projects but remained under denominational control.[34]

Increasingly Adventist educators and church leaders came to believe that governments were willing to help sectarian schools because they recognized them as a public service. It was less expensive to grant financial assistance than erecting and staffing additional government schools. Each region was left to determine its own course of action on the basis of local conditions, with the overarching principle that public money should never force an Adventist school to compromise its identity.

---

[1]This passage about academic freedom based on Sidney Allen, "Academic Freedom," (*Journal of True Education,* April 1963), p. 8, 9; Keld J. Reynolds, "Some Observations on Academic Freedom," (*ibid.*, March-April 1965), pp. 16-19; Earle Hilgert, "Academic Freedom," (*ibid.*, February-March 1967), pp. 16-19; Reuben Hilde, "A Look at Academic Freedom," (*ibid.*, Summer 1969), pp. 14, 15; Minutes, College and University Administrators Meeting, August 2-5, 1965, AST, RG 51; "A Statement on Academic Freedom in SDA Schools," *ibid.*; "To What Degree Can Critical Thinking Be Promoted, or Even Permitted, on an Adventist Campus?" *ibid.*; Board of Higher Education, "Academic Freedom in Seventh-day Adventist Colleges and Universities," *ibid.*; Minutes, Board of Higher Education, June 18, 1972, *ibid.*; John Whitehead, "Academic Freedom and the Rights of Religious Faculty," online version, www.leaderu.com: George Marsden, "Liberating Academic Freedom," *ibid.*; interview by *Atlantic Monthly*, George Marsden, "A truly multicultural society," (*Atlantic online*, October 2000); Wendi Maloney, "Religion and the Academy," (*Academe online*, January-February, 2001); "Academic Freedom and Tenure," AAUP online version; "Developments Relating to Censure," (*Academe online*, January-February 2003); "A Statement on Theological and Academic Freedom and Accountability," official position statement, General Conference of SDA, online version, www.advenist.org.

[2]General Conference Minutes, October 25, 1964; "A Statement on Academic Freedom in SDA Schools," AST, RG 51.

[3]Valentine, *Shaping of Adventism*, pp. 49-51; VandeVere, *Wisdom Seekers*, p. 81.

[4]The introductory note to the twenty-seven fundamental beliefs of the Seventh-day Adventist church reads: "Seventh-day Adventists accept the Bible as their only creed and hold certain fundamental beliefs to be the teaching of the Holy Scriptures. These beliefs, as set forth here, constitute the church's understanding and expression of the teaching of Scripture. Revision of these statements may be expected at a General Conference session when the church is led by the Holy Spirit to a fuller understanding of Bible truth or finds better language in which to express the teachings of God's Holy Word." See online edition, www.advenist.org.

[5]For data about science education and evolution see *General Conference Bulletin*, 1926, no. 12, p. 228; 1930, no. 14, p. 239; "Report of the Conference of Teachers of Science and Mathematics, August 18-30, 1942," AST, RG 51; reports of meetings of science and math teachers, 1947, 1952, 1956, ibid.; H. W. Clark, "Adventist Science Teaching and Post-War Problems," (1947) ibid.; John Beltz, "Student Attitudes Toward Evolution," (1964) ibid.; Gary Land, "God's Second Book: Adventist Education and the Sciences," (*Journal of Adventist Education*, Summer 2002); *Adventist Review*, October 25, 2001; March 21, 2002; Ronald L. Numbers, *The Creationists.* (New York: A. A. Knopf, 1992); Schwarz and Greenleaf, *Light Bearers*, pp. 434-438.

[6]*General Conference Bulletin*, 1930, no. 14, p. 239.

[7]*Adventist Review*, October 25, 2001.

[8]*Adventist Review*, October 7, 2004, p. 41.

[9]"An Affirmation of Creation," *ibid.*, November 11, 2004.

[10]Humberto Rasi, "Integrating Faith in the Classroom," in *Maturing of Adventism*, Edison Samaraj, ed. (Pune, India: Oriental Watchman Publishing House, 1998), p.23.

[11]Interview, Humberto Rasi, February 7, 2002; Humberto Rasi, "Integrating Faith in the Classroom," *ibid.*, pp. 1-26; Humberto Rasi, comp. *Christ in the Classroom: Adventist Approaches to the Integration of Faith and Learning*, vols. 1-26B (Silver Spring, MD: Institute for Christian Teaching, 1991-2001); email messages Rasi to Greenleaf, December 29, 2004.

[12]*General Conference Bulletin*, 1895, no. 2, p. 514.

[13]D. Lois Burnett, "Federal Aid to Nursing Education," *(Journal of True Education*, February 1944), pp. 18, 19.

[14]For a list of actions by the General Conference pertaining to government aid to education, see Robert Nixon, compiler, "Church-State Relationships in the United States: Compilation of Actions and Policies of the General Conference and the North American Division," unpublished document in the Office of General Counsel, General Conference of Seventh-day Adventists.

[15]Charles B. Hirsch, "Government Aid to Education–and Control," June 12, 1965, AST, RG 51.

[16]For differing opinions in the debate as it occurred among Adventists, see Charles Fleming, Jr., "Federal Support Is Not Coercive," (*Spectrum*, Autumn 1969), pp. 53-60; Loyed R. Simmons, "Federal Support Is Intrusive," (*ibid.*), pp. 45-52; Alonzo L. Baker, "Should Adventists Take Federal Aid For Their Schools?" (*ibid.*, Winter 1969), pp. 33-40; Clifford L. Jaqua, "Should Church Schools Receive Government Aid," (*Journal of Adventist Education*, October 1977), pp. 16-18, 24, 25; Robert L. Reynolds, "Government Intrusion in Higher Education," (*ibid.*, February-March 1980), pp. 14, 15, 27-29; Gary M Ross, "The Federal Government's Impact on Adventist Colleges," (*ibid.*, February-March 1984), pp. 15-17, 42.

[17]Roland R. Hegstad, "Government Aid to Education–Pitfalls, Snares, Principles, and Policies," in *Public Funds and Private Education: Issues of Church and State*, D. S. Penner, ed. (Silver Spring, MD.: Board of Education, K-12, Board of Higher Education), 1991, pp. 55-70.

[18]T. S. Geraty, compiler, "Federal Obligations to SDA Colleges & Universities, Fiscal Year 1971," *ibid.*; "NAD Higher Education, 1976-1977," four statistical tables, *ibid.*; three tables: "Church funds," "Government," "Student funds," 1978, *ibid.*

[19]General Conference Minutes, October 20, 1972.

[20]See the papers presented at this meeting in D. S. Penner, ed., *Public Funds and Private Education: Issues of Church and State* (Silver Spring, MD.: Board of Education, K-12, Board of Higher Education), 1991.

[21]This aspect of the issue of government aid received attention at Clackamas, which both Mitchell Tyner and Robert Nixon reemphasized in interviews on February 20, 2002 and February 25, 2002, respectively.

[22]*Columbia Union College v. Edward O. Clarke, Jr., et. al.* 2001, United States Court of Appeals, Fourth Circuit. Copy in the Office of General Counsel, General Conference of Seventh-day Adventists. See also Sasha Ross, "As the Court Turns," (*Spectrum*, spring 2002), pp. 20-29; Nicholas P. Miller, "A Question of Credibility: Columbia Union College and the Pursuit of State Funding," *ibid.*, pp. 30-36; Mitchell A. Tyner, "A Question of Equity: Columbia Union College and the Pursuit of Fairness," *ibid.*, pp. 37-44. For an old but informative discussion of the shifting winds of legal tests applied to government aid to sectarian schools, see Dale E. Twomley, *Parochiaid and the Courts* (Berrien Springs, MI: Andrews University Press, 1979). Chapter 12 especially applies.

[23]North American Division Committee Minutes, October 14, 1971.

[24]For this passage about Australia see Lester D. Devine, "State Aid for Education in Australia: An Overview," in Penner, *Public Funds and Private Education*, pp. 31-40; Anthony Potts, "Public and Private Schooling in Australia–Historical and Contemporary Considerations," wwwhistory.ac.uk/projects/elec/: Australian Council of State School Organizations, "Six myths about private schools in Australia," media@qtu.as..au: "D.O.G.S and the High Court Case," Internet homepage, Australian Council for Defence of Government Schools; *Attorney General (Vict.); ex rel. Black v. the Commonwealth*, "Australian High Court Cases," www.austlii.edu.au/cass/cth/high_ct. See also, "Australasian Division, Summary of Education Funding, 1977," AST, RG 51; "Constraints on the Acceptance of Government Funds for the Operation of Seventh-day Adventist Schools in the South Pacific Division," Office of General Counsel, General Conference of Seventh-day Adventists.

[25]Lester D. Devine, "State Aid for Education in Australia: An Overview," in Penner, *Public Funds and Private Education*, p. 40.

[26]*Proceedings of the Educational and Missionary Volunteer Departments of the General Conference of Seventh-day Adventists in World Convention, p. 189*; *General Conference Bulletin*, 1930, no. 7, p. 127.

[27]"Summary on Government Aid," [1966?], AST, RG 51; J. F. Ashlock to M. E. Loewen, January 20, 1965, "Compilation of Actions and Policies," Office of General Counsel, General Conference of Seventh-day Adventists; statement by George W. Brown re: Caribbean Union, *ibid.*

[28]J. F. Ashlock to M. E. Loewen, January 20, 1965, *ibid.*

[29]This passage on Africa taken from "Survey and Report of the Committee on Government Educational Grants-in-aid as adopted by the East African Union, April 1955," AST, RG 51; "A Memorial to The General Conference of Seventh-day Adventists and the Southern African Division," April 1955, ibid.; F. G. Reid to Roland R. Hegstad, March 16, 1962, ibid; E. D. Hanson to W. R. Beach, February 26, 1965, *ibid.*; "Educational Problems–East African Union," [1965?], *ibid.*; interview, Garland Dulan, February 11, 12, 2002.

[30]*General Conference Bulletin*, 1958, no. 3, p. 60.

[31]*World Report*, 2000: tables for each division.

[32]*Ibid.*; interview, Humberto Rasi, February 7, 2002.

[33]Quoted in Steinweg, *Without Fear or Favor,"* p. 154.

[34]Interviews: Jonathan Gallagher, February 27, 2002; John Graz, February 28, 2002; email message, Rasi to Greenleaf, December 29, 2004.

# CHALLENGES OF MODERNIZATION

The challenges that Adventist education faced from academic freedom and government aid were primarily external in origin, but from within serious questions also developed during the latter half of the twentieth century. The number of post-secondary institutions reached nearly a hundred by the end of the 1990s, and with this growth came financial dilemmas that made systematic regulation of tertiary education increasingly problematical. Opinions differed about the balance between centralized and local control. Perennial debate took place about the breadth of curricula, how high higher education should reach, and more pragmatically, how much post-secondary education the denomination could afford. Questions arose about the identity of Adventist schools of higher learning, and denominational educators speculated about how urbanization and new economic realities impacted their traditional philosophy of practical education. Also problematical was the matter of reconciling technological change to Adventist philosophy of education and accommodating to its ensuing financial burdens.

All of these questions intertwined, creating a tangle that prevented anyone from dealing with any single issue without affecting the others. These problems forced Adventist educators to rethink the purpose of denominational education in order to adapt long accepted principles to new conditions. In the end they found themselves restating Adventist philosophy of education in terms amenable to the twenty-first century.

### Development of Distance Education

One of the more impressive changes took place in the denomination's correspondence school which began as Fireside Correspondence School in 1909. Its name changed to Home Study Institute and then to Home Study International, both of which were known as Home Study in common Adventist parlance. For most of its life Home Study, or HSI, functioned quietly as a convenient source of academic credit for Adventist students at all levels who did not have access to a denominational school. By the end of the 1980s HSI operated branch offices in Singapore, the Philippines, Australia, India, and England. The school received an injection of new life in 1989 when Joseph Gurubatham became its eighth president. Almost immediately he organized the institution into three divisions: Home Study Elementary School, Home Study High School, and Griggs University, the post-secondary section named after Frederick Griggs who founded Fireside Correspondence School. In 1990 Griggs University began offering a limited number of accredited degrees in religion and business, mainly to international students.

Records showed that as Home Study entered the twenty-first century more than 300,000 students had studied under its auspices. During the 1990s it became an aggressive center of distance education. It collaborated with Columbia Union College to offer degrees through that institution's external degree program and began actively to enroll non-Adventist students from the million and a half in the home-school population in the United States. HSI also became the source for online curriculum in more than twenty public school systems in the United States. Gurubatham took his place among the circle of North American college presidents and when Adventist colleges and universities formed a consortium in 2002, he became its executive officer, a part-time salaried position funded from dues paid by the member institutions.[1]

## Offices of Development and Fund Raising

Financial issues were a major concern in the latter half of the century. Between the end of World War II and 1980 aging college campuses in the United States underwent extensive rebuilding, replacing old structures in order to accommodate successively higher enrollments and to meet new standards in education. Of the three leading sources of institutional revenue–student fees, profits from institutional industries, and church subsidies–income from the students was much larger than the other two combined. Adventist schools were tuition driven and depended on progressively larger numbers of students to help pay their bills, but plummeting enrollments beginning about 1980 sent college presidents and business managers reeling to find relief from the tide of red ink that was sure to follow. Already institutional industries had become less productive and contributed fewer dollars to college operating budgets. Some schools had sold off many of their auxiliary operations because they were losing money.

Before enrollment began its downturn, Milton Murray, a graduate of La Sierra College who had become a skilled fund raiser, joined the General Conference to begin a new denominational venture, Philanthropic Service for Institutions, which became a mentoring office for advancement programs among Adventist institutions. For the first time in the history of Adventist education, organized fund raising became a serious part of institutional administration. Murray promoted active solicitation of gifts, issued incentives and nationwide plans for consistent programs of giving by alumni, and helped schools to establish active development offices.

These ideas caught on, and during the five years prior to 1985 Adventist higher education in North America gleaned $45,000,000 from voluntary sources. During the next five years the figure rose to about $88,000,000. Murray retired before the 1995 General Conference session, but not before he had revolutionized the concept of planned giving and fund raising among Adventist institutions. As part of his legacy endowments became common to Adventist schools.[2]

On the threshold of the twenty-first century every tertiary institution in North America and many secondary schools as well as some schools beyond North America had organized sophisticated and permanent development offices that had accumulated millions in endowments and other financial support, all of which brought improved stability to Adventist education. Murray did not resolve all the financial problems of Adventist education, but his consistent leading finally pushed institutional fund raising into the twentieth century and produced a source of income that otherwise donors would have spent elsewhere.

The idea of endowments for Adventist schools was a new idea. Typically, denominational schools at all levels had depended on church subsidies to provide the margin of solvency, and some pointed out that this practice was better than an endowment, which necessarily would have to be of astronomical proportions to furnish the same amount of money that the church pumped into its education program. Taken as a group, the newly established endowments did not eliminate the need for subsidies or become a panacea for operational expenses for Adventist post-secondary institutions, but nonetheless, fund raising in general provided an increasing proportion of institutional budgets.[3]

At the same time while the absolute dollar value of subsidies from parent organizations to the colleges consistently increased during the latter half of the century its proportional value in the total institutional operating budgets remained small and sometimes shrank. This diminishing dependence upon direct support from the church gave rise to a growing sense of independence on post-secondary campuses, which some church leaders saw as a contributing factor to the steady decline of centralized control of a denominational system of education and a potential threat to the Adventist identity of higher education.

## A Centralized System Based on Shared Control

The question of control and systematization of denominational education was probably the overshadowing problem during the years after 1945. Events in the debate about these issues harked back to the beginnings of educational organization in 1901. By 1905 the General Conference adopted plans to standardize curriculum, textbooks, and some teaching materials. Also in effect was the policy to establish a post-secondary institution in each union and assign elementary and secondary schools to the conferences. A stream of students flowing upward through the post-secondary institution would tie the system together. Administratively, the schools operated under an arrangement of shared control in which the General Conference held the upper hand in order to maintain a system. Policy making was centralized at the world headquarters while the conferences and unions owned and administered the schools. In no way was this *modus operandi* meant to be an open door for autonomy among post-secondary institutions.[4]

During the first three decades of the century these practices prevailed. College boards functioned as subsidiaries of the unions and elementary and secondary schools operated under the auspices of departments of education in the unions and local conferences. With ever growing seriousness, conferences assumed responsibility for maintaining a corps of credentialed teachers, assuming responsibility for the financial solvency of church schools and academies, and administering accreditation criteria. The entire structure of education was under the administrative thumb of the General Conference whose task it was to maintain the framework and refine it according to developing needs.[5]

That this organizational model applied to Adventist education around the world was a given. Denominational leaders encouraged schools in the world fields to contextualize their programs, but they also expected educational leaders to pattern their organization after the North American system. Ideally, schools were to be rural and industrial as broadly construed, curricula were to embody Adventist beliefs, and lower schools would prepare students for additional study at higher levels until they reached a training school in the union or division. The entire system revolved around the dual purpose of teaching Adventism to students and preparing church workers. The apparatus of control was inherent in the 1923 world convention of Adventist education at Colorado Springs. The exemplary role of North American organization was patently clear two years later in 1925 when the Department of Education conducted an educational conference in China, the largest such gathering outside North America up to that time.

The most serious questions of shared control occurred at the post-secondary level where the first substantial test cropped up in 1913. Unable to find answers to perennial financial problems in North American schools, the General Conference Department of Education attempted to limit the number of post-secondary institutions in the United States and Canada and determine the extent of curricular offerings, but resistance choked off these proposals. Among the leading dissenters were some of the union presidents who were *ex officio* chairmen of college boards. A similar situation occurred during the Great Depression. These events were defining moments for the education system, demonstrating not only the practical limits of authority of the General Conference Department of Education but also that union conference presidents in North America could and would block organizational change among the colleges if they believed their territorial interests were at stake.

Additional challenges to centralized policies of control of education surfaced during the 1920s and continued into the 1930s as Adventists debated the implications of regional accreditation. General Conference personnel were more prone to oppose accreditation than were union presidents and college administrators whose wall of resistance was visibly porous, if not non-existent in some cases. The *modus operandi,* giving unions ownership and immediate control of colleges, that had emerged from the General Conference sessions of 1901 and 1903 had taken an unforeseen turn. By the time the accreditation issue had run its course, postsecondary education in North America was showing definite signs of a nascent independence. Shared control was tilting more steeply toward the unions.

## Adventist Accrediting Practices

The Association of Seventh-day Adventist Colleges and Secondary Schools, renamed in 1943 as the Association of Seventh-day Adventist Institutions of Higher Education and Secondary Schools, did not succeed in sidestepping regional and professional accreditation bodies, but it became the single most influential factor in maintaining a system of Adventist education. In 1932 the General Conference recognized the Board of Regents as the source of standards and policies which, after ratification by the General Conference, would become the "operating policies for all member institutions."[6]

Using the Board of Regents as the enforcing agency, the General Conference Department of Education established a single set of measurements for education, and by repeatedly updating these criteria, it applied progressively stricter standards to elementary and secondary schools through departments of education in the unions and conferences. The Board of Regents worked directly with postsecondary schools. Denominational accreditation originally applied to North American schools only, but in 1954 the Association broadened its influence to include schools in the world fields. Newbold College became the first Adventist institution outside North America to fulfill denominational accreditation criteria in 1970, more than a decade after it affiliated with Columbia Union College.[7]

The Board of Regents continued into the mid-1990s as the leading systematizing agent within Adventist education. As membership swelled in the world fields and more secondary and tertiary schools arose, denominational accreditation became standard procedure. During the 1990s the Board of Regents changed its name to a more universal term, the Accrediting Association of Seventh-day Adventist Schools, Colleges and Universities, most often shortened to the Adventist Accrediting Association or its acronym, AAA. Briefly, some hoped again that this denominational agency would replace the need for regional accreditation, but that goal proved elusive. In the United States some states recognized denominational accreditation at the elementary and secondary levels as more thorough than criteria of the state governments; however, at post-secondary levels regional accreditation bodies in the United States and governments in the world fields remained the principal sources of recognition. By the end of the century the AAA often concentrated on matters of specific denominational interest during an accreditation process while leaving other matters to regional accrediting bodies.[8]

### Challenges to the System and the Board of Higher Education

As effective as denominational accreditation became, it did not solve other problems of systematization from which Adventist postsecondary education chafed, particularly in the United States. Four trends contributed to this friction: the emergence of graduate education, the soaring cost of education, an infectious competition among institutions of higher learning, and the growing predisposition in the unions to resist centralized influences.

Graduate education began inauspiciously in the mid-1930s with advanced studies in theology, but not until the late 1950s did Adventist leaders take serious note of its impact. Several postsecondary institutions introduced their own limited graduate programs, some of which predated those at Andrews and Loma Linda, but the universities raised the stakes of academic achievement in Adventist circles and added a new dimension to the tradition of each North American union owning a complete educational track from the first grade through the baccalaureate level. With the advent of graduate schools, colleges no longer represented the final step in denominational education. Questions arose spontaneously about the relationship of postsecondary institutions to each other as well as to the two universities.

A Commission on Higher Education, established in 1961, and a Commission on Graduate Education tried to design a rational mold in which to recast Adventist postsecondary institutions, but before the end of the 1960s rivalry among colleges for both students and academic reputation was rife. In 1967 a subcommittee of the reconstituted Commission on Higher Education concluded that conditions had reached a crisis, declaring that the denomination was unable to halt the cost of higher education that had been spiraling upward because of numerous causes, including graduate education and increasingly higher salaries and benefits. The report held out few options. In order to avoid both government aid on the one hand and obsolescence on the other if the schools sat idle in the face of change, the group advocated a restructuring of denominational support as the only means of survival.[9]

Discussions among church leaders and educators during the next year focused on the need for improved systematization as one of the key factors to rein in costs and competition. To a large extent at the behest of union presidents as well as college administrations, a new entity was born, the Board of Higher Education, chaired by the president of the North American Division but under the daily operation of an executive secretary.

The Board of Regents continued as the denominational accrediting body while the new BHE concentrated on managing higher education in North America. As such it became a body of the North American Division rather than another standing committee of the General Conference Department of Education. Its crucial duty was to develop a master plan of higher education in North America and to "recommend or approve the establishment or discontinuance of universities, colleges, schools, college divisions, programs, majors, institutions, departments, branches, campuses and other units as may be indicated by the master plan." The BHE was to "maintain general overview of the system of higher education." It was a tall order.[10]

In his first major report to the BHE in 1972, the executive secretary, Frederick E. J. Harder, who left his post as dean of the graduate school at Andrews University to assume his new position, demonstrated that he took the tasks of systematization seriously. During the previous months the BHE had ruled on curricular issues at five institutions, not all of them positively. Harder called for institutions to plan curricular change according to BHE reports based on disclosures of financial information that administrators had heretofore regarded as institutionally private. Although he spoke in the context of academic freedom for teachers, he announced his agreement with the principle that institutional independence is never absolute.

*F. E. J. Harder, first executive director of the Board of Higher Education. The BHE constituted a major attempt to organize Seventh-day Adventist higher education in the North America into a system.*

The Board of Higher Education did not maintain this robust beginning. A seventy-year accumulation of administrative traditions was not easy to sweep away by a single speech and by the mid-1970s it became apparent that the BHE would not fulfill the purposes that church leaders and educators expressed when it was born.

The weakness of the BHE showed up quickly in 1972 when both Loma Linda and Andrews universities submitted proposals to offer doctoral programs in education. The subcommittee charged with investigating both campuses recommended a rejection of Loma Linda's proposal. In language rarely equaled in denominational records for bluntness, the recommendation reminded members of the BHE that regulatory policies already prohibited competing doctoral degrees in Adventist institutions. Further, it categorized LLU's accreditation in education as insufficient, declared that a doctoral program in education was inconsistent with Loma Linda's mission, chided educators who would not take a 2,000-mile plane trip for doctoral studies at Andrews, and warned the BHE that it would become a laughingstock if it did not make a hard decision that its own policies already dictated. Notwithstanding this inflammatory rhetoric, Loma Linda University began offering doctorates in education within two years, inexplicably with the approval of the BHE.

One of the major driving forces behind the Board of Higher Education was systematization to manage costs, which translated into cutting out duplication of programs, but this incident demonstrated that, despite their earlier claims for the need of new financial and other managerial policies, officers of institutions were unwilling to relinquish their decision-making power. In resolving basic issues pertaining to their own goals, colleges and universities tended to rely more on the authority of their boards rather than to comply with policies of a centralized system.

From the late 1960s into the 1990s the relationship among the colleges remained politely darwinian as institutions sought to attract higher enrollments by dismantling their longstanding territorial distinctions and adding new and sometimes thinly veiled competing programs. Colleges and universities openly recruited students from anywhere. There was also a consciousness that the idea of system had gone awry. For the Adventist public there was no shortage of speculation about solutions. Suggestions ranged from a radical reduction in the number of institutions through consolidation and closure to a virtual release of postsecondary institutions from all controls which would permit all of them to go it alone. A sense prevailed that Adventist higher education in North America was plunging ahead, but with an unclear destination. Some doubted it had a destination, at least at the moment.[11]

In 1992 the North American Division attempted to clear the air by approving a recommendation originating with the college presidents that recognized institutional boards of trustees as the ultimate voice of authority in operating postsecondary schools. Some saw the action as a demise, others as a new beginning, but arguably, it was one of the concluding steps in a trend that began in 1903 when A. G. Daniells and W. C. White concurred that the General Conference should not have any schools, publishing plants, and hospitals, and that the unions and conferences should assume the responsibility of owning and operating denominational institutions. By 1992 shared control of postsecondary schools that the General Conference had once dominated had gravitated into the hands of the owners.[12]

Associated with the independence movement of higher education in North America was a groundswell among educators for a thorough overhaul of the salary schedule. Frequent arguments surfaced that Adventist postsecondary schools lost the service of highly qualified personnel because the traditional salary policy offered them substantially less than they could earn elsewhere in the education market. Agitation set in for a separate remuneration plan for teachers, thus reducing the denominational salary policy to ministers.

The North American salary schedule prescribed relatively low earnings but granted a tax-free package of benefits that included generous health coverage and professional development allowances. The amounts varied from institution to institution, but depending on individual needs, the value of these combined perquisites could amount to thousands of dollars annually. As the twenty-first century began no clear resolution of this issue was in sight, but tertiary schools, acting on the strength of their newly authorized independence, began to experiment with salary plans that increased the income of post-secondary faculty.

The Board of Higher Education survived until the mid-1990s. It never achieved the reality of its original hope, living on with steadily declining strength and finally dying from natural causes–it ceased to function meaningfully and became irrelevant. Replacing it was a Higher Education Cabinet with membership consisting of institutional presidents, board chairmen, and other selected General Conference personnel experienced in education who exercised only perfunctory checks on institutional independence. They functioned more as coordinators than regulators and provided only minimal accountability to the central authority of the church.

## Association of Adventist Colleges and Universities

Some characterized the organization of Adventist higher education in North America as unstable. At best it was fluid. In 2002 college presidents, in consultation with other denominational personnel, organized the Association of Adventist Colleges and Universities, a consortium to fill the vacuum left by the absence of any clear central direction for North American higher education as an establishment. The formal organizational document affirmed the legal individuality of Adventist colleges and universities and pledged their commitment to the mission of the North American Division. The institutions agreed to the ideal of a "seamless fabric" of Adventist higher education, a kind of educational free trade atmosphere in which students could move about with minimal regulation.

The most promising aspect of this action was its spontaneous nature, which recognized that systematization, imposed from centralized authority, had not survived well, but that group organization of some kind was necessary. It was a tacit admission that colleges and universities had more to gain and nothing to lose by acting in voluntary concert rather than in rivalry. The Association's opening statement sounded idealistic and, if achieved, beneficial to the participating campuses, but only time would tell if postsecondary institutions could live up to their own new standard of individual units functioning separately but with mutual helpfulness after decades of competition.[13]

## Ministerial Education and System

Although the boards of postsecondary schools officially became the ultimate controlling authority over higher education in North America, elements of a system remained. One of the most important was the pattern of centralized control over ministerial education that had evolved from the early years of the century when theological programs began to crystallize. The General Conference strongly influenced the formation of theological education by spelling out essential curricular elements. Although programs differed from school to school, baccalaureate ministerial courses resembled each other.

With the arrival of the Theological Seminary, a General Conference institution designated as the world center for Adventist men of cloth, the undergraduate schools became the preparatory phase of ministerial preparation and correlated their programs with the advanced school. Even after a master's degree became the standard credential for ministers, many college graduates continued to enter directly into pastoral work, but the percentage of ministers with graduate degrees steadily increased. The colleges functioned in a prescribed supportive role to the finishing school. Although not formalized in a written statement, this organizational principle was understood to be the bedrock condition of ministerial preparation.

With the appearance of graduate degrees in theology in the world fields the Theological Seminary no longer held the distinction of the sole source of ministerial education. In 1994 the Annual Council voted that ministerial education was the province of the General Conference working through the world divisions, and placed all graduate programs in theology under the aegis of either the "respective division," or, in the case of the Theological Seminary, the General Conference. Institutional discretion was not to direct graduate education in religion. The purpose of this policy was to "strengthen the worldwide unity and mission focus of these programs." By placing the divisions of the General Conference in charge of ministerial education in their territories, the church defined its inherent right to determine how its clergy would be prepared. It also recognized the legitimacy of the seminaries in the world fields, which had grown up as children of the Theological Seminary.[14]

The first serious challenge to this policy occurred two years later in 1996 when the board of Southern College in Tennessee voted to inaugurate a master's degree in pastoral training. The decision of the Tennessee college board gave rise to a bundle of questions. In the religion department an admitted dissatisfaction with the Theological Seminary had been smouldering for years, stoked by accusations of liberal theological tendencies on the Michigan campus. The action by Southern College placed the school in competition with the official ministerial education program instead of the preparatory role it was to play according to denominational policy. The action also challenged church policy by implying that in North America, unions instead of the division determined ministerial education.

Funding for the proposed graduate degree came from private sources, demonstrating that financial backing could be more influential in theological education than denominational policy. In addition, the action raised the question of loyalty among union presidents who were willing to approve a policy when voting as members of the General Conference Committee, but who would take a contradictory position when they returned to chair the boards of their schools.

In the eyes of church leaders the implications of this action were troubling, for they struck one of the most tender spots of Adventist education, the preparation of ministers. The issues added up to what was probably the most serious challenge to the denominational policy of centralized control over the preparation of ministers. Appeals by the North American Division and the General Conference Department of Education slowed but did not stop the graduate degree at Southern College, which in the process changed its name to Southern Adventist University, a result of a parallel decision to enter the field of graduate education.

With the inauguration of a separate graduate program of ministerial education in Tennessee, the last meaningful vestige of centralized control of postsecondary schools disappeared. La Sierra University followed in 2002 with a program of graduate studies in theology. To distinguish its programs from those at other Adventist institutions, the Theological Seminary advertised its graduate degrees for ministers as the only ones approved by the North American Division.

**International Board of Ministerial and Theological Education**

Meanwhile, another ingredient complicated the discussion about what authority controlled ministerial education. Since 1929 the Adventist accrediting system approved or disapproved of institutions as a complete unit, but at the 1998 Annual Council the church took its first step in specialized accreditation by establishing basic criteria for religion departments in all postsecondary schools around the world. The action called the new process "endorsement," but its practical distinction from accreditation was hardly noticeable.

In compliance with the 1994 action confirming ministerial education to be a General Conference responsibility, an International Board of Ministerial and Theological Education, or IBMTE, would give global oversight to pastoral training and each division would organize a branch of the IMBTE to handle questions within its own territory. Coordination between the Adventist Accrediting Association and the division boards of ministerial education linked the two bodies.[15]

The reaction was mixed and debate was immediate. Eventually all the divisions except North America organized boards as the policy prescribed. The presidents of colleges in the United States resisted the endorsement plan, asserting that the policy which gave their boards of trustees ultimate governing authority also applied to theological education and that the new policy was an invasion into the details of campus administration which would adversely impact accreditation. They also declared that processes of accountability built into board control and the criteria of the Adventist Accrediting Association constituted sufficient regulatory authority over ministerial education.

The critical issue was the endorsement process for individual teachers that allowed division boards of ministerial and theological education to screen religion teachers according to criteria established by the international board, which in turn would declare personnel eligible for employment or deserving dismissal. Endorsement would recur on a five-year cycle and would include a signed statement from each individual reaffirming his or her agreement with the published fundamental doctrines of the church. Criticism charged that this endorsement plan impinged on North American traditions of academic freedom by transferring selection of employees and due process from the institution to the divisions of the General Conference.

Some further argued that the policy put trained theologians more or less on trial when instead the church should be relying on them to assist in determining the biblical integrity of Adventist doctrines. Because Seventh-day Adventists taught that biblical understanding was an expanding continuum, theologians on college campuses believed that religion departments were an appropriate place for theological discussions.

For their part, church leaders were more interested in the colleges as sites for ministerial preparation than as centers of theological debate. The General Conference had long since established a Biblical Research Institute, led by recognized theologians drawn from academe, who spent their full time in theological study, and while not proscribing active academicians from this process, church leaders preferred that doctrinal debate should take place under the controlled circumstances of the BRI rather than to spill into college classrooms and publications. The possibility of deviant theology probably helped to inspire the original notion of endorsement, but the proposal focused more on the need to ensure the unity of theological programs in the face of trends toward decentralized control. The heart of the issue was to uphold the long accepted prerogative of the church to determine the preparation of its own ministers.

The newly published *Handbook of Seventh-day Adventist Ministerial and Theological Education* allowed alternative methods of endorsing religion teachers, but required the ministerial board in the division where disagreement with the policy occurred to offer a substitute plan. In North America no ministerial board existed. Prolonged negotiation between the General Conference and the North American colleges did not resolve the controversy.

Complicating the issue was the need to agree upon separate arrangements for General Conference institutions that did not fall under the auspices of a division. Griggs University, Andrews University, Loma Linda University, Oakwood College, and the Adventist International Institute of Advanced Studies in the Philippines constituted this group. Loma Linda did not offer ministerial education, but its academic organization included a faculty of religion with the largest cluster of professors in any Adventist school in North America outside the Theological Seminary. Because four of the five General Conference institutions affected by the policy were in North America they lent moral support to the union schools in the United States, but in October 2003 the General Conference institutions had formulated an alternate plan designed especially for them which the IBMTE accepted. Essentially, because the chairpersons of the boards of these schools and other members of the boards were General Conference personnel, these institutions by definition fulfilled the requirements spelled out in the *Handbook.*

The disagreement with the North American campuses rested on methodology to accomplish a valid objective. College presidents could not and did not try to gainsay the right of the church to regulate the preparation of its own ministry but consistently resisted what they believed to be invasive policies of institutional management. General Conference leaders held North American schools accountable to prepare an alternative plan and gave institutions time to negotiate out of the impasse, but as late as 2004 the issue remained unresolved.[16]

## Issues in Higher Education and World System

The debate over central control of theology was part of the broader issue of systematization and identity of denominational schools worldwide. World systematization strengthened during the 1970s when a Board of Theological Education became the clearinghouse for proposals to establish degree programs for ministers in the world fields. This body became an important part of the controlling authority over the growth of Adventist education outside North America, impacting the academic ambience of entire campuses by requiring fields of instruction beyond theology to develop a genuine post-secondary character in order to maintain academic balance throughout the institution. In most cases denominational recognition of a training school as a four-year, postsecondary institution originated with the institution's capability to offer baccalaureate education in theology. The spread of denominational accreditation roughly coincided with the appearance of degree programs in theology in the world fields.

Associated with this movement were criteria of regional accrediting bodies in the United States that required compliance from schools outside North America if they wished to qualify as an affiliated institution. Of singular influence was the North Central Association to which Andrews University belonged. During the heyday of affiliations, the 1970s and 1980s, these controls functioned effectively, but with the mushrooming of Adventist higher education outside the United States–nearly a score of new denominational colleges and universities emerged during the 1990s—a reexamination of the process became imperative. Affiliations had been a crutch for many Adventist schools in the developing world, but these institutions found it necessary to generate their own academic reputations according to regulatory authority in their own countries, and organic connections with a North American school became less important, if not a hindrance in some cases.

By the late 1980s all matters relating to Adventist postsecondary education beyond North America converged on the International Board of Education which was similar to the North American Board of Higher Education but with global authority. Recognition by the Adventist Accrediting Association kept alive aspects of systematization affecting the identity of denominational schools and educational procedures.

Although denominational accreditation was not a perfect process, it had proven through the years to be effective, especially in developing countries. In contrast to developed countries in the West where Adventist schools functioned on the periphery of the public education establishment, developing states often leaned on private education to lift literacy rates and lead in professional training. These countries lacked strong educational traditions and the resources to build quality school systems on short notice.

Adventist schools, backed by an international church and monitored by its own demonstrably effective international accrediting body, earned high marks in many young countries even though they would fall short of accepted standards in an economically advanced nation. Frequently these schools enrolled large numbers of non-Adventist students in keeping with a long denominational practice of utilizing schools as a mission outreach. Many of these schools also employed non-Adventist teachers, sometimes in increasing numbers to keep pace with expanding enrollment. Because of these circumstances, many Adventist schools substituted for a public education system. By the late years of the twentieth century some governments in the developing world requested Adventists to take over or establish new schools as a public service.[17]

All of this was a mixed blessing. A commendable standing in the public eye was flattering and as old as Adventist education in the non-Christian world beginning with Cecil Rhodes, who perceived Christian schools as a more effective means to accomplish social change than the colonial government itself. The image that Rhodes attached to Adventist schools in particular followed wherever churchmen established education on the frontiers. But flattering as they were, proposals by developing countries to operate schools solely as a public service brought heavy pressure to the church and its philosophy and policies of education. Apprehension that non-Adventist content could creep into denominational education prompted fears that secularism would invade Adventist campuses.

General Conference President Jan Paulsen recognized education as a symbol of "Christ's victory over evil," and he spoke out for "a variety of structures" to meet church needs resulting from unparalleled growth in parts of the world. But he tempered his remarks with a reminder that the church should make the distinction between mission and social development.[18]

In response to these conditions and other concerns including financial support of education, the unique identity of Adventist schools, and the breakdown of a sense of system, especially in the United States, a

General Conference Commission on Higher Education went into action in the year 2000. Its function was to examine the nature and purposes of Adventist postsecondary schools and to gather information upon which to recommend a global plan to guide the development of colleges and universities. The very existence of the commission belied the conviction that the notion of system was not yet dead. After more than four years of discussions, the commission still had more unresolved issues than answers; one of its leading tasks was to engender compliance with denominational policies by the unions, the entities that owned and operated postsecondary institutions. In simple terms, the commission sought ways to redress the question of shared control.[19]

A practical tool began in 2000 when the General Conference Department of Education established the Adventist Professionals' Network, or APN. In collaboration with the secretariat of the General Conference, Adventist Development and Relief Agency, and Andrews and Loma Linda universities, APN established a data base of thousands of names of Adventists with college and university degrees in about 150 countries who may be available to fill employment vacancies around the world.[20]

## The Debate over Adventist Philosophy of Education

The commission could not avoid debate about Adventist philosophy of education, especially as it touched matters such as identity, purpose, and control. Both explicitly and implicitly the philosophy of Adventist education had been central in much of the debate about education during the decades following World War II, but in the verbal sparring from the 1960s onward differences between tradition and philosophy were not always clear. In 1976 Raymond Moore, an educational administrator with experience in both the United States and Asia, published *Adventist Education at the Crossroads*, in which he insinuated that the primary problem with Adventist schools was their departure from several aspects of their original philosophy, among them the agricultural work programs. For corrective measures he advocated revamping denominational schools, reorganizing curricula and extracurricular programs, and setting enrollment caps to conform to economic efficiency. His prescription also called for a possible twelve-month operating schedule for secondary schools.

Four years later Reuben Hilde, an associate director in the General Conference Department of Education, replied with *Showdown: Can SDA Education Pass the Test?*, a book that defended changes in Adventist education during the twentieth century but at the same time admitted to a long list of shortcomings. Under Hilde's scrutinizing eye denominational schools probably merited a C+ or a B-, but he balanced his observations by explaining circumstances surrounding many of the problems church-sponsored schools faced in late twentieth century America that were absent during earlier decades. Pointing out some of the wrong impressions by which Adventists commonly judged their schools, he was quick to identify what he believed to be one of the worst problems: church members, some of them leaders, who had strong convictions about education and supported them with one-sided quotes from Ellen White, claiming to follow the "blueprint," a term mistakenly attributed to Ellen White that generations of Adventists used synonymously with her philosophy of education.[21]

The primary target of Moore's remarks was Adventist boarding schools, mostly in North America, where student labor would be a meaningful feature of campus life. By contrast, Hilde aimed his comments for the most part at both elementary and secondary schools, also in North America. Even compensating for this difference, the two authors were poles apart philosophically. While Moore called for radical change back to a previous ideal, Hilde urged adaptation of Adventist principles to the needs of contemporary society. Hilde was in a position to effect the changes he thought were necessary and during the 1970s he led the North American Division in the development of a reorganized K-12 curriculum that included production of new reading and Bible textbooks, both critical to the identity of Adventist education. Newer science texts were also part of later upgrading.

Following on the heels of Hilde's reforms was the dissolution of the historic "special relationship" that the North American Division maintained with the General Conference and its consequent alignment with the other world divisions. As North America developed its new role during the 1980s and 1990s, a new North American Department of Education set about to establish a different identity for grades K-12 by creating a Ministry of Teaching credential for teachers (until then they had received credentials as a missionary), continuing curriculum development, updating code books and policies, and conducting regular administrative conventions. The crowning event in this process was a gathering of approximately 6,500 teachers in grades K-12 in Dallas, Texas in 2000, probably the largest assembly of Adventist educators in Adventist history. Again, these developments served as models to the rising tide of elementary and secondary education in the world fields, especially in the developing countries.

Before Hilde wrote his defense of Adventist education, George Knight, church historian and educator, destroyed many of the favorite illusions that shaped Adventist ideas about their schools. His *Myths of Adventism* did not focus on education exclusively, but he devoted many chapters to denominational schools whose problems were becoming a conversation piece in church circles. The ink had hardly dried on Hilde's book when Knight added a scholarly touch to the debate by publishing two more books; one, a study that examined Adventist philosophy of education in the light of nineteenth-century America and the second an edited collection of informative biographical sketches of influential leaders in Adventist education.

The obvious conclusion from Knight's books was that denominational education had always faced changing times and Adventist educators themselves were never unanimous when applying educational philosophy to new conditions. Adventist philosophy was an evolving thing and the so-called "blueprint" as such existed only in one's fantasy although Ellen White's pronouncements were still basic to denominational education.[22]

With decades of conflicting debate behind them, more than 250 Adventist educators and church leaders convened an International Conference on the Philosophy of Seventh-day Adventist Education at Andrews University in April 2001. The task of forging a philosophical statement that would fit schools in all world fields was not simple, but it was necessary as a beginning point for the work of the Commission on Higher Education. In essence, the finished document declared that knowledge is best understood in the context of the Christian worldview consisting of both supernatural and natural orders; it upheld biblical teachings about the nature of humans as sinful beings in need of salvation from sin, and committed schools to prepare students for both eternity and productive lives on this earth, including active involvement in the work of the church. More specifically, the statement summarized basic outcomes for education at the elementary, secondary, and tertiary levels.[23]

As Adventist education entered the twenty-first century after nearly 130 years of experimenting, struggling, and reorganizing, perhaps one could ask if the Adventist world could expect anything more than these essentials and how different they were from the principles in Ellen White's "Proper Education" of 1872. One could also ask how well Adventist schools exemplified the ideals that inspired denominational educators to develop one of the largest sectarian programs of education in the world.

Of all the shades of meaning that six or seven generations of Adventists have drawn from their understanding of denominational philosophy of education, a few common denominators remained constant. In 1872 Ellen White advocated separate schools for Adventists for two fundamental reasons: to inculcate spiritual values based on

*Participants in the Faith and Learning Seminar, 1998, conducted on the campus of the University of Eastern Africa, Baraton, Kenya. Humberto Rasi, co-founder, leading promoter and organizer of the seminars, stands at the far right. The seminars were intended to help teachers in Adventist postsecondary schools around the world to cultivate philosophical perceptions of knowledge compatible with a Christian worldview.*

truth as Seventh-day Adventists understand the Bible and to prepare people to become active participants in spreading the biblical message of salvation. Scripture stood at the center. These two purposes and their focal point presupposed philosophical assumptions about the nature of humankind, the source of moral values, the existence of the created universe of which the world is a part, the origins and forms of knowledge, how information is acquired and utilized, and why an organized understanding of all these questions is superior to ignorance.

During the 130 years after Goodloe Harper Bell began the first denominationally sponsored school, Adventist education developed distinctive features about these assumptions and expressed its underlying reason for being. In the beginning its character was appropriate to the nineteenth century. As historian George Knight claimed, changes in the trappings of Adventist education were necessary both with the passage of time and as schools spread to different cultural and politico-economic environments. It was not surprising that disagreements arose when educators engineered change or adaptations while seeking to retain the essential philosophy on which Adventist schools were founded.

Critics charged that Adventist schools lost the key to their identity because student labor programs that were once so prominent, particularly in agriculture, became rare in the twenty-first century. As modern life and schools became more oriented to urban living, agriculture declined in importance. North American schools methodically sold off most of their enterprises as economic conditions made student labor and viable institutional industries not only obsolete but financial drains as well, especially those in agriculture.

Practical education remained, however, by virtue of the heavy emphasis of Adventist higher education on job preparation. The nineteenth-century movement to promote practical education was in part a reaction against a college education in the classics, which produced a specie of academic degree that lost its appeal as the twentieth century unfolded. Vestiges of the classics remain in the traditional liberal arts, but in most denominational institutions education and job preparation became nearly synonymous, which is a far more pragmatic definition of college education than that of the 1870s and the era of Battle Creek College.

Vast differences exist among Adventist schools but so do the environments in which the schools exist. As denominational education spread and elaborations on the original "Proper Education" appeared, Adventist educators learned that in order to implement effective curricula and instructional techniques they had to adapt to the societies they served. This kind of change did not damage fundamental philosophical constants, but required repackaging for different markets.

At the beginning of the twenty-first century one of the most perplexing questions was the extent to which denominational schools could or should parallel non-Adventist education to serve the interests of an expanding denominational population. Adventist educators have not found pat answers to this issue, which has left details in the hands of institutional authorities to decide to the best of their understanding within the framework of Adventist philosophy, their decision-making authority, and the limits of their resources.

Another question that became increasingly serious at the end of the century was how to attract Adventist students to Adventist schools. Statistics showed that after the mid-1960s Adventist schools were losing out to non-Adventist institutions. For twenty years after 1945 about one in four Adventists worldwide attended a denominational school; between 1965 and the year 2000 the proportion dropped steadily to less than one in ten.

Without specific studies to determine the cause of decline explanations become speculative. An instructive example occurred in the United States where the academy, or secondary school, which constituted one of the largest components of denominational education in the region of the Adventist world with the largest student population, became an endangered specie after the 1970s. In 1971 more than 20,000 secondary students enrolled in North American academies and intermediate schools; in the year 2000 the figure dropped to 14,000 even though supporting membership more than doubled from 440,000 to about 923,000.[24]

Educators attributed this decline to several causes, most often citing the steeply rising cost of denominational education, but also of importance was a widespread opinion that parents and students alike appeared more willing than were previous generations of Adventists to view the broader curricular opportunities in public schools as evidence of better education than the narrower offerings in church-sponsored schools. It appeared that families not only in North America but in many parts of the world tended to place less stress on spiritual values when deciding where their children would attend school. As a practical matter, however, it is questionable that Adventist schools could accommodate an enrollment increase that at the end of the century would have raised the student population exponentially if the proportion of Adventists returned to its 1945 level.[25]

With this trend clearly in view, in 1987 the General Conference Department of Education joined the Adventist Chaplaincy Ministries Department and the Youth Department to create new approaches to minister to Adventist students in public colleges and universities, who by 2004 numbered a quarter million, or about three times the enrollment in denominational institutions. Guided by AMiCUS, short for Adventist Ministry to/with College and University Students, this initiative conducts seminars and conferences around the world to nurture faith and loyalty among Adventist students in intellectually hostile environments. In 1989 it began publication of *College and University Dialogue*, a magazine discussing issues of intellectual concern to Adventists, published three times annually in parallel editions–English, French, Portuguese and Spanish. The Department of Education circulates *Dialogue* free in more than a hundred countries.[26]

A debate has remained since the days of Battle Creek College about which purpose of Adventist education–to perpetuate Adventist beliefs in the church's young or to educate denominational workers– is primary and how to balance the two. "Proper Education" admitted of no conflict, but church leaders did not always agree among themselves or with educators about how the two purposes related to each other. In the early years of denominational schools, a smaller number of courses produced higher percentages of graduates seeking denominational employment, but with their broader curricula at the end of the twentieth century Adventist postsecondary schools enrolled proportionately fewer students in worker-preparation courses.

This trend led to the easy conclusion that preparation of church employees has become secondary to education itself and that academic pursuits have obscured the real reason for Adventist education. But not to be overlooked is the fact that as the church became more complex it depended on a wider variety of professionals than in pre-World War II years, which in part justified the increased number of career options for students. Because the church could employ only a fraction of the graduates of Adventist schools, the majority of students sought jobs elsewhere. In turn, educators concluded that the church benefitted from an expanding proportion of laity, professionally prepared on Adventist campuses.

Encouraging news came from the student missionary and task force programs which furnished incontrovertible evidence that commitment and old-fashioned missionary service were not dead letters in Adventist education, in spite of unprecedented emphasis on careers and professionalism. The idea of sending college students to church outposts around the world to assume genuine mission duties materialized spontaneously at Washington Missionary College in 1959, and later became an integral part of the denomination's youth movement. At first the practice was exclusively North American, where some influential church leaders responded with tolerant attitudes that were considerably less than enthusiastic.

*One of the ways the General Conference Department of Education advanced the dignity of the teaching profession was to award a Medallion of Merit to individuals who performed outstanding service. Born in 1874, a child of freed Black slaves, Anna Knight attended Battle Creek College and later established schools for Black children in Mississippi, her native state. She served a long and distinguished career as a teacher, nurse, and Bible worker in India and the United States. In 1971 she received the Medallion of Merit for her life of exemplary and selfless service.*

But the practice hung on and by the end of the century student volunteerism on Adventist campuses had become a global habit. The urge to contribute to the Adventist movement compelled hundreds of students annually from schools circling the world to interrupt their education to participate in short-term mission service or task force assignment in some corner of the world, sometimes filling a vacancy in a struggling secondary school or some other institution. Many secondary schools adapted the idea to what came to be called mission trips, projects lasting one or two weeks during which teenagers traveled to remote spots to build schools and churches. The monetary value of student volunteerism was beyond calculation.

Eventually the youth volunteer program became an integrated part of the Adventist Volunteer Center, an office directed by an associate secretary of the General Conference which organizes volunteerism for the entire denomination.[27]

The status of Adventist higher education at the end of the twentieth century has prompted contemplation on an observation by Wheaton College historian Mark Noll who declares that although intellectuality in evangelical education has been typically weak, it is gathering strength. There is little question that Adventist institutions of higher learning, and to some extent secondary schools as well, have provided a spawning ground for thought and reflection that did not exist in pre-World War II days. The constantly broadening range of academic offerings which developed on North American campuses and which has spread to schools in the world fields, gave both Adventist educators and students alike a chance to think about how they as educated professionals and committed Christians could live relevantly in the world and contribute to the world but not be of the world.

Probably many Adventists did not give this issue a second thought, nor did the conclusions of those who did think about it stun the academic world, but to the thoughtful Adventist the terms *missionary, witnessing*, and *salt of the earth* assumed new philosophical meaning that the founders of denominational schools had not dreamed of. It was not mere coincidence that this question grew in importance as the mood of Adventism became less apocalyptic and more socially conscious. In the process, the church did not yield any ground in its belief in the second advent of Christ and the resultant evangelistic implications for church members, but the church showed more awareness that while people still occupy this planet, there is a Christian obligation to ameliorate the human condition. This mentality brought a willingness to engage in self-criticism, produced a growing awareness of the complexity of Scriptures, and encouraged a desire for higher education and a respect for study.[28]

One of the most striking evidences of this mentality showed up in the church's adoption of the 2004 statement, "An Affirmation of Creation" which congratulated denominational scientists for their contributions to an understanding of the Scriptures and encouraged them to continue their probing despite the tensions that might arise over unanswerable questions. The Annual Council was in good company. That unanswerable question did not endanger faith was the same rationale that Galilei Galileo echoed in his seventeenth-century response to the ecclesiastical prohibition slapped upon him to prevent further discussion of the Copernican view of the universe, which contradicted the officially approved Ptolemaic system. Declaring that God has given humans the right to argue about the universe and he urged "Let us then exercise these activities permitted to us and ordained by God, that we may *recognize and thereby so much the more admire His greatness, however much less fit we may find ourselves to penetrate the profound depths of His infinite wisdom."*(italics supplied)[29]

Also playing a role in the growing intellectual atmosphere of Adventist education was the *Journal of Adventist Education,* the Department of Education quarterly that traced its roots to September 1909 when editor Frederick Griggs' *Christian Education* made its debut. In 1922 the periodical changed to a lengthy name reflecting the belief that Adventist education was a combination of both the home and school. In 1939 it became the *Journal of True Education* and finally *Journal of Adventist Education* in 1967, a less exclusive name more reminiscent of Griggs' original title. As postsecondary and graduate education circled the Adventist world, writers and editors presented increasingly thoughtful penetrations of their profession. For its professionalism the periodical earned recognition and awards from the journalism fraternity. At the end of the century, it was blanketing most of the world of Adventist education with editions in French, Spanish, and Portuguese as well as English.

Philosophically, from Battle Creek College to Sahmyook University Adventist education has proposed that human life is part of a created moral universe which speaks to God's glory even though we can only begin to understand it. Adventist teachers have upheld the Bible as the authoritative communication of God to His created beings on this earth. Adventist education has consistently taught that sin exists which in itself constitutes a cosmic struggle between good and evil and that individuals choose and are responsible for the loyalty they exercise on either side of this conflict. Adventist schools have fostered an understanding and acceptance of salvation through faith in Jesus. Adventist campuses have pointed students to their responsibility as propagators of these convictions. Adventist education has upheld the dignity of the individual. It has maintained that useful labor is as valuable as knowledge and that successful humans should have skills in both. And Adventist education has argued that the human body deserves respect because its spiritual, physical, social and intellectual capacities are best realized in a state of good health.

In the year 2003 nearly 1,300,000 students were receiving this instruction from approximately 65,700 teachers in more than 6,700 schools at all levels. Burgeoning membership had brought administrative decentralization to the church and the system of education as church leaders conceived it at the beginning of the century gave way to a network of schools. But a system remained as expressed in a common concept of education founded upon a universal philosophy, basic mission, and commitment to its ideals. Through an established accrediting process and an international board with regulatory authority, these aspects of systematization enabled Adventist schools to retain a remarkable continuity not only among their partners in the network but with their heritage.

Whether in the simple classrooms of a remote elementary school or in the research laboratories of Loma Linda University, Adventist education had made its mark. It did not compile a perfect record, but "Proper Education" had worked. Despite their critics and their imperfections and shortcomings, and in ways that H. R. Salisbury could never envision, Seventh-day Adventist schools continued to inspire their students to have a passion for the world.

---

[1]*General Conference Bulletin*, 1990, no. 7, p. 27; *ibid.*, 1995, no. 10, p. 10; *ibid.*, 2000, no. 6, p. 15.

[2]*General Conference Bulletin*, 1985, no. 6, p. 22; *ibid.*, 1990, no. 8, p. 22. For the complete story of Murray's career, see Ronald Alan Knott, *The Makings of an Philanthropic Fund-raiser* (San Francisco: Jossey-Boss Publishers, 1992).

[3]Email, Richard Osborn to Floyd Greenleaf, August 3, 2004.

[4]*Ibid.*, 1903, no. 5, p. 67; no. 7, pp. 100, 101; no. 10, pp. 158-160.

[5]*Ibid.*, 1903, no. 12, pp. 177-183; 1905, no. 4, pp. 19, 20.

[6]General Conference Minutes, October 19, 1932.

[7]Joseph G. Smoot, "Accreditation: Quality in the SDA College," (*Journal of Adventist Education,* February-March 1983), p. 44.

[8]Email, Humberto Rasi to Floyd Greenleaf, October 23, 1997; email, Richard Osborn to Floyd Greenleaf, August 3, 2004.

[9]Sources for the passage about the Board of Higher Education are "Report of Sub-Committee of the Commission on Higher Education," December 1, 1967, AST, RG 51; Betty Stirling, "What Is the North American Division Board of Higher Education?" (*Journal of Adventist Education*, December 1975-January 1976), pp. 21-24; Minutes of the Board of

Higher Education, October 15, 1970, AST; *ibid.*, June 18, 1972; *ibid.*, January, 1973; interviews, A. C. McClure, January 23 and April 8, 2002; email interview, Richard Osborn, May 28, 2002; "Higher Educational Policies," www.nadeducation.adventist.org.

[10]Minutes of the Board of Higer Education, October 14, 1970, AST.

[11]For a sampling of these suggestions see Wilfred M Hillock, "Tuition Rates in Seventh-day Adventist Colleges" (*Spectrum*, summer 1969), pp.44-49; Donald R. McAdams, "Free the College Boards: Toward a Pluralism of Excellence," (*ibid.*, summer 1985, pp. 27-35; Malcolm Russell, "Break Up the College Cartel," (*ibid.*), pp. 36-44; Frank A. Knittel, "Merge 14 North American colleges into two? Yes!" (*ibid.*, January 1997), pp. 20-28; Lawrence T. Geraty, "Merge 14 North American colleges into two? No!" (*ibid.*), pp. 29-35; George H. Akers, "Can the Adventist church support two North American universities?" *Adventist Reveiw*, October 5, 1989; Charles B. Hirsch, "The Future of SDA Higher Education," (*Journal of Adventist Education*, December 1984-January 1985).

[12]North American Division Minutes, October 14, 1992.

[13]"Code of Regulations," email, Richard Osborn to Floyd Greenleaf, May 27, 2002.

[14]General Conference Minutes, October 6, 7, 1994; interview, Humberto Rasi, February 27, 2002.

[15]See *Handbook of Seventh-day Adventist Ministerial and Theological Education* (Silver Spring, MD: International Board of Ministerial and Theological Education, 2001); interview, Humberto Rasi, February 27, 2002.

[16]Bonnie Dwyer, "G. C. Approves Proposal to Control Theological Education and Theologians with 'Endorsement' Policy," (*Spectrum*, Winter, 1999), pp. 70-76; Douglas Morgan, "Targeting Higher Education" (*ibid.*, Autumn 2001), pp. 69-73; Press Conference, Jan Paulsen, General Conference Executive Dining Room, October 10, 2002, www.adventist.org; email, Garland Dulan to Floyd Greenleaf, January 11, 2005.

[17]*Adventist Review*, North American edition, October 2001, p. 24.

[18]*Ibid.*, September 25, 2001; "New Commission Will Aim to 'Keep Ahead of Challenges' Facing Higher Education Worldwide," ANN, October 1, 2000, www.adventist.org.

[19]Interview, Garland Dulan, November 29, 2004.

[20]Email message, Rasi to Greenleaf, December 29, 2004.

[21]Raymond E. Moore, *Adventist Education at the Crossroads* (Mountain View, CA: Pacific Press Publishing Association, 1976). Reuben Hilde, *Showdon: Can SDA Education Pass the Test*? (Washington, D.C.: Review and Herald Publishing Association, 1980).

[22]George R. Knight, ed. *Early Adventist Educators* (Berrien Springs, MI: Andrews University Press, 1983); *Myths in Adventism* (Washington, D.C.: Review and Herald Publishing Association, 1985); *Philosophy and Education: An Introduction in Christian Perspective*, 2nd ed. (Berrien Springs, MI: Andrews University Press, 1989)

[23]"A Statement of Seventh-day Adventist Educational Philosophy," (*Journal of Adventist Education*, April-May 2002), insert.

[24]Figures adapted from *Statistical Report*, 1971, *SDA Yearbook*, 2001, and *World Report 2000.*

[25]"Global Adventist Education: Statistics 1945-2000," General Conference Department of Education.

[26]Email message, Rasi to Greenleaf, December 29, 2004.

[27]For a vivid description of the beginnings of the student missionary program see Donna June Evans, *Mosaic of Adventure* (Nashville, TN: Southern Publishing Association, 1976).

[28]Noll, *Scandal*, p. 213.

[29]Galileo Galilei, *Dialogue Concerning the Two Chief World Systems–Ptolmaic and Copernican*, Stilman Drake, trans. (Los Angeles: University of California Press, 1967), p. 464.

# Heads of Seventh-day Adventist Education

The following have served as head of Seventh-day Adventist education with varying titles of "secretary," "chairman," or since 1974, "director":

1887-1897 — W. W. Prescott
1897-1901 — L. A. Hoopes
1901-1902 — J. H. Kellogg
1902-1903 — W. W. Prescott
1903-1904 — L. A. Hoopes
1904-1910 — Frederick Griggs
1910-1913 — H. R. Salisbury
1913-1915 — J. L. Shaw
1915-1918 — Frederick Griggs
1918-1930 — W. E. Howell
1930-1933 — C. W. Irwin
1933-1936 — W. E. Nelson
1936-1946 — H. A. Morrison
1946-1966 — E. E. Cossentine
1966-1974 — Charles B. Hirsch
1974-1980 — Walton J. Brown
1980-1985 — Charles R. Taylor
1985-1990 — George H. Akers
1990-2003 — Humberto Rasi
2003- — C. Garland Dulan

# BIBLIOGRAPHY


## Books

*60 Years of Progress: Walla Walla College.* College Place, WA: Walla Walla College Press, 1952.

Aamodt, Terrie Dopp. *Bold Venture: A History of Walla Walla College.* College Place, WA: Walla Walla College, 1992.

Anderson, Emma, *et. al.* Adelaide B. Evans, ed. *With Our Missionaries in China.* Mountain View, CA: Pacific Press Publishing Association, 1920.

Anderson, W. H. *On the Trail of Livingstone.* Mountain View, CA: Pacific Press Publishing Association, 1919.

Baker, Alonzo. *My Sister Alma and I.* Mountain View, CA: Pacific Press Publishing Association, 1980.

Booth, Ernest S. *Biology: the Story of Life.* Mountain View, CA: Pacific Press Publishing Association, 1950.

Brown, Walton J., compiler. *Chronology of Seventh-day Adventist Education.* Washington, D.C.: Department of Education, General Conference of Seventh-day Adventists, 1972.

—. *Oh Mi C. A.!* Self-published, 1990.

Bull, Malcolm and Keith Lockhart. *Seeking a Sanctuary: Seventh-day Adventism & the American Dream.* San Francisco: Harper & Row, Publishers, 1989.

Cadwallader, E. M. *A History of Seventh-day Adventist Education.* Lincoln, NE: Union College Press, 1958.

Camargo Vieira, Ruy Carlos de. *Vida E Obra de Guilherme Stein Jr.* Sao Paulo, Brazil: Casa Publicadora, 1995.

Carpenter, Joel A. and Kenneth W. Shipps, eds. *Making Higher Education Christian.* Grand Rapids: Christian University Press, 1987.

Chapman, Muriel. *Mission of Love: A Century of Seventh-day Adventist Nursing.* Silver Spring, MD: Association of Seventh-day Adventist Nursing, 2000.

Christian, L. H. *The Fruitage of Spiritual Gifts.* Washington, D.C.: Review and Herald Publishing Association, 1947.

—. *Sons of the North.* Mountain View, CA: Pacific Press Publishing Association, 1942.

Clapham, Noel, ed. *Seventh-day Adventists in the South Pacific 1885-1985.* Warburton, Victoria, Australia: Signs Publishing Company, 1985.

Cooper, Emma Howell. *The Great Advent Movement*, 5th ed. Washington, D. C.: Review and Herald Publishing Association, 1957.

*The Chronicle of Southwestern Adventist College.* 1984. No editor or publisher listed.

*Data Book of the Commission on Seventh-day Adventist Education in Africa*. Silver Spring, MD: General Conference Department of Education, 1995.

Delafield, D. A. *Ellen G. White in Europe*. Washington, D.C.: Review and Herald Publishing Association, 1975.

Dick, Everett. *Union, College of the Golden Cords*. Lincoln, NE: Union College Press, 1967.

Dudley Charles Edward, Sr. *"Thou Who Hath Brought Us . . ."* vols. I, II. Brushton, NY: TEACH Services, 1997.

—. *Thou Who Hast Brought Us Thus Far On Our Way*, book three, vol. three. Nashville: Dudley Publications, 2000.

Edwards, Josephine Cunnington. *Malinki of Malawi*. Mountain View, CA: Pacific Press Publishing Association, 1978.

Evans, Donna June. *Mosaic of Adventure*. Nashville, TN: Southern Publishing Association, 1976.

Ferch, Arthur J., ed. *Symposium on Adventist History in the South Pacific: 1885-1918*. Warburton, Victoria, Australia: Signs Publishing Company, 1986.

Fernando, Donald M., ed. *75th Anniversary: Lakpahana Adventist College*. Mailapitiya, Sri Lanka: Lakpahana Publishing House, 1998.

Fernando, R. S. *The Isles Shall Not Wait*. Colombo, Sri Lanka: Associated Newspapers of Ceylon, 1987.

Fiedler, Dave. *Hindsight: Seventh-day Adventist History in Essays and Extracts*. Hagerstown, MD: Review and Herald Graphics, 1996.

Ford, Herbert. *Affair of the Heart*. Nashville, TN: Southern Publishing Association, 1970.

—. *For the Love of China: The Life Story of Denton E. Rebok*. Mountain View, CA: Pacific Press Publishing Association, 1971.

*From Vision to Reality 1905-1980*. Loma Linda, CA: Loma Linda University, 1980.

Gandhi, Mohandas K. *Gandhi, an Autobiography: the Story of My Experiments with Truth*. Mahadev Desai, trans. Boston: Beacon Press, 1993 ed.

Gardner, Elva B. and J. Mabel Wood. *SMC: A School of His Planning*. Chattanooga, TN: Board of Trustees, 1972.

Gish, Ira, ed. *A Pictorial History of Madison College: School of Divine Origin, 1904-1964*. Clarksville, TN: Madison College Alumni Association, 1986.

— and Harry Christman. *Madison: God's Beautiful Farm*. Mountain View, CA: Pacific Press Publishing Association, 1979.

Graybill, Ronald D. *E. G. White and Church Race Relations*. Washington, D.C.: Review and Herald Publishing Association, 1970.

Greenleaf, Floyd. *The Seventh-day Adventist Church in Latin America and the Caribbean*, 2 vols. Berrien Springs, MI: Andrews University Press, 1992.

*Handbook for the Approval of New Degree Programs and Institutional Upgrading in Seventh-day Adventist Colleges and Universities*, 1995 ed. Silver Spring, MD: International Board of Education, General Conference of Seventh-day Adventists.

*Handbook of Accreditation for Colleges and Universities.* Silver Spring, MD: General Conference Department of Education, 1998.

*Handbook of Seventh-day Adventist Ministerial and Theological Education.* Silver Spring, MD: General Conference of Seventh-day Adventists, 2001.

Hansen, Louis A. *From So Small a Dream.* Nashville, TN: Southern Publishing Association, 1968.

Hartlapp, Johannes, ed. *Chronik Freidensau.* Friedensau: Theologische Hochschule, 1999.

Haussler, Doris Holt. *From Immigrant to Emissary.* Nashville: Southern Publishing Association, 1969.

Hertogs, Drusilla. *Ruth Gorle, Makhumalo: Mother of Teachers.* Published by the author, no date.

Hilde, Reuben. *Showdon: Can SDA Education Pass the Test?* Washington, D.C.: Review and Herald Publishing Association, 1980.

Hodgen, Maurice. *School Bells and Gospel Trumpets: A Documentary History of Seventh-day Adventist Education in North America.* Loma Linda, CA: Adventist Heritage Publications, Loma Linda University Press, 1978.

Hook, Milton. *Avondale: Experiment on the Dora.* Cooranbong, New South Wales, Australia: Avondale Academic Press, 1998.

Jacques, John Godfrey. *Escape from Siberian Exile.* Mountain View, CA: Pacific Press Publishing Association, 1921.

Jenson, George Roos. *Spicer Memorial College . . . a Dynamic Demonstration of an Ideal.* Poona, India: Oriental Watchman Publishing House, 1965.

Jordan, Ann Devereaux. *Seventh-Day Adventists.* New York: Hippocrene Books, 1988.

Loewen, Gertrude. *Crusader for Freedom: the Story of Jean Nussbaum.* Nashville: Southern Publishing Association, 1969.

Knight, Anna. *Mississippi Girl: An Autobiography.* Nashville: Southern Publishing Association, 1952.

Knight, George R., ed. *Early Adventist Educators.* Berrien Springs, MI: Andrews University Press, 1983.

—. *Myths in Adventism.* Washington, D.C.: Review and Herald Publishing Association, 1985.

—. *Philosophy and Education: An Introduction in Christian Perspective*, 2nd ed. Berrien Springs, MI: Andrews University Press, 1989.

Knott, Ronald Alan. *The Makings of an Philanthropic Fundraiser.* San Francisco: Jossey-Boss Publishers, 1992.

Kulakov, Mikhail. *God's Soviet Miracles.* Boise, ID: Pacific Press Publishing Association, 1993.

Land, Gary, ed. *The World of Ellen White.* Washington, D.C.: Review and Herald Publishing Association, 1987.

Loughborough, J. N. *Rise and Progress of Seventh-day Adventists.* Battle Creek: General Conference Association of Seventh-day Adventists, 1892.

Maxwell, C. Mervyn. *Tell It to the World: the Story of Seventh-day Adventists.* Mountain View, CA: Pacific Press Publishing Association, 1977.

McKibbin, Alma E. *Step by Step.* Washington, D.C.: Review and Herald Publishing Association, 1964.

Mitchell, David. *Seventh-Day Adventists.* New York: Vantage Press, 1958.

Moore, Mary Hunter. *They That Be Teachers.* Nashville, TN: Southern Publishing Association, 1937.

Moore, Raymond E. *Adventist Education at the Crossroads.* Mountain View, CA: Pacific Press Publishing Association, 1976.

—. *China Doctor.* New York: Harper & Brothers, 1961.

—. *Mitchibiki.* Washington, D. C.: Review and Herald Publishing Association, 1956.

Neff, Merlin. *For God and C. M. E.* Mountain View, CA: Pacific Press Publishing Association, 1964.

—. *Invincible Irishman: A Biography of Percy T. Magan.* Mountain View, CA: Pacific Press Publishing Association, 1964.

Abridged edition of *For God and C. M. E.*

Noll, Mark A. *The Scandal of the Evangelical Mind.* Grand Rapids: William B. Eerdmans Publishing Company, 1994.

Numbers, Ronald L. *The Creationists.* New York: A. A. Knopf, 1992.

Oliver, Barry, Alex Currie, and Doug Robertson, eds. *Avondale and the South Pacific: 100 years of mission.* Cooranbong, New South Wales, Australia: Avondale Academic Press, 1997.

Olsen, M. E. *Origin and Progress of Seventh-day Adventists.* Washington, D. C.: Review and Herald Publishing Association, 1925.

Oss, John. *Mission Advances in China.* Nashville: Southern Publishing Association, 1949.

Penner, D. S., ed. *Public Funds and Private Education: Issues of Church and State.* Silver Spring, MD: Board of Education, K-12, Board of Higher Education, 1991.

Perry, Walter. *The Open University.* San Francisco: Jossey-Bass Publishers, 1977.

Pettibone, Dennis. *A Century of Challenge: the History of Southern College, 1892-1992.* Collegedale, TN: College Board of Trustees, College Press, 1992.

Phillips, Glenn O. I. *The Making of A Christian College: Caribbean Union College, 1927-1977.* Port-of-Spain, Trinidad: The College Press, 1977.

Phipps, Barbara. *Test Tubes and Chalk Dust: the Story of Burton H. Phipps.* Berrien Springs, MI: University Printers, 1976.

Price, George McCready. *The Geological-Ages Hoax.* New York: Fleming H. Revell Company, 1931.

—. *The Modern Flood Theory of Geology.* New York: Fleming H. Revell Company, 1935.

—. *The New Geology.* Mountain View, CA: Pacific Press Publishing Association, 1923.

—. *The Phantom of Organic Evolution.* New York: Fleming H. Revell Company, 1924.

—. *Q. E. D., or New Light on the Doctrine of Creation.* New York: Fleming H. Revell Company, 1932.

*Proceedings of the Educational and Missionary Volunteer Departments of the General Conference of Seventh-day Adventists in World Convention.* Washington, D.C.: Review and Herald Publishing Association, 1923.

Purdon, Rowena. *That New England School.* South Lancaster, MA: College Press, 1956.

Quimby, Paul with Norma Youngberg. *Yankee on the Yangkze.* Nashville: Southern Publishing Association, 1976.

Reavis, D. W. *I Remember.* Washington, D.C.: Review and Herald Publishing Association, n.d.

Reiber, Milton T. *Graysville, Battle Creek of the South, 1888-1988.* Collegedale, TN: n.d.

Reid, George W. *The Sound of Trumpets: Americans, Adventists, and Health Reform.* Washington, D.C.: Review and Herald Publishing Association, 1982.

Reynolds, Louis B. *We Have Tomorrow: the Story of American Adventists with an African Heritage.* Washington, D.C.: Review and Herald Publishing Association, 1984.

*Report of the Blue Ridge Educational Convention, August 17-25, 1937.* Washington, D.C.: General Conference Department of Education, n.d.

Robertson, John J. *A. G. Daniells: the Making of a General Conference President.* Mountain View, CA: Pacific Press Publishing Association, 1977.

Robinson, Dores E. *The Story of Our Health Message*, 3rd ed. Nashville, TN: Southern Publishing Association, 1965.

Samaraj, Edison, ed. *Images 1893-1993: the Seventh-day Adventist Church in Southern Asia.* Pune, India: Oriental Watchman Publishing House, 1993.

—. *The Challenging Years 1990-1995: Images II.* Pune, India: Oriental Watchman Publishing House, 1995.

—. *Maturing of Adventism.* Pune, India: Oriental Watchman Publishing House, 1998.

Schaefer, Richard A. *Legacy, Daring to Care: the Heritage of Loma Linda.* Loma Linda, CA: Legacy Publishing Company, 1990.

Schwarz, Richard W. *John Harvey Kellogg, M.D.* Nashville, TN: Southern Publishing Association, 1970.

—. *Light Bearers to the Remnant.* Mountain View, CA: Pacific Press Publishing Association, 1979.

—. and Floyd Greenleaf. *Light Bearers: a History of the Seventh-day Adventist Church.* Nampa, ID: Pacific Press Publishing Association, 2000.

Seventh-day Adventist Encyclopedia, rev. ed. Washington, D.C.: Review and Herald Publishing Association, 1976, 1996.

Small, Carol, ed. *Diamond Memories.* Loma Linda, CA: Alumni Association, School of Medicine, 1984.

Spalding, A. W. *Captains of the Host.* Washington, D.C.: Review and Herald Publishing Association, 1949.

—. *Christ's Last Legion.* Washington, D.C.: Review and Herald Publishing Association, 1949.

—. *Origin and History of Seventh-day Adventists*, 4 vols. Washington, D.C.: Review and Herald Publishing Association, 1961. The four-volume set is a revised edition of the original two-volume set.

Stahl, F. A. *In the Land of the Incas.* Mountain View, CA: Pacific Press Publishing Association, 1920.

Steinweg, Virginia. *Without Fear or Favor: the Life of M. L. Andreasen.* Washington, D.C.: Review and Herald Publishing Association, 1979.

Sutherland, E. A. *Studies in Christian Education.* No date or location.

Swomley, John M., Jr. *Religion, the State & the Schools.* New York: Pegasus, 1968.

Syme, Eric. *A History of SDA Church-State Relations in the United States.* Mountain View, CA: Pacific Press Publishing Association, 1973.

Thurston, Claude, chairman of book project. *Sixty Years of Progress: Walla Walla College.* College Place, WA: College Press, 1952.

Timm, Alberto R., ed. *Instituto Adventista de Ensino Campus 2: 15 Anos de Historia.* Engenheiro Coelho, SP: Imprensa Universitaria Adventista, 1999.

Toppenberg, Valdemar E. *Africa Has My Heart.* Mountain View, CA: Pacific Press Publishing Association, 1958.

Twomley, Dale E. *Parochiad and the Courts.* Berrien Springs, MI: Andrews University Press, 1979.

Utt, Richard. *From Vision to Reality, 1905-1980: Loma Linda University.* Loma Linda, CA: Loma Linda University Press, 1980.

—. *Uncle Charlie: a Biography of Charles Elliott Weniger.* Mountain View, CA: Pacific Press Publishing Association, 1978.

Utt, Walter. *A Mountain, a Pickax, a College.* Angwin, CA: Alumni Association of Pacific Union College, 1968.

Valentine, Gilbert M. *The Shaping of Adventism: the Case of W. W. Prescott.* Berrien Springs, MI: Andrews University Press, 1992.

VandeVere, Emmett K. *Rugged Heart: the Story of George I. Butler.* Nashville, TN: Southern Publishing Association, 1979.

—. *The Wisdom Seekers.* Nashville, TN: Southern Publishing Association, 1972.

—. compiler. *Windows.* Nashville, TN: Southern Publishing Association, 1975.

Vasquez, Manuel. *The Untold Story: 100 Years of Hispanic Adventism, 1899-1999.* Nampa, ID: Pacific Press Publishing Association, 2000.

Were, Eric. *No Devil Strings: the Story of Kata Rangoso.* Mountain View, CA: Pacific Press Publishing Association, 1970.

Westphal, F. H. *Pioneering in the Neglected Continent.* Nashville: Southern Publishing Association, 1927.

White, Arthur L. *Ellen G. White*, 6 vols. Washington, D.C.: Review and Herald Publishing Association, 1981-1986.

White, Ellen G. *Counsels to Parents and Teachers.* Mountain View, CA: Pacific Press Publishing Association, 1913, 1943.

—. *Counsels to Writers and Editors.* Nashville, TN: Southern Publishing Association, 1946.

—. *Education.* Mountain View, CA: Pacific Press Publishing Association, 1903, 1942.

—. *Fundamentals of Christian Education.* Nashville, TN: Southern Publishing Association, 1923.

—. *The Southern Work.* Washington, D.C.: Review and Herald Publishing Association, 1966.

—. *Testimonies to the Church*, 9 vols. Mountain View, CA: Pacific Press Publishing Association, 1948.

Wilcox, E. H. *In Perils Oft.* Nashville: Southern Publishing Association, 1961.

## Early Adventist Textbooks

Cady, M. E. *Bible Nature Series*, 3 vols. Mountain View, CA: Pacific Press Publishing Association, 1908, 1910, 1913.

—. *True Education Reader, Book Seven.* Mountain View, CA: Pacific Press Publishing Association, 1907.

*The Gospel Primer.* New York: International Tract Society, 1895.

Kellogg, J. H. *First Book in Physiology and Hygiene.* New York: Harper and Brothers, 1887, 1888.

—. *Second Book in Physiology and Hygiene.* New York: American Book Company, 1894.

McKibbin, Alma E. *Bible Lessons in Old Testament History, Book One.* Mountain View, CA: Pacific Press Publishing Association, 1909.

—. *Bible Lessons in Old Testament History, Book Two.* Mountain View, CA: Pacific Press Publishing Association, 1915.

—. *Bible Lessons: the Life of Christ, Book Three.* Mountain View, CA: Pacific Press Publishing Association, 1909.

—. *Bible Lessons: the Acts of the Apostles; Plan of Salvation, Book Four.* Mountain View, CA: Pacific Press Publishing Association, 1912.

Price, George McCready. *A Testbook of General Science for Secondary Schools.* Mountain View, CA: Pacific Press Publishing Association, 1917.

Sutherland, E. A. *The Bible Reader, Number One*, rev. ed. Berrien Springs, MI: Advocate Publishing Co., 1903.

—. *The Mental Arithmetic for Home and School.* Battle Creek, MI: Review and Herald Publishing Association, 1901.

True Education Reader Series:

Hale, Katherine B. *Indoors with God's Book, Primer.* Mountain View, CA: Pacific Press Publishing Association, 1924.

—. *True Education Reader, Book Two.* Mountain View, CA: Pacific Press Publishing Association, 1907, 1925.

Peck, Sarah Elizabeth. *True Education Reader, Book Three.* Mountain View, CA: 1907.

—. *True Education Reader, Fourth Grade.* Mountain View, CA: Pacific Press Publishing Association, 1931.

—. *True Education Reader, Book Five.* Mountain View, CA: Pacific Press Publishing Association, 1907.

—. *True Education Reader, Book Six.* Mountain View, CA: Pacific Press Publishing Association, 1912.

## Periodicals and Annual Publications

*Academe* (Internet editions)

*Advent Survey*

*Adventist Heritage.* Citations of specific authors found in endnotes.

*Adventist Review* (including all previous names of this paper).

*Adventist Yearbook*

*Australasian Union Conference Record*

*Directory of Seventh-day Adventist Colleges and Universities*

*Eastern African Division Outlook*

*Far Eastern Division Outlook*

*Focus*

*General Conference Bulletin*

*Journal of Adventist Education* (including its predecessor, *Journal of True Education*). Citations of specific authors found in endnotes.

*Light,* including its predecessor, *Northern Light* (official paper of the Northern European Division and Trans-European Division)

*Missionary Magazine*

Rasi, Humberto, comp. *Christ in the Classroom: Adventist Approaches to the Integration of Faith and Learning*, vols. 1-26B. Silver Spring, MD: Institute for Christian Teaching, 1991-2001.

*Southern African Division Outlook*

*Southern Asia Tidings*

*Spectrum.* Citations of specific authors found in endnotes.

*Statistical Report*

*Trans-Africa Division Outlook*

*World Report: Adventist Education Around the World*: Silver Spring, MD: General Conference of Seventh-day Adventists, Department of Education

## Institutional Catalogs

Adventist College of Professional Studies (Surat, India)
Adventist International Institute of Advanced Studies (Philippines)
Adventist International School (Sri Lanka)
Adventist University of the Philippines (Philippines)
Andrews University (United States)
Antillian Adventist University (Puerto Rico)
Avondale College (Australia)
Canadian University College (Canada)
Central Philippine Adventist College (Philippines)
Haitian Adventist University (Haiti)
Helderberg College (South Africa)
Hong Kong Adventist College (China)
La Sierra University (United States)
Middle East College (Lebanon)
Mission College (Thailand)
Myanmar Union Adventist Seminary (Myanmar)
Newbold College (England)
Oakwood College (United States)
Pacific Union College (United States)
Pakistan Adventist Seminary (Pakistan)
Sahmyook Nursing & Health College (Korea)
Sahmyook University (Korea)
Saleve Adventist University (France)
Southwestern Adventist University (United States)
Spicer Memorial College (India)
Tanzania Adventist College (Tanzania)
University of Eastern Africa, Baraton (Kenya)
Universidad de Montemorelos (Mexico)
Yugoslavian Training School (Yugoslavia)

## Articles

Australian Council of State School Organizations. "Six myths about private schools in Australia," media@qtu.asn.au

Brereton, Virginia Lieson. "The Bible Schools and Conservative Evangelical Higher Education, 1880-1940," in *Making Higher Education Christian*, Joel A. Carpenter and Kenneth W. Shipps, eds. Grand Rapids: Christian University Press, 1987. pp. 110-136.

Holsinger, M. Paul. "The Oregon School Bill Controversy, 1922-1925," *Pacific Historical Review*, XXXVII (1968), pp. 327-341.

Jorgenson, Lloyd P. "The Oregon School Law of 1923: Passage and Sequel," *Catholic Historical Review*, LIV (1968), pp. 445-466.

Knight, George R. "The Transformation of Education," in *The World of Ellen*

*White*, Gary Land, ed. Washington, D.C.: Review and Herald Publishing Association, 1987. pp. 161-175.

Potts, Anthony, "Public and Private Schooling Australia–Historical and Contemporary Considerations," www.history.ac.uk/projects/elec

Reynolds, Keld J. "The Church under Stress, 1931-1960," in *Adventism in America*, Gary Land, ed. Grand Rapids: William B. Eerdmans Publishing Co., 1986. pp. 170-207.

Smith, Timothy. "Introduction: Christian Colleges and American Culture," in Carpenter and Shipps, *ibid.* pp. 1-15.

Thompson, Ida E. "Bethel Girls' School," in *With Our Missionaries in China,* Emma Anderson, *et. al.* Mountain View, CA: Pacific Press Publishing Association, 1920, pp. 43-63.

## Archival and Unpublished Materials

"An Affirmation of Creation," the International Faith & Science Conferences 2002-2004. Report of the Organizing Committee to the General Conference Executive Committee through the office of the General Conference President, September 10, 2004.

Ashlock, George S. "The Establishment of White Seventh-day Adventist Elementary Schools in the United States, 1853-1900." M.S. thesis, University of Tennessee, 1959.

Australian High Court Cases, www.austlii.edu.au/au/cases/cth/high_ct

Cady, Marion Ernest. "Seventh Day Adventist Denominational Schools on the Pacific Coast." M.A. thesis, University of California, 1916.

*Columbia Union College v. John J. Oliver, Jr., et. al.*, 2001, United States Court of Appeals, Fourth District. Copy in Office of General Counsel, General Conference of Seventh-day Adventists.

Correspondence: Joyce and Eric Juriansz to Friends of Lakpahana, March 27, 1998; Paul Essig to Joyce and Eric Juriansz, August 20, 1998. Library, Lakpahana Adventist College and Seminary.

Crane, E. A. "I Remember Sri Lanka." Unpublished manuscript, Library, Lakpahana Adventist College and Seminary.

Haloviak, Bert. "A Brief Sketch of SDA Ministerial Training." Unpublished manuscript.

Kelly-Little, Mary. "Development of the Elementary Schools of Seventh-day Adventists in the United States." M.A. thesis, University of Washington, 1932.

Minutes of the Board of Higher Education, General Conference Archives.

Minutes of the Commission on Higher Education, General Conference Archives.

Minutes of the General Conference Committee, General Conference Archives.

Minutes of the International Board of Education, General Conference Archives.

Nixon, Robert, comp. Church-State Relationships in the United States: Compilation of Actions and Policies of the General Conference and North American Division. Office of General Counsel, General Conference of Seventh-day Adventists.

Official Statements, www.adventist.org

Pohlman, Edward. W. "First the Blade, Then the Ear." Unpublished article from the collection of Gordon Christo, Spicer Memorial College, Pune, India (later published in *Eastern Tidings*, September 15, 1945).

Record Group 51, General Conference Department of Education, General Conference Archives.

Robinson, A. W. "Partial Account of Our Ceylon Experience." Library, Lakpahana Adventist College and Seminary.

### Interviews and Correspondence

U. D. Aloysius, W. D. Joseph, Peter Munasinghe, J. Willy Reith, combined interview, Colombo, Sri Lanka, May 21, 2002.

Bert B. Beach, telephone conversation, March 10, 2002.

Enrique Becerra, Silver Spring, MD, February 13, 2002.

Pavle Borovic, Englewood, FL, July 30, 2003.

Dae Yun Cho, Seoul, Korea, June 4, 2002.

Barbara Choi, Hong Kong, May 14, 2002.

G. J. Christo, Hosur, India, May 26, 2002.

Gordon Christo, Pune, India, May 28, 2002; email, June 15, 2004.

Daniel Chuah, Hong Kong, May 14, 2002.

Y. K. Chung, Seoul, Korea, June 4, 2002.

Justus Devadas, Hosur, India, May 24, 2002.

Garland Dulan, Silver Spring, MD, February 11, 12, 2002; November 29, 2004.

Karen Essig, Mailapitiya, Sri Lanka, May 23, 2002.

Paul Essig, Mailapitiya, Sri Lanka, May 22, 2002.

H. G. M. Fernando, Colombo, Sri Lanka, 22, 2002.

R. S. Fernando, Kandy, Sri Lanka, May 23, 2002.

John Fowler, Silver Spring, MD, February 7, 13, 2002; Silang, Cavite, Philippines, May 19, 2002.

Samuel M. Gaikwad, Pune, India, May 27, 2002.

Jonathan Gallagher, Silver Spring, MD, February 27, 2002.

John Graz, Silver Spring, MD, February 28, 2002.

Daniel Heinz, email, July 4-7, 2003.

Si Young Kim, Seoul, Korea, June 4, 2002.

Oliver Koh, Silang, Cavite, Philippines, May 17, 2002.

Ezras Lakra, Hosur, India, May 24, 2002.

Anna Lee, Hong Kong, May 15, 2002.

Andrea Luxton, email, July 11, 2004; January 11, 2005.

H. H. Lyu, Seoul, Korea, June 4, 2002.

Harry Mayden, Takoma Park, MD, February 27, 2002.
Alfred McClure, Punta Gorda, FL, January 23, April 8, 2002.
Julian Melgosa, Silang, Cavite, Philippines, May 18, 2002.
Liberato B. Moises, Silang, Cavite, Philippines, May 17, 2002.
D. K. Nam, Seoul, Korea, June 5, 2002.
Robert Nixon, Silver Spring, MD, February 25, 2002.
M. K. Oh, Seoul, Korea, June 5, 2002.
Richard Osborn, email, May 28, 2002; August 3, 2004.
Dong Seung Park, Seoul, Korea, June 4, 2002.
Tim Poirier, Silver Spring, MD, email, January 14, 2005.
Humberto Rasi, Silver Spring, MD, February 6, 7, 27, 2002; email, November 3 and December 29, 2004.
Vicente Rodriguez, Macon, GA, correspondence April 12, 2002.
Elizabeth Role, Silang, Cavite, Philippines, May 17, 2002.
Mr. and Mrs. Y. R. Samaraj, joint interview, Hosur, India, May 25, 2002.
Jin Hong Shin, Seoul, Korea, June 4, 2002.
Kei Hoon Shin, Seoul, Korea, June 4, 2002.
Milton Siepman, Punta Gorda, FL, January 8, 2002.
Charles Tidwell, Punta Gorda, FL, conducted by email, January 2-29, 2002.
Mitchell Tyner, Silver Spring, MD, February 20, 2002.
Masaji Uyeda, Koyang City, Korea, June 3, 2002.

# Index

*(Page numbers in bold type refer to photo illustrations.)*

T